CW01083077

Yamaha XT660R, XT660X, XT660Z Ténéré & MT-03
Service and Repair Manual

by Matthew Coombs

Models covered

(4910-296)

XT660X 2004 to 2011
XT660R 2004 to 2011
XT660Z Ténéré 2009 to 2011
MT-03 2006 to 2011

ABCDE
FGHIJ
KLMNO
PQRST

© Haynes Publishing 2011

A book in the Haynes Service and Repair Manual Series

ISBN: **978 1 84425 910 6**

British Library Cataloguing in Publication Data
A catalogue record for this book is available from the British Library.

Printed in the USA

Haynes Publishing
Sparkford, Yeovil, Somerset BA22 7JJ, England

Haynes North America, Inc
861 Lawrence Drive, Newbury Park, California 91320, USA

Haynes Publishing Nordiska AB
Box 1504, 751 45 Uppsala, Sweden

Contents

LIVING WITH YOUR YAMAHA

Introduction
Yamaha – Musical instruments to motorcycles	Page	0•4
Acknowledgements	Page	0•8
About this manual	Page	0•8
Identification numbers	Page	0•9
Buying spare parts	Page	0•9
Safety first!	Page	0•10
Model development and bike spec	Page	0•17

Pre-ride checks
Coolant level	Page	0•11
Engine oil level	Page	0•12
Suspension, steering and drive chain	Page	0•13
Brake fluid levels	Page	0•14
Legal and safety	Page	0•15
Tyres	Page	0•16

MAINTENANCE

Routine maintenance and servicing
Specifications	Page	1•1
Lubricants and fluids	Page	1•2
Maintenance schedule	Page	1•3
Component locations	Page	1•4
Maintenance procedures	Page	1•8

Contents

REPAIRS AND OVERHAUL

Engine, transmission and associated systems

Engine, clutch and transmission	Page	**2•1**
Cooling system	Page	**3•1**
Engine management system	Page	**4•1**

Chassis components

Frame and suspension	Page	**5•1**
Brakes, wheels and final drive	Page	**6•1**
Bodywork	Page	**7•1**

Electrical system

	Page	**8•1**

Wiring diagrams

	Page	**8•36**

REFERENCE

Tools and Workshop Tips	Page	**REF•2**
Security	Page	**REF•20**
Lubricants and fluids	Page	**REF•23**
Conversion factors	Page	**REF•26**
MOT Test Checks	Page	**REF•27**
Storage	Page	**REF•32**
Fault Finding	Page	**REF•35**
Technical Terms Explained	Page	**REF•44**

Index

	Page	**REF•48**

Yamaha
Musical instruments to motorcycles

**The FS1E -
first bike of many sixteen year olds in the UK**

The Yamaha Motor Company

The Yamaha name can be traced back to 1889, when Torakusu Yamaha founded the Yamaha Organ Manufacturing Company. Such was the success of the company, that in 1897 it became Nippon Gakki Limited and manufactured a wide range of reed organs and pianos.

During World War II, Nippon Gakki's manufacturing base was utilised by the Japanese authorities to produce propellers and fuel tanks for their aviation industry. The end of the war brought about a huge public demand for low cost transport and many firms decided to utilise their obsolete aircraft tooling for the production of motorcycles. Nippon Gakki's first motorcycle went on sale in February 1955 and was named the 125 YA-1 Red Dragonfly. This machine was a copy of the German DKW RT125 motorcycle, featuring a single cylinder two-stroke engine with a four-speed gearbox. Due to the outstanding success of this model the motorcycle operation was separated from Nippon Gakki in July 1955 and the Yamaha Motor Company was formed.

The YA-1 also received acclaim by winning two of Japan's biggest road races, the Mount Fuji Climbing race and the Asama Volcano race. The high level of public demand for the YA-1 led to the development of a whole series of two-stroke singles and twins.

Having made a large impact on their home market, Yamahas were exported to the USA in 1958 and to the UK in 1962. In the UK the signing of an Anglo-Japanese trade agreement during 1962 enabled the sale of Japanese lightweight motorcycles and scooters in Britain. At that time, competition between the many motorcycle producers in Japan had reduced numbers significantly and by the end of the sixties, only the big-four which are familiar with today remained.

Yamaha Europe was founded in 1968 and based in Holland. Although originally set up to market marine products, the Dutch base is now the official European Headquarters and distribution centre. Yamaha motorcycles are built at factories in Holland, Denmark, Norway, Italy, France, Spain and Portugal. Yamahas are imported into the UK by Yamaha Motor UK Ltd, formerly Mitsui Machinery Sales (UK) Ltd. Mitsui and Co. were originally a trading house, handling the shipping, distribution and marketing of Japanese products into western countries. Ultimately Mitsui Machinery Sales was formed to handle Yamaha motorcycles and outboard motors.

Based on the technology derived from its motorcycle operation, Yamaha have produced many other products, such as automobile and lightweight aircraft engines, marine engines and boats, generators, pumps, ATVs, snowmobiles, golf cars, industrial robots, lawnmowers, swimming pools and archery equipment.

Two-strokes first

Part of Yamaha's success was a whole string of innovations in the two-stroke world. Autolube engine lubrication, torque induction, multi-ported engines, reed valves and power valves kept their two-strokes at the forefront of technology. Many advances were achieved with the use of racing as a development laboratory. They went to the USA in the late 1950s with an air-cooled 250cc twin but didn't hit the GPs until the early 1960s when Fumio Ito scored a hat-trick of sixth places in the Isle of Man TT, the Dutch TT and the Belgian GP. This experiment gave rise to the idea of the over-the-counter racer, an idea that became reality in the TD1, the first in an unmatched series of two-stroke racers that were the standard issue for privateers at national and international level for years and helped Yamaha develop their road engines. While privateers raced the twins, Yamaha built the outrageously complicated vee-four 250 for Phil Read and followed it with a vee-four 125 that Bill Ivy lapped the Isle of Man on at over 100mph! When the FIM regulations were changed to limit the smaller GP classes to two cylinders, these exotic bikes died but set the scene for an unparalleled dynasty of mass-produced racers based on the same technology as the road bikes.

In the 1960s and 70s the two-stroke engined YAS3 125, YDS1 to YDS7 250 and YR5 350 formed the core of Yamaha's range. By the mid-70s they had been superseded by the RD (Race-Developed) 125, 250, and 350 range of two-stroke twins, featuring improved 7-port engines with reed valve induction. Braking

was improved by the use of an hydraulic brake on the front wheel of DX models, instead of the drum arrangement used previously, and cast alloy wheels were available as an option on later RD models. The RD350 was replaced by the RD400 in 1976.

Running parallel with the RD twins was a range of single-cylinder two-strokes. Used in a variety of chassis types, the engine was used in the popular 50 cc FS1-E moped, the V50 to 90 step-thrus, RS100 and 125, YB100 and the DT trail range.

The TD racers got water-cooling in 1973 to become the TZs, the most successful and numerous over-the-counter racers ever built. That same year, Jarno Saarinen became the first rider to win a 500cc GP on a four-cylinder two-stroke on the new in-line four which was effectively a pair of TZs side-by-side. TZs won everywhere – including the Daytona 200 and 500 races when overbored to 351cc. A 700cc TZ also appeared, one year later taken out to 750cc. Steve Baker won the first Formula 750 world title – one of the precursors of Superbike – on one in 1977. The following year Kenny Roberts won Yamaha's first world 500 title and would be succeeded by Wayne Rainey and Eddie Lawson before Mick Doohan and the NSR500 took over.

The air-cooled single and twin cylinder RD road bikes were eventually replaced by the LC series in 1980, featuring liquid-cooled engines, radical new styling, spiral pattern cast wheels and cantilever rear suspension (Yamaha's Monoshock). Of all the LC models, the RD350LC, or RD350R as it was later known, has made the most impact in the market. Later models had YPVS (Yamaha Power Valve System) engines, another first for Yamaha – this was essentially a valve located in the exhaust ports which was electronically operated to alter port timing to achieve maximum power output. The RD500LC was the largest two-stroke made by Yamaha and differed from the other LCs by the use of its vee-four cylinder engine.

With the exception of the RD350R, now manufactured in Brazil, the LC range has been discontinued. Two-stroke engined models have given way to environmental pressure, and thus with a few exceptions, such as the TZR125 and TZR250, are used only in scooters and small capacity bikes.

The Four-strokes

Yamaha concentrated solely on two-stroke models until 1970 when the XS1 was produced, their first four-stroke motorcycle. It was perhaps Yamaha's success with two-strokes that postponed an earlier

The distinctive paintwork and trim of the RD models

move into the four-stroke motorcycle market, although their work with Toyota during the 1960s had given them a sound base in four-stroke technology.

The XS1 had a 650 cc twin-cylinder SOHC engine and was later to become known as the XS650, appearing also in the popular SE custom form. Yamaha introduced a three cylinder 750 cc engine in 1976, fitted in a sport-tourer frame and called the XS750, TX750 in the USA . The XS750 established itself well in the sport tourer class and remained in production with very few changes until uprated to 850 cc in 1980.

Other four-strokes followed in 1976, with the introduction of the XS250/360/400 series twins. The XS range was strengthened in 1978 by the four-cylinder XS1100.

The 1980s saw a new family of four-strokes, the XJ550, 650, 750 and 900 Fours. Improvements over the XS range amounted to a slimmer DOHC engine unit due to the relocation of the alternator behind the cylinders, electronic ignition and uprated braking and suspension systems. Models were available mainly in standard trim, although custom-styled Maxims were produced especially for the US market. The XJ650T was the first model from Yamaha to have a turbo-charged engine. Although these early XJ models have now been discontinued, their roots live on in the XJ600S and XJ900S Diversion (Seca II) models.

The FZR prefix encompasses the pure

The XS650 led the way for Yamaha's four-stroke range

sports Yamaha models. With the exception of the 16-valve FZR400 and FZR600 models, the FZ/FZR750 and FZR1000 used 20-valve engines, two exhaust valves and three inlet valves per cylinder. This concept was called Genesis and gave improved gas flow to the combustion chambers. Other features of the new engine were the use of down-draught carburetors and the engine's inclined angle in the frame, plus the change to liquid-cooling.

Yamaha's XS750 was produced from 1976 to 1982 and then uprated to 850 cc

Lightweight Deltabox design aluminium frames and uprated suspension improved the bikes's handling. The Genesis engine lives on in the YZF750 and 1000 models.

The Genesis concept was the basis of Yamaha's foray into four-stroke racing, first with a bike known simply as 'The Genesis', an FZ750 motor in a TT Formula 1 bike with which the factory attempted to steal the Honda RVF750's thunder at important events like the Suzuka 8 Hours and the Bol d'Or although they never fielded it for a whole World Championship season. That had to wait for the advent of the World Superbike Championship, although there was no full works team until 1995, instead it was left to individual importers to support teams. It was the Australian Dealer Team Yamaha which scored the factory's first World Superbike win in the series debut year of 1988. The rider? Mick Doohan. Slightly, embarrassingly, it was the steel framed FZ750 rather than the FZR homologation special that won races. The OW01 was a race winner, mainly in the hands of Fabrizio Pirovano, the factory's most successful Superbike racer with ten victories, but national success in the UK, Japan, and in the Daytona 200 has not been translated into World Championships for any of Yamaha's 750s.

The vee-twin engine has been the mainstay of the XV Virago range. Since 1981 XVs have been produced in 535, 700, 750, 920, 1000 and 1100 engine sizes, all using the same basic air-cooled sohc vee-twin engine. Other uses of vee engines have been in the XZ550 of the early 1980s, the XVZ12 Venture and the mighty VMX-12 V-Max.

Yamaha has always been a sporting-orientated company whose motto could be 'Racing Improves the Breed', so it's no surprise that the latest generation of lightweight sportsters are at the cutting edge of performance on and off the track. The R6 won more races than any other machine in the inaugural year of the World Supersports Championship, the R7 won a race in its debut year in World Superbike in the hands of the mercurial Noriyuki Haga, and the mighty 1000cc R1 ended Honda's domination of the Isle of Man F1 TT when David Jefferies won three races in a week in 1999.

A new family of four-strokes was released in 1980 with the introduction of the XJ range

Pioneering Single

It's difficult to overstate what an important bike the very first XT Yamaha was. Back in the mid-1970s when the big single-cylinder four-stroke motorcycle was all but extinct and regarded as the preserve of Luddite enthusiasts of obscure, vibratory British bikes, Yamaha produced the XT500. This was Yamaha's first four-stroke single and its impact can be judged from the fact that there is an XT 500 in Honda's museum at the Twin-Ring Motegi circuit. Not surprisingly, there aren't many non-Hondas in there, mainly because the Honda company made most of the landmark motorcycles in the recent history of powered two-wheeled transport. I also seem to recall a DT Yamaha in there – that's one of the slightly earlier two-stroke trail bikes. In various capacities, the DT range

were the best of the little trail bikes much favoured by learners, trail riders and club enduro competitors. But it did not follow that a big four-stroke would be equally successful. However, the pared down spec and slightly retro look gave the XT a credibility which, allied to a considerably smaller price tag than contemporary middleweight four-cylinder UJMs, hit a spot with the market.

When in 1979 a Yamaha won the inaugural Paris-Dakar Rally and the following year filled the first four places, Europe's love affair with the XT really started. The UK never quite got big trail bikes, nowadays more poetically labelled as 'adventure touring' but France, Italy and Germany bought them in record-breaking numbers. Yamaha really started exploiting their rally-raid success in 1983 with the first Ténéré. Basically, it was an XT500 with an enormous, 28-litre petrol tank to ape

The 2005 XT660R

The 2010 XT660X

The 2008 XT660Z Ténéré

The 2008 MT-03

the look of the desert racers. British bikers venturing abroad, especially to the 24-hour races at Le Mans and the Bol d'Or, were astonished to see that every other motorcycle they came across was a Ténéré. And if you went on holiday somewhere exotic you were bound to come across a party of Germans on Ténérés. I was on holiday in Djerba, a Tunisian island near the border with Libya in the early '80s and sure enough the only big bikes I saw was a brace of Munich-registered Ténérés.

On the back of massive interest in the Paris-Dakar, the XT evolved steadily. The advent of the Ténéré in '83 also saw the engine taken out to 600cc. Following rally-raid fashion, a twin-headlamp fairing arrived in '88 and by '91 the air-cooled four-valve motor gave way to a five-valve water-cooled lump. There was always a plain-Jane XT alongside the big-tanked Ténéré. By 1999 interest in the

Paris-Dakar had waned from obsession to polite interest and the Ténéré quietly slipped out of the range.

However, BMW with their GS range changed the emphasis subtly from the desert-race-replica to the go-anywhere adventure tourer and this time the British market got it, as the sales figures and waiting lists show. So the XT660 reappeared in 2004 using a new four-valve, fuel-injected motor. The Z-model Ténéré followed in 2009 with big tank, long-travel suspension and the capability of dealing with gentle off-road going – a proper adventure tourer. There isn't really a proper trailbike in the range, the X-model is a supermotard bike. This is a fashion that has always been going to catch on big time but never has. Nevertheless, the lowered XT running proper road tyres and 17-inch wheels is a brilliant city and back-roads bike. The R looks like a trail bike but is really a slightly

cheaper and slightly less radical version of the X.

Back in 1978 Yamaha put the XT500 motor into a pure road chassis and produced the SR500, the last of the air-cooled thumpers. This deliberately retro styled roadster became a massive cult hit in Japan (where it was the SR400) and did respectable business in Europe. A less successful sports style model, the SZR660, followed in 1996 and used the 5-valve liquid-cooled engine from the XT. This time Yamaha decided not to use the SR designation and put the new XT in a thoroughly modern roadster called the MT-03.

Not many model names or concepts have a lifetime of nearly 30 years like the Ténéré. The emphasis of the bike may have changed but the bike still carries the banner for that most fundamental of motorcycle layouts, the four-stroke single.

Acknowledgements

Our thanks are due to Bransons Motorcycles of Yeovil who supplied the machines featured in the illustrations throughout this manual. We would also like to thank NGK Spark Plugs (UK) Ltd for supplying the colour spark plug condition photographs, the Avon Rubber Company for supplying information on tyre fitting and Draper Tools Ltd for some of the workshop tools shown.

Thanks are also due to Julian Ryder who wrote the introduction and to Yamaha Motor (UK) Ltd. who supplied model photographs.

About this Manual

The aim of this manual is to help you get the best value from your motorcycle. It can do so in several ways. It can help you decide what work must be done, even if you choose to have it done by a dealer; it provides information and procedures for routine maintenance and servicing; and it offers diagnostic and repair procedures to follow when trouble occurs.

We hope you use the manual to tackle the work yourself. For many simpler jobs, doing it yourself may be quicker than arranging an appointment to get the motorcycle into a dealer and making the trips to leave it and pick it up. More importantly, a lot of money can be saved by avoiding the expense the shop must pass on to you to cover its labour and overhead costs. An added benefit is the sense of satisfaction and accomplishment that you feel after doing the job yourself.

References to the left or right side of the motorcycle assume you are sitting on the seat, facing forward.

We take great pride in the accuracy of information given in this manual, but motorcycle manufacturers make alterations and design changes during the production run of a particular motorcycle of which they do not inform us. No liability can be accepted by the authors or publishers for loss, damage or injury caused by any errors in, or omissions from, the information given.

Illegal copying

Frame and engine numbers

The frame number is stamped into the right-hand side of the steering head and is repeated on the VIN plate rivetted to the frame under the seat. The engine number is stamped into the top of the crankcase and is visible from the right-hand side. Both of these numbers should be recorded and kept in a safe place so they can be given to law enforcement officials in the event of a theft. There is also a model code label stuck to the frame under the seat. The throttle body has an ID number stamped into its body.

The frame and engine numbers, model and colour codes should also be kept in a handy place (such as with your driver's licence) so they are always available when purchasing parts.

The procedures in this manual identify models by their model name (e.g. XT-R, XT-X, XT-Z, or MT-03), and where necessary, by their production year (e.g. 2004 to 2006 XT-R models). The production year is also linked to the four-digit model code, e.g. 11D2 which can be found on the model code label and in certain countries it is linked to model code letter, e.g. XT660R(S) indicating 2004.

Letter	Production year
S	2004
T	2005
V	2006
W	2007
X	2008
Y	2009
Z	2010
A	2011

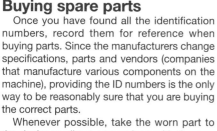

The VIN plate is rivetted to the frame cross-member under the seat

The frame number is stamped into the right-hand side of the steering head

Buying spare parts

Once you have found all the identification numbers, record them for reference when buying parts. Since the manufacturers change specifications, parts and vendors (companies that manufacture various components on the machine), providing the ID numbers is the only way to be reasonably sure that you are buying the correct parts.

Whenever possible, take the worn part to the dealer so direct comparison with the new component can be made. Along the trail from the manufacturer to the parts shelf, there are numerous places that the part can end up with the wrong number or be listed incorrectly.

The two places to purchase new parts for your motorcycle – the franchised or main dealer and the parts/accessories store – differ in the type of parts they carry. While dealers can obtain every single genuine part for your motorcycle, the accessory store is usually limited to normal high wear items such as chains and sprockets, brake pads, spark plugs and cables, and to tune-up parts and various engine gaskets, etc. Rarely will an accessory outlet have major suspension components, camshafts, transmission gears, or engine cases.

Used parts can be obtained from breakers yards for roughly half the price of new ones, but you can't always be sure of what you're getting. Once again, take your worn part to the breaker for direct comparison, or when ordering by mail order make sure that you can return it if you are not happy.

Whether buying new, used or rebuilt parts, the best course is to deal directly with someone who specialises in your particular make.

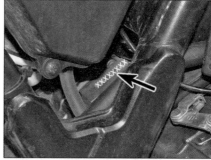

The label stuck to the frame under the seat provides the 4-digit model codel, a production code and the single letter indicates the colour code

The engine number is stamped into the top of the crankcase

Professional mechanics are trained in safe working procedures. However enthusiastic you may be about getting on with the job at hand, take the time to ensure that your safety is not put at risk. A moment's lack of attention can result in an accident, as can failure to observe simple precautions.

There will always be new ways of having accidents, and the following is not a comprehensive list of all dangers; it is intended rather to make you aware of the risks and to encourage a safe approach to all work you carry out on your bike.

Asbestos

● Certain friction, insulating, sealing and other products - such as brake pads, clutch linings, gaskets, etc. - contain asbestos. Extreme care must be taken to avoid inhalation of dust from such products since it is hazardous to health. If in doubt, assume that they do contain asbestos.

Fire

● Remember at all times that petrol is highly flammable. Never smoke or have any kind of naked flame around, when working on the vehicle. But the risk does not end there - a spark caused by an electrical short-circuit, by two metal surfaces contacting each other, by careless use of tools, or even by static electricity built up in your body under certain conditions, can ignite petrol vapour, which in a confined space is highly explosive. Never use petrol as a cleaning solvent. Use an approved safety solvent.

● Always disconnect the battery earth terminal before working on any part of the fuel or electrical system, and never risk spilling fuel on to a hot engine or exhaust.

● It is recommended that a fire extinguisher of a type suitable for fuel and electrical fires is kept handy in the garage or workplace at all times. Never try to extinguish a fuel or electrical fire with water.

Fumes

● Certain fumes are highly toxic and can quickly cause unconsciousness and even death if inhaled to any extent. Petrol vapour comes into this category, as do the vapours from certain solvents such as trichloro-ethylene. Any draining or pouring of such volatile fluids should be done in a well ventilated area.

● When using cleaning fluids and solvents, read the instructions carefully. Never use materials from unmarked containers - they may give off poisonous vapours.

● Never run the engine of a motor vehicle in an enclosed space such as a garage. Exhaust fumes contain carbon monoxide which is extremely poisonous; if you need to run the engine, always do so in the open air or at least have the rear of the vehicle outside the workplace.

The battery

● Never cause a spark, or allow a naked light near the vehicle's battery. It will normally be giving off a certain amount of hydrogen gas, which is highly explosive.

● Always disconnect the battery ground (earth) terminal before working on the fuel or electrical systems (except where noted).

● If possible, loosen the filler plugs or cover when charging the battery from an external source. Do not charge at an excessive rate or the battery may burst.

● Take care when topping up, cleaning or carrying the battery. The acid electrolyte, evenwhen diluted, is very corrosive and should not be allowed to contact the eyes or skin. Always wear rubber gloves and goggles or a face shield. If you ever need to prepare electrolyte yourself, always add the acid slowly to the water; never add the water to the acid.

Electricity

● When using an electric power tool, inspection light etc., always ensure that the appliance is correctly connected to its plug and that, where necessary, it is properly grounded (earthed). Do not use such appliances in damp conditions and, again, beware of creating a spark or applying excessive heat in the vicinity of fuel or fuel vapour. Also ensure that the appliances meet national safety standards.

● A severe electric shock can result from touching certain parts of the electrical system, such as the spark plug wires (HT leads), when the engine is running or being cranked, particularly if components are damp or the insulation is defective. Where an electronic ignition system is used, the secondary (HT) voltage is much higher and could prove fatal.

Remember...

✗ **Don't** start the engine without first ascertaining that the transmission is in neutral.

✗ **Don't** suddenly remove the pressure cap from a hot cooling system - cover it with a cloth and release the pressure gradually first, or you may get scalded by escaping coolant.

✗ **Don't** attempt to drain oil until you are sure it has cooled sufficiently to avoid scalding you.

✗ **Don't** grasp any part of the engine or exhaust system without first ascertaining that it is cool enough not to burn you.

✗ **Don't** allow brake fluid or antifreeze to contact the machine's paintwork or plastic components.

✗ **Don't** siphon toxic liquids such as fuel, hydraulic fluid or antifreeze by mouth, or allow them to remain on your skin.

✗ **Don't** inhale dust - it may be injurious to health (see Asbestos heading).

✗ **Don't** allow any spilled oil or grease to remain on the floor - wipe it up right away, before someone slips on it.

✗ **Don't** use ill-fitting spanners or other tools which may slip and cause injury.

✗ **Don't** lift a heavy component which may be beyond your capability - get assistance.

✗ **Don't** rush to finish a job or take unverified short cuts.

✗ **Don't** allow children or animals in or around an unattended vehicle.

✗ **Don't** inflate a tyre above the recommended pressure. Apart from overstressing the carcass, in extreme cases the tyre may blow off forcibly.

✔ **Do** ensure that the machine is supported securely at all times. This is especially important when the machine is blocked up to aid wheel or fork removal.

✔ **Do** take care when attempting to loosen a stubborn nut or bolt. It is generally better to pull on a spanner, rather than push, so that if you slip, you fall away from the machine rather than onto it.

✔ **Do** wear eye protection when using power tools such as drill, sander, bench grinder etc.

✔ **Do** use a barrier cream on your hands prior to undertaking dirty jobs - it will protect your skin from infection as well as making the dirt easier to remove afterwards; but make sure your hands aren't left slippery. Note that long-term contact with used engine oil can be a health hazard.

✔ **Do** keep loose clothing (cuffs, ties etc. and long hair) well out of the way of moving mechanical parts.

✔ **Do** remove rings, wristwatch etc., before working on the vehicle - especially the electrical system.

✔ **Do** keep your work area tidy - it is only too easy to fall over articles left lying around.

✔ **Do** exercise caution when compressing springs for removal or installation. Ensure that the tension is applied and released in a controlled manner, using suitable tools which preclude the possibility of the spring escaping violently.

✔ **Do** ensure that any lifting tackle used has a safe working load rating adequate for the job.

✔ **Do** get someone to check periodically that all is well, when working alone on the vehicle.

✔ **Do** carry out work in a logical sequence and check that everything is correctly assembled and tightened afterwards.

✔ **Do** remember that your vehicle's safety affects that of yourself and others. If in doubt on any point, get professional advice.

● If in spite of following these precautions, you are unfortunate enough to injure yourself, seek medical attention as soon as possible.

Coolant level

Before you start:

✔ Make sure you have a supply of coolant available (a mixture of 50% distilled water and 50% corrosion inhibited ethylene glycol anti-freeze is needed).

> ⚠ **Warning: DO NOT remove the radiator pressure cap to add coolant. Topping up is done via the coolant reservoir tank filler. DO NOT leave open containers of coolant about, as it is poisonous.**

✔ Always check the coolant level when the engine is cold.
Caution: Do not run the engine in an enclosed space such as a garage or workshop.
✔ Support the motorcycle upright on level ground.
✔ The coolant reservoir is located on the right-hand side – the level lines are visible without removing any bodywork.

Bike care:

● Use only the specified coolant mixture. It is important that the correct proportion of anti-freeze is used in the system all year round, and not just in the winter. Do not top the system up using only water, as the system will become too diluted.
● Do not overfill the reservoir tank. If the coolant is significantly above the FULL level line at any time, the surplus should be siphoned or drained off to prevent the possibility of it being expelled out of the overflow hose.
● If the coolant level falls steadily, check the system for leaks (see Chapter 1). If no leaks are found and the level continues to fall, it is recommended that the machine is taken to a Yamaha dealer for a pressure test.

XT-R and XT-X models

  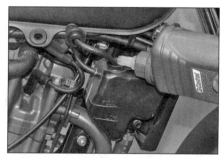

1 The coolant level should lie between the FULL and LOW level lines (arrowed) that are marked on the reservoir.

2 If the coolant level is on or below the LOW line, remove the fuel tank right-hand cover (see Chapter 7), then remove the reservoir filler cap.

3 Top the reservoir up with the recommended coolant mixture to the FULL level line, using a suitable funnel if required. Fit the cap. Install the fuel tank cover.

XT-Z models

1 The coolant level should lie between the FULL and LOW level lines (arrowed) that are marked on the reservoir.

2 If the coolant level is on or below the LOW line, remove the radiator right-hand cover (see Chapter 7), then remove the reservoir filler cap.

3 Top the reservoir up with the recommended coolant mixture to the FULL level line, using a funnel if required. Fit the cap. Install the radiator cover.

MT-03 models

1 The coolant level should lie between the FULL and LOW level lines (arrowed) that are marked on the reservoir.

2 If the coolant level is on or below the LOW line, remove the reservoir filler cap.

3 Top the reservoir up with the recommended coolant mixture to the FULL level line, using a suitable funnel if required. Fit the cap.

Engine oil level

Before you start:
✔ Start the engine and let it warm up for 10 to 15 minutes, then turn it off.
Caution: Do not run the engine in an enclosed space such as a garage or workshop.
✔ Support the motorcycle upright on level ground. Allow it to stand for a few minutes for the oil level to stabilise.

The correct oil:
● Modern, high-revving engines place great demands on their oil. It is very important that the correct oil for your bike is used.
● Always top up with a good quality motorcycle oil of the specified type and viscosity and do not overfill the engine. Do not use engine oil designed for car use.

Oil type	API grade SG or higher
Oil viscosity	SAE 10W30 or 10W40

Caution: Do not use chemical additives or oils graded CD or higher or labelled 'ENERGY CONSERVING' – such additives or oils could cause clutch slip.

Bike care:
● If you have to add oil frequently, check the engine joints, oil seals and gaskets, and the oil pipes from the frame or tank, for oil leakage. If not, the engine could be burning oil, in which case there will be white smoke coming out of the exhaust (see *Fault Finding*).

XT models

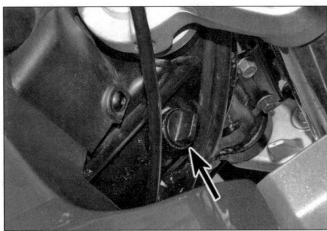

1 The oil level dipstick is incorporated with the oil filler cap (arrowed), which is on the right-hand side of the frame headstock.

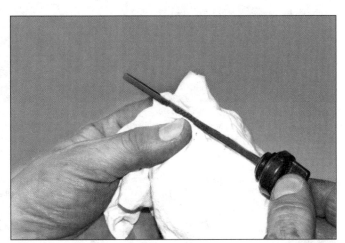

2 Unscrew the cap and wipe the dipstick clean.

3 Insert the dipstick so that the cap contacts the threads, but do not screw it in.

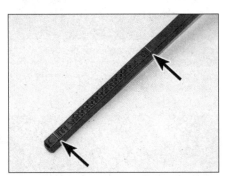

4 Remove the dipstick and check the oil mark – it should lie between the upper and lower level lines (arrowed).

5 If the level is on or below the lower line, top up the engine with the recommended grade and type of oil to bring the level almost up to the upper line. Do not overfill.

Note: *On completion, make sure the O-ring on the underside of the cap is in good condition and properly seated. Fit a new one if necessary. Wipe it clean and smear new oil onto it. Fit the cap, making sure it is secure in the frame. Run the engine for a few minutes, then turn it off and wait a few minutes, then re-check the level.*

MT-03 models

1 The oil level dipstick is incorporated with the oil filler cap (arrowed), which is in the tank below the radiator.

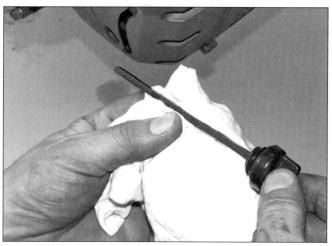

2 Unscrew the cap and wipe the dipstick clean.

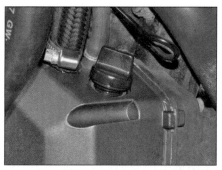

3 Insert the dipstick so that the cap contacts the threads, but do not screw it in.

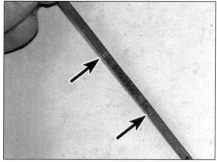

4 Remove the dipstick and check the oil mark – it should lie between the upper and lower level lines (arrowed).

5 If the level is on or below the lower line, top up the engine with the recommended grade and type of oil to bring the level almost up to the upper line. Do not overfill.

Note: *On completion, make sure the O-ring on the underside of the cap is in good condition and properly seated. Fit a new one if necessary. Wipe it clean and smear new oil onto it. Fit the cap, making sure it is secure in the cover. Run the engine for a few minutes, then turn it off and wait a few minutes, then re-check the level.*

Suspension, steering and drive chain

Suspension and Steering:
● Check that the front and rear suspension operates smoothly without binding (see Chapter 1).
● Check that the steering moves smoothly from lock-to-lock.

Final drive:
● Check that the chain isn't too loose or too tight, and adjust it if necessary (see Chapter 1).
● If the chain looks dry, lubricate it (see Chapter 1).

Brake fluid levels

> ⚠ **Warning: Brake hydraulic fluid can harm your eyes and damage painted surfaces, so use extreme caution when handling and pouring it and cover surrounding surfaces with rag. Do not use fluid that has been standing open for some time, as it is hygroscopic (absorbs moisture from the air) which can cause a dangerous loss of braking effectiveness.**

Before you start:

✔ The front brake fluid reservoir is on the right-hand handlebar.
✔ The rear brake fluid reservoir is above the clutch cover on the right-hand side.
✔ Make sure you have the correct hydraulic fluid. DOT 4 is recommended.
✔ Wrap a rag around the reservoir to ensure that any spillage does not come into contact with painted surfaces.

Bike care:

● The fluid in the reservoir will drop as the brake pads wear down. If the fluid level is low check the brake pads for wear (see Chapter 1), and replace them with new ones if necessary (see Chapter 6). Do not top the reservoir(s) up until the new pads have been fitted, and then check to see if topping up is still necessary – when the caliper pistons are pushed back to accommodate the extra thickness of the pads some fluid will be displaced back into the reservoir.

● If either fluid reservoir requires repeated topping-up there is a leak somewhere in the system, which must be investigated immediately.

● Check for signs of fluid leakage from the hydraulic hoses and/or brake system components – if found, rectify immediately (see Chapter 6).

● Check the operation of both brakes before taking the machine on the road; if there is evidence of air in the system (spongy feel to lever or pedal), it must be bled (see Chapter 6).

FRONT

1 Set the handlebars so the reservoir is level and check the fluid level through the window in the front or back (according to model) of the reservoir body – it must be above the LOWER level line (arrowed).

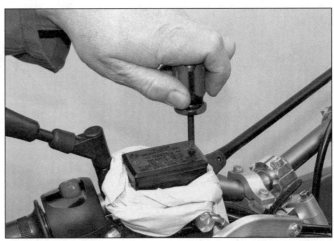

2 If the level is on or below the LOWER line, undo the two reservoir cover screws and remove the cover, diaphragm plate (where fitted), and diaphragm.

3 Top up with new clean DOT 4 hydraulic fluid, until the level is up to the marker (arrowed) on the inside of the reservoir. Do not overfill and take care to avoid spills (see **Warning**).

4 Wipe any moisture off the diaphragm with a tissue.

5 Ensure that the diaphragm is correctly seated before fitting the plate (where fitted) and cover. Secure the cover with its screws.

REAR

1 The rear brake fluid level is visible through the reservoir body – it must be between the UPPER and LOWER level lines (arrowed).

2 If the level is on or below the LOWER line unscrew the reservoir bolt (arrowed), then unscrew the cap and remove the diaphragm plate and diaphragm.

3 Top up with new clean DOT 4 hydraulic fluid, until the level is up to the UPPER line. Do not overfill and take care to avoid spills (see **Warning**).

4 Wipe any moisture off the diaphragm with a tissue.

5 Ensure that the diaphragm is correctly seated before fitting the plate and cap.

Legal and safety

Lighting and signalling:

● Take a minute to check that the headlight, tail light, brake light, licence plate light (XT-Z and MT-03 models), instrument lights and turn signals all work correctly.
● Check that the horn sounds when the button is pressed.
● A working speedometer, graduated in mph, is a statutory requirement in the UK.

Safety:

● Check that the throttle grip rotates smoothly when opened and snaps shut when released, in all steering positions. Also check for the correct amount of freeplay (see Chapter 1).
● Check that the brake lever and pedal, clutch lever and gearchange lever operate smoothly. Lubricate them at the specified intervals or when necessary (see Chapter 1).
● Check that the engine shuts off when the kill

switch is operated. Check the starter interlock circuit (see Chapter 1).
● Check that sidestand return springs hold the stand up securely when retracted.

Fuel:

● This may seem obvious, but check that you have enough fuel to complete your journey. If you notice signs of fuel leakage – rectify the cause immediately.
● Ensure you use the correct grade fuel – unleaded, minimum 95 RON

Tyres

Tyre tread depth:
● At the time of writing UK law requires that tread depth must be at least 1 mm over 3/4 of the tread breadth all the way around the tyre, with no bald patches. Many riders, however, consider 2 mm tread depth minimum to be a safer limit. Yamaha recommend a minimum of 1.6 mm. Refer to the tyre tread legislation in your country.
● Many tyres now incorporate wear indicators in the tread. Identify the location marking on the tyre sidewall to locate the indicator bar and replace the tyre if the tread has worn down to the bar.

The correct pressures:
● The tyres must be checked when **cold**, not immediately after riding. Note that incorrect tyre pressures will cause abnormal tread wear and unsafe handling. Low tyre pressures may cause the tyre to slip on the rim or come off.
● Use an accurate pressure gauge. Many forecourt gauges are wildly inaccurate. If you buy your own, spend as much as you can justify on a quality gauge.
● Proper air pressure will increase tyre life and provide maximum stability and ride comfort.

Tyre care:
● Check the tyres carefully for cuts, tears, embedded nails or other sharp objects, and excessive wear. Riding a motorcycle with excessively worn tyres is extremely hazardous, as traction and handling are directly affected.
● Check the condition of the tyre valve and ensure the dust cap is in place.
● Pick out any stones or nails which may have become embedded in the tyre tread. If left, they will eventually penetrate through the casing and cause a puncture.
● If tyre damage is apparent, or unexplained loss of pressure is experienced, seek the advice of a tyre fitting specialist without delay.

XT660-R

	Front	Rear
Rider only	29 psi (2.0 Bar)	29 psi (2.0 Bar)
Rider and pillion	29 psi (2.0 Bar)	33 psi (2.3 Bar)
Off-road	29 psi (2.0 Bar)	29 psi (2.0 Bar)

XT660-X

	Front	Rear
Rider only	30 psi (2.1 Bar)	30 psi (2.1 Bar)
Rider and pillion	32 psi (2.2 Bar)	33 psi (2.3 Bar)

XT660-Z Ténéré

	Front	Rear
Rider only	30 psi (2.1 Bar)	33 psi (2.3 Bar)
Rider and pillion	33 psi (2.3 Bar)	36 psi (2.5 Bar)
Off-road	29 psi (2.0 Bar)	29 psi (2.0 Bar)

MT-03

	Front	Rear
Rider only	30 psi (2.1 Bar)	33 psi (2.3 Bar)
Rider and pillion	33 psi (2.3 Bar)	36 psi (2.5 Bar)

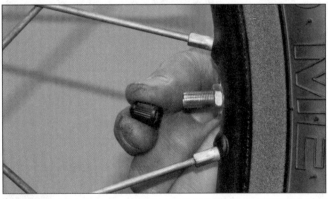

1 Remove the dust cap from the valve and do not forget to fit it after checking the pressure.

2 Check the tyre pressures when the tyres are cold.

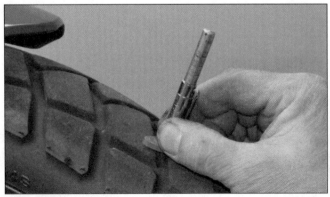

3 Measure tread depth at the centre of the tyre using a depth gauge.

4 Tyre tread wear indicator (A) and its location marking (B) on the edge or sidewall (according to manufacturer).

XT660R

The XT660R was launched in 2004. It has a single cylinder liquid-cooled engine. Drive to the single overhead camshaft which actuates the four valves via a pair of rocker arms is by chain from the left-hand end of the crankshaft. A balancer shaft driven directly off the crankshaft keeps things smooth. It has a dry-sump lubrication system with the oil stored in the frame. The clutch is a conventional wet multi-plate unit and the gearbox is 5-speed constant mesh. Drive to the rear wheel is by chain and sprockets. The engine has an electric starter motor.

The fuel injection system supplies pressurised fuel from a pump housed within the tank via a single injector and throttle body. An electronic ignition system ignites the mixture via a single spark plug. Twin exhausts incorporate catalytic converters. In 2007 an oxygen sensor was added.

The steel frame uses the engine as a stressed member. Front suspension is by oil-damped 41 mm telescopic forks. Rear suspension is by a single shock absorber via a three-way linkage and box-section steel swingarm that pivots through the frame.

Wheels are steel rimmed with wire spokes.

The front and rear brake systems are hydraulic disc brakes, with a twin piston sliding caliper at the front and a single piston sliding caliper at the rear.

XT660X

The XT660X supermotard style bike was also launched in 2004. It uses the same engine/transmission unit and engine management system as the XT660R described above.

The steel frame uses the engine as a stressed member. Front suspension is by oil-damped 43 mm telescopic forks. Rear suspension is by a single shock absorber via a three-way linkage and box-section steel swingarm that pivots through the frame. In 2007 the swingarm was changed to one of aluminium construction.

Wheels are steel rimmed with wire spokes.

The front and rear brake systems are hydraulic disc brakes, with a four opposed-piston caliper at the front and a single piston sliding caliper at the rear.

XT660Z Ténéré

The Adventure sports XT660Z was launched in 2009. It uses the same engine/transmission unit and engine management system as the XT660R and X models.

The steel frame uses the engine as a stressed member. Front suspension is by oil-damped telescopic forks. Rear suspension is by a single shock absorber via a three-way linkage and aluminium swingarm that pivots through the frame. A large capacity 22 litre fuel tank enables long ranges to be covered.

Wheels are steel rimmed with wire spokes. The front and rear brake systems are hydraulic disc brakes, with two twin piston sliding calipers at the front and a single piston sliding caliper at the rear.

MT-03

The MT-03 is a completely new design of street bike following in the steps of the larger-engine MT-01 it was launched in 2006. It uses the 660cc engine from the above models, but carries the engine oil in a separate fuel tank rather than in the frame.

The fuel injection system supplies pressurised fuel from a pump housed within the tank via a single injector and throttle body. An electronic ignition system ignites the mixture via a single spark plug. Twin exhausts incorporate a catalytic converter. In 2007 an oxygen sensor was added.

The steel frame uses the engine as a stressed member. Front suspension is by oil-damped telescopic forks. Rear suspension is by a single shock absorber and aluminium swingarm that pivots through the frame.

Wheels are 5-spoke alloys.

The front and rear brake systems are hydraulic disc brakes, with two twin piston sliding calipers at the front and a single piston sliding caliper at the rear.

Bike spec

Engine

Type	Four-stroke, single cylinder
Capacity	660 cc
Bore	100.0 mm
Stroke	84.0 mm
Compression ratio	10.0 to 1
Lubrication	Dry sump
Cooling system	Liquid-cooled
Clutch	Wet multi-plate
Transmission	Five-speed constant mesh
Final drive	Chain and sprockets
Camshaft	SOHC, chain-driven
Fuel system	Single throttle body with single injector
Exhaust system	Two-into-two
Ignition system	Transistorised

Chassis

XT660R

Frame type	Steel
Rake and Trail	27.25°, 107.0 mm
Fuel tank	
Capacity (including reserve)	15 litres
Reserve volume (when fuel warning light comes on)	approx. 5 litres
Front suspension	
Type	41 mm oil-damped telescopic forks
Wheel travel	225 mm
Rear suspension	
Type	Single shock absorber, rising rate linkage, box-section steel swingarm
Wheel travel	200 mm
Adjustment	Spring pre-load
Wheels	
Front	21 inch steel spoke
Rear	17 inch steel spoke
Tyres	
Front	90/90-21M/C 54S or 54T tubed
Rear	130/80-17M/C 65S or 65T tubed
Front brake	Single disc with twin piston sliding caliper
Rear brake	Single disc with single piston sliding caliper

XT660X

Frame type	Steel
Rake and Trail	26.00°, 94.0 mm
Fuel tank	
Capacity (including reserve)	15 litres
Reserve volume (when fuel warning light comes on)	approx. 5 litres
Front suspension	
Type	43 mm oil-damped telescopic forks
Wheel travel	200 mm
Rear suspension	
Type	Single shock absorber, rising rate linkage, box-section steel or aluminium swingarm (according to year)
Wheel travel	191 mm
Adjustment	Spring pre-load
Wheels	17 inch steel spoke
Tyres	
Front	120/70-R17M/C 58H or 120/70-ZR17M/C 58W tubed
Rear	160/60-R17M/C 69H or 160/60-ZR17M/C 69W tubed
Front brake	Single disc with four piston opposed caliper
Rear brake	Single disc with single piston sliding caliper

XT660Z Ténéré

Frame type	Steel
Rake and Trail	28.00°, 113.0 mm
Fuel tank	
Capacity (including reserve)	23 litres
Reserve volume (when fuel warning light comes on)	approx. 6.7 litres
Front suspension	
Type	Oil-damped telescopic forks
Wheel travel	210 mm
Adjustment	Spring pre-load
Rear suspension	
Type	Single shock absorber, rising rate linkage, aluminium swingarm
Wheel travel	200 mm
Adjustment	Spring pre-load
Wheels	
Front	21 inch steel spoke
Rear	17 inch steel spoke
Tyres	
Front	90/90-21M/C 54S or 54T tubed
Rear	130/80-17M/C 65S or 65T tubed
Front brake	Twin discs with twin piston sliding calipers
Rear brake	Single disc with single piston sliding caliper

Chassis (continued)

MT-03

Frame type	Steel
Rake and Trail.	26.00°, 97.0 mm

Fuel tank
Capacity (including reserve)	15 litres
Reserve volume (when fuel warning light comes on)	approx. 4.25 litres

Front suspension
Type	Oil-damped telescopic forks
Wheel travel	130 mm

Rear suspension
Type	Single shock absorber, aluminium swingarm
Wheel travel	120 mm
Adjustment	Spring pre-load
Wheels	17 inch 5 spoke alloys

Tyres
Front	120/70-ZR17M/C 58W or 120/70-R17M/C 58H, tubeless
Rear	160/60-ZR17M/C 69W or 160/60-R17M/C 69H, tubeless
Front brake.	Twin discs with twin piston sliding calipers
Rear brake	Single disc with single piston sliding caliper

Dimensions and weights

	XT660R	XT660X – 2004 to 2006	XT660X – 2007-on	XT660Z Ténéré	MT-03
Overall length	2240 mm	2150 mm	2175 mm	2246 mm	2070 mm
Overall width.	845 mm	865 mm	860 mm	864 mm	860 mm
Overall height	1230 mm	1210 mm	1170 mm	1477 mm	1115 mm
Wheelbase	1505 mm	1490 mm	1490 mm	1490 mm	1420 mm
Seat height	865 mm	870 mm	875 mm	896 mm	805 mm
Ground clearance.	210 mm	205 mm	205 mm	260 mm	200 mm
Weight (wet)	181 kg	186 kg	186 kg	208.5 kg	195 kg

Chapter 1
Routine maintenance and servicing

Contents

	Section		Section
Air filter	18	Fuel system	4
Air induction system check	5	General lubrication	14
Battery	17	Idle speed	3
Brake fluid level check	see *Pre-ride checks*	Nuts and bolts	15
Brake system	10	Spark plug	2
Clutch	7	Sidestand and starter safety circuit	16
Coolant level check	see *Pre-ride checks*	Steering head bearings	13
Cooling system	9	Suspension	12
Drive chain and sprockets	1	Throttle cables	6
Engine oil and filter	8	Tyre checks	see *Pre-ride checks*
Engine oil level check	see *Pre-ride checks*	Valve clearances	19
Engine wear assessment	see Chapter 2	Wheels, wheel bearings and tyres	11

Degrees of difficulty

Easy, suitable for novice with little experience	**Fairly easy,** suitable for beginner with some experience	**Fairly difficult,** suitable for competent DIY mechanic	**Difficult,** suitable for experienced DIY mechanic	**Very difficult,** suitable for expert DIY or professional

Specifications

Engine

Spark plug type	NGK CR7E
Spark plug electrode gap	0.7 to 0.8 mm
Engine idle speed	
XT-R and XT-X models	
2004 to 2006 models	1300 to 1500 rpm
2007-on models	1400 to 1500 rpm
XT-Z models	1400 to 1600 rpm
MT-03 models	
2006 model	1300 to 1500 rpm
2007-on models	1400 to 1600 rpm
Valve clearances (COLD engine)	
Intake valves	0.09 to 0.13 mm
Exhaust valves	0.16 to 0.20 mm

Chassis

Brake pad friction material minimum thickness	1.0 mm
Clutch cable freeplay	10 to 15 mm
Drive chain slack	
XT-R and XT-X models	40 to 55 mm
XT-Z models	50 to 60 mm
MT-03 models	40 to 50 mm
Drive chain stretch limit (see text)	240.5 mm
Throttle cable freeplay	3 to 5 mm
Rear brake pedal height (see text)	
XT-R and XT-X models	12 mm
XT-Z models	26.8 mm
MT-03 models	14.5 mm
Tyre pressures (cold)	see *Pre-ride checks*

Lubricants and fluids

Engine oil . . . . SAE 10W/30 or 10W/40 motorcycle oil, API grade SG or higher
Engine oil capacity
   XT models
      Oil change. . . . . 2.5 litres
      Oil and filter change . . . . 2.6 litres
      Following engine overhaul . . . . 2.9 litres
   MT-03 models
      Oil change. . . . . 3.0 litres
      Oil and filter change . . . . 3.1 litres
      Following engine overhaul . . . . 3.4 litres
Coolant type. . . . . 50% distilled water, 50% corrosion inhibited ethylene glycol anti-freeze
Coolant capacity
   XT-R and XT-X models
      Radiator and engine . . . . 1.0 litre
      Reservoir. . . . . 0.25 litre
   XT-Z models
      Radiator and engine . . . . 1.2 litre
      Reservoir. . . . . 0.5 litre
   MT-03 models
      Radiator and engine . . . . 1.0 litre
      Reservoir. . . . . 0.25 litre
Brake fluid . . . . DOT 4
Drive chain . . . . Chain lubricant suitable for O-ring chains, or engine oil
Steering head bearings . . . . Lithium based multi-purpose grease
Bearing seal lips . . . . Lithium based multi-purpose grease
Gearchange lever/rear brake pedal/footrest pivots . . . . Lithium based multi-purpose grease
Clutch lever pivot . . . . Lithium based multi-purpose grease
Sidestand pivot . . . . Lithium based multi-purpose grease
Throttle twistgrip. . . . . Lithium based multi-purpose grease
Front brake lever pivot and piston tip . . . . Silicone grease
Cables . . . . Cable lubricant

Torque settings

Camshaft sprocket cover bolts . . . . 10 Nm
Cooling system drain bolt . . . . 10 Nm
Engine oil drain plugs/bolt
   XT models
      Crankcase drain plug . . . . 30 Nm
      Oil tank drain plug. . . . . 18 Nm
      Oil filter housing drain bolt . . . . 10 Nm
      Oil filter housing cover bolts. . . . . 10 Nm
   MT-03 models
      Crankcase drain plug . . . . 30 Nm
      Oil tank drain plug. . . . . 30 Nm
      Oil filter housing drain bolt . . . . 10 Nm
      Oil filter housing cover bolts. . . . . 10 Nm
Engine oil pressure check bolt . . . . 5 Nm
Fork clamp bolts (top yoke) . . . . 23 Nm
Frame tensioning bar bolts (MT-03 models). . . . . 30 Nm
Rear axle nut
   XT models. . . . . 105 Nm
   MT-03 models. . . . . 150 Nm
Spark plug . . . . 13 Nm
Steering head bearing adjuster nut (using Yamaha tool)
   XT-R and XT-X models
      Initial setting . . . . 43 Nm
      Final setting . . . . 7 Nm
   XT-Z models
      Initial setting . . . . 45 Nm
      Final setting . . . . 7 Nm
   MT-03 models
      Initial setting . . . . 52 Nm
      Final setting . . . . 18 Nm
Steering stem nut
   XT models. . . . . 130 Nm
   MT-03 models. . . . . 110 Nm
Valve clearance adjuster cover bolts . . . . 10 Nm

Note: *The Pre-ride checks outlined in the owner's manual cover those items which should be inspected before every ride. Also perform the pre-ride inspection at every maintenance interval (in addition to the procedures listed). The intervals listed below are the intervals recommended by the manufacturer for the models covered in this manual.*

Pre-ride

☐ See *'Pre-ride checks'* at the beginning of this manual.

After the initial 600 miles (1000 km)

Note: *This check is usually performed by a Yamaha dealer after the first 600 miles (1000 km) from new. Thereafter, maintenance is carried out according to the following intervals of the schedule.*

Every 300 miles (500 km) – XT models

Every 500 miles (800 km) – MT-03 models

☐ Check, adjust, clean and lubricate the drive chain (Section 1)

Every 6000 miles (10,000 km)

☐ Check the spark plug (Section 2)
☐ Check and adjust the engine idle speed (Section 3)
☐ Check the fuel system and hoses (Section 4)
☐ Check the air induction system (Section 5)
☐ Check and adjust the throttle cables (Section 6)
☐ Check and adjust the clutch cable (Section 7)
☐ Change the engine oil (Section 8)
☐ Check the cooling system (Section 9)
☐ Check the brake system and brake light switch operation (Section 10)
☐ Check the brake pads for wear (Section 10)
☐ Check the condition of the wheels, wheel bearings and tyres (Section 11)
☐ Check the front and rear suspension (Section 12)
☐ Check and adjust the steering head bearings (Section 13)
☐ Lubricate the clutch and brake levers, brake pedal, sidestand pivot, and the throttle cables (Section 14)
☐ Check the tightness of all nuts, bolts and fasteners (Section 15)
☐ Check the sidestand and starter interlock circuit (Section 16)
☐ Check the battery (Section 17)

Every 12,000 miles (20,000 km) or 12 months

Carry out all the items under the 6000 mile (10,000 km) check, plus the following:

☐ Fit a new spark plug (Section 2)
☐ Fit a new air filter element (Section 18)
☐ Check and adjust the valve clearances (Section 19)
☐ Change the engine oil and fit a new filter (Section 8)
☐ Re-grease the steering head bearings (Section 13)

Every 30,000 miles (50,000 km)

☐ Re-grease the swingarm bearings (Section 12)

Every two years

☐ Change the brake fluid (Section 10)

Every three years

☐ Change the coolant (Section 9)

Every four years

☐ Fit new brake hoses (Section 10)

Non-scheduled maintenance

☐ Fit new fuel system hoses (Section 4)
☐ Change the front fork oil (Section 12)

XT-R right side

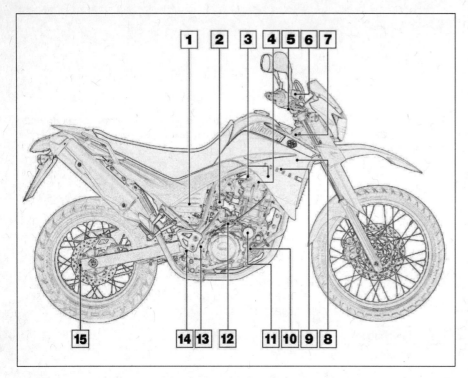

1 Air filter
2 Rear brake fluid reservoir
3 Valve clearance adjuster covers
4 Spark plug
5 Throttle cable upper adjuster
6 Front brake fluid reservoir
7 Engine oil filler/dipstick
8 Radiator pressure cap
9 Coolant reservoir and filler cap
10 Coolant drain bolt
11 Engine oil filter
12 Clutch cable lower adjuster
13 Rear brake light switch
14 Rear brake pedal height adjuster
15 Drive chain adjuster

XT-R left side

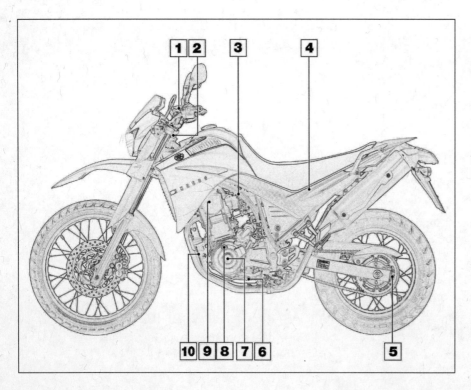

1 Clutch cable upper adjuster
2 Steering head bearing adjuster
3 Throttle cable lower adjuster
4 Battery
5 Drive chain adjuster
6 Engine crankcase oil drain bolt
7 Crankshaft end cap
8 Timing inspection cap
9 Camshaft sprocket cover
10 Engine oil tank drain bolt

XT-X right side

1   Air filter
2   Rear brake fluid reservoir
3   Valve clearance adjuster covers
4   Spark plug
5   Throttle cable upper adjuster
6   Front brake fluid reservoir
7   Engine oil filler/dipstick
8   Radiator pressure cap
9   Coolant reservoir and filler cap
10 Coolant drain bolt
11 Engine oil filter
12 Clutch cable lower adjuster
13 Rear brake light switch
14 Rear brake pedal height adjuster
15 Drive chain adjuster (aluminium
    swingarm type)

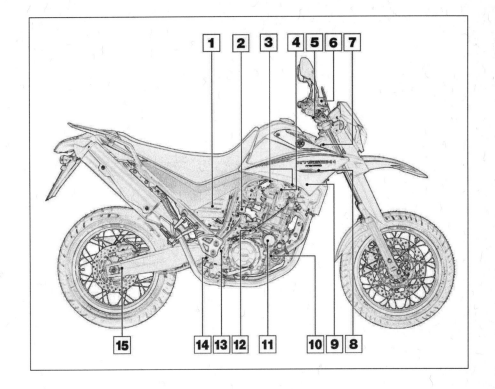

XT-X left side

1   Clutch cable upper adjuster
2   Steering head bearing adjuster
3   Throttle cable lower adjuster
4   Battery
5   Drive chain adjuster (aluminium
    swingarm type)
6   Engine crankcase oil drain bolt
7   Crankshaft end cap
8   Timing inspection cap
9   Camshaft sprocket cover
10 Engine oil tank drain bolt

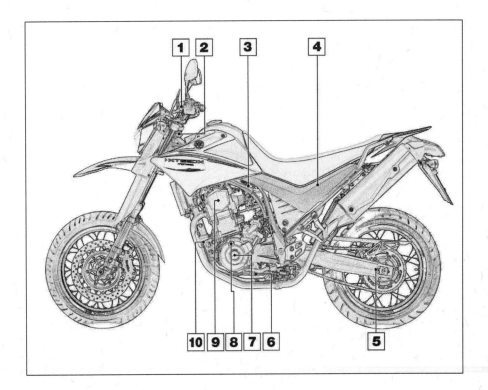

XT-Z right side

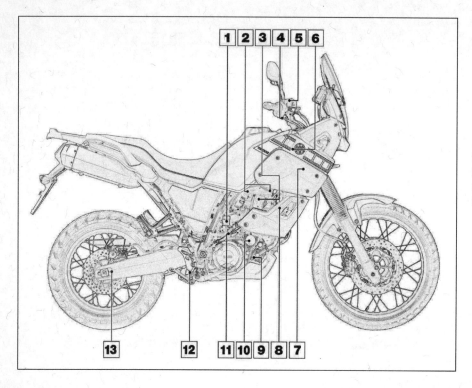

1   Rear brake fluid reservoir
2   Valve clearance adjuster covers
3   Spark plug
B   Throttle cable upper adjuster
5   Front brake fluid reservoir
6   Engine oil filler/dipstick
B   Radiator pressure cap
B   Coolant reservoir and filler cap
9   Coolant drain bolt
10 Engine oil filter
11 Clutch cable lower adjuster
12 Rear brake pedal height adjuster
13 Drive chain adjuster

XT-Z left side

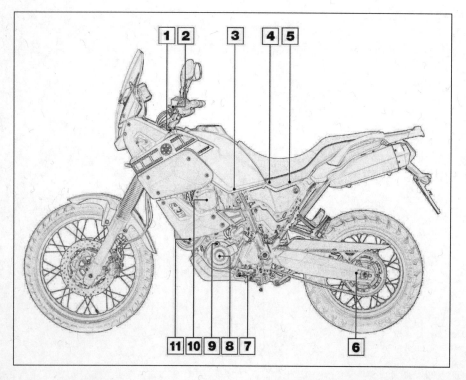

1   Steering head bearing adjuster
2   Clutch cable upper adjuster
3   Throttle cable lower adjuster
4   Air filter
5   Battery
6   Drive chain adjuster
7   Engine crankcase oil drain bolt
8   Crankshaft end cap
9   Timing inspection cap
10 Camshaft sprocket cover
11 Engine oil tank drain bolt

MT-03 right side

1 Rear brake fluid reservoir
2 Valve clearance adjuster covers
3 Spark plug
4 Front brake fluid reservoir
5 Throttle cable upper adjuster
6 Radiator pressure cap
7 Engine oil filler/dipstick
8 Coolant reservoir and filler cap
9 Coolant drain bolt
10 Engine oil filter
11 Clutch cable lower adjuster
12 Rear brake pedal height adjuster
13 Drive chain adjuster

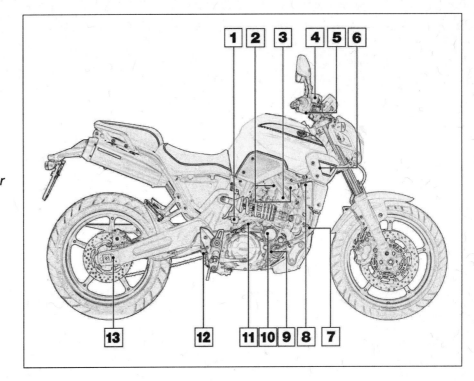

MT-03 left side

1 Clutch cable upper adjuster
2 Steering head bearing adjuster
3 Throttle cable lower adjuster
4 Air filter
5 Drive chain adjuster
6 Engine crankcase oil drain bolt
7 Crankshaft end cap
8 Timing inspection cap
9 Engine oil tank drain bolt
10 Camshaft sprocket cover
11 Battery

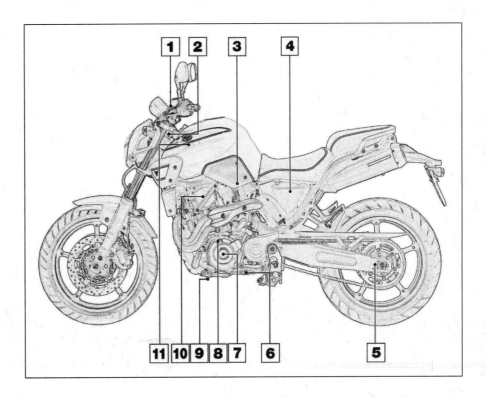

1 This Chapter is designed to help the home mechanic maintain his/her motorcycle for safety, economy, long life and peak performance.

2 Deciding where to start or plug into the routine maintenance schedule depends on several factors. If your motorcycle has been maintained according to the warranty standards and has just come out of warranty, start routine maintenance as it coincides with the next mileage or calendar interval. If you have owned the machine for some time but have never performed any maintenance on it, start at the nearest interval and include some additional procedures to ensure that nothing important is overlooked. If you have just had a major engine overhaul, then start the maintenance routine from the beginning. If you have a used machine and have no knowledge of its history or maintenance record, combine all the checks into one large service initially and then settle into the specified maintenance schedule.

3 Before beginning any maintenance or repair, clean the bike thoroughly, especially around the oil filter, valve cover, body panels, drive chain, suspension, wheels, etc. Cleaning will help ensure that dirt does not contaminate the engine and will allow you to detect wear and damage that could otherwise easily go unnoticed.

4 Certain maintenance information is sometimes printed on labels attached to the motorcycle. If the information on the labels differs from that included here, use the information on the label.

1 Drive chain and sprockets

Check chain slack

1 As the chain stretches with wear, adjustment is necessary. A neglected drive chain won't last long and will quickly damage the sprockets. Routine chain adjustment and lubrication isn't difficult and will ensure maximum chain and sprocket life.

2 To check the chain, place the bike on its sidestand. Make sure the transmission is in neutral. Make sure the ignition switch is OFF.

3 Measure the amount of up-and-down movement in the chain midway between the two sprockets, then compare your measurement to that listed in this Chapter's Specifications **(see illustration)**. Since the chain will rarely wear evenly roll the bike forward so that another section of chain can be checked; do this several times to check the

entire length of chain, and mark the tightest spot.

Caution: Riding the bike with excess slack in the chain could lead to damage.

4 In some cases where lubrication has been neglected, corrosion and dirt may cause the links to bind and kink, which effectively shortens the chain's length and makes it tight **(see illustration)**. Thoroughly clean and work free any such links, then highlight them with a marker pen or paint. Take the bike for a ride.

5 After the bike has been ridden, repeat the measurement for slack in the highlighted area. If the chain has kinked again and is still tight, replace it with a new one (see Chapter 6). A rusty, kinked or worn chain will damage the sprockets and can damage transmission bearings. If in any doubt as to the condition of a chain, it is far better to install a new one than risk damage to other components and possibly yourself.

6 Check the entire length of the chain for damaged rollers, loose links and pins, and missing O-rings, and replace it with a new one if necessary. **Note:** *Never fit a new chain onto old sprockets, and never use the old chain if you fit new sprockets – replace the chain and sprockets as a set.*

7 Inspect the drive chain slider on the front of the swingarm for excessive wear and damage and replace it with a new one if necessary.

Adjust chain slack

8 Set the tightest spot of the chain at the centre of its bottom run.

9 On all XT-R models and 2004 to 2006 XT-X models slacken the rear axle nut **(see illustration)**. Slacken the locknut on the adjuster on each side of the swingarm **(see illustration)**. To reduce chain slack turn the adjuster on each side evenly clockwise. To increase chain slack turn the adjuster on each side of the swingarm anti-clockwise then push the wheel forwards in the swingarm until it butts. Adjust the chain as required until the amount of freeplay specified is obtained at

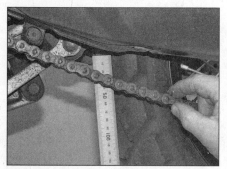

1.3 Push up on the chain and measure the slack

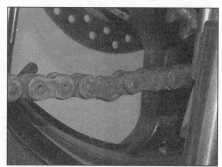

1.4 Neglect has caused the links in this chain to kink

1.9a Slacken the axle nut (arrowed)

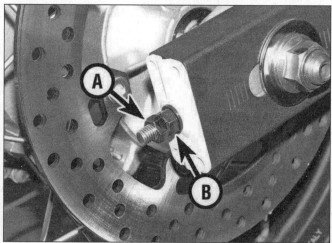

1.9b Slacken the locknut (A) on each side, then turn each adjuster nut (B) as required

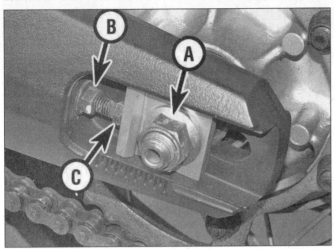

1.10 Slacken the axle nut (A), then slacken the locknut (B) on each side and turn each adjuster bolt (C) by an equal amount

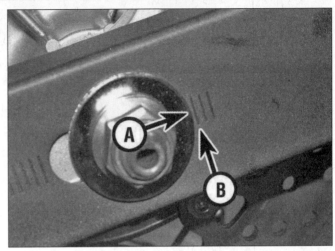

1.11a Chain adjustment marker edge (A) and index lines (B) – XT-R and 2004 to 2006 XT-X models

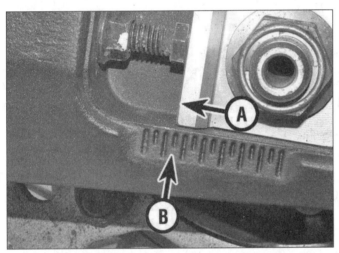

1.11b Chain adjustment marker edge (A) and index lines (B) – 2007-on XT-X and all XT-Z and MT-03 models

1.13 Tighten the axle nut to the specified torque

the centre of the bottom run of the chain (see Step 3). Now refer to Step 11 and check the wheel alignment.

10 On 2007-on XT-X models and all XT-Z and MT-03 models slacken the rear axle nut **(see illustration)**. Slacken the locknut on the adjuster on each side of the swingarm. To reduce chain slack turn the adjuster on each side evenly anti-clockwise. To increase chain slack turn the adjuster on each side of the swingarm clockwise then push the wheel forwards in the swingarm until it butts. Adjust the chain as required until the amount of freeplay specified at the beginning of the Chapter is obtained at the centre of the bottom run of the chain (see Step 3). Now refer to Step 11 and check the wheel alignment.

11 Following adjustment, check that each chain adjustment marker is in the same position relative to the index lines on the swingarm **(see illustrations)**. It is important the alignment is the same on each side otherwise

the rear wheel will be out of alignment with the front. Also make sure that the wheel is pushed fully forward so it butts. If there is a difference in the positions, adjust one of them so that its position is exactly the same as the other. Check the chain freeplay again and readjust if necessary.

12 From time to time check the amount of chain stretch (Steps 16 to 19).

13 When adjustment is complete, counter-hold the adjusters to prevent them turning and tighten the locknuts **(see illustration 1.9b or 1.10)**. Tighten the axle nut to the torque setting specified at the beginning of the Chapter for your model **(see illustration)**. Recheck the adjustment as above, then make sure the wheel turns freely.

Clean and lubricate the chain

14 If required, wash the chain using a dedicated aerosol cleaner, or in paraffin (kerosene) or a suitable non-flammable or high flash-point solvent that will not damage the

O-rings, using a soft brush to work any dirt out if necessary – specially shaped chain cleaning brushes are available from good suppliers **(see illustration)**. Wipe the cleaner off the chain and allow it to dry. If the chain is excessively dirty remove it from the machine and allow it to soak in the paraffin or solvent for a maximum of ten minutes (see Chapter 6).

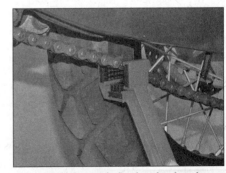

1.14 Using a chain cleaning brush

1.15 Apply the lubricant to the overlapping sections of the sideplates

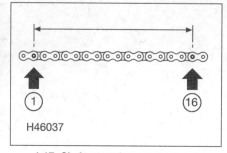

H46037

1.17 Chain stretch measurement

Measure a 15-link section – between the 1st and 16th pins

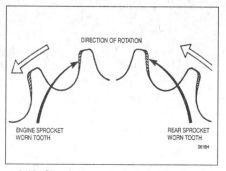

DIRECTION OF ROTATION

ENGINE SPROCKET WORN TOOTH

REAR SPROCKET WORN TOOTH

0618H

1.19 Check the sprockets in the areas indicated

Caution: Don't use petrol (gasoline), an unsuitable solvent (such as benzene) or other cleaning fluids which might damage the internal sealing properties of the chain. Don't use high-pressure water to clean the chain. The entire process shouldn't take longer than ten minutes, otherwise the O-rings could be damaged.

15 The best time to lubricate the chain is after the motorcycle has been ridden. When the chain is warm, the lubricant will penetrate the joints between the side plates better than when cold. **Note:** *Yamaha specifies engine oil or an aerosol chain lube that it is suitable for O-ring (sealed) chains; do not use any other*

Apply the lubricant to the top of the lower chain run, so centrifugal force will work the oil into the chain when the bike is moving. After applying lubricant, let it soak in a few minutes before wiping off any excess.

⚠️ *Warning: Take care not to get any lubricant on the rear tyre or brake disc. If any of the lubricant inadvertently contacts them, clean it off thoroughly using a suitable solvent or dedicated brake cleaner before riding the machine.*

chain lubricants – the solvents could damage the chain's sealing rings. Apply the lubricant to the area where the sideplates overlap – not the middle of the rollers **(see illustration)**.

Check drive chain stretch

16 Measure the amount of chain stretch as follows:

17 Adjust the chain as described in Steps 9 to 11 until all slack is taken up, but not so much that the chain is taut. Measure a 15 link section along the bottom run of the chain as shown **(see illustration)**. Rotate the rear wheel so that several sections of the chain can be measured, then calculate the average and compare it to the stretch limit specified at the beginning of the Chapter. If the chain stretch measurement exceeds the service limit it must be replaced with a new one (see Chapter 6).

18 If the chain is good, reset the adjusters so that there is the correct amount of freeplay (see Steps 9 to 13).

Caution: Never fit a new chain onto old sprockets, and never use the old chain if you fit new sprockets – replace the chain and sprockets as a set.

Check sprocket wear

19 Remove the front sprocket cover (see Chapter 6). Check the teeth on the front

sprocket and the rear sprocket for wear **(see illustration)**. If the sprocket teeth are worn excessively, replace the chain and both sprockets with a new set. Check that the sprocket fasteners are tight (refer to Chapter 6 Specifications for torque settings).

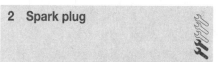

2   Spark plug

Check and adjustment

1 Make sure your spark plug socket is the correct size (16 mm hex) before attempting to remove the plug – a suitable one is supplied in the motorcycle's tool kit, which on XT-R and X models is under the seat, on XT-Z models is in the recess in the back of the fuel tank, and on MT-03 models is in the underside of the seat. Refer to Chapter 7 to remove the seat.

2 Pull the cap off the spark plug **(see illustration)**.

3 Clean the area around the base of the spark plug to prevent any dirt falling into the engine.

4 Using either the plug removing tool supplied in the bike's toolkit or a deep spark plug socket, unscrew and remove the plug from the cylinder head **(see illustration)**.

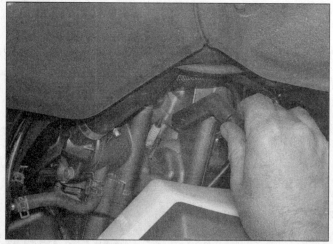

2.2 Pull the cap off the spark plug

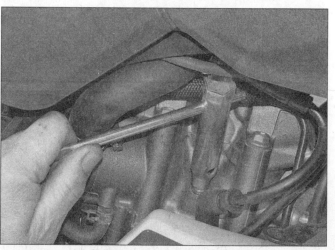

2.4 Unscrew and remove the plug

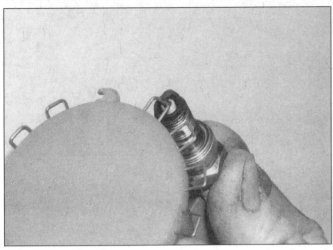
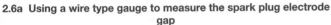

2.6a Using a wire type gauge to measure the spark plug electrode gap

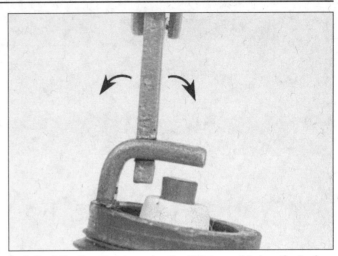

2.6b Adjusting the gap using the fitting provided on the tool

5 Check the condition of the electrodes, referring to the spark plug reading chart at the end of this manual if signs of contamination are evident.
6 Clean the plug with a wire brush. Examine the tips of the electrodes; if a tip has rounded off, the plug is worn. Measure the gap between the two electrodes using a feeler gauge or a wire type gauge **(see illustration)**. The gap should be as given in the Specifications at the beginning of this chapter; if necessary adjust the gap by bending the side electrode **(see illustration)**.
7 Check the threads, the washer and the ceramic insulator body for cracks and other damage.
8 If the plug is worn or damaged, or if any deposits cannot be cleaned off, replace the plug with a new one. If in any doubt as to the condition of the plug replace it with a new one – the expense is minimal.
9 Thread the plug into the cylinder head until the washer seats **(see illustration)**. Since the

cylinder head is made of aluminium, which is soft and easily damaged, thread the plug as far as possible by hand. Once the plug is finger-tight, the job can be finished with a spanner on the tool supplied or a socket drive **(see illustration 2.4)**. If a new plug is being installed, tighten it by 1/2 a turn after the washer has seated. If the old plug is being reused, tighten it by 1/4 turn after the washer has seated, or if a torque wrench can be applied, tighten the spark plug to the torque setting specified at the beginning of the Chapter.
10 Fit the spark plug cap, making sure it locates correctly onto the plug **(see illustration 2.2)**.

HAYNES HINT *Stripped plug threads in the cylinder head can be repaired with a Heli-Coil insert – see 'Tools and Workshop Tips' in the Reference section.*

Renewal

11 At the prescribed interval, whatever the condition of the existing spark plug, remove the plug as described above and install a new one.

3 Idle speed

1 The idle speed should be checked at the specified interval. It should also be checked and if necessary adjusted after the valve clearances have been adjusted, and after fitting a new air filter.
2 The engine should be at normal operating temperature, which is usually reached after 10 to 15 minutes of stop-and-go riding. Make sure the transmission is in neutral.
3 The idle speed adjuster is a screw located on the left-hand side of the throttle body **(see illustration)**. With the engine running, turn

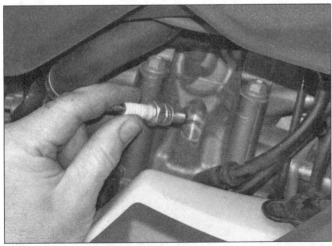

2.9 Thread the plug into the head by hand to prevent cross-threading

3.3 Idle speed adjuster screw (arrowed)

5.2 Air induction system control valve (arrowed)

6.4 Throttle cable freeplay is measured in terms of twistgrip rotation

the screw until the engine idles at the speed specified at the beginning of the Chapter. Turn the screw clockwise to increase idle speed, and anti-clockwise to decrease it.

4 Snap the throttle open and shut a few times, then recheck the idle speed. If necessary, repeat the adjustment procedure. On completion check and adjust throttle cable freeplay (Section 6).

5 If a smooth, steady idle can't be achieved, and if not already done, check the spark plug, air filter element and valve clearances (Sections 2, 18 and 19).

6 If the idle speed cannot be set, or if there is a problem with cold starting or fast running when warm, it is possible there is a fault with the fast idle unit – the unit incorporates a plunger that reacts to the temperature of coolant that circulates around it. The unit is part of the throttle body and is not available separately – see Chapter 4, section 11.

4 Fuel system

Warning: Petrol (gasoline) is extremely flammable, so take extra precautions when you work on any part of the fuel system. Don't smoke or allow open flames or bare light bulbs near the work area, and don't work in a garage where a natural gas-type appliance is present. If you spill any fuel on your skin, rinse it off immediately with soap and water. When you perform any kind of work on the fuel system, wear safety glasses and have a fire extinguisher suitable for a Class B type fire (flammable liquids) on hand.

1 Remove the fuel tank (see Chapter 4).

2 Check all the hoses to/from the fuel tank, the throttle body, the air filter housing and crankcase breather system, and the air induction system (see Section 5), for signs of cracks, leaks, deterioration or damage. In particular check that there are no leaks from the fuel supply hose or hose unions. Make

sure each hose is secure on its union at each end and retained by a clamp. Replace any hose that is cracked or deteriorated with a new one – refer to Chapter 4 if required.

3 Check the fuel tank for signs of fuel leakage. If the joint between the fuel pump and the tank is leaking, make sure the bolts are tight, to the torque setting specified if you have the correct tools (see Chapter 4); if the leak persists remove the pump and fit a new seal (see Chapter 4).

4 Inspect the fuel rail and injector for signs of leakage. Remove the injector and fit new seals if necessary (see Chapter 4).

5 Air induction system

1 To reduce the amount of unburned hydrocarbons released in the exhaust gases, an air induction system is fitted. Under normal running conditions the system allows filtered air to be drawn into the exhaust where it mixes with the exhaust gases, causing any unburned particles of the fuel in the mixture to be burnt. This process changes a considerable amount of hydrocarbons and carbon monoxide into relatively harmless carbon dioxide and water.

2 The control valve, mounted under the fuel tank, is actuated by electronically by the ECU **(see illustration)**. Under normal operating conditions, the valve is open allowing air from the filter housing to be drawn through via a reed valve and into the air passage through the cylinder head to the exhaust port. The reed valve prevents the flow of exhaust gases back up the cylinder head passage and into the air filter housing.

3 The system is not adjustable and requires little maintenance. On XT-R and XT-X models remove the right-hand fuel tank cover (see Chapter 7). On XT-Z and MT-03 models remove the fuel tank (see Chapter 4). Check that the hoses are not kinked or pinched, are in good condition and are securely connected at each

end. Replace any hoses that are cracked, split or generally deteriorated with new ones.

4 Refer to Chapter 4 for further information on the system and for checks if it is believed to be faulty.

6 Throttle cables

1 With the engine off, make sure the throttle grip rotates smoothly and freely from fully closed to fully open with the front wheel turned at various angles, and returns without resistance from fully open to fully closed when released.

2 If the throttle sticks, this is probably due to a cable fault. Remove the cables (see Chapter 4) and lubricate them (see Section 14). Check that the inner cables slide freely and easily in the outer cables. If not, replace the cables with new ones.

3 With the cables removed, make sure the throttle twistgrip rotates freely on the handlebar – dirt combined with a lack of lubrication can cause the action to be stiff. If necessary remove the handlebar end-weight (see Chapter 5), then slide the twistgrip off the handlebar. Clean any old grease from the bar and the inside of the tube. Smear lithium-based grease onto the bar, then refit the twistgrip. When re-fitting the end-weight make sure there is a 1 to 3 mm gap between the grip and the weight. Install the cables, making sure they are correctly routed (see Chapter 4). If this fails to improve the operation of the throttle, the cables must be replaced with new ones. Note that in very rare cases the fault could lie in the throttle body (see Chapter 4).

4 With the throttle operating smoothly, and after the idle speed has been checked and if necessary adjusted (Section 3), check for a small amount of freeplay in the cable, measured in terms of the amount of twistgrip rotation before the throttle opens, and compare the amount to that listed in this Chapter's Specifications **(see illustration)**. If

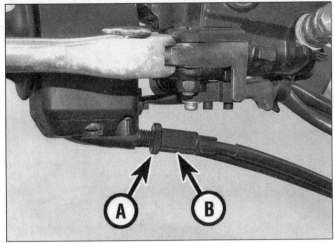

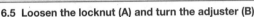

6.5 Loosen the locknut (A) and turn the adjuster (B)

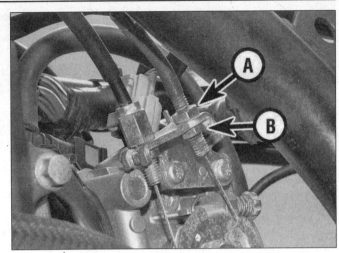

6.7 Loosen the locknut (A) and reset the adjuster nut (B)

it's incorrect, adjust the cables to correct it as follows.

5 Initially adjust freeplay using the adjuster in the throttle opening cable where it leaves the throttle pulley housing on the handlebar. Loosen the locknut and turn the adjuster in or out as required until the specified amount of freeplay is obtained (see this Chapter's Specifications), then retighten the locknut **(see illustration)**.

6 If the adjuster has reached its limit of adjustment, reset it to its start point by turning it fully in, so that freeplay is at a maximum. The adjuster at the throttle body end is on the left-hand side and is fairly accessible on XT-R and XT-X models, but on XT-Z and MT-03 remove the fuel tank for best access (see Chapter 4).

7 The opening cable is the rear cable in the bracket. Slacken the locknut until the adjuster nut is free, then thread the adjuster nut up or down as required, until the specified amount of freeplay is obtained, then locate the adjuster nut so it is captive under the bracket and tighten the locknut **(see illustration)**.

Subsequent adjustments can be made at the throttle end when required. If the cable cannot be adjusted as specified, replace it with a new one (see Chapter 4). Check that the throttle twistgrip operates smoothly and snaps shut quickly when released.

⚠️ **Warning: Turn the handlebars all the way through their travel with the engine idling. Idle speed should not change. If it does, the cables may be routed incorrectly. Correct this condition before riding the bike.**

7 Clutch

1 Check that the clutch lever operates smoothly and without undue resistance.
2 If the clutch lever operation is heavy or stiff, remove the cable (see Chapter 2) and lubricate it (see Section 14). Check that the inner cable slides freely and easily in the outer cable. If the cable is still stiff, replace it with a

new one. Install the lubricated or new cable (see Chapter 2).

3 With the cable operating smoothly, check that it is correctly adjusted. Periodic adjustment is necessary to compensate for wear in the clutch plates and stretch of the cable. Check that the amount of freeplay at the clutch lever end is within the range specified at the beginning of the Chapter **(see illustration)**.

4 If adjustment is required, pull the rubber boot off the adjuster in the lever bracket. Loosen the adjuster lockring, then turn the adjuster in or out until the required amount of freeplay is obtained **(see illustration)**. To reduce freeplay, thread the adjuster out of the bracket. To increase freeplay, thread the adjuster into the lever bracket.

5 Make sure that the slot in the adjuster and the lockring, are not aligned with the slot in the lever bracket – these slots are to allow removal of the cable, and if they are all aligned while the bike is in use the cable could jump out. Also make sure the adjuster is not threaded too far

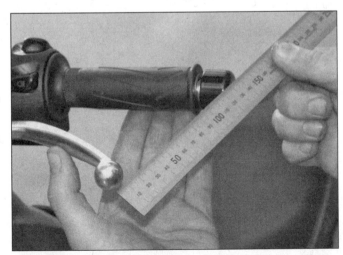

7.3 Measure the amount of freeplay at the clutch lever end as shown

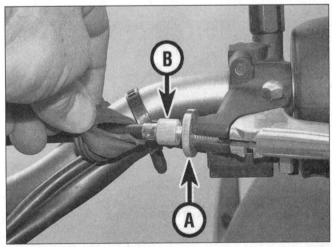

7.4 Slacken the lockring (A) and turn the adjuster (B) in or out as required

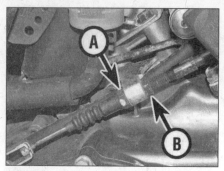

7.6 Slacken the locknut (A) and turn the adjuster (B) in or out as required

8.2a Remove the seat and retrieve the chute . . .

out of the bracket so that it is only held by a few threads – this will leave it unstable and the threads could be damaged. Tighten the lockring on completion, then refit the rubber boot.

6 If all the adjustment has been taken up at the lever, thread the adjuster all the way into the bracket to give the maximum amount of freeplay, then back it out about one turn (exactly how much will depend on the position

of the slots) – this resets the adjuster to its start point. Now set the correct amount of freeplay using the adjuster on the right-hand side of the engine **(see illustration)**. Slacken the locknut, then turn the adjuster nut as required until the freeplay at the lever end is as specified. Tighten the locknut on completion. Subsequent adjustments can now be made using the lever adjuster only.

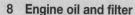

8 Engine oil and filter

> **Warning: Be careful when draining the oil, as the exhaust pipe, the engine, and the oil itself can cause severe burns.**

Oil change

1 Consistent routine oil changes are the single most important maintenance procedure you can perform. The oil not only lubricates the internal parts of the engine, transmission and clutch, but it also acts as a coolant, a cleaner, a sealant, and a protector. Because of these demands, the oil takes a terrific amount

> **HAYNES HINT** *Saving a little money on the difference in cost between a good oil and a cheap oil won't pay off if the engine is damaged.*

8.2b . . . and locate it as shown to prevent oil getting on the exhaust

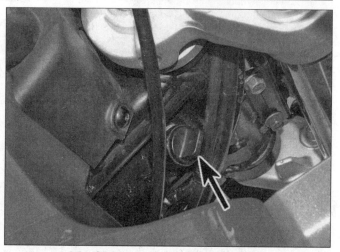

8.3a Oil filler cap (arrowed) – XT models

8.3b Oil filler cap (arrowed) – MT-03 models

8.4a Unscrew the crankcase drain plug (arrowed) . . .

of abuse and should be replaced as specified with new oil of the recommended type and quantity (see Specifications).

2 Before changing the oil, warm up the engine so the oil will drain easily. Place the bike on its sidestand on level ground. On XT-Z models remove the sump guard (see Chapter 7). Prepare a clean drain tray for catching the oil – note that the oil must be drained from the crankcase, the oil tank and from the filter housing, so unless you have a large tray you will need more than one. XT-R and XT-X models come with a drain chute (located under the seat next to the toolkit) that fits under the drain bolt and prevents oil coating the exhaust **(see illustrations)**.

3 Position the drain tray(s) below the engine. Unscrew the oil filler cap to vent the crankcase and to act as a reminder that there is no oil in the engine **(see illustrations)**. Check the condition of the O-ring and replace it with a new one if it is damaged or worn.

4 Unscrew the crankcase drain plug and allow the oil to flow into the drain tray **(see illustrations)**. Unscrew the oil tank drain plug and allow the oil to flow into the drain tray(s)

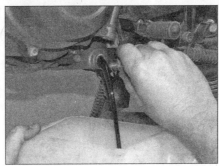

8.4b . . . and allow the oil to completely drain

8.4c Oil tank drain plug (arrowed) – XT models

(see illustrations). Unscrew the oil filter housing drain bolt and allow the oil to flow into the drain tray(s) **(see illustration)**. Check the condition of the sealing washers on the drain plugs and replace them with new ones if they damaged or worn – it is highly advisable to use new ones whatever the condition of the old ones. You may have to cut the old ones off, depending on the type fitted.

5 If you are fitting a new oil filter do so now (see Steps 13 to 16).

6 When the oil has completely drained, fit the plugs into the crankcase and oil tank, preferably using new sealing washers, and tighten them to the torque settings specified at the beginning of the Chapter **(see illustrations)**. If you have not fitted a new filter fit the filter housing drain bolt and tighten to the specified torque.

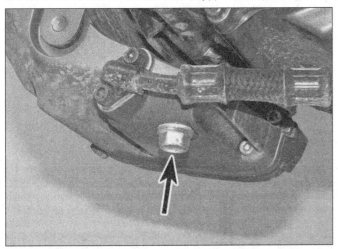

8.4d Oil tank drain plug (arrowed) – MT-03 models

8.4e Filter housing drain bolt (arrowed)

8.6a Fit the drain plugs with their sealing washers . . .

8.6b . . . preferably using new ones

8.9a Slacken the check bolt (arrowed) . . .

8.9b . . . and make sure oil seeps past the threads

7 The new engine oil must be added in two stages. First add 1.9 litres of oil on XT models, and 2 litres on MT-03 models. Fit the filler cap (see illustration 8.3a or b).

8 Start the engine and blip the throttle five or six times so the engine runs fast, but not so it exceeds the red line. Shut it off, wait a few minutes, then add the rest of the oil – on XT models add 0.6 litre if the filter hasn't been changed, 0.7 litre with a new filter, or 1.0 litre following a complete engine overhaul; on MT-03 models add 1.0 litre if the filter hasn't been changed, 1.1 litre with a new filter, or 1.4 litres following a complete engine overhaul.

9 Because an engine oil pressure switch and warning light are not fitted, it is advisable to check that oil is flowing as it should – to do this slacken the pressure check bolt on the top of the filter housing (see illustration). Start the engine and let it idle – oil should start to weep from the bleed hole fairly quickly (see illustration). If no oil appears after one minute stop the engine immediately, then check the filter, oil passages and oil pump (see Chapter 2).

If oil appears as it should, tighten the bolt to the specified torque setting, continue to warm the engine up for several minutes, then shut it off and check the level on the dipstick (see Pre-ride checks).

10 Check around the drain plugs and bolt for leaks. If a leak is evident and a new washer was not used, you will have to drain the oil again and fit a new washer. If a new washer was used then make sure the plug is tightened to the correct torque setting using a torque wrench. If one is not available tighten the plug a little more but take great care not to overtighten it and strip the threads – if in doubt ask a dealer to check using a torque wrench. On XT-Z models install the sump guard (see Chapter 7).

11 The old oil drained from the engine cannot be re-used and should be disposed of properly. Check with your local refuse disposal company, disposal facility or environmental agency to see whether they will accept the used oil for recycling. Don't pour used oil into drains or onto the ground.

> **HAYNES HiNT**
> Check the old oil carefully – if it is very metallic coloured, then the engine is experiencing wear from break-in (new engine) or from insufficient lubrication. If there are flakes or chips of metal in the oil, then something is drastically wrong internally and the engine will have to be disassembled for inspection and repair. If there are pieces of fibre-like material in the oil, the clutch is experiencing excessive wear and should be checked.

Oil and filter change

12 The filter must be changed at every second oil change. Drain the oil as described in Steps 2 to 4.

13 Unscrew the remaining two filter housing cover bolts and remove the cover (see illustration). Withdraw the filter (see illustration). Clean the cover and housing using a clean lint-free cloth.

8.13a Unscrew the bolts (arrowed) . . .

8.13b . . . and remove the filter

8.15a Fit the cover O-ring . . .

8.15b . . . and the drain bolt O-ring

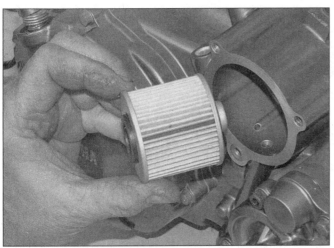

8.16a Fit the new filter . . .

8.16b . . . then fit the cover

14 Remove the O-rings from the cover and drain bolt hole and replace them with new ones if they are damaged, deformed or deteriorated **(see illustrations 8.15a and b)**. Note that it is advisable to fit new ones whatever the apparent condition of the existing ones.
15 Fit the cover O-ring into its grove and the drain bolt O-ring into its recess, preferably using new ones, and making sure they are correctly seated **(see illustrations)**.
16 Fit the new filter into the housing with the rubber end facing out **(see illustration)**. Fit the cover and tighten the bolts, including the

drain bolt, to the torque setting specified at the beginning of the chapter **(see illustration)**.
17 Refill the engine with oil (see Steps 6 to 10).

9 Cooling system

Check

⚠️ *Warning: The engine must be cool before beginning this procedure.*

1 Check the coolant level in the reservoir (see *Pre-ride checks*).
2 Check the entire cooling system for evidence of leaks – remove the fuel tank covers or other panels as required according to model (see Chapter 7). Examine each rubber coolant hose along its entire length. Look for cracks, abrasions and other damage. Squeeze each

hose at various points to see whether they are dried out or hard **(see illustration)**. They should feel firm, yet pliable, and return to their original shape when released. If necessary, replace them with new ones (see Chapter 3).
3 Check for evidence of leaks at each cooling system hose connection, and around the water pump and the thermostat housing, and the

9.2 Check the hoses for cracks and hardening

9.3a Check around the pump (arrowed) . . .

9.3b . . . the thermostat housing (arrowed) . . .

inlet union to the engine (see illustrations). If the pump cover, thermostat housing cover or inlet union is leaking, check that the bolts are tight. If they are, remove the cover or union as required and replace the gasket or O-ring with a new one (see Chapter 3).

4 To prevent leakage of coolant from the cooling system to the lubrication system and vice versa, two seals are fitted on the pump shaft. The coolant seal on the water pump side is of the mechanical type which bears on the rear face of the impeller. The oil seal, which is mounted behind the mechanical seal is of the normal feathered lip type. On the underside of the pump housing there is a drain hole. If either seal fails, the drain allows the coolant or oil to escape. If on inspection the drain shows signs of leakage remove the pump and replace the seals and bearing with new ones (see Chapter 3).

5 Check the radiator on the front of the engine for leaks and other damage (see illustration). Leaks in the radiator leave tell-tale scale

deposits or coolant stains on the outside of the core below the leak. If leaks are noted, remove the radiator (see Chapter 3) and have it repaired or replace it with a new one – do not use a liquid leak stopping compound to try to repair leaks.

6 Check the radiator grille and fins for mud, dirt and insects, which may impede the flow of air through it. Clean the grille if necessary. If the fins are dirty, remove the radiator (see Chapter 3) and clean it using water or low pressure compressed air directed through the fins from the inner side of the radiator. If the fins are bent or distorted, straighten them carefully with a screwdriver. If the air flow is restricted by bent or damaged fins over more than 20% of the radiator's surface area, replace the radiator with a new one.

⚠️ Warning: Do not remove the pressure cap when the engine is hot. It is good practice to cover the cap with a heavy cloth and turn the cap slowly anti-clockwise. If you hear a

hissing sound (indicating that there is still pressure in the system), wait until it stops, then continue turning the cap until it can be removed.

7 On XT-R and XT-X models remove the retainer from the radiator pressure cap (see illustration). Remove the pressure cap from the radiator filler neck by turning it anti-clockwise until it reaches the stop. Now press down on the cap and continue turning it until it can be removed (see illustration).

8 Check the condition of the coolant in the system. If it is rust-coloured or if accumulations of scale are visible, drain, flush and refill the system with new coolant (see below). Check the antifreeze content of the coolant with an antifreeze hydrometer. The system must have the correct coolant mixture (see Specifications) – if the coolant is too weak (too little anti-freeze) there will not be adequate protection against freezing and corrosion, and if it is too strong the ability to cool the engine is reduced. If the hydrometer

9.3c . . . and the inlet union on the front of the engine

9.5 Check around the radiator for leaks and damage

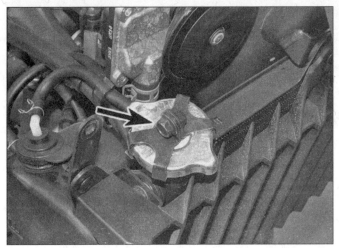

9.7a Unscrew the bolt (arrowed) and remove the retainer

9.7b Remove the pressure cap as described

indicates an incorrect mixture, drain, flush and refill the system (see below).

9 Check the cap seal for cracks and other damage. If in doubt about the pressure cap's condition, have it tested by a Yamaha dealer or fit a new one.

10 Fit the cap by turning it clockwise until it reaches the first stop then push down on it and continue turning until it can turn no further. On XT-R and XT-X models fit the retainer onto the pressure cap **(see illustration 9.7a)**. Start the engine and let it reach normal operating temperature, then check for leaks again. As the coolant temperature increases, the electric fan mounted on the back of the radiator should come on automatically and the temperature should begin to drop. If it does not, refer to Chapter 3 and check the fan and fan circuit.

11 If the coolant level is consistently low, and no evidence of leaks can be found, have the entire system pressure checked by a Yamaha dealer.

Change the coolant

⚠️ *Warning: Allow the engine to cool completely before performing this maintenance operation. Also, don't allow anti-freeze to come into contact with your skin or the painted surfaces of the motorcycle. Rinse off spills immediately with plenty of water. Anti-freeze is highly toxic if ingested. Never leave anti-freeze lying around in an open container or in puddles on the floor; children and pets are attracted by its sweet smell and may drink it. Check with local authorities (councils) about disposing of anti-freeze. Many communities have collection centres which will see that anti-freeze is disposed of safely. Anti-freeze is also combustible, so don't store it near open flames.*

Draining

12 On XT-R and XT-X models remove the fuel tank right-hand cover and on MT-03 models remove the fuel tank right-hand trim panel

(see Chapter 7). On XT-Z models remove the sump guard (see Chapter 7) and the fuel tank (see Chapter 4).

13 On XT-R and XT-X models remove the retainer from the radiator pressure cap **(see illustration 9.7a)**. Remove the pressure cap from the top of the radiator by covering it with a heavy cloth and turning it anti-clockwise until it reaches a stop **(see illustration 9.7b)**. If you hear a hissing sound (indicating there is still pressure in the system), wait until it stops. Now press down on the cap and continue turning the cap until it can be removed. Also remove the coolant reservoir cap.

14 Position a suitable container beneath the water pump on the right-hand side of the engine. Unscrew the drain bolt from the pump and allow the coolant to completely drain **(see illustrations)**. Check the condition of the sealing washer and replace it with a new one if it is damaged or deformed – retain the original washer for use during flushing if required, but

9.14a Unscrew the drain bolt (arrowed) . . .

9.14b . . . and allow the coolant to drain

9.15 Displace the reservoir and tip the coolant out

9.23 Fit the drain bolt using a new sealing washer

note that a new washer should be fitted before refilling the system with coolant.

15 Also empty the reservoir, either by displacing it (see Chapter 3) and tipping the contents into the container, or by pumping the contents out if a suitable hand pump is available **(see illustration)**.

Flushing

16 Flush the system with clean tap water by inserting a hose in the radiator filler neck. Allow the water to run through the system until it is clear and flows out cleanly. If the radiator is extremely corroded, remove it (see Chapter 3) and have it cleaned by a specialist. Also flush the reservoir, then install it or fit the hose back onto its union as required according to model.

17 Clean the drain hole in the pump then fit the drain bolt using the old sealing washer.

18 Fill the cooling system via the radiator with clean water mixed with a flushing compound **(see illustration 9.24)**. Make sure the flushing compound is compatible with aluminium components, and follow the manufacturer's instructions carefully. Fit the radiator cap.

19 Start the engine and allow it to reach normal operating temperature. Let it run for about ten minutes.

20 Stop the engine. Let it cool for a while, then cover the pressure cap with a heavy rag and turn it anti-clockwise to the first stop, releasing any pressure that may be present in the system. Once the hissing stops, push down on the cap and remove it completely.

21 Drain the system once again.

22 Fill the system with clean water and repeat Steps 19 to 21.

Refilling

23 Fit the cooling system drain bolt using a new sealing washer and tighten it to the torque setting specified at the beginning of the Chapter **(see illustration)**.

24 Fill the system to the base of the radiator filler neck with the proper coolant mixture (see this Chapter's Specifications) **(see illustration)**. **Note:** *Pour the coolant in slowly to minimise the amount of air entering the system, and when full carefully waggle the bike from side to side to dislodge any trapped air. Fill the reservoir to the FULL line (see Pre-ride checks).*

25 Start the engine and allow it to idle for 2 to 3 minutes. Flick the throttle twistgrip part open 3 or 4 times, so that the engine speed rises to approximately 4000 to 5000 rpm, then stop the engine. Any air trapped in the system should bleed back to the radiator filler neck.

26 If necessary, top up the coolant level to the base of the radiator filler neck, then fit the pressure cap. Also top up the coolant reservoir to the FULL line.

27 Start the engine and allow it to reach normal operating temperature, then shut it off. Let the engine cool then remove the pressure cap as described in Step 13. Check that the coolant level is still up to the base of the upper radiator filler neck. If it's low, add the specified mixture until it reaches the base of the filler neck. Refit the cap. On XT-R and XT-X

9.24 Fill the system with the specified coolant mix

models fit the retainer onto the cap **(see illustration 9.7a)**.

28 Check the coolant level in the reservoir and top up if necessary.

29 Check the system for leaks. On XT-R and XT-X models install the fuel tank cover and on MT-03 models install the fuel tank trim panel (see Chapter 7). On XT-Z models install the sump guard (see Chapter 7) and the fuel tank (see Chapter 4).

30 Do not dispose of the old coolant by pouring it down the drain. Instead pour it into a heavy plastic container, cap it tightly and take it into an authorised disposal site or service station – see **Warning** at the beginning of this Section.

10 Brake system

Brake system check

1 A routine general check of the brake system will ensure that any problems are discovered and remedied before the rider's safety is jeopardised. Check the brake pads for wear (see below), and make sure the fluid level in each reservoir is correct (see *Pre-ride checks*).

2 Make sure all brake component fasteners are tight. Check the brake lever and pedal for improper or rough action, excessive play, bends, and other damage. Replace any damaged parts with new ones (see Chapter 6). Clean and lubricate the lever and pedal pivots if their action is stiff or rough (see Section 14). If the lever or pedal is spongy, bleed the brakes (see Chapter 6).

3 Twist and flex the hoses while looking for cracks, bulges and seeping hydraulic fluid. Check extra carefully around the areas where the hoses connect with the banjo fittings,

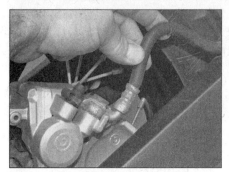

10.3 Twist and flex the hoses to check for cracks and deterioration

as these are common areas for hose failure **(see illustration)**. Inspect the banjo fittings connected to the brake hoses. If the fittings are rusted, scratched or cracked, fit new hoses.

4 Make sure the brake light comes when the

front brake lever is pulled in. If not, first check the bulb or LED (see Chapter 8, Section 6). If the bulb or LED is good, check the switch (see Chapter 8) – the switch is not adjustable.

5 Make sure the brake light is activated just before the rear brake takes effect. On XT-R and XT-X models the switch is adjustable – if adjustment is necessary, hold the switch and turn the adjuster nut on the switch body until the brake light is activated when required **(see illustration)**. If the brake light comes on too late or not at all, turn the nut clockwise (when looked at from the top) so the switch threads up out of the bracket. If the brake light comes on too soon or is permanently on, turn the nut anti-clockwise so the switch threads down into the bracket. If the switch doesn't operate the brake light, check it (see Chapter 8). On XT-Z and MT-03 models the switch is actuated hydraulically and cannot be adjusted. If the brake light fails to operate properly, and the

bulb is good, check the switch (see Chapter 8).

6 On XT-Z and MT-03 models the front brake lever has a span adjuster which alters the distance of the lever from the handlebar. Each setting is identified by a number on the adjuster which aligns with the triangular index mark on the lever **(see illustration)**. Push the lever away from the handlebar and turn the adjuster ring until the setting which best suits the rider is obtained, then release the lever **(see illustration)**. Position 1 gives the largest span, 5 the smallest. Do not set the adjuster between the defined settings.

7 The height of the rear brake pedal in relation to the top of the footrest should be as specified at the beginning of the Chapter, or to suit the rider's preference if required **(see illustration)**. To adjust the height slacken the clevis locknut on the master cylinder pushrod, then turn the pushrod using a spanner on

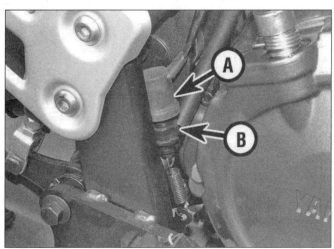

10.5 Hold the rear brake light switch body (A) and turn the adjuster nut (B) as required

10.6a Brake lever span adjuster – the setting number must align with the index mark (arrowed)

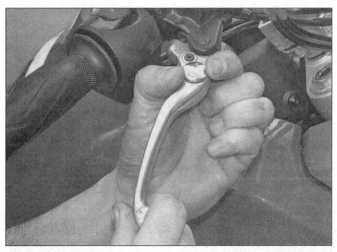

10.6b Push the lever forwards and turn the adjuster as required

10.7a Check the height of the rear brake pedal

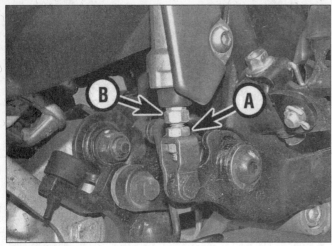

10.7b Slacken the locknut (A) and turn the pushrod (B) to adjust pedal height

10.8a Front brake pad friction material (arrowed)

the hex at the top of the rod until the pedal is at the desired height **(see illustration)**. On completion tighten the locknut.

Brake pad wear check

8 Each brake pad has wear indicators in the form of cut-outs in the friction material or raised sections on the material backing. The wear indicators on the front pads are not easily visible, but the amount of friction material left is. Look from below the front caliper, and from behind the rear caliper, but note that an accumulation of road dirt and brake dust could make the indicators difficult to see **(see illustrations)**. If the pad has reached the wear limit then new pads must be fitted (see Chapter 6).

9 If the indicators aren't visible, then visually check the amount of friction material remaining. Yamaha specify a minimum thickness of 1 mm. Replace the pads with new ones before they have worn to the minimum thickness (see Chapter 6). On the front caliper(s) also check that the pads are wearing evenly – uneven wear is indicative of a sticking piston, in which

case the caliper should be overhauled (see Chapter 6).

10 If the pads are dirty or if you are in doubt as to the amount of friction material remaining, remove them for inspection (see Chapter 6). If the pads are excessively worn, check the brake discs (see Chapter 6).

Brake fluid change

11 The brake fluid should be changed at the prescribed interval or whenever a master cylinder or caliper overhaul is carried out. Refer to Chapter 6, Section 11 for details. Ensure that all the old fluid is pumped from the hydraulic system and that the level in the fluid reservoir is checked and the brakes tested before riding the motorcycle.

Brake hoses

12 The hoses will deteriorate with age and should be replaced with new ones regardless of their apparent condition (see Chapter 6).
13 Always replace the banjo union sealing washers with new ones when fitting new hoses. Refill the system with new brake fluid and bleed the system as described in Chapter 6.

11 Wheels, wheel bearings and tyres

Wire spoke wheels – XT models

1 Visually check the spokes for damage and corrosion. A broken or bent spoke must be replaced with a new one immediately because the load taken by it will be transferred to adjacent spokes which may in turn fail. Check the tension in the spokes by tapping each one lightly with a screwdriver and noting the sound produced – each should make the same sound of the correct pitch. Properly tensioned spokes will make a sharp pinging sound, loose ones will produce a lower pitch dull sound and tight ones will be higher pitched. If a spoke needs adjustment turn the adjuster at the rim using a spoke adjustment tool or an open-ended spanner **(see illustration)**.
2 Unevenly tensioned spokes will promote rim misalignment – refer to information on wheel runout in Chapter 6 and seek the advice of a

10.8b Rear brake pad wear limit lines (arrowed)

11.1 Turn the adjuster (arrowed) to set spoke tension

11.7 Checking for play in the rear wheel bearings

12.2 Compress and release the front suspension

Yamaha dealer or wheel building specialist if the wheel needs realigning, which it may well do if many spokes are unevenly tensioned. Check front and rear wheel alignment as described in Chapter 6. Check that any wheel balance weights are fixed firmly to the wheel rim. If you suspect that a weight has fallen off, have the wheel rebalanced by a motorcycle tyre specialist.

Cast wheels – MT-03 model

3 Cast wheels are virtually maintenance free, but they should be kept clean and checked periodically for cracks and other damage. Also check the wheel runout and alignment (see Chapter 6). Never attempt to repair damaged cast wheels; they must be replaced with new ones if damaged. Check that any wheel balance weights are fixed firmly to the wheel rim. If you suspect that a weight has fallen off, have the wheel rebalanced by a motorcycle tyre specialist.

Tyres

4 Check the tyre condition and tread depth thoroughly – see *Pre-ride checks*.
5 Make sure the valve cap is in place and tight. Check the valve for signs of damage. If tyre deflation occurs and it is not due to a slow puncture the valve core may be loose or it could be leaking past the seal – remove the cap and make sure the core is tight; if it is tight then it could be leaking – unscrew the core from the valve housing using a core removal tool and thread a new one in its place. A tool can be made quite easily by cutting a slot into the threaded end of a bolt using a hacksaw – the bolt must fit inside the valve housing and the slot must be deep enough to locate around the flat sides of the core and grip it.

Wheel bearings

6 Wheel bearings will wear over a considerable mileage and should be checked periodically to avoid handling problems.
7 Support the motorcycle upright using

an auxiliary stand so that the wheel being examined is off the ground. When checking the front wheel bearings turn the handlebars to full lock on one side so you have something to push against. Check for any play in the bearings by pushing and pulling the wheel against the hub (see illustration). Also rotate the wheel and check that it turns smoothly and without any grating noises.
8 If any play is detected in the hub, or if the wheel does not rotate smoothly (and this is not due to brake or chain drag), remove the wheel and inspect the bearings for wear or damage (see Chapter 6).

12 Suspension

1 The suspension components must be maintained in top operating condition to ensure rider safety. Loose, worn or damaged suspension parts decrease the motorcycle's stability and control.

Front suspension check

2 While standing alongside the motorcycle, apply the front brake and push on the handlebars to compress the forks several

12.3 Lift the gaiters off the outer tubes on XT-Z models

times (see illustration). See if they move up-and-down smoothly without binding. If binding is felt, the forks should be disassembled and inspected (see Chapter 5).
3 Inspect the fork inner tubes for scratches, corrosion and pitting which will cause premature seal failure – if the damage is excessive, new tubes should be fitted (see Chapter 5). On XT-Z models you will need to raise the gaiters off the fork outer tubes for inspection (see illustration).
4 Inspect the area above the dust seal for signs of oil leakage, then carefully lever the seal up using a flat-bladed screwdriver and inspect the area around the fork seal (see illustration). If leakage is evident, the seals must be replaced with new ones (see Chapter 5). If there is evidence of corrosion between the seal retaining ring and its groove in the fork outer tube spray the area with a penetrative lubricant, otherwise the ring will be difficult to remove if needed. Press the dust seal back into the top of the fork outer tube on completion.
5 Check the tightness of the fork clamp bolts in the yokes, and the fork top bolts, to be sure none have worked loose, referring to the illustrations and torque settings specified in Chapter 5.

12.4 Check for oil leakage and corrosion on the inner tube above and below the dust seal

12.8 Checking for play in the swingarm bushes

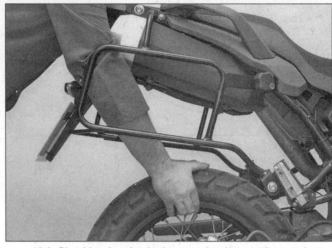

12.9 Checking for play in the rear shock mountings and suspension linkage (XT models)

Rear suspension check

6 Inspect the rear shock absorber for fluid leakage and tightness of the mountings. If leakage is found, the shock must be replaced with a new one (see Chapter 5).

7 With the aid of an assistant to support the bike, compress the rear suspension several times. It should move up-and-down freely without binding. If any binding is felt, the worn or faulty component must be identified and checked (see Chapter 5). The problem could be due to either the shock absorber, the suspension linkage on XT models, or the swingarm pivot.

8 Support the motorcycle on an auxiliary stand so that the rear wheel is off the ground. Grab the swingarm and rock it from side-to-side – there should be no discernible movement at the rear **(see illustration)**. If there's a little movement or a slight clicking can be heard, inspect the tightness of the swingarm and shock absorber, and on XT models the suspension linkage, mounting bolts and nuts, referring to the torque settings specified at the beginning of Chapter 5, and re-check for movement.

9 Next, grasp the top of the rear wheel and pull it upwards – there should be no discernible freeplay before the shock absorber(s) compress **(see illustration)**. Any freeplay felt in either check indicates worn bushes or bearings in the shock absorber or swingarm, or on XT models the suspension linkage. The worn components must be identified and replaced with new ones (see Chapter 5).

10 To make an accurate assessment of the swingarm bearings, remove the rear wheel (see Chapter 6) and the bolt securing the suspension linkage or shock absorber (according to model) to the swingarm (see Chapter 5). Grasp the rear of the swingarm with one hand and place your other hand at the junction of the swingarm and the frame. Try to move the rear of the swingarm from side-to-side. Any wear (play) in the bushes

should be felt as movement between the swingarm and the frame at the front. If there is any play, the swingarm will be felt to move forward and backward at the front (not from side-to-side). If there is any play in the swingarm remove it for inspection (see Chapter 5).

Front fork oil change

11 Although there is no set interval for changing the fork oil, note that the oil will degrade over a period of time and lose its damping qualities. Refer to Chapter 5 for details of fork removal, oil draining and refilling. The forks do not need to be completely disassembled to change the oil.

Rear suspension lubrication

12 Remove the swingarm, clean and re-grease the pivot bolt, spacers and bearings (see Chapter 5).

---

13 Steering head bearings

Freeplay check and adjustment

1 Steering head bearings can become dented, rough or loose during normal use of the machine. In extreme cases, worn or loose steering head bearings can cause steering wobble – a condition that is potentially dangerous. .

Check

2 Raise the front wheel off the ground using an auxiliary stand placed under the engine – on XT-R and XT-X models do not take the weight of the bike through the exhaust pipes, and on XT-Z models remove the sump guard (see Chapter 7). Always make sure that the bike is properly supported and secure.

3 Point the front wheel straight-ahead and slowly move the handlebars from lock to lock. Any dents or roughness in the bearing races

will be felt and if the bearings are too tight the bars will not move smoothly and freely. Again point the wheel straight-ahead, and tap the front of the wheel to one side. The wheel should 'fall' under its own weight to the limit of its lock, indicating that the bearings are not too tight (take into account the restriction that cables and wiring may have). Check for similar movement to the other side.

4 Next, grasp the bottom of the forks and gently pull and push them forward and backward **(see illustration)**. Any looseness or freeplay in the steering head bearings will be felt as front-to-rear movement of the forks. If play is felt, adjust the bearings as described below.

> **HAYNES HINT** *Make sure you are not mistaking any movement between the bike and stand, and between the stand and the ground, for freeplay in the bearings. Do not pull and push the forks too hard – a gentle movement is all that is needed. Freeplay between the fork inner and outer tubes due to worn bushes can also be misinterpreted as steering head bearing play – do not confuse the two.*

13.4 Checking for play in the steering head bearings

13.6 Unscrew the nut and withdraw the bolt on each side

13.8a Fork clamp bolts (arrowed) – XT models

Adjustment

5 Cover the fuel tank and its covers in some rag, or if preferred as a precaution, remove the fuel tank (see Chapter 4) – though not actually necessary, this will prevent the possibility of damage should a tool slip.

6 On MT-03 models remove the instrument cluster (see Chapter 8). Undo the top turn signal bracket bolt on each side **(see illustration)**.

7 Displace the handlebars from the top yoke and support them clear on some rag (see Chapter 5).

8 Slacken fork clamp bolt(s) in each side of the top yoke **(see illustrations)**. Unscrew the steering stem nut and remove it along with its washer **(see illustration)**.

9 Gently ease the top yoke upwards off the fork tubes and position it clear, using a rag to protect the tank or other components **(see illustration)**.

10 Remove the tabbed lock washer, noting how it fits **(see illustration)**. Unscrew and remove the locknut using a C-spanner if required – though it should only be finger-tight **(see illustration)**. Remove the rubber washer **(see illustration)**.

11 To adjust the bearings as specified

by Yamaha, a special service tool (Pt. No. 90890-01403) and a torque wrench are required. If the tool is available, first slacken the adjuster nut, then tighten it to the initial torque setting specified at the beginning of the Chapter, making sure the torque wrench arm is at 90° to the tool arm **(see illustration 9.15 in Chapter 5)**. Now slacken the nut again, then tighten it to the final torque setting specified. Check that the steering is still able to move freely from side to side, but that all freeplay is eliminated.

12 If the Yamaha tool is not available, use a C-spanner to slacken the adjuster nut slightly until pressure is just released, then tighten it

13.8b Fork clamp bolt (arrowed) – MT-03 models

13.8c Unscrew the steering stem nut . . .

13.9 . . . and lift the yoke off the forks

13.10a Remove the lockwasher . . .

13.10b . . . the locknut . . .

13.10c . . . and the rubber washer

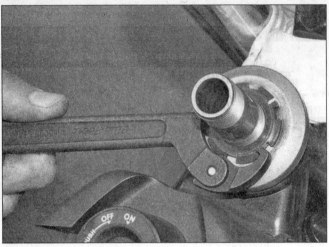

13.12 Using a C-spanner to tighten the head bearing adjuster nut

13.14 Fit the nut with its washer and tighten to the specified torque

until all freeplay is removed, then tighten it a little more **(see illustration)**. This pre-loads the bearings. Now slacken the nut, then tighten it again, setting it so that all freeplay is just removed, yet the steering is able to move freely from side to side. To do this tighten the nut only a little at a time, and after each tightening repeat the checks outlined above (Steps 2 to 4) until the bearings are correctly set. The object is to set the adjuster nut so that the bearings are under a very light loading, just enough to remove any freeplay.

Caution: Take great care not to apply excessive pressure because this will cause premature failure of the bearings.

13 With the bearings correctly adjusted, fit the rubber washer, then the locknut **(see illustrations 13.10c and b)**. Tighten the locknut finger-tight, then tighten it further until its notches align with those in the adjuster nut. If necessary, counter-hold the adjuster nut and tighten the locknut using a C-spanner until the notches align, but make sure the adjuster nut does not turn as well. Fit the tabbed lock washer so that the tabs fit into the notches in both the locknut and adjuster nut **(see illustration 13.10a)**.

14 Fit the top yoke onto the steering stem **(see illustration 13.9)**. Fit the washer and steering stem nut and tighten the nut to the

torque setting specified at the beginning of the Chapter **(see illustration)**. Now tighten the fork clamp bolts to the specified torque setting **(see illustration 13.8a or b)**.

15 Install the handlebars (see Chapter 5).

16 On MT-03 models fit the turn signal bracket bolts **(see illustration 13.6)**, and install the instrument cluster (see Chapter 8).

17 Check the bearing adjustment as described above and re-adjust if necessary.

18 Install the fuel tank and covers if removed (see Chapter 4).

Lubrication

19 Over time the grease in the bearings will be dispersed or will harden allowing the ingress of dirt and water.

20 At the specified interval disassemble the steering head and clean and re-grease the bearings (see Chapter 5, Section 9).

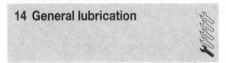

14 General lubrication

1 The controls, cables, footrest pivots, clutch and brake lever pivots, brake pedal pivot and sidestand pivots are exposed to the elements, and so need to be checked and lubricated

periodically to ensure safe and trouble-free operation.

Pivot points

2 In order for the lubricant to be applied where it will do the most good, the component should be disassembled (see Chapters 5 and 6). The lubricant recommended by Yamaha for each application is listed at the beginning of the Chapter. If chain or cable lubricant is being used, it can be applied to the pivot joint gaps and will usually work its way into the areas where friction occurs, so less disassembly of the component is needed (however it is always better to do so and clean off all corrosion, dirt and old lubricant first). If motor oil or light grease is being used, apply it sparingly as it may attract dirt (which could cause the controls to bind or wear at an accelerated rate).

Cables

Special tool: *A cable lubricating adapter is necessary for this procedure* **(see illustration 14.3c)**.

3 To lubricate the cables, disconnect the relevant cable at its upper end, then lubricate it with a pressure adapter and aerosol lubricant **(see illustrations)**. See Chapter 4 for throttle cable removal procedure, and Chapter 2 for the clutch cable.

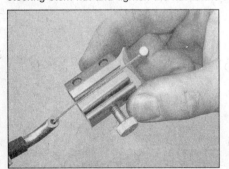

14.3a Fit the cable into the adapter . . .

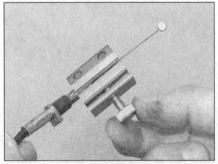

14.3b . . . and tighten the screw to seal it in . . .

14.3c . . . then apply the lubricant using the nozzle provided inserted in the hole in the adapter

18.2 Undo the screws (arrowed) and remove the cover

18.3 Withdraw the filter from the housing

15 Nuts and bolts

1 Since vibration of the machine tends to loosen fasteners, all nuts, bolts, screws, etc. should be periodically checked for proper tightness.

2 Pay particular attention to the following, referring to the relevant Chapter:

Spark plug
Engine oil drain plugs and bolt
Lever and pedal bolts
Footrest and stand bolts
Engine mounting bolts/nuts
Shock absorber and suspension linkage (XT models) bolts/nuts; swingarm pivot bolt/nut
Handlebar clamp bolts
Front fork clamp bolts (top and bottom yoke), and fork top bolts
Steering stem nut
Front axle
Rear axle nut
Front and rear sprocket nuts
Brake caliper and master cylinder mounting bolts
Brake hose banjo bolts and caliper bleed valves
Brake disc bolts
Exhaust system bolts/nuts

3 If a torque wrench is available, use it along with the torque settings given at the beginning of this and other Chapters.

16 Sidestand and starter safety circuit

1 Check the stand springs for damage and distortion. The springs must be capable of retracting the stand fully and holding it retracted when the motorcycle is in use. If a spring is sagged or broken it must be replaced with a new one.

2 Lubricate the stand pivot regularly (see Section 14).

3 Check the stand and its mount for bends and cracks. Stands can often be repaired by welding.

4 The starter safety circuit, comprising the neutral switch, the clutch switch and the sidestand switch, prevents the engine from being started unless it is in neutral, or if it is in gear unless the clutch lever is pulled in and the sidestand is up. Check the circuit is working correctly.

5 If the circuit does not operate as described, check the neutral switch, the clutch switch, the sidestand switch where fitted, the circuit diode, and the wiring between them (see Chapter 8).

17 Battery

1 All models covered in this manual are fitted with a sealed MF (maintenance free) battery. **Note:** *Do not attempt to remove the battery caps to check the electrolyte level or battery specific gravity.* Removal will damage the caps, resulting in electrolyte leakage and battery damage. All that should be done is to check that the terminals are clean and tight and that the casing is not damaged or leaking. See Chapter 8 for further details.

2 If the machine is not in regular use, disconnect the battery and give it a refresher charge every month to six weeks (see Chapter 8).

18 Air filter

Caution: If the machine is continually ridden in wet or dusty conditions, the filter should be cleaned between service intervals, or replaced with a new one more often than specified.

Caution: If the machine is continually ridden in wet conditions or at full throttle, the air filter housing drain should be checked more frequently.
Caution: Never run the engine without an air filter.

XT-R and XT-X models

1 Remove the right-hand side cover (see Chapter 7).

2 Undo the air filter cover screws and remove the cover **(see illustration)**.

3 Withdraw the filter, noting how it fits **(see illustration)**.

4 Make sure the cover seal is in good condition and properly seated – fit a new one if necessary. Fit the new filter into the housing, then fit the cover and secure it with its screws.

5 Install the side cover (see Chapter 7).

6 To clean the filter in between replacement intervals tap it on a hard surface to dislodge any dirt, then use compressed air to blow through it, directing the air in the opposite way to normal flow, i.e. from the front side to the rear **(see illustration 18.18)**.

7 Check the air filter housing drain for residue **(see illustration)**. If necessary place some rag under the drain, then release the clamp

18.7 Check the drain collector (arrowed) for residue

18.9 Undo the screws (arrowed) and remove the duct

18.10 Withdraw the filter from the housing

18.11 Fit the new filter then fit the duct

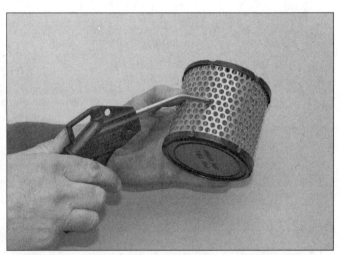

18.13 Direct the air in the opposite direction to normal flow as shown

18.14 Check the drain hose for residue

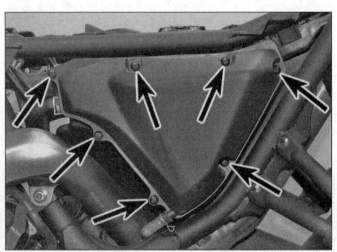

18.15 Undo the screws (arrowed) and remove the cover

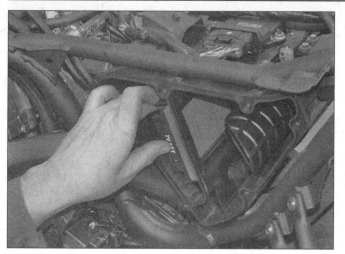

18.16 Withdraw the filter from the housing

18.17a Make sure the seal (arrowed) is in good condition and correctly seated

and remove the collector. Allow any residue to drain from the housing, and clean out the collector.

XT-Z models

8 Remove the seat (see Chapter 7).
9 Undo the air duct screws and remove the duct (see illustration).
10 Withdraw the filter from the housing (see illustration).
11 Fit the new filter into the housing, making sure it is properly seated. Fit the air intake duct and secure it with its screws (see illustration).
12 Install the seat (see Chapter 7).
13 To clean the filter in between replacement intervals tap it on a hard surface to dislodge any dirt, then use compressed air to blow through it, directing the air in the opposite way to normal flow, i.e. from the outside to the centre (see illustration).
14 Check the air filter housing drain hose

for residue (see illustration). Place some rag under the drain, then remove the hose plug and allow any residue to drain.

MT-03 models

15 Undo the air filter cover screws and remove the cover (see illustration).
16 Withdraw the filter, noting how it fits (see illustration).
17 Make sure the cover seal is in good condition and properly seated – fit a new one if necessary (see illustration). Fit the new filter into the housing, then fit the cover and secure it with its screws (see illustration).
18 To clean the filter in between replacement intervals tap it on a hard surface to dislodge any dirt, then use compressed air to blow through it, directing the air in the opposite way to normal flow, i.e. from the front side to the rear (see illustration).
19 Check the air filter housing drain for residue (see illustration). Place some rag

18.17b Fit the new filter then fit the cover

under the drain, then release the clamp and remove the collector. Allow any residue to drain from the housing, and clean out the collector. Also check the drain hose for residue (see illustration 18.14). Place some rag under the drain, then remove the hose plug and allow any residue to drain.

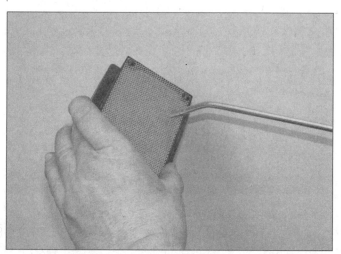

18.18 Direct the air in the opposite direction to normal flow as shown

18.19 Check the drain collector (arrowed) for residue

19.3 Unscrew the bolts (arrowed) and remove the bar

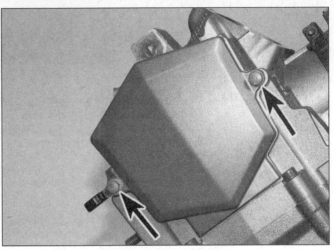

19.5a Unscrew the bolts (arrowed) and remove the sprocket cover

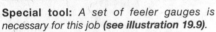

19 Valve clearances

Special tool: *A set of feeler gauges is necessary for this job (see illustration 19.9).*
1 The engine must be completely cool for this maintenance procedure.
2 Remove the fuel tank (see Chapter 4).
3 On XT-Z models remove the left-hand radiator cover (see Chapter 7). On MT-03 models remove the frame tensioning bar **(see illustration)**. If required for best access remove the radiator (see Chapter 3).
4 Remove the spark plug (see Section 2).
5 Unscrew the camshaft sprocket cover bolts and remove the cover **(see illustration)**. Unscrew the valve clearance adjuster cover

bolts and remove the covers **(see illustration)**. Discard the O-rings – new ones must be used.
6 Unscrew the timing inspection cap and the crankshaft end cap from the alternator cover on the left-hand side of the engine **(see illustration)**. Check the condition of the cap O-rings and replace them with new ones if necessary.
7 To check the valve clearances the engine must be turned so the piston is at top dead centre (TDC) on its compression stroke so that the valves are closed.
8 Turn the engine anti-clockwise using a suitable socket on the alternator rotor nut until the index line on the rotor aligns with the notch in the inspection hole, and the index line on the camshaft sprocket aligns with the pointer on the top of the cylinder head **(see illustrations)**. **Note:** *Do not

confuse the index line on the rotor with one of the upright lines on the H mark that comes just before it as you turn the engine.* There should now be some freeplay in each rocker arm (i.e. they are not contacting the valve stem) **(see illustration)**. If the index line on the sprocket is at the bottom, rotate the engine anti-clockwise one full turn (360°) until the index line on the rotor again aligns with the pointer inside the inspection hole – the index line on the sprocket will now be at the top.
9 With the engine in this position, check the clearance of each valve by inserting a feeler gauge of the same thickness as the correct valve clearance (see Specifications) in the gap between the rocker arm and the valve stem **(see illustration)**. The intake valves are on the back of the cylinder head and the exhaust valves are on the front. The gauge should be

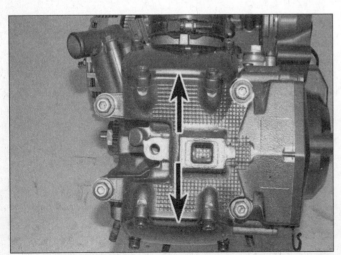

19.5b Unscrew the adjuster cover bolts and remove the covers (arrowed)

19.6 Remove the crankshaft end cap (A) and the timing inspection cap (B)

19.8a Turn the engine anti-clockwise using the nut . . .

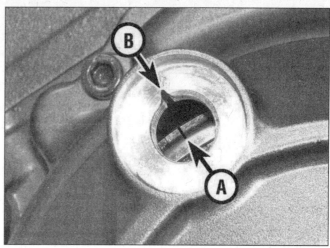

19.8b . . . until the line (A) on the rotor aligns with the notch (B) . . .

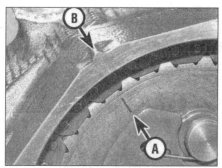

19.8c . . . and the line (A) on the camshaft sprocket aligns with the pointer (B)

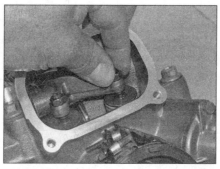

19.8d There should be some discernible up-and-down freeplay in each rocker

19.9 Insert the feeler gauge between the base of the adjuster on the arm and the top of the valve stem as shown

a firm sliding fit – you should feel a slight drag when you pull the gauge out.

10 If the gap (clearance) is either too wide or too narrow, slacken the locknut on the adjuster in the rocker arm **(see illustration)**. Turn the adjuster as required using a screwdriver, until the gap is as specified and the feeler gauge is a sliding fit **(see illustration)**. Hold the adjuster still and tighten the locknut. Recheck the clearance after tightening the locknut.

11 When the clearances are correct fit the camshaft sprocket and adjuster covers using

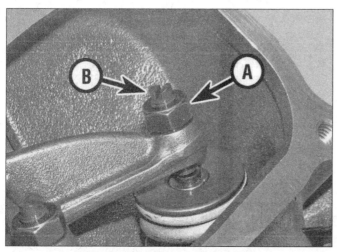

19.10a Locknut (A) and adjuster (B) . . .

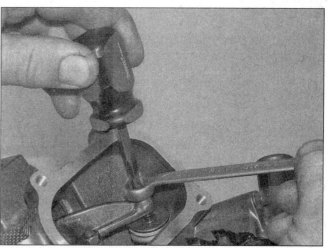

19.10b . . . turn the adjuster until the gap is correct, then hold the adjuster while tightening the locknut

19.11a **Fit the sprocket cover using a new O-ring smeared with grease . . .**

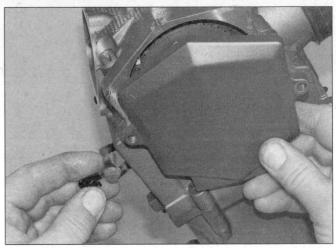

19.11b **. . . and do not forget the wire guide with the front bolt**

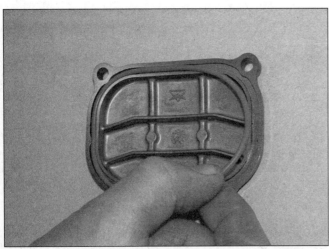

19.11c **Fit each adjuster cover using a new O-ring smeared with grease**

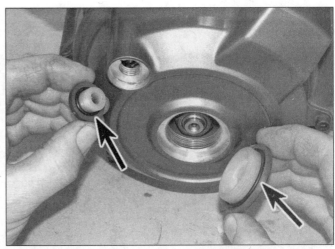

19.12 **Fit the caps using new O-rings (arrowed) if required and smear them with grease**

new O-rings smeared with grease and tighten the bolts to the torque setting specified at the beginning of the Chapter, not forgetting the wiring clamp with the sprocket cover front bolt **(see illustrations)**.

12 Fit the timing inspection cap and crankshaft end cap using new O-rings if required, and smear the O-rings with grease **(see illustration)**.

13 Install the spark plug (Section 2), and the fuel tank (Chapter 4). Install the radiator if removed (see Chapter 3).

14 On XT-Z models install the left-hand radiator cover (see Chapter 7). On MT-03 models fit the frame tensioning bar and tighten the bolts to the specified torque.

15 Check and adjust the idle speed (see Section 3).

Chapter 2
Engine, clutch and transmission

Contents

	Section			Section
Alternator	see Chapter 8		General information	1
Balancer shaft	24		Idle speed check and adjustment	see Chapter 1
Cam chain tensioner	6		Neutral switch	see Chapter 8
Camshaft and rocker arms	7		Oil and filter change	see Chapter 1
Cam chain, tensioner blade and guide blade	8		Oil level check	see Pre-ride checks
Clutch	15		Oil pump and strainer	19
Clutch cable	16		Piston	12
Clutch check	see Chapter 1		Piston rings	13
Component access	2		Right-hand crankcase cover	17
Crankcases and bearings	22		Running-in procedure	28
Crankcase separation and reassembly	21		Selector drum and forks	27
Crankshaft and connecting rod	23		Spark plug	see Chapter 1
Cylinder block	11		Starter clutch and gears	14
Cylinder head removal and installation	9		Starter motor	see Chapter 8
Cylinder head and valve overhaul	10		Transmission shaft overhaul	26
Engine disassembly and reassembly general information	5		Transmission assembly removal and installation	25
Engine removal and installation	4		Valve clearance check and adjustment	see Chapter 1
Engine wear assessment	3		Water pump	see Chapter 3
Gearchange mechanism	20		Water pump, primary drive and balancer shaft gears	18

Degrees of difficulty

| **Easy,** suitable for novice with little experience | 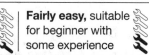 | **Fairly easy,** suitable for beginner with some experience | | **Fairly difficult,** suitable for competent DIY mechanic | | **Difficult,** suitable for experienced DIY mechanic | | **Very difficult,** suitable for expert DIY or professional | |

Specifications

General

Type	Four-stroke single
Capacity	660 cc
Bore	100.0 mm
Stroke	84.0 mm
Compression ratio	10.0 to 1
Cylinder compression	92.4 psi (6.5 Bar) @ 800 rpm
Cooling system	Liquid-cooled
Lubrication	Dry sump, dual rotor trochoid pump
Clutch	Wet multi-plate
Transmission	Five-speed constant mesh
Final drive	Chain and sprockets

Camshafts and rockers

Intake lobe height	
Standard	43.488 to 43.588 mm
Service limit (min)	43.338 mm
Exhaust lobe height	
Standard	43.129 to 43.229 mm
Service limit (min)	43.029 mm
Runout (max)	0.03 mm
Rocker arm bore diameter	
Standard	12.000 to 12.018 mm
Service limit (min)	12.036 mm
Rocker arm shaft diameter	
Standard	11.981 to 11.991 mm
Service limit (min)	11.955 mm
Rocker arm-to-shaft clearance	
Standard	0.009 to 0.037 mm
Service limit (min)	0.081 mm

Cylinder head

Warpage (max)	0.03 mm

Valves, guides and springs

Valve clearances	see Chapter 1
Stem diameter	
Intake valve	
Standard	5.975 to 5.990 mm
Service limit (min)	5.945 mm
Exhaust valve	
Standard	5.960 to 5.975 mm
Service limit (min)	5.930 mm
Guide bore diameter – intake and exhaust valves	
Standard	6.000 to 6.012 mm
Service limit (max)	6.05 mm
Stem-to-guide clearance	
Intake valve	
Standard	0.010 to 0.037 mm
Service limit	0.08 mm
Exhaust valve	
Standard	0.025 to 0.052 mm
Service limit	0.10 mm
Valve stem runout (max)	0.010 mm
Valve head diameter	
Intake valve	37.9 to 38.1 mm
Exhaust valve	31.9 to 32.1 mm
Valve face width	1.91 to 2.62 mm
Seat width in head	
Standard	1.0 to 1.2 mm
Service limit (max)	1.6 mm
Valve spring free length – intake and exhaust valves	
Standard	40.38 mm
Service limit (min)	38.36 mm
Valve spring tilt (max)	1.8 mm

Cylinder bore

Standard . . . .   100.000 to 100.010 mm
Ovality (out-of-round) (max) . . . .   0.05 mm
Taper (max) . . . .   0.05 mm
Cylinder compression
   Standard . . . .   92.4 psi (6.5 Bar)
   Maximum . . . .   99.6 psi (7 Bar)
   Minimum . . . .   85.3 psi (6 Bar)

Piston

Piston diameter . . . .   99.955 to 99.970 mm (measured 10 mm up from skirt, at 90° to piston pin axis)
Piston-to-bore clearance
   Standard . . . .   0.030 to 0.055 mm
   Service limit (min) . . . .   0.13 mm
Piston pin diameter
   Standard . . . .   22.991 to 23.000 mm
   Service limit (min) . . . .   22.971 mm
Piston pin bore diameter in piston
   Standard . . . .   23.004 to 23.015 mm
   Service limit (max) . . . .   23.045 mm
Piston pin-to-piston pin bore clearance
   Standard . . . .   0.004 to 0.024 mm
   Service limit . . . .   0.074 mm

Piston rings

Ring end gap (installed)
   Top ring
      Standard . . . .   0.20 to 0.35 mm
      Service limit (max) . . . .   0.60 mm
   Second ring
      Standard . . . .   0.35 to 0.50 mm
      Service limit (max) . . . .   0.85 mm
   Oil ring side-rail
      Standard . . . .   0.20 to 0.70 mm
Ring-to-groove clearance
   Top ring
      Standard . . . .   0.030 to 0.080 mm
      Service limit (max) . . . .   0.13 mm
   Second ring
      Standard . . . .   0.030 to 0.070 mm
      Service limit (max) . . . .   0.11 mm
   Oil ring side-rail . . . .   0.060 to 0.150 mm

Clutch

Friction plates
   Type 1   4
   Type 2   2
   Type 3   1
Plain plates   7
Friction plate thickness
   Type 1 (ID 119 mm, notched tab)
      Standard . . . .   2.90 to 3.10 mm
      Service limit (min) . . . .   2.80 mm
   Type 2 (ID 119 mm)
      Standard . . . .   2.92 to 3.08 mm
      Service limit (min) . . . .   2.80 mm
   Type 3 (ID 128 mm)
      Standard . . . .   2.90 to 3.10 mm
      Service limit (min) . . . .   2.80 mm
Plain plate thickness . . . .   1.5 to 1.7 mm
Plain plate warpage (max) . . . .   0.20 mm
Spring free length
   Standard . . . .   55.6 mm
   Service limit (min) . . . .   52.82 mm

Oil pump

2004 to 2006 models

Inner rotor tip-to-outer rotor clearance (max)

    Standard . . . .   0.07 to 0.12 mm

    Service limit (max) . . . .   0.20 mm

Outer rotor-to-housing clearance

    Standard . . . .   0.03 to 0.08 mm

    Service limit (max) . . . .   0.15 mm

Rotor end-float

    Standard . . . .   0.03 to 0.08 mm

    Service limit (max) . . . .   0.15 mm

2007-on models

Inner rotor tip-to-outer rotor clearance (max)

    Standard . . . .   0.03 to 0.08 mm

    Service limit (max) . . . .   0.16 mm

Outer rotor-to-housing clearance

    Standard . . . .   0.19 to 0.15 mm

    Service limit (max) . . . .   0.22 mm

Rotor end-float

    Standard . . . .   0.03 to 0.08 mm

    Service limit (max) . . . .   0.15 mm

Crankshaft and connecting rod

Crankshaft runout (max) . . . .   0.04 mm

Crankshaft width (see text) . . . .   74.95 to 75.00 mm

Connecting rod big-end side clearance

    Standard . . . .   0.35 to 0.65 mm

    Service limit (max) . . . .   1.0 mm

Connecting rod big-end radial clearance

    Standard . . . .   0.010 to 0.025 mm

    Service limit (max) . . . .   0.05 mm

Connecting rod small-end freeplay . . . .   0.16 0.40 mm

Transmission

Gear ratios (no. of teeth)

    Primary reduction . . . .   2.083 to 1 (75/36)

    Final reduction

        XT models . . . .   3.000 to 1 (45/15)

        MT-03 models . . . .   3.133 to 1 (47/15)

    1st gear . . . .   2.500 to 1 (30/12)

    2nd gear . . . .   1.625 to 1 (26/16)

    3rd gear . . . .   1.150 to 1 (23/20)

    4th gear . . . .   0.909 to 1 (20/22)

    5th gear . . . .   0.769 to 1 (20/26)

Shaft runout (max) . . . .   0.08 mm

Selector drum and forks

Selector fork end thickness . . . .   5.76 to 5.89 mm

Torque settings

Air induction system pipe bolts . . . .   10 Nm

Balancer shaft nut (securing balancer driven gear) . . . .   70 Nm

Cam chain tensioner blade bolts . . . .   8 Nm

Cam chain tensioner cap bolt . . . .   20 Nm

Cam chain tensioner mounting bolts . . . .   10 Nm

Camshaft/rocker shaft retainer bolts . . . .   10 Nm

Camshaft sprocket cover bolts . . . .   10 Nm

Camshaft sprocket bolts . . . .   20 Nm

Clutch cable holder bolts . . . .   10 Nm

Clutch cover bolts . . . .   10 Nm

Clutch nut . . . .   90 Nm

Clutch spring bolts . . . .   9 Nm

Coolant inlet union bolts . . . .   10 Nm

Crankcase bolts . . . .   10 Nm

Torque settings (continued)

Crankshaft nut (securing drive gears)	80 Nm
Cylinder block bolts	
Top bolts	
Initial setting	15 Nm
Final setting	50 Nm
Side bolts	10 Nm
Cylinder head bolts	
Top bolts	50 Nm
Front/rear bolts	45 Nm
Side bolts	10 Nm
Engine mounting bolt nuts	
XT-R and XT-X 2004 to 2006 models	
Front bracket-to-frame	73 Nm
Front bracket-to-engine	73 Nm
Rear mounting bolt	73 Nm
Upper bracket-to-frame	73 Nm
Upper bracket-to-engine	55 Nm
XT-R and XT-X 2007-on models and XT-Z models	
Rear mounting bolt	65 Nm
Front bracket-to-frame	65 Nm
Front bracket-to-engine	65 Nm
Upper bracket-to-frame	65 Nm
Upper bracket-to-engine	55 Nm
MT-03 models	
Adjuster nut	18 Nm
Rear mounting bolt	65 Nm
Front bracket-to-frame	65 Nm
Front bracket-to-engine	65 Nm
Upper bracket-to-frame	65 Nm
Upper bracket-to-engine	55 Nm
Tensioning bar bolts	30 Nm
Gearchange lever pinch bolt	
XT-R and XT-X models	16 Nm
XT-Z and MT-03 models	20 Nm
Gearchange shaft centralising spring locating pin	22 Nm
Oil feed and return pipe union bolts	10 Nm
Oil pressure check bolt	5 Nm
Oil pump assembly screw	7 Nm
Oil pump/inner baffle plate bolts	10 Nm
Oil strainer bolts	10 Nm
Oil transfer pipe banjo bolts	20 Nm
Oil transfer pipe retaining bolt	10 Nm
Outer baffle plate bolts	4 Nm
Right-hand crankcase cover bolts	10 Nm
Right-hand footrest bracket bolts	
XT-R and XT-X models	48 Nm
MT-03 models	
Footrest bracket bolt	65 Nm
Master cylinder bolts	23 Nm
Swingarm pivot bolt nut	92 Nm
Starter clutch bolts	30 Nm
Transmission input shaft bearing retainer bolts	10 Nm
Transmission output shaft oil seal retainer bolts	10 Nm
Valve clearance adjuster cover bolts	10 Nm

1 General information

The engine/transmission unit is a liquid-cooled single cylinder of unit construction. The four valves are operated by rocker arms actuated by a single overhead camshaft which is chain driven off the left-hand end of the crankshaft. The crankshaft drives a single balancer shaft. The crankcase divides vertically.

The crankcase incorporates a dry sump, pressure-fed lubrication system which uses a dual rotor trochoidal oil pump that is gear-driven off the back of the clutch. Oil is filtered by a standard cartridge filter and by a strainer in the sump.

There is a gear driven water pump.

The alternator is on the left-hand end of crankshaft. The crankshaft position sensor triggers for the ignition timing are on the outside of the alternator rotor, and the sensor is mounted in the alternator cover along with the stator.

Power from the crankshaft is routed to the transmission via the clutch. The clutch is of the wet, multi-plate type and is gear-driven off the crankshaft. The clutch is operated by cable. The transmission is a five-speed constant-mesh unit. Final drive to the rear wheel is by chain and sprockets.

2 Component access

Operations possible with the engine in the frame

The components and assemblies listed below can be removed without having to remove the engine from the frame. If however, a number of areas require attention at the same time, removal of the engine is recommended.

    Camshaft and rockers
    Clutch
    Right-hand crankcase cover
    Water pump, primary drive and balancer
      shaft gears
    Oil pump
    Gearchange mechanism
    Alternator
    Starter clutch
    Cam chain, tensioner and blades
    Starter motor
    Transmission output shaft oil seal (see
      Section 25)

Operations requiring engine removal

It is necessary to remove the engine from the frame to gain access to the following components.

    Cylinder head
    Cylinder block and piston
    Crankshaft, connecting rod and bearings
    Transmission shafts and bearings
    Selector drum and forks
    Balancer shaft
    Oil strainer

3 Engine wear assessment

Cylinder compression check

Special tool: *A compression gauge is required to perform this test.*

1 Poor engine performance may be caused by leaking valves, incorrect valve clearances, a leaking head gasket, or worn pistons, piston

3.5a Fit an adapter onto the gauge hose . . .

rings or cylinder walls. A cylinder compression check will highlight these conditions and can also indicate the presence of excessive carbon deposits in the cylinder head.

2 The only tools required are a compression gauge (with an M10 x 1.0 mm threaded adapter to fit the spark plug hole in the cylinder head) and a spark plug socket. Depending on the outcome of the initial test, a squirt-type oil can may also be needed.

3 Make sure the valve clearances are correctly set (see Chapter 1).

4 Run the engine until it is at normal operating temperature. Remove the spark plug (see Chapter 1). Fit the plug back into the plug cap and earth (ground) the plug against the engine away from the plug hole – if the plug is not grounded the ignition system could be damaged.

5 Fit the gauge along with any necessary adapter into the spark plug hole **(see illustrations)**.

6 With the ignition switch ON, the throttle held fully open and the spark plug earthed (grounded), turn the engine over on the starter motor until the gauge reading has built up and stabilised **(see illustration)**.

7 Compare the reading on the gauge to the cylinder compression figures listed at the beginning of the Chapter.

8 If the reading is low, it could be due to a worn cylinder bore, piston or rings, failure of the head gasket, loose cylinder head bolts, or worn valve seats. To determine which is the cause, pour a small quantity of engine oil into the spark plug hole to seal the rings, then repeat the compression test. If the figures are

3.5b . . . then thread the adapter and gauge into the spark plug hole

noticeably higher the cause is a worn cylinder, piston or rings. If there is no change the cause is probably a leaking head gasket or worn valve seats, but could also be due to a holed piston or broken ring(s).

9 If the reading is high there could be a build-up of carbon deposits in the combustion chamber. Remove the cylinder head and scrape all deposits off the piston and the cylinder head.

Engine oil pressure check

10 If there is any doubt about the performance of the engine lubrication system an oil pressure check must be carried out. The check provides useful information about the state of wear of the engine.

11 Check the engine oil level and make sure it is correct, and make sure the correct grade oil is being used (see Pre-ride checks). Make sure there is no obvious oil leakage from anywhere around the engine, and that the drain plugs and bolt are tight (see Chapter 1). Loosen the oil pressure check bolt on the top of the oil filter housing **(see illustration)**. Have some rag to hand to catch the oil which should come out of the hole.

12 Start the engine and allow it idle, and watch the pressure check hole – oil should seep out around the bolt threads quite soon after starting the engine **(see illustration)**. When the oil appears stop the engine. If no oil has appeared after one minute stop the engine immediately.

13 If no oil comes out the pressure is significantly lower than it should be or non-existent, either the oil pump or its drive mechanism is faulty, the filter is blocked, an oil

3.6 Hold the throttle open and turn the engine over

3.11 Slacken the check bolt (arrowed) . . .

3.12 . . . and make sure oil seeps past the threads

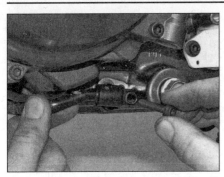

4.11a Unscrew the bolt and detach the oil pipe. . .

4.11b . . . and remove the O-ring and dowel

4.12 Release the clamp and detach the hose

4.13a Release the clamps (arrowed) and detach the hoses

4.13b Unscrew the bolt (arrowed) on the left . . .

4.13c . . . and the bolts (arrowed) on the right and remove the oil tank

passage is blocked, or there is other engine damage. Begin diagnosis by checking the oil filter, then the oil pump (see Section 19). If those items check out okay, the engine needs to be overhauled to clean out all oil passages and to clean the oil strainer.

14 Tighten the oil pressure check bolt to the torque setting specified at the beginning of the Chapter.

4	Engine removal and installation

Caution: The engine is heavy. Engine removal and installation should be carried out with the aid of an assistant; personal injury or damage could occur if the engine falls or is dropped.

Removal

1 Support the bike upright on level ground using axle stands under the bottom of the frame or passenger footrest brackets, or tie the rear of the bike up using a hoist or support frame – you cannot support the bike using a rear paddock stand because the swingarm pivots through the engine. Work can be made easier by raising the machine to a suitable working height on a hydraulic ramp or a suitable platform. Make sure the motorcycle is secure and will not topple over, and tie the front brake lever to the handlebar to prevent it rolling forwards.

2 On XT-Z models remove the sump guard and radiator covers (see Chapter 7).

3 If the engine is dirty, particularly around its mountings, wash it thoroughly. This will make work much easier and rule out the possibility of caked on lumps of dirt falling into some vital component.

4 Drain the engine oil and coolant (see Chapter 1).

5 Disconnect the leads from the battery (see Chapter 8). On XT-Z and MT-03 models remove the regulator/rectifier (see Chapter 8).

6 Remove the fuel tank (see Chapter 4).

7 Remove the radiator along with its hoses, noting their routing (see Chapter 3). On XT-Z models remove the coolant reservoir along with its hoses, again noting their routing (see Chapter 3).

8 Remove the exhaust system (see Chapter 4).

9 Remove the throttle body (see Chapter 4). Plug the intake on the engine with clean rag.

10 Remove the ignition coil (see Chapter 4).

4.14 Release the clamp (arrowed) and detach the hose

Remove the air induction system (AIS) control valve (see Chapter 4).

11 Unscrew the bolt securing the oil feed pipe to the left-hand side of the engine **(see illustration)**. Detach the pipe and remove the dowel **(see illustration)**. Discard the O-ring – a new one must be used.

12 On XT-models release the clamp securing the oil feed hose to its union on the frame downtube and detach the hose **(see illustration)**.

13 On MT-03 models release the clamp and detach the oil return hose from the top of the oil tank **(see illustration)**. Unscrew the tank mounting bolts and remove the tank **(see illustrations)**.

14 Release the clamp and detach the oil hose from the return pipe on the back of the engine **(see illustration)**.

15 Detach the oil tank breather hose from the engine **(see illustration)**. Free the crankcase

4.15a Release the clamp (arrowed) and detach the breather hose

4.15b Free the peg from its grommet then detach the hose (arrowed) and remove the chamber

4.16 Unscrew the bolt (arrowed) and detach the lead

breather chamber from the bracket and detach it from the hose **(see illustration)**.

16 Detach the clutch cable from the engine (see Section 16, Step 2). Position the cable clear of the engine. On MT-03 models unscrew the cable bracket rear bolt, detach the earth lead, then replace the bolt **(see illustration)**.

17 Disconnect the alternator, crankshaft position (CKP) sensor, neutral switch, sidestand switch and speed sensor wiring connectors **(see illustrations)**. Disconnect the wiring connector from the engine coolant temperature (ECT) sensor **(see illustration)**.

18 Unscrew the sidestand bracket bolts and remove the stand assembly **(see illustrations)**.

4.17a Alternator, CKP sensor, neutral switch, sidestand switch and speed sensor wiring connectors – XT-R and XT-X models

4.17b Alternator, CKP sensor, neutral switch and sidestand switch wiring connectors . . .

4.17c . . . and speed sensor wiring connector – XT-Z models

4.17d Alternator, CKP sensor, neutral switch and sidestand switch wiring connectors (arrowed) . . .

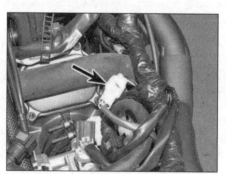

4.17e . . . and speed sensor wiring connector (arrowed) – MT-03 models

4.17f Disconnect the ECT sensor connector

4.18a Sidestand bracket bolts (arrowed) – XT-R and XT-X models

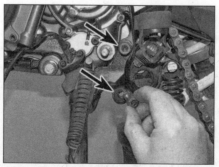

4.18b Sidestand bracket bolts (arrowed) – XT-Z models

4.18c Sidestand bracket bolts (arrowed) – MT-03 models

4.20a Unscrew the nut and detach the lead . . .

4.20b . . . then unscrew the bolt (arrowed) and detach the lead

19 Remove the gearchange lever and rear brake pedal (see Chapter 5).
20 If required, remove the starter motor (see Chapter 8). If you want to leave the starter motor in situ, pull back the rubber cover on its terminal, then unscrew the nut and disconnect the lead (see illustration). Also unscrew the earth lead bolt (see illustration). Secure the leads clear of the engine.
21 If required remove the front sprocket (see Chapter 6). Remove the swingarm (see Chapter 5). If you haven't removed the front sprocket slip the drive chain off it.
22 Position an hydraulic or mechanical jack under the engine with a block of wood between them (see illustration). Make sure the jack is centrally positioned so the engine will not topple in any direction when the last mounting bolt is removed. Raise the jack to take the weight of the engine, but make sure it is not lifting the bike and taking the weight of that as well. The idea is to support the engine so that there is no pressure on any of the mounting bolts once they have been slackened, so they can be easily withdrawn. Note that it may be necessary to alter the position of the jack as some of the bolts are removed to relieve the stress transferred to the other bolts.

XT-R and XT-X models

Note: *Note from which side the engine mounting bolts and bracket bolts are fitted, and keep any washers with their bolts.*

23 Unscrew the nuts on the engine front mounting bolts and on the bolts securing the front bracket to the frame (see illustration 4.29a). Withdraw the bolts and remove the bracket (see illustration 4.29c).
24 Unscrew the nut on the rear mounting bolt (see illustration 4.30).
25 Unscrew the nuts on the engine upper mounting bolt and on the bolts securing the upper brackets to the frame and remove the left-hand bracket (see illustrations 4.28b and c). Withdraw the engine bolt, leaving the right-hand bracket held by the bolts into the frame (see illustration 4.28d).
26 Check that the engine is properly supported by the jack. Check that all wiring, cables and hoses are free and clear.
27 Withdraw the rear mounting bolt (see illus-

tration 4.32).Carefully lower the jack, supporting the engine and keeping it clear of the frame. With the aid of an assistant remove the jack from under the engine and remove the engine from the right-hand side (see *Caution* above).

XT-Z models

Note: *Note from which side the engine mounting bolts and bracket bolts are fitted, and keep any washers with their bolts.*
28 Remove the caps from the upper mounting bracket nuts (see illustration). Unscrew the nuts on the engine upper mounting bolt and on the bolts securing the upper brackets to the frame and remove the left-hand bracket (see illustrations). Withdraw the engine bolt, leaving the right-hand bracket held by the bolts into the frame (see illustration).

4.22 Support the engine on a jack

4.28a Remove the caps from the nuts . . .

4.28b . . . then unscrew the nuts . . .

4.28c . . . remove the left-hand bracket . . .

4.28d . . . and withdraw the engine bolt

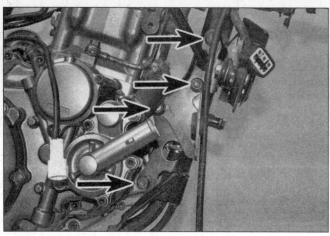

4.29a Unscrew the nuts (arrowed) . . .

4.29b . . . then displace and secure the regulator/rectifier/horn bracket

4.29c Withdraw the bolts and remove the front bracket

29 Unscrew the nuts on the engine front mounting bolts and on the bolts securing the front bracket to the frame **(see illustration)**. Displace the regulator/rectifier/horn bracket and tie it up to the frame **(see illustration)**. Withdraw the bolts and remove the front bracket **(see illustration)**.

30 Unscrew the nut on the rear mounting bolt **(see illustration)**.

31 Check that the engine is properly supported by the jack. Check that all wiring, cables and hoses are free and clear.

32 Withdraw the rear mounting bolt **(see illustration)**.Carefully lower the jack, supporting the engine and keeping it clear of the frame. With the aid of an assistant remove

the jack from under the engine and remove the engine (see *Caution* above).

MT-03 models

Note: *Note from which side the engine mounting bolts and bracket bolts are fitted, and keep any washers with their bolts. An alignment tool, Part No. 90890-11097, is required.*

33 Unscrew the frame tensioning bar bolts and remove the bar **(see illustration)**.

34 Slacken the adjuster nut in the swingarm pivot in the left-hand side of the frame using the alignment tool so it is at least 2 mm clear of the engine.

35 Remove the caps from the upper mounting bracket nuts **(see illustration 4.28a)**. Unscrew the nuts on the engine upper mounting bolt and on the bolts securing the upper brackets to the frame and remove the left-hand bracket **(see illustration 4.28b and c)**. Withdraw the engine bolt, leaving the right-hand bracket held by the bolts into the frame **(see illustration 4.28d)**.

36 Unscrew the nuts on the engine front mounting bolts and on the bolts securing the front bracket to the frame **(see illustration 4.29a)**. Withdraw the bolts and remove the bracket **(see illustration 4.29c)**.

37 Unscrew the nut on the rear mounting bolt **(see illustration 4.30)**.

38 Check that the engine is properly

supported by the jack. Check that all wiring, cables and hoses are free and clear.

39 Withdraw the rear mounting bolt **(see illustration 4.32)**.Carefully lower the jack, supporting the engine and keeping it clear of the frame. With the aid of an assistant remove the jack from under the engine and remove the engine (see *Caution* above).

Installation

40 Manoeuvre the engine into position in the frame and support it with a jack. Align all the mounting bolt holes, making sure that all cables and wiring are correctly routed and do not get trapped. Note that it may be necessary to adjust the jack as some of the bolts are installed and tightened to realign the other bolt holes.

41 On MT-03 models insert the alignment tool (see **Note** in the removal procedure above) through the adjuster nut in the left-hand side of the frame and through to the right-hand side of the frame.

42 Referring to the relevant illustrations and in reverse order of the removal procedure, fit all the mounting bolts and brackets, inserting the bolts from the same side from which they were removed. Fit all the nuts and tighten them finger-tight. Now refer to the tightening procedure below for your model, counter-holding the bolts and tightening the nuts in the

4.30 Unscrew the nut

4.32 Withdraw the rear bolt and the engine is free

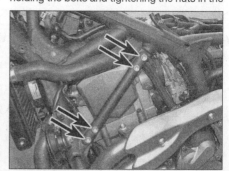

4.33 Unscrew the bolts (arrowed) and remove the bar

correct sequence and to the torque settings specified at the beginning of the Chapter.

XT-R and XT-X models

43 Front bracket-to-frame bolt nuts.
44 Front bracket-to-engine bolt nuts.
45 Rear mounting bolt nut.
46 Upper bracket-to-frame bolt nuts.
47 Upper bracket-to-engine bolt nut.

XT-Z models

48 Rear mounting bolt nut.
49 Front bracket-to-frame bolt nuts.
50 Front bracket-to-engine bolt nuts.
51 Upper bracket-to-frame bolt nuts, front nut first.
52 Upper bracket-to-engine bolt nut.

MT-03 models

53 Tighten the adjuster nut in the left-hand side of the frame to the specified torque setting using a torque wrench on the alignment tool.
54 Rear mounting bolt nut.
55 Front bracket-to-frame bolt nuts.
56 Front bracket-to-engine bolt nuts.
57 Upper bracket-to-frame bolt nuts, front nut first.
58 Upper bracket-to-engine bolt nut.
59 Remove the alignment tool.
60 Fit the frame tensioning bar and tighten the bolts to the specified torque setting **(see illustration 4.33)**.

All models

61 Remove the jack from under the engine.
62 The remainder of the installation procedure is the reverse of removal, noting the following points, and referring to the relevant illustrations in the removal procedure, and to the relevant Chapters where directed:
● Use new gaskets on the exhaust header pipes.
● Use a new O-ring smeared with grease on the oil feed pipe union dowel **(see illustration 4.11b)**. Clean the threads of the bolt and apply a suitable non-permanent thread locking compound then tighten the bolt to the specified torque.
● Clean the threads of the sidestand bracket bolts and apply fresh threadlock.
● Make sure all wires, cables and hoses are correctly routed and connected, and secured by any clips or ties.
● Refill the engine with the specified oil and coolant to the correct level (see Chapter 1).

● Adjust throttle and clutch cable freeplay.
● Adjust the drive chain (see Chapter 1).
● Start the engine and check that there are no oil or coolant leaks. Adjust the idle speed (see Chapter 1).

---

5 Engine disassembly and reassembly general information

1 Before beginning the engine overhaul, read through the related procedures to familiarise yourself with the scope and requirements of the job. Overhauling an engine is not all that difficult, but it is time consuming. Check on the availability of parts and make sure that any necessary special tools are obtained in advance.
2 Most work can be done with a decent set of typical workshop hand tools, although a number of precision measuring tools are required for inspecting parts to determine if they are worn.
3 To ensure maximum life and minimum trouble from a rebuilt engine, everything must be assembled with care in a spotlessly clean environment.

Disassembly

4 Before disassembling the engine, thoroughly clean its external surfaces. This will prevent contamination of the engine internals, and will also make the job a lot easier and cleaner. A high flash-point solvent, such as paraffin (kerosene) can be used, or better still, a proprietary engine degreaser such as Gunk. Use old paintbrushes and toothbrushes to work the solvent into the various recesses of the casings. Take care to exclude solvent or water from the electrical components and intake and exhaust ports.

 Warning: The use of petrol (gasoline) as a cleaning agent should be avoided because of the risk of fire.

5 When clean and dry, position the engine on the workbench, leaving suitable clear area for working. Gather a selection of small containers, plastic bags and some labels so that parts can be grouped together in an easily identifiable manner. Also get some paper and a pen so that notes can be taken. You will also

need a supply of clean rag, which should be as absorbent as possible.
6 Before commencing work, read through the appropriate section so that some idea of the necessary procedure can be gained. When removing components note that great force is seldom required, unless specified (checking the specified torque setting of the particular bolt being removed will indicate how tight it is, and therefore how much force should be needed). In many cases, a component's reluctance to be removed is indicative of an incorrect approach or removal method – if in any doubt, re-check with the text.
7 When disassembling the engine, keep 'mated' parts together (including gears, valves, etc, that have been in contact with each other during engine operation). These 'mated' parts must be reused or replaced as an assembly.
8 A complete engine strip should be done in the following general order with reference to the appropriate Sections.

Remove the cylinder head
Remove the cylinder block and piston
Remove the starter motor (see Chapter 8)
Remove the clutch
Remove the water pump
Remove the oil pump
Remove the gearchange mechanism
Remove the alternator and starter clutch (see Chapter 8)
Remove the cam chain and tensioner blade
Separate the crankcase halves
Remove the transmission shafts and selector drum and forks
Remove the crankshaft and balancer shaft

Reassembly

9 Reassembly is accomplished by reversing the general disassembly sequence.

---

6 Cam chain tensioner

Note: *The cam chain tensioner can be removed with the engine in the frame. If the engine has been removed, ignore the steps which do not apply.*

Removal

1 On XT-Z models remove the left-hand radiator cover (see Chapter 7) and the exhaust shield, but for best access you need to remove the intermediate section of the exhaust, which means removing the complete system (see Chapter 4).
2 On MT-03 models remove the exhaust system (see Chapter 4). Release the oil return hose clamp and detach the hose from the pipe **(see illustration)** – wrap the end of the hose in some rag to catch any residual oil.
3 Set the piston at TDC on the compression stroke (see Section 7, Steps 3 to 5).
4 Unscrew the tensioner cap bolt and remove the spring **(see illustration)**. Discard the sealing washer as a new one must be used.

6.2 Release the clamp (arrowed) and detach the hose

6.4 Unscrew the cap bolt (arrowed)

6.5 Unscrew the bolts and remove the tensioner

6.10 Release the ratchet and push the plunger in

6.11 Install the tensioner using a new gasket and tighten the mounting bolts to the specified torque

6.12 Fit the spring and cap using a new sealing washer

5 Unscrew the tensioner mounting bolts and withdraw the tensioner from the engine **(see illustration)**.
6 Remove the gasket and discard it – a new one must be used on installation.
7 Remove all traces of old gasket from the tensioner and cylinder block mating surfaces.

Inspection

8 Lift the ratchet on the plunger and check that the plunger moves smoothly and freely in and out of the body **(see illustration 6.10)**. With the plunger extended and the ratchet locked make sure you cannot push the

plunger into the body. Replace the tensioner with a new one if there are any faults.

Installation

9 Ensure the tensioner and cylinder block mating surfaces are clean and dry.
10 Lift the ratchet on the plunger and push the plunger fully into the body **(see illustration)**.
11 Fit a new gasket onto the tensioner body with the beaded side facing the tensioner **(see illustration)**. Fit the tensioner and tighten the bolts to the torque setting specified at the beginning of the Chapter **(see illustration 6.5)**.

12 Fit a new sealing washer and the spring onto the tensioner cap bolt, then insert the spring and tighten the bolt to the specified torque **(see illustration)** – as the spring is compressed you should hear the plunger push out over the ratchet mechanism to tension the chain.
13 Turn the engine anti-clockwise through two full turns and check again that all the timing marks still align (see Section 7) **(see illustrations 7.5a, b and c)**. Refit the camshaft sprocket cover, timing inspection cap and crankshaft end cap (see Section 7, Steps 31 and 32).
14 On MT-03 models fit the oil hose onto the return pipe and secure it with the clamp **(see illustration 6.2)**.
15 On XT-Z and MT-03 models, install the exhaust system components as required according to model (see Chapter 4).

7 Camshaft and rocker arms

Note: *The camshaft and rockers can be removed with the engine in the frame.*

Removal

1 Remove the fuel tank (see Chapter 4). On XT-Z models remove the left-hand radiator cover (see Chapter 7). On MT-03 models remove the frame tensioning bar **(see illustration 4.33)**. For best access remove the radiator (see Chapter 3).
2 Remove the spark plug (see Chapter 1).
3 Unscrew the camshaft sprocket cover bolts and remove the cover **(see illustration)**. Unscrew the valve clearance adjuster cover bolts and remove the covers **(see illustration)**. Discard the O-rings – new ones must be used.
4 Unscrew the timing inspection cap and the crankshaft end cap from the alternator cover on the left-hand side of the engine **(see**

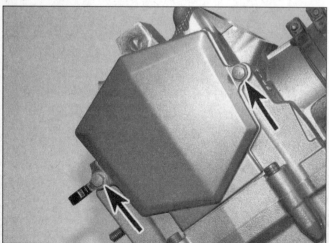

7.3a Unscrew the bolts (arrowed) and remove the sprocket cover

7.3b Unscrew the adjuster cover bolts and remove the covers (arrowed)

7.4 Remove the crankshaft end cap (A) and the timing inspection cap (B)

7.5a Turn the engine anti-clockwise using the nut . . .

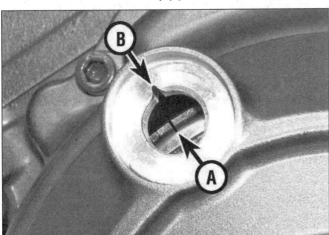

7.5b . . . until the line (A) on the rotor aligns with the notch (B) . . .

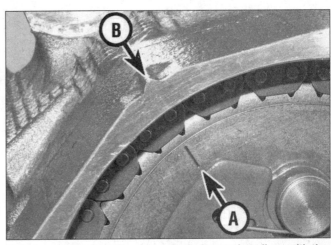

7.5c . . . and the line (A) on the camshaft sprocket aligns with the pointer (B)

illustration). Check the condition of the cap O-rings and replace them with new ones if necessary.

5 The engine must be turned so the piston is at top dead centre (TDC) on its compression stroke so that the valves are closed. Turn the engine anti-clockwise using a suitable socket on the alternator rotor nut until the index line on the rotor aligns with the notch in the inspection hole, and the index line on the camshaft sprocket aligns with the

pointer on the top of the cylinder head (see illustrations). Note: *Do not confuse the index line on the rotor with one of the upright lines on the* H *mark that comes just before it as you turn the engine.* There should now be some freeplay in each rocker arm (i.e. they are not contacting the valve stem) (see illustration). If the index line on the sprocket is at the bottom, rotate the engine anti-clockwise one full turn (360°) until the index line on the rotor again aligns with the pointer inside the inspection

hole – the index line on the sprocket will now be at the top.

6 Remove the cam chain tensioner (see Section 6).

7 Counter-hold the alternator rotor nut and unscrew the cam chain sprocket bolts (see illustration). Slip the sprocket off the end of the camshaft, noting how it locates, and disengage it from the chain (see illustration). You can let the cam chain drop into the tunnel – it can be hooked out later using a magnet or

7.5d There should be some discernible up-and-down freeplay in each rocker

7.7a Unscrew the bolts (arrowed) . . .

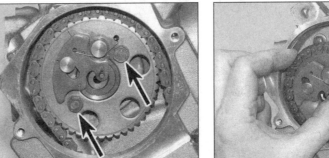

7.7b . . . and remove the sprocket

7.8 Unscrew the bolts (arrowed) and remove the retainer

7.9a Thread the adapter into the shaft . . .

7.9b . . . then fit the slide-hammer and draw the shaft out . . .

7.9c . . . and remove the rocker arm

7.10 Use a screwdriver located as shown to tap the camshaft out

piece of wire, or if preferred secure it with a piece of wire.

8 Unscrew the camshaft/rocker shaft retainer bolts and remove the retainer, noting how it locates **(see illustration)**.

9 Mark each rocker arm according to its location in the holder. To remove the rocker arm shafts you need a slide-hammer to pull them out. Thread a 6 mm adapter with a 1 mm pitch thread into the end of the rocker arm shaft being removed, then fit the slide-hammer attachment and jar the shaft out **(see illustrations)**. If you don't have the necessary tools you can trying using a normal bolt and a pair of pliers on the bolt, but on the engine photographed the shafts were too tight. After removing the shaft remove the rocker arm, then slide the rocker back onto its shaft to prevent mixing up – both shafts are identical and are therefore interchangeable, but the

arms are different. Repeat the procedure for the other rocker arm and shaft.

10 Withdraw the camshaft from the cylinder head – the cut-out in its end must be at the top for the lobes to clear the opening **(see illustration 7.20b)**. If necessary tap the camshaft out using a screwdriver located on the recessed section between the lobes so you are tapping against the edge of the outer lobe **(see illustration)**. If required withdraw the decompression mechanism shaft from the camshaft and remove the pin **(see illustration 7.20a)**.

11 While the camshaft is out do not rotate the crankshaft – the chain may bind. Place a rag over the cylinder head.

Inspection

12 Clean the camshaft, rockers and

shafts. Blow the oil passages through with compressed air.

13 Check the camshaft bearings **(see illustrations)** – they must run smoothly, quietly and freely, and there should be no excessive play between the inner and outer races, or between the inner race and the camshaft, or between the outer race and the cylinder head. The inner bearing is available on its own so can be replaced with a new one. The outer bearing behind the sprocket flange is not available separately – if it is worn a new camshaft must be fitted.

14 Check the camshaft lobes for heat discoloration (blue appearance), score marks, chipped areas, flat spots and pitting. Measure the height of each lobe with a micrometer **(see illustration)** and compare the results to the minimum height listed in this Chapter's Specifications. If damage is noted or wear is excessive, the camshaft must be replaced with a new one.

15 Check the amount of camshaft runout by supporting each end on V-blocks, and measuring any runout using a dial gauge. If the runout exceeds the specified limit the camshaft must be replaced with a new one.

16 Check the action of the decompression mechanism weight on the sprocket, making sure it moves smoothly and freely against the spring and returns when released **(see illustration)**. Also

> **HAYNES HiNT** *Refer to Tools and Workshop Tips in the Reference section for details of how to read a micrometer and dial gauge.*

7.13 Check the bearings (arrowed) on the camshaft

7.14 Measure the height of the camshaft lobes with a micrometer

7.16 Check the action of the weight and look for wear and damage on the shaft (A) and decompression pin (B)

7.17a Check the contacting surfaces of the rocker arm rollers and camshafts . . .

7.17b . . . and of the adjusters and valve stems

7.18a Check for freeplay between the arm and the shaft . . .

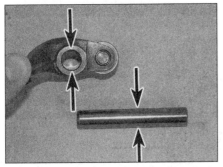

7.18b . . . and measure the internal diameter of the bore and the external diameter of the shaft

7.20a Fit the pin (arrowed) and the shaft, and turn the shaft to make sure the pin moves

7.20b Slide the shaft into the head . . .

check all contacting surfaces between the weight locating pin, the shaft and the decompression pin.

17 Check the rocker arm rollers for heat discoloration (blue appearance), score marks, chipped areas, flat spots and pitting where they contact the camshaft lobes, and make sure they turn freely **(see illustration)**. Similarly check the bottom of each clearance adjuster and the top of each valve stem **(see illustration)**. If damage is noted or wear is excessive, the rocker arms, camshaft and valves must be replaced with new ones as required.

18 Check for freeplay between each rocker arm and its shaft **(see illustration)**. The arms should move freely with a light fit but no appreciable freeplay. If necessary measure the internal diameter of the arm bores and the corresponding diameter of the shaft

and calculate the difference (clearance) to determine the extent of wear **(see illustration)**. Replace the arms and/or shafts with new ones if they are worn beyond their specifications. Check that the fork shaft holes in the holder are neither worn nor damaged.

19 Except in cases of oil starvation, the cam chain should wear very little. If the chain has stretched excessively, which makes it difficult to maintain proper tension, or if it is stiff or the links are binding or kinking, replace it with a new one. Refer to Section 8 for replacement. Check the sprocket for wear, cracks and other damage, and replace it with a new one if necessary. If the sprocket teeth are worn, the cam chain is also worn, and so probably is the sprocket on the crankshaft. If severe wear is apparent, the entire engine should be disassembled for inspection.

Installation

20 If removed fit the decompression mechanism pin and shaft into the camshaft, and make sure the pin moves up and down as you turn the shaft **(see illustration)**. Lubricate the camshaft bearings with clean engine oil and the camshaft lobes with molybdenum disulphide oil. Slide the camshaft, with the cut-out in its end at the top, fully into the head and locate the inner bearing in its housing, then use a drift to tap it home **(see illustrations)**. Make sure the decompression shaft and pin are still correctly in place. Align the camshaft so the cut-out in its end is pointing up, aligned with the pointer on the top of the head **(see illustration)**.

21 Lubricate one rocker shaft and its rocker arm bore with molybdenum disulphide oil (a 50/50 mixture of molybdenum disulphide grease and engine oil). Thread a 6 mm bolt into the shaft **(see illustration)**. Fit the shaft into its bore and

7.20c . . . and tap it until it seats

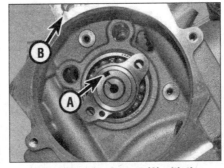

7.20d Align the cut-out (A) with the pointer (B)

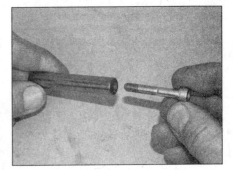

7.21a Fit a bolt into the shaft . . .

7.21b . . . and tap it part-way in . . .

7.21c . . . then position the rocker arm and tap the shaft fully in

7.22 Fit the retainer plate

tap it far enough in to hold it but not so far that it protrudes from the inner side of the first bore (see illustration). Position the rocker arm in its location in the head, with the adjusters on the outside and the contact roller located against the camshaft lobe, then tap the shaft all the way through using a hammer on the bolt head (see illustration). Repeat for the other arm and shaft.
22 Make sure both rocker shafts and the camshaft are fully inserted in the head. Clean the threads of the retainer bolts then apply a suitable non-permanent thread locking compound, then fit the retainer and tighten the bolts to the torque setting specified at the beginning of the Chapter (see illustration).

7.24a Hook the chain out . . .

23 Check that the index line on the alternator rotor aligns with the notch in the inspection hole (see illustration 7.5b). Make sure the cut-out in the camshaft is at the top aligned with the pointer on the head (see illustration 7.20d). Turn the decompression mechanism shaft so the cut-out faces back (see illustration 7.24c).
24 Draw the chain out of the tunnel if you let it drop (see illustration). Engage the cam chain sprocket with the chain (see illustration), making sure the index line on the camshaft sprocket is aligned with the pointer on the top of the cylinder head (see illustration 7.5c), the crankshaft does not rotate, the front run of the chain between the sprockets is tight and that any slack is in the rear run so it will be taken up by the tensioner, then fit the sprocket onto the flange, locating the pin on the decompression mechanism weight in the cut-out in the shaft, and aligning the sprocket bolt holes (see illustration).
25 Fit the cam chain sprocket bolts and lightly tighten them (see illustration 7.7a).
26 Use a piece of wooden dowel or other suitable tool to press on the back of the cam chain tensioner blade via the tensioner bore in the cylinder block to ensure that any slack in the cam chain is taken up and

transferred to the rear run of the chain. At this point check that the timing marks are still in exact alignment as described in Step 5 (see illustrations 7.5b and c). Note that it is easy to be slightly out (one tooth on the sprocket) without the marks appearing drastically out of alignment. If the marks are out unscrew the sprocket bolts and slide the sprocket off the camshaft, then reposition the sprocket in the chain as required, fit the sprocket back into the chain and onto the camshaft, and check the marks again (see illustration 7.7b).
Caution: If the marks are not aligned exactly as described, the valve timing will be incorrect and the valves may strike the piston, causing extensive damage to the engine.
27 Install the cam chain tensioner (see Section 6).
28 Turn the engine anti-clockwise through two full turns and check again that all the timing marks still align (see Step 5) (see illustrations 7.5a, b and c).
29 Counter-hold the alternator rotor nut and tighten the camshaft sprocket bolts to the specified torque setting.
30 Check the valve clearances and adjust them if necessary (see Chapter 1).

7.24b . . . then fit the sprocket . . .

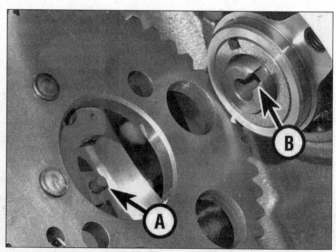

7.24c . . . locating the pin (A) in the cut-out (B)

31 When the clearances are correct fit the camshaft sprocket and adjuster covers using new O-rings smeared with grease and tighten the bolts to the torque setting specified at the beginning of the Chapter, not forgetting the wiring clamp with the sprocket cover front bolt **(see illustrations)**.
32 Fit the timing inspection cap and crankshaft end cap using new O-rings if required, and smear the O-rings with grease **(see illustration)**.
33 Install the spark plug, the radiator if removed (Chapter 3) and the fuel tank (Chapter 4).
34 On XT-Z models install the left-hand radiator cover (see Chapter 7). On MT-03 models fit the frame tensioning bar and tighten the bolts to the specified torque **(see illustration 4.33)**.
35 Check and adjust the idle speed (see Chapter 1).

8 Cam chain, tensioner blade and guide blade

Note: *The cam chain and its blades can be removed with the engine in the frame.*

Removal

Cam chain

1 Remove the camshaft sprocket (see Section 7).
2 Remove the tensioner blade (Steps 4 to 6).
3 Draw the cam chain off the crankshaft sprocket and out of the engine **(see illustration)**.

Tensioner blade

4 Remove the cylinder head (see Section 9).
5 Remove the alternator rotor and starter clutch (see Chapter 8).
6 Unscrew the tensioner blade bolts, then draw the blade out of the top of the cylinder block **(see illustrations)**.

Guide blade

7 Remove the cylinder head (see Section 9).
8 Draw the guide blade out of the top of the cylinder block, noting how it locates **(see illustration)**.

Inspection

Cam chain

9 Check the chain for binding, kinks and any obvious damage and replace it with a new one if necessary. Check the camshaft and crankshaft sprocket teeth for wear and replace the cam chain, camshaft sprocket and crankshaft with a new set if necessary – the drive sprocket on the crankshaft is part of the crankshaft and is not available separately.

Tensioner and guide blades

10 Check the sliding surface and edges of the blades for excessive wear, deep grooves,

7.31a Fit the sprocket cover using a new O-ring smeared with grease . . .

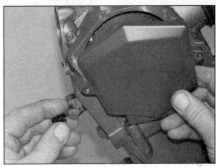

7.31b . . . and do not forget the wire guide with the front bolt

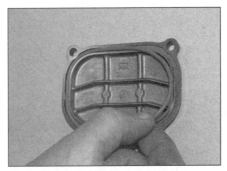

7.31c Fit each adjuster cover using a new O-ring smeared with grease

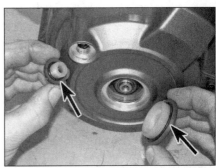

7.32 Fit the caps using new O-rings (arrowed) if required and smear them with grease

8.3 Removing the cam chain

8.6a Unscrew the bolts (arrowed) . . .

8.6b . . . and withdraw the tensioner blade

8.8 Draw the guide blade out, noting how it locates

8.11a The cam chain fits around the outer set of teeth

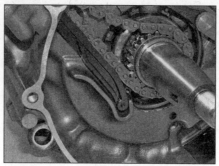

8.11b Make sure the bottom locates in its seat . . .

8.11c . . . and the lugs locate in the cut-outs

cracking and other obvious damage, and replace them with new ones if necessary.

Installation

11 Installation of the chain and blades is the reverse of removal. Note that the cam chain locates around the outer set of teeth on the crankshaft – the inner set is not a sprocket **(see illustration)**. Make sure the bottom of the guide blade sits in its seat and the lugs near its top locate in the cut-outs in the cylinder block **(see illustrations)**. Tighten the tensioner blade bolts to the torque setting specified at the beginning of the Chapter.

9 Cylinder head

Note: *To remove the cylinder head the engine must be removed from the frame.*

Removal

1 Remove the engine from the frame (see Section 4).

2 Unscrew the oil transfer pipe banjo bolts and retaining bolt and remove the pipe **(see illustration)**. Discard the sealing washers – new ones must be used.

3 Unscrew the air induction system pipe bolts and remove the pipe **(see illustration)**. Discard the gasket, noting how it fits **(see illustration 9.19)**.

4 Remove the camshaft sprocket (see Section 7, Steps 2 to 7). If required also remove the camshaft and rocker arms, but note that you can do this after removing the head. Remove the thermostat if required (see Chapter 3).

5 The cylinder head is secured by eight bolts – two on the side of the cam chain tunnel, one at the front and one at the rear, and four on the top. Unscrew the bolts on the side first,

then those on the front and back, noting the washers **(see illustrations)**. Now unscrew the top bolts 1/4 a turn at a time in a criss-cross pattern until they are all loose, then remove them, noting which fits where as they are different lengths, and noting the washers **(see illustration)**. Discard all the washers as new ones must be used.

6 Pull the cylinder head up off the block **(see illustration)**. If the head is stuck, tap around the joint faces with a soft-faced mallet. Do not attempt to free it by inserting a screwdriver between the head and block mating surfaces – you'll damage them.

7 Remove the cylinder head gasket and discard it as a new one must be used **(see illustration 9.11)**. If they are loose, remove the dowels from the cylinder block or the underside of the cylinder head.

8 Check the cylinder head gasket and the mating surfaces on the cylinder head and

9.2 Unscrew the bolts (arrowed) and remove the oil pipe

9.3 Unscrew the bolts (arrowed) and remove the air induction pipe

9.5a Unscrew the bolts (arrowed) on the side . . .

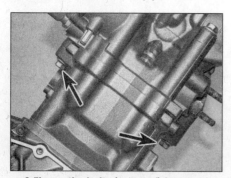

9.5b . . . the bolts (arrowed) front and back . . .

9.5c . . . and the bolts (arrowed) on the top

9.6 Carefully lift the head up off the block

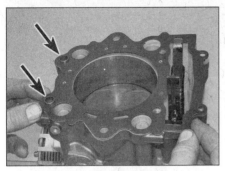

9.11 Fit the dowels (arrowed) then lay the new gasket on the block

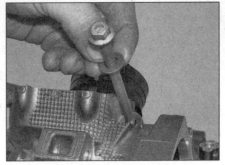

9.13a Fit the top bolts with new sealing washers, lubricated as described . . .

9.13b . . . and the same for the front and rear bolts

cylinder block for signs of leakage, which could indicate warpage. Refer to Section 10 and check the cylinder head gasket surface for warpage.

9 Clean all traces of old gasket material from the cylinder head and cylinder block. Also clean off any carbon deposits from the combustion chamber. If a scraper is used, take care not to scratch or gouge the soft aluminium. Be careful not to let any of the gasket material fall into the cylinder bore or the oil passages.

Installation

10 Lubricate the cylinder bore with engine oil. If removed, fit the dowels into the cylinder block (see illustration 9.11). Make sure the cam chain guide blade is correctly seated (see Section 8).

11 Ensure both cylinder head and cylinder block mating surfaces are clean. Lay the new head gasket over the cam chain blades and onto the block, locating it over the dowels and making sure all the holes are correctly aligned (see illustration). Never reuse the old gasket.

12 Carefully fit the cylinder head over the cam chain blades and onto the block, making sure it locates correctly onto the dowels (see illustration 9.6).

13 Apply engine oil to the threads, under the heads and onto both sides of the new sealing washers on the top, front and rear bolts. Fit the washers onto the bolts with their rounded side facing the underside of the bolt head. Fit the bolts and tighten them finger-tight – the longer top bolts fit on the left-hand side of the head (see illustrations). Apply engine oil to the threads and under the heads of the side bolts and tighten them finger-tight (see illustration 9.5a).

14 Now tighten the top bolts evenly and a little at a time in the numerical sequence shown to the torque setting specified at the beginning of the Chapter (see illustration).

15 Now tighten the front and rear bolts evenly and a little at a time to the specified torque setting.

16 Finally tighten the side bolts to the specified torque setting.

17 Install the camshaft and rocker arms if removed and not already done, then the camshaft sprocket (see Section 7). Fit the thermostat if removed (see Chapter 3).

18 Fit a new gasket onto the air induction system pipe (see illustration). Fit the pipe onto the cylinder head and tighten the bolts to the specified torque setting (see illustration).

19 Fit the oil transfer pipe using new sealing washers on each side of each union and tighten the banjo bolts finger-tight (see illustration). Fit the retaining bolt and tighten to the specified torque setting (see illustration 9.2). Now tighten the banjo bolts to the specified torque.

20 Install the engine (see Section 4).

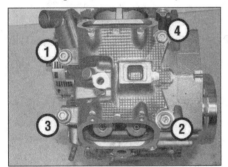

9.14 Tighten the bolts as described in the numerical sequence shown

9.18a Fit a new gasket, making sure its clips locate correctly . . .

10 Cylinder head and valve overhaul

1 Because of the complex nature of this job and the special tools and equipment required, most owners leave servicing of the valves, valve seats and valve guides to a professional. However, you can make an initial assessment of whether the valves are seating correctly, and therefore sealing, by tilting the head and pouring a small amount of solvent into each of the valve ports in turn. If the solvent leaks past either valve into the combustion chamber area the valve is not seating correctly and sealing.

2 With the correct tools (a valve spring compressor is essential – make sure it is suitable for motorcycle work), you can also remove the valves and associated components from the cylinder head, clean them and check them for wear to assess the extent of the work needed, and, unless seat cutting or guide replacement is required, grind in the valves and reassemble them in the head.

3 A dealer service department or specialist can replace the guides and re-cut the valve seats.

9.18b . . . then fit the pipe onto the head

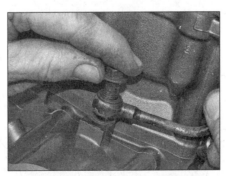

9.19 Fit the oil pipe using new sealing washers on each side of each union

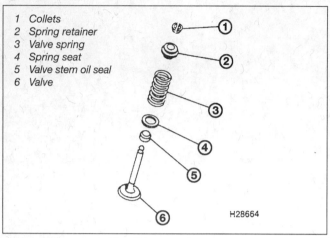

1 Collets
2 Spring retainer
3 Valve spring
4 Spring seat
5 Valve stem oil seal
6 Valve

H28664

10.5 Valve components

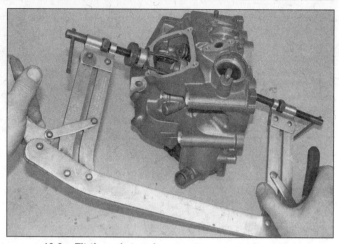

10.6a Fit the valve spring compressor as shown . . .

10.6b . . . making sure it locates correctly both on the top of the spring retainer . . .

10.6c . . . and on the bottom of the valve

10.7a Remove the collets . . .

4 After the valve service has been performed, be sure to clean the head very thoroughly before installation to remove any metal particles or abrasive grit that may still be present from the valve service operations. Use compressed air, if available, to blow out all the holes and passages.

Disassembly

5 Before proceeding, arrange to label and store the valves along with their related components in such a way that they can be returned to their original locations without getting mixed up **(see illustration)**. Labelled plastic bags or a plastic container with four compartments are ideal.

6 Compress the valve spring on the first valve with a spring compressor, making sure it is correctly located onto each end of the valve assembly **(see illustration)** – on the top of the valve the adaptor needs to be about the same size as the spring retainer – if it is too small it will be difficult to remove and install the collets **(see illustration)**. On the underside of the head make sure the plate on the compressor only contacts the valve and not the soft aluminium of the head **(see illustration)** – if the plate is too big for the valve, use a spacer between them. Do not compress the springs any more than is absolutely necessary.

7 Remove the collets, using a magnet or a screwdriver with a dab of grease on it **(see illustration)**. Carefully release the valve spring compressor and remove the spring retainer, noting which way up it fits, the spring and the valve **(see illustrations)**. If the valve binds in the guide and won't pull through, push it back into the head and deburr the area around the collet groove with a very fine file or whetstone **(see illustration)**.

8 Pull the valve stem seal off the top of the valve guide with pliers and discard it (the

10.7b . . . the spring retainer and spring . . .

10.7c . . . and the valve

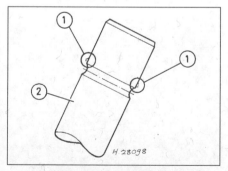

H 28098

10.7d If the valve stem (2) won't pull through the guide, deburr the area (1) above the collet groove

10.8a Pull the seal off the valve stem . . .

10.8b . . . then remove the spring seat

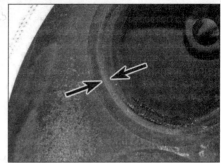

10.15 Measure the valve seat width

old seals should never be reused) **(see illustration)**. Remove the spring seat noting which way up it fits **(see illustration)**.

9 Repeat the procedure for the other valves. Remember to keep the parts for each valve together so they can be reinstalled in the same location.

10 Clean the cylinder head with solvent and dry it thoroughly. Compressed air will speed the drying process and ensure that all holes and recessed areas are clean. **Note:** *Do not use a wire brush mounted in a drill motor to clean the combustion chambers as the head material is soft and may be scratched or eroded away by the wire brush.*

11 Clean all of the valve springs, collets, retainers and spring seats with solvent and dry them thoroughly. Do the parts from one valve at a time so that no mixing of parts occurs.

12 Scrape and clean off any deposits that may have formed on the valve.

Inspection

13 Inspect the head very carefully for cracks and other damage. If cracks are found, a new head is required.

14 Using a precision straight-edge and a feeler gauge set to the warpage limit listed in the specifications at the beginning of the Chapter, check the head gasket mating surface for warpage. Take six measurements, one along each side and two diagonally across. If the head is warped beyond the limit specified at the beginning of this Chapter, consult a Yamaha dealer or take it to a specialist repair shop for an opinion, though be prepared to have to buy a new one.

15 Examine the valve seats in the combustion chamber. If they are pitted, cracked or burned, the head will require work beyond the scope of the home mechanic. Measure the valve seat width and compare it to this Chapter's Specifications **(see illustration)**. If it exceeds the service limit, or if it varies around its circumference, overhaul is required.

16 Working on one valve and guide at a time, measure the valve stem diameter **(see illustration)**. Clean the valve's guide using a guide reamer to remove any carbon build-up. Now measure the inside diameter of the guide (at both ends and in the centre of the guide) with a small bore gauge, then

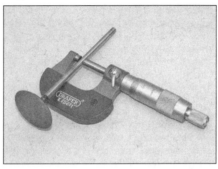

10.16a Measure the valve stem diameter with a micrometer

measure the gauge with a micrometer **(see illustration)**. Measure the guide at the ends and at the centre to determine if they are worn in a bell-mouth pattern (more wear at the ends). Subtract the stem diameter from the valve guide diameter to obtain the valve stem-to-guide clearance. If the stem-to-guide clearance is greater than listed in this Chapter's Specifications, replace whichever component is beyond its specification limits with a new one – take the head to a specialist for valve guide replacement. If the valve guide is within specifications, but is worn unevenly, it should be replaced with a new one. Repeat for the other valves.

17 Carefully inspect each valve face, stem and collet groove area for cracks, pits and burned spots **(see illustration)**.

18 Rotate the valve and check for any obvious indication that it is bent, in which case

10.16b Measure the valve guide with a small bore gauge, then measure the bore gauge with a micrometer

it must be replaced with a new one – if you are not sure place the valve stem in V-blocks and check for runout using a dial gauge. Check the end of the stem for pitting and excessive wear. The presence of any of the above conditions indicates the need for valve servicing.

19 Check the end of the valve spring for wear and pitting. Measure the spring free length and compare them to the specifications **(see illustration)**. If any spring is shorter than specified it has sagged and must be replaced with a new one. Also place the spring upright on a flat surface and check it for bend by placing a ruler against it, or alternatively lay it against a set square. If the bend in any spring exceeds the specified limit, it must be replaced with a new one.

20 Check the spring seats, retainers and collets for obvious wear and cracks. Any questionable parts should not be reused, as

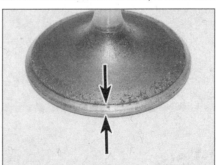

10.17 Measure the valve face width

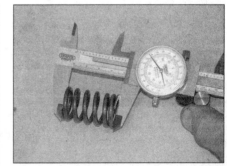

10.19 Measure the free length of the valve springs and check them for bend

10.23 Apply small dabs of the paste around the circumference of the valve

10.24a Using a valve lapping tool

10.24b Make sure the contact areas are as described

extensive damage will occur in the event of failure during engine operation.

21 If the inspection indicates that no overhaul work is required, the valve components can be reinstalled in the head.

Reassembly

22 Unless a valve service has been performed, before installing the valves in the head they should be ground in (lapped) to ensure a positive seal between the valves and seats. This procedure requires coarse and fine valve grinding compound and a valve grinding tool (either hand-held or drill driven – note that some drill-driven tools specify using only a fine grinding compound). If a grinding tool is not available, a piece of rubber or plastic hose can be slipped over the valve stem (after the valve has been installed in the guide) and used to turn the valve.

23 Apply a small amount of coarse grinding

compound to the valve face **(see illustration)**. Smear some molybdenum disulphide oil (a 50/50 mixture of molybdenum disulphide grease and engine oil) to the valve stem, then slip the valve into the guide **(see illustration 10.27)**. Note: *Make sure each valve is installed in its correct guide and be careful not to get any grinding compound on the valve stem.*

24 Attach the grinding tool to the valve and rotate the tool between the palms of your hands **(see illustration)**. Use a back-and-forth motion (as though rubbing your hands together) rather than a circular motion (i.e. so that the valve rotates alternately clockwise and anti-clockwise rather than in one direction only). If a motorised tool is being used, take note of the correct drive speed for it – if your drill runs too fast and is not variable, use a hand tool instead. Lift the valve off the seat and turn it at regular intervals to distribute the grinding compound properly. Continue the grinding procedure until the valve

face and seat contact area is of uniform width, and unbroken around the entire circumference **(see illustration and 10.15)**.

25 Carefully remove the valve and wipe off all traces of grinding compound, making sure none gets in the guide. Use solvent to clean the valve and wipe the seat area thoroughly with a solvent soaked cloth.

26 Repeat the procedure with fine valve grinding compound, then use solvent to clean the valve and flush the guide, and wipe the seat area thoroughly with a solvent soaked cloth. Repeat the entire procedure for the other valves. On completion thoroughly clean the entire head again, then blow through all passages with compressed air. Make sure all traces of the grinding compound have been removed before assembling the head.

27 Working on one valve at a time, coat the valve stem with molybdenum disulphide oil (a 50/50 mixture of molybdenum disulphide grease and engine oil), then slide it into its guide **(see illustration)**. Check that the valve moves up-and-down freely in the guide.

28 Lay the spring seat in place in the cylinder head with its shouldered side facing up **(see illustration)**.

29 Fit a new valve stem seal over the stem and onto the guide, using finger pressure, a stem seal fitting tool or an appropriate size deep socket, to push the seal squarely onto the top of the valve guide until it is felt to clip into place **(see illustrations)**.

30 Next fit the spring, with the painted end up so the closer-wound coils face down into the cylinder head **(see illustration)**. Fit the

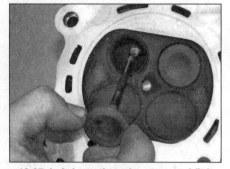

10.27 Lubricate the valve stem and fit it into the guide

10.28 Fit the spring seat shouldered side up

10.29a Fit a new valve stem seal . . .

10.29b . . . and press it squarely into place using a deep socket of the appropriate size

10.30a Fit the spring . . .

spring retainer, with its shouldered side facing down so that it fits into the top of the spring **(see illustration)**.

31 Apply a small amount of grease to the collets to help hold them in place. Compress the valve spring with a spring compressor, making sure it is correctly located onto each end of the valve assembly (see Step 6) **(see illustrations 10.6a and b)**. Do not compress the spring any more than is necessary to slip the collets into place. Locate each collet in turn into the groove in the valve stem using a screwdriver with a dab of grease on it **(see illustration)**. Carefully release the compressor, making sure the collets seat and lock in the retaining groove **(see illustration)**.

32 Repeat the procedure for the other valves.

33 Support the cylinder head on blocks so the valves can't contact the work surface, then tap the end of each valve stem lightly to make sure the collets have seated in their grooves **(see illustration)**.

HAYNES HINT *Check for proper sealing of the valves by pouring a small amount of solvent into each of the valve ports. If the solvent leaks past any valve into the combustion chamber the valve grinding operation on that valve should be repeated.*

34 After the cylinder head and camshaft have been installed, check the valve clearances and adjust as required (see Chapter 1).

11 Cylinder block

Note: *To remove the cylinder block the engine must be removed from the frame.*

Removal

1 Remove the cylinder head (see Section 9).
2 Draw the cam chain guide blade out of the top of the block, noting how it locates **(see illustration 8.8)**.
3 If required remove the coolant inlet union (see Chapter 3).
4 The cylinder block is secured by six bolts – two on the side of the cam chain tunnel, and four on the top. Unscrew the bolts on the

10.30b . . . then fit the retainer shouldered side down

10.31b After releasing the compressor make sure the collets remain seated

side first **(see illustration)**. Now unscrew the top bolts 1/4 a turn at a time in a criss-cross pattern until they are all loose, then remove them, noting which fits where as they are different lengths, and noting the washers **(see illustration)**. Discard the washers as new ones must be used.

5 Pull the cylinder block up off the crankcase, supporting the piston so the connecting rod does not knock against the engine **(see illustration)**. If the block is stuck, tap around the joint faces with a soft-faced mallet. Do not attempt to free it by inserting a screwdriver between the block and crankcase mating surfaces – you'll damage them.

6 Remove the base gasket and discard it as a new one must be used. If they are loose, remove the dowels from the crankcase or the underside of the cylinder block **(see illustration 11.14)**.

7 Stuff some clean rag into the cam chain

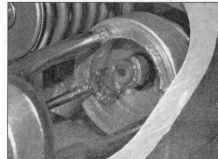
10.31a Use grease to stick each collet in place

10.33 Tap the top of each valve stem to seat the collets

tunnel and around the connecting rod to protect and support it and the piston and to prevent anything falling into the engine.

8 Clean all traces of old gasket material from the cylinder block and crankcase. If a scraper is used, take care not to scratch or gouge the soft aluminium. Be careful not to let any of the gasket material fall into the engine.

Inspection

Note: *Do not attempt to separate the cylinder liner from the cylinder block. The liner is made of aluminium with its bore plated to provide a wear resistant surface – reboring is not possible.*

9 Check the cylinder wall carefully for scratches and score marks.

10 Using a telescoping bore gauge and a micrometer, check the dimensions of the cylinder to assess the amount of wear, taper and ovality. Measure near the top (but below

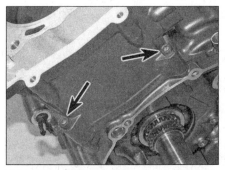
11.4a Unscrew the bolts (arrowed) on the side . . .

11.4b . . . and the bolts (arrowed) on the top

11.5 Carefully lift the block up off the crankcase

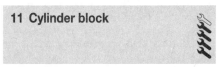

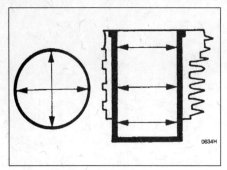

11.10a Measure the cylinder bore in the directions shown . . .

11.10b . . . using a telescoping gauge, then measure the gauge with a micrometer

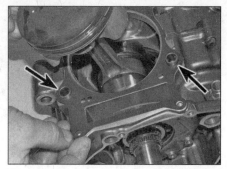

11.14 Lay the new gasket over the dowels (arrowed) and onto the crankcase

the level of the top piston ring at TDC), centre and bottom (but above the level of the oil ring at BDC) of the bore, both parallel to and across the crankshaft axis **(see illustrations)**. Compare the results to the specifications at the beginning of the Chapter. If the cylinder is worn, oval or tapered beyond the service limit it must be replaced with a new one – do not re-bore the cylinder as oversize sets of pistons and rings are not available from Yamaha. If a new cylinder block is fitted also fit a new piston and rings.

11 If the precision measuring tools are not available, take the cylinder block to a Yamaha dealer or specialist motorcycle repair shop for assessment and advice.

Installation

12 Check that the mating surfaces of the cylinder block and crankcase are free from oil or pieces of old gasket.

13 If removed, fit the dowels into the crankcase and push them firmly home **(see illustration 11.14)**.

14 Remove the rags from around the piston and the cam chain tunnel, taking care not to let the connecting rod fall against the rim of the crankcase. Lay the new base gasket in place, locating it over the dowels **(see illustration)**. The gasket can only fit one way, so if all the holes do not line up properly it is the wrong way round. Never re-use the old gasket.

15 Ensure the piston ring end gaps are positioned correctly before fitting the cylinder block **(see illustration 13.10)**. If possible, have an assistant to support the cylinder block while the piston rings are fed into the bore.

16 Rotate the crankshaft so that the piston is at its highest point (top dead centre). It is useful to place a support under the piston so that it remains at TDC while the block is fitted, otherwise the downward pressure will turn the crankshaft and the piston will drop. Lubricate the cylinder bore, piston and piston rings with clean engine oil.

17 Carefully lower the block onto the piston until the crown fits into the bore, holding the underside of the piston if you are not using a support to prevent it dropping, and making sure it enters the bore squarely and does not get cocked sideways **(see illustration 11.5)**.

18 Carefully compress and feed each ring into the bore as the cylinder is lowered **(see illustration)**. If necessary, use a soft mallet to gently tap the cylinder down, but do not use force if it appears to be stuck as the piston and/or rings may be damaged.

19 When the piston and rings are correctly located in the bore, remove the support if used then press the cylinder block down onto the base gasket, making sure the dowels locate.

20 Apply engine oil to the threads, under the heads and onto both sides of the new sealing washers on the top bolts. Fit the washers

onto the bolts with their rounded side facing the underside of the bolt head. Fit the bolts and tighten them finger-tight – the longer bolts fit on the left-hand side of the block **(see illustration)**. Apply engine oil to the threads and under the heads of the side bolts and tighten them finger-tight **(see illustration 11.4a)**.

21 Tighten all the top bolts to the initial torque setting specified at the beginning of the Chapter. Now tighten them to the final torque setting.

22 Tighten the side bolts to the specified torque setting.

23 Turn the crankshaft to check that everything moves as it should.

24 If removed fit the coolant inlet union (see Chapter 3).

25 Install the cam chain guide blade, making sure the bottom of the blade sits in its seat and the lugs near its top locate in the cut-outs in the cylinder block **(see illustrations 8.8 and 8.11b and c)**.

26 Install the cylinder head (see Section 9).

12 Piston

Note: To remove the piston the engine must be removed from the frame.

11.18 Carefully feed each ring into the bore as you lower the block

11.20 Fit the top bolts with new sealing washers lubricated as described

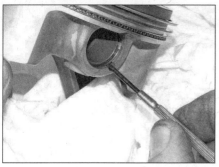

12.3a Prise out the circlip using a suitable tool in the notch . . .

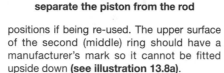

12.3b . . . then push out the pin and separate the piston from the rod

12.10 Measure the piston ring-to-groove clearance with a feeler gauge

Removal

1 Remove the cylinder block (see Section 11). Check that the holes into the crankcase and the cam chain tunnel are completely blocked with rag.
2 Note that the piston crown has a punch mark on its front (exhaust) side, though the mark is likely to be invisible until the piston is cleaned (see illustration 12.15).
3 Carefully prise out the circlip on one side of the piston using needle-nose pliers or a small flat-bladed screwdriver inserted into the notch (see illustration). Push the piston pin out from the other side to free the piston from the connecting rod (see illustration). Remove the other circlip and discard them as new ones must be used.

> **HAYNES HINT** *If the piston pin is a tight fit in the piston bosses, heat the piston using a heat gun – this will expand the piston sufficiently to release its grip on the pin. If the piston pin is particularly stubborn, extract it using a drawbolt tool, but be careful not to mark the pin's bearing surfaces in the piston.*

4 Using your thumbs or a piston ring removal and installation tool, carefully remove the rings from the pistons (see illustrations 13.9, 13.8a and b, 13.6c, b and a). Do not nick or gouge the piston in the process. Carefully note which way up each ring fits and in which groove as they must be installed in their original

positions if being re-used. The upper surface of the second (middle) ring should have a manufacturer's mark so it cannot be fitted upside down (see illustration 13.8a).
5 Scrape all traces of carbon from the top of the piston. A hand-held wire brush or a piece of fine emery cloth can be used once most of the deposits have been scraped away. Do not, under any circumstances, use a wire brush mounted in a drill motor to remove deposits from the piston; the piston material is soft and will be eroded away by the wire brush.
6 Use a piston ring groove cleaning tool to remove any carbon deposits from the ring grooves. If a tool is not available, a piece broken off an old ring will do the job. Be very careful to remove only the carbon deposits. Do not remove any metal and do not nick or gouge the sides of the ring grooves.
7 Once the deposits have been removed, clean the piston with solvent and dry it thoroughly. Make sure the oil return holes below the oil ring groove are clear.

Inspection

8 Carefully inspect the piston for cracks around the skirt, at the pin bosses and at the ring lands. Normal piston wear appears as even, vertical wear on the thrust surfaces. If the skirt is scored or scuffed, the engine may have been suffering from overheating and/or abnormal combustion, which caused excessively high operating temperatures. Also check that the circlip grooves are not damaged.
9 A hole in the top of the piston, in one

extreme, or burned areas around the edge of the piston crown, indicate that pre-ignition or knocking under load have occurred. If you find evidence of any problems the cause must be corrected or the damage will occur again (see *Fault Finding* in the Reference section).
10 Measure the piston ring-to-groove clearance by laying each piston ring in its groove and slipping a feeler gauge in beside it (see illustration). Make sure you have the correct ring for the groove (see Step 4). Check the clearance at three or four locations around the groove. If the clearance is greater than specified, replace both the piston and rings as a set. If new rings are being used, measure the clearance using the new rings. If the clearance is greater than that specified, the piston is worn and must be replaced with a new one.
11 Check the piston-to-bore clearance by measuring the bore (see Section 11), then measure the piston 10 mm up from the bottom of the skirt and at 90° to the piston pin axis (see illustration). Refer to the Specifications at the beginning of the Chapter and subtract the piston diameter from the bore diameter to obtain the clearance. If it is greater than the specified figure, the piston must be replaced with a new one (assuming the bore itself is within limits).
12 Apply clean engine oil to the piston pin, insert it into the piston and check for any freeplay between the two (see illustration). Measure the pin external diameter at each end, and the pin bore in the piston (see illustration). Calculate the difference to obtain

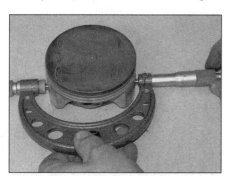

12.11 Measure the piston diameter with a micrometer at the specified distance from the bottom of the skirt

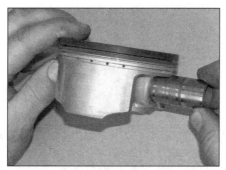

12.12a Fit the pin into the piston and check for any freeplay

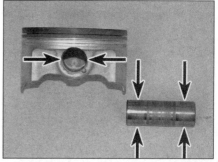

12.12b Measure the external diameter of each end of the pin and the internal diameter of the bore in the piston on each side

12.12c Fit the pin into the connecting rod and check for any freeplay

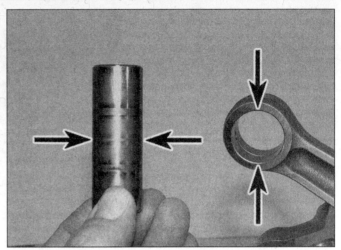

12.12d Measure the external diameter of the middle of the pin and the internal diameter of the small-end of the connecting rod

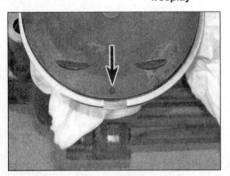

12.15 Fit the piston with the punch mark to the front of the engine

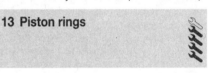

12.16 Use new circlips and make sure they locate correctly

just enough to fit them in the piston, and make sure they are properly seated in their grooves with the open end away from the removal notch.

17 Install the cylinder block (see Section 11).

13 Piston rings

Inspection

1 It is good practice to replace the piston rings with a new set when an engine is being overhauled. Before installing the new rings, check the end gaps with the rings installed in the bore, as follows.

2 Insert the top ring into the bottom of the bore and square it up with the bore walls by pushing it in with the top of the piston (see illustrations). The ring should be about 40 mm below the top edge of the bore. Slip a feeler gauge between the ends of the ring and compare the measurement to the specifications at the beginning of the Chapter (see illustration).

3 If the gap is larger or smaller than specified, double check to make sure that you have the correct ring before proceeding; excess end gap is not critical unless it exceeds the service

the piston pin-to-piston pin bore clearance. Compare the result to the specifications at the beginning of the Chapter. If the clearance is greater than specified, replace the components that are worn beyond their specified limits with new ones. Repeat the check and measurements between the middle of the pin and the connecting rod small-end (see illustrations).

Installation

13 Inspect and install the piston rings (see Section 13).

14 Lubricate the piston pin, the piston pin bore and the connecting rod small-end bore

with molybdenum disulphide oil (a 50/50 mixture of molybdenum disulphide grease and clean engine oil).

15 When fitting the piston onto the connecting rod make sure the punch mark on the piston crown faces the exhaust side (front) of the engine (see illustration).

16 Fit a *new* circlip into one side of the piston (do not reuse old circlips). Line up the piston on the connecting rod with the mark at the front and insert the piston pin from the other side (see illustration 12.3b). Secure the pin with the other *new* circlip (see illustration). When fitting the circlips, compress them only

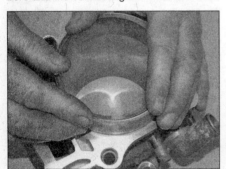

13.2a Fit the ring in the bore . . .

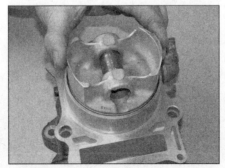

13.2b . . . and set it square using the piston . . .

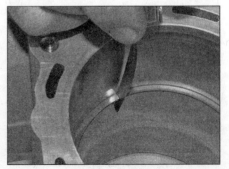

13.2c . . . then measure the end gap using a feeler gauge

13.6a Fit the oil ring expander in its groove . . .

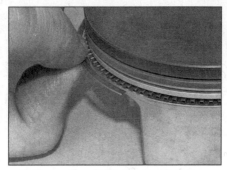

13.6b . . . then fit the lower side rail . . .

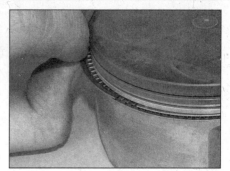

13.6c . . . and the upper side rail on each side of it

13.8a Note the letters on the middle ring which must face up

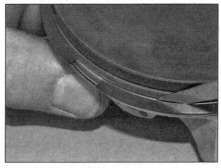

13.8b Install the middle ring . . .

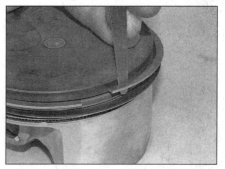

13.9 . . . and the top ring as described

limit. If the gap is too small, the ring ends may come in contact with each other during engine operation, which can cause serious damage.

4 Repeat the procedure for the second (middle) ring but not the oil control ring side-rails and expander ring.

5 If the service limit is exceeded with new rings, check the bore for wear (see Section 12).

Installation

6 Fit the oil control ring (lowest on the piston) first. It is composed of three separate components, namely the expander and the upper and lower side-rails. Slip the expander into the groove, making sure the ends don't overlap, then fit the lower side-rail **(see illustrations)**. Do not use a piston ring installation tool on the side-rails as they may be damaged. Instead, place one end of the side-rail into the groove between the expander and the ring land. Hold it firmly in place and slide a finger around the piston while pushing the rail into the groove. Next, fit the upper side-rail in the same manner **(see illustration)**. Check that the ends of the expander have not overlapped.

7 After the three oil ring components have been installed, check to make sure that both the upper and lower side-rails can be turned smoothly in the ring groove.

8 Fit the second (middle) ring next. Make sure that the identification letters RN near the end gap are facing up **(see illustration)**. Fit the ring into the middle groove in the piston **(see illustration)**. Do not expand the ring any

more than is necessary to slide it into place. To avoid breaking the ring, use a piston ring installation tool.

9 Finally, fit the top ring in the same manner into the top groove in the piston **(see illustration)**.

10 Once the rings are correctly installed,

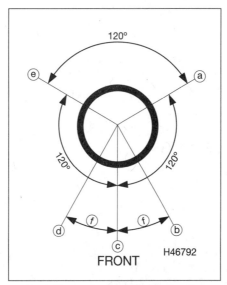

13.10 Piston ring installation details – stagger the ring end gaps as shown

a   Top ring
b   Upper side rail
c   Oil ring expander
d   Lower side rail
e   Second ring
f   20 mm at piston edge

check they move freely without snagging and stagger their end gaps as shown **(see illustration)**.

14 Starter clutch and gears

Note: *The starter clutch can be removed with the engine in the frame. If the engine has been removed, ignore the steps which do not apply.*

Check

1 The operation of the starter clutch can be checked while it is in situ. Remove the starter motor (see Chapter 8). Check that the starter damper gear is able to rotate freely anti-clockwise as you look at it via the starter motor aperture, but locks and turns the engine when rotated clockwise. If not, the starter clutch is faulty and should be removed for inspection.

Removal

2 Remove the alternator rotor and starter driven gear (see Chapter 8) – the starter clutch is bolted to the back of it.

Inspection, disassembly and reassembly

3 With the rotor face down on a workbench, check that the starter driven gear rotates freely anti-clockwise and locks against the

14.3a Check the operation of the starter clutch as described

14.3b Withdraw the driven gear

14.4 Check the sprags and hub for wear and damage

14.5 Starter clutch bolts (arrowed)

14.6 Check the bearing and the bearing surfaces (arrowed) in the gear and on the shaft for wear

rotor clockwise **(see illustration)**. If it doesn't, remove the starter driven gear, rotating it anti-clockwise as you do **(see illustration)**.

4 Check the condition of the sprags and the corresponding surface on the driven gear hub **(see illustration)**. If the sprags are damaged, marked or flattened at any point, replace the starter clutch with a new one.

5 To remove the starter clutch from the back of the alternator rotor hold the rotor using a holding strap and unscrew the three bolts, noting the washers **(see illustration)**. Clean the threads of the bolts. On installation apply a suitable non-permanent thread locking compound to the bolts, then fit them with

their washers and tighten them to the torque setting specified at the beginning of the Chapter.

6 Check the needle bearing and its bearing surfaces in the starter driven gear hub and on the crankshaft **(see illustration)**. Replace the bearing with a new one if necessary.

7 Check the teeth of the starter driven gear, the idle/reduction gear, the damper gear and starter motor drive shaft. Replace the gears and/or starter motor if worn or chipped teeth are discovered on related gears. Also check the idle/reduction gear shaft for damage, and check that the gear is not a loose fit on it. Check the shaft ends and the bores they run

in for wear, and similarly check the damper gear shaft ends, bores and thrust washers.

Installation

8 Install the starter driven gear components and alternator rotor (see Chapter 8).

15 Clutch

Note: *The clutch can be removed with the engine in the frame. If the engine has been removed, ignore the steps which don't apply.*

Removal

1 Drain the engine oil (see Chapter 1).
2 Detach the clutch cable (see Section 16, Step 2). Position the cable clear.
3 Working evenly in a criss-cross pattern, slacken then unscrew the clutch cover bolts **(see illustration)**. Remove the cover, pressing down on the rear brake pedal for clearance, and being prepared to catch any residual oil. Remove the gasket and discard it **(see illustration 15.30a)**. Remove the two dowels from either the cover or the crankcase if they are loose. **Note:** *For improved access to the clutch, remove the complete right-hand cover (Section 17).*
4 Working in a criss-cross pattern, gradually slacken the clutch spring bolts until pressure is released **(see illustration)**. To prevent

15.3 Unscrew the bolts (arrowed) and remove the cover

15.4 Unscrew the bolts (arrowed) as described

15.5 Draw the plates out as a pack and keep them in order

15.7a Bend back the lockwasher tab . . .

15.7b . . . then lock or hold the clutch and unscrew the nut – this shows a commercially available holding tool

15.10 Draw the clutch housing off the shaft

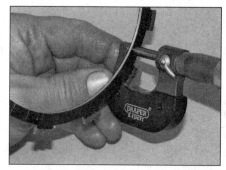

15.11 Measuring clutch friction plate thickness

the clutch from turning, cover it with a rag and hold it securely – the bolts are not very tight. If available, have an assistant hold the clutch while you unscrew the bolts. Remove the bolts, springs and the pressure plate, noting the pull rod fitted in the bearing **(see illustrations 15.28 and 15.27a)**.

5 Remove the clutch friction and plain plates, noting how they fit and keeping them in order **(see illustration)**. Note how the inner friction plate has a larger internal diameter so it seats around the anti-judder spring and spring seat. If you are replacing the plates with new ones and no further disassembly of the clutch is intended, refer to Steps 11-on and follow the relevant inspection procedures, then refer to Steps 24-on to fit the new plates.

6 Remove the anti-judder spring and spring seat, noting which way round they fit **(see illustrations 15.23b and a)**.

7 Bend the clutch nut lockwasher tab off the nut **(see illustration)**. To unscrew the clutch nut, the input shaft must be locked – this can be done in several ways: if the engine is in the frame, engage 5th gear and have an assistant hold the rear brake on hard with the rear tyre in firm contact with the ground; alternatively, and if the engine has been removed, the Yamaha service tool (Pt. No. 90890-04086) or a commercially available clutch holding tool (as shown) can be used to stop the clutch centre from turning **(see illustration)**. Unscrew the nut and remove the washer **(see illustrations 15.22b and a)**. Check the condition of the washer and replace it with a new one if necessary – Yamaha specify to use a new one.

8 Slide the clutch centre off the shaft **(see illustration 15.21b)**.

9 Slide the thrust washer off the shaft **(see illustration 15.21a)**.

10 Slide the clutch housing off the shaft **(see illustration)**.

Inspection

11 After an extended period of service the clutch friction plates will wear and promote clutch slip. Measure the thickness of each friction plate using a Vernier calliper, making sure you apply the correct specification to each plate – the outer two plates are type 1, then next two are type 2, the next two are type 1, and the innermost plate is type 3 **(see illustration)**. If any plate has worn to or beyond the service limits given in the Specifications at the beginning of the Chapter, or if any of the plates smell burnt or are glazed,

the friction plates must be replaced with a new set.

12 The plain plates should not show any signs of excess heating (bluing). Check for warpage using a flat surface and feeler gauges **(see illustration)**. If any plate exceeds the maximum permissible amount of warpage, or shows signs of bluing, all plain plates must be replaced with a new set.

13 Measure the free length of each clutch spring using a Vernier caliper **(see illustration)**. Place each spring upright on a flat surface and check it for bend by placing a ruler against it, or alternatively lay it against a set square. If any spring is below the minimum free length specified or if the bend in any spring is excessive, replace all the springs as a set.

14 Inspect the friction plate tabs and the clutch housing slots for burrs and indentations on the edges **(see illustration)**. Similarly

15.12 Check the plain plates for warpage

15.13 Measure the free length of the clutch springs and check them for bend

15.14a Check the friction plate tabs and housing slots . . .

15.14b . . . and the plain plate teeth and centre slots as described

15.15 Check the bearing surfaces on the bush (arrowed) and the shaft

15.16a Check the pressure plate bearing . . .

check for wear between the inner teeth of the plain plates and the slots in the clutch centre **(see illustration)**. Wear of this nature will cause clutch drag and slow disengagement during gear changes as the plates will snag when the pressure plate is lifted. With care a small amount of wear can be corrected by dressing with a fine file, but if this is excessive the worn components should be replaced with new ones.

15 Inspect the bearing surfaces of the clutch housing bush and the input shaft **(see illustration)**. If there are any signs of excessive wear (the oil retention dimples should be visible), pitting or other damage the affected parts must be replaced with new ones.

16 Check the pressure plate and ball bearing for signs of wear or damage and make sure the bearing turns smoothly and freely **(see illustration)**. Check the teeth on the pull rod and the corresponding teeth on the release mechanism shaft for wear and damage **(see illustration)**. Replace any parts necessary with new ones.

17 Check the release mechanism shaft in the clutch cover for a smooth action. If the action is stiff or rough, remove the E-clip and washer then withdraw the shaft, noting how the spring ends locate **(see illustrations)**. Clean and check the oil seal and the bearings in the cover, and the bearing surfaces on the shaft **(see illustration)**. The seal can be replaced by levering it out with a seal hook or screwdriver. The bearings must be driven out using a punch or pulled out – refer to *Tools and Workshop Tips* in the reference section

for more information. Fit the new bearings and seal, using a suitable socket to drive them in if necessary **(see illustrations)**. Lubricate the bearings with molybdenum disulphide oil (a 50/50 mixture of molybdenum disulphide grease and engine oil) and the seal lips with grease before installing the shaft and fitting the washer and E-clip **(see illustration)**. Make sure the return spring ends locate correctly **(see illustration)**.

18 Check the teeth of the primary driven gear and oil pump drive gear on the back of the clutch housing and the corresponding teeth of the primary drive gear on the crankshaft and the oil pump driven gear **(see illustration 15.15)**. Replace the clutch housing and/or primary drive gear and/or oil pump driven gear with a new one if worn or chipped teeth

15.16b . . . and the pull rod and shaft teeth

15.17a Release the E-clip and remove the washer . . .

15.17b . . . then withdraw the shaft

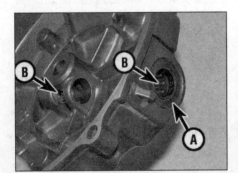

15.17c Check the seal (A) and the bearings (B)

15.17d Do not forget the washer (arrowed) and seat the E-clip in its groove

15.17e Make sure the spring ends (arrowed) locate correctly

15.20 Turn the oil pump driven gear with your finger to align the teeth if necessary

15.21a Fit the thrust washer onto the splines . . .

15.21b . . . then slide the clutch centre on

are discovered – refer to Section 18 for the primary drive gear and Section 19 for the oil pump gear. Check for any rotational play between the primary driven gear and the clutch housing and replace the housing with a new one if any is evident.

Installation

19 Remove all traces of old gasket from the crankcase and clutch cover surfaces.
20 Smear the bush in the centre of the clutch housing with clean engine oil **(see illustration 15.15)**. Slide the housing onto the shaft making sure that the teeth of the oil pump drive gear and primary driven gear on the back of the housing engage with those of the oil pump driven gear and primary drive gear **(see illustration)**.

21 Slide the thrust washer onto the shaft, followed by the clutch centre **(see illustrations)**.
22 Fit the lockwasher, preferably using a new one, and locating its locking tab in the cut-out **(see illustration)**. Lubricate the threads on the end of the input shaft with clean oil. Thread the clutch nut on **(see illustration)**. Using the method employed on removal to lock the input shaft, tighten the nut to the torque setting specified at the beginning of the Chapter **(see illustration)**. Bend the rim of the washer up against one of the flats on the nut to lock it **(see illustration)**.
23 Fit the anti-judder spring seat into the clutch centre, then fit the spring with its OUTSIDE mark facing out so that its outer

edge is raised off the seat and facing outwards **(see illustrations)**.
24 There are three different types of friction plate and they must be installed in the correct order. There are four Type 1 plates, two Type 2 plates, and one Type 3 plate. The Type 1 and 2 plates are distinguishable by the colour code (Type 2) or notched surface (Type 1) on one of the tabs. The type 3 plate has a larger internal diameter. The plain plates are all identical, and there must be a plain plate between each pair of friction plates. Now identify the two slots on the clutch housing with posts marked with triangles and turn the housing to position them at the top.
25 Coat each clutch plate with engine oil prior to installation, then build up the plates

15.22a Locate the washer tab in the cut-out (arrowed)

15.22b Thread the nut on . . .

15.22c . . . and tighten it to the specified torque

15.22d Bend the washer tab up against the nut

15.23a Fit the spring seat and spring . . .

15.23b . . . with the OUTSIDE mark on the spring facing out

15.25a Fit the friction plate with the larger internal diameter first . . .

15.25b . . . then a plain plate

15.25c Fit the notched tab into the right-hand of the two marked slots

15.25d The installed plate pack should be as shown

15.27a Fit the pressure plate with the pull rod . . .

another Type 1 friction plate and plain plate in the same way, then fit the two Type 2 friction plates alternating with plain plates, then fit another Type 1 friction plate and plain plate as before, then fit the final Type 1 friction plate, locating the notched tab in the shallow left-hand slot of the two marked with triangles **(see illustration)**.

26 Lubricate the bearing and pull rod and fit them into the pressure plate if removed.

27 Fit the pressure plate, making sure the castellations locate in the clutch centre **(see illustrations)**. Hold the pressure plate and check for any gaps between the clutch plates – there should be none; if there are, it means the pressure plate has not located properly.

28 Lubricate the clutch spring bolt threads with oil, then fit the springs and bolts and tighten the bolts evenly and a little at a time in a criss-cross sequence to the specified torque **(see illustration)**.

29 Turn the pull rod so the teeth face to the rear.

30 Fit the two dowels into the crankcase if removed, then fit a new gasket, locating it over the dowels **(see illustration)**. Fit the cover with the release mechanism arm pointing to the rear, making sure the pull rod and shaft teeth engage correctly, in which case the arm will move forwards as the cover is seated **(see illustration)**. Install all the bolts finger-tight, then tighten them evenly and a little at a time in a criss-cross pattern to the specified torque.

31 Check the alignment of the release mechanism arm – with the arm pushed forward the punch mark should align with that on the cover **(see illustration)**. If they

15.27b . . . engaging the castellations on the inner face with the slots of the clutch centre

15.28 Fit the springs and tighten the bolts as described

as follows. First fit the Type 3 friction plate with the larger internal diameter, seating it around the anti-judder spring and spring seat **(see illustration)**, then fit a plain plate **(see**

illustration**)**, then fit a Type 1 friction plate, locating the notched tab in the right-hand of the two slots marked with triangles **(see illustration)**, then fit a plain plate, then fit

15.30a Locate the new gasket over the dowels (arrowed) . . .

15.30b . . . then fit the cover

15.31 Push the arm forwards and when it can go no further the punch marks should align

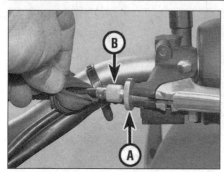

16.1 Pull back the boot, slacken the lockring (A) and turn the adjuster (B) in

do not align, either remove the cover and reposition the shaft/arm to compensate before refitting the cover, or remove the circlip and washer from the top of the shaft, then slide the arm and spring up off the shaft, realign the arm, then refit all components, making sure the spring ends locate correctly.

32 Connect the clutch cable (see Section 16).

33 Fill the engine with the correct amount and type of oil (see Chapter 1).

16 Clutch cable

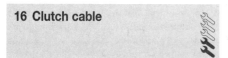

1 Pull the rubber boot off the adjuster at the handlebar end of the cable. Fully slacken the lockring, then thread the adjuster fully in **(see illustration)**. This provides freeplay in the cable and resets the adjuster to the beginning of its span.

2 Bend the retaining tab in the release arm up **(see illustration)**. Slacken the nuts securing the clutch cable in the bracket on the engine, slip the cable out of the bracket and free the end from the release arm **(see illustrations)**.

3 Align the slots in the adjuster and lockring at the handlebar end of the cable with that in the lever bracket, then pull the outer cable end from the socket in the adjuster and release the inner cable from the lever **(see illustrations)**.

16.2a Bend the retaining tab up

16.2c ... then slip the cable out of the bracket ...

 HAYNES HiNT *Before removing the cable from the bike, tape the lower end of the new cable to the upper end of the old cable. Slowly pull the lower end of the old cable out, guiding the new cable down into position. Using this method will ensure the cable is routed correctly.*

Remove the cable from the machine, noting its routing.

4 Installation is the reverse of removal. Apply grease to the cable ends. Make sure the cable is correctly routed. Adjust the amount of clutch lever freeplay (see Chapter 1). Do not forget to bend the tab against the cable end in the release arm **(see illustration)**.

16.2b Draw the boot off and slacken the nuts (arrowed) ...

16.2d ... and detach the end from the arm

17 Right-hand crankcase cover

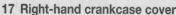

Note: *The cover can be removed with the engine in the frame. If the engine has been removed ignore the Steps which don't apply.*

Removal

1 Drain the engine oil and remove the oil filter. Drain the coolant (see Chapter 1). Detach the clutch cable (see Section 16, Step 2). Position the cable clear.

2 Remove the water pump (see Chapter 3).

3 On XT-R and XT-X models unscrew the rear master cylinder reservoir bolt **(see**

16.3a Free the outer cable from the adjuster ...

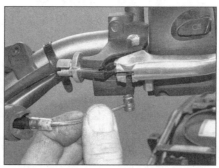

16.3b ... and the inner cable from the lever

16.4 Bend the retaining tab down to secure the cable

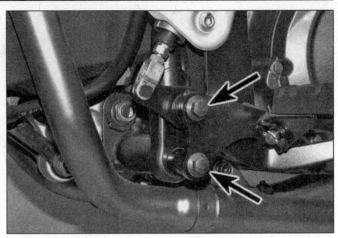

17.3a Unscrew the reservoir bolt (A) and cut the cable-tie (B)

17.3b Unscrew the bolts (arrowed) and displace the assembly

illustration). Cut the cable-tie securing the rear brake light switch wire to the frame. Unscrew the right-hand footrest bracket bolts and displace the footrest bracket/brake pedal/master cylinder assembly, securing it clear of the crankcase cover and making sure no strain is placed on the brake hose or switch wiring (see illustration).

4 On XT-Z models remove the rear brake pedal (see Chapter 5).

5 On MT-03 models, if the clutch has been

removed you only need to remove the brake pedal (see Chapter 5). If the clutch is in place, remove the split pin and washer from the clevis pin securing the brake pedal to the master cylinder pushrod, then withdraw the pin and detach the pushrod (see illustration). Discard the split pin – a new one must be used. Unscrew the master cylinder bolts and displace the master cylinder assembly (see illustration). Unscrew the nut on the left-hand end of the swingarm pivot and remove the

washer (see illustration). Note the nut is self-locking and Yamaha specify to use a new one. Unscrew the bolt on the bottom of the footrest bracket on the right-hand side (see illustration). Grasp the bracket and draw it off the frame, bringing the swingarm pivot with it, just enough so there is clearance for the crankcase cover whilst leaving the swingarm properly supported.

6 Unscrew the oil transfer pipe banjo bolts (see illustration). Discard the sealing washers

17.5a Remove the split pin and washer (arrowed) then withdraw the clevis pin

17.5b Unscrew the master cylinder bolts (arrowed)

17.5c Unscrew the nut (arrowed) and remove the washer

17.5d Unscrew the bolt (arrowed), then draw the bracket away from the frame as described

17.6 Unscrew the oil pipe banjo bolts (arrowed)

17.7 Unscrew the bolts (arrowed) and remove the cover

17.8a Unscrew the bolts (arrowed) and remove the retainer

– new ones must be used. If you are removing the crankcase cover as part of a complete engine overhaul then also detach the rear pipe from the crankcase and remove it.

7 Working evenly in a criss-cross pattern, slacken then unscrew the cover bolts, noting the position of the cable bracket, and on MT-03 models of the earth lead secured with it **(see illustration and 4.16)**. Remove the cover, being prepared to catch any residual oil. Remove the gasket and discard it **(see**

illustration 17.9a)**. Remove the two dowels from either the cover or the crankcase if they are loose.

Installation

8 Remove all traces of old gasket from the crankcase and cover surfaces. Unscrew the oil seal retainer bolts and remove the retainer **(see illustration)**. Lever the oil seal out and replace it with a new one **(see illustrations)**. Clean the threads of the retainer bolts and

apply fresh threadlock. Make sure the check valve ball moves in when pressed and springs back out when released **(see illustration)**.

9 Fit the two dowels into the crankcase if removed, then fit a new gasket, locating it over the dowels **(see illustration)**. Fit the cover **(see illustration)**. Install all the bolts finger-tight, then tighten them evenly and a little at a time in a criss-cross pattern to the torque setting specified at the beginning of the Chapter.

17.8b Lever the oil seal out . . .

17.8c . . . and replace it with a new one

17.8d Check the action of the valve ball

17.9a Fit a new gasket onto the dowels (arrowed) . . .

17.9b . . . then fit the cover

18.3 Water pump/primary drive/balancer drive gears nut (A), balancer driven gear nut (B). Note the alignment of the punch marks (C) between the balancer gears

10 Fit new sealing washers on each side of each oil transfer pipe union and tighten the banjo bolts to the specified torque setting (see illustration 9.19).
11 On XT-R and XT-X models fit the footrest bracket/brake pedal/master cylinder assembly and tighten the bolts to the specified torque (see illustration 17.3b). Secure the reservoir with its bolt and the brake light switch wire with a new cable-tie (see illustration 17.3a).
12 On XT-Z models install the brake pedal (see Chapter 5).
13 On MT-03 models, if displaced relocate the footrest bracket/brake pedal/master cylinder assembly. Fit the footrest bracket bolt and a new swingarm pivot bolt nut and tighten them and the master cylinder bolts to the specified torque settings (see illustrations 17.5d,

18.6a Lock the gears at the top . . .

18.7a Unscrew the nut and remove the lockwasher . . .

18.5a Bend the lockwasher tabs back . . .

c, and b). Align the master cylinder clevis with the brake pedal, then insert the clevis pin, fit the washer and a new split pin, then bend its ends round to secure it (see illustration 17.5a). Otherwise install the brake pedal (see Chapter 5).
14 Install the water pump (see Chapter 3).
15 Fit a new the oil filter and replenish the engine oil and coolant (see Chapter 1). Connect the clutch cable (see Section 16).

18 Water pump, primary drive and balancer shaft gears

Note: The gears can be removed with the engine in the frame.

Removal

1 Remove the spark plug (see Chapter 1).

18.6b . . . or at the bottom as required and described when unscrewing the nuts

18.7b . . . the slotted washer . . .

18.5b . . . to free the nuts

2 Remove the right-hand crankcase cover (see Section 17).
3 The water pump, primary drive and balancer shaft drive gears are secured by a nut on the end of the crankshaft and the balancer shaft driven gear is secured by a nut on the end of the balancer shaft (see illustration). Each nut has a lockwasher behind it – note that new lockwashers should be used on installation.
4 Turn the crankshaft clockwise using a spanner or socket on the crankshaft nut and align the punch marks on the balancer shaft drive and driven gears (see illustration 18.3).
5 Bend back the lockwasher tab on the nut being unscrewed (see illustrations).
6 To unscrew the nuts you need to lock the gears to prevent them turning – to do this wedge a stout piece of rag or rolled up strap, or if available a piece of aluminium plate as shown (DO NOT use steel), between the teeth of the balancer shaft drive and driven gears where they mesh at the top when unscrewing the water pump, primary drive and balancer shaft drive gear nut, and at the bottom when unscrewing the balancer shaft driven gear nut (see illustrations). With the gears locked slacken the nut(s). Remove the rag, strap or plate.
7 Unscrew the crankshaft nut and remove the lockwasher and slotted washer, noting how they locate, then slide the water pump, primary drive and balancer shaft drive gears off the end of the shaft, noting how they locate on the key (see illustrations). Remove the key from

18.7c . . . the water pump drive gear . . .

18.7d ... the primary drive gear ...

18.7e ... and the balancer drive gear

18.7f Draw the key from its slot ...

the slot in the shaft (see illustration). Slide the thrust washer off shaft (see illustration).

8 Unscrew the balancer shaft nut and remove the lockwasher, noting how it locates, then slide the balancer shaft driven gear off the end of the shaft, noting how it locates on the key (see illustrations). Remove the key from the slot in the shaft (see illustration).

Installation

9 Fit the short key into the slot in the balancer shaft (see illustration 18.8c). Slide the balancer driven gear onto the shaft with the punch mark facing out, seating the slot in the gear over the key (see illustration 18.8b). Fit a new lockwasher, locating the inward facing tab in the slot in the gear (see illustration 18.8a). Smear clean engine oil onto the threads and tighten the nut finger-tight.

10 Slide the thrust washer onto the crankshaft (see illustration 18.7g). Fit the long key into the slot in the crankshaft (see illustration 18.7f).

Slide the balancer drive gear onto the shaft with the punch mark facing out (see illustration 18.7e), aligning the mark with that on the driven gear, turning the shaft(s) as required, and seating the slot in the gear over the key (see illustration). Slide the primary drive gear on with its shouldered side facing in, seating the slot in the gear over the key (see illustration 18.7d). Finally slide the water pump drive gear on (see illustration 18.7c). Slide the slotted washer on, locating the slot around the key (see illustration 18.7b). Fit a new lockwasher, locating the inward facing tab between the ends of the slotted washer (see illustration 18.7a). Smear molybdenum disulphide oil (a 50/50 mixture of molybdenum disulphide grease and engine oil) onto the threads and tighten the nut finger-tight.

11 Wedge the stout piece of rag, strap or aluminium plate where the balancer drive and driven gear teeth mesh at the bottom to tighten the nut on the crankshaft, and at the

top to tighten the nut on the balancer shaft (see illustrations 18.6b and a) – tighten both nuts to the torque settings specified at the beginning of the Chapter. Bend the lockwasher tabs up against the nuts (see illustrations).

12 Install the right-hand crankcase cover (see Section 17) and the spark plug (see Chapter 1).

18.7g ... then slide the thrust washer off

18.8a Unscrew the nut and remove the lockwasher ...

18.8b ... and the balancer driven gear

18.8c Draw the key from its slot

18.10 Make sure the punch marks on the balancer gears align

18.11a Bend the lockwasher tabs up ...

18.11b ... to secure the nuts

19 Oil pump and strainer

Note: *The oil pump can be removed with the engine in the frame. The oil strainer can only be accessed once the crankcases have been separated.*

Oil pump

Removal

1 Remove the right-hand crankcase cover (see Section 17).

2 Unscrew the outer baffle plate bolts and remove the plate **(see illustration)**.

3 Release the circlip securing the pump gear and slide the gear off the shaft **(see illustrations)**. Discard the circlip – a new one should be used.

4 Unscrew the oil pump bolts and remove the inner baffle plate and the pump **(see illustration)**.

5 Remove the gasket and discard it – a new one must be used **(see illustration 19.20a)**. Remove the O-rings from the oil passages and discard them **(see illustration 19.19)** – new ones must be used.

Inspection

Note: *Before removing the rotors note the punch marks and which way they face. Refitting the rotors in their original positions will ensure that mated surfaces continue to run together. Note that individual components*

19.2 Unscrew the bolts (arrowed) and remove the outer plate

19.3a Release the circlip . . .

19.3b . . . and remove the gear

19.4 Unscrew the bolts (arrowed) and remove the inner plate and the pump

are not available for the pump – it comes as an assembly.

6 Undo the screw on the back of the pump, then remove the inner cover and feed pump outer and inner rotors, noting which way round

they fit, and the drive pin **(see illustrations)**. Remove the centre cover and the locating pins **(see illustrations)**. Remove the scavenge pump outer and inner rotors, noting which way round they fit, and the drive pin **(see**

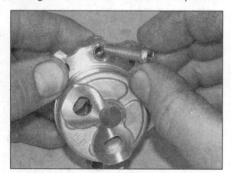

19.6a Undo the screw . . .

19.6b . . . remove the inner cover . . .

19.6c . . . the feed pump outer rotor . . .

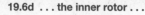

19.6d . . . the inner rotor . . .

19.6e . . . and the drive pin

19.6f Remove the centre cover . . .

19.6g . . . and the locating pins

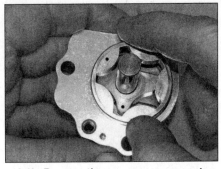

19.6h Remove the scavenge pump outer rotor . . .

19.6i . . . the inner rotor . . .

19.6j . . . and the drive pin

19.6k Draw the shaft out

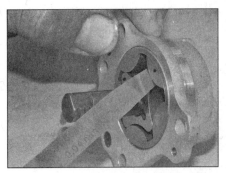

19.9 Measure the inner rotor tip-to-outer rotor clearance as shown

illustrations). Withdraw the shaft from the outer cover.
7 Clean all the components in solvent.
8 Inspect the pump body and rotors for scoring and wear. If any damage, scoring or uneven or excessive wear is evident, replace the pump with a new one.
9 Fit the scavenge pump inner and outer rotors into the front cover with the punch marks facing out. Fit the shaft into the inner rotor. Measure the clearance between the inner rotor tip and the outer rotor with a feeler gauge and compare it to the service limit listed in the specifications at the beginning of the Chapter **(see illustration)**. If the clearance measured is greater than the maximum listed, replace the pump with a new one.
10 Measure the clearance between the outer rotor and the pump housing with a feeler gauge

and compare it to the maximum clearance listed in the specifications at the beginning of the Chapter **(see illustration)**. If the clearance measured is greater than the maximum listed, replace the pump with a new one.
11 Lay a straight-edge across the rotors and the pump housing and, using a feeler gauge, measure the rotor end-float (the gap between the rotors and the straight-edge **(see illustration)**. If the clearance measured is greater than the maximum listed, replace the pump with a new one.
12 Repeat the measurement procedure for the feed pump rotors and inner cover.
13 Check the pump drive and driven gears, shaft and drive pins, and the seals in the centre and outer covers, for wear and damage, and replace the pump with a new one if necessary **(see illustration)**.

14 If the pump is good, make sure all the components are clean, then lubricate them with new engine oil.
15 Fit the shaft through the outer cover with the grooved end facing out **(see illustration 19.6k)**. Fit the drive pin, then fit the scavenge pump inner rotor, locating the cut-outs over the drive pin ends, and then the outer rotor, with the punch marks facing away from the front cover **(see illustrations 19.6j, i and h)**.
16 Fit the locating pins into the outer cover then fit the centre cover onto the pins **(see illustrations 19.6g and f)**.
17 Fit the drive pin **(see illustration 19.6e)**. Fit the feed pump inner rotor with the punch mark facing the centre cover, locating the cut-outs over the drive pin ends, then fit the outer rotor **(see illustrations 19.6d and c)**. Fit the inner cover and tighten the assembly

19.10 Measure the outer rotor-to-body clearance as shown

19.11 Measure rotor end-float as shown

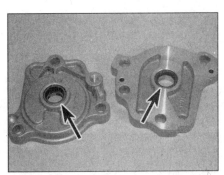

19.13 Check the seals (arrowed) in the covers

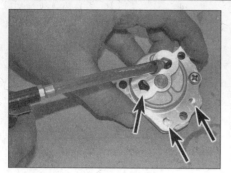

19.18 Prime the pumps with oil via the inlet and outlet holes

19.19 Fit a new O-ring onto each passage

19.20a Fit a new gasket . . .

screw to the torque setting specified at the beginning of the Chapter **(see illustrations 19.6b and a)**.

18 Rotate the pump shaft by hand and check it turns the rotors smoothly and freely. Fill the pump with clean engine oil via the holes **(see illustration)**.

Installation

19 Fit new O-rings smeared with grease onto the oil passages **(see illustration)**.

20 Fit the pump using a new gasket, then fit the inner baffle plate and tighten the bolts to the torque setting specified at the beginning of the Chapter **(see illustrations)**.

21 Slide the gear onto the pump shaft and secure it using a new circlip, fitting it with its rounded side facing the gear and making

sure it locates correctly in the groove **(see illustrations 19.3b and a)**.

22 Clean the threads of the outer baffle plate bolts. Apply a suitable non-permanent thread locking compound to the threads, then fit the plate and tighten the bolts to the specified torque setting **(see illustration)**.

23 Install the right-hand crankcase cover (see Section 17).

Oil strainer

Removal

24 Remove the engine from the frame (see Section 4).

25 Separate the crankcase halves (see Section 21).

26 Unscrew the strainer bolts and remove

the strainer and its gasket **(see illustration)**. Discard the gasket – a new one must be used.

Inspection

27 Clean the strainer with solvent, removing any debris caught in the gauze **(see illustration)**. Check the gauze for splits and holes and replace the strainer with a new one if necessary.

Installation

28 Clean the threads of the strainer bolts. Fit the strainer using a new gasket **(see illustration)**. Apply a suitable non-permanent thread locking compound to the bolt threads and tighten the bolts to the torque setting specified at the beginning of the Chapter.

29 Assemble the crankcase halves (see Section 21).

19.20b . . . then locate the pump and fit the top bolt . . .

19.20c . . . then fit the inner plate and bottom bolts

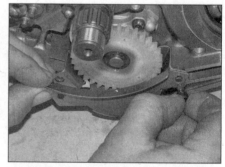

19.22 Apply threadlock to the outer plate bolts

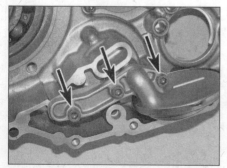

19.26 Unscrew the bolts (arrowed) and remove the strainer

19.27 Clean and check the strainer gauze (arrowed)

19.28 Fit the strainer using a new gasket

20.3 Remove the E-clip and washer from the left-hand end of the shaft

20.5a Partially withdraw the shaft/arm assembly, noting how it fits . . .

20.5b . . . then unhook the spring and withdraw the complete shaft/arm assembly

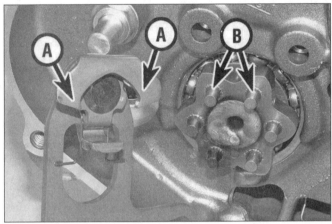

20.6a Check the selector arm pawls (A) and cam plate pins (B)

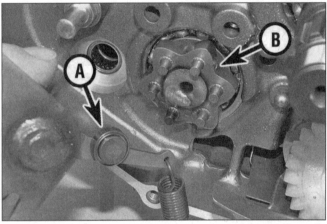

20.6b Check the stopper arm roller (A) and cam plate detents (B)

20 Gearchange mechanism

Note: *The gearchange mechanism can be removed with the engine in the frame. If the engine has been removed, ignore the steps which don't apply.*

Removal

1 Make sure the transmission is in neutral. Remove the clutch (see Section 15) and the right-hand crankcase cover (see Section 17).
2 Remove the gearchange lever (see Chapter 5).
3 Remove the E-clip and washer from the left-hand end of the gearchange shaft **(see illustration)**.
4 Note how the gearchange shaft centralising spring ends fit on each side of the locating pin in the casing, how the pawls on the selector arm locate onto the pins on the selector drum cam plate, and how the stopper arm roller locates in the neutral detent in the cam.
5 Grasp the shaft/selector arm assembly and partially withdraw it from the crankcase, then unhook the stopper arm spring and remove the complete shaft/selector arm/stopper arm assembly, noting the washer **(see illustrations)**.

Inspection

6 Check the selector arm for cracks, distortion and wear of its pawls, and check for any corresponding wear on the pins on the selector drum cam plate **(see illustration)**. Also check the stopper arm roller and the detents in the cam plate for any wear or damage, and make sure the roller turns freely **(see illustration)**. Replace any components that are worn or damaged with new ones – the selector drum cam is an integral part of the drum (see Section 27).
7 Inspect the shaft centralising spring and the stopper arm return spring for fatigue, wear or damage **(see illustration 20.9)**. The return spring can be replaced with a new one, but the centralising spring is not listed as being

available but is part of the shaft. Also check the movement of the pawl plate – make sure it is smooth and returns to centre from the pressure of its spring **(see illustration)**. The pawl plate and its spring are also part of the shaft and not available separately.
8 Check the gearchange shaft is straight and look for damage to the splines. If the shaft is bent you can attempt to straighten it, but if the splines are damaged the shaft must be replaced with a new one.
9 If required slide the washer and stopper arm assembly off the shaft, then release the circlip and slide it and the washer and the stopper arm off the collar, noting how they **(see illustration)**. Reassemble the shaft in reverse order.

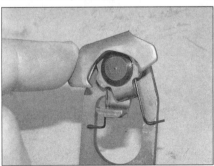

20.7 Make sure the pawl plate moves smoothly and centres correctly

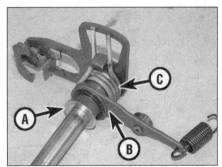

20.9 Washer (A), stopper arm assembly (B) and centralising spring (C)

20.11a Lever the old seal out

20.11b Check the bearing (arrowed) in each side of the crankcase

20.11c Press the new seal into its bore

20.13a Slide the shaft into its bore . . .

20.13b . . . and locate the stopper arm and its spring

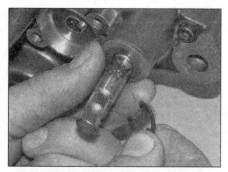

20.15 Slide the washer on then fit the E-clip into the groove

10 Check the centralising spring locating pin in the crankcase is tight. If necessary unscrew it, clean the threads, apply a suitable non-permanent thread locking compound and tighten it to the torque setting specified at the beginning of the Chapter.

11 Check the condition of the shaft oil seal in the left-hand side of the crankcase. If it is damaged, deteriorated or shows signs of leakage it must be replaced with a new one, though it is advisable to fit a new one whatever the apparent condition. Lever out the old seal with a seal hook or screwdriver **(see illustration)**. With the seal removed check the bearing behind it, and also the bearing in the right-hand side of the crankcase **(see illustration)**. Replace them with new ones if necessary – you will have to pull them out using an internal expanding knife-edge puller with slide-hammer attachment. Press or drive the new bearings squarely into place using a bearing driver or suitable socket. Press the new seal in using your fingers, a driver or socket **(see illustration)**.

Installation

12 Apply some oil to the shaft bearings in the crankcase and some grease to the lips of the gearchange shaft oil seal in the left-hand side of the crankcase **(see illustrations 20.11a and b)**.

13 Check that the shaft centralising spring is properly positioned and the inner washer is on the shaft **(see illustration 20.9)**. Slide the shaft into place and push it most of the way in, then locate the stopper arm roller into the

neutral detent on the cam and fit the return spring onto its post **(see illustrations)**. Push the shaft all the way in, locating the selector arm pawls onto the pins and the centralising spring ends onto each side of the locating pin in the crankcase **(see illustration 20.5a)**.

14 Check that all components are correctly positioned.

15 Fit the washer and the E-clip **(see illustration)**. Install the gearchange lever (see Chapter 5). Check the action of the gearchange mechanism.

16 Install the right-hand crankcase cover (see Section 17). Install the clutch (see Section 15).

21 Crankcase separation and reassembly

Note: *To separate the crankcase halves, the engine must be removed from the frame.*

Separation

1 To access the crankshaft and connecting rod assembly, balancer shaft, transmission shafts, selector drum and forks, and their bearings, the crankcase must be split into its two halves.

2 Before the crankcases can be separated the following components must be removed:
Starter motor (Chapter 8)
Neutral switch (Chapter 8)
Speed sensor (Chapter 4)
Cylinder head (Section 9)
Cylinder block (Section 11)

Piston (Section 12)
Alternator (Chapter 8)
Cam chain and blades (Section 8)
Clutch (Section 15)
Right-hand crankcase cover (Section 17)
Water pump, primary drive and balancer shaft gears (section 18)
Oil pump (Section 19)
Gearchange mechanism (Section 20)

3 Make a cardboard template punched with holes to match all the bolts in each crankcase half – as each crankcase bolt is removed, store it in its relative position in the template, along with the wiring clamps **(see illustration)**. This will ensure all bolts, of which there are six different sizes, are installed in the correct location on reassembly.

4 Unscrew the crankcase bolts evenly, a little at a time and in a criss-cross sequence until they are finger-tight, then remove them – there

21.3 Make a cardboard template like the one shown to store the bolts

21.4a Right-hand crankcase bolts (arrowed)

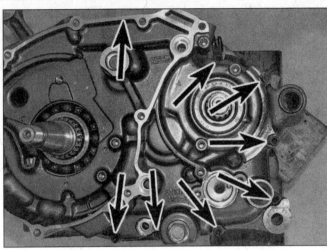

21.4b Left-hand crankcase bolts (arrowed)

are six bolts in the right-hand side and eight in the left **(see illustrations)**.

5 Holding both halves of the crankcase place the engine on its left-hand side, laying it on wooden blocks so the shaft ends are clear of the bench. Carefully lift the right crankcase half off the left half **(see illustration)** – if necessary use a screwdriver inserted in the leverage points to initially separate the halves, along with a soft-faced mallet if necessary to tap around the joint and on the right-hand ends of the crankshaft, balancer shaft and transmission input shaft to ensure they remain in the left-hand crankcase. **Note:** *If the halves do not separate easily, make sure all fasteners have been removed. Do not try and separate the halves by levering against the crankcase mating surfaces as they are easily scored and will leak oil in the future if damaged.* The right-hand crankcase half will come away leaving the crankshaft, balancer shaft, transmission shafts and selector drum and forks in the left-hand half.

6 Remove the two locating dowels from the crankcase if they are loose – they could be in either half **(see illustration 21.13)**. Also remove the oil passage dowel and its O-ring **(see illustration 21.12)** – discard the O-ring, a new one must be used. Remove the oil pipe and discard its O-rings **(see illustrations 21.14b and a)**. Remove the oil strainer (see Section 19).

7 Refer to Sections 22 to 27 for the removal of the main components housed within the crankcases.

Reassembly

8 Remove all traces of sealant from the crankcase mating surfaces. Clean the oil pipe with solvent, making sure the small holes are clear, and blow it through with compressed air.

9 Clean then install the oil strainer (see Section 19).

10 Refer to Sections 22 to 27 for the installation of the main components housed within the crankcases.

11 Double check that all components and

their bearings, and the transmission output shaft and balancer shaft oil seals are in place in the left-hand crankcase half, and that all bearings and the bearing retainer are in the right-hand half.

12 Fit the oil passage dowel with a new O-ring smeared with grease into the right-hand crankcase half **(see illustration)**.

13 If removed, fit the two locating dowels into the right-hand crankcase half **(see illustration)**.

14 Fit a new O-ring smeared with grease into the groove on each end of the oil pipe, then fit the cut away end of the pipe into the left-hand crankcase, locating the cut section against the flat side of its bore **(see illustrations)**.

21.5 Carefully separate the crankcase halves

21.12 Fit the oil passage dowel with a new O-ring (arrowed)

21.13 Make sure the locating dowels (arrowed) are fitted

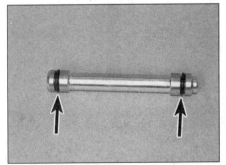

21.14a Fit a new O-ring (arrowed) onto each end of the pipe . . .

21.14b . . . then fit the pipe into the crankcase, aligning the flats so the pipe seats fully

21.16 Apply the sealant to the perimeter mating surface, making sure none blocks the oil passages

15 Generously lubricate the crankshaft and transmission shaft bearings and gears and the selector fork shafts and fork ends and the tracks in the selector drum with clean engine oil, then use a rag soaked in high flash-point solvent to wipe over the mating surfaces of both crankcase halves to remove all traces of oil.

16 Apply a small amount of suitable sealant (Yamaha-Bond 1215 or equivalent RTV sealant – ask your dealer) to the mating surface of the right-hand crankcase half as shown, avoiding the oil gallery **(see illustration)**.

Caution: Apply the sealant only to the mating surfaces. Do not apply an excessive amount as it will ooze out when the case halves are assembled and may obstruct oil passages. Do not apply the sealant close to any of the oil passages.

17 Check again that all components are in position. Carefully fit the right-hand crankcase half down onto the left-hand half, making sure the shaft ends, oil pipe and dowels all locate correctly **(see illustration 21.5)**.

18 Check that the right-hand crankcase half is correctly seated. Clean the threads of all the crankcase bolts. Fit the six bolts into the right-hand crankcase and tighten them finger-tight **(see illustration 21.4a)**. Grasp both halves of the crankcase and turn the engine over.

Caution: The crankcase halves should fit together without being forced. If the casings are not correctly seated, remove the right-hand crankcase half and investigate the problem. Do not attempt to pull them together using the crankcase bolts as the casing will crack and be ruined.

19 Install the eight left-hand crankcase bolts, along with the wiring clamps, and tighten them finger-tight **(see illustration 21.4b)**. Set the engine upright. Now tighten all the bolts evenly and a little at a time in a criss-cross sequence to the torque setting specified at the beginning of the Chapter.

20 With all crankcase fasteners tightened, check that the crankshaft, balancer shaft and transmission shafts rotate smoothly and easily. Check that the transmission shafts rotate freely and independently in neutral, then rotate the selector drum cam by hand and select each gear in turn whilst rotating the input shaft. If

there are any signs of undue stiffness, tight or rough spots, poor or incorrect gear selection, or of any other problem, the fault must be rectified before proceeding further.

21 Install all other removed assemblies in a reverse of the sequence given in Step 2.

22 Crankcases and bearings

Crankcases

1 After the crankcases have been separated, remove the crankshaft and balancer shaft, the selector drum and forks and the transmission shafts, referring to the relevant Sections of this Chapter.

2 Clean the crankcases thoroughly with new solvent and dry them with compressed air. Blow out all oil passages with compressed air.

3 Remove all traces of old gasket sealant from the mating surfaces. Clean up minor damage to the surfaces with a fine sharpening stone or grindstone.

Caution: Be very careful not to nick or gouge the crankcase mating surfaces or oil leaks will result. Check both crankcase halves very carefully for cracks and other damage.

4 Small cracks or holes in aluminium castings can be repaired with an epoxy resin adhesive as a temporary measure or with one of the low temperature welding kits. Permanent repairs can only be done by TIG (tungsten inert gas or heli-arc) welding, and only a specialist in this process is in a position to advise on the economy or practical aspect of such a repair. If any damage is found that can't be repaired, replace the crankcase halves as a set.

5 Damaged threads can be economically reclaimed using a diamond section wire insert, for example of the Heli-Coil type (though there are other makes), which are easily fitted after drilling and re-tapping the affected thread.

6 Sheared studs or screws can usually be removed with extractors, which consist of a tapered, left-hand thread screw of very hard steel. These are inserted into a pre-drilled hole in the stud, and usually succeed in dislodging the most stubborn stud or screw. If a stud has sheared above its bore line, it can be removed using a conventional stud extractor which avoids the need for drilling.

 Refer to Tools and Workshop Tips for details of installing a thread insert and using screw extractors.

7 Install all components and assemblies, referring to the relevant Sections of this and the other Chapters, before reassembling the crankcase halves.

Bearing information

8 The crankshaft, balancer shaft, and transmission shaft bearings should all be

replaced with new ones as part of a complete engine overhaul, or individually as required due to wear or failure.

9 Bearing failure occurs mainly because of lack of lubrication, the presence of dirt or other foreign particles, overloading the engine, break-up of one or more of the bearing components due to fatigue, or corrosion. Regardless of the cause of bearing failure, it must be corrected before the engine is reassembled to prevent it from happening again.

10 The bearings should rotate smoothly, freely and quietly, there should be no rough spots, and there should be no excessive play between the inner and outer races, or between the inner race and the shaft it fits on, or between the outer race and its housing in the crankcase.

11 Dirt and other foreign particles get into the engine in a variety of ways. They may be left in the engine during assembly or they may pass through filters or breathers, then get into the oil and from there into the bearings. Metal chips from machining operations and normal engine wear are often present. Abrasives are sometimes left in engine components after reconditioning operations, especially when parts are not thoroughly cleaned using the proper cleaning methods. The best prevention for this cause of bearing failure is to clean all parts thoroughly and keep everything spotlessly clean during engine reassembly. Regular oil changes in accordance with the specified schedule are also essential.

12 Lack of lubrication or lubrication breakdown has a number of interrelated causes. Excessive heat (which thins the oil), overloading and oil leakage all contribute to lubrication breakdown. Blocked oil passages will starve a bearing of lubrication and destroy it.

13 Riding habits can have a definite effect on bearing life. Full throttle low, speed operation, or labouring the engine, puts very high loads on bearings. Short trip riding leads to corrosion of bearings, as insufficient engine heat is produced to drive off the condensed water and corrosive gases produced. These products collect in the engine oil, forming acid and sludge. As the oil is carried to the engine bearings, the acid attacks and corrodes the bearing material.

14 Incorrect bearing installation during engine assembly will lead to bearing failure as well. To avoid bearing problems, clean all parts thoroughly before reassembly, and lubricate the new bearings with clean engine oil during installation.

Bearing removal and installation

Note: *If the correct bearing removal and installation tools are not available take the crankcases and crankshaft to a Yamaha dealer for removal and installation of the bearings – do not risk damaging either the cases or the crankshaft.*

Crankshaft (main) bearings

15 If the crankshaft (main) bearings have failed, excessive rumbling and vibration will

22.17 Right-hand main bearing (arrowed)

22.19 Left-hand main bearing (arrowed)

22.24a Heat the housing . . .

be felt when the engine is running. If only one bearing has failed, it is best to replace both with new ones.

16 Separate the crankcase halves (Section 21) and remove the crankshaft (Section 23).

17 The right-hand main bearing is in the crankcase **(see illustration)**. To remove the bearing heat the housing with a hot air gun, then tap the bearing out from the outside of the crankcase using a bearing driver or a suitable socket **(see illustrations 22.24a and b)**.

18 Smear the outside of the new bearing with clean oil and fit it with its marked side towards the inside of the engine, then heat the housing again and drive the bearing squarely in until it seats using a driver or socket that bears only on the outer race **(see illustration 22.25)**.

19 The left-hand bearing is part of the left-hand crankshaft web and is not available separately **(see illustration)**. If the bearing has failed either a complete new crankshaft assembly, which includes the connecting rod and big-end bearing, or a new left-hand web must be fitted. Note that if the main bearing is worn it is quite likely that the connecting rod big-end bearing is also worn. Balance up the respective costs of the complete unit against the cost of just the left-hand web plus that of having to disassemble then reassemble the crankshaft components, which requires special equipment and a degree of skill and accuracy to separate and reset the crankshaft webs correctly on the crankpin.

Connecting rod (big-end) bearing

20 If the connecting rod (big-end) bearing has failed, there will be a pronounced knocking noise when the engine is running, particularly under load and increasing with engine speed. Refer to Section 23, Step 7 for checks that can be made.

21 The bearing is available separately, but the work required to separate the crankshaft webs is complex – see Step 19, balancing the costs of the new bearing and the work involved against the cost of a new assembled crankshaft. If you do fit a new crankshaft you should also fit a new right-hand main bearing (Steps 17 and 18).

Balancer shaft bearings

22 If the balancer bearings have failed, excessive rumbling and vibration will be felt when the engine is running.

23 Separate the crankcase halves (Section 21) and remove the balancer shaft (Section 24).

24 To remove the right-hand bearing from the crankcase, heat the bearing housing from the outside of the crankcase with a hot air gun, then tap the bearing out from the outside of the crankcase using a bearing driver or a suitable socket **(see illustrations)**.

25 Smear the outside of the new bearing with clean oil and fit it with its marked side towards the inside of the engine, then heat the housing again and drive the bearing squarely in until it seats using a driver or socket that bears only on the outer race **(see illustration)**.

26 To remove the left-hand bearing from the crankcase, heat the bearing housing with a hot air gun until the bearing drops out **(see illustration)**. If it doesn't come out, an expanding knife-edge bearing puller with slide-hammer attachment is required. Heat the bearing housing with a hot air gun, then fit the expanding end of the puller behind the bearing, then turn the puller to expand it and lock it **(see illustration 22.34a)**. Attach the slide-hammer to the puller, then hold the crankcase firmly down and operate the slide-hammer to jar the bearing out **(see illustration 22.34b)**.

27 Lever out the oil seal from the behind the bearing using a seal hook or screwdriver, noting which way round it fits. Fit a new oil seal, pressing it in with your fingers or using a suitable driver or socket to drive it in. Smear the seal lips with grease.

28 Smear the outside of the new bearing with clean oil and fit it with its marked side towards the inside of the engine, then heat the housing again and drive the bearing squarely in until it seats using a driver or socket that bears only on the outer race **(see illustration 22.25)**.

Transmission shaft bearings

29 If the transmission bearings have failed, excessive rumbling and vibration will be felt when the engine is running.

30 Separate the crankcase halves (Section 21) and remove the transmission shafts and the output shaft oil seal (Section 25).

31 Unscrew the input shaft right-hand

22.24b . . . then drive the bearing out from the outside

22.25 Drive the new bearing in using a socket or driver on the outer race

22.26 Left-hand balancer shaft bearing (arrowed)

22.31 Unscrew the bolts (arrowed) and remove the plate

22.34a Fit the expander behind the inner race of the bearing . . .

22.34b . . . then fit the slide-hammer and jar the bearing out

bearing retainer plate bolts and remove the retainer **(see illustration)**.

32 To remove the input shaft bearing from the right-hand crankcase and the output shaft bearing from the left-hand crankcase, heat the bearing housing with a hot air gun, then tap the bearing out from the outside of the crankcase using a bearing driver or a suitable socket **(see illustrations 22.24a and b)**.

33 Smear the outside of the new bearing with clean oil and fit it with its marked side towards the inside of the engine, then heat the housing again and drive the bearing squarely in until it seats using a driver or socket that bears only on the outer race **(see illustration 22.25)**.

34 To remove the input shaft bearing from the left-hand crankcase and the output shaft bearing from the right-hand crankcase, heat

the bearing housing with a hot air gun until the bearing drops out. If it doesn't come out, an expanding knife-edge bearing puller with slide-hammer attachment is required. Heat the bearing housing with a hot air gun, then fit the expanding end of the puller behind the bearing, then turn the puller to expand it and lock it **(see illustration)**. Attach the slide-hammer to the puller, then hold the crankcase firmly down and operate the slide-hammer to jar the bearing out **(see illustration)**.

35 Smear the outside of the new bearing with clean oil and fit it with its marked side towards the inside of the engine, then heat the housing again and drive the bearing squarely in until it seats using a driver or socket that bears only on the outer race **(see illustration 22.25)**.

36 Clean the threads of the bearing retainer

plate bolts. Apply a suitable non-permanent thread locking compound to the threads, then fit the plate with the OUT mark facing out and tighten the bolts to the torque setting specified at the beginning of the Chapter **(see illustration 22.31)**.

23 Crankshaft and connecting rod

Note: *To remove the crankshaft the engine must be removed from the frame and the crankcase halves separated.*

Removal

1 Remove the engine from the frame (see Section 4) and separate the crankcase halves (see Section 21).

2 Remove the balancer shaft (see Section 24).

3 The crankshaft needs to be pressed out of the left-hand crankcase. You could use either the Yamaha tool (part No. 90890-01135) or a suitable equivalent set-up as shown **(see illustration)** – the studs threads into the holes in the crankcase, the nut on the end of the crankshaft protects it, and turning the centre bolt pushes the crankshaft out. On the engine photographed it was found that the bearing was so tight in the crankcase that this set-up pushed the crankshaft through the bearing, rather than pushing the bearing and crankshaft out as one and thus disturbing the position of the bearing on the crankshaft. It is preferable to use the alternative method shown comprising a piece of steel tube against the inner race of the bearing, therefore pushing the bearing out of the crankshaft and bringing the crankshaft with it without any danger of disturbing their relative positions **(see illustration)**.

Inspection

4 Clean the crankshaft with solvent. If available, blow the crank dry with compressed air. Check the cam chain sprocket for wear or damage **(see illustration)**. If any of the teeth are excessively worn, chipped or broken, the crankshaft must be replaced with a new one.

5 Place the crankshaft on V-blocks and check for runout using a dial gauge **(see**

23.3a This set-up is equivalent to the Yamaha special tool

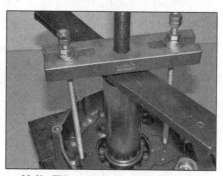

23.3b This set-up works better if the bearing is tight in the crankcase . . .

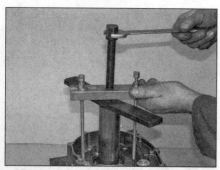

23.3c . . . hold the cross-piece while turning the bolt to prevent anything getting out of line

23.4 Check the teeth of the cam chain sprocket (arrowed)

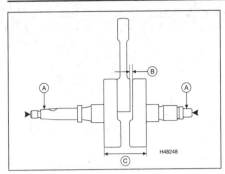

23.5 Crankshaft measurement points

A *Runout*
B *Connecting rod side clearance*
C *Width across webs*

23.6 Measuring the connecting rod side clearance

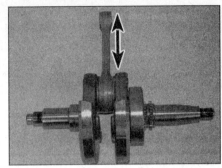

23.7 Check for any radial play in the big-end bearing

illustration). Compare the reading to the maximum specified at the beginning of the Chapter. If the runout exceeds the limit, the crankshaft must be replaced with a new one.
6 Measure the connecting rod side clearance (the gap between the connecting rod big-end and the crankshaft web) with a feeler gauge **(see illustration)**. If the clearance is greater than the service limit listed in this Chapter's Specifications, replace the crankshaft with a new one.
7 Hold the crankshaft still and check for any radial (up and down) play in the big-end bearing by pushing and pulling the rod against the crank **(see illustration)**. If a dial gauge is available measure the amount of radial play and compare the reading to the maximum specified at the beginning of the Chapter. If the play exceeds the limit, the bearing must be replaced with a new one (see Section 22, Step 21).
8 Refer to Section 12, Step 12 and check the connecting rod small-end and piston pin for wear.
9 Have the rod checked for twist and bend by a Yamaha dealer if you are in doubt about its straightness.
10 Refer to Section 22 and check the crankshaft (main) bearings.
11 Measure the width of the crankshaft from between the outer edge of each web **(see illustration)**. Replace the crankshaft assembly with a new one if it is not within the specified limits.

Installation

12 The crankshaft can be drawn into the left-hand crankcase using the Yamaha tools part Nos. 90890-01274, 01275, 04130 and 04144. Set the tool up as shown, making sure it is central to the shaft axis, then heat the area around the bearing housing with a hot air gun to ease installation and draw the crankshaft in until it seats **(see illustration)**. However we found that if the crankcase was hot enough, either by heating it with a hot air gun or placing it in the oven, and the bearing was cold enough, either by using a freeze spray on the bearing or putting the whole crankshaft in the freezer, the crankshaft fitted with only a small amount of persuasion with a hammer via a suitable drift against the outer race of the bearing, turning the crankshaft as required to expose different sections of

the rim so the bearing goes in square **(see illustrations)** – DO NOT strike the end of the crankshaft and DO NOT use excessive force. The advantage of this method is there is no force transmitted through the bearing itself. Whichever method you use, make sure the connecting rod is positioned so it sits in the opening for the cylinder bore, and make sure the outer race of the bearing is seated against the crankcase so there is no gap between them **(see illustration)**. If you do not have the tools or experience required take the crankcase and crankshaft to a dealer or engine specialist.
13 Install the balancer shaft (see Section 24).
14 Reassemble the crankcase halves (see Section 21).

23.11 Check the width of the crankshaft as shown

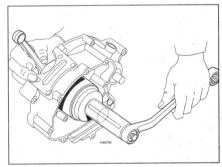

23.12a Installing the crankshaft using the Yamaha special tool

23.12b Fit the cold bearing (A) into the hot bearing housing (B) . . .

23.12c . . . then tap round the inner race using a suitable drift . . .

23.12d . . . until the bearing seats

24.2 Removing the balancer shaft

25.2a Unscrew the bolts (arrowed) and remove the retainer

25.2b Slide the spacer off the shaft

24 Balancer shaft

Note: *To remove the balancer shaft the engine must be removed from the frame and the crankcases separated.*

Removal

1 Remove the engine from the frame (see Section 4) and separate the crankcase halves (see Section 21).
2 Lift balancer shaft out of the crankcase **(see illustration)**.

Inspection

3 Clean the balancer shaft with solvent. If available, blow it dry with compressed air. Check the balancer drive and driven gears for wear or damage. If any of the gear teeth are excessively worn, chipped or broken, the gears must be replaced with a new set.
4 Refer to Section 22 and check the balancer shaft bearings.

Installation

5 Carefully fit the balancer shaft into the left-hand crankcase, locating the shaft end in the bearing and seal **(see illustration 24.2)**.
6 Reassemble the crankcase halves (see Section 21).

25 Transmission assembly and output shaft oil seal

Note: *To remove the transmission shafts the engine must be removed from the frame and the crankcases separated.*

Transmission assembly

Removal

1 Remove the engine from the frame (see Section 4).
2 Undo the oil seal retainer bolts and remove the retainer **(see illustration)**. Slide the spacer off the output shaft **(see illustration)**.

3 Separate the crankcase halves (see Section 21).
4 Grasp the input shaft and output shaft and the selector drum and forks together and lift the assembly out of the crankcase **(see illustration)**. If the shafts are stuck, use a soft-faced hammer and gently tap on their ends.
5 Before removing the selector drum and forks, note that each fork carries an identification letter **(see illustration)**. The right-hand fork has R, the centre fork C, and the left-hand fork L, with all marks facing the right-hand side of the engine. If no letters are visible, mark them yourself using a felt pen. The R and L forks fit into the output shaft, and the C fork fits into the input shaft.
6 Remove the selector drum, then remove the forks **(see illustrations 25.19, 18, 17 and 16)**.

25.4 Lift the transmission shafts and selector drum and forks out together

25.7 Remove the O-ring

7 Remove the O-ring from the left-hand of the output shaft **(see illustration)** – a new one must be fitted.
8 Prise the output shaft oil seal out of the left-hand crankcase using a seal hook or screwdriver **(see illustration)** – a new one must be fitted.
9 Refer to Section 22 and check the transmission shaft bearings.
10 Refer to Section 26 and check the transmission shafts – if necessary, the shafts can be disassembled and new components fitted.
11 Refer to Section 27 and check the selector drum and forks.

Installation

12 Grease the lips of the new seal. Press or drive the seal into its housing until its outer

25.5 Each fork is marked with an identification letter

25.8 Remove and discard the oil seal

25.12 Drive the new seal in, setting it flush with the rim

25.13 Fit a new O-ring (arrowed) into the groove in the shaft

25.14 Lay the shafts together correctly engaged

face is flush with the housing rim – using a piece of wood across the seal is a good way to achieve this **(see illustration)**.

13 Fit a new O-ring smeared with grease into the groove in the left-hand end of the output shaft **(see illustration)**.

14 Join the shafts together on the bench so their related gears are engaged **(see illustration)**.

15 Lubricate the ends of each selector fork and fork shaft and the guide pins with oil.

16 Locate the output shaft fork, marked L, in its pinion groove **(see illustration)**.

17 Locate the input shaft fork, marked C, in its pinion groove **(see illustration)**.

18 Locate the output shaft fork, marked R, in its pinion groove **(see illustration)**.

19 Position the selector drum, fitting the fork guide pins into their tracks **(see illustration)**.

20 Grasp the shafts and the selector drum and forks together **(see illustration)**. Fit them into the left-hand crankcase, locating the shaft ends in the bearings and bores **(see illustration 25.4)**.

21 Make sure the transmission and selector fork shafts are correctly seated and all related components are correctly engaged.

22 Position the gears in the neutral position and check the shafts are free to rotate easily and independently (i.e. the input shaft can turn whilst the output shaft is held stationary) before proceeding further. Also check that each gear can be selected by turning the input shaft with one hand and the selector drum with the other.

23 Reassemble the crankcase halves (see Section 21).

24 Lubricate the spacer inside and out with

grease then slide it onto the output shaft with the more chamfered end facing in, twisting it as you do to ease its entry into the seal and over the O-ring **(see illustration 25.2b)**.

25 Clean the threads of the seal retainer bolts. Apply a small amount of suitable sealant (Yamaha-Bond 1215 or equivalent RTV sealant – ask your dealer) to the bolt threads, then fit the retainer and tighten the bolts to the torque setting specified at the beginning of the Chapter **(see illustration)**.

Output shaft oil seal

26 If there is evidence of leakage from the oil seal in normal use it can be replaced with a new one without having to remove the transmission assembly.

27 Remove the front sprocket (see Chapter 6).

25.16 Fit the L fork . . .

25.17 . . . then C fork . . .

25.18 . . . and the R fork

25.19 Lay the drum onto the forks, locating the guide pins in their tracks

25.20 Grasp the assembly, making sure everything is correctly positioned and engaged

25.25 Clean the bolts and apply sealant before fitting the plate

When disassembling the transmission shafts, place the parts on a long rod or thread a wire through them to keep them in order and facing the proper direction

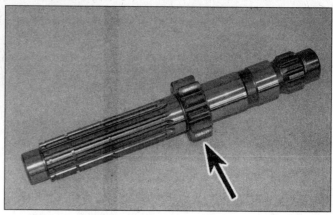

26.7 1st gear pinion (arrowed) is part of the input shaft

28 Undo the oil seal retainer bolts and remove the retainer (see illustration 25.2a). Slide the spacer off the shaft (see illustration 25.2b).
29 Push one side of the seal in so it tilts then prise out the other side. Remove the O-ring from the shaft and fit a new one (see illustration 25.7).
30 Wrap some insulating tap around the end of the shaft. Grease the lips of the new seal. Slide the seal over the shaft and press it into its housing. Press or drive the seal in until its outer face is flush with its housing (see illustration 25.12). Remove the tape.
31 Lubricate the spacer inside and out with grease then slide it onto the shaft with the more chamfered end facing in, twisting it as you do to ease its entry into the seal and over the O-ring (see illustration 25.2b).
32 Clean the threads of the seal retainer bolts. Apply a small amount of suitable sealant (Yamaha-Bond 1215 or equivalent RTV sealant – ask your dealer) to the bolt threads, then fit the retainer and tighten the bolts to the torque setting specified at the beginning of the Chapter (see illustration 25.25).

26 Transmission shaft overhaul

1 Remove the transmission assembly from the crankcase and remove the selector drum and forks (see Section 25). Always disassemble the transmission shafts separately to avoid mixing up the components.

Input shaft

Disassembly

2 Remove the circlip securing the 2nd gear pinion then slide the pinion off the shaft (see illustrations 26.20b and a).
3 Slide the tabbed lockwasher off the shaft, then turn the slotted splined washer to offset the splines and slide it off the shaft, noting how they fit together (see illustrations 26.19c and a).
4 Slide the 5th gear pinion and its splined

bush off the shaft, followed by the splined washer (see illustrations 26.18c, b and a).
5 Remove the circlip securing the 3rd gear pinion, then slide the pinion off the shaft (see illustrations 26.17b and a).
6 Remove the circlip securing the 4th gear pinion, then slide the splined washer and the pinion off the shaft (see illustrations 26.16c, b and a).
7 The 1st gear pinion is integral with the shaft (see illustration).

Inspection

8 Check the gear teeth for cracking, chipping, pitting and other obvious wear or damage. Any pinion that is damaged as such must be replaced with a new one.
9 Inspect the dogs and the dog holes in the gears for cracks, chips, and excessive wear especially in the form of rounded edges (see illustration). Make sure mating gears engage properly. Replace the paired gears as a set if necessary.
10 Check for signs of scoring or bluing on the pinions, bush and shaft (see illustration). This could be caused by overheating due to inadequate lubrication. Replace any damaged pinions with new ones.
11 Check that each pinion moves freely on the shaft or bush but without undue freeplay.
12 The shaft is unlikely to sustain damage unless the engine has seized, placing an unusually high loading on the transmission, or

the machine has covered a very high mileage. Check the surface of the shaft, especially where a pinion turns on it, and replace the shaft if it has scored or picked up, or if there are any cracks. Damage of any kind can only be cured by replacement. Using V-blocks and a dial gauge check the shaft for runout – replace the shaft with a new one if it exceeds the specified limit.
13 Check the washers and circlips and replace any that are bent or appear weakened or worn. Use new ones if in any doubt. Note that it is good practice, and specified by Yamaha, to use new circlips when overhauling the transmission shafts.

Reassembly

14 Wash all of the components in clean solvent and dry them off. Check that all the oil holes and passages are clear.
15 During reassembly, apply molybdenum disulphide oil (a 50/50 mixture of molybdenum disulphide grease and clean engine oil) to the mating surfaces of the shaft and pinions. When fitting the circlip, do not expand its ends any further than is necessary, and position them between the raised splines as shown in the photos. Fit the circlip so that its chamfered side faces away from the thrust side, i.e. towards the pinion it secures.
16 Slide the 4th gear pinion onto the shaft with its dog holes facing away from the

26.9 Check the dogs and dog holes for rounding and wear

26.10 Check all related components for wear and damage

26.16a Slide the 4th gear pinion . . .

26.16b . . . and the splined washer onto the shaft . . .

26.16c . . . and secure them with the circlip . . .

26.16d . . . making sure it locates properly in its groove

26.17a Slide the 3rd gear pinion onto the shaft . . .

26.17b . . . then fit the circlip . . .

integral 1st gear **(see illustration)**. Slide the splined washer onto the shaft, then fit the circlip, making sure that it locates correctly in the groove in the shaft **(see illustrations)**.

17 Slide the 3rd gear pinion onto the shaft with the selector fork groove facing the 4th gear pinion **(see illustration)**. Fit the circlip, making sure that it locates correctly in the groove **(see illustrations)**.

18 Slide the splined washer onto the shaft, followed by the 5th gear pinion splined bush **(see illustrations)**. Slide the 5th gear pinion onto the bush, making sure its dogs face the 3rd gear pinion **(see illustration)**.

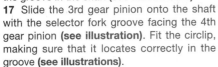

26.17c . . . making sure it locates properly in its groove

26.18a Slide the splined washer onto the shaft . . .

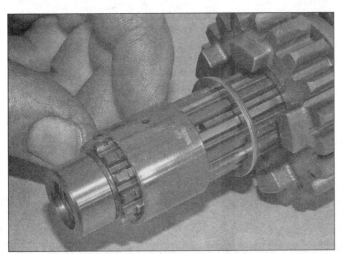

26.18b . . . followed by the 5th gear pinion bush . . .

26.18c . . . then fit the 5th gear pinion onto the bush

26.19a Slide the slotted washer on . . .

26.19b . . . locking it against the splines . . .

26.19c . . . then slide the tabbed washer on . . .

26.19d . . . locating the tabs in the slots

29.20a Slide the 2nd gear pinion on . . .

26.20b . . . then fit the circlip . . .

19 Slide the slotted splined washer onto the shaft and locate it in its groove, then turn it in the groove so that the splines on the washer align with the splines on the shaft and secure the washer in the groove **(see illustrations)**. Slide the tabbed lockwasher onto the shaft and locate the tabs in the slots in the outer rim of the splined washer **(see illustrations)**.
20 Slide the 2nd gear pinion onto the end of the shaft with the recessed face outermost **(see illustration)**. Fit the circlip making sure that it locates correctly in the groove **(see illustrations)**.
21 Check that all components have been correctly installed **(see illustration)**.

Output shaft

Disassembly

22 Remove the circlip securing the 1st gear pinion then slide the thrust washer off the shaft **(see illustrations 26.33b and a)**. Slide the 1st gear pinion **(see illustration 26.32)** and the 4th gear pinion **(see illustration 26.31)** off the shaft.
23 Remove the circlip securing the 3rd gear pinion, then slide the splined washer and the 3rd gear pinion off the shaft **(see illustrations 26.30c, b and a)**.
24 Slide the 5th gear pinion off the shaft **(see illustration 26.29)**.
25 Remove the circlip securing the 2nd gear

pinion, then slide the splined washer and the pinion off the shaft **(see illustrations 26.28c, b and a)**.

Inspection

26 Wash all of the components in clean solvent and dry them off. Check that all the oil holes and passages are clear. Refer to Steps 8 to 13.

Reassembly

27 During reassembly, apply molybdenum disulphide oil (a 50/50 mixture of molybdenum disulphide grease and clean engine oil) to the mating surfaces of the shaft, pinions and bushes. When installing the circlips, do not

26.20c . . . making sure it locates properly in its groove

26.21 The complete input shaft should be as shown

26.28a Slide the 2nd gear pinion onto the shaft . . .

26.28b . . . followed by the splined washer . . .

26.28c . . . and secure them with the circlip . . .

26.28d . . . making sure it locates in the groove

26.29 Slide the 5th gear pinion onto the shaft

26.30a Slide the 3rd gear pinion onto the shaft . . .

expand the ends any further than is necessary. Install the stamped circlips so that their chamfered side faces away from the thrust side, i.e. towards the pinion it secures.

28 Slide the 2nd gear pinion onto the shaft with its dog holes facing away from the rib it butts against, followed by the splined washer (see illustrations). Fit the circlip, making sure it is locates correctly in its groove in the shaft (see illustrations).

29 Slide the 5th gear pinion onto shaft with its selector fork groove facing away from the 2nd gear pinion (see illustration).

30 Slide the 3rd gear pinion onto the shaft with its dog holes facing away from the 5th gear pinion (see illustration). Slide the splined washer on, then fit the circlip, making sure it is locates correctly in its groove in the shaft (see illustrations).

26.30b . . . followed by the splined washer . . .

26.30c . . . and secure them with the circlip . . .

31 Slide the 4th gear pinion onto the shaft with its selector fork groove facing the 3rd gear pinion (see illustration).

32 Slide the 1st gear pinion onto the shaft

with its recessed face and raised centre section facing the 4th gear pinion (see illustration).

33 Slide the thrust washer onto the shaft then

26.30d . . . making sure it locates in the groove

26.31 Slide the 4th gear pinion onto the shaft

26.32 Slide the 1st gear pinion onto the shaft

26.33a Slide the washer onto the shaft . . .

26.33b . . . then fit the circlip . . .

26.33c . . . making sure it locates in the groove

26.34 The complete output shaft should be as shown

fit the circlip, making sure it is locates correctly in its groove **(see illustrations)**.

34 Check that all components have been correctly installed **(see illustration)**.

27 Selector drum and forks

Note: *To remove the selector drum and forks the engine must be removed from the frame and the crankcases separated.*

Removal

1 Remove the engine (see Section 4) and separate the crankcase halves (see Section 21).

2 Refer to Section 25 and remove the transmission assembly.

Inspection

3 Inspect the selector forks for any signs of wear or damage, especially around the fork ends where they engage with the groove in the pinion. Check that each fork fits correctly in its pinion groove **(see illustration)**. Measure the thickness of each fork end and replace them with new ones if worn below the specified thickness **(see illustration)**. Check closely to see if the forks are bent. If the forks are in any way damaged they must be replaced with new ones.

4 Check that the fork shaft ends and their holes in the casings are neither worn nor

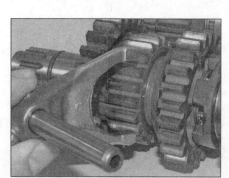
27.3a Check the fit of each fork in its pinion . . .

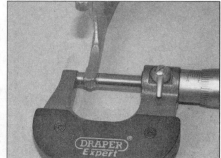
27.3b . . . and measure the thickness of each end

27.4 Check the fit and feel of each shaft in its bore

27.6 Check the guide pins and their grooves in the drum

27.7 Selector drum bearing (arrowed)

27.8a Check the plunger in the drum . . .

27.8b . . . and the contact (arrowed) in the switch

damaged and the shafts are a smooth sliding fit with no freeplay **(see illustration)**.
5 Check each selector fork shaft is straight. A bent rod will cause difficulty in selecting gears and make the gearchange action heavy. Replace the shaft with a new one if it is bent.
6 Inspect the selector drum tracks and selector fork guide pins for signs of wear or damage **(see illustration)**. If either component shows signs of wear or damage the fork(s) and drum must be replaced with new ones.
7 Check that the selector drum bearing rotates smoothly and freely, and check the fit of the plain end in its bore in the crankcase **(see illustration)**. Replace the drum and/or crankcases with new ones if they are worn.
8 Check the neutral switch contact plate, plunger and spring, and also check the contacts on the switch **(see illustrations)**. Make sure the plunger moves in and out freely. Replace any damaged or worn parts with new ones – to remove the plate undo the screw, noting that the plunger is under pressure from

the spring. Clean the threads of the screw and apply a suitable non-permanent thread locking compound on installation.

Installation

9 Refer to Section 25 and install the selector drum/forks and transmission shafts as an assembly.
10 Reassemble the crankcase halves (see Section 21).

28 Running-in procedure

1 Make sure the engine oil and coolant levels are correct (see *Pre-ride checks*). Make sure there is fuel in the tank.
2 Turn the engine kill switch to the ON position and shift the gearbox into neutral. Turn the ignition ON.
3 Start the engine and allow it to run at a

moderately fast idle until it reaches operating temperature.
4 If a lubrication failure is suspected, stop the engine immediately and try to find the cause. If an engine is run without oil, even for a short period of time, severe damage will occur.
5 Check carefully that there are no oil or coolant leaks and make sure the transmission and controls, especially the brakes, function properly before road testing the machine.
6 Treat the machine gently for the first few miles to make sure oil has circulated throughout the engine and any new parts installed have started to seat.
7 Even greater care is necessary if a new piston and rings or a new cylinder block have been fitted, and the bike will have to be run in as when new. This means greater use of the transmission and a restraining hand on the throttle – for the first 600 miles (1000 km) avoid prolonged use above 4500 rpm and 1/3 throttle opening. From 600 to 1000 miles (1000 to 1600 km) avoid prolonged use above 6000 rpm and 1/2 throttle opening. There's no point in keeping to any set speed limit – the main idea is to keep from labouring the engine, but making sure you vary engine speed and load within those limits. Gradually increase performance, and do not run the engine for more than an hour without letting it cool down for five to ten minutes. Experience is the best guide, since it's easy to tell when an engine is running freely.
8 Upon completion of the road test, and after the engine has cooled down completely, recheck the valve clearances (see Chapter 1) and check the engine oil and coolant levels (see *Pre-ride checks*).

Chapter 3
Cooling system

Contents

	Section
Coolant change	see Chapter 1
Coolant hoses and unions	8
Coolant level check	see Pre-ride checks
Coolant reservoir	7
Cooling fan and fan relay	2
Cooling system checks	see Chapter 1

	Section
General information	1
Radiator	5
Temperature warning light and ECT sensor	3
Thermostat	4
Water pump	6

Degrees of difficulty

Easy, suitable for novice with little experience	**Fairly easy,** suitable for beginner with some experience	**Fairly difficult,** suitable for competent DIY mechanic	**Difficult,** suitable for experienced DIY mechanic	**Very difficult,** suitable for expert DIY or professional

Specifications

Coolant

Mixture type and capacity	see Chapter 1

ECT sensor

Resistance @ 20°C	2.28 to 2.63 K-ohms
Resistance @ 80°C	300 to 330 ohms

Thermostat

Opening temperature	71°C
Fully open	85°C
Valve lift	8 mm (min)

Radiator

Cap valve opening pressure	16 to 20 psi (1.1 to 1.4 Bar)

Torque settings

Coolant inlet union bolts	10 Nm
ECT sensor	18 Nm
Thermostat cover bolts	10 Nm
Water pump bolts	10 Nm
Water pump outlet pipe bolt	10 Nm

1 General information

The cooling system uses a water/anti-freeze coolant to carry away excess heat from the engine and maintain as constant a temperature as possible. The cylinder is surrounded by a water jacket from which the heated coolant is circulated by thermo-syphonic action in conjunction with a water pump, which is driven by gear off the crankshaft. The hot coolant passes upwards to the thermostat and through to the radiator. The coolant flows across the core of the radiator, then to the water pump and back to the engine. Coolant is also circulated around the fast idle plunger in the throttle body.

A thermostat is fitted in the cylinder head to prevent the coolant flowing when the engine is cold, therefore accelerating the speed at which the engine reaches normal operating temperature. The ECT (engine coolant temperature) sensor mounted in the cylinder head transmits information to the ECU (electronic control unit). If the engine gets too hot the ECU actuates the cooling fan on the back of the radiator via a relay to draw extra air through, and if necessary turns on the temperature warning light in the instrument cluster.

The complete cooling system is partially sealed and pressurised, the pressure being controlled by a valve contained in the spring-loaded radiator cap. By pressurising the coolant the boiling point is raised, preventing premature boiling in adverse conditions. The overflow pipe from the system is connected to a reservoir into which excess coolant is expelled under pressure. The discharged coolant automatically returns to the radiator by the vacuum created when the engine cools.

⚠️ **Warning:** *Do not remove the pressure cap from the radiator when the engine is hot. Scalding hot coolant and steam may be blown out under pressure, which could cause serious injury. When the engine has cooled, place a thick rag, such as a towel, over the pressure cap; slowly rotate the cap anti-clockwise to the first stop – on XT-R and XT-X models*
first remove the retainer from the radiator pressure cap. This procedure allows any residual pressure to escape. When the steam has stopped escaping, press down on the cap while turning it anti-clockwise and remove it.

Caution: Do not allow anti-freeze to come in contact with your skin or painted surfaces of the motorcycle. Rinse off any spills immediately with plenty of water. Anti-freeze is highly toxic if ingested. Never leave anti-freeze lying around in an open container or in puddles on the floor; children and pets are attracted by its sweet smell and may drink it. Check with the local authorities about disposing of used anti-freeze. Many communities will have collection centres which will see that anti-freeze is disposed of safely.

Caution: At all times use the specified type of anti-freeze, and always mix it with distilled water in the correct proportion. The anti-freeze contains corrosion inhibitors which are essential to avoid damage to the cooling system. A lack of these inhibitors could lead to a build-up of corrosion which would block the coolant passages, resulting in overheating and severe engine damage. Distilled water must be used as opposed to tap water to avoid a build-up of scale which would also block the passages.

2 Cooling fan and relay

1 If the engine is overheating and the cooling fan does not come on, first check the cooling fan fuse (see Chapter 8). If the fuse is good, check the relay (see Steps 2 to 6). If the fuse and relay are good check the fan motor (Steps 10 and 11).

Cooling fan relay

Check

2 On XT-R and XT-X models remove the right-hand side panel (see Chapter 7), on XT-Z models remove the battery (see Chapter 8), and on MT-03 models remove the seats (see Chapter 7). Displace the relay and disconnect its wiring connector **(see illustrations)**.

3 Set a multimeter to the ohms x 1 scale and connect it across the brown and blue wire terminals on the relay. There should be no continuity (infinite resistance). Using a fully-charged 12 volt battery and two insulated jumper wires, connect the positive (+) terminal of the battery to the red/white wire terminal on the relay, and the negative (–) terminal to the green/yellow wire terminal on the relay. At this point the relay should be heard to click and the multimeter read 0 ohms (continuity). If this is the case the relay is proved good. If the relay does not click when battery voltage is applied and still indicates no continuity (infinite resistance) across its terminals, it is faulty and must be replaced with a new one.

4 If the relay is good, check for battery voltage at the brown wire in the wiring connector with the ignition switch OFF, and at red/white wire in the wiring connector with the ignition switch ON. If there is no voltage, check the wiring to the connector for continuity, referring to *Electrical System Fault Finding* at the beginning of Chapter 8 and the relevant wiring diagram at the end of it. If voltage is present, check that there is continuity in the green/yellow wire to the ECU wiring connector, and in the blue wire to the fan motor connector. There should be continuity in all wires.

5 If the fan is on the whole time, pull the relay off its connector. The fan should stop. If it does, the relay is defective and must be replaced with a new one.

6 If the fan works but is suspected of cutting in at the wrong temperature, check the ECT sensor (see Section 3).

Removal and installation

7 On XT-R and XT-X models remove the right-hand side panel (see Chapter 7), on XT-Z models remove the battery (see Chapter 8), and on MT-03 models remove the seats (see Chapter 7).

8 Displace the relay and disconnect its wiring connector **(see illustration 2.2a, b or c)**.

9 Installation is the reverse of removal.

Cooling fan

Check

10 The cooling fan is on the back of the radiator. On XT-R, XT-X and MT-03 models remove the fuel tank (see Chapter 4). On

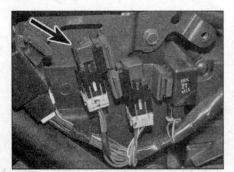
2.2a Cooling fan relay (arrowed) – XT-R and XT-X models

2.2b Cooling fan relay (arrowed) – XT-Z models

2.2c Cooling fan relay (arrowed) – MT-03 models

XT-Z models remove the fuel tank left-hand cover (see Chapter 7). Trace the wiring from the fan and disconnect the connector **(see illustrations)**.

11 Using a 12 volt battery and two jumper wires with suitable connectors, connect the battery positive (+) lead to the blue wire terminal on the fan side of the wiring connector, and the battery negative (–) lead to the black wire terminal on the connector. Once connected the fan should operate. If it does not, and the connector and the wiring between it and the motor is good, then the fan motor is faulty. Individual components are not available – replace the fan assembly with a new one.

Removal and installation

 Warning: The engine must be completely cool before carrying out this procedure.

12 Remove the radiator (see Section 5).
13 Undo the screws and remove the fan assembly **(see illustration)** – on XT-Z models note the spacers between the fan and the radiator and the collars inserted from the front that the screws thread into.
14 Installation is the reverse of removal.

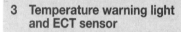

3 Temperature warning light and ECT sensor

Temperature warning light

Note: *If the warning light comes on during normal use stop the engine and check the coolant level in the reservoir (see Pre-ride checks).*

1 The circuit consists of the ECT sensor mounted in the cylinder head and the warning light LED in the instrument cluster. When the ignition is first switched on the LED should come on for a few seconds then go out – if it doesn't, refer to Chapter 8 and check the LED.
2 If the LED is good connect the positive (+) probe of a voltmeter to the yellow/blue (XT-R and XT-X models), red/green (XT-Z models) or green/red (MT-03 models) wire terminal in the loom side of the instrument cluster wiring connector and the negative (-) probe to the black/white wire terminal. Turn the ignition switch ON and check the voltage – there should be 5 volts. If not check for continuity in the wire to the ECU and check for continuity to earth in the black/white wire.
3 If the wiring is good check the ECT sensor (see below).

ECT sensor
Check

4 Remove the sensor (see Steps 7 and 8 below).
5 Fill a small heatproof container with the specified coolant mix and place it on a stove. Connect the probes of an ohmmeter to the terminals on the sensor **(see illustration)**.

2.10a On XT-R and XT-X models the cooling fan wiring connector is among the cluster on the left-hand side

2.10c Cooling fan wiring connector (arrowed) – MT-03 models

Using some wire or other support suspend the sensor in the coolant so that just the sensing head and the threads are submerged, and with the head a minimum of 40 mm above the bottom of the container. Also place a thermometer in the coolant so that its bulb is close to the sensor. **Note:** *None of the components should be allowed to directly touch the container.*

 Warning: This must be done very carefully to avoid the risk of personal injury.

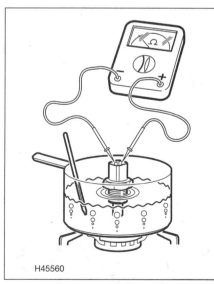
3.5 ECT sensor test set-up

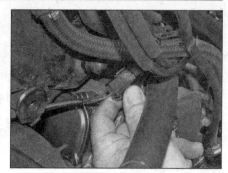
2.10b Cooling fan wiring connector – XT-Z models

2.13 Fan assembly mounting screws (arrowed) – XT-Z shown

6 Begin to heat the coolant, stirring it gently. At 20°C the meter reading should be as specified at the beginning of the Chapter. As the temperature reaches around 80°C, turn the heat down and maintain the temperature steady for three minutes. The meter reading should be as specified at the beginning of the Chapter. If you were to continue heating the coolant (noting that it will boil at just over 100°C) the resistance should drop further as temperature rises.

Removal and installation

 Warning: The engine must be completely cool before carrying out this procedure.

7 Drain the cooling system (see Chapter 1). The sensor is mounted in the back of the cylinder head on the right-hand side **(see illustration)**.
8 Disconnect the sensor wiring connector. Unscrew and remove the sensor, and discard the sealing washer.

3.7 ECT sensor location (arrowed)

4.3 Release the clamps (arrowed) and detach the hoses

4.4 Unscrew the bolts (arrowed) and detach the cover . . .

9 Fit a new sealing washer onto the sensor. Fit the sensor and tighten it to the torque setting specified at the beginning of the Chapter. Connect the wiring.

10 Refill the cooling system (see Chapter 1) and check the coolant level (see *Pre-ride checks*).

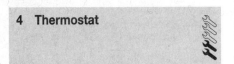

4 Thermostat

Note: *Where single-use crimped hose clamps are used they can be replaced with multi-use screw clamps if required – this prevents having to also obtain special pliers to crimp the single-use clamps.*

1 The thermostat is automatic in operation and should give many years service without requiring attention. In the event of a failure, the valve will probably jam open, in which case the engine will take much longer than normal to warm up. Conversely, if the valve jams shut, the coolant will be unable to circulate and the engine will overheat. Neither condition is acceptable, and the fault must be investigated promptly.

Removal

 Warning: The engine must be completely cool before carrying out this procedure.

4.5 . . . then withdraw the thermostat from the housing

2 Drain the cooling system (see Chapter 1). The thermostat housing is in the back of the cylinder head on the right-hand side.

3 If required release the hose clamps and detach the hoses **(see illustration)**.

4 Unscrew the cover bolts and detach it from the cylinder head **(see illustration)**.

5 Withdraw the thermostat, noting how it fits **(see illustration)**.

6 Remove the O-ring and discard it **(see illustration 4.11)** – a new one must be used.

Check

7 Examine the thermostat visually before carrying out the test. If it remains in the open position at room temperature, it should be replaced with a new one.

8 Suspend the thermostat by a piece of wire in a container of cold water. Place a thermometer in the water so that the bulb is close to the thermostat **(see illustration)**. Heat the water, noting the temperature when the thermostat opens, and compare the result with the specifications given at the beginning of the Chapter. Also check the amount the valve opens after it has been heated for a few minutes and compare the measurement to the specifications. If the readings obtained differ from those given, the thermostat is faulty and must be replaced with a new one.

9 In the event of thermostat failure, if the thermostat is permanently closed, as an

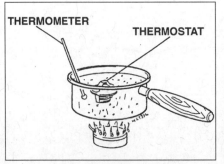

4.8 Thermostat testing set-up

emergency measure only it can be removed and the machine used without it (this is better than leaving it in as the engine will overheat). If it is permanently open you are better to leave it in. In both cases take care when starting the engine from cold as it will take much longer than usual to warm up. Ensure that a new unit is installed as soon as possible.

Installation

10 Fit the thermostat into the housing with the hole at the top **(see illustration 4.5)**.

11 Fit the cover using a new O-ring smeared with grease **(see illustration)**. Tighten the cover bolts to the torque setting specified at the beginning of the Chapter **(see illustration 4.4)**.

12 If detached fit the hoses and secure them with the clamps **(see illustration 4.3)**. Refill the cooling system (see Chapter 1) and check the coolant level (see *Pre-ride checks*).

5 Radiator

Note: *If the radiator is being removed as part of the engine removal procedure, detach the hoses from their unions on the engine rather than on the radiator and remove the radiator complete with its hoses. Note the routing of the hoses.*

4.11 Fit the cover using a new O-ring

5.3a Detach the hoses (arrowed) from the right-hand side of the radiator . . .

5.3b . . . and the hose from the left-hand side

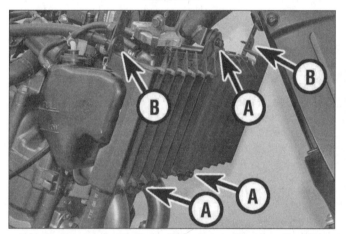

5.4a Radiator mounting bolts (A), radiator grille trim clips (B) – XT-R/X

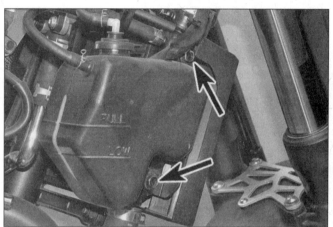

5.4b Reservoir mounting bolts (arrowed)

Note: *Where single-use crimped hose clamps are used they can be replaced with multi-use screw clamps if required – this prevents having to obtain special pliers to crimp the single-use clamps.*

Removal

 Warning: The engine must be completely cool before carrying out this procedure.

1 Drain the cooling system (see Chapter 1). On XT-R and XT-X models remove the fuel tank covers (see Chapter 7). On XT-Z models remove the radiator covers (see Chapter 7) and the fuel tank (see Chapter 4). On MT-03 models remove the fuel tank right-hand trim panel (see Chapter 7).

2 Disconnect the fan wiring connector **(see illustration 2.10a, b or c)**.

3 Slacken the clamps securing the hoses to the radiator and detach them **(see illustrations)**.

4 On XT-R and XT-X models unscrew and remove the radiator mounting bolts and

remove the radiator with its grille and the coolant reservoir **(see illustration)**. If required release the trim clips and remove the grille, then unscrew the bolts and remove the reservoir **(see illustration)**.

5 On XT-Z models undo the radiator mounting screws and remove the grille, then ease the radiator up to free the mounting lug on the bottom from its grommet and remove the radiator, taking care not to catch the fins on anything **(see illustrations)**.

6 On MT-03 models unscrew and remove the

5.5a Undo the screws (arrowed) . . .

5.5b . . . remove the grille . . .

5.5c . . . then draw the radiator up to free the lug from the grommet – XT-Z

5.6a Radiator mounting bolts (arrowed) –
MT-03

5.6b Radiator cover screws (arrowed) –
they also secure the reservoir

radiator mounting bolts and washers, then ease the radiator up to free the mounting lug on the bottom from its grommet, and remove the radiator with its end covers and the coolant reservoir, taking care not to catch the fins on anything **(see illustration)**. If required undo the screw and remove the covers and reservoir **(see illustration)**.

7 Note the arrangement of the collars and rubber grommets in the radiator mounts. Replace the grommets with new ones if they are damaged, deformed or deteriorated.

8 Check the radiator for signs of damage and clear any dirt or debris that might obstruct airflow and inhibit cooling. If the radiator fins are badly damaged or broken the radiator must be replaced with a new one. To enable full examination and cleaning, remove the cooling fan from the radiator (see Section 2).

Installation

9 Installation is the reverse of removal, noting the following.

● Ensure the coolant hoses are in good condition (see Chapter 1), and are securely retained by their clamps, using new ones if necessary.

● Make sure the rubber grommets and collars are correctly fitted.

● Make sure that the fan wiring is securely connected.

● On completion refill the cooling system as described in Chapter 1 and check the coolant level (see *Pre-ride checks*).

Pressure cap check

10 If problems such as overheating or loss of coolant occur, check the entire system as described in Chapter 1. The radiator cap opening pressure should be checked by a Yamaha dealer with the special tester required to do the job. If the cap is defective, replace it with a new one.

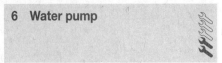

6 Water pump

Note: *Where single-use crimped hose clamps are used they can be replaced with multi-use screw clamps if required – this prevents having to obtain special pliers to crimp the single-use clamps.*

Check

1 Refer to Chapter 1, Section 9.

Removal

2 Drain the engine oil and coolant (see Chapter 1).

3 Release the clamps securing the hoses to the unions on the pump and detach the hoses **(see illustrations)**.

4 Unscrew the bolts as required to either just remove the cover, and then if required the pump, or to remove the pump complete with the cover attached **(see illustrations)**.

5 Remove and discard the pump body O-ring and cover gasket according to method – new ones must be used **(see illustrations 6.22 and 6.23)**. If required unscrew the outlet pipe bolt and remove the pipe **(see illustration)**. Discard the O-ring – a new one must be used.

6.3a Slacken the clamp (arrowed) and
detach the inlet hose

6.3b Also slacken either the outlet hose
top or bottom clamp (arrowed), according
to ease of access on your model

6.4a To remove the cover unscrew all the
bolts (arrowed), and to remove the pump
complete with the cover unscrew the three
bolts (A)

6.4b Removing the cover by itself

6.4c Removing the pump after removing
the cover

6.5 Outlet pipe bolt (arrowed)

6.7a Release the circlip . . .

6.7b . . . and remove the gear . . .

6.7c . . . the drive pin . . .

Inspection

6 To check the pump impeller bearing, wiggle the impeller back-and-forth and turn it by hand. If there is excessive movement, or the bearing is noisy or rough when turned, the bearing must be replaced with a new one. Also check the bearing referring to *Tools and Workshop Tips* (Section 5) in the *Reference* section.

7 Remove the circlip securing the driven gear on the pump shaft **(see illustration)**. Remove the gear, the drive pin and the washer **(see illustrations)**. Withdraw the impeller **(see illustration)**. Discard the circlip – a new one must be used.

8 Check the condition of the impeller and shaft. If there are signs of wear or other damage, the impeller must be replaced with a new one. Check the condition of the rubber damper and its holder on the rear face of the impeller. Do not remove them from the shaft unnecessarily, as they cannot be reused. If they are damaged or deteriorated replace them with new ones – Yamaha do not list the damper and holder as being available separately, but they come as part of the seal kit along with the mechanical seal. To replace them, lever off the old ones with a flat-bladed screwdriver **(see illustration)**. Apply coolant to the new ones and press them squarely

6.7d . . . and the washer . . .

6.7e . . . then withdraw the impeller

down the shaft on to the back of the impeller, making sure they are flush with their housing rim **(see illustration)**.

9 Check the condition of the seals and bearing. Refer to Steps 12 to 19 to fit new ones.

10 Inspect the pump body for corrosion or a build-up of scale and clean with steel wool as necessary, then rinse the pump body in running clean water.

11 Lubricate the impeller shaft with coolant and slide it into the pump body **(see illustration 6.7e)**. Fit the washer, the drive pin and the gear, locating the cut-outs on its

inner face over the drive pin ends **(see illustrations 6.7d, c and b)**. Secure the gear with a new circlip, pushing on the impeller to compress the mechanical seal and expose the groove **(see illustration 6.7a)**. Turn the impeller by hand and check it turns as it should.

Seal and bearing replacement

12 Remove the impeller (see Step 7).

13 Drive the bearing and oil seal out using a drift from the outer side of the pump **(see illustration)**.

14 Drive the mechanical seal out using a

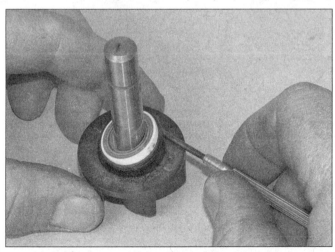

6.8a Lever the rubber damper and holder out . . .

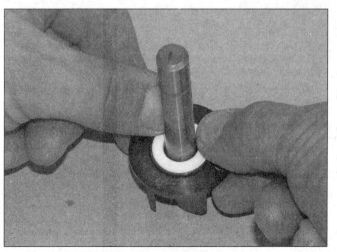

6.8b . . . and press the new ones in

6.13 Drive the bearing and oil seal out using a drift

6.14a Use a socket . . .

6.14b . . . to drive the mechanical seal out

6.16 Fit the new seal as described . . .

6.17a . . . then fit the new bearing . . .

6.17b . . . using a socket on the outer race to drive it in

suitable socket from the inner side of the pump **(see illustrations)**.

15 Clean any traces of sealant from around the mechanical seal seat with a suitable solvent.

16 Apply a smear of coolant to the outside of the new oil seal. Push the new seal in from the inner (bearing) side with the marked side facing down and set it below the rim so the bearing will not touch it **(see illustration)**.

17 Drive the bearing into the pump using a suitable driver or socket bearing on the outer race until it is seated **(see illustration)**.

18 Smear Yamaha Bond 1215 or a suitable equivalent to the mechanical seal seat. Press the new mechanical seal into the pump body using the set-up shown or a suitable equivalent **(see illustrations)**. Do not drive the seal in using a socket and hammer.

6.18a Find a suitable piece of tubing to fit onto the rim of the seal . . .

6.18b . . . and inside the first recess of the seal housing

6.18c Set up a method of pressing the new seal in, such as using a puller as shown

6.18d Position the new seal in the pump . . .

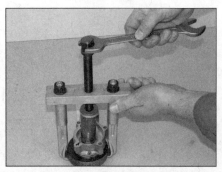

6.18e . . . then press the seal in . . .

6.18f . . . until the rim seats

6.21 Fit the outlet pipe using a new O-ring

6.22 Fit a new O-ring into the groove

6.23 Fit a new gasket onto the cover, using the bolts to hold it in place

19 Fit the impeller (see Step 11).

Installation

20 Clean all traces of old gasket off the pump and cover mating surfaces – if using a scraper take care not to gouge the surface.
21 If removed fit a new O-ring smeared with grease onto the outlet pipe (see illustration). Fit the pipe into the pump and tighten the bolt to the torque setting specified at the beginning of the Chapter.
22 Fit a new O-ring smeared with grease into the groove in the pump (see illustration). Fit the pump into the crankcase, making sure the O-ring does not dislodge, and fitting the outlet hose onto its union (see illustration 6.4c). Tighten the outlet hose clamp (see illustration 6.3b).
23 Fit the cover using a new gasket and tighten the bolts evenly and a little at a time in a criss-cross sequence to the specified torque setting (see illustration).

24 Fit the coolant inlet hose onto the pump and secure it with the clamp (see illustration 6.3a).
25 Refill the cooling system and replenish the engine oil (see Chapter 1).

7 Coolant reservoir

1 The coolant reservoir is located on the right-hand side. Obtain a suitable container to tip the coolant into.
2 On XT-R and XT-X models remove the fuel tank covers (see Chapter 7). Release the trim clips securing the grille to the radiator, then unscrew the radiator screws and remove the grille, and refit the screws finger-tight to secure the radiator (see illustration 5.4a). Remove the reservoir filler cap and detach the

overflow hose (see illustration). Unscrew the reservoir mounting bolts and tip the coolant into the container (see illustration 5.4b).
3 On XT-Z models remove the radiator right-hand cover (see Chapter 7). Detach the top hose (see illustration). Unscrew the reservoir mounting bolts, then remove the cap and tip the contents of the reservoir into the container (see illustrations). Detach the bottom hose.
4 On MT-03 models remove the reservoir filler cap and detach the hose (see illustration). Remove the radiator right-hand cover (see Chapter 7) – the bolts also secure the reservoir (see illustration 5.6b). Tip the coolant into the container.
5 Installation is the reverse of removal. Refill the reservoir to the FULL level line with the specified coolant mixture (see Pre-ride checks).

7.2 Remove the cap and detach the hose (arrowed)

7.3a Detach the hose (arrowed)

7.3b Unscrew the bolts (arrowed) . . .

7.3c . . . and drain the reservoir . . .

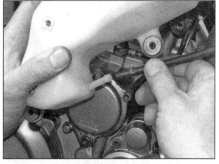
7.3d . . . then detach the bottom hose

7.4 Remove the cap and detach the hose (arrowed)

8 Coolant hoses and unions

Note: *Where single-use crimped hose clamps are used they can be replaced with multi-use screw clamps if required – this prevents having to obtain special pliers to crimp the single-use clamps.*

Removal

1 Before removing a hose, drain the coolant (see Chapter 1).

2 Use a screwdriver to release or slacken the larger-bore hose clamps, then slide them back along the hose and clear of the union spigot **(see illustrations 6.3a and b)**. The smaller-bore hoses are secured by spring clamps which can be expanded by squeezing their ears together with pliers.

Caution: The radiator unions are fragile. Do not use excessive force when attempting to remove the hoses.

8.4 Coolant inlet union bolts (arrowed)

3 If a hose proves stubborn, release it by rotating it on its union before working it off. If all else fails, cut the hose with a sharp knife. Whilst this means replacing the hose with a new one – it is preferable to buying a new radiator.

4 The inlet union to the engine can be removed by unscrewing its bolts **(see illustration)**. If the union is removed, the O-ring must be replaced with a new one.

Installation

5 Slide the clamps onto the hose and then work the hose on to its union as far as the spigot where present.

> **HAYNES HINT** *If the hose is difficult to push on its union, soften it by soaking it in very hot water, or alternatively a little soapy water on the union can be used as a lubricant.*

6 Rotate the hose on its unions to settle it in position before sliding the clamps into place and tightening them securely.

7 If the inlet union has been removed, fit a new O-ring smeared with grease into the groove. Fit the union and tighten the bolts to the torque setting specified at the beginning of the Chapter.

8 Refill the cooling system with fresh coolant (see Chapter 1) and check the coolant level (see *Pre-ride checks*).

Chapter 4
Engine management system

Contents
	Section
Air filter .... see Chapter 1	
Air filter housing 8	
Air induction system (AIS) 14	
Catalytic converter 15	
Clutch switch .... see Chapter 8	
Electronic control unit (ECU) 18	
Engine management system description 5	
Engine management system fault diagnosis 6	
Engine management system components 7	
Exhaust system 13	
Fast idle unit 11	
Fuel gauge or warning light and level sensor .... see Chapter 8	
Fuel hose renewal .... see Chapter 1	
Fuel rail and injector 10	
Fuel pump and relay 4	
Fuel pressure check 3	

	Section
Fuel system check .... see Chapter 1	
Fuel tank 2	
General information and precautions 1	
Idle speed check .... see Chapter 1	
Ignition switch .... see Chapter 8	
Ignition coil and spark plug cap 17	
Ignition system check 16	
Ignition timing 19	
Immobiliser system 20	
Neutral switch .... see Chapter 8	
Sidestand switch .... see Chapter 8	
Spark plug .... see Chapter 1	
Starter circuit cut-off relay (in relay unit) .... see Chapter 8	
Throttle cable check and adjustment .... see Chapter 1	
Throttle body 9	
Throttle cables 12	

Degrees of difficulty

Easy, suitable for novice with little experience	Fairly easy, suitable for beginner with some experience	Fairly difficult, suitable for competent DIY mechanic	Difficult, suitable for experienced DIY mechanic	Very difficult, suitable for expert DIY or professional

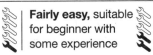

Specifications

Fuel

Grade	Unleaded. Minimum 95 RON
Fuel tank capacity	
XT-R and XT-X	
Capacity (including reserve)	15 litres
Reserve volume (when fuel warning light comes on)	approx. 5 litres
XT-Z	
Capacity (including reserve)	23 litres
Reserve volume (when bottom segment of gauge flashes)	approx. 6.7 litres
MT-03	
Capacity (including reserve)	15 litres
Reserve volume (when fuel warning light comes on)	approx. 4.25 litres

Fuel injection system

Throttle body
  XT-R and XT-X
    2004 to 2006 models

Type	Mikuni 44EHS
ID mark	5VK1 00

    2007-on models

Type	Mikuni 44EHS
ID mark	5VK8 10

  XT-Z

Type	Mikuni 44EHS-8/5B
ID mark	5YK2 11

  MT-03
    2004 to 2006 models

Type	Mikuni 44EHS/5B
ID mark	5YK1 00

    2007-on models

Type	Mikuni 44EHS-8
ID mark	5YK2 10
Idle speed	see Chapter 1
Air induction system (AIS) control valve resistance	18 to 22 ohms @ 20°C
Crankshaft position (CKP) sensor resistance	192 to 288 ohms @ 20°C

Engine coolant temperature (ECT) sensor resistance

Resistance @ 20°C	2.28 to 2.63 K-ohms
Resistance @ 80°C	300 to 330 ohms
Fuel injector resistance	12 ohms @ 20°C
Fuel pressure (at idle speed)	46 psi (3.31 Bar)
Intake air pressure (IAP) sensor output voltage	3.4 to 3.8 volts

Intake air temperature (IAT) sensor resistance

@ 20°C	2.21 to 2.69 K-ohms
@ 80°C	290 to 354 ohms
Speed sensor voltage	0.6 to 4.8 V fluctuating
Throttle position (TP) sensor maximum resistance	4.0 to 6.0 K-ohms
Throttle position (TP) sensor resistance range	0 to 6.0 K-ohms

Tip-over (TO) sensor output voltage

Sensor upright	0.4 to 1.4V
Sensor tilted	3.7 to 4.4V

Ignition system

Spark plugs	see Chapter 1
Primary winding resistance	3.4 to 4.6 ohms @ 20°C
Secondary winding resistance (without cap)	10.4 to 15.6 K-ohms @ 20°C
Spark plug cap resistance	approx 10 K-ohms @ 20°C

Torque settings

Exhaust system
  XT-R and XT-X models

Downpipe flange nuts	20 Nm
Downpipe joint clamp bolt	12 Nm
Downpipe mounting bolts	27 Nm
Downpipe mounting bracket bolts	23 Nm
Silencer clamp bolts	20 Nm
Silencer mounting bolts	27 Nm

  XT-Z and MT-03 models

Downpipe flange nuts	20 Nm
Intermediate pipe clamp bolts	18 Nm
Intermediate pipe mounting bolt	25 Nm
Silencer clamp bolt	18 Nm
Silencer mounting bolts	22 Nm

Fuel pump retaining ring bolts

XT-R and XT-X models	4 Nm
XT-Z and MT-03 models	7 Nm

Fuel tank bolt(s)

XT-R and XT-X models	10 Nm
XT-Z models	20 Nm
MT-03 models	10 Nm
Oxygen (O2) sensor	45 Nm

1 General information and precautions

Fuel system

The fuel supply system consists of the fuel tank, an internal and integrated fuel pump, filter, pressure regulator and level sensor, the fuel hose, fuel injector, throttle body, and throttle cables. The injection system supplies fuel and air to the engine via a single throttle body. The injector is operated by the Electronic Control Unit (ECU) using the information obtained from the sensors it monitors (refer to Section 5 for more information on the operation of the fuel injection system). Cold start idle speed is controlled by the fast idle unit that reacts to the temperature of engine coolant that is circulated around it.

Air is drawn into the throttle body via an air filter fitted in a housing behind the throttle body.

The exhaust system contains a catalytic converter, and on models produced from 2007-on an oxygen sensor.

XT-R, XT-X and MT-03 models have a low fuel warning light in the instrument cluster, actuated by a level sensor that is part of the fuel pump inside the fuel tank – when the warning light comes on there is 5 litres of fuel left on XT-R and XT-X models, and 4.25 litres on MT-03 models.

XT-Z models have a fuel gauge in the instrument cluster, actuated by a level sensor that is part of the fuel pump inside the fuel tank – when the bottom segment starts to flash there is 6.7 litres of fuel left. At this point a function of the trip meter (F-TRIP) displays the distance travelled since the segment started to flash.

Ignition system

All models are fitted with a fully transistorised electronic ignition system which, due to its lack of mechanical parts, is totally maintenance-free. The system comprises a set of triggers, a crankshaft position (CKP) sensor, electronic control unit (ECU), and ignition coil (refer to Wiring Diagrams at the end of Chapter 8 for details).

The ignition triggers, which are on the alternator rotor on the left-hand end of the crankshaft, magnetically operate the crankshaft position sensor as the crankshaft rotates. The sensor sends a signal to the electronic control unit, which then supplies the ignition coil with the power necessary to produce a spark at the plug.

The ECU incorporates an electronic advance system.

The system has a starter safety circuit, comprising the neutral switch, the clutch switch, and the sidestand switch, that prevents the engine from being started unless it is in neutral, or if it is in gear unless the clutch lever is pulled in and the sidestand is up.

Because of their nature, the individual ignition system components can be checked but not repaired. If ignition system troubles occur, and the faulty component can be isolated, the only cure for the problem is to replace the part with a new one. Keep in mind that most electrical parts, once purchased, cannot be returned. To avoid unnecessary expense, make very sure the faulty component has been positively identified before buying a replacement part.

Note that there is no provision for adjusting the ignition timing.

Precautions

⚠️ **Warning: Petrol (gasoline) is extremely flammable, so take extra precautions when you work on any part of the fuel system. Always remove the battery (see Chapter 8). Don't smoke or allow open flames or bare light bulbs near the work area, and don't work in a garage where a natural gas-type appliance is present. If you spill any fuel on your skin, rinse it off immediately with soap and water. When you perform any kind of work on the fuel system, wear safety glasses and have a fire extinguisher suitable for a class B type fire (flammable liquids) on hand.**

Residual pressure will remain in the fuel feed hose and fuel injector after the motorcycle has been used. Before disconnecting any fuel hose, ensure the ignition is switched OFF and have some rag handy to catch any fuel. It is vital that no dirt or debris is allowed to enter the fuel system. Any foreign matter could result in injector damage or malfunction. Ensure the ignition is switched OFF before disconnecting or reconnecting any fuel injection system wiring connector. If a connector is disconnected or reconnected with the ignition switched ON, the electronic control unit (ECU) may be damaged.

Always perform service procedures in a well-ventilated area to prevent a build-up of fumes.

Never work in a building containing a gas appliance with a pilot light, or any other form of naked flame. Ensure that there are no naked light bulbs or any sources of flame or sparks nearby.

Do not smoke (or allow anyone else to smoke) while in the vicinity of petrol (gasoline) or of components containing it. Remember the possible presence of vapour from these sources and move well clear before smoking.

Check all electrical equipment belonging to the house, garage or workshop where work is being undertaken (see the Safety first! section of this manual). Remember that certain electrical appliances such as drills, cutters etc, create sparks in the normal course of operation and must not be used near petrol (gasoline) or any component containing it. Again, remember the possible presence of fumes before using electrical equipment.

Always mop up any spilt fuel and safely dispose of the rag used.

Any stored fuel that is drained off during servicing work must be kept in sealed containers that are suitable for holding petrol (gasoline), and clearly marked as such; the containers themselves should be kept in a safe place. Note that this last point applies equally to the fuel tank if it is removed from the machine; also remember to keep its filler cap closed at all times.

Read the Safety first! section of this manual carefully before starting work.

2 Fuel tank

⚠️ **Warning: Refer to the precautions given in Section 1 before starting work.**

Draining

1 The best way to drain the tank is to use a pump, cheaply available at any good parts shop.
2 Remove the filler cap, insert the suction end of the pump in the tank and the expulsion end into a container suitable and large enough for storing the fuel, then operate the pump, moving the suction nozzle around all the extremities of the tank, until empty **(see illustration)**. Refit the filler cap.

Removal

XT-R and XT-X models

3 Remove the seat, the side panels and the fuel tank covers (see Chapter 7).
4 Make sure the fuel filler cap is secure. Unscrew the fuel tank bolt and remove the plate and upper rubber support **(see illustration)**.
5 Lift the back of the tank, noting the lower

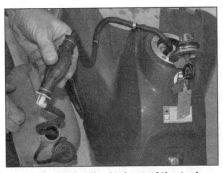
2.2 Pumping the fuel out of the tank

2.4 Unscrew the bolt and remove the plate and rubber

2.5 Lift the back of the tank and support or hold it

2.6 Disconnect the pump wiring connectors (arrowed)

rubber support, and either support it using a block of wood or hold it steady with one hand **(see illustration)**.
6 Disconnect the fuel pump wiring connectors **(see illustration)**.

7 Have a rag ready to catch any residual fuel. Slide the fuel hose connector cover across, then press the clips in and pull the hose off its union **(see illustrations)**.
8 Draw the tank back and remove it **(see**

illustration). Do not rest it on the fuel pump base.
9 Inspect the tank mounting rubbers for signs of damage or deterioration and replace them with new ones if necessary.

XT-Z models

10 Remove the seat, the cockpit covers and the fuel tank covers (see Chapter 7). Remove the bracket from each side of the tank **(see illustration)**.
11 Make sure the fuel filler cap is secure. Unscrew the fuel tank rear bolts and remove the bracket, washers and sleeves **(see illustrations)**. Unscrew the front bolts – note the collars in the rubber mounts **(see illustration)**.
12 Detach the breather/overflow hose **(see illustration)**.
13 Lift the back of the tank and support it using a block of wood **(see illustration)**.

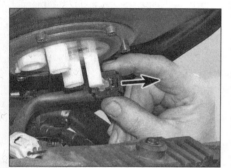

2.7a Draw the clip off the connector . . .

2.7b . . . then press the clips in and pull the hose off

2.8 Carefully remove the tank

2.10 Unscrew the bolts (arrowed) and remove the bracket from each side

2.11a Unscrew the bolts and remove the bracket . . .

2.11b . . . and the washers and sleeves

2.11c Unscrew the front bolt on each side

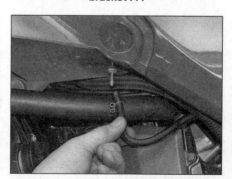

2.12 Detach the breather/overflow hose

2.13 Lift and support the tank

2.14 Disconnect the pump wiring connectors (arrowed)

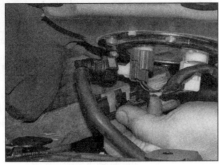

2.15a Remove the cover from the connector . . .

2.15b . . . then press the clips in . . .

14 Disconnect the fuel pump wiring connectors **(see illustration)**.

15 Remove the fuel hose connector cover **(see illustration)**. Have a rag ready to catch any residual fuel. Press the blue clips in and pull the hose off its union **(see illustrations)**.

16 Draw the tank back and remove it **(see illustration)**. Do not rest it on the fuel pump base.

17 Inspect the tank mounting rubbers for signs of damage or deterioration and replace them with new ones if necessary. If required remove the

MT-03 models

18 Remove the seat and the fuel tank covers (see Chapter 7).

19 Make sure the fuel filler cap is secure. Unscrew the fuel tank rear bolt and remove the plate **(see illustration)**. Unscrew the front bolts **(see illustrations)**. Lift the back of the tank and support it.

20 Disconnect the fuel pump wiring connectors **(see illustration)**.

21 Remove the fuel hose connector cover **(see illustration 2.15a)**. Have a rag ready to catch any residual fuel. Press the blue clips in and pull the hose off its union **(see illustrations 2.15b and c)**.

22 Detach the breather and overflow hoses **(see illustration)**.

23 Draw the tank back and remove it. Note the collars in the brackets, and remove

2.15c . . . and pull the hose off

2.16 Carefully remove the tank

2.19a Unscrew the bolt (arrowed) and remove the plate

2.19b Unscrew the bolt (arrowed) on each side . . .

2.19c . . . using a socket extension through the hole in the bracket

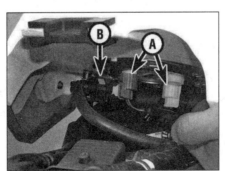

2.20 Disconnect the pump wiring connectors (A). Fuel hose connector (B)

2.22 Detach the hoses (arrowed)

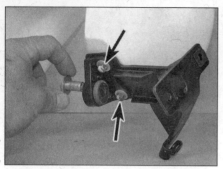

2.23a Note the collars, and remove the brackets by unscrewing the bolts (arrowed)

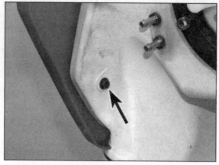

2.23b Undo the screw (arrowed) on the inside . . .

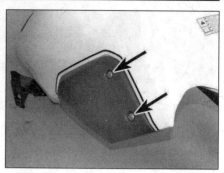

2.23c . . . and the screws (arrowed) on the outside and remove the trim panels

the brackets if required **(see illustration)**. Remove the side trim panels if required **(see illustrations)**.

24 Inspect the tank mounting rubbers for signs of damage or deterioration and replace them with new ones if necessary.

Installation

25 Installation is the reverse of removal, noting the following:

● *Make sure the tank rubbers and mounting parts are correctly fitted.*
● *Make sure the fuel hose is fully pushed onto the union until the clips locate, then on XT-R and XT-X models push the connector cover across **(see illustration)**, and on XT-Z and MT-03 models fit the connector cover **(see illustration 2.15a)**. Make sure the breather and overflow hoses are correctly fitted as required according to model.*
● *Make sure the wiring connectors are securely connected.*
● *Tighten the tank mounting bolt(s) to the torque settings specified at the beginning of the Chapter.*
● *Start the engine and check that there is no sign of fuel leakage, then turn it off.*

Fuel tank storage, cleaning and repair

26 If the fuel tank is removed from the bike, it should not be placed in an area where sparks or open flames could ignite the fumes coming out of the tank. Be especially careful inside garages where a natural gas-type appliance

2.25 Push the cover across the connector – XT-R and XT-X models

is located, because the pilot light could cause an explosion.

27 All repairs to metal fuel tanks (XT-R and XT-X) should be carried out by a professional who has experience in this critical and potentially dangerous work. Even after cleaning and flushing of the fuel system, explosive fumes can remain and ignite during repair of the tank.

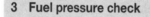

3 Fuel pressure check

Special Tool: *A fuel pressure gauge is required for this procedure.*

1 To check the fuel pressure, a suitable gauge and adapter hose (Yamaha part. Nos. 90890-03153 and 90890-03176) are needed. Raise and support the fuel tank (see Section 2).

2 Have a rag ready to catch any residual fuel. Disconnect the fuel hose from the throttle body (see Section 9).

3 Connect the gauge assembly between the hose and the injector.

4 Start the engine and check the pressure with the engine idling. It should be as specified at the beginning of this Chapter.

5 Turn the ignition OFF and remove the gauge assembly, using a rag to catch any residual fuel.

6 Reconnect the fuel hose (see Section 9).

7 If the pressure is too low, check for a leak in the fuel supply system, including the injector

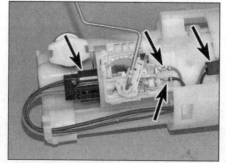

4.2 Make sure all the pump wiring and connectors (arrowed) are secure

and its holder. If there is no leakage the pressure regulator could be faulty, the pick-up in the pump could be blocked, or the pump could be faulty. The pressure regulator is part of the pump. Refer to Section 4 to check the pump.

8 If the pressure is too high, either the pressure regulator or the fuel pump check valve is faulty or the injector could be clogged. The pressure regulator is incorporated in the fuel pump; check the pump and injector.

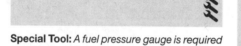

4 Fuel pump and relay

Fuel pump

Check

1 The fuel pump is located inside the fuel tank. When the ignition is switched ON, it should be possible to hear the pump run for a few seconds until the system is up to pressure. If you can't hear anything, first make sure the battery is charged and the fuel injection fuse is good (see Chapter 8).

2 Next refer to Section 2 and raise the fuel tank, then disconnect the green wiring connector from the pump **(see illustration 2.6, 2.14 or 2.20)**. Using a fully charged 12V battery connect the positive (+) terminal to the red/blue wire terminal in the pump side of the connector using an auxiliary lead, and connect the negative (-) terminal to the black wire terminal – the pump should operate. If it doesn't, remove it (see below) and check that all its wiring and connectors are secure **(see illustration)**. If they are, replace the pump with a new one.

3 Next check for continuity in the red/blue wire to the relay unit connector for continuity, and check for continuity in the black wire to earth – see Step 10 to access the relay unit. If there is a fault in either case check the wiring, connectors and terminals in the pump circuit for physical damage or loose or corroded connections and rectify as necessary (see *Electrical System Fault Finding* and the *Wiring Diagrams* in Chapter 8). If all is good check the relay (Steps 10 to 12).

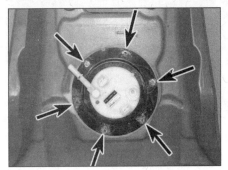

4.5a Unscrew the bolts (arrowed) and remove the ring – XT-Z model shown

Removal

4 Disconnect the battery (see Chapter 8). Drain and remove the fuel tank (see Section 2). Place the tank upside down on a suitable work surface, resting it on plenty of rag.

5 Note which way the fuel hose union points. Unscrew the pump bolts and remove the retaining ring **(see illustration)**. Carefully withdraw the pump from the tank **(see illustration)**. Remove the pump seal and discard it – a new one must be fitted **(see illustration)**. Do not disassemble the pump.

Installation

6 Ensure the pump and tank mating surfaces are clean and dry. Fit a new sealing ring onto the base of the pump, making sure the flat side seats against the pump flange **(see illustration 4.5c)**.

7 Fit the pump assembly into the tank, aligning the fuel hose union as noted on removal **(see illustration 2.6, 2.14 or 2.20)**. Fit the retaining

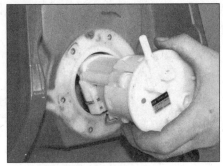

4.5b Carefully withdraw the pump . . .

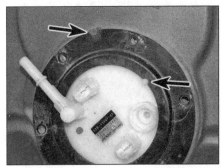

4.7a Fit the retaining ring, locating the cut-out(s) over the projection(s) (arrowed)

ring, locating the cut-out in its inner rim over the projection on the pump base, and where fitted the cut-out in its outer rim over the projection on the tank **(see illustration)**. Fit the bolts and tighten them evenly and a little at a time in the numerical sequence shown to the torque setting

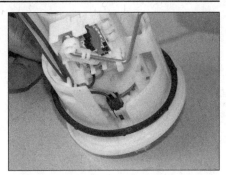

4.5c . . . and remove the sealing ring

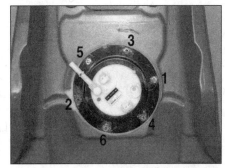

4.7b Tighten the bolts in the correct numerical sequence to the specified torque

specified at the beginning of the Chapter **(see illustration)** – note that the sequence is relative to the position of the fuel hose union, rather than the position of the fuel tank.

8 Install the fuel tank. Pour in some fuel and check for any leakage around the pump.

9 Connect the battery (see Chapter 8).

Fuel pump relay

10 Make sure the ignition is OFF. To access the relay unit on XT-R and XT-X models remove the right-hand side panel (see Chapter 7), on XT-Z models remove the seat (see Chapter 7), and on MT-03 models remove the battery (see Chapter 8), then remove the battery box **(see illustrations)**. The relay unit contains the fuel pump relay and starter circuit cut-off relay and diodes **(see illustrations)**. The fuel pump relay also provides power for the fuel injector.

11 Displace the relay and disconnect the wiring connector **(see illustration)**. Move the relay assembly to the bench for testing.

4.10a Relay unit (arrowed) – XT-R and XT-X models

4.10b Relay unit (arrowed) – XT-Z models

4.10c Unscrew the bolts (arrowed) and remove the box . . .

4.10d . . . to access the relay unit (arrowed) – MT-03 models

4.11 Displace the relay and disconnect the wiring connector

12 Using an ohmmeter or continuity tester, connect the positive (+) probe to the brown wire terminal on the relay unit and the negative (-) probe to the red/blue wire terminal **(see illustration)**. There should be no continuity. Using a fully-charged 12V battery and some jumper leads, connect the positive (+) terminal of the battery to the red/black wire terminal on the relay unit, and the negative (–) terminal to the blue/red wire terminal. There should now be continuity between the brown and red/blue wire terminals. If the relay does not test as described, replace the rely unit with a new one.

5 Engine management system description

1 The management system consists of the fuel injection circuit and the electronic control circuit.

2 The fuel circuit consists of the tank with internal integrated pump/pressure regulator/filter, level sensor, the fuel hose, the throttle body and injector. Fuel is pumped under pressure from the tank to the injector via the filter and pressure regulator. Operating pressure is maintained by the pump and pressure regulator. The injector sprays pressurised fuel into the intake duct where it mixes with air controlled by the throttle body and vaporises, before entering the cylinder where it is compressed and ignited by the spark plug.

3 The electronic control circuit consists of the electronic control unit (ECU), which operates and co-ordinates both the fuel injection and ignition systems via the relay unit (containing the fuel pump relay and the starter circuit cut-off relay), and the various sensors which provide the ECU with information on engine operating conditions.

4 The electronic control unit (ECU) monitors signals from the following sensors:

● Intake air temperature (IAT) sensor
● Intake air pressure (IAP) sensor
● Throttle position (TP) sensor
● Crankshaft position (CKP) sensor
● Engine coolant temperature (ECT) sensor
● Tip-over (TO) sensor
● Oxygen (O2) sensor (fitted from 2007-on)

5 Based on the information it receives, the ECU calculates the appropriate ignition and fuel requirements of the engine. By varying the length of the electronic pulse it sends to the injector, the ECU controls the length of time the injector is held open and thereby the amount of fuel that is supplied to the engine. Fuel supply varies according to the engine's needs for starting, warming-up, idling, cruising and acceleration. In the event of the machine falling over, the tip-over sensor cuts power to the fuel and ignition systems.

6 The engine trouble warning light should come on for a short time when the ignition is switched ON, then go out – this serves as a check that the circuit is working correctly. If not, check the instrument cluster (see Chapter 8).

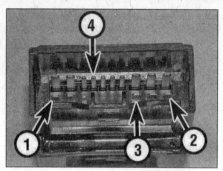

4.12 Fuel pump relay test connections

1 *Brown wire terminal – meter positive*
2 *Red/blue wire terminal – meter negative*
3 *Red/black wire terminal – battery positive*
4 *Blue/red wire terminal – battery negative*

7 The fuel injection system has its own fault diagnosis function (Section 6). In the event of a problem the engine trouble warning light in the instrument cluster comes on or flashes and any fault codes are stored in the ECU. The ECU will determine whether the engine can still be run safely. If it can, a back-up mode substitutes the sensor signal with a fixed signal, restricting performance but allowing the bike to be ridden home or to a dealer. When this occurs, the engine trouble warning light in the instrument cluster will come on and stay on. In some cases the engine will continue to run after the fault has been registered, but once stopped the engine will not be able to be restarted. If the fault is serious, the fuel injection system will be shut down and the engine will not run. When this occurs, the engine management warning light will flash while the start switch is being pressed.

8 On XT-R and XT-X models, after the engine has been stopped, the two digit fault code will appear on the instrument cluster LCD multi-function display – make a note of the number displayed. The code is also stored in the ECU memory. The diagnostic function of the instrument cluster can be used to assess the function of the sensor or actuator related to the fault code displayed – see Section 6.

9 On XT-Z and MT-03 models, after the engine has been stopped, the fault code is displayed as a series of timed flashes of the warning light – see Section 6. The code is also stored in the ECU memory. Yamaha produce a diagnostic tool (part No. 90890-03182) that, among other things, can be used to assess the function of the sensor or actuator related to the fault code displayed – see Section 6.

6 Engine management system fault diagnosis

Note: *The engine trouble warning light comes on for a short time when the ignition is turned ON. If the light does not come on, check the LED (see Chapter 8).*

1 The system incorporates a self-diagnostic function whereby most faults, when they occur, are identified by a two digit fault code, which is displayed on the instrument cluster LCD multi-function display on XT-R and XT-X models, and as a series of flashes of the engine trouble warning light in the instrument cluster on XT-Z and MT-03 models, after the engine has been stopped. The code(s) is/are stored in the ECU memory until a deletion operation is performed (see Step 14).

2 In the case of a minor fault in the system, the warning light will come on and stay on and the engine will continue to run, and may be able to be restarted (depending on the fault), enabling the machine to be ridden, although performance will be significantly reduced. In the case of a major fault the warning light will flash while the start switch is being pressed, or if already running the engine will stop and not be able to be restarted – this applies to fault codes 12, 19, 30, 33, 41 and 50 (refer to Table 1).

3 If a fault code is displayed refer to the table below to identify the faulty component and the appropriate diagnostic code (where given). If a diagnostic code is given you can use the diagnostic mode of the instrument cluster or the diagnostic tool (see below), to assess the function of the sensor or actuator concerned. If a diagnostic code is not given for a particular fault code (i.e. 12), refer to Section 7 and check the component as described.

4 Certain faults will not activate the warning light and are not subject to a fault code, but have a related a diagnostic code. If the engine does not run correctly but no warning light and fault code are shown, check the diagnostic code and details given in the table that relate to the fault, then use the diagnostic mode of the instrument cluster or the diagnostic tool (see Step 2 or 3 according to model), to assess the function of the sensor or actuator concerned.

5 If on XT-Z and MT-03 models the diagnostic tool is not available just use the details given in the table and the relevant procedure(s) in Section 7, or if necessary take the bike to a Yamaha dealer equipped with the tool.

6 If the system as a whole rather than just an individual component does not seem to function check the fuses and the relay unit connector, and the relays in the unit – refer to Chapter 8 for the fuses and starter circuit cut-off relay, and Section 4 for the fuel pump relay.

XT-R and XT-X models

7 The two digit fault code will appear on the instrument cluster LCD multi-function display – make a note of the number displayed, then compare the fault code displayed with those in Table 1 to identify the faulty component and the appropriate diagnostic code (where given).

8 If a diagnostic code is not given for a particular fault code (i.e. 12 or 24), refer to Section 7 and check the component as

Table 1 Engine management system fault codes – all models

Fault code	Faulty component – symptoms	Possible causes	Diagnostic code (according to model)
12	Crankshaft position sensor – engine will stop and will not restart	Faulty wiring or wiring connector Damaged or improperly installed sensor or timing rotor Faulty ECU	–
13	Intake air pressure sensor – engine will run, air pressure signal fixed at 101 kPa (kilopascals)	Faulty wiring or wiring connector Damaged or faulty sensor	03 or D03
14	Intake air pressure sensor hose system – engine will run, air pressure signal fixed at 101 kPa (kilopascals)	Hose system detached, pinched or blocked Faulty ECU	03 or D03
15	Throttle position sensor – engine will run, sensor signal fixed fully open	Faulty wiring or wiring connector Damaged or improperly installed sensor Faulty ECU	01 or D01
16	Throttle position sensor – engine will run, sensor signal fixed fully open	Throttle position sensor stuck Faulty ECU	01 or D01
19	ECU input – engine will not run	Faulty blue/black wire or wiring connector Faulty ECU	20 or D20
21	Coolant temperature sensor – engine will run, coolant temperature fixed at 80°C	Faulty wiring or wiring connector Damaged or improperly installed sensor Faulty ECU	06 or D06
22	Intake air temperature sensor – engine will run, intake temperature fixed at 20°C	Faulty wiring or wiring connector Damaged or improperly installed sensor Faulty ECU	05 or D05
24	Oxygen sensor – engine will run	Faulty wiring or wiring connector Damaged or improperly installed sensor Faulty ECU	–
30	Tip-over sensor – engine will not run, fuel system turned OFF	Machine overturned Faulty ECU	08 or D08
31	Oxygen sensor detects continuously lean air/fuel ratio – engine will run	Low fuel pressure Clogged injector Faulty wiring or wiring connector Damaged or improperly installed sensor Faulty ECU	–
32	Oxygen sensor detects continuously rich air/fuel ration – engine will run (2007-on models)	High fuel pressure Faulty injector Faulty wiring or wiring connector Damaged or improperly installed sensor Faulty ECU	–
33	Ignition coil – engine will not run	Faulty wiring or wiring connector Damaged ignition coil Faulty ignition cut-off circuit Faulty ECU	30 or D30
41	Tip-over sensor – engine will not run, fuel system turned OFF	Faulty wiring or wiring connector Damaged sensor Faulty ECU	08 or D08
42	Speed sensor/neutral switch – engine will run, signal fixed in fifth gear	Damaged speed sensor/neutral switch (see Chapter 8 for neutral switch) Faulty wiring or wiring connector Faulty ECU	07 or D07 21 or D21
43	ECU not reading battery voltage – engine will run, signal fixed at 12V	Faulty fuel pump relay in relay unit Faulty wiring or wiring connector Faulty ECU	09 or D09 50 or D50
44	Carbon monoxide density in exhaust gas incorrect – engine will run	Error writing CO to EPROM Faulty ECU	60 or D60
46	Abnormal power supply to FI system (fuel pump/starter circuit cut-off) relay – engine will run	Faulty wiring or wiring connector Faulty charging system	09 or D09
50	ECU malfunction – fault code may not be displayed, engine will continue to run, but will not restart	Faulty wiring or wiring connector Damaged ECU	–
Er-1 Er-2 Er-3 Er-4	No communication or unreadable communication between ECU and instrument cluster – wiring harness, injection system component wiring connector, instrument cluster or ECU fault, engine will not run	Faulty wiring or wiring connector Damaged instrument cluster Damaged ECU	–

Table 2 Fuel system diagnostic codes and data – all models

Diagnostic code	Issue	Action required	Data displayed
01 or D01	Throttle angle	Check angle data displayed with throttle fully closed Check angle data displayed with throttle fully open	0 – 125 degrees Fully closed – 15 to 17° Fully open – 97 to 100°
03 or D03	Intake air pressure	Turn the engine stop switch ON and crank the engine using the starter motor to generate a pressure difference	Actual pressure with engine still*, then with it cranking
05 or D05	Intake air temperature	Check the temperature** in the air filter housing and compare with data displayed	Intake air temperature
06 or D06	Coolant temperature	Check the temperature*** of the engine coolant and compare with data displayed	Engine coolant temperature
07 or D07	Vehicle speed sensor pulse	Turn the rear wheel in the normal direction of rotation and check pulses are generated and displayed	0 to 199 (number of recorded pulses, returns to 0 on reaching 199)
08 or D08	Tip-over sensor	Check the operation of the tip-over sensor	Machine upright – 0.4 to 1.4V Laid over – 3.7 to 4.4V
09 or D09	Voltage supply to fuel system	Turn the engine stop switch ON and check battery voltage (see Chapter 8)	Normally around 12V
20 or D20	Sidestand switch	Select a gear position other than neutral then move stand up and down	Stand retracted – ON Stand down – OFF
21 or D21	Neutral switch	Check the operation of the neutral switch by selecting neutral then selecting a gear. Also refer to Chapter 8	Gearbox in neutral – ON In gear – OFF
30 or D30	Ignition coil	Check the operation of the ignition coil – setting the engine kill switch from OFF to ON will generate five sparks in the coil and the engine management warning light comes on. Check for the sparks by removing the plugs and checking as described in Section 16	–
36 or D36	Fuel injector	Check the operation of the fuel injector – setting the engine kill switch from OFF to ON will generate five pulses in the injector and the engine management warning light comes on. Check for the pulses using a sounding rod	–
48 or D48	Air induction system	Check the operation of the air induction system control valve – setting the engine kill switch from OFF to ON will actuate the valve's solenoid five times and the engine management warning light comes on. You should be able to hear the solenoid – refer to Section 14 for access and further checks	–
50 or D50	Fuel pump relay	Check the operation of the relay – setting the engine kill switch from OFF to ON will actuate the relay five times and the engine management warning light comes on. You should be able to hear the relay click – refer to Section 4 for access and further checks	–
51	Cooling fan relay	Check the operation of the radiator cooling fan relay – setting the engine kill switch from OFF to ON will actuate the relay five times and the engine management warning light comes on. You should be able to hear the relay – refer to Chapter 3 for access and further checks	–
52	Headlight relay	Check the operation of the headlight relay – setting the engine kill switch from OFF to ON will actuate the relay five times and the engine management warning light comes on. You should be able to hear the relay and the light should come on – refer to Chapter 8 for access and further checks	–
60	EEPROM		01 00 when no fault
61	Fault code history		12 to 61 00 when no fault
62	Fault code history erasure		00 to 17
70	Control number	Programme control number displayed	00 to 255

* If an atmospheric pressure gauge is not available, use 101.3 kPa (kilopascals) (760 mmHg, 30 inHg) as the standard
** If possible, check the temperature next to the sensor, otherwise use the ambient temperature as the standard
*** Check the temperature of the coolant as close as possible to the sensor

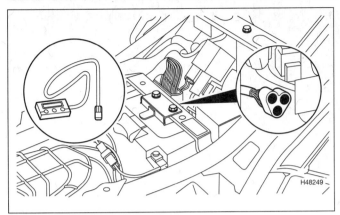

6.11a Diagnostic tool connection – XT-Z models

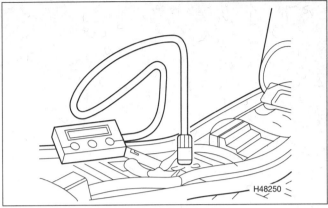

6.11b Diagnostic tool connection – MT-03 models

described. If a diagnostic code is given set the instrument cluster to diagnostic mode as follows: make sure the ignition switch is OFF and set the kill switch to RUN. Disconnect the fuel pump wiring connector (see Section 2). Simultaneously press and hold the SELECT and RESET buttons on the instrument cluster, then turn the ignition switch ON, and keep the SELECT and RESET buttons pressed for at least 8 seconds. All display segments disappear, and either DIAG or CO will be displayed – if CO is displayed press the SELECT button to change to DIAG. Confirm the selection by pressing the SELECT and RESET buttons simultaneously for 2 seconds. Set the engine kill switch to OFF.

9 Use the SELECT or RESET button to find the appropriate diagnostic code on the display. The SELECT button displays the code numbers in ascending order, the RESET button displays the numbers in descending order. In the case of a sensor related diagnostic code the appropriate sensor test specifications are displayed. Compare the diagnostic code with Table 2 to identify the test action required. Compare the test results to any data displayed on the meter for that diagnostic code. In the case of an actuator related diagnostic code set the engine kill switch to RUN to test the actuator relevant to the code displayed. To cancel the diagnostic mode, turn the ignition switch OFF.

XT-Z and MT-03 models

10 All fault codes are displayed as a series of flashes of the engine trouble warning light. The first number of any code is indicated by long (1 second) flashes with 1.5 second intervals, the number of flashes representing the number of the code. The second number of any code is indicated by short (0.5 second) flashes with 0.5 second intervals, the number of flashes representing the number of the code. For example fault code 15 comprises one long flash and five short flashes, and fault code 43 comprises four long flashes and three short flashes. If there is more than one code the lowest number is indicated first. Make a

note of the number displayed, then compare the fault code displayed with those in Table 1 to identify the faulty component and the appropriate diagnostic code (where given). If a diagnostic code is not given for a particular fault code (i.e. 12 or 24), refer to Section 7 and check the component as described.

11 If a diagnostic code is given, and you have access to the Yamaha diagnostic tool (part No. 90890-03182), connect the tool and set it to diagnostic mode as follows: make sure the ignition switch is OFF and set the kill switch to RUN. Remove the seat(s) (see Chapter 7). Remove the cap from the diagnostic tool wiring connector and connect the tool **(see illustrations)**. Press and hold the MODE button on the tool, then turn the ignition switch ON. DIAG will be displayed on the tool and the LED should be green – if CO is displayed press the UP button to change to DIAG. Confirm the selection by pressing the MODE button.

12 Use the UP or DOWN button to find the appropriate diagnostic code on the display. The UP button displays the code numbers in ascending order, the DOWN button displays the numbers in descending order. In the case of a sensor related diagnostic code the appropriate sensor test specifications are displayed. Compare the diagnostic code with Table 2 to identify the test action required. Compare the test results to any data displayed on the meter for that diagnostic code. In the case of an actuator related diagnostic code set the engine kill switch to OFF and then to RUN to test the actuator relevant to the code displayed. To cancel the diagnostic mode, turn the ignition switch OFF.

13 Once the fault has been corrected, confirm that the fault code is no longer displayed by turning the ignition (main) switch OFF and then ON again. If the code is no longer displayed the repair is complete.

14 To delete the fault code from the ECU memory, follow the procedure in Step 2 or 3 to set-up the diagnostic mode, then enter code 62. The total number of stored codes will be displayed (00 to 17). Turn the engine kill switch ON, or if already ON turn it OFF them ON, to

delete the stored codes – the display should then show 00.

7 Engine management system components

1 If a fault is indicated in any of the system components, first check the wiring and connectors between the appropriate component and the ECU (refer to *Electrical System Fault Finding* at the beginning of Chapter 8, and to the *Wiring diagrams* at the end of Chapter 8). A continuity test of all wires will locate a break or short in any circuit. Inspect the terminals inside the wiring connectors and ensure they are not loose, bent, broken or corroded. Spray the inside of the connectors with a proprietary electrical terminal cleaner or protector before reconnection. If the system as a whole rather than just an individual component does not seem to function check the fuses and the relay unit connector, and the relays in the unit – refer to Chapter 8 for the fuses and starter circuit cut-off relay, and Section 4 for the fuel pump relay.

2 It is possible to undertake most checks on system components using a multimeter and comparing the results with the specifications at the beginning of the Chapter. **Note:** *Different meters may give slightly different results to those specified even though the component being tested is not faulty – do not consign a component to the bin before having it double-checked.* However, some faults will only become evident when a component is tested with specialised equipment, in which case the checks should be undertaken by a Yamaha dealer.

3 If after a thorough check the source of a fault has not been identified, it is possible that the ECU itself is faulty. Yamaha provides no test specifications for the ECU. In order to determine conclusively that the unit is defective, it should be substituted with a known good one. If the problem is rectified, the original unit is faulty.

7.5a The wiring connector is behind left-hand side panel on XT-R and XT-X models

7.5b CKP sensor wiring connector is behind the reservoir on XT-Z models

7.5c CKP sensor wiring connector is behind regulator/rectifier on MT-03 models (arrowed)

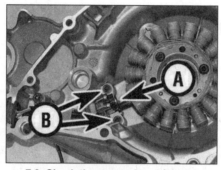

7.6 Check the sensor head (A) and bolts (B)

Intake air pressure (IAP) sensor

Check

9 Remove the fuel tank (see Section 2). The sensor is on the right-hand side (see illustrations).

10 For fault code 13, first check the wiring and connectors as in Step 1. Next, using a voltmeter or multimeter set to the volts (DC) scale, insert the positive (+) probe of the meter into the pink/white wire terminal in the back of the connector, with the connector still connected, and insert the negative (-) probe into the black/blue terminal. Turn the ignition ON and measure the sensor output voltage. Turn the ignition OFF.

11 If the voltage is not as specified at the beginning of the chapter, replace the sensor with a new one (Step 14).

12 For fault code 14, check the condition of the vacuum hose between the underside of the sensor and the throttle body. If the hose is cracked or perished replace it with a new one. Make sure it is not kinked, pinched or trapped, and is a tight fit on the union at each end.

13 After installing the new sensor, for fault code 13 turn the ignition switch ON, and for fault code 14 run the engine at idle speed, to reinstate the system, then check the fault code has been erased by turning the ignition switch OFF and then ON again. If the code is no longer displayed the repair is complete.

Removal and installation

14 Remove the fuel tank (see Section 2). The sensor is on the right-hand side (see illustration 7.9a, b or c). Disconnect the wiring connector and the vacuum hose from the sensor. Undo the nuts (XT models) or bolts (MT-03 models) and remove the sensor. On installation, ensure the wiring connector terminals are clean and that the vacuum hose is a tight fit on the sensor union.

Intake air temperature (IAT) sensor

Check

15 On XT-R and XT-X models the sensor is in the left-hand side of the air filter housing, remove the left-hand side panel for access (see Chapter 7). On XT-Z models the sensor is in the top of the air filter housing, remove the

Crankshaft position (CKP) sensor

Check

4 Make sure the ignition is OFF. On XT-R and XT-X models remove the left-hand side panel (see Chapter 7). On MT-03 models displace the regulator/rectifier (see Chapter 8).

5 The crankshaft position sensor is in the alternator cover on left-hand side of the engine. Trace the wiring from the top if the cover and disconnect it at the 2-pin connector (see illustrations). Using an ohmmeter or multimeter set to the ohms x 100 scale, measure the resistance between the terminals on the sensor side of the connector. If the result is not as specified at the beginning of the chapter, replace the sensor with a new one (Step 7).

6 If the result is good, and you have checked the wiring and connectors as described in Step 1, remove the alternator cover (see Chapter 8) and check whether the sensor head is fouled or the sensor has come loose on its mounts (see illustration).

Removal and installation

7 Make sure the ignition is OFF. Remove the alternator cover, then remove the stator and CKP sensor from it (see Chapter 8) – the stator and CKP sensor come as an integrated assembly along with the wiring sub-loom, including the neutral switch wire.

8 After installing the new sensor, turn the engine over on the starter motor to reinstate the system, then check the fault code has been erased by turning the ignition switch OFF and then ON again. If the code is no longer displayed the repair is complete.

7.9a IAP sensor (arrowed) - XT-R and XT-X models

7.9b IAP sensor (arrowed) - XT-Z models

7.9c IAP sensor (arrowed) – MT-03 models

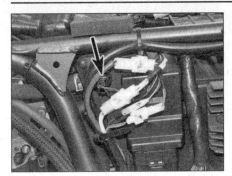

7.17a IAT sensor (arrowed) - XT-R and XT-X models

7.17b IAT sensor (arrowed) - XT-Z models

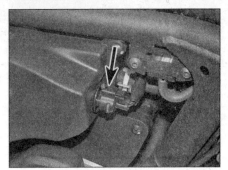

7.17c IAT sensor (arrowed) – MT-03 models

fuel tank for access (see Section 2). On MT-03 models the sensor is in the right-hand side of the air filter housing.

16 Make sure the ignition is OFF. First check the wiring and connectors as in Step 1.

17 Disconnect the wiring connector from the sensor (see illustrations). Using an ohmmeter or multimeter set to the ohms x 100 scale, connect the positive (+) probe to the brown/white wire terminal in the sensor and the negative (-) probe to the black/blue wire terminal and measure the resistance. If the result is not as specified at the beginning of the chapter (20°C value) replace the sensor with a new one.

18 After installing the new sensor, turn the ignition switch ON to reinstate the system, then check the fault code has been erased by turning the ignition (main) switch OFF and then ON again. If the code is no longer displayed the repair is complete.

Removal and installation

19 The sensor is mounted in the air filter housing (see illustration 7.17a, b or c) – see Step 15 for access. Make sure the ignition is OFF. Disconnect the wiring connector, then pull the sensor out (see illustration).

Throttle position (TP) sensor

Check

20 Make sure the ignition is OFF. The throttle position sensor is on the right-hand side of the throttle body (see illustration).

21 First check the wiring and connectors as in Step 1. Also make sure the sensor assembly

is not loose on the throttle body – if it is refer to the installation and adjustment procedure (Steps 27 to 29). Also check that the throttle twistgrip turns smoothly and freely form fully closed to fully open.

22 Undo the screws and remove the sensor (see illustration 7.20). Using an ohmmeter or multimeter set to the K-ohm scale, connect the positive (+) probe to the blue wire terminal in the sensor, and the negative (-) probe to the black/blue terminal. If the maximum resistance is not as specified at the beginning of the chapter replace the sensor with a new one.

23 Next connect the positive (+) probe to the yellow wire terminal, and the negative (-) probe to the black/blue terminal. Slowly turn the sensor rotor using a screwdriver in the slot to mimic the opening and closing of throttle and check that the resistance changes in proportion with the amount and rate of opening/closing – if there is no change or there are abrupt changes replace the sensor with a new one. Also check that the resistance range from fully closed to fully open is as specified.

24 After installing the new sensor, for fault code 15 turn the ignition switch ON, and for fault code 16 run the engine first at idle speed and then quickly open and close the throttle so the engine races but does not exceed the red line, to reinstate the system, then check the fault code has been erased by turning the ignition switch OFF and then ON again. If the code is no longer displayed the repair is complete.

Removal, installation and adjustment

25 The throttle position sensor is mounted on the right-hand side of the throttle body. Make

sure the ignition is OFF. Disconnect the wiring connector (see illustration).

26 Undo the screws and remove the sensor (see illustration 7.20).

27 Fit the sensor onto the throttle body, locating the throttle shaft tab in the slot, and lightly tighten the screws, so the sensor is held but can be turned. Connect the wiring connector.

28 Start the engine and make sure the idle speed is correct (see Chapter 1).

29 To check the adjustment (position) of the sensor, insert the positive (+) probe of a voltmeter meter into the yellow wire terminal in the back of the connector, with the connector still connected, and insert the negative (-) probe into the black/blue terminal. Turn the ignition ON and measure the voltage, and adjust the position of the sensor as required by turning it until the voltage is 0.63 to 0.73 volts. Tighten the screws.

Engine coolant temperature (ECT) sensor

30 The sensor is in the back of the cylinder head on the right-hand side (see illustration 7.20). First check the wiring and connectors as in Step 1.

31 Refer to Chapter 3, Section 3 for checking, removal and installation details.

Tip-over sensor

Check

32 On XT-R and XT-X models the sensor is above the crankcase breather chamber on the back of the engine, displace the rear brake

7.19 Pull the sensor out of its rubber grommet

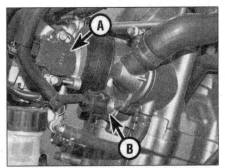

7.20 Throttle position sensor (A); coolant temperature sensor (B)

7.25 Disconnect the wiring connector from the sensor

7.32a On XT-R and XT-X unscrew the bolt (arrowed) and displace the reservoir . . .

7.32b . . . to access the TO sensor

7.32c Tip-over sensor (arrowed) – XT-Z

7.32d Tip-over sensor (arrowed) – MT-03

master cylinder reservoir for access (see illustrations). On XT-Z models the sensor is under the rear sub-frame cross-piece (see illustration), remove the seat for access (see Chapter 7). On MT-03 models the sensor is under the rider's seat (see illustration), remove the seats for access (see Chapter 7).

33 Make sure the ignition is OFF. First check the wiring and connectors as in Step 1. Also make sure the sensor is not loose on its mounts.

34 Displace the sensor (see Step 38) leaving the wiring connected.

35 Using a voltmeter or multimeter set to the volts (DC) scale, insert the positive (+) probe of the meter into the yellow/green wire terminal in the back of the connector, with the connector still connected, and insert the negative (-) probe into the black/blue terminal. Turn the ignition ON. Hold the sensor in its normal position when the bike is upright with the UP mark facing up, then tilt it 65° to one side and then the other. Turn the ignition OFF.

36 If the voltage is not as specified at the beginning of the chapter when the sensor is upright and tilted over, replace the sensor with a new one. Note the top surface of the sensor is marked UP.

37 After installing the new sensor, turn the ignition switch ON to reinstate the system, then check the fault code has been erased by turning the ignition switch OFF and then ON again. If the code is no longer displayed the repair is complete.

Removal and installation

38 On XT-R and XT-X models the sensor is above the crankcase breather chamber on the back of the engine, displace the rear brake master cylinder reservoir for access (see illustrations 7.32a and b). On XT-Z models the sensor is under the rear sub-frame cross-piece (see illustration 7.32c), remove

the seat for access (see Chapter 7). On MT-03 models the sensor is under the rider's seat (see illustration 7.32d), remove the seats for access (see Chapter 7).

39 Make sure the ignition is OFF. Undo the bolts securing the sensor, noting the washers. Displace the sensor and disconnect the wiring connector. Note the top surface of the sensor is marked UP – make sure this mark is on top when installing the sensor.

Speed sensor

Check

40 Make sure the ignition is OFF. First check the wiring and connectors as in Step 1.

41 Support the machine on an auxiliary stand so the rear wheel is off the ground. On XT-R and XT-X models remove the left-hand side cover (see Chapter 7) to access the connector (see illustration 7.5a). On XT-Z and MT-03 models remove the fuel tank (see Section 2) to access the connector (see illustrations).

42 The sensor is on the back of the crankcase on the left-hand side (see illustration). Trace the wiring from the sensor to the three-pin wiring connector. Using a voltmeter or multimeter set to the volts (DC) scale, insert the positive (+) probe of the meter into the pink wire terminal in the back of the connector, with the connector still connected, and insert the negative (-) probe into the black/white terminal. Turn the ignition switch ON, select a gear and rotate the rear wheel by hand in its normal direction of rotation. As the engine turns, the output voltage should fluctuate between the two levels given in the specifications at the beginning of the Chapter. Turn the ignition OFF.

43 If the voltage is not as specified, replace the sensor with a new one.

44 After installing the new sensor, take the bike for a ride making sure you exceed 20 mph (30 kmh) to reinstate the system, then check the fault code has been erased by turning the ignition switch OFF and then ON again. If the code is no longer displayed the repair is complete.

Removal and installation

45 The sensor is on the back of the crankcase on the left-hand side (see illustration 7.42). Make sure the ignition is OFF.

7.41a Speed sensor connector – XT-Z

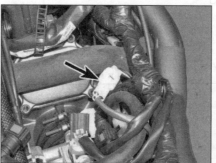

7.41b Speed sensor connector (arrowed) – MT-03

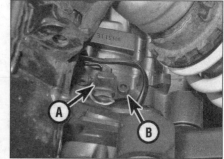

7.42 Speed sensor (A) and its bolt (B)

7.48 Fit a new O-ring smeared with grease

7.49a Oxygen sensor (arrowed - behind guard) – XT-R and XT-X models

7.49b Oxygen sensor (arrowed) – XT-Z models

7.53 Oxygen sensor wiring connector (arrowed)

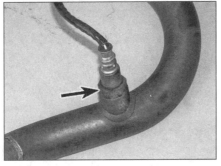

7.55a Unscrew the sensor using a spanner on the hex (arrowed) . . .

7.55b . . . or using a special socket that accommodates the wiring

46 On XT-R and XT-X models remove the left-hand side cover (see Chapter 7) to access the connector **(see illustration 7.5a)**. On XT-Z and MT-03 models remove the fuel tank (see Section 2) to access the connector **(see illustrations 7.41a or b)**.

47 Trace the wiring from the sensor and disconnect it at the three-pin wiring connector. Undo the bolt securing the sensor to the crankcase and withdraw the sensor **(see illustration 7.42)**. Discard the O-ring – a new one must be used.

48 On installation, apply grease to the new O-ring, and make sure the wiring is correctly routed and the connector terminals are clean and the pins are not damaged **(see illustration)**.

Oxygen (O2) sensor – 2007-on

Check

49 The sensor is fitted in the left-hand exhaust downpipe **(see illustrations)**. Make sure the ignition is OFF. First check the wiring and connectors as in Step 1.

50 No test details are given for the O2 sensor itself. Depending on the fault code given, before fitting a new sensor check the fuel pressure (see Section 3), and then if necessary the fuel pump and the injector (Sections 4 and 10).

51 After installing the new sensor, run the engine at idle speed to reinstate the system, then check the fault code has been erased by turning the ignition switch OFF and then ON again. If the code is no longer displayed the repair is complete.

Removal and installation

Note: *The oxygen sensor is delicate and will not work if dropped or knocked, or if any cleaning materials are used on it. Ensure the exhaust system is cold before proceeding. To tighten the sensor to the correct torque setting a special socket is required to accommodate the sensor wiring – you can get one from a good tool supplier (measure the size of the hex first).*

52 The sensor is fitted in the left-hand exhaust downpipe. Make sure the ignition is OFF and the engine is cold.

53 On XT-R and XT-X models remove the fuel tank (see Section 2). Trace the wiring from the sensor and disconnect it at the connector **(see illustration)**. Release the wiring from any ties and feed it back to the sensor, noting its routing. Unscrew the sensor guard bolts and remove the guard **(see illustration 7.49a)**.

54 On XT-Z and MT-03 models remove the left-hand exhaust downpipe (see Section 13).

55 Unscrew the oxygen sensor and remove it from the exhaust system **(see illustrations)**.

56 Installation is the reverse of removal. Tighten the sensor to the torque setting specified at the beginning of the Chapter – to do this the socket shown **(see illustration 7.55b)** is needed.

Fuel injector

57 Refer to Section 10.

Ignition coil

58 Refer to Section 17.

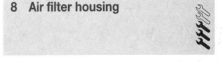

8 Air filter housing

Removal

XT-R and XT-X models

1 Make sure the ignition is OFF. Remove the seat, the side panels and the rear cowl (see Chapter 7).

2 Remove the battery (see Chapter 8).

3 Remove the fuel tank (see Section 2).

4 Remove the silencers (see Section 13).

5 Remove the rear wheel (see Chapter 6).

6 Disconnect the tail light and turn signal wiring connectors **(see illustration)**. Release the wiring from any ties and feed it back to the tail unit, noting its routing.

8.6 Disconnect the wiring connectors (arrowed)

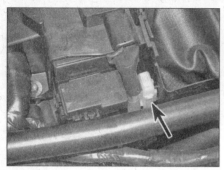
8.7 Displace the fuseholder (arrowed)

8.8a Unscrew the top bolts (arrowed) . . .

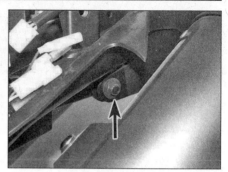
8.8b . . . and the bolt (arrowed) on each side . . .

8.8c . . . and remove the tail unit

8.9a Remove the oil chute and toolkit, then unscrew the bolts (arrowed) . . .

8.9b . . . the screw (arrowed) . . .

8.9c . . . and the bolts (arrowed) to release the undertray

7 Displace the fuseholder from the front of the undertray **(see illustration)**.

8 Unscrew the tail unit bolts, noting the collars with the side bolts, and remove the unit **(see illustrations)**.

9 Remove the toolkit and oil chute, then unscrew the bolts on the frame cross-piece **(see illustration)**. Undo the screw in the centre and bolts at the back and remove the undertray **(see illustrations)**.

10 Displace or remove the ECU (see Section 18), the IAT sensor (see Section 7), the fusebox, starter relay and the regulator/ rectifier (see Chapter 8), from the left-hand side of the housing **(see illustration)**.

11 Remove the air filter (see Chapter 1). Remove the resonance chamber from the top of the air duct **(see illustration)**.

12 Detach all the hoses from the front of the air filter housing, noting which fits where.

13 Unscrew the nut and remove the washer from the upper drive chain roller bolt, then withdraw the bolt and remove the roller, noting the collar and the bush.

14 Slacken the air intake duct clamp screw, noting the orientation of the clamp and how it

8.10 Displace or remove all components from the left-hand side of the housing

8.11 Remove the resonance chamber

8.14a Unscrew the top bolts (arrowed) . . .

8.14b . . . and the bolt (arrowed) . . .

8.14c . . . on each side

8.18 Undo the screws (arrowed) and remove the cover

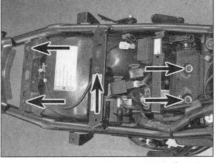

8.20 Unscrew the bolts (arrowed) and move the tray back a little

8.21a Slacken the clamp screw (arrowed) . . .

locates **(see illustration 8.21a)**. Unscrew the air filter housing bolts, noting which fits where and the arrangement of the washers, collars and grommets, and draw the housing out the back **(see illustrations)**.

XT-Z models

15 Make sure the ignition is OFF. Remove the seat (see Chapter 7).
16 Remove the fuel tank (see Section 2). Remove the air filter (see Chapter 1).
17 Displace or remove the IAT sensor (see Section 7).
18 Remove the cover from the left-hand side of the housing **(see illustration)** – check the condition of the seal and replace it with a new one if necessary.
19 Detach all the hoses from the front and underside of the air filter housing, three on the right and one on the left.

20 Remove the battery (see Chapter 8). Unscrew the five undertray bolts and move it back **(see illustration)** – there is not much movement in it but the small amount is enough.
21 Slacken the air intake duct clamp screw, noting the orientation of the clamp and how it locates **(see illustration)**. Unscrew the air filter housing bolts, noting which fits where and the arrangement of the collars and grommets, and draw the housing out to the right **(see illustrations)**.

MT-03 models

22 Make sure the ignition is OFF. Remove the seat (see Chapter 7).
23 Remove the fuel tank (see Section 2).
24 Displace or remove the IAT sensor and tip-over sensor (see Section 7).
25 Detach all the hoses from the front of the air filter housing, noting which fits where.

26 Slacken the air intake duct clamp screw, noting the orientation of the clamp and how it locates **(see illustration 8.21a)**. Unscrew the air filter housing bolts and screws, noting the arrangement of the collars and grommets, and draw the housing out the left-hand side **(see illustration)**.
27 If required remove the cover(s) from each side of the housing – check the condition of the seals and replace them with new ones if necessary.
28 If required remove the air filter (see Chapter 1).

Installation

29 Installation is the reverse of removal. Make sure the air duct clamp indent is located over the rib on the duct. Make sure all hoses and wiring are securely and correctly connected.

8.21b . . . then unscrew the bolts (arrowed) . . .

8.21c . . . and draw the housing out

8.26 Undo the bolts and the screws (arrowed) and draw the housing out

9.2 Detach the vacuum hose

9.3 Disconnect the injector wiring connector

9.6 Either clamp the hoses (arrowed) or drain the coolant before detaching them

9 Throttle body

> ⚠ **Warning: Refer to the precautions given in Section 1 before starting work.**

Removal

1 Remove the fuel tank (see Section 2). Remove the air filter housing (see Section 8).
2 Detach the IAP sensor vacuum hose from the intake duct **(see illustration)**.
3 Disconnect the injector wiring connector **(see illustration)**.
4 Disconnect the throttle position sensor wiring connector **(see illustration 7.25)**.
5 Detach the throttle cables (Section 12).
6 Clamp the coolant inlet and outlet hoses to the fast idle unit **(see illustration)** – if you

don't have any hose clamps drain the coolant (see Chapter 1). Detach the hoses from the fast idle unit.
7 Fully slacken the clamp screw securing the throttle body to the intake duct – note the orientation of the clamp **(see illustration)**.
8 Ease the throttle body out of the duct and remove it **(see illustration)**.
9 If required slacken the intake duct clamp screw and detach it from the cylinder head – note the orientation of the clamp and how it locates, and how the duct locates on the cylinder head.
Caution: Do not snap the throttle valve from fully open to fully closed once the cable has been disconnected because this can lead to engine idle speed problems.
Caution: Tape over or stuff clean rag into the intake duct or cylinder head (according to what has been removed) to prevent anything from falling in.

10 Check the air and intake duct rubbers for signs of cracking or deterioration and replace with new one(s) if necessary.
11 If required slide the fuel hose cover across to reveal the clips, then press the clips in and pull the hose off its union **(see illustrations)**. If required detach the air hose. If required remove the throttle position sensor (Section 7) and the fuel rail and injector (Section 10). Do not remove the fast idle unit.

Cleaning

Caution: Use only a dedicated cleaner or petroleum-based solvent for cleaning. Do not use caustic cleaners.
12 Clean the throttle body using a petrol based cleaner – do not use a caustic cleaner.
13 Loosen and remove any varnish and other deposits using a nylon-bristle brush – do not use any metallic or pointed tool to clean passages. Rinse then dry with compressed air, blowing out all of the passages.

Inspection

14 Check the throttle body and intake duct for cracks, distorted sealing surfaces and other damage. If any defects are found, replace the faulty component with a new one.
15 Make sure the butterfly valve moves smoothly and returns under spring pressure. Make sure valve is not distorted or loose on its shaft.

Installation

16 Installation is the reverse of removal, noting the following:
● Remove the tape/plug from the intake adapter or cylinder head.

9.7 Slacken the clamp screw (arrowed) . . .

9.8 . . . and remove the throttle body

9.11a Slide the cover across . . .

9.11b . . . then depress the clips . . .

9.11c . . . and detach the hose

9.16 Push the cover across

10.3 Checking injector resistance

3 Disconnect the injector wiring connector **(see illustration 9.3)**. Connect an ohmmeter or multimeter set to the ohms x 1 scale between the terminals on the injector and check the resistance – it should be as specified at the beginning of the Chapter **(see illustration)**. If not the injector is probably faulty.

Removal

4 Remove the fuel tank (see Section 2).
5 Have a rag ready to catch any residual fuel. Slide the fuel hose cover across, then press the clips in and pull the hose off its union on the fuel injector **(see illustrations 9.11a, b and c)**.
6 Disconnect the fuel injector wiring connector **(see illustration 9.3)**.
7 Undo the screws securing the fuel rail **(see illustration)**. Lift the fuel rail and injector off the throttle body **(see illustration)**.
8 Remove the seal from the injector seat in the throttle body **(see illustration 10.7b)** – a new one must be used.
9 If required carefully pull the injector out of the fuel rail **(see illustration)**. Remove the O-ring from the top of the injector – a new one must be used.

Installation

10 Installation is the reverse of removal, noting the following:
● Fit a new O-ring onto the top of the injector **(see illustration)**.
● Fit a new seal into the injector seat in the throttle body **(see illustration)**.
● Carefully push the injector into the fuel rail, making sure the O-ring does not dislodge **(see illustration 10.9)**.
● Make sure the injector seats correctly in the throttle body.
● Push the fuel hose connector fully onto the union on the fuel injector until the clips locate **(see illustration 9.11c)**, then push the cover across **(see illustration 9.16)**.
● Make sure the wiring connector is securely connected **(see illustration 9.3)**.
● Run the engine and check that the fuel system is working correctly, with no leaks, before taking the machine out on the road.

● If detached push the fuel hose connector fully onto the union on the fuel injector until the clips locate **(see illustration 9.11c)**, then push the connector cover across **(see illustration)**.
● Make sure the intake duct is correctly located with the slot on its inside located over the rib on the intake duct, and locate the indent in the clamp over the rib on the outside **(see illustration 9.7)**. Make sure the throttle body is pushed all the way into the duct and located with its rib in the slot, and the indent in the clamp is over the rib on the duct.
● Make sure the wiring connectors and hoses are securely connected.
● If the throttle position sensor was removed make sure it is correctly adjusted before tightening the screws (see Section 7).
● Check the operation of the throttle and adjust the cable as necessary (see Chapter 1).

● Refill the cooling system if drained (see Chapter 1).
● Run the engine and check that the fuel system is working correctly before taking the machine out on the road. Check the idle speed and adjust if necessary (see Chapter 1).

10 Fuel rail and injector

Warning: Refer to the precautions given in Section 1 before starting work.

Check

1 Remove the fuel tank (see Section 2).
2 First refer to Section 7, Step 1, and check the wiring and connectors.

10.7a Undo the screws . . .

10.7b . . . and remove the injector. Remove and discard the seal (arrowed)

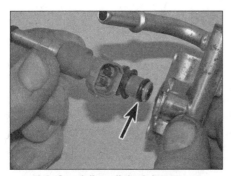

10.9 Carefully pull the injector out. Remove and discard the O-ring (arrowed)

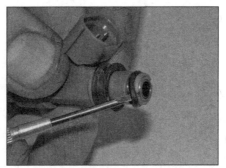

10.10a Fit a new O-ring . . .

10.10b . . . and a new seal

12.2a Slacken the locknut . . .

12.2b . . . release the cable from the bracket . . .

12.2c . . . and detach the opening cable end

12.2d Unscrew the hex and release the cable from the bracket . . .

12.2e . . . then detach the closing cable end

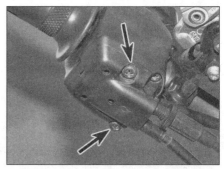

12.4a Undo the screws (arrowed) . . .

11 Fast idle unit

 Warning: Refer to the precautions given in Section 1 before starting work.

1 If the idle speed cannot be set, or if there is a problem with cold starting or fast running when warm, it is possible there is a fault with the fast idle unit – the unit, located on the underside of the throttle body, incorporates a plunger that reacts to the temperature of coolant that circulates around it.

2 The unit is part of the throttle body and is not available separately, and Yamaha advise that the unit should not be removed from the throttle body. If all other possible causes of the problem have been investigated (throttle cable, idle speed adjuster mechanism, fuel pump, injector, throttle body butterfly valve, fuel hose, fuel injection system sensors, etc) and no faults have been found it is likely the unit is faulty, in which case the throttle body must be replaced with a new one.

3 The unit is part of the throttle body and is not available separately – see Section 9.

12 Throttle cables

 Warning: Refer to the precautions given in Section 1 before proceeding.

Removal

1 Remove the fuel tank (see Section 2).

2 Slacken the opening cable locknut until the adjuster nut is free, then slip the cable out of the bracket (**see illustrations**). Detach the cable end from the throttle cam (**see illustration**). Slacken the closing cable hex until the nut is free, then slip the cable out of the bracket (**see illustration**). Detach the cable end from the throttle cam (**see illustration**).

3 Withdraw the cables from the machine, carefully noting the correct routing – you can tie string to the ends which can be drawn through with the cables and then used as a guide to draw the new cables in.

4 Undo the cable holder screws on the underside of the switch housing on the handlebar and remove the holder (**see illustrations**). Undo the remaining switch housing screw and detach the top half (**see illustrations**). Detach the cable ends from the pulley in the housing, then draw the cables

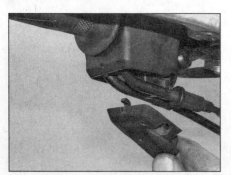

12.4b . . . and remove the holder

12.4c Undo the housing screw . . .

12.4d . . . split the housing . . .

12.4e . . . detach the cable ends . . .

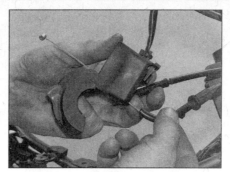

12.4f . . . and draw the cables out

12.4g Remove the locating piece from the housing

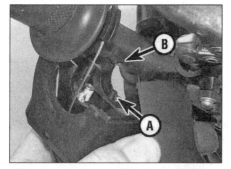

12.5a Locate the peg (A) in the hole (B) . . .

12.5b . . . and make sure the washer (arrowed) is on the outside

12.5c Make sure the cable elbows are correctly located

out of the housing **(see illustrations)**. Note the locating piece in the bottom half of the switch housing and remove it for safekeeping **(see illustration)**.

Installation

5 Fit the locating piece into the bottom half of the switch housing **(see illustration 12.4g)**. Fit the cables into the switch housing **(see illustration 12.4f)**. Lubricate the cable ends with multi-purpose grease and fit them into the throttle pulley **(see illustration 12.4e)**. Fit the housing halves onto the handlebar, locating the peg in the bottom half in the hole in the handlebar, and making sure the washer is between the housing and the twistgrip, not inside the housing **(see illustrations)**. Fit and tighten the front housing screw **(see illustration 12.4c)**. Make sure the cable elbows are correctly positioned **(see illustration)**. Fit the holder, locating the tab in the slot, and tighten

the screws **(see illustrations 12.4b and a)**.
6 Loosen the lockring on the cable adjuster and turn the adjuster fully in **(see illustration)**. Feed the cables through to the throttle body, making sure they are correctly routed – if used on removal tie the string to the ends and pull them through. The cables must not interfere with any other component and should not be kinked or bent sharply.
7 Lubricate the cable ends with multi-purpose grease. Fit the closing cable end into its socket, then locate the cable in the bracket and fully tighten the hex, making sure the nut locates correctly **(see illustrations 12.2e and d)**.
8 Thread the locknut on the opening cable fully up the threads. Fit the opening cable end into its socket, then locate the cable in the bracket, seated on the locknut, and thread the adjuster nut up under the bracket as far as possible, then pull the cable up to seat the adjuster nut captive under the bracket and

tighten the locknut down onto the bracket **(see illustrations 12.2c, b and a)**.
9 Adjust the cable freeplay (see Chapter 1). Operate the throttle to check that it opens and closes freely. Turn the handlebars back and forth to make sure the cable doesn't cause the steering to bind.
10 Start the engine and check that the idle speed does not rise as the handlebars are turned. If it does, the throttle cables are routed incorrectly. Correct the problem before riding the motorcycle.
11 Install the fuel tank (see Section 2).

13 Exhaust system

> **Warning: If the engine has been running the exhaust system will be very hot. Allow the system to cool before carrying out any work.**

HAYNES HINT *Before starting work on the exhaust system spray all the exposed nuts, mounting bolts and clamp bolts with penetrating fluid – they are prone to corrosion.*

XT-R and XT-X models

Silencer removal

1 Slacken the silencer clamp bolt **(see illustration)**.

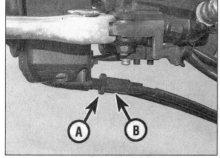

12.6 Slacken the lockring (A) and turn the adjuster (B) in

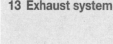

13.1 Silencer clamp bolts (arrowed)

13.2 Silencer mounting bolts (arrowed)

13.7 Unscrew the bolt (arrowed) on each side

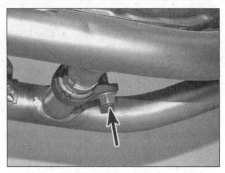

13.9 Joint pipe clamp bolt (arrowed)

2 Unscrew the silencer mounting bolts **(see illustration)**. Ease the silencer out of the downpipe. If required remove the shields from the silencer.
3 Check the condition of the sealing ring, either in the end of the silencer pipe or on the end of the downpipe, and replace it with a new one if it is damaged or deformed or no longer sealing correctly.

Downpipe assembly removal

4 Remove the fuel tank covers (see Chapter 7).
5 If required remove the silencers (see above). If not slacken the silencer clamp bolts **(see illustration 13.1)**.

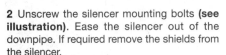

13.13 Disconnect the wiring connectors (arrowed)

6 Disconnect the oxygen sensor wiring connector on 2007-on models **(see illustration 7.53)**. Feed the wiring down to the sensor, noting its routing. If required remove the sensor (see Section 7).
7 Unscrew the rear mounting bolts **(see illustration)**.
8 Unscrew the nuts securing the header pipes to the cylinder head **(see illustration 13.21a)**. Draw the flanges off the studs and manoeuvre the downpipe assembly out of the head and the silencers if not removed.
9 If required slacken the joint pipe clamp bolt and separate the downpipes **(see illustration)**.

13.14a Unscrew the bolts (arrowed) . . .

10 If required unscrew the downpipe bracket bolts and detach it from the frame.
11 Remove the sealing ring from each port in the cylinder head and discard them as new ones must be used **(see illustration 13.22)**. If the downpipes have been separated check the condition of the joint pipe sealing ring and replace it with a new one if it is damaged or deformed or no longer sealing correctly.

> **HAYNES HINT** *Yamaha specify to always use a new sealing ring but it is very easy to damage a new one when fitting it. If the old one is definitely reusable you may as well leave it.*

XT-Z models

Silencer removal

12 Remove the seat (see Chapter 7).
13 Disconnect the tail light and turn signal wiring connectors **(see illustration)**. Release the wiring from any ties.
14 Unscrew the rear mudguard/licence plate/tail light holder bolts and remove the complete assembly, drawing the wiring out **(see illustrations)**.

13.14b . . . and remove the assembly, drawing the wiring through

13.14c Note the collars (arrowed) in the underside of the carrier and the top of the tail unit

13.15 Slacken the clamp bolt (arrowed)

13.16a Unscrew the bolts (arrowed) . . .

13.16b . . . and remove the silencer

15 Slacken the silencer clamp bolt **(see illustration)**.
16 Unscrew the silencer mounting bolts,

13.18 Unscrew the bolts (arrowed) and remove the shield

noting the washers **(see illustration)**. Ease the silencer out of the intermediate pipe **(see illustration)**. If required remove the shields from the silencer.
17 Check the condition of the sealing ring, either in the end of the silencer pipe or on the end of the intermediate pipe, and replace it with a new one if it is damaged or deformed or no longer sealing correctly.

Downpipe removal

18 Remove the radiator covers and fuel tank left-hand cover (see Chapter 7). Remove the intermediate pipe shield **(see illustration)**.
19 Remove the left-hand downpipe first. When removing the left-hand downpipe, disconnect the oxygen sensor wiring connector **(see illustration)**. Feed the wiring down to the sensor, freeing it from its guides and noting its routing.

20 Slacken the intermediate pipe clamp bolt **(see illustration)**.
21 Unscrew the nuts securing the pipe to the cylinder head **(see illustration)**. Draw the flanges off the studs and manoeuvre the downpipe out of the head and intermediate pipe **(see illustration)**.
22 Remove the sealing ring from the port in the cylinder head and discard it as a new one must be used **(see illustration)**. Check the condition of the intermediate pipe sealing ring and replace it with a new one if it is damaged or deformed or no longer sealing correctly.

Intermediate pipe removal

23 Remove the silencer and the downpipes.
24 Detach the hose from the front of the air filter housing **(see illustration)**.
25 For best clearance remove the clamps

13.19 Disconnect the sensor wiring connector

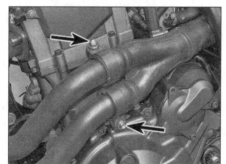

13.20 Intermediate pipe clamp bolts (arrowed)

13.21a Downpipe flange nuts (arrowed)

13.21b Removing the left-hand downpipe

13.22 Dig the sealing ring out of each port

13.24 Detach the hose (arrowed) from the air filter housing and move aside

13.25a Remove the clamps if required for better clearance

13.25b Unscrew the bolt (arrowed) . . .

13.25c . . . and manoeuvre the pipe out

from the pipes **(see illustration)**. Unscrew the intermediate pipe mounting bolt and manoeuvre the pipe out the back **(see illustrations)**.

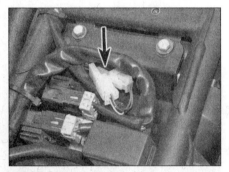

13.28 Disconnect the wiring connectors (arrowed)

26 Refer to Steps 17 and 22.

MT-03 models

Silencer removal

27 Remove the seats (see Chapter 7).
28 Disconnect the tail light and turn signal wiring connectors **(see illustration)**. Release the wiring from any ties.
29 Unscrew the rear mudguard/licence plate/tail light holder bolts and remove the complete unit, drawing the wiring out **(see illustrations)**.
30 Slacken the silencer clamp bolt **(see illustration)**.
31 Unscrew the silencer mounting bolts, noting the washers **(see illustration 13.16a)**. Ease the silencer out of the intermediate pipe

(see illustration 13.16b). If required remove the shields from the silencer.
32 Check the condition of the sealing ring, either in the end of the silencer pipe or on the end of the intermediate pipe, and replace it with a new one if it is damaged or deformed or no longer sealing correctly.

Downpipe removal

33 Remove the intermediate pipe shield **(see illustration)**.
34 Remove the left-hand downpipe first. On 2007 models onward, when removing the left-hand downpipe, remove the fuel tank (see Section 2, then displace the starter relay and disconnect the oxygen sensor wiring connector **(see illustration)**. Feed the wiring down to the sensor, noting its routing.

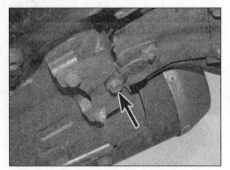

13.29a Unscrew the bolt (arrowed) on the underside . . .

13.29b . . . and the bolt (arrowed) on each side . . .

13.29c . . . and remove the assembly, drawing the wiring through

13.30 Slacken the clamp bolt (arrowed)

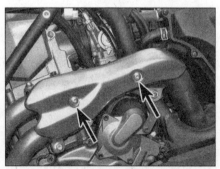

13.33 Undo the screws (arrowed) and remove the shield

13.34 Displace the relay (A) for best access to the connectors inside the boot (B)

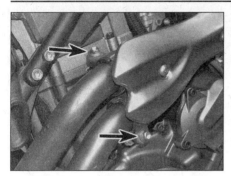

13.35 Intermediate pipe clamp bolts (arrowed)

13.42 Intermediate pipe bolt (arrowed)

13.44 Fit a new sealing ring into each port

35 Slacken the intermediate pipe clamp bolt **(see illustration)**.

36 Unscrew the nuts securing the header pipe to the cylinder head **(see illustration 13.21a)**. Draw the flanges off the studs and manoeuvre the downpipe out of the head and intermediate pipe **(see illustration 13.21b)**.

37 Remove the sealing ring from the port in the cylinder head and discard it as a new one must be used **(see illustration 13.22)**. Check the condition of the intermediate pipe sealing ring and replace it with a new one if it is damaged or deformed or no longer sealing correctly.

38 If required on later models, remove the oxygen sensor (see Section 7).

Intermediate pipe removal

39 Either remove the silencer or the downpipes or both as required or preferred.

40 If not already done remove the intermediate pipe shield **(see illustration 13.33)**.

41 Slacken the clamp bolt(s) as required according to what has already been removed.

42 Unscrew the intermediate pipe mounting bolt and manoeuvre the pipe out **(see illustration)**.

43 Refer to Steps 32 and 37.

Installation – all models

44 Installation is the reverse of removal, noting the following:

● Replace any damaged, deformed or deteriorated mounting bolts, nuts, washers collars and rubbers with new ones. Make sure the collars are fitted in the rubbers.

● Use a new sealing ring in each cylinder head port, and dab them with grease to stick them in place **(see illustration)**.

● Use a new sealing ring in each pipe joint if required.

● Apply a smear of copper grease to all nuts and bolts to prevent them from seizing up. Tighten the nuts/bolts to the torque settings specified at the beginning of the Chapter.

● Where applicable, refer to Section 7 for installation of the oxygen sensor if removed, and do not forget to reconnect the oxygen sensor wiring connector **(see illustration 7.53, 13.19 or 13.34)**. Make sure the wiring is correctly routed.

● Run the engine and check the system for leaks.

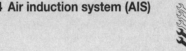

14 Air induction system (AIS)

Function

1 The air induction system uses exhaust gas pulses to suck fresh air into the exhaust ports, where it mixes with hot combustion gases. The extra oxygen causes continued combustion, allowing unburnt hydrocarbons to burn off, thereby reducing emissions. The system comprises the control valve, incorporating an air cut-off valve and a reed valve, and the hoses and pipe linking it to the air filter housing and the cylinder head. The cut-off valve, responding to signals from the ECU, controls the flow of air from the air filter housing, allowing air to flow during warm-up, and when idling after the engine reaches normal operating temperature. The valve shuts off the flow of air from the air filter housing when the engine reaches normal operating temperature and is being ridden (i.e. not idling). If the coolant temperature drops below normal, the valve opens and air is added to aid combustion and raise the gas temperature inside the exhaust system. The reed valve allows the flow of air in one direction only, opening when there is negative pressure, and preventing exhaust gases flowing back into the cut-off valve and air filter housing.

2 Refer to Chapter 1, Section 5, for a check of the system.

14.4a Air should flow in the direction shown

Testing

3 Remove the control valve from the motorcycle (see below). Clean the air filter hose union.

4 Check the operation of the system by blowing through the air filter housing hose union; air should flow freely through the control valve and reed valves **(see illustration)**. Apply battery voltage (12 volts) across the valve terminals and repeat the check **(see illustration)**; no air should flow through the control valve. Disconnect the battery. If the valve does not behave as described check its resistance (Step 6).

5 Now suck on the air filter hose union; you should not be able to suck air back up the hose, indicating the reed valve is closing and sealing correctly. If you can suck air through, remove the valve for cleaning (see Step 13), then test it again. Replace the valve with a new one if necessary.

6 Check the resistance of the cut-off valve windings by connecting an ohmmeter to the connector terminals and compare the reading obtained to that given in the Specifications at the beginning of the chapter **(see illustration 14.4b)**. Replace the valve with a new one if faulty.

Removal and installation

7 On XT-R and XT-X models remove the fuel tank right-hand cover (see Chapter 7) and the ignition coil (see Section 17).

8 On XT-Z models remove the fuel tank (see Section 2) and the ignition coil (see Section 17).

14.4b Connect a battery to the terminals (arrowed)

14.10a AIS control valve wiring connector (arrowed) – XT-R and XT-X

14.10b AIS control valve wiring connector – XT-Z

14.10c AIS control valve wiring connector (arrowed) – MT-03

9 On MT-03 models remove the fuel tank (see Section 2) and the battery (see Chapter 8), then remove the battery box (see illustration 4.10c).
10 Disconnect the wiring connector from the valve (see illustrations).
11 Release the hose clamps (see illustration). Remove the valve from its bracket, detaching the hoses as you do (see illustration).
12 Installation is the reverse of removal.
13 To remove the reed valve unscrew the cover bolts and remove the cover (see illustration). Remove the reed valve, noting which way round it fits.

14.11a Release the clamps (arrowed) and slide them down . . .

14 Installation is the reverse of removal. Make sure the reed valve and housing are clean and correctly fitted. Clean the threads of the cover bolts and apply a suitable non-permanent thread locking compound.

15 Catalytic converter

General information

1 A catalytic converter is incorporated in the exhaust system to minimise the level of exhaust pollutants released into the atmosphere. It is an open-loop system with no feedback to the ECU.
2 The catalytic converter consists of a canister containing a fine mesh impregnated with a catalyst material, over which the hot exhaust gases pass. The catalyst speeds up the oxidation of harmful carbon monoxide, unburned hydrocarbons and soot, effectively reducing the quantity of harmful products released into the atmosphere via the exhaust gases.

Precautions

3 The catalytic converter is a reliable and

simple device which needs no maintenance in itself, but there are some facts of which an owner should be aware if the converter is to function properly for its full service life.
● DO NOT use leaded or lead replacement petrol (gasoline) – the additives will coat the precious metals, reducing their converting efficiency and will eventually destroy the catalytic converter.
● Always keep the ignition and fuel systems well-maintained in accordance with the manufacturer's schedule – if the fuel/air mixture is suspected of being incorrect have it checked on an exhaust gas analyser.
● If the engine develops a misfire, do not ride the bike at all (or at least as little as possible) until the fault is cured.
● DO NOT use fuel or engine oil additives – these may contain substances harmful to the catalytic converter.
● DO NOT continue to use the bike if the engine burns oil to the extent of leaving a visible trail of blue smoke.
● Avoid bump-starting the bike unless absolutely necessary.

14.11b . . . then remove the valve, detaching the hoses

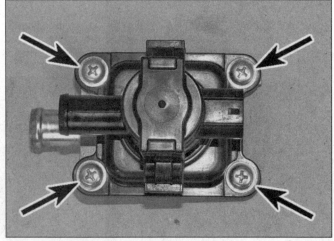

14.13 Undo the screws (arrowed) and remove the cover to access the reed valve

16 Ignition system check

16.2 Pull the cap off the spark plug

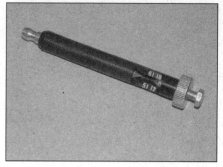

16.4 A typical spark gap testing tool

⚠ **Warning: The energy levels in electronic systems can be very high. On no account should the ignition be switched on whilst the plug or plug cap is being held. Shocks from the HT circuit can be most unpleasant. Secondly, it is vital that the engine is not turned over with the plug cap removed, and that the plug is soundly earthed (grounded) when the system is checked for sparking. The ignition system components can be seriously damaged if the HT circuit becomes isolated.**

1 As no means of adjustment is available, any failure of the system can be traced to failure of a system component or a simple wiring fault. Of the two possibilities, the latter is by far the most likely. In the event of failure, check the system in a logical fashion, as described. First make sure the battery is fully charged and a related fuse has not blown (see Chapter 8).

2 Next pull the cap off the spark plug **(see illustration)**. Fit a spare spark plug that is known to be good into the cap and lay the plug against the cylinder head with the threads contacting it. If necessary, hold the spark plug with an insulated tool.

⚠ **Warning: Do not remove the spark plug from the engine to perform this check – atomised fuel being pumped out of the open spark plug hole could ignite, causing severe injury! Make sure the plug is securely held against the engine – if it is not earthed when the engine is turned over, the ECU could be damaged.**

3 Check that the transmission is in neutral, then turn the ignition switch ON, set the kill switch to RUN, and turn the engine over on the starter motor. If the system is in good condition a regular, fat blue spark should be evident at the plug electrodes. If the spark appears thin or yellowish, or is non-existent, further investigation will be necessary. Turn the ignition off.

4 The ignition system must be able to produce a spark which is capable of jumping at least a 6 mm gap. Simple ignition spark gap testing tools are commercially available – follow the manufacturer's instructions **(see illustration)**.

5 If the test results are good the entire ignition system can be considered good. If the spark appears thin or yellowish, or is non-existent, further investigation is necessary.

6 Ignition faults can be divided into two categories, namely those where the ignition system has failed completely, and those which are due to a partial failure. The likely faults are listed below, starting with the most probable source of failure. Work through the list systematically, referring to the subsequent sections for full details of the necessary checks and tests, and to the *Wiring Diagrams* at the end of Chapter 8. **Note:** *Before checking*

the following items ensure that the battery is fully charged and that all fuses are in good condition.

● *Loose, corroded or damaged wiring connections, broken or shorted wiring between any of the component parts of the ignition system (see Chapter 8).*
● *Faulty HT lead or spark plug cap, faulty spark plug, dirty, worn or corroded plug electrodes, or incorrect gap between electrodes.*
● *Faulty neutral, clutch or sidestand switch, or safety circuit diodes (see Chapter 8).*
● *Faulty engine kill switch (see Chapter 8).*
● *Faulty tip-over sensor.*
● *Faulty crankshaft position sensor or damaged trigger.*
● *Faulty ignition coil.*
● *Faulty ignition switch (see Chapter 8).*
● *Faulty electronic control unit (ECU).*

7 If the above checks don't reveal the cause of the problem, have the ignition system tested by a Yamaha dealer.

17 Ignition coil and spark plug cap

Check

1 On XT-R, XT-X and MT-03 models remove the fuel tank (see Section 2). On XT-Z models remove the fuel tank right-hand cover (see Chapter 7). Check the coil visually for loose or damaged connectors and terminals, loose mountings, cracks and other damage **(see illustrations)**.

2 Make sure the ignition is off.

3 Disconnect the primary wiring connectors **(see illustration)**. Pull the cap off the spark plug **(see illustration 16.2)**.

17.1a Ignition coil (arrowed) – XT-R and XT-X models

17.1b Ignition coil (arrowed) – XT-Z models

17.1c Ignition coil (arrowed) – MT-03 models

17.3 Disconnect the coil primary wiring connectors (arrowed)

17.4 Testing the coil primary resistance

17.5a To test the coil secondary resistance unscrew the cap from the lead . . .

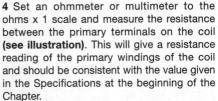

17.5b . . . and connect the multimeter leads between the red/black primary circuit terminal and the spark plug lead end

17.6 Measuring the resistance of the spark plug cap

4 Set an ohmmeter or multimeter to the ohms x 1 scale and measure the resistance between the primary terminals on the coil **(see illustration)**. This will give a resistance reading of the primary windings of the coil and should be consistent with the value given in the Specifications at the beginning of the Chapter.

5 To check the condition of the secondary windings, set the meter to the K-ohm scale. Unscrew the plug cap from the end of the HT lead **(see illustration)**. Connect the positive (+) meter probe to the primary terminal for the red/black wire on the coil, and insert the other probe in the end of the HT lead **(see illustration)**. If the reading obtained is not within the range shown in the Specifications, the coil is defective.

6 If the readings are as specified, measure the

resistance of the spark plug cap by connecting the meter probes between the HT lead socket and the spark plug contact **(see illustration)**. If the reading obtained is not as specified, replace the spark plug cap with a new one.

Removal and installation

7 On XT-R, XT-X and MT-03 models remove the fuel tank (see Section 2). On XT-Z models remove the fuel tank right-hand cover (see Chapter 7).

8 Disconnect the primary wiring connectors from the coil **(see illustration 17.3)**. Pull the cap off the spark plug **(see illustration 16.2)**.

9 Unscrew the bolts, noting the nuts and washers as fitted according to model, and remove the coil **(see illustration 17.1a, b or c)**.

10 Installation is the reverse of removal.

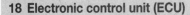

18 Electronic control unit (ECU)

Check

1 If the tests shown in the preceding or following Sections have failed to isolate the cause of an ignition fault, it is possible that the electronic control unit itself is faulty. No test details are available with which the unit can be tested. The best way to determine whether it is faulty is to substitute it with a known good one, if available. Otherwise, take the unit to a Yamaha dealer for assessment.

2 Before condemning the ECU make sure the wiring connector terminals are clean and none of the wires have broken.

Removal and installation

3 On XT-R and XT-X models remove the left-hand side panel (see Chapter 7) to access the ECU, and on XT-Z and MT-03 models remove the seat(s) (see Chapter 7), and on XT-Z the battery (see Chapter 8). Make sure the ignition is off.

4 Unscrew the nuts or bolts (according to model), displace the ECU and disconnect the wiring connector **(see illustrations)**.

5 Installation is the reverse of removal. Make sure the wiring connector is securely connected.

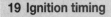

19 Ignition timing

General information

1 Since no provision exists for adjusting the ignition timing and since no component is subject to mechanical wear, there is no need for regular checks: only if investigating a fault such as a loss of power or a misfire, should the ignition timing be checked.

2 The ignition timing is checked dynamically (engine running) using a stroboscopic lamp. The inexpensive neon lamps should be adequate in theory, but in practice may produce a pulse of such low intensity that the

18.4a Electronic control unit (arrowed) – XT-R and XT-X models

18.4b Electronic control unit (arrowed) – XT-Z models

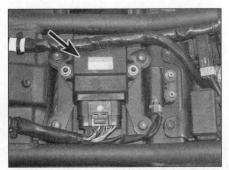

18.4c Electronic control unit (arrowed) – MT-03 models

timing mark remains indistinct. If possible, one of the more precise xenon tube lamps should be used, powered by an external source of the appropriate voltage. **Note:** *Do not use the machine's own battery, as an incorrect reading may result from stray impulses within the machine's electrical system.*

Check

3 Warm the engine up to normal operating temperature, then stop it.
4 Unscrew the timing inspection cap from the alternator cover on the right-hand side of the engine **(see illustration)**.
5 The mark on the timing rotor which indicates the firing point at idle speed is an 'H' **(see illustration)**. The static timing mark with which this should align is the notch in the inspection hole.

 The timing marks can be highlighted with white paint to make them more visible under the stroboscope light.

6 Connect the timing light to the HT lead as described in the manufacturer's instructions.
7 Start the engine and aim the light at the inspection hole.
8 With the machine idling at the specified speed, the mark on the rotor should align with the static timing mark.
9 Slowly increase the engine speed whilst observing the mark – it should appear to move clockwise, increasing in relation to the engine speed until it reaches full advance (no identification mark).
10 As already stated, there is no means of adjustment of the ignition timing on these machines. If the ignition timing is incorrect, or suspected of being incorrect, one of the ignition system components is at fault, and the system must be tested as described in the preceding Sections of this Chapter.
11 Fit the timing inspection cap using a new O-ring smeared with grease.

20 Immobiliser system

General information

1 The immobiliser system will only allow the machine to be started if the correct registered key is used to turn the ignition ON. The system consists of a transponder which is part of the ignition key, a receiver which is fitted around the ignition switch **(see illustration 20.27a and b)**, and the electronic control unit (ECU).
2 When the ignition is switched ON, the ECU sends power through the receiver to the transponder. The transponder sends a coded signal back through the receiver to the ECU. If the signal sent by the transponder matches the signal stored in the ECU memory, the

19.4 Unscrew the timing inspection cap (arrowed)

immobiliser indicator light in the instrument cluster (marked by a key symbol) comes on for about a second, then goes out, and the ECU allows the engine to be started. If the key code signal is not recognised, or if there is a fault in the system, the indicator light flashes. If the light flashes, refer to the fault diagnosis and troubleshooting Sections below. Likewise if the light does not come on at all. When the ignition is switched OFF the immobiliser light will start to flash after thirty seconds, indicating the system is enabled. The light will stop flashing after 24 hours but the system remains enabled.
3 The ECU can store the codes for up to three registered keys, two of which are standard use keys with black casings, and one is a code re-registering key with a red casing. They keys should be kept separately (i.e. not on the same key-ring) as the proximity of another key to the one being used in the switch can lead to the signal from it being jammed, and the bike will not start. The key has a built in transponder which can be damaged if the key is dropped or knocked, gets too hot, is too close to a magnetic object, or is submerged in water. If all the keys are lost, the ECU must be replaced with a new one, so always make sure you have one spare key. If a new key is obtained, it must be registered into the system before the bike can be started.
Caution: If you lose a key, or suspect it has been stolen, immediately re-register your code re-registering key and your remaining key – this will cancel the registration of the key that has been lost (or possibly stolen) which means that it will not be possible to start the bike using that key.
If all three keys are lost, or if the ignition switch is faulty, a new ECU, immobiliser unit and lock set must be fitted. If either the immobiliser or ECU is faulty either unit can be replaced on its own.

Standard key registration procedure

Note: *This must be done when a key is lost and a new one is obtained, or after a new 'code re-registering key' has been registered.*
4 Obtain a new key from a Yamaha dealer, and have it cut to match the original key.

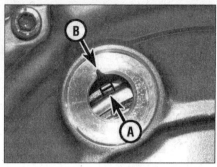

19.5 Ignition timing mark (A) and the notch (B)

5 Turn the ignition switch ON using the code re-registering key, then turn it OFF within 5 seconds, and then within 5 seconds turn it ON with the key you wish to register. The immobiliser indicator light should flash on and off every half second. This indicates that the system is in registration mode. At this point the registration of the other existing standard key will have been cancelled, so this will also have to be registered.
6 To register the second key, turn the ignition OFF and remove the first key, placing it well away from the receiver, and within 5 seconds insert the second key into the switch and turn it ON. Turn the ignition OFF and remove the key. If the light stops flashing, more than 5 seconds have elapsed and the system is no longer in registration mode, in which case start again.
7 On completion turn the ignition OFF and remove the key. After five seconds the light will stop flashing and the system is no longer in registration mode.
8 Check that both registered keys can start the motorcycle.

Code re-registering key registration procedure

Note: *This must be done when a new ECU or immobiliser receiver is fitted.*
9 Obtain a new key from a Yamaha dealer, and have it cut to match the original key.
10 Turn the ignition switch ON using the new code re-registering key. The immobiliser light will come on for about one second, then go out, indicating that the key has been registered.
11 Check that the key can start the motorcycle.
12 Now register the standard keys as described in Steps 4 to 8.

Installing a new ECU

13 Install the ECU (see Section 19).
14 Turn the ignition switch ON using the code re-registering key. This registers the key to the new ECU.
15 Check that the key can start the motorcycle.
16 Now register the standard keys as described in Steps 4 to 8.

Installing a new immobiliser

17 Remove the old immobiliser receiver from the ignition switch and fit the new one (see Step 27).

18 Turn the ignition switch ON using the code re-registering key. This registers the key to the new immobiliser.

19 Check that the key can start the motorcycle.

20 Now register the standard keys as described in Steps 4 to 8.

Fault diagnosis

21 If there is a fault in the system, the immobiliser indicator light in the instrument cluster (marked by a key symbol) flashes in a particular series that relates to a particular fault code. All fault codes are two-digit. The first number of any code is indicated by long (1 second) flashes with 1.5 second intervals, the number of flashes representing the number of the code. The second number of any code is indicated by short (0.5 second) flashes with 0.5 second intervals, the number of flashes representing the number of the code. For example fault code 53 comprises five long flashes and three short flashes. Thereafter there is a 3 second gap before the series is repeated in the case of a single fault code, or before the series gives the second fault code, and so on.

Troubleshooting procedure

22 If fault code 51 or 52 is shown, first check that none of the other registered keys are close to the receiver. If they are, remove them and try the ignition again.

23 If any fault code is shown, first check the fuses and the wiring and connectors between the immobiliser receiver, ignition switch and the ECU (see *Electrical System Fault Finding* in Section 2 of Chapter 8 and the *Wiring diagrams* at the end of it). A continuity test of all wires will locate a break or short in any circuit. Inspect the terminals inside the wiring connectors and ensure they are not loose, bent or corroded. Spray the inside of the connectors with a proprietary electrical terminal cleaner before reconnection. Also make sure the battery is in good condition and that the ignition switch is not faulty (see Chapter 8).

24 Remove the fuel tank (see Section 2). Trace the wiring from the receiver on the

20.27a On XT-Z and MT-03 remove the shroud

20.27b Immobiliser receiver screws (arrowed) – XT-R and XT-X

Fault code	Symptoms	Possible causes
51	Signal from key not being received by immobiliser	Interference from other keys or magnet Faulty key transponder Faulty immobiliser receiver
52	Code from key not recognised by receiver	Interference from other key Unregistered key being used
53	Signal from immobiliser not being received by ECU	Faulty wiring or wiring connector Faulty immobiliser receiver Faulty ECU
54	Code from immobiliser not recognised by ECU	Faulty wiring or wiring connector Immobiliser unregistered to ECU – code re-registering key not registered Faulty immobiliser receiver Faulty ECU
55	Key registration error	Same key being registered twice
56	Code from immobiliser not recognised by ECU	Faulty wiring or wiring connector Faulty immobiliser receiver Faulty ECU

ignition switch and disconnect it at the 6-pin wiring connector. Using a voltmeter, connect the positive (+) probe to the red/green wire terminal on the loom side of the connector and the negative (–) probe to the black wire terminal indicated. Turn the ignition ON – there should be battery voltage. If no voltage was recorded refer to the wiring diagrams and check the red/green circuit to its power source, and check the black wire for continuity to earth. If there is voltage the immobiliser receiver is probably faulty and must be replaced with a new one.

25 If the immobiliser LED or the LCD display in the instrument cluster do not come on, refer to Chapter 8 and check the instrument cluster.

26 If all indications are that either the immobiliser or the ECU are faulty, it is worth having them checked by a Yamaha dealer before buying replacements.

Replacement

27 To replace the receiver, remove the fuel tank (see Chapter 7). Trace the wiring from the receiver on the ignition switch and disconnect it at the 6-pin wiring connector. Feed the wiring back to the receiver, freeing it from any ties and noting its routing. On XT-Z and MT-03 models remove the ignition switch shroud **(see illustration)**. Undo the screws and remove the receiver, noting how it fits **(see illustration)**.

28 To replace the ECU see Section 18.

Chapter 5
Frame and suspension

Contents

	Section
Footrests, brake pedal and gearchange lever	3
Fork overhaul	8
Fork oil change	7
Fork removal and installation	6
Frame inspection and repair	2
General information	1
Handlebars and levers	5
Handlebar switches	see Chapter 8
Rear shock absorber	11
Rear suspension linkage (XT models)	12

	Section
Sidestand	4
Stand lubrication	see Chapter 1
Sidestand switch	see Chapter 8
Steering head bearing check and adjustment	see Chapter 1
Steering head bearings	10
Steering stem	9
Suspension adjustment	14
Suspension check	see Chapter 1
Swingarm	13

Degrees of difficulty

| **Easy,** suitable for novice with little experience | 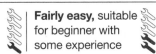 | **Fairly easy,** suitable for beginner with some experience | | **Fairly difficult,** suitable for competent DIY mechanic | | **Difficult,** suitable for experienced DIY mechanic | | **Very difficult,** suitable for expert DIY or professional | |

Specifications

Front forks

Fork oil type	10W oil fork oil
Fork oil capacity	
XT-R models	640 cc
XT-X models	600 cc
XT-Z models	650 cc
MT-03 models	570 cc
Fork oil level*	
XT-R models	125 mm
XT-X models	125 mm
XT-Z models	145 mm
MT-03 models	95 mm
Fork spring free length (min)	
XT-R models	
Standard	633 mm
Service limit	620 mm
XT-X models	
Standard	593 mm
Service limit	581 mm
XT-Z models	
Standard	580 mm
Service limit	572 mm
MT-03 models	
Standard	376 mm
Service limit	368 mm
Fork tube runout limit	0.2 mm

Oil level is measured from the top of the tube with the fork spring removed and the inner tube fully compressed.

Torque settings

Clutch lever assembly clamp bolt(s)
    XT-R and XT-X models . . . . 7 Nm
    XT-Z models . . . . 10 Nm
    MT-03 models. . . . . 10 Nm
Footrest bracket bolts – XT-R and XT-X models . . . . 48 Nm
Footrest bracket bolts – MT-03 models
    2006 models. . . . . 65 Nm
    2007-on models . . . . 100 Nm
Fork damper rod bolt . . . . 30 Nm
Fork top bolt. . . . . 18 Nm
Fork clamp bolts
  XT-R and XT-X models
    Top and bottom yoke bolts. . . . . 23 Nm
  XT-Z models
    Top yoke bolts . . . . 23 Nm
    Bottom yoke bolts . . . . 21 Nm
  MT-03 models
    Top and bottom yoke bolts. . . . . 28 Nm
Front brake master cylinder clamp bolts
    XT models. . . . . 7 Nm
    MT-03 models. . . . . 10 Nm
Gearchange lever pinch bolt
    XT-R and XT-X models . . . . 16 Nm
    XT-Z and MT-03 models . . . . 20 Nm
Handlebar clamp bolts . . . . 23 Nm
Handlebar end-weight bolts – XT-R and XT-X models. . . . . 7 Nm
Handlebar end-weights – XT-Z models . . . . 25 Nm
Handlebar end-weight bolts – MT-03 models . . . . 23 Nm
Handlebar holder nuts . . . . 32 Nm
Rear brake pedal pivot bolt – XT-Z and MT-03 models . . . . 48 Nm
Rear master cylinder/heel plate bolts. . . . . 23 Nm
Rear shock absorber
  XT-R and XT-X models
    Top bolt/nut. . . . . 59 Nm
    Bottom bolt/nut. . . . . 42 Nm
  XT-Z models
    Top bolt/nut. . . . . 60 Nm
    Bottom bolt/nut. . . . . 45 Nm
  MT-03 models
    Rear bolt/nut. . . . . 50 Nm
    Front bolt . . . . 155 Nm
    Crossbar bolt . . . . 155 Nm
Rear suspension linkage bolts/nuts
    XT-R and XT-X models . . . . 59 Nm
  XT-Z models
    Linkage arm-to-frame bolt/nut . . . . 60 Nm
    Linkage rod bolts/nuts . . . . 50 Nm
Sidestand bracket bolts
    XT models. . . . . 63 Nm
  MT-03 models
    2006 models. . . . . 63 Nm
    2007-on models . . . . 100 Nm
Sidestand pivot bolt nut
    XT models. . . . . 56 Nm
    MT-03 models. . . . . 46 Nm
Steering head bearing adjuster nut
  XT-R and XT-X models
    Initial setting . . . . 43 Nm
    Final setting . . . . 7 Nm
  XT-Z models
    Initial setting . . . . 45 Nm
    Final setting . . . . 7 Nm
  MT-03 models
    Initial setting . . . . 52 Nm
    Final setting . . . . 18 Nm
Steering stem nut
    XT models. . . . . 130 Nm
    MT-03 models. . . . . 110 Nm
Swingarm pivot bolt nut . . . . 92 Nm
Swingarm adjuster bolt – XT-Z models . . . . 8 Nm

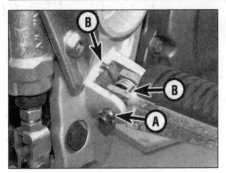

3.1 Remove the split pin (A) and withdraw the pivot pin, noting how the spring ends (B) locate – MT-03 shown

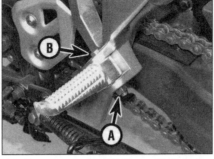

3.2 Unscrew the nut (A) then withdraw the bolt (B) – XT models

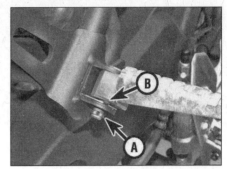

3.3 Remove the split pin (A) and withdraw the pivot pin, noting how the detent plate, ball and spring (B) locate – MT-03

1 General information

The steel frame uses the engine as a stressed member.

Front suspension is by oil-damped telescopic forks, and rear suspension is by a single shock absorber (on XT models via a rising rate linkage) with a swingarm that pivots through the engine and frame.

On XT-R and XT-X models the shock absorber has adjustable spring pre-load.

On XT-Z models the front forks and shock absorber have adjustable spring pre-load.

On MT-03 models the shock absorber has adjustable spring pre-load.

2 Frame inspection and repair

1 The frame should not require attention unless accident damage has occurred. In most cases, fitting a new frame is the only satisfactory remedy for such damage. Frame specialists have the jigs and other equipment necessary for straightening a frame to the required standard of accuracy, but even then there is no simple way of assessing to what extent it may have been over-stressed.

2 After a high mileage, examine the frame closely for signs of cracking or splitting at the welded joints. Loose engine mounting bolts can cause ovaling or fracturing of the mounting points. Minor damage can often be repaired by specialised welding, depending on the extent and nature of the damage.

3 Remember that a frame that is out of alignment will cause handling problems. If, as the result of an accident, misalignment is suspected, it will be necessary to strip the machine completely so the frame can be thoroughly checked.

3 Footrests, brake pedal and gearchange lever

Footrests

1 To remove a rider's footrest, straighten and remove the split pin from the bottom of the footrest pivot pin, then withdraw the pin and remove the footrest, noting how the return spring ends locate (see illustration). Discard the split pin.

2 To remove a passenger footrest on XT models, unscrew the nut, then withdraw the bolt and remove the footrest, collecting the washer(s), detent plate, ball, spring and collar as fitted according to model, noting how they fit (see illustration).

3 To remove a passenger footrest on MT-03 models, straighten and remove the split pin from the bottom of the footrest pivot pin, then withdraw the pin and remove the footrest, collecting the detent plate, ball and spring, noting how they fit (see illustration).

4 If required and where fitted remove the rubber from the peg by undoing the screw(s) or bolt(s) on the underside (see illustration) – new rubbers are available.

5 Installation is the reverse of removal. Apply a small amount of multi-purpose grease to the pivot pin. Use new split pins on the pivot pins, and bend the ends round the pivot pin.

Brake pedal
XT-R and XT-X models

6 Remove the split pin and washer from the clevis pin securing the brake pedal to the master cylinder pushrod, then withdraw the pin and detach the pushrod (see illustration). Discard the split pin – a new one must be used.

7 Unhook the brake light switch spring and the pedal return spring from the pedal (see illustration).

8 Unscrew the pivot bolt and bracket bolt and draw the pedal off its pivot (see illustration).

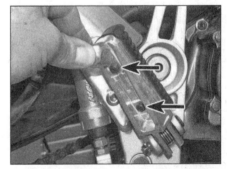

3.4 Footpeg rubber screws (arrowed)

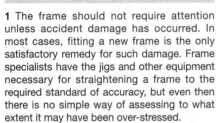

3.6 Remove the split pin (A) and withdraw the clevis pin (B)

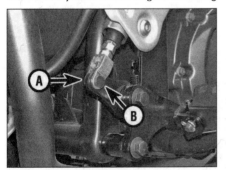

3.7 Unhook the switch spring (arrowed) and the pedal return spring

3.8 Unscrew the bolts, displace the bracket assembly and remove the pedal

3.10a Remove the split pin . . .

3.10b . . . and the washer, then withdraw the clevis pin

3.11a Unscrew the pivot bolt, detach the pedal and remove the washer . . .

3.11b . . . and the spring

3.12 Withdraw, clean and check the bush and its O-rings

9 Installation is the reverse of removal, noting the following:

● Clean all old grease off the pedal pivot and apply fresh grease.
● Tighten the footrest bracket bolts to the torque settings specified at the beginning of the Chapter.
● Clean all old grease off the clevis pin and apply fresh grease. Use a new split pin and bend the ends round to secure it.
● Check the operation of the rear brake, and the brake light switch (see Chapter 1).

XT-Z models

10 Remove the split pin and washer from the clevis pin securing the brake pedal to the master cylinder pushrod, then withdraw the pin and detach the pushrod **(see illustrations)**. Discard the split pin – a new one must be used.

11 Unscrew the pedal pivot bolt and remove the pedal along with the return spring, noting how its ends locate, and the washer **(see illustrations)**.

12 Withdraw the pedal pivot bush and clean off old grease **(see illustration)**. Replace the O-rings with new ones if damaged, deformed or deteriorated. Check for excess play between the bush and the pedal and fit a new bush if necessary.

13 Installation is the reverse of removal, noting the following:

● Clean off any old grease from the bush and pivot bolt. Apply grease to the outside and inside of the bush and to the O-rings, and the pivot bolt shank **(see illustration 3.12)**.
● Make sure the return spring ends locate correctly **(see illustration)**.
● Clean all old grease off the clevis pin and apply fresh grease. Use a new split pin and bend the ends round to secure it **(see illustration 3.10a)**.

MT-03 models

14 Remove the split pin and washer from the clevis pin securing the brake pedal to the master cylinder pushrod, then withdraw the pin and detach the pushrod **(see illustration)**. Discard the split pin – a new one must be used.

15 Unhook the pedal return spring **(see illustration 3.14)**.

16 Unscrew the pedal pivot bolt nut and remove the washer, withdraw the bolt and remove the pedal **(see illustration 3.14)**.

17 Withdraw the pedal pivot bush and clean off the old grease **(see illustration 3.12)**. Replace the O-rings with new ones if damaged, deformed or deteriorated. Check for excess play between the bush and the pedal and fit a new bush if necessary.

3.13 Make sure the return springs ends (arrowed) are correctly located

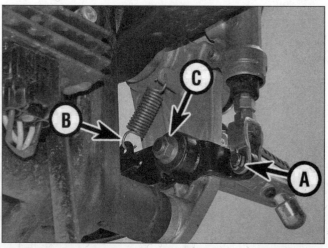

3.14 Remove the split pin (A) and withdraw the clevis pin, then unhook the spring (B). Pedal pivot bolt nut (C)

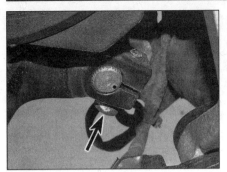

3.19a Note the alignment of the lever, then unscrew the bolt (arrowed) . . .

3.19b . . . and draw the lever off

Withdraw the pivot bolt and remove the stand.

Installation

4 Installation is the reverse of removal. Apply grease to the pivot bolt shank. Counter-hold the bolt while tightening the nut to the torque setting specified at the beginning of the Chapter.
5 Reconnect the springs, and on MT-03 models the spring link plate, and check that they hold the stand securely up when not in use **(see illustration 4.2a or b)** – an accident could occur if the stand extends while the machine is in motion. Check the operation of the switch (see Chapter 1).

18 Installation is the reverse of removal, noting the following:
● Clean off any old grease from the bush and pivot bolt. Apply grease to the outside and inside of the bush and to the O-rings, and the pivot bolt shank **(see illustration 3.12)**.
● Clean all old grease off the clevis pin and apply fresh grease. Use a new split pin and bend the ends round to secure it.

Gearchange lever

19 Mark the alignment of the punch mark on the gearchange shaft with the lever **(see illustration)**. Unscrew the pinch bolt and slide the lever off the shaft **(see illustration)**.
20 On installation align the mark you made on the lever with the punch mark on the shaft. Clean the threads of the pinch bolt, then apply a suitable non-permanent thread locking

compound to the threads and tighten the bolt to the specified torque.

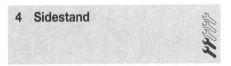

4 Sidestand

Note: *Centrestands are available as optional equipment on certain models.*

Removal

1 Support the bike on an auxiliary stand.
2 Unhook the stand springs, and on MT-03 models the spring link plate **(see illustrations)**.
3 Unscrew the nut from the pivot bolt and remove the washer **(see illustrations)**.

5 Handlebars and levers

Handlebar removal

Note: *If required, for example if the top yoke is being removed to access the steering head bearings, the handlebars can be displaced from the tops of the forks without detaching any of the assemblies from them – see Step 13 only. Support the assembly on some rag to protect all surfaces. Also wrap rag around the brake master cylinder, and keep it upright if possible.*
1 As a precaution, remove the fuel tank (see Chapter 4). Though not actually necessary, this will prevent the possibility of damage should a tool slip. Before removing the assemblies from the handlebars make a note of their position and alignment on the bar, making marks where necessary, so everything can be installed in the same position. Look for any existing alignment marks, usually in the form of a punch mark aligned with the mating surfaces of clamps.
2 Remove the mirrors (see Chapter 7).
3 Release any ties from the handlebars, noting what is secured and how it is routed. Remove the end-weight from each end of the handlebar **(see illustration)**.

4.2a Sidestand spring arrangement – XT models

4.2b Sidestand spring arrangement – MT-03 models

4.3a Pivot bolt nut (arrowed) – XT models

4.3b Pivot bolt nut (arrowed) – MT-03 models

5.3 Handlebar end-weight (arrowed)

5.4 Release each switch by pressing up the clip (arrowed) and drawing the switch out

5.5a Brake light switch connectors (arrowed)

5.5b Clutch switch connector (arrowed)

5.6 Unscrew the master cylinder clamp bolts (arrowed) and displace the assembly

5.7 Slide the twistgrip off

5.8 Undo the screws (arrowed) and split the housing

4 On XT-R and XT-X models press the clip up on the underside of the brake light switch and clutch switch and draw the switches out of their housings (see illustration).

5 On XT-Z and MT-03 models disconnect the brake light switch and clutch switch wiring connectors (see illustrations).

6 Unscrew the brake master cylinder assembly clamp bolts and position the assembly clear of the handlebar, wrapping it in some rag, and making sure no strain is placed on the hydraulic hose (see illustration). Keep the master cylinder reservoir upright to prevent possible fluid leakage.

7 Refer to Chapter 4 and detach the throttle cables from the twistgrip – this involves detaching the switch housing. Slide the twistgrip off (see illustration).

8 Undo the left-hand switch housing screws and displace the switch (see illustration).

9 Remove the grip from the left-hand end of the handlebar – if it has been glued on or is stuck feed a wooden or plastic tool up the inside and move it round the bar to release it, and if available squirt some compressed air up. At worst you will have to cut the grip off and fit a new one.

10 Detach the clutch cable (see Chapter 2).

11 On XT models unscrew the clutch lever bracket clamp bolts and remove the lever assembly (see illustration).

12 On MT-03 models unscrew the clutch lever bracket clamp bolt and slide the assembly off the handlebar (see illustration).

13 Where fitted carefully prise the blanking caps out of the handlebar clamp bolts (see

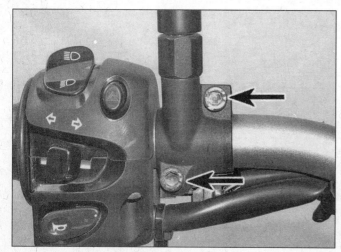

5.11 Unscrew the clamp bolts (arrowed) and displace the assembly

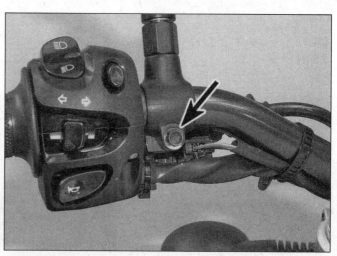

5.12 Unscrew the bolt (arrowed) and slide the clutch lever bracket off

5.13a Remove the blanking caps where fitted

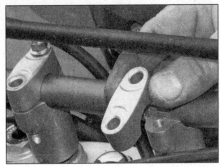

5.13b Unscrew the bolts and remove the clamps . . .

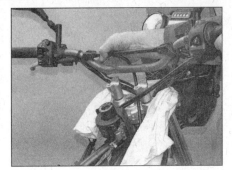

5.13c . . . and remove or displace the handlebars

5.14 Unscrew the nut (arrowed) to free the holder from the yoke

5.15a Handlebar alignment punch mark (arrowed) – XT-Z models

5.15b Fit the clamps with the arrows pointing to the front

illustration). Unscrew the handlebar clamp bolts and remove the clamps, then displace or remove the handlebars **(see illustrations)**.

14 If required unscrew the handlebar holder nuts on the underside of the yoke and remove the washers **(see illustration)**. Lift the holders off the yoke and remove the washer(s) or bracket (fitted with the left-hand holder on XT-R and XT-X models), and on MT-03 models the dampers.

Installation

15 Installation is the reverse of removal, noting the following.
● If removed fit the handlebars holders and associated components (see Step 14), and tighten the nuts to the torque setting specified at the beginning of the Chapter.
● Make sure the handlebars are central, and align the punch mark with the clamp mating surfaces **(see illustration 5.15a)**.

● Fit the clamps with the arrow pointing to the front or the punch mark at the front according to model, and tighten the front bolt first, then the rear, to the torque setting specified at the beginning of the Chapter **(see illustration 5.15b)**.
● Fit the front brake master cylinder bracket clamp with the UP mark facing up and with the clamp mating surfaces aligned with the punch mark **(see illustration 5.6)**. Tighten the top clamp bolt first, and tighten the bolts to the torque setting specified for your model. Also align the clutch lever bracket clamp mating surfaces with the punch mark, and tighten the bolt(s) to the specified torque **(see illustration 5.11 or 5.12)**.
● Refer to Chapter 4 to fit the throttle cables.
● When fitting the switch housings, locate the peg in the hole in the handlebar.

● When fitting the handlebar end-weights make sure there is a 1 to 4 mm gap between them and the grips. Tighten the end weights themselves or the bolts to the specified torque setting according to model.
● Check and adjust clutch and throttle cable freeplay (see Chapter 1).

Levers

16 To remove the front brake lever, undo the lever pivot bolt locknut, then undo the pivot screw and remove the lever **(see illustration)**.
17 To remove the clutch lever, loosen the cable adjuster lockring then thread the adjuster into the bracket to provide freeplay in the cable **(see illustration)**. Undo the lever pivot bolt locknut, then undo the pivot bolt and remove the lever, detaching the cable nipple as you do **(see illustration)**.

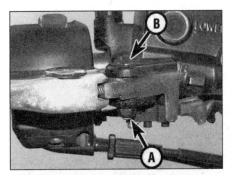

5.16 Unscrew the nut (A), then undo the screw (B) and remove the lever

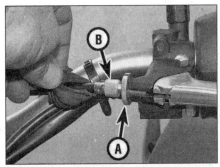

5.17a Pull back the boot then slacken the lockring (A) and thread the adjuster (B) in

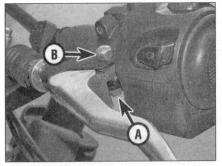

5.17b Unscrew the locknut (A) then undo the pivot bolt (B) and remove the lever

18 Installation is the reverse of removal, noting the following.

- Apply silicone grease to the contact area between the front brake master cylinder pushrod tip and the brake lever.
- Apply lithium or molybdenum grease to the pivot bolt shafts and the contact areas between the lever and its bracket.
- Make sure the levers move smoothly and freely.
- Adjust clutch cable freeplay (see Chapter 1).

6 Fork removal and installation

Removal

1 Note the routing of the cables, hose and wiring around the forks. Mark each fork according to the side it fits on. Note the setting of the top of the fork in respect to the upper surface of the top yoke (see illustration 6.10).

2 Remove the front wheel (see Chapter 6).

3 On XT-R and XT-X models remove the fork protector and the upper and lower mudguards, and the front cowl assembly (see Chapter 7). Release the brake hose guide (see illustration).

4 On XT-Z models remove the front mudguard, and for best access to the clamp bolts in the top yoke remove the cockpit covers (see Chapter 7). Release the brake hose guide (see illustration).

5 On MT-03 models remove the front mudguard (see Chapter 7). Carefully prise the blanking caps out of the clamps bolts in the bottom yoke (see illustration).

Release the brake hose guide (see illustration).

6 Working on one fork at a time, slacken the fork clamp bolt(s) in the top yoke (see illustrations).

7 If the fork is to be disassembled, or if the fork oil is being changed, slacken the fork top bolt (see illustration 6.11).

8 Slacken the fork clamp bolt(s) in the bottom yoke (see illustration or 6.5a). Remove the fork by twisting it and pulling it down (see illustration).

> **HAYNES HINT** *If the fork legs are seized in the yokes, spray the area with penetrating oil and allow time for it to soak in before trying again.*

Installation

9 Remove all traces of corrosion from the fork tube and the yokes. Make sure you install the forks the correct way round as marked on removal. On XT-Z models if removed make sure the fork gaiter is fitted but do not tighten the clamp as its position needs to set first.

10 Slide the fork up through the bottom yoke and into the top yoke, making sure all cables, hoses and wiring are routed on the correct side of the fork (see illustration 6.8b). Set the top of the fork inner tube flush with the upper

6.3 Unscrew the bolts (arrowed) . . .

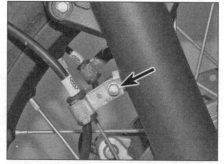
6.4 . . . and free the brake hose clamps

6.5a Remove the blanking caps from the clamp bolts in the bottom yoke

6.5b Unscrew the bolt (arrowed) and free the hose

6.6a Top yoke fork clamp bolts (arrowed) – XT models

6.6b Top yoke fork clamp bolt (arrowed) – MT-03 models

6.8a Bottom yoke fork clamp bolts (arrowed) – XT models

6.8b Draw the fork down and out of the yokes

6.10 Set the top of the tube flush with the yoke

6.11 If necessary tighten the top bolt

6.13 Seat the gaiter up against the yoke and tighten the clamp

surface of the top yoke (see illustration). Tighten the clamp bolt(s) in the bottom yoke to the torque setting specified at the beginning of the Chapter (see illustration 6.8a or 6.5a).

11 If the fork has been dismantled or if the fork oil was changed, tighten the fork top bolt to the specified torque setting (see illustration).

12 Tighten the fork clamp bolt(s) in the top yoke to its specified torque setting (see illustration 6.6a or b).

13 Install the remaining components in a reverse of the removal procedure according to model, referring to the relevant Chapters. On XT-Z models if necessary seat the gaiters under the bottom yoke and tighten the clamp screws (see illustration). Check the operation of the front forks and brake before taking the machine out on the road.

7 Fork oil change

1 After a high mileage the fork oil will deteriorate and its damping and lubrication qualities will be impaired. Always change the oil in both fork legs.

2 Remove the fork – make sure that the top bolt is loosened while the fork is still clamped in the bottom yoke (see Section 6).

3 On XT-Z models slacken the gaiter clamp and slide the gaiter up off the fork (see illustration).

4 Support the fork leg in an upright position and unscrew the fork top bolt from the top of the inner tube – the bolt is under pressure from the fork spring; use a ratchet tool so it does not need to be removed from the bolt as you unscrew it, and maintain some downward pressure on it, particularly as you come to the end of the threads, or alternatively hold the

7.3 Slacken the screw (arrowed) and remove the gaiter

tool still and twist the fork tube to unthread it from the bolt (see illustration).

5 Slide the fork inner tube down. On XT-Z and MT-03 models remove the spacer. On all models remove the washer and the spring (see illustrations). Wipe any excess oil off the spring and spacer. If the top bolt O-ring is damaged or deteriorated fit a new one (see illustration 7.9).

6 Invert the fork leg over a suitable container and pump the fork to expel as much oil as possible (see illustration). Support the fork upside down in the container and allow it to drain for a few minutes. If the fork oil contains

7.4 Unscrew the fork top bolt using a ratchet tool

7.5 Remove the spacer where fitted, the washer and the spring

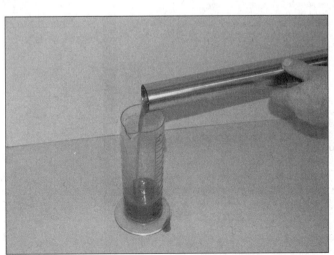

7.6 Invert the fork over a container and tip the oil out

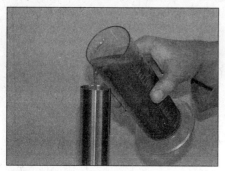

7.7a Pour the oil into the top of the tube and distribute and bleed it as described . . .

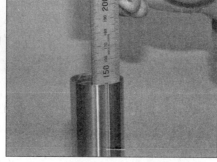

7.7b . . . then measure the level as described using a ruler

7.8a Fit the spring . . .

7.8b . . . and the washer, and where fitted the spacer

7.9 Smear the O-ring (arrowed) with oil before fitting the top bolt

metal particles inspect the fork bushes for wear (see Section 8).

7 Slowly pour in the specified quantity of the specified grade of fork oil, then pump the fork several times to distribute it evenly **(see illustration)**. Slide the inner tube down until it seats then measure the oil level from the top of the tube **(see illustration)**. Add or subtract oil until it is at the level specified at the beginning of this Chapter.

8 Fit the spring into the fork with its closer-wound coils at the top **(see illustration)**. Draw the inner tube up until it is flush with the top of the spring, then fit the washer **(see illustration)**. On XT-Z and MT-03 models lift the tube some more and fit the spacer.

9 Smear some fork oil onto the top bolt O-ring, using a new one if necessary **(see illustration)**. Fully extend the inner tube and fit the top bolt into it, compressing the spring

as you do, and thread it in (making sure it does not cross-thread), keeping downward pressure on the spring, using a ratchet tool or by turning the tube while holding the bolt still as on removal **(see illustration 7.4)**. Lightly tighten the top bolt at this stage – tighten it to the specified torque setting when the fork leg is being installed and is securely held in the bottom yoke (see Section 6).

10 Install the fork (see Section 6).

8 Fork overhaul

Disassembly

1 Remove the fork – make sure that the top bolt is loosened while the leg is still

clamped in the bottom yoke (see Section 6). Always dismantle the fork legs separately to avoid interchanging parts and thus causing an accelerated rate of wear. Store all components in separate, clearly marked containers.

2 On MT-03 models remove the fork protector from the top of the outer tube, noting how it locates.

3 Lay the fork flat on the bench, hold it down and slacken the damper rod bolt in the base of the outer tube **(see illustration)**. If the bolt does not slacken but instead the rod turns with the bolt inside the fork, try compressing the fork so that more pressure is exerted on the damper rod head, or if available use an air-ratchet. Otherwise, follow Step 4, then use the Yamaha holding tool (part No 90890-01460), located in the shaped top of the damper rod on a long extension, or a broom handle or piece of wooden dowel rounded at the end, inserted in the fork and pressed against the top of the damper rod to hold it.

4 Refer to Section 7, Steps 3 to 6 and drain the oil from the fork.

5 Remove the damper cartridge bolt and its copper sealing washer from the bottom of the outer tube **(see illustration)**. Discard the sealing washer as a new one must be used on reassembly. Tip the damper rod out **(see illustration)**.

6 Carefully prise out the dust seal from the top of the outer tube **(see illustration)**.

7 Carefully prise out the oil seal retaining clip,

8.3 Slacken the damper rod bolt

8.5a Unscrew and remove the damper rod bolt . . .

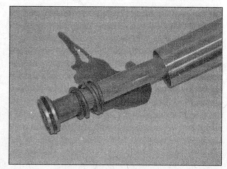

8.5b . . . then tip the damper rod out of the inner tube

8.6 Prise out the dust seal using a
flat-bladed screwdriver

8.7 Prise out the retaining clip using a
flat-bladed screwdriver

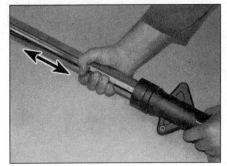

8.8a Repeatedly draw the tubes apart . . .

8.8b . . . until the seal and bush are
displaced

8.10 Tip the oil lock piece (arrowed) out

8.13a Check the working surface
(arrowed) of each bush for wear

taking care not to scratch the surface of the inner tube **(see illustration)**.

8 To separate the inner and outer tubes it is necessary to displace the top bush and oil seal from the top of the outer tube. The bottom bush on the inner tube will not pass through the top bush, and this can be used to good effect. Grasp the inner tube in one hand and the outer tube in the other and compress them slightly, then pull them apart so that the bottom bush strikes the top bush **(see illustration)**. Repeat this operation until the top bush and seal are tapped out **(see illustration)**.

9 Slide the oil seal, the oil seal washer and top bush off the inner tube, noting which way up they fit. Discard the oil seal and the dust seal as new ones must be used. Do not remove the bottom bush from the inner tube unless it is being replaced with a new one (see Step 13).

10 Tip the damper rod oil lock piece out of the outer tube **(see illustration)**.

Inspection

11 Clean all parts in solvent and blow them dry with compressed air, if available. Check the inner fork tube for score marks, scratches, flaking of the chrome finish and excessive or abnormal wear – the tubes can be re-chromed by a specialist if required (they must be hard-chromed). Look for dents in the outer tube and replace the tubes in both forks if any are found. Check the fork seal seat for nicks, gouges and scratches. If damage is evident, leaks will occur.

12 Check the inner tube for runout using V-blocks and a dial gauge. If the amount of runout exceeds the service limit specified, the tube should be replaced with a new one.

⚠️ *Warning: If the tube is bent or exceeds the runout limit, it should not be straightened; replace it with a new one.*

13 Check the working surface of each bush for wear **(see illustration)** – the surface should be Teflon grey all over. If the Teflon has worn to expose the material below replace the bushes with new ones. To remove the bottom bush from the inner tube carefully lever its ends apart using a screwdriver and slide it out of its recess **(see illustration)**.

14 Check the springs (both the main spring and the rebound spring on the damper rod) for cracks and other damage. Measure the main spring free length and compare the measurement to the specifications at the beginning of the Chapter **(see illustration)**. If it is defective or sagged below the service limit, replace the main springs in both forks with new ones. Never replace only one spring.

15 Check the damper rod, and in particular the ring in its head, for damage and wear, and replace it with a new one if necessary **(see illustration)**. Check the oil lock piece for damage.

8.13b To remove the bottom bush lever its
ends apart

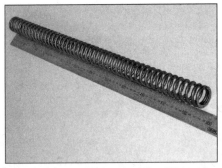

8.14 Measure the free length of the main
fork spring

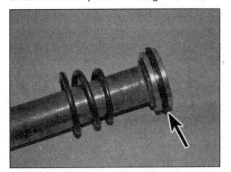

8.15 Check the rod and spring for damage
and the ring (arrowed) for wear

8.17a Slide the damper rod into the top of the tube . . .

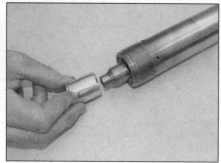

8.17b . . . so it protrudes from the bottom, then fit the oil lock piece

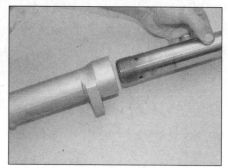

8.18 Fit the inner tube into the outer tube

Reassembly

16 If removed fit the bottom bush into its recess in the bottom of the inner tube (see illustration 8.13b). Apply a smear of the specified clean fork oil to the bush.

17 If removed, fit the rebound spring onto the damper rod, and fit the ring into its groove in the head (see illustration 8.15). Slide the damper rod into the top of the inner tube and all the way down so it protrudes from the bottom (see illustration). Fit the oil lock piece onto the bottom of the rod, then push the rod back into the tube so the oil lock piece fits into the bottom (see illustration).

18 Lay the fork flat on the bench. Slide the inner tube fully into the outer tube (see illustration).

19 Clean the threads of the damper rod bolt. Fit a new copper sealing washer onto the damper bolt and apply a few drops of a suitable non-permanent thread locking compound (see illustration). Fit the bolt into the bottom of the slider and tighten it to the specified torque setting (see illustration). If the damper rod rotates inside the tube as you tighten the bolt, either use the same holding method as on disassembly (Step 3), or wait until the fork is fully reassembled and tighten it then (the pressure of the spring on the head of the damper rod should prevent it from turning, especially if you compress the fork).

20 Apply a smear of the specified clean fork oil to the inner surface of the top bush. Slide the bush down the inner tube and seat it in the top of the outer tube (see illustration). Slide the oil seal washer onto the bush (see illustration).

21 Support the fork upright. Using a suitable drift with tape wrapped around it to prevent scratching the chrome, carefully drive the bottom bush fully and squarely into its recess, moving it round to exert even pressure – the oil seal washer prevents damaging the rim of the bush (see illustration). Make sure the bush enters the recess squarely. It is best to make sure that the fork inner tube is withdrawn as much as possible from the tube so that any accidental scratching is confined to the area that does not affect the oil seal.

22 Lift the washer to check the bush is seated fully and squarely in its recess in the outer tube, then wipe the recess clean and re-seat the washer (see illustration).

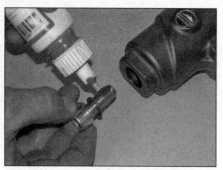

8.19a Fit a new sealing washer and apply threadlock . . .

8.19b . . . and tighten the damper rod bolt to the specified torque

8.20a Slide the top bush down and into the outer tube . . .

8.20b . . . then seat the washer on the bush . . .

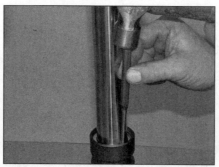

8.21 . . . and drive the bush in and onto its seat

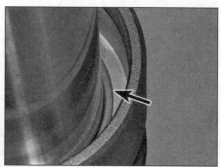

8.22 Make sure the bush (arrowed) is fully driven in

8.23a Smear grease into the oil seal lip recess

8.23b Slide the seal down and into the outer tube . . .

8.23c . . . and press or drive it in and onto its seat

8.23d Make sure the retaining clip groove (arrowed) is fully exposed

8.24 Fit the retaining clip in its groove . . .

8.25 . . . then press the dust seal in

23 Apply a smear of grease to the oil seal lips **(see illustration)**. Slide the seal onto the tube with its marked side facing up **(see illustration)**. Drive the seal into place as described in Step 20 until the retaining clip groove is visible **(see illustrations)**.

24 Fit the retaining clip, making sure it is correctly located in its groove **(see illustration)**.

25 Lubricate the lips of the new dust seal then slide it down the fork tube and press it into position **(see illustration)**.

26 Refer to Section 7, Steps 7 to 9 and fill the fork with oil and finish reassembly.

27 If the damper rod bolt requires tightening (see Step 19), place the fork upside down on the floor, using a rag to protect it, then have an assistant compress the fork so that maximum

spring pressure is placed on the damper rod head while tightening the bolt to the specified torque setting.

28 Install the fork (see Section 6).

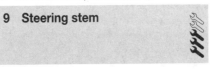

9 Steering stem

Removal

1 Cover the fuel tank and its covers in some rag, or if preferred as a precaution, remove the fuel tank (see Chapter 4) – though not actually necessary, this will prevent the possibility of damage should a tool slip.

2 Remove the front forks (see Section 6).

3 Displace the handlebars from the top yoke

(see Section 5) and support them clear on some rag **(see illustration)**.

4 On MT-03 models remove the headlight/turn signal assembly and the instrument cluster (see Chapter 8).

5 If you want to remove the top yoke completely rather than just displace it, trace the wiring from the ignition switch and immobiliser receiver and disconnect it at the connectors – if not already done you will need to remove the fuel tank for access. Feed the wiring back to the switch, freeing it from any clips and ties and noting its routing.

6 Detach the brake hose holder from the bottom yoke.

7 On XT-Z models if required detach the tow-hook/handle from the bottom yoke **(see illustration)**.

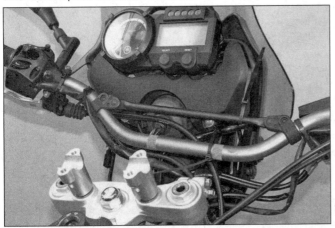

9.3 Displace and secure the handlebar assembly

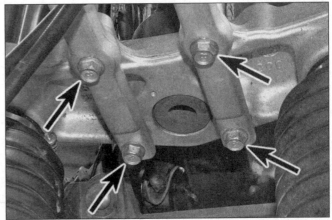

9.7 Unscrew the bolts (arrowed) and remove the handle

9.8a Unscrew the nut and remove the washer . . .

9.8b . . . then lift the yoke up off the stem

9.10a Unscrew the adjuster nut . . .

9.10b . . . and remove the bearing cover . . .

9.10c . . . then draw the bottom yoke/ steering stem out of the steering head

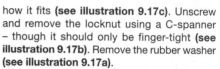
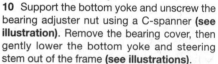

8 Unscrew and remove the steering stem nut, and remove the washer (see illustration). Lift the top yoke up off the steering stem and either

rest it on some rag or remove it if the wiring has been disconnected (see illustration).
9 Remove the tabbed lock washer, noting

how it fits (see illustration 9.17c). Unscrew and remove the locknut using a C-spanner – though it should only be finger-tight (see illustration 9.17b). Remove the rubber washer (see illustration 9.17a).
10 Support the bottom yoke and unscrew the bearing adjuster nut using a C-spanner (see illustration). Remove the bearing cover, then gently lower the bottom yoke and steering stem out of the frame (see illustrations).
11 Remove the upper bearing from the top of the steering head (see illustration). The lower bearing is an interference fit on the stem (see illustration).
12 Clean all old grease from the bearings and races using solvent or paraffin, then check them for wear or damage as described in Section 10.
Note: *Do not attempt to remove the races from the steering head or the lower bearing from the steering stem unless they are to be replaced with new ones (see Section 10).*

Installation

13 Smear a liberal quantity of multi-purpose grease onto the bearing races and bearings.
14 Carefully lift the steering stem/bottom yoke up through the steering head and support it (see illustration 9.10c). Fit the upper bearing into the top of the steering head, then fit the bearing cover (see illustrations). Thread the adjuster nut onto the steering stem and tighten it finger-tight (see illustration).
15 To adjust the bearings as specified by Yamaha, a special service tool (Pt. No.90890-

9.11a Remove the upper bearing from the top of the head

9.11b The lower bearing is tight on the steering stem

9.14a Fit the upper bearing . . .

9.14b . . . the bearing cover . . .

9.14c . . . and the adjuster nut

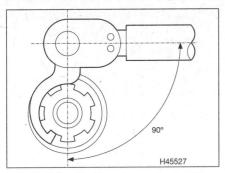

9.15 Using the Yamaha service tool to tighten the adjuster nut

9.16 Tightening the adjuster nut using a C-spanner

9.17a Fit the rubber washer . . .

9.17b . . . then tighten the locknut as described . . .

9.17c . . . and fit the tabs on the washer into the aligned notches

9.18 Tighten the steering stem nut to the specified torque

01403) and a torque wrench are required. If the tool is available, tighten the adjuster nut to the initial torque setting specified at the beginning of the Chapter, making sure the torque wrench arm is at 90° to the tool arm **(see illustration)**. Now slacken the nut, then tighten it to the final torque setting specified. Make sure that the steering stem is able to move freely from lock-to-lock.

16 If the Yamaha tool is not available, using a C-spanner tighten the adjuster nut until all freeplay is removed, then tighten it a little more **(see illustration)**. This pre-loads the bearings. Now slacken the nut, then tighten it again, setting it so that all freeplay is just removed, yet the steering is able to move freely from side to side.

Caution: Take great care not to apply excessive pressure because this will cause premature failure of the bearings.

17 Fit the rubber washer, then the locknut **(see illustrations)**. Tighten the locknut finger-tight, then tighten it further until its notches align with those in the adjuster nut. If necessary, counter-hold the adjuster nut and tighten the locknut using a C-spanner until the notches align, but make sure the adjuster nut does not turn as well. Fit the tabbed lock washer so that the tabs fit into the notches in both the locknut and adjuster nut **(see illustration)**.

18 Fit the top yoke onto the steering stem **(see illustration 9.8b)**. Fit the steering stem nut with its washer and tighten it finger-tight

(see illustration 9.8a). Temporarily install one of the forks to align the top and bottom yokes, and secure it by tightening the bottom yoke clamp bolts only (see Section 6). Now tighten the steering stem nut to the torque setting specified at the beginning of the Chapter **(see illustration)**.

19 Install the remaining components in a reverse of the removal procedure, referring to the relevant Sections or Chapters where required, and to the torque settings specified at the beginning of the Chapter. Make sure the wiring, cables and hose are correctly routed.

20 Refer to the freeplay check procedure in Chapter 1 to make a final assessment of the bearings with the leverage and inertia of all components taken into account, and if necessary readjust.

10 Steering head bearings

Inspection

1 Remove the steering stem (see Section 9).
2 Clean all traces of old grease from the bearings and races using paraffin or solvent, and check them for wear or damage.
3 The outer races in the steering head should be polished and free from indentations (see

illustration). Make sure each bearing turns smoothly and freely on its inner race. Inspect the bearing rollers for signs of wear, damage or discoloration. If there are any signs of wear on any of the above components both upper and lower bearing assemblies must be replaced with a new set. Only remove the outer races in the steering head and the lower bearing on the steering stem if they need to be replaced with new ones – do not reuse them once they have been removed.

Replacement

4 The outer races are an interference fit in the steering head – you may be able to tap them out using a suitable drift located on the exposed inner lip of the race **(see**

10.3 Check the outer races for wear and damage

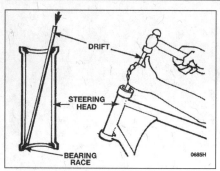

10.4 Drive the bearing races out with a brass drift or screwdriver locating it on the exposed inner rim of the race

10.5a Locate the adapter behind the rim of the race and expand it to lock it . . .

10.5b . . . then fit the slide-hammer and jar the race out

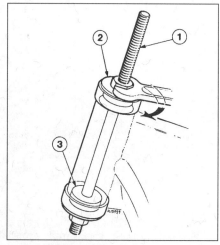

10.6 Drawbolt arrangement for fitting steering stem bearing races

1 Long bolt or threaded bar
2 Thick washer
3 Guide for lower race

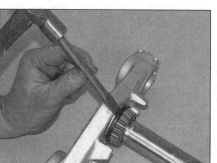

10.7a Remove the lower bearing race using a cold chisel . . .

10.7b . . . and screwdrivers . . .

illustration). Tap firmly and evenly around each race to ensure that it is driven out squarely. Curve the end of the drift slightly to improve access if necessary.
5 Alternatively, remove the races using a slide-hammer type bearing extractor (see illustrations) – these can often be hired from tool shops.

6 Press the new outer races into the head using a drawbolt arrangement (see illustration), or drive them in using a large diameter tubular drift (to do this the bike must be solidly supported as all the force needs to be transmitted to the race). Make sure that the drawbolt washer or drift (as applicable) bears only on the outer edge of the race and does not contact the

HAYNES **HiNT** *Installation of new bearing outer races is made much easier if the races are left overnight in the freezer. This causes them to contract slightly making them a looser fit. Alternatively, use a freeze spray on the races just before you install them.*

working surface. Alternatively, have the races installed by a Yamaha dealer equipped with the bearing race installation tools.
7 Only remove the lower bearing from the steering stem if a new one is being fitted. To remove the race, first thread the steering stem nut onto the top to protect the threads and position the yoke on its front for stability, then tap under it using a cold chisel to dislodge it (see illustration). Next use two screwdrivers placed on opposite sides to work the race free, using blocks of wood to improve leverage and protect the yoke (see illustration). If the race is firmly in place it will be necessary to use a puller (see illustration). Take the steering stem to a Yamaha dealer if required.
8 Where fitted remove the dust seal from the bottom of the stem and replace it with a new one. Smear the new one with grease.
9 Fit the new lower bearing onto the steering stem. Tap the new race into position using a length of tubing with an internal diameter slightly larger than the steering stem so that it locates on the inner race of the bearing (see illustration).
10 Install the steering stem (see Section 9).

11 Rear shock absorber

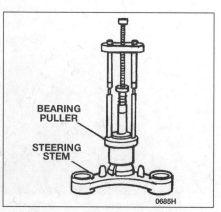

10.7c . . . or a puller if necessary

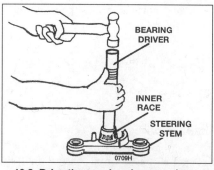

10.9 Drive the new bearing on using a suitable bearing driver or a length of pipe that bears only against the inner race and not against the rollers or cage

⚠ *Warning: Do not attempt to disassemble the shock absorber. Improper disassembly could result in serious injury. No individual components are available for it.*

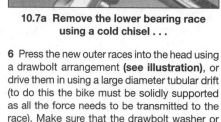
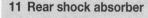

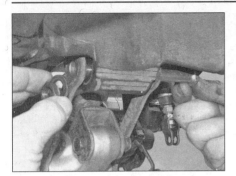

11.3 Unscrew the nut, withdraw the bolt and swing the rods down

11.4 Unscrew the nut, withdraw the bolt and swing the arm down

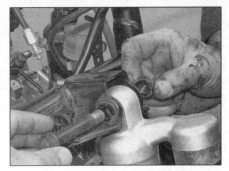

11.5a Unscrew the nut, withdraw the bolt . . .

Removal

1 Support the motorcycle using an auxiliary stand or stands so that no weight is transmitted through any part of the rear suspension – tie the front brake lever to the handlebar to ensure the bike can't roll forward. Position a support under the rear wheel or swingarm so that it does not drop when the suspension is detached, but also making sure that the weight of the machine is off the rear suspension so that it is not compressed. Note the fitted direction of all bolts.

XT models

2 On XT-R and XT-X models remove the air filter housing (see Chapter 4).
3 Unscrew the nut and remove the washer on the bolt securing the linkage rods to the swingarm. Withdraw the bolt and swing the rods down.
4 Unscrew the nut and remove the washer (where fitted) on the bolt securing the shock absorber to the linkage arm **(see illustration)**. Withdraw the bolt with its washer (where fitted) and swing the arm down off the shock absorber.
5 Unscrew the nut on the shock absorber upper mounting bolt **(see illustration)**. Support the shock then withdraw the bolt, on XT-R and XT-X models noting how the plate washer locates. Raise the swingarm and draw the shock absorber down and manoeuvre it out – on XT-Z models twist the shock so the reservoir is at the front **(see illustration)**.

11.5b . . . and remove the shock absorber

MT-03 models

6 Unscrew the crossbar bolt and remove the shaped washer, noting how it locates **(see illustration)**.
7 Unscrew the bolt securing the front of the shock absorber and remove the crossbar **(see illustration)**.
8 Unscrew the nut on the rear bolt. Withdraw the bolt and remove the shock absorber.

Inspection

9 Inspect the body of the shock absorber for obvious physical damage and the spring for looseness, cracks or signs of fatigue.
10 Inspect the damper rod for signs of bending, pitting and oil leakage **(see illustration)**.
11 On XT-Z models inspect the gas cylinder for damage.
12 Inspect the pivot bush in the top mounting

11.6 Unscrew the bolt (arrowed) and remove the special washer

for wear **(see illustration)** – it is not available as a spare part so if worn a new shock absorber must be fitted.
13 On XT models refer to Section 12 and inspect the exposed seals and bearings in the linkage arm. If there is evidence of wear, damage, dirt or corrosion remove the complete linkage assembly as described and remove the seals, clean and check the bearings and either re-grease them or fit new ones as required, then fit new seals – do not forget the linkage rod pivot in the underside of the swingarm.
14 On MT-03 models remove the collars from the swingarm mount. Check the seals and ball joint – if there is evidence of wear, damage, dirt or corrosion lever the seals out, clean and check the ball joint, making sure it moves smoothly and freely, and either re-grease it or fit a new one as required – drive the old

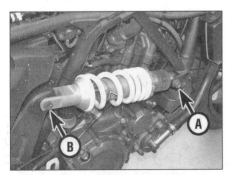

11.7 Unscrew the front bolt (A), then the rear bolt (B)

11.10 Check for signs of oil and pitting on the rod (arrowed)

11.12 Check the bush (arrowed) in the top mount

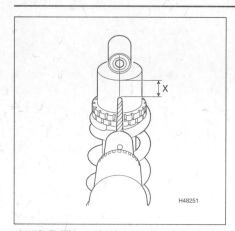

11.18 Drilling point in rear shock body for gas disposal

*X = 15 to 20 mm on XT-Z and MT-03 models,
X = 30 to 60 mm on XT-R and XT-X models*

one out using a suitable driver or socket, and draw the new one in using a drawbolt (see *Tools and Workshop Tips* in the Reference section), setting it centrally in the bore (there should 5 to 5.5 mm between it and the rim of the bore on each side). Fit new seals, pressing them in with your fingers or tapping them in if necessary.

15 Ensure that the spring pre-load adjusting ring is clean and free to rotate; inspect the indents on the ring for wear.

16 The shock cannot be dismantled for the replacement of parts. If it is worn or damaged, it must be replaced with a new one.

12.4a Fit washers between the coils as shown . . .

12.4c Unscrew the nut . . .

Installation

17 Installation is the reverse of removal, noting the following:
● Apply multi-purpose lithium grease to all pivot points and the mounting bolt shanks, and on XT models to the seal lips in the linkage arm (if not already done).
● On XT models install all components and tighten the bolts and nuts finger-tight at first, then tighten the bolts/nuts to the torque settings specified for your model at the beginning of the Chapter.
● On MT-03 models make sure the collars are fitted in the rear mount. Make sure the special washer fitted with the crossbar rear bolt is correctly positioned and rotate it clockwise so it butts correctly as the bolt is tightened. Install all components and tighten the bolts and nuts finger-tight at first, then tighten the bolts/nuts to the torque settings specified at the beginning of the Chapter, tightening the rear bolt/nut first, then the front bolt, then the crossbar bolt.

Shock absorber disposal

18 Before disposing of an old shock absorber, you should release the nitrogen gas from the top. To do this, make a drill point roughly mid-way between the upper or front mount and the top of the spring using a centre punch **(see illustration)**. Mount the shock in a vice. Drill a hole using a sharp 2 or 3 mm drill bit to release the gas – it is best to cover the shock and drill and avert your face to prevent the possibility of injury, making sure the material

12.4b . . . then unhook and remove the spring

12.4d . . . withdraw the bolt and sleeve and remove the roller

used does not get caught in the chuck as it spins.

19 If you doubt your ability to carry this out safely, take the shock to a Yamaha dealer or suspension specialist for disposal.

 Warning: Wear protective eyewear and be very careful when releasing the gas pressure – it is possible for fine debris particles to be released with it, and as the pressure is high these could damage you eyes if done carelessly.

12 Rear suspension linkage (XT models)

Removal

1 Support the motorcycle using an auxiliary stand or stands so that no weight is transmitted through any part of the rear suspension – tie the front brake lever to the handlebar to ensure the bike can't roll forward. Position a support under the rear wheel or swingarm so that it does not drop when the suspension is detached, but also making sure that the weight of the machine is off the rear suspension so that it is not compressed. Note the fitted direction of all bolts.

2 Unscrew the nuts and remove the washers on the bolts securing the linkage rods to the linkage arm and swingarm **(see illustration 11.3)**. Withdraw the bolts and remove the rods.

3 Unscrew the nut and remove the washer where fitted on the bolt securing the shock absorber to the linkage arm **(see illustration 11.4)**. Withdraw the bolt with its washer where fitted and swing the arm down off the shock absorber.

4 If a centrestand is fitted you need to remove the left-hand spring – before doing so fit lots of thick washers between the coils to keep the spring expanded, making it easier to unhook **(see illustrations)**. Now unscrew the nut (doubling as the spring hook point where fitted) on the lower chain roller, withdraw the bolt and remove the roller, noting the sleeve **(see illustrations)**.

5 Unscrew the nut, remove the washer, and withdraw the bolt securing the linkage arm to the frame and detach the arm **(see illustrations)**.

12.5a Unscrew the nut and remove the washer . . .

12.5b . . . then withdraw the bolt and remove the linkage arm

12.6a Withdraw the sleeves . . .

12.6b . . . then lever the seals out

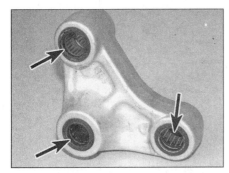

12.8 Check the bearings (arrowed) in the linkage arm and swingarm

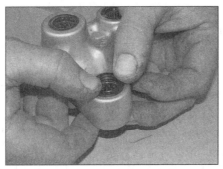

12.11a Press the new seals in . . .

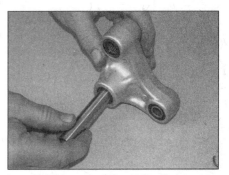

12.11b . . . then insert the sleeves

Inspection

6 Withdraw the sleeves from the bearings in each pivot of the linkage arm and from the linkage rod mount in the swingarm, noting which fits where **(see illustration)**. Lever out the bearing seals **(see illustration)**. Thoroughly clean all components with a suitable solvent, removing all traces of dirt, corrosion and grease.

7 Inspect all components closely, looking for obvious signs of wear such as heavy scoring, or for damage such as cracks or distortion. Inspect the bolt holes in the linkage plates for elongation.

8 Check the condition of the needle roller bearings in the linkage arm and in the linkage plate mounting in the swingarm **(see illustration)**. Refer to *Tools and Workshop Tips* (Section 5) in the Reference section for more information on bearings. Slip each collar back into its bearing and check that there is not an excessive amount of freeplay between the two components.

9 Worn bearings can be drifted or drawn out of their bores, but note that once removed needle bearings cannot be reused; new bearings should be obtained before work commences. Before removing any bearing or bush measure and note its set depth in the bore. The new bearings should be pressed or drawn into their bores rather than driven into position. In the absence of a press, a suitable drawbolt tool can be made up as described in *Tools and Workshop Tips* in the Reference section. When fitting the new bearings make sure they

are central in their bores, and where there are two bearings in the same bore make sure the set depth is equal on each side – on XT-R and XT-X models the needle bearing for the shock absorber mount should be recessed by 4 to 5 mm from the rim of the bore, and the bearings in the other mounts, including the swingarm, by 7.2 to 8.2 mm; on XT-Z models the needle bearings in the frame mount of the linkage arm should be recessed by 3.5 to 4 mm from the rim of the bore, the bearing in the shock absorber mount by 4.5 mm, and the bearings for the linkage rods in the arm and swingarm by 5 mm.

10 Lubricate the needle bearings, sleeves and seals with multi-purpose lithium grease.

11 Press the new seals squarely into place with the marked side facing out **(see illustration)**. Fit the sleeves **(see illustration)**.

13.3 Chainguard bolts (arrowed) – XT-X shown

Installation

12 Installation is the reverse of removal, noting the following:
● If not already done, withdraw the sleeves from the arm and the linkage rod mount in the swingarm then clean the seals and needle bearings and apply lithium-based grease **(see illustration 12.11b)**.
● Install all nuts and bolts finger-tight only until all components are in position, then tighten the nuts to the torque setting specified for your model at the beginning of the Chapter.

13 Swingarm

Removal

1 Support the motorcycle using an auxiliary stand or stands so that no weight is transmitted through any part of the rear suspension – tie the front brake lever to the handlebar to ensure the bike can't roll forward. Position a support under the rear wheel or swingarm so that it does not drop when the suspension is detached, but also making sure that the weight of the machine is off the rear suspension so that it is not compressed. Note the fitted direction of all bolts.

2 Remove the rear wheel (see Chapter 6).

XT-R and XT-X models

3 Undo the bolts securing the chainguard and remove it, noting how it fits **(see illustration)**.

13.4 Unscrew the bolts (arrowed) to free the brake hose

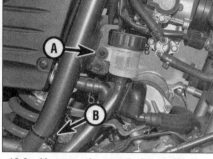

13.6a Unscrew the reservoir bolt (A) and cut the cable-tie (B)

13.6b Unscrew the bolts (arrowed) and displace the assembly

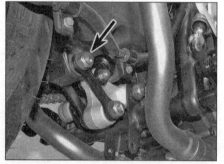

13.7 Unscrew the nut (arrowed), withdraw the bolt and detach the rods

13.10 Unscrew the bolt (arrowed) to free the brake hose

4 Free the brake hose from the swingarm (see illustration). Secure the caliper clear.

5 Check the heel plate fitted on the left-hand side of the bike – on early models it partially covers the swingarm pivot cap, in which case remove it.

6 Unscrew the rear master cylinder reservoir bolt (see illustration). Cut the cable-tie securing the rear brake light switch wire to the frame. Unscrew the right-hand footrest bracket bolts and displace the footrest/brake

pedal/master cylinder assembly, supporting it clear of the swingarm pivot and making sure no strain is placed on the brake hose or switch wiring (see illustration).

7 Unscrew the nut and remove the washer on the bolt securing the linkage rods to the swingarm (see illustration). Withdraw the bolt and swing the rods down off the arm.

8 Remove the cap from each end of the swingarm pivot. Unscrew the swingarm pivot bolt nut (see illustration 13.13a). Withdraw the pivot bolt, then manoeuvre the swingarm out of the frame (see illustration 13.13b). Note the nut is self-locking and Yamaha specify to use a new one.

9 If required unscrew the chain slider bolt, noting the collar, and remove the slider from the front of the swingarm. Check the condition of the slider and replace it with a new one if necessary. Also check the chain roller guides fitted on the frame.

XT-Z models

10 Free the brake hose from the swingarm (see illustration).

11 Undo the screws securing the chainguard and remove it, noting how it fits (see illustrations). Release the trim clips securing the splash guard (see illustrations).

12 Unscrew the nut and remove the washer on the bolt securing the linkage rods to the swingarm (see illustration 11.3). Withdraw the bolt and swing the rods down off the arm.

13 Unscrew the swingarm pivot bolt nut (see illustration). Withdraw the pivot bolt with its

13.11a Unscrew the bolt (arrowed) at the back . . .

13.11b . . . and the two (arrowed) at the front to release the guard

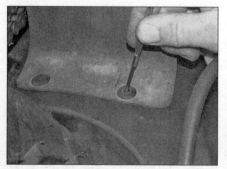

13.11c Push the centre of the trim clip in . . .

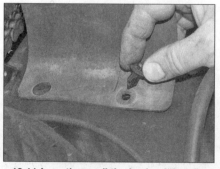

13.11d . . . then pull the body of the clip out

13.13a Unscrew the nut (arrowed) . . .

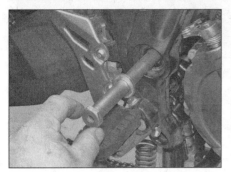

13.13b . . . then withdraw the pivot bolt

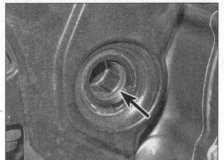

13.13c Turn the adjuster (arrowed) anti-clockwise . . .

13.13d . . . using a 15 mm hex key if available or 15 mm nut/bolt arrangement as shown . . .

13.13e . . . then remove the swingarm

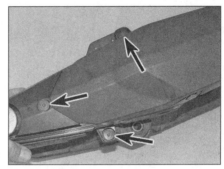

13.14a Undo the screws (arrowed) . . .

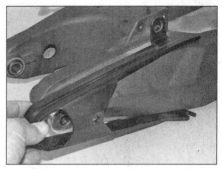

13.14b . . . and remove the chain slider

washer (see illustration). Using a 15 mm hex key or nut/bolt arrangement turn the adjuster bolt in the right-hand side of the frame anti-clockwise to back it off the swingarm, then manoeuvre the swingarm out of the frame (see illustrations). Note the pivot bolt nut is self-locking and Yamaha specify to use a new one.

14 If required undo the chain slider screws and remove the slider from the front of the swingarm (see illustrations). Check the condition of the slider and replace it with a

new one if necessary. Also check the chain roller guides fitted on the frame.

MT-03 models

15 Remove the rear shock absorber (see Section 11).
16 Undo the screws securing the chainguard/rear hugger, noting the collars, and remove it, noting how it fits (see illustrations).
17 Free the brake hose from the swingarm (see illustration).
18 Displace the sidestand switch, then unscrew the sidestand bracket bolts and

13.16a Undo the screw (arrowed) on the underside . . .

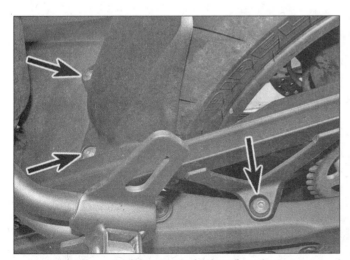

13.16b . . . and the screws (arrowed) on the top

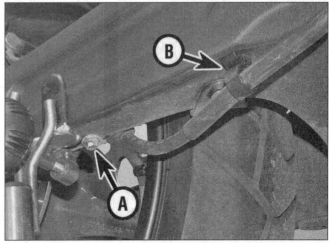

13.17 Unscrew the bolt (A) and release the clip (B)

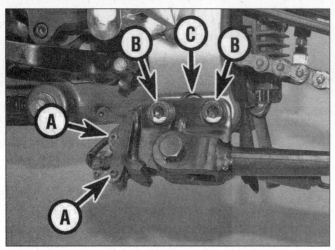

13.18 Unscrew the bolts (A) and displace the switch, then the bolts (B) and remove the stand, to access the bolt (C)

13.19a Unscrew the nut (arrowed), remove the washer and draw the bracket off

remove the stand **(see illustration)**. Unscrew the footrest bracket bolt.

19 Unscrew the swingarm pivot bolt nut and remove the washer **(see illustration)**. Remove the footrest bracket assembly, noting the spacer between the bottom and the frame. Withdraw the pivot bolt with its washer, then manoeuvre the swingarm out of the frame **(see illustration)**. Note the nut is self-locking and Yamaha specify to use a new one.

20 If required undo the chain slider screws and remove the slider from the front of the swingarm. Check the condition of the slider and replace it with a new one if necessary.

Inspection

21 Remove the pivot cap from each side, noting the seal on XT models or the washer on MT-03 models **(see illustration)**.

22 Thoroughly clean the swingarm, removing all traces of dirt, corrosion and grease.

23 Inspect the swingarm closely, looking for obvious signs of wear such as heavy scoring, and cracks or distortion due to accident damage.

24 Withdraw the sleeves from the pivots and check the pivot components (bearings, bushes and grease seals as fitted, according

to model) **(see illustrations)**. If necessary replace any worn components with new ones. First lever out the old grease seals where fitted **(see illustration)**.

25 Worn bearings and bushes can be driven or drawn out of their bores, but note that once removed needle bearings cannot be re-used; new parts should be obtained before work commences. Before removing any bearing or bush measure and note its set depth in the bore. The new bearings should be pressed or drawn into their bores rather than driven into position. In the absence of a press, a suitable drawbolt tool can be made up as described in *Tools and Workshop Tips* in the Reference section. Set each bearing and bush as noted on removal of the old ones – on XT-R and XT-X models the needle bearings should be recessed by 4 mm from the rim of the bore, and the bushes by 8 mm; on XT-Z models the needle bearings should be recessed by 12 mm from the rim of the bore, and the bushes by 8 mm; on MT-03 models the needle bearings should be recessed by 9 mm from the rim of the bore.

26 Lubricate the needle bearings, collars and seals with multi-purpose lithium grease.

27 Press the new seals squarely into place with the marked side facing out

13.19b Withdraw the pivot bolt (arrowed) and remove the swingarm

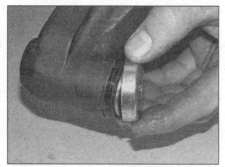

13.21 Remove the pivot cap, noting the seal or washer according to model

13.24a Withdraw the sleeves . . .

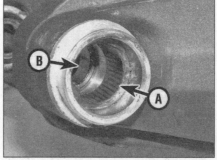

13.24b . . . and check the bearings (A) and bushes (B) as fitted

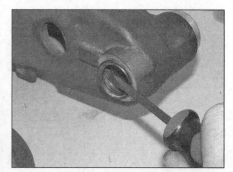

13.24c Lever the grease seals out

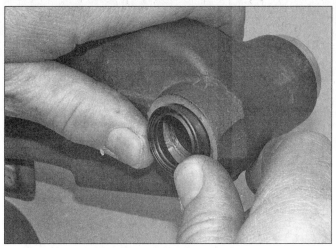

13.27a Fit new grease seals . . .

13.27b . . . and on XT models new pivot cap seals

13.29a Initially insert the bolt from the left . . .

13.29b . . . to support the arm while tightening the adjuster bolt

(see illustration). Insert the sleeves (see illustration 13.24a). On XT models fit new pivot cap seals if necessary (see illustration).

28 Check the swingarm pivot bolt is straight by rolling it on a flat surface such as a piece of plate glass (first wipe off all old grease and remove any corrosion using wire wool). Replace the bolt with a new one if it is bent.

Installation

29 Installation is the reverse of removal, noting the following:
- If not already done, withdraw the sleeves then clean the seals and needle bearings and bushes as fitted according to model and apply lithium-based grease (see illustrations 13.24a and b).
- On XT-Z models position the swingarm in the frame then slide the pivot bolt in from the left far enough to support it, but not the whole way through so you can get a tool in the adjuster bolt (see illustration 13.29a). Tighten the adjuster bolt to the torque setting specified at the beginning of

the Chapter (see illustration 13.29b). Now withdraw the pivot bolt from the left and slide it back through from the right (see illustration 13.13b).
- Use a new self-locking nut on the pivot bolt and tighten it to the torque setting specified at the beginning of the Chapter (see illustration 13.29c).
- On XT models tighten the suspension

13.29c Use a new self-locking nut

linkage rod bolt/nut to the torque setting specified for your model.
- On XT-R and XT-X models tighten the right-hand footrest bracket bolts to the specified torque setting.
- On MT-03 models refer to Section 11 to install the shock absorber. Tighten the footrest bracket bolt and sidestand bracket bolts to the specified torque settings – first the clean the bolts threads, then apply some fresh threadlock.

14 Suspension adjustment

Note: Refer to the Owner's Manual supplied with the machine for recommended front and rear suspension settings to suit loading.
Caution: Never attempt to turn an adjuster beyond the minimum or maximum setting.

14.2 Fork pre-load adjuster (arrowed) –
XT-Z

14.4a Shock absorber pre-load adjuster
(arrowed) – XT-R and XT-X

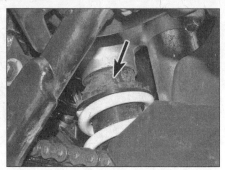

14.4b Shock absorber pre-load adjuster
(arrowed) – XT-Z

14.6 Loosen the locking ring (A) then turn
the adjuster ring (B)

Front forks – XT-Z models

1 The front forks are adjustable for spring pre-load.
2 Spring pre-load is adjusted using a suitable hex key in the adjuster on the top of each fork **(see illustration)**. The amount of pre-load is indicated by the number of turns out anti-clockwise from the fully turned in (maximum pre-load) position. The standard position is 22 full turns out anti-clockwise. The maximum number of turns out (minimum pre-load) is 27. Turn the adjuster clockwise to increase pre-load, and anti-clockwise to decrease it. Always make sure both adjusters are set equally.

Rear shock absorber

XT models

3 The rear shock absorber is adjustable for spring pre-load.
4 Spring pre-load is adjusted using a suitable C-spanner (one is provided in the bike's toolkit) to turn the adjuster ring on the top of the shock absorber **(see illustrations)**. There are five positions on XT-R and XT-X models and nine positions on XT-Z models. Position 1 is the minimum setting, position 4 is the standard setting, and position 5 or 9 (according to model) is the maximum. Align the setting required with the adjustment stopper.

MT-03 models

5 The rear shock absorber is adjustable for spring pre-load. The rear wheel must be raised off the ground using an auxiliary stand. Tie the front brake lever to the handlebar to prevent the bike rolling forwards.
6 Spring pre-load is adjusted by loosening the locking ring on the front of the shock absorber then turning the adjuster ring using the tool provided in the toolkit or a suitable equivalent **(see illustration)**. Thread the adjuster ring towards the rear of the shock absorber (compressing the spring) to increase pre-load and to the front of the shock absorber to decrease it. The amount of pre-load is measured in terms of the installed length of the spring. The maximum length of the spring (or minimum amount of pre-load) should not be more than 174.5 mm. The standard length is 170 mm. The minimum length of the spring (or maximum amount of pre-load) should not be less than 165.5 mm. Tighten the locking ring securely against the adjuster ring after making an adjustment.

Chapter 6
Brakes, wheels and final drive

Contents

	Section
Brake fluid level check . . . . see *Pre-ride checks*	
Brake hoses and fittings.	10
Brake light switches . . . . see Chapter 8	
Brake pad wear check . . . . see Chapter 1	
Brake system bleeding and fluid change.	11
Brake system check. . . . . see Chapter 1	
Drive chain	18
Drive chain check, adjustment, cleaning and lubrication see Chapter 1	
Front brake caliper(s)	3
Front brake disc(s)	4
Front brake master cylinder	5
Front brake pads	2
Front wheel.	14
General information	1
Rear brake caliper	7
Rear brake disc	8
Rear brake master cylinder	9
Rear brake pads.	6
Rear sprocket coupling/rubber dampers	20
Rear wheel	15
Sprockets.	19
Tyres	17
Tyre pressure, tread depth and condition. . . . . . . see *Pre-ride checks*	
Wheel bearing check . . . . see Chapter 1	
Wheel bearings.	16
Wheel alignment check	13
Wheel check. . . . . see Chapter 1	
Wheel inspection and repair.	12

Degrees of difficulty

Easy, suitable for novice with little experience 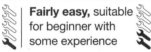	Fairly easy, suitable for beginner with some experience	Fairly difficult, suitable for competent DIY mechanic	Difficult, suitable for experienced DIY mechanic	Very difficult, suitable for expert DIY or professional

Specifications

Front brake

Brake fluid type	DOT 4
Brake pad friction material minimum thickness.	1.0 mm
Caliper bore ID	
XT-R models	32 and 30 mm
XT-X models	34 and 30 mm
XT-Z models	28 mm
MT-03 models.	30.16 and 25.40 mm
Master cylinder bore ID	
XT-R and XT-X models	12.7 mm
XT-Z and MT-03	16.0 mm
Disc thickness	
XT models	
Standard.	4.5 mm
Service limit (min)	4.0 mm
MT-03 models	
Standard.	5.0 mm
Service limit (min)	4.5 mm
Disc maximum runout	
XT-R and XT-X models	0.15 mm
XT-Z and MT-03 models	0.10 mm

Rear brake

Brake fluid type	DOT 4
Brake pad friction material minimum thickness.	1.0 mm
Caliper bore ID	34 mm
Master cylinder bore ID	12.7 mm
Disc thickness	
Standard.	5.0 mm
Service limit (min)	4.5 mm
Disc maximum runout	0.15 mm

Wheels

Maximum wheel runout (front and rear)
  XT-R and XT-X models
    Axial (side-to-side) . . . . 2.0 mm
    Radial (out-of-round). . . . . 2.0 mm
  XT-Z models
    Axial (side-to-side) . . . . 0.8 mm
    Radial (out-of-round). . . . . 1.2 mm
  MT-03 models
    Axial (side-to-side) . . . . 0.5 mm
    Radial (out-of-round). . . . . 1.0 mm
Maximum axle runout (front and rear) . . . . 0.25 mm

Tyres

Tyre pressures . . . . see *Pre-ride* checks
Tyre sizes*
  XT-R
    Front . . . . 90/90-21M/C 54S or 54T tubed
    Rear . . . . 130/80-17M/C 65S or 65T tubed
  XT-X
    Front . . . . 120/70-R17M/C 58H or 120/70-ZR17M/C 58W tubed
    Rear . . . . 160/60-R17M/C 69H or 160/60-ZR17M/C 69W tubed
  XT-Z
    Front . . . . 90/90-21M/C 54S or 54T tubed
    Rear . . . . 130/80-17M/C 65S or 65T tubed
  MT-03
    Front . . . . 120/70-ZR17M/C 58W or 120/70-R17M/C 58H, tubeless
    Rear . . . . 160/60-ZR17M/C 69W or 160/60-R17M/C 69H, tubeless
Refer to the owners handbook or the tyre information label on the swingarm for approved tyre brands.

Final drive

Drive chain slack and lubricant . . . . see Chapter 1
Drive chain type
  XT-R and XT-X models . . . . DAIDO DID520VP (110 links)
  XT-Z models . . . . Regina 520 ZRA (110 links)
  MT-03 models. . . . . Regina 520 ZRA (112 links)
Sprocket sizes (No. of teeth)
  XT models
    Front (engine) sprocket. 15
    Rear (wheel) sprocket. 45
  MT-03 models
    Front (engine) sprocket. 15
    Rear (wheel) sprocket. 47

Torque settings

Brake caliper bleed valves
  XT models. . . . . 14 Nm
  MT-03 models
    Front caliper . . . . 6 Nm
    Rear caliper. . . . . 14 Nm
Brake disc bolts
  XT-R and XT-X models
    Front disc . . . . 23 Nm
    Rear disc. . . . . 13 Nm
  XT-Z models
    Front discs . . . . 18 Nm
    Rear disc. . . . . 14 Nm
  MT-03 models
    Front discs . . . . 18 Nm
    Rear disc. . . . . 30 Nm
Brake hose banjo bolts. . . . . 30 Nm
Brake light switch – XT-Z and MT-03 models. . . . . 24 Nm
Front axle
  XT-R and XT-X models . . . . 59 Nm
  XT-Z models . . . . 60 Nm
  MT-03 models. . . . . 72 Nm

Torque settings (continued)

Front axle clamp bolt(s)
XT-R and XT-X models . . . . 18 Nm
XT-Z models . . . . 18 Nm
MT-03 models . . . . 14 Nm
Front caliper mounting bolts
XT-R and XT-Z models . . . . 40 Nm
XT-X models . . . . 40 Nm
MT-03 models . . . . 40 Nm
Front caliper slider bolts – MT-03 models . . . . 40 Nm
Front master cylinder clamp bolts
XT models . . . . 7 Nm
MT-03 models . . . . 10 Nm
Front sprocket cover bolts . . . . 10 Nm
Front sprocket nut . . . . 120 Nm
Rear axle nut
XT models . . . . 105 Nm
MT-03 models . . . . 150 Nm
Rear master cylinder bolts . . . . 23 Nm
Rear sprocket nuts . . . . 70 Nm

1 General information

All models have hydraulic brake systems at the front and the rear.

XT660-R models have a twin piston sliding caliper at the front and a single piston sliding caliper at the rear.

XT660-X models have a four opposed-piston caliper at the front and a single piston sliding caliper at the rear.

XT660-Z and MT-03 models have two twin piston sliding calipers at the front and a single piston sliding caliper at the rear.

The drive to the rear wheel is by chain and sprockets.

All XT models have steel spoked wheels with tubed tyres. MT-03 models have cast alloy wheels with tubeless tyres.

Caution: Disc brake components rarely require disassembly. Do not disassemble components unless absolutely necessary. If an hydraulic brake hose is loosened or disconnected, the union sealing washers must be replaced with new ones and the system bled upon reassembly. Do not use solvents on internal brake components. Solvents will cause the seals to swell and distort. Use only clean brake fluid of the correct type for cleaning. Use care when working with brake fluid as it can injure your eyes and it will damage painted surfaces and plastic parts.

2 Front brake pads

Warning: The dust created by the brake system is harmful to your health. Never blow it out with compressed air and don't inhale any of it. An approved filtering mask should be worn when working on the brakes.
Note: Do not operate the brake lever while the pads are out of the caliper.
1 For greater freedom of movement release the brake hose guide from the fork **(see illustrations)**.

2.1a On XT-R and XT-X unscrew the bolts (arrowed)

2.1b On XT-Z unscrew the bolt (arrowed)

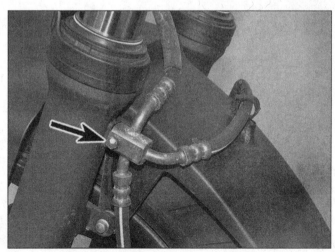
2.1c On MT-03 unscrew the bolt (arrowed)

2.2a Unscrew the bolts (arrowed) and slide the caliper off the disc

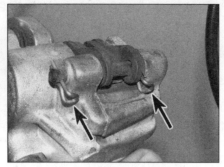

2.2b Remove the clips (arrowed) . . .

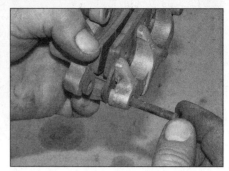

2.2c . . . then withdraw the pin . . .

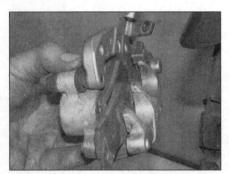

2.2d . . . and remove the pads

2.2e Slide the caliper off the bracket

2 On XT-R and XT-Z models unscrew the caliper mounting bolts and slide the caliper off the disc **(see illustration)**. Remove the clips securing the pad pin **(see illustration)**. Withdraw the pin and remove the pads **(see illustrations)**. Slide the caliper off the bracket **(see illustration)**.

3 On XT-X models unscrew the caliper mounting bolts and slide the caliper off the disc **(see illustration)**. Remove the clips securing the pad pins **(see illustration)**. Withdraw the pins and remove the pad spring and the pads **(see illustrations)**.

4 On MT-03 models unscrew the caliper slider bolts **(see illustration)**. Lift the caliper up off the bracket. Remove the pads from the bracket, noting how they fit **(see illustration)**.

2.3a Unscrew the bolts (arrowed) and slide the caliper off the disc

2.3b Remove the clips (arrowed) . . .

2.3c . . . then withdraw the pins and remove the spring (arrowed) . . .

2.3d . . . and remove the pads

2.4a Unscrew the bolts (arrowed) and lift the caliper off . . .

2.4b . . . and remove the pads

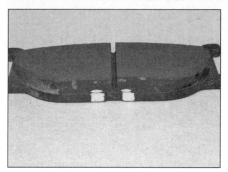

2.5 Check the surface of the friction material and the extent of wear

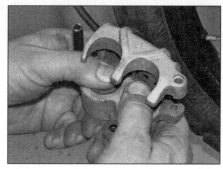

2.9a Push the piston(s) in using one of the methods described . . .

2.9b . . . or using a purpose built commercial tool

5 Inspect the surface of each pad for contamination and check that the friction material has not worn beyond its service limit (see Chapter 1, Section 10) **(see illustration)**. If either pad is worn down to, or beyond, the service limit wear indicator, is fouled with oil or grease, or heavily scored or damaged, fit a set of new pads. If required measure the thickness of the friction material to determine the extent of wear – the service limit is 1 mm. **Note:** *It is not possible to degrease the friction material; if the pads are contaminated in any way they must be replaced with new ones.*

6 If the pads are in good condition clean them carefully, using a fine wire brush which is completely free of oil and grease to remove all traces of road dirt and corrosion. Using a pointed instrument, dig out any embedded particles of foreign matter. If required, spray with a dedicated brake cleaner to remove any dust.

7 Check the condition of the brake disc(s) (see Section 4).

8 Remove all traces of corrosion from the pad pin(s) and check for wear and damage. Fit new ones if necessary.

9 Clean around the exposed section of the pistons to remove any dirt or debris that could cause the seals to be damaged. If new pads are being fitted, now push the pistons all the way back into the caliper to create room for them; if the old pads are still serviceable push the pistons in a little way. To push the pistons back use finger pressure or a piece of wood as leverage, or place the old pads back in the

caliper and use a metal bar or a screwdriver inserted between them, or use grips and a piece of wood, with rag or card to protect the caliper body **(see illustration)**. Alternatively obtain a proper piston-pushing tool from a good tool supplier **(see illustration)**. If there is too much brake fluid in the reservoir It may be necessary to remove the master cylinder reservoir cover, plate and diaphragm and siphon some out (see *Pre-ride) checks*. If a piston is difficult to push back, remove the bleed valve cap, then attach a length of clear hose to the bleed valve and place the open end in a suitable container, then open the valve and try again (see Section 11). Take great care not to draw any air into the system. If in doubt, bleed the brake afterwards.

10 If a piston appears seized, apply the brake lever and check whether the piston

in question moves at all – first block or hold the other piston(s) using wood or cable-ties. If the piston moves out but can't be pushed back in the chances are there is some hidden corrosion stopping it. If it doesn't move at all, or to fully clean and inspect the pistons, disassemble the caliper and overhaul it (see Section 3).

11 On XT-R, XT-Z and MT-03 models clean off all traces of corrosion and hardened grease from the slider pins and from their rubber boots **(see illustrations)**. Replace the boots with new ones if they are damaged, deformed or deteriorated. On XT-R and XT-Z models make sure each slider pin is tight. Apply a smear of silicone-based grease to the boots and slider pins. Make sure the pad guide(s) and pad spring are correctly located on the bracket **(see illustrations)**.

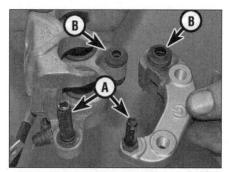

2.11a Slider pins (A) and their boots (B) – XT-R and XT-Z

2.11b Slider pin boots (arrowed) – MT-03

2.11c Make sure the pad guide(s) (arrowed) . . .

2.11d . . . and pad spring (XT-R and Z) . . .

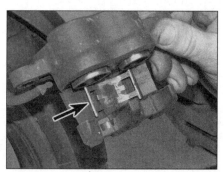

2.11e . . . are correctly in place (MT-03)

2.12a Make sure the pad locates correctly against the guide

2.12b Slide the caliper onto the disc and fit the bolts

14 On MT-03 models smear some copper grease onto the back of each pad. Fit the pads into the bracket with the friction material facing each side of the disc, making sure they locate correctly against the guides **(see illustrations)**. Slide the caliper onto the bracket and over the pads **(see illustration)**. Fit the slider bolts and tighten them to the torque setting specified at the beginning of the Chapter.
15 Fit the brake hose guide **(see illustration 2.1a, b or c)**.
16 Operate the brake lever until the pads contact with the disc. Check the level of fluid in the hydraulic reservoir and top-up if necessary (see *Pre-ride checks*).
17 Check the operation of the front brake before riding the motorcycle.

12 On XT-R and XT-Z models slide the caliper onto the bracket, making sure each boot seats correctly around the base of its pin **(see illustration 2.2e)**. Smear some copper grease onto the back of each pad and the pad retaining pins. Fit the pads, making sure they locate correctly against the guide on the bracket **(see illustration)**. Press the pads up against the spring to align the holes and insert the pad pin **(see illustration 2.2c)**. Secure the pin with the clips **(see illustration 2.2b)**. Slide the caliper onto the disc making sure the pads locate correctly on each side **(see illustration)**. Fit the caliper mounting bolts and

tighten them to the torque setting specified at the beginning of the Chapter.
13 On XT-X models smear some copper grease onto the back of each pad and to the pad retaining pins. Fit the pads into the caliper, then fit the spring with the arrow pointing in the direction of normal disc rotation **(see illustrations)**. Insert the pins and secure them with the clips **(see illustrations 2.3c and b)**. Slide the caliper onto the disc making sure the pads locate correctly on each side. Fit the caliper mounting bolts and tighten them to the torque setting specified at the beginning of the Chapter **(see illustration 2.3a)**.

3 Front brake caliper(s)

Note: *Brake caliper seals and pistons are only available for MT-03 models – on XT models if a piston has seized or if there is fluid leaking past the seals a new caliper must be installed.*

⚠️ *Warning: If a caliper is being completely removed, or on MT-03 models if a caliper is in need of*

2.13a Fit the pads . . .

2.13b . . . then fit the spring with the arrow pointing in the direction of rotation

2.14a Fit the pads . . .

2.14b . . . making sure they seat correctly against the brackets

2.14c Fit the caliper over the pads and fit the bolts

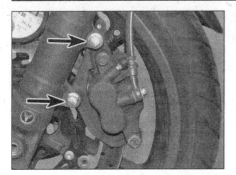

3.1 Unscrew the bolts (arrowed) and slide the caliper assembly off the disc

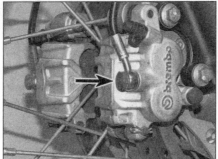

3.2a Brake hose banjo bolt (arrowed) – XT-R and XT-Z

3.2b Brake hose banjo bolt (arrowed) – XT-X

an overhaul, it is best to drain all old brake fluid from the system, then fill with new fluid after the overhaul (see Section 11). On MT-03 models overhaul of the brake calipers must be done in a spotlessly clean work area to avoid contamination and possible failure of the brake hydraulic system components. Do not, under any circumstances, use petroleum-based solvents to clean brake parts. Use clean DOT 4 brake fluid, dedicated brake cleaner or denatured alcohol only, as described. To prevent damage from spilled brake fluid, always cover paintwork when working on the braking system.

Removal

Note: *Do not operate the brake lever while the caliper is off the disc.*

1 If the caliper is just being displaced from the forks as part of the wheel removal procedure release the brake hose guide from the fork to give more freedom of movement **(see illustration 2.1a, b or c)**, then unscrew the mounting bolts and slide the caliper off the disc **(see illustration 2.2a or 2.3a for XT models and 3.1 for MT-03)**. Tie the caliper back out of the way.

2 If the caliper is being completely removed, or on MT-03 models overhauled, unscrew the brake hose banjo bolt and detach the banjo union, noting its alignment with the caliper **(see illustrations)**. If the brake fluid has not been drained seal the banjo union – a good way of doing this is to place a piece of rubber over each side of the union (we used some

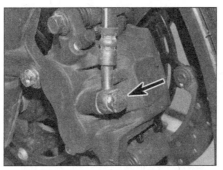

3.2c Brake hose banjo bolt (arrowed) – MT-03

3.2d Using a spring clamp and rubber caps to prevent fluid loss

rubber blanking caps), and clamp them in place using a spring clamp **(see illustration)**. Alternatively wrap plastic foodwrap around the banjo union and secure the hose in an upright position to minimise fluid loss. Discard the sealing washers, as new ones must be fitted on reassembly.

3 Unscrew the caliper mounting bolts and slide the caliper off the disc **(see illustration 2.2a or 2.3a for XT models and 3.1 for MT-03)**.

4 If required remove the brake pads (see Section 2, Step 2, 3 or 4 according to model).

Overhaul – MT-03 models

Note: *If the caliper is being overhauled (usually due to sticking piston(s) or fluid leaks) read through the entire procedure first and make sure that you have obtained all the new parts required, including some new DOT 4 brake fluid.*

5 Clean the exterior of the caliper and bracket with denatured alcohol or brake system cleaner. Have some clean rag ready to catch any spilled brake fluid. Clean off all traces of corrosion. Clean off any hardened grease from the slider pins and their rubber boots. Replace the boots with new ones if they are damaged, deformed or deteriorated **(see illustration)**.

6 Make sure the bleed valve is tight. To remove the pistons, cover them and the caliper with rag and apply compressed air gradually and progressively, starting with a fairly low pressure, to the fluid inlet in the caliper and allow the pistons to ease out of the bores **(see illustrations)**. If one is being pushed out before the other, you may need to block that one so more pressure is applied to the sticking one, but do not use your fingers. Always make sure the caliper is covered, with the pistons pointing down onto the bench so they cannot fly out and hit something.

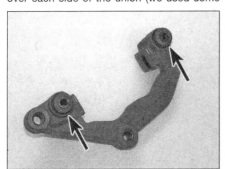

3.5 Replace the boots (arrowed) with new ones if necessary

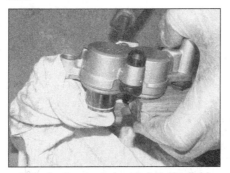

3.6a Apply compressed air to the fluid passage . . .

3.6b . . . until the piston is displaced

3.8 Remove the seals and discard them

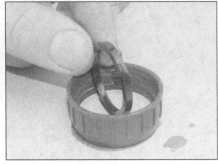

3.11a Lubricate the new piston seal with brake fluid . . .

3.11b . . . then fit it into its groove . . .

3.12 . . . followed by the new dust seal

7 If a piston is stuck in its bore due to corrosion, find a suitable bolt to block the fluid inlet banjo bolt bore and thread it in, then unscrew the bleed valve and apply the air via the bleed valve bore in the caliper (its narrower passage will allow more air pressure to be applied to the piston). Do not try to remove a piston by levering it out or by using pliers or other grips. If the piston has completely seized you may have to replace the caliper with a new one.

8 Note that two sizes of piston are used in each caliper (see Specifications at the beginning of this Chapter) – mark each piston and the caliper body to ensure that the pistons (if being reused) can be matched to their

original bores on reassembly. Remove the dust seals and the piston seals from the piston bores using a soft wooden or plastic tool to avoid scratching the bores **(see illustration)**. Discard the seals as new ones must be fitted.

9 Clean the pistons and bores with clean brake fluid. If compressed air is available, blow it through the fluid galleries in the caliper to ensure they are clear (make sure it is filtered and unlubricated).

Caution: Do not, under any circumstances, use a petroleum-based solvent to clean brake parts.

10 Inspect the caliper bores and pistons for signs of corrosion, nicks and burrs and loss of plating. If surface defects are present, the pistons and/or the caliper assembly must be replaced with new ones.

11 Lubricate the new piston seals with new brake fluid and fit them into the inner (large) grooves in the caliper bores **(see illustrations)**. Note that there are two sizes of bore in each caliper and care must therefore be taken to ensure that the correct size seals are fitted to the correct bores (see Specifications). The same applies when fitting the new dust seals and pistons.

12 Lubricate the new dust seals with new brake fluid and fit them into the outer grooves in the caliper bores **(see illustration)**.

13 Lubricate the pistons with new brake fluid

and fit them, closed-end first, into the caliper bores, taking care not to displace the seals **(see illustration)**. Using your thumbs, push the pistons squarely all the way in.

14 Apply a smear of silicone-based grease to the boots and slider pins **(see illustration 3.5)**.

Installation

15 If removed, install the brake pads (see Section 2, Step 5-on, as required).

16 Slide the caliper onto the brake disc, making sure the pads locate correctly on each side **(see illustration 2.12b)**. Install the caliper mounting bolts and tighten them to the torque setting specified at the beginning of the Chapter.

17 If detached, connect the brake hose to the caliper, using new sealing washers on each side of the banjo fitting **(see illustration)**. Locate the hose elbow between or against the lug(s) on the caliper where present according to model **(see illustration 3.2a, b or c)**. Tighten the banjo bolt to the specified torque setting.

18 Fit the brake hose guide **(see illustration 2.1a, b or c)**.

19 Top up the hydraulic reservoir with DOT 4 brake fluid (see *Pre-ride checks*) and bleed the system as described in Section 11. Check that there are no fluid leaks and test the operation of the brake before riding the motorcycle.

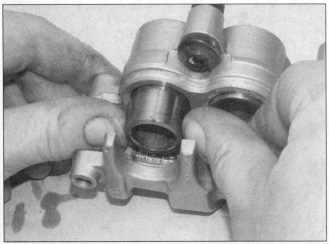

3.13 Fit the piston and push it all the way in

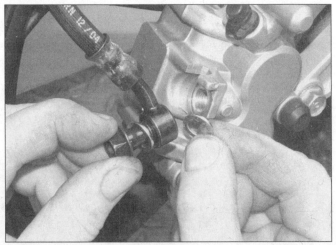

3.17 Always use new sealing washers and align the hose as noted on removal

4.2 Measure the thickness of the disc

4.3 Checking disc runout with a dial gauge

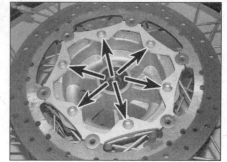

4.5 Brake disc bolts (arrowed) –
XT-Z shown

4 Front brake disc(s)

Inspection

1 Inspect the surface of the disc for score marks and other damage. Light scratches are normal after use and won't affect brake operation, but deep grooves and heavy score marks will reduce braking efficiency and accelerate pad wear. If a disc is badly grooved it must be replaced with a new one.
2 The disc must not be machined or allowed to wear down to a thickness less than the service limit as listed in this Chapter's Specifications. The minimum thickness may also be stamped on the disc. Check the thickness of the disc in the middle of the pad contact area using a micrometer **(see illustration)** – do not measure across the rim of the disc with a ruler. Replace the disc with a new one if necessary, noting that both discs should be renewed on XT-Z and MT-03 models with two front discs.
3 To check if the disc is warped, position the bike on an auxiliary stand with the front wheel raised off the ground. Mount a dial gauge to the fork leg, with the gauge plunger touching the surface of the disc about 10 mm from the outer edge **(see illustration)**. Rotate the wheel and watch the gauge needle, comparing the reading with the limit listed in the Specifications at the beginning of this Chapter. If the runout is greater than the service limit, check the wheel bearings for

play (see Chapter 1). If the bearings are worn, install new ones (see Section 16) and repeat this check. If the disc runout is still excessive, remove the disc (Steps 4 and 5) and check for corrosion where it seats on the hub and clean it up if necessary. You can also try moving the disc around the wheel one bolt hole at a time and after each movement rechecking for runout. In most cases a new disc will have to be fitted.

Removal

4 Remove the wheel (see Section 14).
Caution: Don't lay the wheel down and allow it to rest on the disc – the disc could become warped. Set the wheel on wood blocks so the wheel rim supports the weight of the wheel.
5 If you are not replacing the disc with a new one, mark the relationship of the disc to the wheel, so it can be installed in the same position. Unscrew the disc bolts, loosening them evenly and a little at a time in a criss-cross pattern to avoid distorting the disc, then remove the disc **(see illustration)**.

Installation

6 Before installing the disc, make sure there is no dirt or corrosion where it seats on the hub. If the disc does not sit flat when it is bolted down, it will appear to be warped when checked or when the front brake is used.
7 Fit the disc onto the wheel with its marked side facing out, aligning the previously applied matchmarks (if you're reinstalling the original disc), and making sure the arrow points in the direction of normal rotation.

8 Clean the threads of the disc mounting bolts, then apply a suitable non-permanent thread locking compound. Fit the bolts and tighten them evenly and a little at a time in a criss-cross pattern to the torque setting specified at the beginning of this Chapter. Clean the disc using acetone or brake system cleaner. If a new disc has been fitted, remove any protective coating from its working surfaces and fit new brake pads.
9 Install the front wheel (see Section 14).
10 Check the operation of the brake before riding the motorcycle.

5 Front brake master cylinder

⚠ *Warning: If the brake master cylinder is in need of an overhaul it is best to drain all old brake fluid from the system, then fill with new fluid after the overhaul (see Section 11). Overhaul must be done in a spotlessly clean work area to avoid contamination and possible failure of the brake hydraulic system components. Do not, under any circumstances, use petroleum-based solvents to clean brake parts. Use clean DOT 4 brake fluid, dedicated brake cleaner or denatured alcohol only, as described. To prevent damage from spilled brake fluid, always cover paintwork when working on the braking system.*

Removal

Note: *If the master cylinder is being overhauled (usually due to sticking or poor action, or fluid leaks) read through the entire procedure first and make sure that you have obtained all the new parts required, including some new DOT 4 brake fluid.*
1 On XT-R and XT-X models press the clip up on the underside of the brake light switch and draw the switch out of its housing **(see illustration)**. On XT-Z and MT-03 models disconnect the brake light switch wiring connectors **(see illustration)**.
2 If the master cylinder is being overhauled, follow Steps 3 to 7. If the master cylinder is just being displaced, follow this Step only: unscrew

5.1a On XT-R and XT-X press up on the clip (arrowed) and withdraw the switch

5.1b On XT-Z and MT-03 disconnect the brake light switch wires (arrowed)

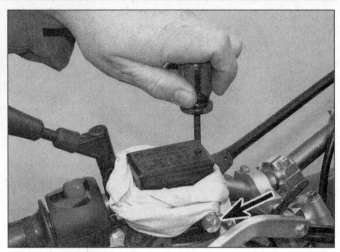

5.2 Unscrew the bolts (arrowed) and remove the master cylinder and its clamp

5.4 Slacken the cover screws. Brake hose banjo bolt (arrowed)

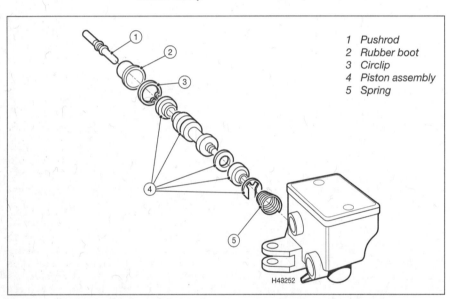

1 Pushrod
2 Rubber boot
3 Circlip
4 Piston assembly
5 Spring

H48252

5.8 Front brake master cylinder components – XT-Z and MT-03 models

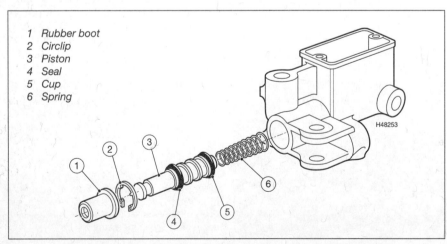

1 Rubber boot
2 Circlip
3 Piston
4 Seal
5 Cup
6 Spring

H48253

5.9 Front brake master cylinder components – XT-R and XT-X models

the master cylinder clamp bolts and remove the back of the clamp, noting how it fits, then position the master cylinder assembly clear of the handlebar **(see illustration)**. Ensure no strain is placed on the hydraulic hose. Keep the reservoir upright to prevent air entering the system.

3 Remove the brake lever (see Chapter 5). Remove the mirror (see Chapter 7).

4 Slacken the reservoir cover screws **(see illustration)**.

5 Unscrew the brake hose banjo bolt and detach the banjo union, noting its alignment with the master cylinder **(see illustration 5.4)**. If the brake fluid has not been drained seal the banjo union – a good way of doing this is to place a piece of rubber over each side of the union (we used some rubber blanking caps), and clamp them in place using a spring clamp **(see illustration 3.2d)**. Alternatively wrap plastic foodwrap around the banjo union and secure the hose in an upright position to minimise fluid loss. Discard the sealing washers, as new ones must be fitted on reassembly.

6 Unscrew the master cylinder clamp bolts and remove the back of the clamp, noting how it fits, then lift the master cylinder and reservoir away from the handlebar **(see illustration 5.2)**.

7 Remove the reservoir cover, diaphragm plate where fitted, and diaphragm. Drain the brake fluid from the master cylinder and reservoir into a suitable container. Wipe any remaining fluid out of the reservoir with a clean rag.

Overhaul

8 On XT-Z and MT-03 models remove the pushrod from the rubber boot, noting how it locates **(see illustration)**. If required remove the brake light switch.

9 Carefully remove the rubber boot from the master cylinder **(see illustration)**.

10 Depress the piston and use circlip pliers to remove the circlip, then slide out the piston assembly and the spring, noting how they fit. If they are difficult to remove, apply low pressure compressed air to the brake fluid outlet. Lay the parts out in the proper order to prevent confusion during reassembly.

11 Clean the master cylinder bore with clean brake fluid. If compressed air is available, blow it through the fluid galleries to ensure they are clear (make sure the air is filtered and unlubricated).

Caution: Do not, under any circumstances, use a petroleum-based solvent to clean brake parts.

12 Check the master cylinder bore for corrosion, scratches, nicks and score marks. If damage or wear is evident, the master cylinder must be replaced with a new one. If the master cylinder is in poor condition, then the caliper(s) should be checked as well.

13 All the master cylinder components are included in the rebuild kit **(see illustration 5.8 or 5.9)**. Use all of the new parts, regardless of the apparent condition of the old ones. Lay out the new parts in their correct order according to those removed.

14 Smear the piston, cup and seal and the master cylinder bore with new brake fluid. Slide the piston and spring assembly into the master cylinder. Push the piston in, making sure the lips on the cup and seal do not turn inside out. Fit the circlip over the end of the piston. Push the circlip into its groove, making sure it locates correctly.

15 Smear some silicone grease onto the lips and inside of the rubber boot. On XT-R and XT-X models fit the boot onto the piston so its outer end lip locates in the groove and press the inner rim into place in the end of the cylinder. On XT-Z and MT-03 models press the inner rim into place in the end of the cylinder, then fit the pushrod into the boot, seating its groove in the outer lip.

16 Inspect the reservoir diaphragm and fit a new one if it is damaged or deteriorated.

Installation

17 Attach the master cylinder to the handlebar, aligning the clamp joint with the punch mark, then fit the back of the clamp with its UP mark facing up **(see illustration 5.2)**. Tighten the upper bolt first, then the lower bolt, to the torque setting specified at

the beginning of the Chapter for your model.

18 Connect the brake hose to the master cylinder, using new sealing washers on each side of the banjo fitting. Align the hose as noted on removal and tighten the banjo bolt to the torque setting specified at the beginning of the Chapter.

19 On XT-R and XT-X models align the brake light switch tab with its hole and push the switch in until it clicks into place **(see illustration 5.1a)**. On XT-Z and MT-03 models, fit the switch if removed, and connect the switch wiring connectors **(see illustration 5.1b)**.

20 Install the brake lever (see Chapter 5). Install the mirror (see Chapter 7).

21 Fill the fluid reservoir with new DOT 4 brake fluid (see *Pre-ride checks*). Refer to Section 11 and bleed the air from the system.

22 Check the operation of the brake before riding the motorcycle.

6 Rear brake pads

⚠️ *Warning: The dust created by the brake system is harmful to your health. Never blow it out with compressed air and don't inhale any of it. An approved filtering mask should be worn when working on the brakes.*

Note: *Do not operate the brake pedal while the pads are out of the caliper.*

1 Push the caliper against the disc, all the way across if new pads are being fitted so

6.1 Push the caliper against the disc so the piston is pushed in

the piston is pushed all the way back into the caliper to create room for them **(see illustration)**. It may be necessary to remove the master cylinder reservoir cap, plate and diaphragm and siphon out some fluid (see *Pre-ride checks*). If the piston is difficult to push back, remove the bleed valve cap, then attach a length of clear hose to the bleed valve and place the open end in a suitable container, then open the valve and try again (see Section 11). Take great care not to draw any air into the system. If in doubt, bleed the brakes afterwards. If the caliper is difficult to push in the chances are there is some hidden corrosion stopping it. If it doesn't move at all, or to fully clean and inspect the piston, remove the caliper (see Section 7).

2 Remove the clip securing the pad pin **(see illustration)**. Drive the pin out using a suitable drift and remove the pads **(see illustrations)**.

3 Inspect the surface of each pad for contamination and check that the friction material has not worn beyond its service limit (see Chapter 1, Section 10) **(see illustration)**. If either pad is worn down to, or beyond, the service limit wear indicator, is fouled with oil or grease, or is heavily scored or damaged, fit a new set of pads. If required measure the thickness of the friction material to determine the extent of wear – the service limit is 1 mm. **Note:** *It is not possible to degrease the friction material; if the pads are contaminated in any way they must be replaced with new ones.*

4 If the pads are in good condition clean them carefully, using a fine wire brush which is completely free of oil and grease to remove

6.2a Remove the clip . . .

6.2b . . . then drive the pin out . . .

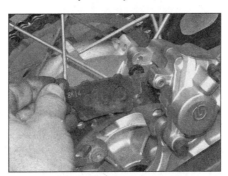

6.2c . . . and remove the pads

6.3 Check the surface of the friction material and the extent of wear

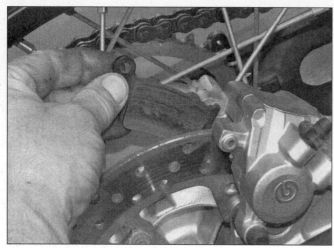

6.8a Fit the pads . . .

6.8b . . . making sure they locate correctly against the guide (arrowed)

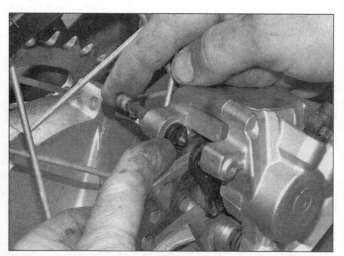

6.8c Align the holes and insert the pin . . .

6.8d . . . driving it all the way in

all traces of road dirt and corrosion. Using a pointed instrument, dig out any embedded particles of foreign matter. If required, spray with a dedicated brake cleaner to remove any dust.

5 Check the condition of the brake disc (see Section 8).

6 Remove all traces of corrosion from the pad pin and check it for wear and damage, replacing it with a new one if necessary.

7 Lightly smear the back of each pad and the pad pin with copper-based grease.

8 Fit the pads, making sure they locate correctly against the guide on the bracket **(see illustrations)**. Press the pads up against the spring to align the holes and insert the pad pin, then drive it home using a suitable drift **(see illustrations)**. Secure the pin with the clip **(see illustration 6.2a)**.

9 Operate the brake pedal until the pads contact with the disc. Check the level of fluid in the hydraulic reservoir and top-up if necessary (see *Pre-ride checks*).

10 Check the operation of the rear brake before riding the motorcycle.

7 Rear brake caliper

⚠️ **Warning:** *If the brake master cylinder is being completely removed it is best to drain all old brake fluid from the system, then fill with new fluid on installation (see Section 11). Do not, under any circumstances, use petroleum-based solvents to clean brake parts. Use clean DOT 4 brake fluid, dedicated brake cleaner or denatured alcohol only, as described. To prevent damage from spilled brake fluid, always cover paintwork when working on the braking system.*

Note: *The brake caliper seals and piston are not available – if the piston has seized or if there is fluid leaking past the seals a new caliper must be installed.*

Removal

Note: *Do not operate the brake pedal while the caliper is off the disc.*

1 If the caliper is being completely removed, unscrew the brake hose banjo bolt and detach the banjo union, noting its alignment with the caliper **(see illustration)**. If the brake fluid

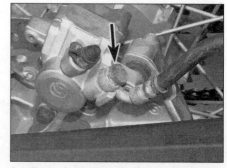

7.1 Brake hose banjo bolt (arrowed) – note its alignment

7.2a Brake hose guide bolts (arrowed) – XT-R and XT-X

7.2b Brake hose guide bolt (arrowed) – XT-Z

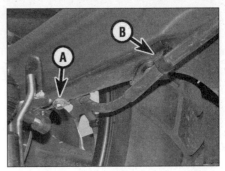

7.2c Brake hose guide bolt (A) and clip (B) – MT-03

has not been drained seal the banjo union – a good way of doing this is to place a piece of rubber over each side of the union (we used some rubber blanking caps), and clamp them in place using a spring clamp **(see illustration 3.2d)**. Alternatively wrap plastic foodwrap around the banjo union and secure the hose in an upright position to minimise fluid loss. Discard the sealing washers, as new ones must be fitted on reassembly.

2 If required, release the brake hose guide(s) from the swingarm **(see illustrations)**.

3 If required remove the brake pads (see Section 6).

4 Remove the rear wheel (see Section 15). Displace the caliper bracket from the swingarm, noting how it locates **(see illustration)**.

Inspection

5 Slide the caliper and bracket apart **(see illustration)**.

6 Clean around the exposed section of the piston to remove any dirt or debris that could cause the seals to be damaged.

7 If the piston appears seized, apply the brake pedal and check whether the piston moves at all. If it moves out but can't be pushed back in the chances are there is some hidden corrosion stopping it. If it doesn't move at all, fit a new caliper.

8 Clean off all traces of corrosion and hardened grease from the slider pins and from their rubber boots **(see illustration)**. Replace the boots with new ones if they are damaged, deformed or deteriorated. Make sure each slider pin is tight. Apply a smear of silicone-based grease to the boots and slider pins.

7.4 Displace the bracket from the swingarm

9 Make sure the pad spring is correctly located in the caliper **(see illustration)**. Make sure the pad guide is correctly located on the bracket **(see illustration)**. Slide the caliper onto the bracket, making sure each boot seats correctly around the base of its pin **(see illustration 7.5)**.

Installation

10 Locate the caliper bracket on the swingarm **(see illustration 7.4)**. Install the rear wheel (see Section 15).

11 If removed install the brake pads (see Section 6).

12 If detached fit the rear brake hose guide(s) onto the swingarm **(see illustration 7.2a, b or c)**.

13 If detached, connect the brake hose to the caliper, using new sealing washers on each side of the fitting, and aligning it as noted on removal **(see illustration 7.1)**. Tighten the

7.5 Slide the caliper off the bracket

banjo bolt to the torque setting specified at the beginning of the Chapter.

14 Top up the hydraulic reservoir with DOT 4 brake fluid (see *Pre-ride checks*) and bleed the system as described in Section 11. Check that there are no fluid leaks and test the operation of the rear brake before riding the motorcycle.

8 Rear brake disc

Inspection

1 Refer to Section 4 of this Chapter, noting that the dial gauge should be attached to the swingarm.

Removal

2 Remove the wheel (see Section 15).

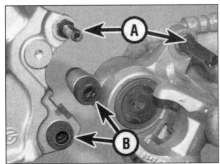

7.8 Clean and check the pins (A) and the boots (B)

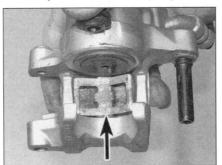

7.9a Make sure the spring (arrowed) . . .

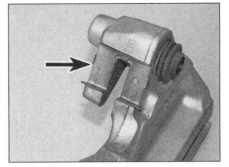

7.9b . . . and the guide (arrowed) are correctly located

8.3 Rear brake disc bolts (arrowed) –
XT-Z shown

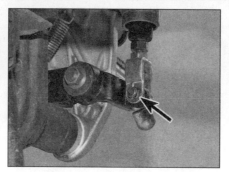

9.1a Straighten and remove the split pin
arrowed

9.1b Remove the washer and withdraw the
clevis pin

Caution: Don't lay the wheel down and allow it to rest on the disc or sprocket – they could become warped. Set the wheel on wood blocks so the wheel rim supports the weight of the wheel.

3 If you are not replacing the disc with a new one, mark the relationship of the disc to the wheel so it can be installed in the same position. Unscrew the disc retaining bolts, loosening them evenly and a little at a time in a criss-cross pattern to avoid distorting the disc, then remove the disc **(see illustration)**.

Installation

4 Before installing the disc, make sure there is no dirt or corrosion where it seats on the hub. If the disc does not sit flat when it is bolted down, it will appear to be warped when checked or when the rear brake is used.

5 Fit the disc on the wheel with its marked side facing out, aligning the previously applied matchmarks (if you're reinstalling the original disc).

6 Clean the threads of the disc mounting bolts, then apply a suitable non-permanent thread locking compound. Install the bolts and tighten them evenly and a little at a time in a criss-cross pattern to the torque setting specified at the beginning of this Chapter. Clean the disc using acetone or brake system cleaner. If a new disc has been installed, remove any protective coating from its working surfaces and fit new brake pads.

7 Install the rear wheel (see Section 16).

8 Check the operation of the rear brake before riding the motorcycle.

9 Rear brake master cylinder

> ⚠ *Warning: If the brake master cylinder is in need of an overhaul it is best to drain all old brake fluid from the system, then fill with new fluid after the overhaul (see Section 11). Overhaul must be done in a spotlessly clean work area to avoid contamination and possible failure of the brake hydraulic system components. Do not, under any circumstances, use petroleum-based solvents to clean brake parts. Use clean DOT 4 brake fluid, dedicated brake cleaner or denatured alcohol only, as described. To prevent damage from spilled brake fluid, always cover paintwork when working on the braking system.*

Removal

Note: *If the master cylinder is being overhauled (usually due to sticking or poor action, or fluid leaks) read through the entire procedure first and make sure that you have obtained all the new parts required, including some new DOT 4 brake fluid.*

1 Remove the split pin and washer from the clevis pin securing the brake pedal to the master cylinder pushrod, then withdraw the

pin and detach the pushrod **(see illustrations)**. Discard the split pin – a new one must be used.

2 Unscrew the bolt securing the fluid reservoir to the frame, then undo the reservoir cap and remove the diaphragm plate and diaphragm **(see illustration)**. Pour the brake fluid into a suitable container. Wipe any remaining fluid out of the reservoir with a clean rag.

3 On XT-R and XT-X models unscrew the brake hose banjo bolt and detach the banjo union, noting its alignment with the master cylinder **(see illustration)**. If the brake fluid has not been drained seal the banjo union – a good way of doing this is to place a piece of rubber over each side of the union (we used some rubber blanking caps), and clamp them in place using a spring clamp **(see illustration 3.2d)**. Alternatively wrap plastic foodwrap around the banjo union and secure the hose in an upright position to minimise fluid loss. Discard the sealing washers, as new ones must be fitted on reassembly.

4 On XT-Z and MT-03 models remove the brake light switch (see Chapter 8).

5 Undo the bolts securing the heel plate and master cylinder and remove the plate and the master cylinder along with the reservoir **(see illustration)**.

Overhaul

6 Release the clip securing the reservoir hose to the union on the master cylinder and detach the hose, being prepared to catch any

9.2 Unscrew the bolt (arrowed), then
displace and drain the reservoir

9.3 Brake hose banjo bolt (arrowed)

9.5 Unscrew the bolts (arrowed) and
remove the master cylinder and reservoir
assembly

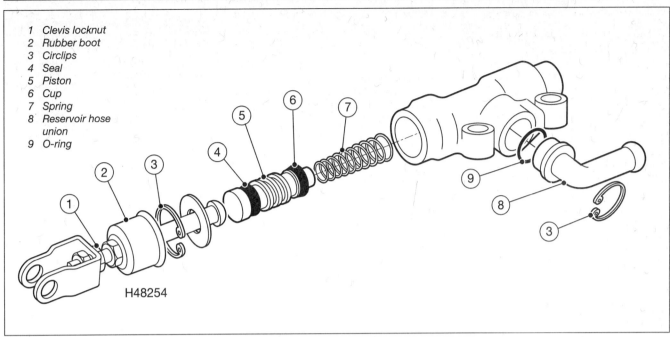

1 Clevis locknut
2 Rubber boot
3 Circlips
4 Seal
5 Piston
6 Cup
7 Spring
8 Reservoir hose
   union
9 O-ring

H48254

9.6 Rear brake master cylinder components

residual fluid **(see illustration)**. Inspect the hose for cracks or splits and replace it with a new one if necessary. If required, release the circlip securing the union and detach it from the master cylinder. Discard the O-ring as a new one must be used.

7 Dislodge the rubber dust boot from the base of the master cylinder and from around the pushrod, noting how it locates. Push the pushrod in and, using circlip pliers, remove the circlip from its groove in the master cylinder and slide out the pushrod assembly, the piston assembly and the spring, noting how they fit. Lay the parts out in order as you remove them to prevent confusion during reassembly.

8 Drive the roll pin out of the bottom of the pushrod. Slacken the locknut on the top of the clevis. Note how far the clevis is threaded up the pushrod, then thread it off, followed by the locknut. Remove the rubber boot and the circlip.

9 Clean the master cylinder bore with clean brake fluid. If compressed air is available, blow it through the fluid galleries to ensure they are clear (make sure the air is filtered and unlubricated).

Caution: Do not, under any circumstances, use a petroleum-based solvent to clean brake parts.

10 Check the master cylinder bore for corrosion, scratches, nicks and score marks. If damage or wear is evident, the master cylinder must be replaced with a new one. If the master cylinder is in poor condition, then the caliper should be checked as well.

11 All the necessary parts are included in the master cylinder rebuild kit. Use all of the new parts, regardless of the apparent condition of the old ones. Lay out the new parts in their

correct order according to those removed.

12 Smear the piston, cup and seal and the master cylinder bore with new brake fluid. Slide the piston and spring assembly into the master cylinder. Make sure the lips on the cup and seal do not turn inside out.

13 Smear some silicone grease onto the lips and inside of the rubber boot and onto the rounded end of the pushrod. Fit the new circlip and rubber boot onto the pushrod, seating the lower lip of the boot in the groove above the hex. Thread the locknut and clevis on. Set the position of the clevis as noted on removal and tighten the locknut securely against it. Drive the roll pin into the hole.

14 Push the piston in using the pushrod and locate the circlip in the groove.

15 Press the rubber boot into place in the end of the cylinder.

16 If removed fit a new fluid reservoir hose union O-ring smeared with brake fluid, then press the union into the master cylinder and secure it with a new circlip. Connect the hose to the union on the master cylinder and secure it with the clip. Check that the hose is secured with a clip at the reservoir end as well. If the clips have weakened, use new ones.

Installation

17 Locate the master cylinder along with the heel plate, then fit the bolts and tighten them to the torque setting specified at the beginning of the Chapter **(see illustration 9.5)**.

18 Align the clevis with the brake pedal, then insert the clevis pin, fit the washer and a new split pin, then bend its ends round to secure it **(see illustrations 9.1b and a)**.

19 On XT-R and XT-X models connect the brake hose to the master cylinder, using new sealing washers on each side of the banjo

fitting, and aligning it as noted on removal **(see illustration 9.3)**. Tighten the banjo bolt to the torque setting specified at the beginning of the Chapter.

20 On XT-Z and MT-03 models install the brake light switch (see Chapter 8).

21 Fit the fluid reservoir onto its mount and tighten the bolt **(see illustration 9.2)**.

22 Fill the fluid reservoir with new DOT 4 brake fluid (see *Pre-ride checks*). Refer to Section 11 and bleed the air from the system.

23 Check the operation of the brake and brake light switch before riding the motorcycle.

10 Brake hoses and fittings

Inspection

1 Brake hose condition should be checked regularly and the hoses replaced with new ones at the specified interval (see Chapter 1).

Removal and installation

2 Drain all old brake fluid from the system (see Section 11).

3 The brake hoses have banjo fittings on each end – with the exception that the rear master cylinder on XT-Z and MT-03 models has the brake light switch to secure the hose rather than a banjo bolt, so you must disconnect the wiring connector before unscrewing it (see Chapter 8). Cover the surrounding area with plenty of rags and unscrew the banjo bolt (or the switch) at each end of the hose, noting the alignment of the fitting with the master cylinder or brake caliper **(see illustrations 3.2a, b and c, 5.4, 7.1 and 9.3)**. Free the hose from any clips or guides and remove it, noting its routing. Discard the sealing washers. **Note:** *Do not operate the brake lever or pedal while a brake hose is disconnected.*

4 Position the new hose, making sure it isn't twisted or otherwise strained, and ensure that it is correctly routed through any clips or guides and is clear of all moving components. Make sure the elbow locates correctly.

5 Check that the fittings align correctly, then install the banjo bolts/brake light switch, using new sealing washers on both sides of the fittings **(see illustrations 3.17)**. Tighten the banjo bolts or the brake light switch to the torque setting specified at the beginning of this Chapter.

6 Refill the system with new DOT 4 brake fluid (see *Pre-ride checks*) and bleed the air from it (see Section 11).

7 Check the operation of the brakes before riding the motorcycle.

11 Brake system bleeding and fluid change

Note: *If bleeding the system using the conventional method does not work sufficiently well, you could try a commercially available vacuum-type brake bleeding tool* **(see illustration 11.17)**, *following the manufacturer's instructions for using the tool.*

Bleeding

1 Bleeding the brakes is simply the process

of removing air from the brake fluid reservoir, the hose and the brake caliper. Bleeding is necessary whenever a brake system hydraulic connection is loosened, after a component or hose is replaced with a new one, or when the master cylinder or caliper is overhauled. Leaks in the system may also allow air to enter, but leaking brake fluid will reveal their presence and warn you of the need for repair.

2 To bleed the brakes, you will need some new DOT 4 brake fluid, a length of clear flexible hose, a small container partially filled with clean brake fluid, some rags, a spanner to fit the brake caliper bleed valve, and possibly help from an assistant. Bleeding kits that include the hose, a one-way valve and a container are available relatively cheaply from a good auto store, and simplify the task as you don't need an assistant.

3 Cover painted components to prevent damage in the event that brake fluid is spilled.

4 Refer to *'Pre-ride checks'* and remove the reservoir cover or cap, diaphragm plate (where fitted) and diaphragm and slowly pump the brake lever (front brake) or pedal (rear brake) a few times, until no air bubbles can be seen floating up from the holes in the bottom of the reservoir. This bleeds the air from the master cylinder end of the line. Temporarily refit the reservoir cover or cap.

5 Pull the dust cap off the bleed valve **(see illustrations)**. If using a ring spanner fit it onto the valve **(see illustration)**. Attach one end of the hose to the bleed valve and, if not using a

HAYNES HiNT *To avoid damaging the bleed valve during the procedure, loosen it and then tighten it temporarily with a ring spanner before attaching the hose. With the hose attached, the valve can then be opened and closed either with an open-ended spanner, or by leaving the ring spanner located on the valve and fitting the hose above it as shown in illustration 11.5e.*

kit, submerge the other end in the clean brake fluid in the container **(see illustration)**.

6 Check the fluid level in the reservoir. Do not allow the fluid level to drop below the lower mark during the procedure.

7 Carefully pump the brake lever or pedal three or four times and hold it in (front) or down (rear) while opening the bleed valve. When the valve is opened, brake fluid will flow out of the caliper into the clear tubing, and the lever will move toward the handlebar, or the pedal will move down. If there is air in the system there will be air bubbles in the brake fluid coming out of the caliper.

8 Tighten the bleed valve, then release the brake lever or pedal gradually. Repeat the process until no air bubbles are visible in the brake fluid leaving the caliper, and the lever or pedal is firm when applied, topping the reservoir up when necessary. On completion, disconnect the hose, then tighten the bleed valve to the torque setting specified at the beginning of this Chapter and install the dust cap.

11.5a Front brake caliper bleed valve – XT-R and XT-Z models

11.5b Front brake caliper bleed valve (arrowed) – XT-X models

11.5c Front brake caliper bleed valve (arrowed) – MT-03 models

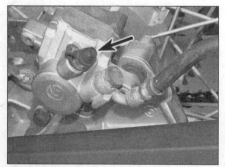
11.5d Rear brake caliper bleed valve (arrowed)

11.5e Fit the ring spanner before connecting the hose

11.5f One of several commercially available one-man bleeding kits

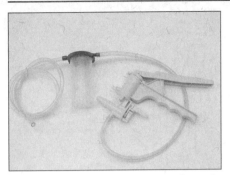

11.17 This tool creates a vacuum to suck the fluid out

9 Top-up the reservoir, then install the diaphragm, diaphragm plate (where fitted), and cover or cap (see *Pre-ride checks*). Wipe up any spilled brake fluid. Check the entire system for fluid leaks.

10 Check the operation of the brakes before riding the motorcycle.

Fluid change

11 Changing the brake fluid is a similar process to bleeding the brakes and requires

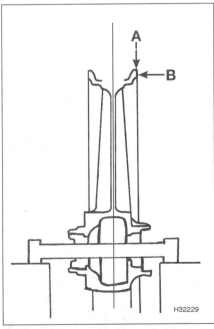

12.2 Check the wheel for radial (out-of-round) runout (A) and axial (side-to-side) runout (B)

the same materials plus a suitable tool (such as a syringe) for siphoning the fluid out of the reservoir. Also ensure that the container is large enough to take all the old fluid when it is flushed out of the system.

12 Follow Steps 3 and 5, then remove the reservoir cover or cap, diaphragm plate (where fitted) and diaphragm and siphon the old fluid out of the reservoir. Wipe the reservoir clean. Fill the reservoir with new brake fluid, then carefully pump the brake lever or pedal three or four times and hold it in (front) or down (rear) while opening the caliper bleed valve. When the valve is opened, brake fluid will flow out of the caliper into the clear tubing, and the lever will move toward the handlebar, or the pedal will move down.

13 Tighten the bleed valve, then release the brake lever or pedal gradually. Keep the reservoir topped-up with new fluid to above the LOWER level at all times or air may enter the system and greatly increase the length of the task. Repeat the process until new fluid can be seen emerging from the caliper bleed valve.

14 Disconnect the hose, then tighten the bleed valve to the specified torque setting and install the dust cap.

15 Top-up the reservoir, then install the diaphragm, diaphragm plate (where fitted), and cover or cap (see *Pre-ride checks*). Wipe up any spilled brake fluid. Check the entire system for fluid leaks.

16 Check the operation of the brakes before riding the motorcycle.

Draining the system for overhaul

17 Draining the brake fluid is again a similar process to bleeding the brakes. Follow the procedure described above for changing the fluid, but quite simply do not put any new fluid into the reservoir – the system fills itself with air instead. An alternative is to use a commercially available vacuum-type brake bleeding tool **(see illustration)** – follow the manufacturer's instructions.

12 Wheel inspection and repair

1 In order to carry out a proper inspection of the wheels, it is necessary to support the bike upright so that the wheel being inspected is raised off the ground. Position the motorcycle on an auxiliary stand. Clean the wheels thoroughly to remove mud and dirt that may interfere with the inspection procedure or

mask defects. Make a general check of the wheels (see Chapter 1) and tyres (see *Pre-ride checks*).

2 Attach a dial gauge to the fork or the swingarm and position its tip against the side of the wheel rim. Spin the wheel slowly and check the axial (side-to-side) runout of the rim **(see illustration)**.

3 In order to accurately check radial (out of round) runout with the dial gauge, remove the wheel from the machine, and the tyre from the wheel. With the axle clamped in a vice and the dial gauge positioned on the top of the rim, the wheel can be rotated to check the runout **(see illustration 12.2)**.

4 An easier, though slightly less accurate, method is to attach a stiff wire pointer to the fork or the swingarm and position the end a fraction of an inch from the wheel rim where the wheel and tyre join. If the wheel is true, the distance from the pointer to the rim will be constant as the wheel is rotated. **Note:** *If wheel runout is excessive, check the wheel bearings very carefully before renewing the wheel.*

5 The wheels should also be inspected for cracks, flat spots on the rim and other damage. Look very closely for dents in the area where the tyre bead contacts the rim. Dents in this area may prevent complete sealing of the tyre against the rim, which leads to deflation of the tyre over a period of time. If damage is evident, or if runout in either direction is excessive, the wheel will have to be renewed. Never attempt to repair a damaged cast alloy wheel.

13 Wheel alignment check

1 Misalignment of the wheels due to a bent frame or forks can cause strange and possibly serious handling problems. If the frame or forks are at fault, repair by a frame specialist or renewal are the only options.

2 To check wheel alignment you will need an assistant, a length of string or a perfectly straight piece of wood and a ruler. A plumb bob or spirit level for checking that the wheels are vertical will also be required.

3 In order to make a proper check of the wheels it is necessary to support the bike in an upright position, using an auxiliary stand. First ensure that the chain adjuster markings coincide on each side of the swingarm (see Chapter 1, Section 1). Next, measure the width of both tyres at their widest points. Subtract the smaller measurement from the larger measurement, then divide the difference by two. The result is the amount of offset that should exist between the front and rear tyres on both sides of the machine.

4 If a string is used, have your assistant hold one end of it about halfway between the floor and the rear axle, with the string touching the back edge of the rear tyre sidewall.

5 Run the other end of the string forward and

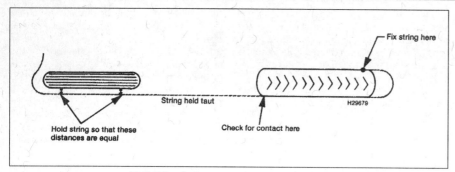

13.5 Wheel alignment check using string

pull it tight so that it is roughly parallel to the floor **(see illustration)**. Slowly bring the string into contact with the front edge of the rear tyre sidewall, then turn the front wheel until it is parallel with the string. Measure the distance from the front tyre sidewall to the string.
6 Repeat the procedure on the other side of the motorcycle. The distance from the front tyre sidewall to the string should be equal on both sides.
7 As previously mentioned, a perfectly straight length of wood or metal bar may be substituted for the string **(see illustration)**.
8 If the distance between the string and tyre is greater on one side, or if the rear wheel appears to be out of alignment, have your machine checked by a Yamaha dealer or frame specialist.
9 If the front-to-back alignment is correct, the wheels still may be out of alignment vertically.
10 Using a plumb bob or spirit level, check the rear wheel to make sure it is vertical. To do this, hold the string of the plumb bob against the tyre upper sidewall and allow the weight to settle just off the floor. If the string touches both the upper and lower tyre sidewalls and is perfectly straight, the wheel is vertical. If it is not, adjust the stand until it is.

11 Once the rear wheel is vertical, check the front wheel in the same manner. If both wheels are not perfectly vertical, the frame and/or major suspension components are bent.

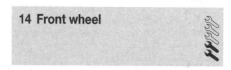
14 Front wheel

Removal

1 Position the motorcycle on an auxiliary stand so that the front wheel is off the ground. Always make sure the motorcycle is properly supported.
2 Displace the front brake caliper(s) (see Section 3). Support the caliper(s) with a cable-tie or a bungee cord so that no strain is placed on the hydraulic hose(s). There is no need to disconnect the hose(s). **Note**: *Do not operate the front brake lever with the caliper(s) removed.*
3 Slacken the axle clamp bolt(s) on the bottom of the right-hand fork **(see illustrations)**. Unscrew the axle **(see illustration 14.11)**.
4 Take the weight of the wheel, then withdraw the axle from the right-hand side **(see**

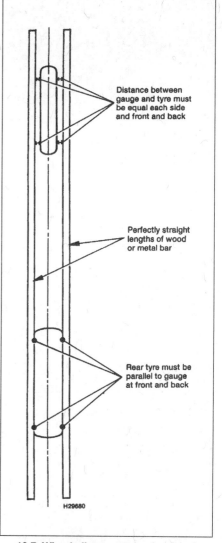

13.7 Wheel alignment check using a straight-edge

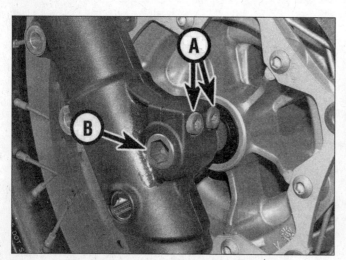

14.3a Axle clamp bolts (A), axle (B) – XT models

14.3b Axle clamp bolt (A), axle (B) – MT-03

14.4 Withdraw the axle and remove the wheel

14.11 Tighten the axle to the specified torque

illustration). Carefully lower the wheel and draw it forwards.

5 On XT models remove the plain spacer from the right-hand side of the wheel and the shouldered spacer from the left **(see illustrations)**. On MT-03 models remove the shouldered spacer from each side of the wheel – they are the same. Clean all dirt and old grease off the spacers, axle and bearing seals.

6 Check the axle is straight by rolling it on a flat surface such as a piece of plate glass (first remove any corrosion using wire wool or a suitable alternative). If the equipment is available, place the axle in V-blocks and measure the runout using a dial gauge. If the axle is bent or the runout exceeds the limit specified at the beginning of the Chapter, replace it with a new one.

7 Check the condition of the wheel bearings (see Section 16).

14.5a On XT models, remove the plain spacer from the right-hand side . . .

Caution: Don't lay the wheel down and allow it to rest on the disc – it could become warped. Set the wheel on wood blocks so the disc doesn't support the weight of the wheel.

Installation

Note: *If a new tyre has been fitted, make sure the directional arrow on the tyre is pointing in the direction of normal rotation of the wheel.*

8 Smear some grease on the inside of the wheel spacers and to the outside where they fit into the dust seals. On XT models fit the plain spacer into the right-hand side of the wheel and the shouldered spacer into the left **(see illustrations 14.5a and b)**. On MT-03 models fit the shouldered spacer into each side of the wheel.

9 Manoeuvre the wheel into position between the forks, on XT-R and XT-X models making sure the brake disc is on the left-hand side. Apply a thin coat of grease to the axle.

10 Lift the wheel into place, making sure the spacers remain in position. Slide the axle in from the right-hand side **(see illustration 14.4)**.

11 Tighten the axle to the torque setting specified at the beginning of the Chapter **(see illustration)**.

12 Install the brake caliper(s) (see Section 3). Apply the front brake a few times to bring the pads back into contact with the disc.

13 Lower the bike so the wheel is on the ground, then hold the front brake on and push

14.5b . . . and the shouldered spacer from the left

down on the handlebars to compress the forks several times to align the right-hand fork on the axle. Now tighten the axle clamp bolt(s) to the specified torque **(see illustration 14.3a or b)** – on XT models tighten the outer bolt first, then the inner bolt, then tighten the outer bolt again.

14 Check for correct operation of the front brake before riding the motorcycle.

---

15 Rear wheel

Removal

1 Position the motorcycle on an auxiliary stand so that the rear wheel is off the ground. Always make sure the motorcycle is properly supported. Create some slack in the chain (see Chapter 1, Section 1).

2 Unscrew the axle nut and remove the washer on models with a steel swingarm, and the adjuster plate on models with an aluminium swingarm, noting how it fits **(see illustrations)**.

3 Take the weight of the wheel, then withdraw the axle, bringing the other washer or adjuster plate with it (again according to swingarm type), and lower the wheel to the ground **(see illustration)**. If the axle is difficult to withdraw, drive it through with a drift, making sure you don't damage the threads.

4 Disengage the chain from the sprocket **(see**

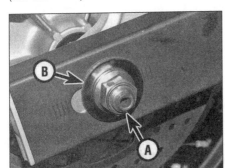

15.2a Axle nut (A) and washer (B) – steel swingarm

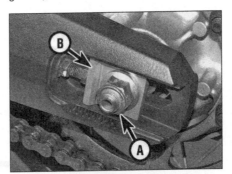

15.2b Axle nut (A) and washer (B) – aluminium swingarm

15.3 Withdraw the axle and lower the wheel

15.4 Disengage the chain and draw the wheel out the back

15.9a Fit the right-hand spacer . . .

15.9b . . . and the left-hand spacer – XT-Z shown

illustration). Draw the wheel back out of the swingarm. Retrieve the spacer from each side of the wheel, noting which fits where as they are different **(see illustrations 15.9a and b)**.

5 If required displace the rear brake caliper with its bracket from the swingarm, noting how it locates, and tie it up or rest it on some rag on the swingarm **(see illustration 7.4)** – release the brake hose guide(s) from the swingarm for extra freedom of movement if required **(see illustration 7.2a, b or c)**. **Note:** *Do not operate the brake pedal while the caliper is off the disc.* **Caution: Do not lay the wheel down and allow it to rest on the disc or the sprocket. Keep it upright, or set the wheel on wood blocks so the disc or the sprocket doesn't support the weight of the wheel.**

6 Clean all old grease off the spacers, caliper bracket and axle.

7 Check the axle is straight by rolling it on a flat surface such as a piece of plate glass (if the axle is corroded, first remove any corrosion with wire wool or a suitable alternative). If the equipment is available, place the axle in V-blocks and check the runout using a dial gauge. If the axle is bent or the runout exceeds the limit specified at the beginning of the Chapter, replace it with a new one.

8 Check the condition of the wheel bearings (see Section 16).

Installation

Note: *If a new tyre has been fitted, make sure the directional arrow on the tyre is pointing in the direction of normal rotation of the wheel.*

9 Apply a smear of grease to the inside of each wheel spacer and also to the ends where they fit in the seals, and to the axle bore in the caliper bracket and the axle. Fit the spacers into the wheel **(see illustrations)**.

10 On XT-R models and XT-X models with a steel swingarm make sure the chain adjusters are correctly fitted inside the ends of the swingarm, then fit the washer onto the axle – note that each washer is marked with a letter that must face out, and the washer marked O fits under the axle head and the washer marked N fits under the axle nut **(see illustration 15.2a)**.

11 On XT-X models with an aluminium swingarm fit the left-hand chain adjuster block onto the axle with the raised section towards the axle head – the axle goes in from the left. On XT-Z and MT-03 models fit the right-hand chain adjuster block onto the axle with the raised section towards the axle head – the axle goes in from the right.

12 If displaced route the brake hose on the inside of the swingarm and fit the guide(s), then locate the caliper bracket on the swingarm **(see illustration 7.2a, b or c and 7.4)**.

13 Manoeuvre the wheel into position between the ends of the swingarm with the sprocket to the left. Engage the drive chain with the sprocket **(see illustration 15.4)**.

14 Lift the wheel into position, making sure the spacers stay in place, the caliper bracket stays in place and the disc locates between the brake pads, and slide the axle

in **(see illustration 15.3)**. On models with an aluminium swingarm make sure the chain adjuster block has its thicker end facing forward against the adjuster bolt head, and the axle head is located against the rear edge of it. Fit the other washer or adjuster plate (according to swingarm type, and with the thicker end of the plate facing forwards) and the axle nut, but leave the nut loose **(see illustrations)**.

15 Check and adjust the drive chain slack (see Chapter 1). On completion tighten the axle nut to the torque setting specified at the beginning of the Chapter **(see illustration)**.

16 Operate the brake pedal several times to bring the pads into contact with the disc. Check the operation of the rear brake carefully before riding the bike.

16 Wheel bearings

Caution: Don't lay the wheel down and allow it to rest on the discs or the sprocket – they could become warped. Set the wheel on wood blocks so the wheel rim supports the weight of the wheel, or keep the wheel upright. Don't operate the brake lever/ pedal with the wheel removed.

Note: *Always replace the wheel bearings in sets, never individually. Avoid using a high pressure cleaner on the wheel bearing area.*

15.14a Make sure the axle head and adjuster plate are correctly located and seated

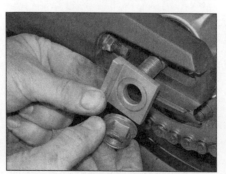

15.14b Fit the washer or adjuster plate and the axle nut

15.15 Tighten the axle nut to the specified torque

16.2 Lever out the bearing seal

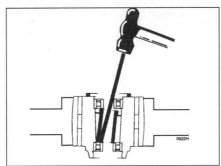

16.4a Locate the drift as shown . . .

16.4b . . . and drive the bearing out

Front wheel bearings

1 Remove the wheel (see Section 14).

2 Lever out the bearing seal from each side of the hub using a flat-bladed screwdriver or a seal hook **(see illustration)**. Take care not to damage the hub. Discard the seals as new ones must be fitted on reassembly.

3 Inspect the bearings – check that the inner race turns smoothly, quietly and freely and that the outer race is a tight fit in the hub. **Note:** *Yamaha recommends that the bearings are not removed unless they are going to be replaced with new ones.*

4 If the bearings are worn, remove them using a metal rod (preferably a brass punch) inserted through the centre of the opposite bearing and locating it on the inner race, pushing the bearing spacer aside to expose it **(see illustration)**. Curve the end of the drift to obtain better purchase if necessary. Strike the drift with a hammer, working evenly around the bearing, to drive it from the hub **(see illustration)**. Remove the spacer which fits between the bearings, noting which way round it fits if shaped at one end. If the bearings are difficult to remove as described, use a puller with slide-hammer attachment (see *Tools and Workshop Tips* in the Reference section).

5 Turn the wheel over and remove the other bearing using the same procedure.

6 Thoroughly clean the hub area of the wheel with a suitable solvent and inspect the bearing seats for scoring and wear. If the seats are damaged, consult a Yamaha dealer before reassembling the wheel.

7 Drive the new bearings into the hub with the marked side facing outwards using a bearing driver or suitable socket that bears on the outer race **(see illustration)** – do not drive the bearings in by the inner race. Make sure the bearing fits squarely and all the way into its seat.

8 Turn the wheel over then install the bearing spacer and the other new bearing.

9 Apply a smear of grease to the new seals, then press them into the hub with your fingers or drive them in using a socket and level them with the rim **(see illustrations)**.

10 Clean the brake disc using acetone or brake system cleaner, then install the wheel (see Section 14).

Rear wheel bearings

11 Remove the wheel (see Section 15). Lift the sprocket coupling out of the hub, noting the spacer inside it **(see illustration 16.22)**.

12 Lever out the bearing seal from the right-hand side of the hub using a flat-bladed screwdriver or a seal hook **(see illustration 16.2)**. Take care not to damage the hub. Discard the seal as a new one should be fitted on reassembly.

13 Inspect the bearings in both sides of the hub – check that the inner race turns smoothly, quietly and freely and that the outer race is a tight fit in the hub. **Note:** *Yamaha recommends that the bearings are not removed unless they are going to be renewed.*

14 If the bearings are worn, remove them using a metal rod (preferably a brass punch)

inserted through the centre of the opposite bearing and locating it on the inner race, pushing the bearing spacer aside to expose it **(see illustration 16.4a)**. Curve the end of the drift to obtain better purchase if necessary. Strike the drift with a hammer, working evenly around the bearing, to drive it from the hub **(see illustration 16.4b)**. Remove the spacer which fits between the bearings, noting which way round it fits if shaped at one end. If the bearings are difficult to remove as described, use a puller with slide-hammer attachment (see *Tools and Workshop Tips* in the Reference section).

15 Turn the wheel over and remove the remaining bearing using the same procedure.

16 Thoroughly clean the hub area of the wheel with a suitable solvent and inspect the bearing seats for scoring and wear. If the seats are damaged, consult a Yamaha dealer before reassembling the wheel.

17 Drive the new bearings into the hub with the marked side facing outwards using a bearing driver or suitable socket that bears on the outer race **(see illustration 16.7)** – do not drive the bearings in by the inner race. Make sure the bearing fits squarely and all the way into its seat.

18 Turn the wheel over then install the bearing spacer and the other new bearing.

19 Apply a smear of grease to the new seal, then press it into the hub with your fingers or drive it in using a socket and level it with the rim **(see illustrations 16.19a and b)**.

20 Check the sprocket coupling/rubber

16.7 Using a socket to drive the bearing in

16.9a Press the new seal into place . . .

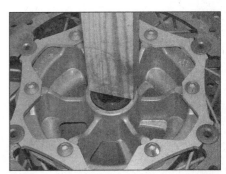

16.9b . . . using a piece of wood across the housing sets the seal flush

16.22 Lift the sprocket coupling off the wheel

16.23a Drive the spacer out of the bearing using a socket . . .

16.23b . . . and remove it from the inside

16.24 Lever out the bearing seal

16.26 Drive the bearing out from the inside

then press it into the coupling with your fingers or drive it in using a socket and level it with the rim **(see illustration)**.

30 Support the sprocket coupling upside down on a socket that bears on the inner race of the bearing. Fit the spacer into the bearing from the inside **(see illustration 16.23b)**, then use a socket to drive it into the bearing **(see illustration)**.

31 Check the sprocket coupling/rubber dampers (see Section 20).

32 Fit the sprocket coupling into the wheel **(see illustration 16.22)**. Install the wheel (see Section 15).

17 Tyres

General information

1 The wheels fitted to all XT models are designed to take tubed tyres only. MT-03 wheels are designed for tubeless tyres only. Tyre sizes are given in the Specifications at the beginning of this Chapter.

2 Refer to the *Pre-ride checks* listed at the beginning of this manual for tyre maintenance, and to Chapter 1 for wheel maintenance, particularly on the spoke wheels fitted to XT models.

Fitting new tyres

3 When selecting new tyres, refer to the tyre information in the Owner's Handbook. Ensure

dampers (see Section 20). Fit the sprocket coupling into the wheel, making sure the spacer is fitted **(see illustration 16.22)**.

21 Install the wheel (see Section 15).

Sprocket coupling bearing

22 Remove the rear wheel (see Section 15). Lift the sprocket coupling out of the hub **(see illustration)**.

23 Drive the spacer out of the bearing using a socket and remove it from the inside of the coupling **(see illustrations)**.

24 Lever out the bearing seal on the outside of the coupling using a flat-bladed screwdriver or a seal hook **(see illustration)**. Take care not to damage the rim of the coupling. Discard the seal as a new one should be fitted on reassembly.

25 Inspect the bearing – check that the inner races turn smoothly, quietly and freely, and

that the outer race is a tight fit in the coupling. **Note:** *Yamaha recommends that the bearing is not removed unless it is going to be replaced with a new one.*

26 Support the coupling on blocks of wood, sprocket side down, and drive the bearing out from the inside using a bearing driver or socket **(see illustration)**.

27 Thoroughly clean the bearing seat with a suitable solvent and inspect it for scoring and wear. If the seat is damaged, consult a Yamaha dealer before reassembling the wheel.

28 Drive the new bearing into the hub with the marked side facing outwards using a bearing driver or suitable socket that bears on the outer race **(see illustration)** – do not drive the bearing in by the inner race. Make sure the bearing fits squarely and all the way into its seat.

29 Apply a smear of grease to the new seal,

16.28 Using a socket to drive the bearing in

16.29 Fit the new seal and level it with the rim of the housing

16.30 Drive the spacer in using a socket

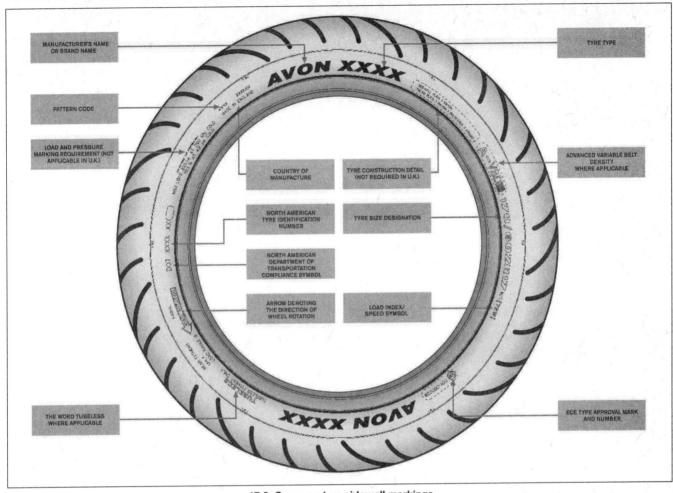

17.3 Common tyre sidewall markings

that front and rear tyre types are compatible, the correct size and correct speed rating; if necessary seek advice from a Yamaha dealer or tyre fitting specialist **(see illustration)**.

4 It is recommended that tyres are fitted by a motorcycle tyre specialist rather than attempted in the home workshop. The specialist will be able to balance the wheels after tyre fitting.

18 Drive chain

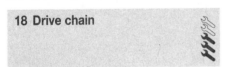

Cleaning

1 Refer to Chapter 1, Section 1, for details of routine cleaning with the chain installed on the sprockets.

2 If the chain is extremely dirty remove it from the motorcycle and soak it in paraffin (kerosene) for approximately five or six minutes, then clean it using a soft brush.

Caution: Don't use gasoline (petrol), solvent or other cleaning fluids which might damage its internal sealing properties.

Don't use high-pressure water. Remove the chain, wipe it off, then blow dry it with compressed air immediately. The entire process shouldn't take longer than ten minutes – if it does, the O-rings in the chain rollers could be damaged.

Removal and installation

3 Before removing the chain you must identify the type fitted. Either an endless chain (for which there is no joining link and must be removed as a complete loop) or a staked master link chain will be fitted. The staked chain can be identified by the master link's side plate identification marks (and usually its different colour), as well as by the staked ends of the link's two pins which look as if they have been deeply centre-punched, instead of peened over as with all the other pins – a special drive chain cutting/staking tool is needed to unstake the link and stake the new one in place.

 Warning: Use ONLY the correct specification chain – ask your Yamaha dealer if in doubt.

Endless chain

4 Remove the swingarm (see Chapter 5).

5 Remove the drive chain.

6 Fit the new chain and all components in reverse order, referring to the relevant Sections and Chapters, and applying torque settings where given. Tension and lubricate the new chain as described in Chapter 1.

Staked master link

 Warning: Use ONLY the correct service tools to secure the staked-type of master link – if you do not have access to such tools, have the chain replaced by a dealer to be sure of having it securely installed.

7 Support the motorcycle so that the rear wheel is off the ground. Tie the front brake on. Locate the joining link in a suitable position to work on by rotating the back wheel.

8 Split the chain at the joining link using the chain cutter, following carefully the manufacturer's operating instructions (see also Section 8 in *Tools and Workshop Tips* in the Reference Section). Remove the chain from the bike, noting its routing around the swingarm.

9 Fit the drive chain around the swingarm and sprockets, leaving the two ends mid-way between the sprockets along the bottom run.

10 Refer to Section 8 in *Tools and Workshop Tips* in the Reference Section. Install the new joining link from the inside with the four O-rings correctly located between the link plate and side plates. Install the new side plate with its identification marks facing out and press it into position. Stake the new link using the drive chain cutting/staking tool, following carefully the instructions of both the chain manufacturer and the tool manufacturer. DO NOT reuse old joining link components.

11 After staking, check the joining link and staking for any signs of cracking. If there is any evidence of cracking, the joining link, O-rings and side plate must be replaced. Make sure the ends are evenly staked. Check that the link pivots freely.

12 Tension and lubricate the new chain as described in Chapter 1.

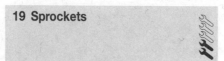

19 Sprockets

Front sprocket cover

1 Unscrew the bolts securing the front sprocket cover and remove it along with the drive chain guide, noting how the wiring is routed **(see illustrations)**. When fitting the cover make sure the wiring is correctly routed **(see illustration)**.

Sprocket check

2 Check the wear pattern on both sprockets (see Chapter 1, Section 1). If the sprocket teeth are worn excessively, replace the chain and both sprockets as a set – worn sprockets can ruin a new drive chain and *vice versa*. Whenever the sprockets are inspected, the drive chain should be inspected also (see Chapter 1).

Sprocket removal and installation

Front sprocket

3 Remove the front sprocket cover (see Step 1). Tie the front brake on using a cable-tie or suitable alternative.

4 Bend back the tabs on the sprocket nut lockwasher **(see illustration)**. Have an assistant apply the rear brake hard, then unscrew the nut and remove the washer. Discard the washer – a new one must be used on reassembly.

5 Adjust the chain so that it is fully slack (see Chapter 1, Section 1). If the rear sprocket is being removed as well, remove the rear wheel now to create full slack (see Section 15). Otherwise disengage the chain from the rear sprocket if required to provide more slack.

19.1a Unscrew the bolts (arrowed) . . .

19.1b . . . and remove the cover and the chain guide

19.1c Make sure the wiring is correctly routed

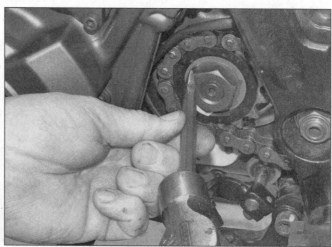
19.4 Bend back the tabs, then unscrew the nut

19.6 Draw the sprocket off the shaft and disengage the chain

19.9a Fit the new washer and the nut and tighten to the specified torque

19.9b Bend the tabs up against the nut

6 Slide the sprocket and chain off the shaft and slip the sprocket out of the chain **(see illustration)**. **Note:** *If the sprocket is not being replaced with a new one, mark its outside face so that it can be installed the same way around.*

7 Engage the new sprocket with the chain and slide it on the shaft **(see illustration 19.7)**.

8 If the rear wheel was removed, change the sprocket now and install the wheel (see Section 15). If the chain was merely disengaged, fit it back onto the rear sprocket. Take up the slack in the chain.

9 Fit the **new** lockwasher, then fit the nut with its shouldered side facing in and tighten it to the torque setting specified at the beginning of this Chapter, applying the rear brake to prevent the sprocket from turning **(see illustration)**. Bend the tabs of the lockwasher up against the nut flats **(see illustration)**.

10 Fit the sprocket cover (see Step 1). Adjust and lubricate the chain following the procedures described in Chapter 1.

Rear sprocket

11 Remove the rear wheel (see Section 15).

12 Unscrew the nuts securing the sprocket to the hub. Remove the sprocket. **Note:** *If the sprocket is not being replaced with a new one, mark its outside face so that it can be installed the same way around.*

13 Check the condition of the sprocket studs and nuts and replace them all with new ones if any are damaged. The studs can be removed using a stud tool, or by threading two nuts onto each stud and locking them together, then unscrewing the stud using the bottom nut. Apply a suitable thread locking compound to the threads of the new studs and tighten them into the sprocket coupling.

14 Fit the sprocket onto the hub with the stamped mark facing out. Fit the nuts and tighten them evenly and in a criss-cross sequence to the torque setting specified at the beginning of the Chapter.

15 Install the rear wheel (see Section 15).

20 Rear sprocket coupling/ rubber dampers

1 Remove the rear wheel (see Section 15). Grasp the sprocket and feel for play between the sprocket coupling and the wheel hub by attempting to twist the sprocket in each direction. Any play indicates worn rubber damper segments.

Caution: Do not lay the wheel down on the disc as it could become warped. Lay the wheel on wooden blocks so that the disc is off the ground.

2 Lift the sprocket coupling out of the hub leaving the rubber dampers in position **(see illustration 16.22)**. Check the coupling for cracks or any obvious signs of damage.

3 Lift the rubber damper segments from the wheel and check them for cracks, hardening and general deterioration **(see illustration)**. Replace them with a new set if necessary.

4 Checking and replacement procedures for the sprocket coupling bearing are in Section 16.

5 Installation is the reverse of removal.

6 Install the rear wheel (see Section 15).

20.3 Check the rubber dampers as described

Notes

Chapter 7
Bodywork

Contents

Section

General information 1
MT-03 models... 4

Section

XT-R and XT-X models 2
XT-Z models 3

Degrees of difficulty

Easy, suitable for novice with little experience | **Fairly easy,** suitable for beginner with some experience | **Fairly difficult,** suitable for competent DIY mechanic | **Difficult,** suitable for experienced DIY mechanic | **Very difficult,** suitable for expert DIY or professional

Specifications

Torque settings

Passenger grab-rail bolts
XT-R and XT-X models .... 23 Nm
XT-Z models .... 25 Nm
MT-03 models.. 24 Nm

1 General information

This Chapter covers the procedures necessary to remove and install the bodywork. Since many service and repair operations on these motorcycles require the removal of the body panels, the procedures are grouped here and referred to from other Chapters.

In the case of damage to the bodywork, it is usually necessary to remove the broken component and replace it with a new (or used) one. The material that the body panels are composed of doesn't lend itself to conventional repair techniques. Note that there are however some companies that specialize in 'plastic welding' and there are a number of DIY bodywork repair kits now available for motorcycles.

When attempting to remove any body panel, first study it closely, noting any fasteners and associated fittings, to be sure of returning everything to its correct place on installation. Once the evident fasteners have been removed, try to withdraw the panel as described but DO NOT FORCE IT – if it will not release, check that all fasteners have been removed and try again.

When installing a body panel, first study it closely, noting any fasteners and associated fittings removed with it, to be sure of returning everything to its correct place. Check that all fasteners are in good condition, including the rubber mounts; replace any faulty fasteners with new ones before the panel is reassembled. Check also that all mounting brackets are straight and repair them or replace them with new ones if necessary before attempting to install the panel.

Tighten the fasteners securely, but be careful not to overtighten any of them or the panel may break (not always immediately) due to the uneven stress.

2.1 Unlock the seat using the ignition key

2.3 Make sure the tab locates under the bracket

2.5a Undo the screws (arrowed) . . .

2 XT-R and XT-X models

Seat

1 Unlock the seat using the ignition key in the lock on the left-hand side panel – turn the key anti-clockwise **(see illustration)**.
2 Lift the back of the seat and draw it back, noting how the tab at the front locates.
3 Installation is the reverse of removal. Make sure the tab at the front locates correctly **(see illustration)**. Push the back of the seat down to engage the lock.

Side panels

4 Remove the seat.

5 To remove the left-hand panel undo the two screws, noting the collar with the lower one **(see illustration)**. Carefully pull the rear away to free the peg from the grommet, then draw the panel back to free the tabs from the fuel tank cover **(see illustration)**.
6 To remove the right-hand panel undo the screw **(see illustration)**. Carefully pull the bottom and rear away to free the pegs from the grommets, then draw the panel back to free the tabs from the fuel tank cover **(see illustration)**.
7 Installation is the reverse of removal. Make sure the grommets are in good condition. Make sure the tabs at the front locate correctly.

Passenger grab-rails

8 Unscrew the bolts and remove the rail **(see illustration)**.

9 Installation is the reverse of removal. Tighten the bolts to the torque setting specified at the beginning of the Chapter.

Rear cowl

10 Remove the seat and the grab-rails.
11 Release and remove the two trim clips by pushing the centre pins in then drawing the bodies out and remove the cowl **(see illustrations)**.
12 Installation is the reverse of removal. To reset the trim clips push the centre pin out so it protrudes from the top, then fit the clip and push the centre pin in flush to secure it.

Fuel tank covers

13 Each side cover is secured by four fasteners. The top cover is secured by the side cover screws, one on each side. Remove the seat (see Step 1).

2.5b . . . then free the peg from the grommet (arrowed) and release the tabs

2.6a Undo the screw (arrowed) . . .

2.6b . . . then free the pegs from the grommets (arrowed) and release the tabs

2.8 Passenger grab-rail bolts (arrowed)

2.11a Release the trim clip (arrowed) on each side by pushing the centre in and drawing the body out . . .

2.11b . . . and remove the cowl

2.14a Release the trim clips (arrowed) at the front . . .

2.14b . . . then undo the screw (arrowed) on the top and the one at the back

2.15a Undo the bolt (arrowed) at the front . . .

14 On all XT-R models and on XT-X models to 2006 release the two trim clips at the front by pushing the centre pins in then drawing the bodies out, then undo the screw on the top and the screw at the back **(see illustrations)**. Carefully pull the bottom of the cover away to release the peg from its grommet and the tab from the side panel **(see illustration 2.15c)**.

15 On XT-X models from 2007-on undo the bolt at the front and the screws on the side **(see illustrations)**. Carefully pull the bottom of the cover away to release the peg from its grommet and the tab from the side panel **(see illustration)**.

16 If both side covers have been removed also remove the top cover.

17 Installation is the reverse of removal. Make sure the grommets are in good condition. To reset the trim clips push the centre pin out so it protrudes from the top, then fit the clip and push the centre pin in flush to secure it.

Front mudguards and fork protector

18 To remove the upper mudguard unscrew the six bolts securing it to the fork protector and the bottom yoke **(see illustration)**. Remove the mudguard, noting the collars fitted in from the top for the bottom yoke bolts **(see illustration)**.

19 To remove the fork protector first remove the upper mudguard. Unscrew the two bolts

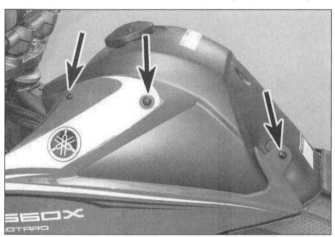

2.15b . . . and the screws (arrowed) on the side

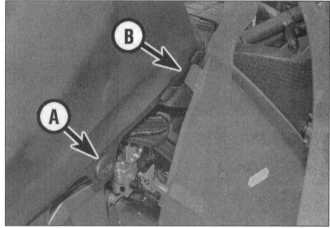

2.15c Release the peg from the grommet (A) and disengage the tab (B)

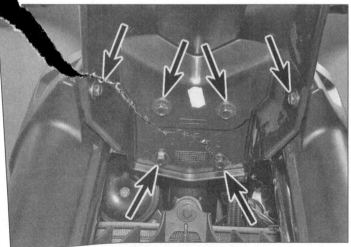

2.18a Unscrew the bolts (arrowed) . . .

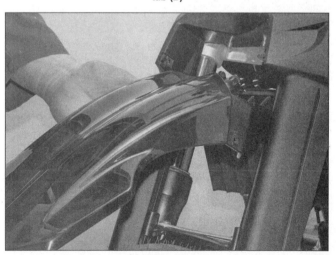

2.18b . . . and remove the upper mudguard

2.19a Unscrew the bolt at the top on each side . . .

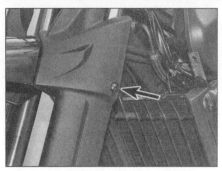

2.19b . . . and the bolt in the middle on each side . . .

2.19c . . . then slide the protector up and remove it . . .

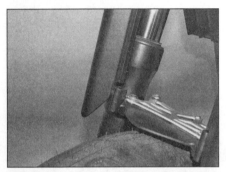

2.19d . . . noting how it locates at the bottom

2.19e Remove the collars for safekeeping

2.21 Unscrew the bolts (arrowed) and remove the lower mudguard

2.24 Disconnect the relevant wiring connectors

on each side, noting the collars, and remove the fork protector **(see illustrations)** – note that the front cowl assembly is secured by the upper bolts and so will be left unsecured. Note the collars for the upper mudguard bolts and remove them for safekeeping **(see illustration)**.

20 To remove the lower mudguard on XT-R models unscrew the two bolts on each side and remove the brackets, then remove the mudguard.

21 To remove the lower mudguard on XT-X models unscrew the bolts, noting the washers, and remove the mudguard **(see illustration)**. If required unscrew the centre bolt and detach the brace from the guard, noting the collars.

22 Installation is the reverse of removal.

Front cowl assembly

23 Remove the fuel tank (see Chapter 4).

24 Disconnect the headlight and instrument wiring connectors and free the wiring from the cable-tie **(see illustration)**.

25 Unscrew the bolt on each side and remove the collar **(see illustration 2.19a)**. Lift the assembly up off the bottom yoke, noting how it locates, then draw the wiring out and remove it **(see illustrations)**.

26 On XT-R models if required remove the screen.

27 Installation is the reverse of removal.

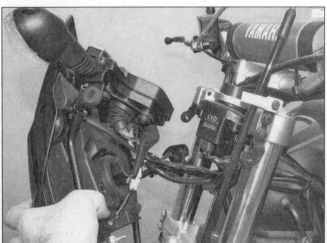

2.25a Lift the assembly off the yoke . . .

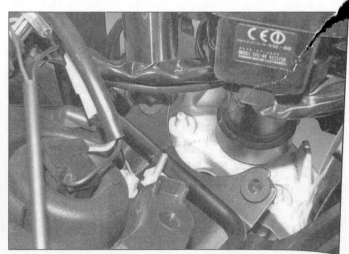

2.25b . . . noting how it locates

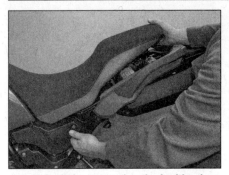

3.1 Unlock the seat using the ignition key

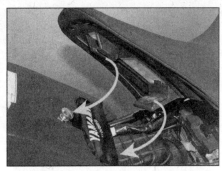

3.3 Make sure the slot locates around the post and the tab locates under the tank

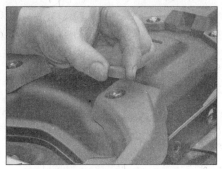

3.5a Remove the blanking caps . . .

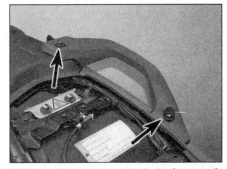

3.5b . . . then unscrew the bolts (arrowed)

3.11a Unscrew the nuts (arrowed) . . .

3.11b . . . and remove the bolts and collars . . .

Mirrors

28 Unscrew the mirror using the hex at the base.
29 Installation is the reverse of removal – make sure the mirror is tight enough to stop it from unscrewing it when moving. If required reposition the mirror by slackening the locknut, turning the mirror as required, then tightening the locknut.

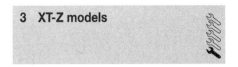

3 XT-Z models

Seat

1 Unlock the seat using the ignition key in the lock on the left-hand side panel **(see illustration)** – turn the key anti-clockwise.
2 Lift the back of the seat and draw it back, noting how the tab and slot at the front locate.
3 Installation is the reverse of removal. Make sure the tab and slot at the front locate correctly **(see illustration)**. Push the back of the seat down to engage the lock.

Passenger grab-rails

4 Remove the seat.
5 Remove the blanking caps from the bolts **(see illustration)**. Unscrew the bolts and remove the rail **(see illustration)**.
6 Installation is the reverse of removal. Tighten the bolts to the torque setting specified at the beginning of the Chapter.

Seat panels

7 Remove the grab-rails.
8 Undo the two screws on the underside and remove the panel.
9 Installation is the reverse of removal.

Luggage rack covers

10 Remove the grab-rails and seat panels.
11 Unscrew the two nuts/bolts and remove the collars **(see illustrations)**. Lift the top cover off, then the main cover **(see illustrations)**.
12 Installation is the reverse of removal.

Fuel tank covers

13 Undo the four screws, noting the washers, and remove the cover **(see illustration)**.
14 Installation is the reverse of removal.

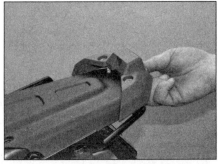

3.11c . . . then remove the top cover . . .

3.11d . . . and the main cover

3.13 Undo the screws (arrowed) and remove the cover

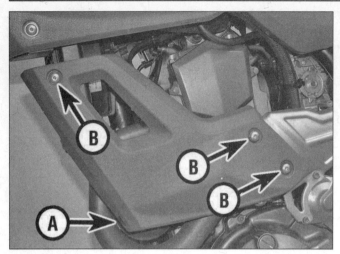

3.15 Release the trim clip (A) then undo the screws (B)

3.18a Undo the screws . . .

Radiator covers

15 Release the trim clip by pushing the centre pin in then drawing the body out **(see illustration)**.
16 Undo the three screws, noting the collars, and remove the cover.
17 Installation is the reverse of removal. To reset the trim clip push the centre pin out so it protrudes from the top, then fit the clip and push the centre pin in flush to secure it.

Cockpit covers

18 Undo the outer screws securing the windshield **(see illustration 3.23)**. Undo the two screws, noting the collars, and lift the cover off the tank, pulling the side of the windshield out for clearance, noting the rubber washers and how the pegs locate, then disconnect the turn signal wiring connectors **(see illustrations)**.
19 Installation is the reverse of removal.

3.18b . . . then lift the cover to free the pegs and remove the washers . . .

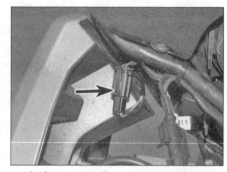

3.18c . . . and disconnect the wiring connector

Front mudguard

20 Undo the screw and the bolt on each side, noting the nuts with the bolt and remove the mudguard **(see illustrations)**. Note the arrangement of the collars and grommets, and make sure the grommets are in good condition.
21 Installation is the reverse of removal.

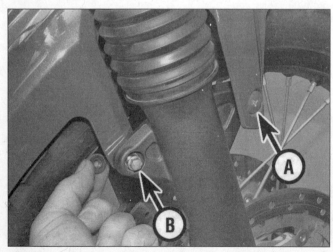

3.20a Undo the screw (A) and the bolt (B), retrieving the nut . . .

3.20b . . . and remove the mudguard

3.23 Undo the three screws (arrowed) on each side to free the windshield

3.24a Unscrew the centre bolt and the bolt (arrowed) on each side . . .

3.24b . . . and remove the cowl

Front cowl

22 Remove the cockpit covers.
23 If required remove the windshield **(see illustration)**.
24 Unscrew the three bolts, noting the collars with the side bolts, and draw the cowl off the headlight **(see illustrations)**.
25 Installation is the reverse of removal.

Mirrors

26 Slacken the base nut then unscrew the mirror **(see illustration)**.
27 Installation is the reverse of removal – position the mirror as required when almost fully screwed in then tighten the locknut.

Sump guard

28 Unscrew the four bolts and remove the guard **(see illustration)**. Note the collars fitted in the grommets for the front mounts – make sure the grommets are in good condition.
29 Installation is the reverse of removal.

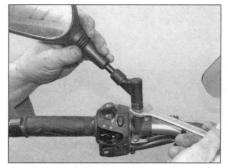

3.26 Slacken the locknut then unscrew the mirror

3.28 Unscrew the two bolts (arrowed) on each side

4	MT-03 models

Seats

1 Unlock the passenger seat using the ignition key in the lock at the back **(see illustration)** – turn the key anti-clockwise. Lift the back of the seat and draw it back, noting how the tab at the front locates **(see illustration)**.
2 Unscrew the bolts securing the rider's seat **(see illustration)**. Lift the seat and draw it back, noting how the tab at the front locates **(see illustration)**.
3 Installation is the reverse of removal. Make sure the tab at the front of each seat locates correctly. Push the back of the passenger seat down to engage the lock.

Passenger grab-rails

4 Unscrew the bolts and remove the rail.
5 Installation is the reverse of removal. Tighten the bolts to the torque setting specified at the beginning of the Chapter.

4.1a Unlock the seat . . .

4.1b . . . then lift it off, noting how the tab locates

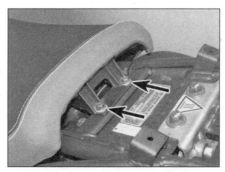

4.2a Unscrew the bolts (arrowed) . . .

4.2b . . . and remove the seat, noting how it locates

4.6 Undo the two screws (arrowed)

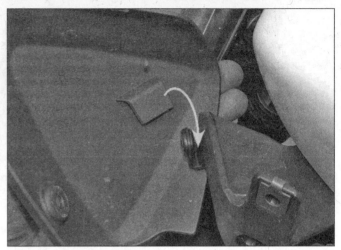

4.7 Locate the tab behind the hook

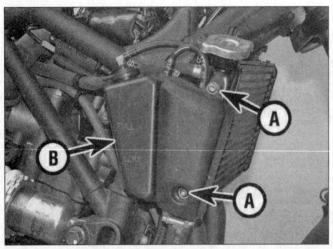

4.8 Unscrew the two bolts (A) and support the reservoir (B) after removing the right-hand cover

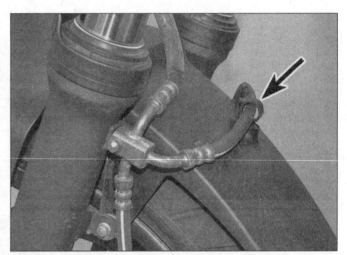

4.10 Release the hose from the clip (arrowed)

Fuel tank covers

6 Undo the two screws and remove the cover **(see illustration)**.

7 Installation is the reverse of removal – make sure the tab on the inner face of the cover locates behind the hook **(see illustration)**.

Radiator covers

8 Unscrew the two bolts, noting the collars with the top bolt, and remove the cover – note that the bolts for the right-hand cover also secure the coolant reservoir, which you will need to support **(see illustration)**.

9 Installation is the reverse of removal.

Front mudguard

10 Release the brake hose clip **(see illustration)**. Unscrew the two bolts on each side, noting there are nuts on the rear bolts and remove the mudguard. Note the arrangement of the collars and grommets, and make sure the grommets are in good condition.

11 Installation is the reverse of removal.

Mirrors

12 Slacken the base nut then unscrew the mirror **(see illustration 3.26)**.

13 Installation is the reverse of removal – position the mirror as required when almost fully screwed in then tighten the locknut.

Chapter 8
Electrical system

Contents

Alternator 29
Battery charging 4
Battery removal, installation and inspection 3
Brake light switches 14
Brake/tail light bulb and licence plate bulb 9
Charging system testing 28
Clutch switch 22
Diodes 23
Electrical system fault finding 2
Fuel gauge or warning light and level sensor 17
Fuses 5
General information 1
Handlebar switches 19
Headlight 8
Headlight bulb(s) and sidelight bulb(s) 7
Horn 24

Ignition switch 18
Ignition system . . . . see Chapter 4
Instrument cluster 15
Instrument and warning light LEDs 16
Lighting system check 6
Neutral switch 20
Regulator/rectifier 30
Relay unit and diodes 23
Sidestand switch 21
Starter motor overhaul 27
Starter motor removal and installation 26
Starter relay 25
Tail light 10
Turn signal assemblies 13
Turn signal bulbs 12
Turn signal circuit check 11

Degrees of difficulty

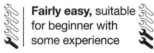

| **Easy,** suitable for novice with little experience | **Fairly easy,** suitable for beginner with some experience | **Fairly difficult,** suitable for competent DIY mechanic | **Difficult,** suitable for experienced DIY mechanic | **Very difficult,** suitable for expert DIY or professional |

Specifications

Battery
Type	Yuasa GT9B-4/GS
Capacity	12 V, 8 Ah
Voltage	
Fully-charged	above 12.8 V
Discharged	12.0 to 12.7 V
Charging rate	0.8 A for 5 to 10 hrs

Bulbs
Headlight	
XT-R and XT-X models	55/60 W x 1
XT-Z models	55 W x 2
MT-03 models	55/60 W x 1
Sidelight	
XT-R and XT-X models	5 W x 1
XT-Z models	5 W x 2
MT-03 models	3 W x 1
Brake/tail light	
XT-R, XT-X and MT-03 models	21/5 W x 1
XT-Z models	LED
Licence plate light (XT-Z and MT-03 models)	5 W
Turn signal lights	10 W x 4
Instrument and warning lights	LED

Charging system

Stator coil resistance	0.224 to 0.336 ohms
Nominal output	14.0 V / 20.8 A @ 5000 rpm
Regulated voltage output	14.1 to 14.9 V @ 5000 rpm
Current leakage	0.1 mA (max)

Fuses

XT-R and XT-X models

Main fuse (in starter relay)	30 A
Fusebox fuses	
No. 1 – Lighting, brake lights, horn	10 A
No. 2 – Headlight	20 A
No. 3 – Ignition	10 A
No. 4 – Fuel injection	10 A
No. 5 – Cooling fan	7.5 A
No. 6 – Immobiliser and instruments	10 A
Sidelight, turn signals (in separate fuse holder)	10 A

XT-Z and MT-03 models

Main fuse (in starter relay)	30 A
Fusebox fuses	
No. 1 – Sidelight, turn signals	10 A
No. 2 – Lighting, brake lights, horn	10 A
No. 3 – Headlight	20 A
No. 4 – Ignition	10 A
No. 5 – Fuel injection	10 A
No. 6 – Cooling fan	7.5 A
No. 7 – Immobiliser and instruments	10 A

Fuel level sensor

Resistance	1.35 to 1.65 K-ohms

Starter motor

Brush length	
Standard	12.5 mm
Service limit (min)	5.0 mm
Commutator diameter	
Standard	28.0 mm
Service limit (min)	27.0 mm
Mica undercut (depth)	0.7 mm
Armature coil resistance	0.025 to 0.035 ohms

Starter relay

Coil resistance	4.18 to 4.62 ohms

Torque settings

Alternator cover bolts	10 Nm
Alternator rotor nut	80 Nm
Alternator stator, CKP sensor and wiring clamp bolts	10 Nm
Brake light switch – XT-Z and MT-03 models	24 Nm
Starter damper gear cover bolts	10 Nm
Starter motor mounting bolts	10 Nm

1 General information

All models have a 12 volt electrical system charged by an alternator with separate regulator/rectifier.

The regulator maintains the charging system output within the specified range to prevent overcharging, and the rectifier converts the ac (alternating current) output of the alternator to dc (direct current) to power the lights and other components and to charge the battery. The alternator rotor is mounted on the left-hand end of the crankshaft.

The starter motor is mounted on the top of the crankcase. The starting system includes the motor, the battery, the relay and the various wires and switches. Some of the switches are part of a starter safety interlock system – see Chapter 1 for further information and checks on the system.

Note: *Keep in mind that electrical parts, once purchased, often cannot be returned. To avoid unnecessary expense, make very sure the faulty component has been positively identified before buying a replacement part.*

2 Electrical system fault finding

1 A typical electrical circuit consists of an electrical component, the switches, relays, etc, related to that component and the wiring and connectors that link the component to the battery and the frame.

2 Before tackling any troublesome electrical circuit, first study the wiring diagram thoroughly to get a complete picture of what makes up that individual circuit. Trouble

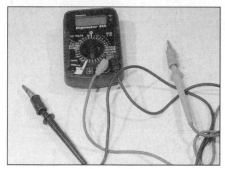

2.4a A digital multimeter can be used for all electrical tests

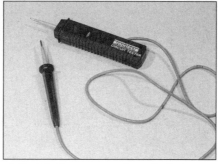

2.4b A battery-powered continuity tester

2.4c A simple test light is useful for voltage tests

spots, for instance, can often be narrowed down by noting if other components related to that circuit are operating properly or not. If several components or circuits fail at one time, chances are the fault lies either in the fuse or in the common earth (ground) connection, as several circuits are often routed through the same fuse and earth (ground) connections.

3 Electrical problems often stem from simple causes, such as loose or corroded connections or a blown fuse. Prior to any electrical fault finding, always visually check the condition of the fuse, wires and connections in the problem circuit. Intermittent failures can be especially frustrating, since you can't always duplicate the failure when it's convenient to test. In such situations, a good practice is to clean all connections in the affected circuit, whether or not they appear to be good – where possible use a dedicated electrical cleaning spray along with sandpaper, wire wool or other abrasive material to remove corrosion, and a dedicated electrical protection spray to prevent further problems. All of the connections and wires should also be wiggled to check for looseness which can cause intermittent failure.

4 If you don't have a multimeter it is highly advisable to obtain one – they are not expensive and will enable a full range of electrical tests to be made. Go for a modern digital one with LCD display as they are easier to use. A continuity tester and/or test light are useful for certain electrical checks as an alternative, though are limited in their usefulness compared to a multimeter **(see illustrations)**.

Continuity checks

5 The term continuity describes the uninterrupted flow of electricity through an electrical circuit. Continuity can be checked with a multimeter set either to its continuity function (a beep is emitted when continuity is found), or to the resistance (ohms / Ω) function, or with a dedicated continuity tester. Both instruments are powered by an internal battery, therefore the checks are made with the ignition OFF. As a safety precaution, always disconnect the battery negative (–) lead before making continuity checks, particularly if ignition switch checks are being made.

6 If using a multimeter, select the continuity

function if it has one, or the resistance (ohms) function. Touch the meter probes together and check that a beep is emitted or the meter reads zero, which indicates continuity. If there is no continuity there will be no beep or the meter will show infinite resistance. After using the meter, always switch it OFF to conserve its battery.

7 A continuity tester can be used in the same way – its light should come on or it should beep to indicate continuity in the switch ON position, but should be off or silent in the OFF position.

8 Note that the polarity of the test probes doesn't matter for continuity checks, although care should be taken to follow specific test procedures if a diode or solid-state component is being checked.

Switch continuity checks

9 If a switch is at fault, trace its wiring to the wiring connectors. Separate the connectors and inspect them for security and condition. A build-up of dirt or corrosion here will most likely be the cause of the problem – clean up and apply a water dispersant such as WD40, or alternatively use a dedicated contact cleaner and protection spray.

10 If using a multimeter, select the continuity function if it has one, or the resistance (ohms) function, and connect its probes to the terminals in the connector **(see illustration)**. Simple ON/OFF type switches, such as brake light switches, only have two wires whereas combination switches, like the handlebar switches, have many wires. Study the wiring

diagram to ensure that you are connecting to the correct pair of wires. Continuity should be indicated with the switch ON and no continuity with it OFF.

Wiring continuity checks

11 Many electrical faults are caused by damaged wiring, often due to incorrect routing or chaffing on frame components. Loose, wet or corroded wire connectors can also be the cause of electrical problems.

12 A continuity check can be made on a single length of wire by disconnecting it at each end and connecting the meter or continuity tester probes to each end of the wire **(see illustration)**. Continuity (low or no resistance – 0 ohms) should be indicated if the wire is good. If no continuity (high resistance) is shown, suspect a broken wire.

13 To check for continuity to earth in any earth wire connect one probe of your meter or tester to the earth wire terminal in the connector and the other to the frame, engine, or battery earth (–) terminal. Continuity (low or no resistance – 0 ohms) should be indicated if the wire is good. If no continuity (high resistance) is shown, suspect a broken wire or corroded or loose earth point (see below).

Voltage checks

14 A voltage check can determine whether power is reaching a component. Use a multimeter set to the dc voltage scale, or a test light. The test light is the cheaper component, but the meter has the advantage of being able to give a voltage reading.

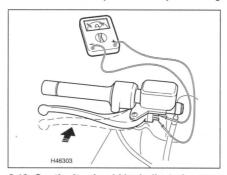

2.10 Continuity should be indicated across switch terminals when lever is operated

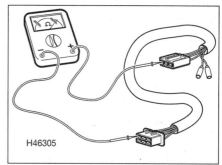

2.12 Wiring continuity check. Connect the meter probes across each end of the same wire

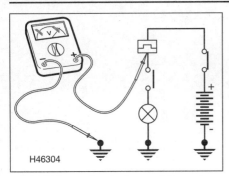

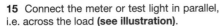

2.15 Voltage check. Connect the meter positive probe to the component and the negative probe to earth

15 Connect the meter or test light in parallel, i.e. across the load **(see illustration)**.

16 First identify the relevant wiring circuit by referring to the wiring diagram at the end of this manual. If other electrical components share the same power supply (i.e. are fed from the same fuse), take note whether they are working correctly – this is useful information in deciding where to start checking the circuit.

17 If using a meter, check first that the meter leads are plugged into the correct terminals on the meter (red to positive (+), black to negative (–)). Set the meter to the dc volts function, where necessary at a range suitable for the battery voltage – 0 to 20 vdc. Connect the meter red probe (+) to the power supply wire and the black probe to a good metal earth (ground) on the motorcycle's frame or directly to the battery negative terminal.

3.1a On XT-R and XT-X models unscrew the bolts (arrowed), lift the retainer and release the tabs at the back

3.1c On MT-03 models remove the cover . . .

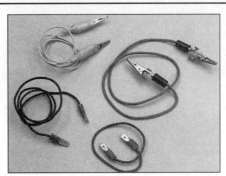

2.23 A selection of insulated jumper wires

Battery voltage should be shown on the meter with the ignition switch, and if necessary any other relevant switch, ON.

18 If using a test light, connect its positive (+) probe to the power supply terminal and its negative (–) probe to a good earth (ground) on the motorcycle's frame. With the switch, and if necessary any other relevant switch, ON, the test light should illuminate.

19 If no voltage is indicated, work back towards the fuse continuing to check for voltage. When you reach a point where there is voltage, you know the problem lies between that point and your last check point.

Earth (ground) checks

20 Earth connections are made either directly to the engine or frame (such as neutral switch, oil pressure switch etc. which only have a

3.1b On XT-Z models unscrew the bolts and remove the retainer

3.1d . . . then unhook the strap

positive feed) or by a separate wire into the earth circuit of the wiring harness. Alternatively a short earth wire is sometimes run from the component directly to the motorcycle's frame.

21 Corrosion is a common cause of a poor earth connection, as is a loose earth terminal fastener.

22 If total or multiple component failure is experienced, check the security of the main earth lead from the negative (–) terminal of the battery, the earth lead bolted to the engine, and the main earth point(s) on the frame. If corroded, dismantle the connection and clean all surfaces back to bare metal. Remake the connection and prevent further corrosion from forming by smearing battery terminal grease over the connection.

23 To check the earth of a component, use an insulated jumper wire to temporarily bypass its earth connection **(see illustration)** – connect one end of the jumper wire to the earth terminal or metal body of the component and the other end to the motorcycle's frame. If the circuit works with the jumper wire installed, the earth circuit is faulty.

24 To check an earth wire first check for corroded or loose connections, then check the wiring for continuity (Step 13) between each connector in the circuit in turn, and then to its earth point, to locate the break.

---

3 Battery removal, installation and inspection

Caution: Be extremely careful when handling or working around the battery. The electrolyte is very caustic and an explosive gas (hydrogen) is given off when the battery is charging.

Removal and installation

1 Make sure the ignition is switched OFF. On XT models remove the seat (see Chapter 7). On MT-03 models remove the fuel tank (see Chapter 4). Remove the battery retainer **(see illustrations)**.

2 Unscrew the negative (–) terminal bolt first and disconnect the lead from the battery **(see illustrations)**. Lift up the insulating cover to

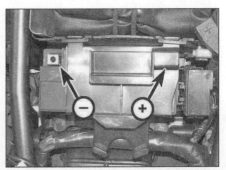

3.2a Negative and positive terminals – XT-R and XT-X

3.2b Negative and positive terminals – XT-Z

3.2c Negative and positive terminals – MT-03

3.3a Removing the battery on XT models

access the positive (+) terminal, then unscrew the bolt and disconnect the lead.

3 Lift the battery from the bike **(see illustrations)**.

4 On installation, clean the battery terminals and lead ends with a wire brush, fine sandpaper or steel wool. Reconnect the leads, connecting the positive (+) terminal first.

 Battery corrosion can be kept to a minimum by applying a layer of battery terminal grease or petroleum jelly (Vaseline) to the terminals after the leads have been connected. DO NOT use a mineral based grease.

5 Install the seat (see Chapter 7) or fuel tank (see Chapter 4).

Inspection and maintenance

6 All models are fitted with a maintenance free (MF) battery that does not require electrolyte level checks and topping up. However, the following checks should still be performed. **Note:** *Do not attempt to remove the battery caps to check the electrolyte level or battery specific gravity. Removal will damage the caps, resulting in electrolyte leakage and battery damage.*

7 Check the battery terminals and leads are tight and free of corrosion. If corrosion is evident, clean the terminals as described in Step 4, then protect them from further corrosion (see *Haynes Hint*).

8 Keep the battery case clean to prevent current leakage, which can discharge the battery over a period of time (especially when it sits unused). Wash the outside of the case with a solution of baking soda and water. Rinse the battery thoroughly, then dry it.

9 Look for cracks in the case and replace the battery with a new one if any are found. If acid has been spilled on the frame or battery box, neutralise it with a baking soda and water solution, dry it thoroughly, then touch up any damaged paint.

10 If the motorcycle sits unused for long periods of time, disconnect the cables from the battery terminals, negative (–) terminal first. Refer to Section 4 and charge the battery once every month to six weeks.

11 Check the condition of the battery by measuring the voltage present at the battery

3.3b Removing the battery on MT-03 models

terminals. Connect the voltmeter positive (+) probe to the battery positive (+) terminal, and the negative (–) probe to the battery negative (–) terminal **(see illustration)**. When fully-charged there should be 12.8 to 13.2 volts present. If the voltage falls much below this remove the battery (see above), and recharge it as described below in Section 4.

4 Battery charging

Caution: Be extremely careful when handling or working around the battery. The electrolyte is very caustic and an explosive gas (hydrogen) is given off when the battery is charging.

1 Remove the battery (see Section 3). Connect the charger to the battery, making sure that the

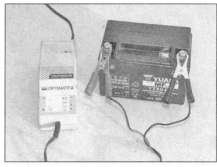

4.1 Battery connected to a motorcycle charger

3.11 Checking battery voltage – connect the meter as shown

positive (+) lead on the charger is connected to the positive (+) terminal on the battery, and the negative (–) lead is connected to the negative (–) terminal. Use of a dedicated motorcycle battery charger is advised **(see illustration)**. These are designed for the maintenance and recovery of motorcycle batteries, in particular catering for the requirements of heavily discharged MF batteries. They are not too expensive, and are a worthwhile investment, especially if the bike is not used over winter. Follow the manufacturer's instructions.

2 Yamaha recommend that the battery is charged at the normal rate specified at the beginning of the Chapter. Exceeding this figure can cause the battery to overheat, buckling the plates and rendering it useless. If a normal domestic charger is used check that after a possible initial peak, the charge rate falls to a safe level **(see illustration)**. If the battery

4.2 Battery connected to a car type charger with built-in ammeter

5.2a Main and spare main fuses (arrowed) – XT-R and XT-X

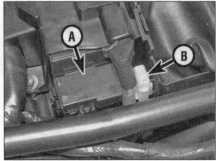
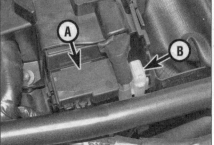

5.2b Fusebox (A) and sidelight fuse holder (B) – XT-R and XT-X

becomes hot during charging **stop**. Further charging will cause damage.

3 If the recharged battery discharges rapidly if left disconnected it is likely that an internal short caused by physical damage or sulphation has occurred. A new battery will be required. A sound item will tend to lose its charge at about 1% per day.

4 Install the battery (see Section 3).

5 If the motorcycle sits unused for long periods of time, charge the battery once every month to six weeks and leave it disconnected.

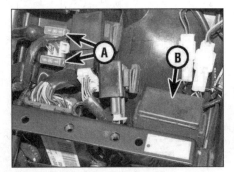

5.3 Main and spare main fuses (A), fusebox (B) – XT-Z

5.4a Main and spare main fuses (arrowed) – MT-03

1 The electrical system is protected by fuses of different ratings (see Specifications at the beginning of the Chapter). The main fuse is in the starter relay. All other fuses are in a fusebox. A spare fuse of each rating except the main fuses is housed in the fusebox, and a spare main fuse is housed in the starter relay holder. If a spare fuse is used, always replace it with a new one so that a spare of each rating is carried on the bike at all times.

2 On XT-R and XT-X models remove the left-hand side panel to access the starter relay (see Chapter 7) **(see illustration)**. Remove the seat to access the fusebox (see Chapter 7) **(see illustration)** – the sidelight fuse is in its own holder next to the fusebox.

3 On XT-Z models remove the seat to access the starter relay and the fusebox (see Chapter 7) **(see illustration)**.

4 On MT-03 models remove fuel tank to access the starter relay (see Chapter 4) **(see illustration)**. Remove the seat to access the fusebox (see Chapter 7) **(see illustration)**.

5 Remove the cap to access the main fuse **(see illustration)**. Unclip the fusebox lid to access the fusebox fuses **(see illustration)**. The fuses are numbered, and the numbers are marked on the fusebox lid **(see illustration)** – refer to the Specifications at the beginning of the Chapter for the function and rating of each fuse. The fuses can be removed and checked visually – if you can't pull the fuse out with your fingertips, use a pair of suitable pliers **(see illustration)**. A

5.4b Fusebox (arrowed) – MT-03

5.5a Remove the cap to access the main fuse and its spare

5.5b Unclip the lid to access the fuses

5.5c The number of each fuse is marked on the lid – cross-refer to the specifications for the function of each fuse

5.5d Pull the fuse out using your fingers or small pliers

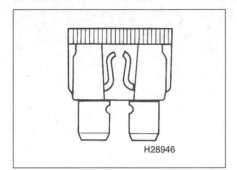

5.5e A blown fuse can be identified by a break in its element

blown fuse is easily identified by a break in the element **(see illustration)**. Each fuse is clearly marked with its rating and must only be replaced by a fuse of the correct rating.

 Warning: Never put in a fuse of a higher rating or bridge the terminals with any other substitute, however temporary it may be. Serious damage may be done to the circuit, or a fire may start.

6 If the new fuse blows immediately check the wiring circuit very carefully for evidence of a short-circuit. Look for bare wires and chafed, melted or burned insulation.

7 Occasionally a fuse will blow or cause an open-circuit for no obvious reason. Corrosion of the fuse ends and fusebox terminals may occur and cause poor fuse contact. If this happens, remove the corrosion with a wire brush or emery paper, then spray the fuse end and terminals with electrical contact cleaner.

6 Lighting system check

1 If a light fails first check the bulb (see relevant Section), the bulb terminals in the holder, and the wiring connector(s). If none of the lights work, check the battery – low voltage indicates either a faulty battery or a defective charging system. Refer to Section 3 for battery checks and Section 28 for charging system tests. Also, check the fuses (Section 5) – if there is more than one problem at the

same time, it is likely to be a fault relating to a multi-function component, such as one of the fuses governing more than one circuit, or the ignition switch. When checking for a blown filament in a bulb, it is advisable to back up a visual check with a continuity test of the filament as it is not always apparent that a bulb has blown. When testing for continuity, remember that on single terminal bulbs it is the metal body of the bulb that is the earth (ground).

Headlight

2 XT-R, XT-X and MT-03 models have one twin filament bulb, one filament for high beam and one for low beam. XT-Z models have two single filament bulbs, one bulb for high beam and one for low beam. If one of the beams fails to work, first check the bulb (see Section 7). If both beams fail to work first check the headlight fuse (see Section 5). If all is good so far, the problem lies in the wiring or connectors, the headlight relay, or the dimmer switch. First make sure the wiring connectors are secure (see Section 7). Next check the relay (Step 3).

3 To check the relay, on XT-R and XT-X models remove the right-hand side panel (see Chapter 7), on XT-Z models remove the battery (see Section 3), and on MT-03 models remove the seats (see Chapter 7). Displace the relay and disconnect its wiring connector **(see illustrations)**. Set a multimeter to the ohms x 1 scale and connect it across the relay's red/blue and blue/white wire terminals. There should be no continuity (infinite resistance). Using a fully-charged 12 volt battery and two insulated jumper wires, connect the positive (+) terminal of the battery to the red/yellow wire terminal, and the negative (–) terminal to the yellow/black wire terminal. At this point the relay should be heard to click and the meter read 0 ohms (continuity). If this is the case the relay is good. If the relay does not click when battery voltage is applied and indicates no continuity (infinite resistance) across its terminals, it is faulty and must be replaced with a new one.

4 If the relay is good, check for battery voltage at the red/yellow and red/blue wire terminals in the relay wiring connector with

the ignition ON. If there is no voltage check the wiring between the connector and the ignition switch via the fusebox. If the voltage is good check the blue/white wire between the relay and the dimmer switch, and then the yellow and green wires from the switch to the headlight for continuity, checking the switch at the same time by alternating it between LO and HI beam while checking for continuity from the blue/white wire through the switch to the green or yellow wire in the switch housing wiring connector according to the position of the switch, referring to Section 19 and the wiring diagrams at the end of the Chapter. Next check the yellow/black wire from the relay to the ECU for continuity. Also make sure that all the terminals and connectors are clean and secure. Repair or renew the wiring or connectors as necessary.

5 If the LO beam does not work, and the bulb is good, check for battery voltage at the green wire terminal on the headlight wiring connector with the ignition ON and the dimmer switch set to LO. If the HI beam does not work, and the bulb is good, check for battery voltage at the yellow wire terminal on the headlight wiring connector with the ignition ON and the dimmer switch set to HI. If voltage is present, check for continuity to earth (ground) in the black wire from the wiring connector. Repair or renew the wiring or connectors as necessary.

Sidelight(s)

6 XT-R, XT-X and MT-03 models have one sidelight bulb, XT-Z models have two sidelight bulbs. If the sidelight, or one of the sidelights on XT-Z models, fails to work, first check the bulb (Section 7). If the bulb is good, or if both sidelights fail on XT-Z models, check the sidelight fuse (see Section 5). If the fuse is good, disconnect the sidelight wiring connector(s), and check for battery voltage at the blue/red wire terminal on the loom side of the connector with the ignition switch ON. If voltage is present, check for continuity to earth (ground) in the black wire from the wiring connector. If no voltage is indicated, check the wiring and connectors in sidelight circuit, referring to the wiring diagrams at the end of this Chapter.

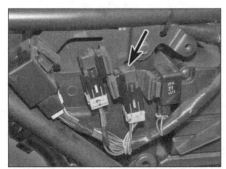

6.3a Headlight relay (arrowed) – XT-R and XT-X

6.3b Headlight relay (arrowed) – XT-Z

6.3c Headlight relay (arrowed) – MT-03

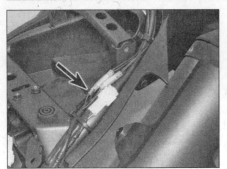

6.7a Tail/brake light and turn signal wiring connectors (arrowed) – XT-R and XT-X

6.7b Tail/brake light, licence plate light, and turn signal wiring connectors (arrowed) – MT-03

6.8 Tail/brake light, licence plate light, and turn signal wiring connectors (arrowed) – XT-Z

Tail light

7 On XT-R, XT-X and MT-03 models if the tail light fails to work, first check the bulb (Section 9). If it is good, remove the seat (see Chapter 7) and disconnect the tail light wiring connector **(see illustrations)**. Check for battery voltage at the blue/red wire terminal on the loom side of the connector with the ignition switch ON. If voltage is present, check for continuity to earth (ground) in the black wire from the wiring connector. If no voltage is indicated, check the wiring and connectors in the tail light circuit, referring to the wiring diagrams at the end of this Chapter.

8 On XT-Z models if the tail light fails to work, remove the seat (see Chapter 7) and disconnect the tail light wiring connector **(see illustration)**. Check the LED by connecting the positive (+) terminal of a 12 volt battery to the blue/red wire terminal in the light unit side of the connector, and the negative (–) terminal to the black wire terminal – the LED should come on. If it doesn't replace the tail light with a new one (see Section 10). If it is good, check for battery voltage at the blue/red wire terminal on the loom side of the connector with the ignition switch ON. If voltage is present, check for continuity to earth (ground) in the black wire from the wiring connector. If no voltage is indicated, check the wiring and connectors in the tail light circuit, referring to the wiring diagrams at the end of this Chapter.

Brake light

9 On XT-R, XT-X and MT-03 models if the brake light fails to work, first check the bulb (Section 9).

If it is good remove the seat (see Chapter 7) and disconnect the tail light wiring connector **(see illustration 6.7a or b)**. Check for battery voltage at the yellow or yellow/green (according to model) wire terminal on the loom side of the connector, first with the front brake lever pulled in, then with the rear brake pedal pressed down. If voltage is present with one brake on but not the other, then the switch or its wiring is faulty. If voltage is present in both cases, check for continuity to earth (ground) in the black wire from the wiring connector. If no voltage is indicated, check the wiring and connectors between the brake light and the switches, then check the switches themselves. Refer to Section 14 for the switch testing procedures, and also to the wiring diagrams at the end of this Chapter.

10 On XT-Z models if the tail light fails to work, remove the seat (see Chapter 7) and disconnect the tail light wiring connector **(see illustration 6.8)**. Check the LED by connecting the positive (+) terminal of a 12 volt battery to the yellow/green wire terminal in the light unit side of the connector, and the negative (–) terminal to the black wire terminal – the LED should come on. If it doesn't replace the tail light with a new one (see Section 10). If it is good, check for battery voltage at the yellow/green wire terminal on the loom side of the connector, first with the front brake lever pulled in, then with the rear brake pedal pressed down. If voltage is present with one brake on but not the other, then the switch or its wiring is faulty. If voltage is present in both cases, check for continuity to earth (ground) in the black wire from the wiring connector. If

no voltage is indicated, check the wiring and connectors between the brake light and the switches, then check the switches themselves. Refer to Section 14 for the switch testing procedures, and also to the wiring diagrams at the end of this Chapter.

Licence plate light – XT-Z and MT-03 models

11 If the licence plate light fails to work, first check whether the tail light is working – they run off the same circuit. If it isn't refer to Step 7. If it is check the bulb (Section 9). If the bulb and tail light are both good check the wire between the connector on the tail light and that on the licence plate light for continuity.

Turn signals

12 See Section 11.

| 7 | Headlight bulb(s) and sidelight bulb(s) | |

Note: *Do not touch the glass of quartz halogen bulbs as skin acids will shorten the bulb's service life. If the bulb is accidentally touched, it should be wiped carefully when cold with a rag soaked in methylated spirit and dried before fitting.*

HAYNES HiNT *Always use a paper towel or dry cloth when handling new bulbs to prevent injury if the bulb should break and to increase bulb life.*

XT-R and XT-X models
Headlight

1 Displace the front cowl assembly (see Chapter 7) – there is no need to remove the fuel tank and disconnect the main wiring connectors unless you want to completely remove the cowl assembly.

2 Disconnect the headlight wiring connector then pull the rubber cover off **(see illustration)**.

3 Release the bulb holder by turning it anti-clockwise then withdraw the bulb, bearing in mind the information in the **Note** above **(see illustration)**.

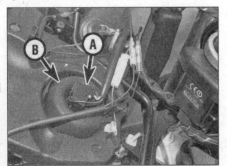

7.2 Disconnect the wiring connector (A) then remove the cover (B)

7.3 Turn the bulb holder (arrowed) anti-clockwise

7.9 Pull the bulb holder (arrowed) out then remove the bulb

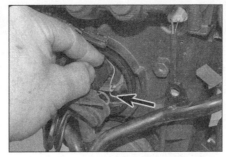

7.13 Remove the cover, disconnect the wiring connector, then release the clip (arrowed)

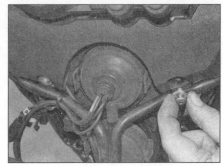

7.17a Undo the screws . . .

7.17b . . . then release the pegs from the grommets and remove the cover

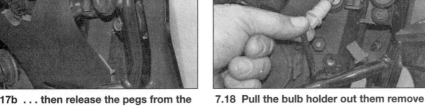

7.18 Pull the bulb holder out them remove the bulb

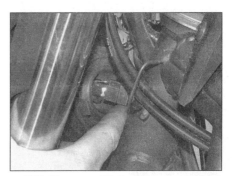

7.23 Disconnect the wiring connector

4 Fit the new bulb and secure it with the holder, turning it clockwise to secure it.

5 Fit the rubber cover then connect the headlight wiring connector **(see illustration 7.2)**.

6 Check the operation of the headlight.

7 Install the front cowl assembly (see Chapter 7).

Sidelight

8 Displace the front cowl assembly (see Chapter 7) – there is no need to remove the fuel tank and disconnect the main wiring connectors unless you want to completely remove the cowl assembly.

9 Carefully pull the sidelight bulb holder out, then carefully pull the bulb out of the holder **(see illustration)**.

10 Fit the new bulb, then fit the holder into the headlight.

11 Check the operation of the sidelight.

12 Install the front cowl assembly (see Chapter 7).

XT-Z models

Headlights

13 To access the top (LO beam) bulb displace the cover, then disconnect the wiring connector **(see illustration)**. Release the bulb retaining clip and withdraw the bulb, bearing in mind the information in the **Note** above.

14 To access the lower (HI beam) bulb displace the cover, then disconnect the wiring connector **(see illustration 7.13)**. Release the bulb holder by twisting it anti-clockwise and remove the bulb, bearing in mind the information in the **Note** above **(see illustration 7.3)**.

15 Fit the new bulb in reverse order. Fit the cover.

16 Check the operation of the headlight.

Sidelights

17 Unscrew the instrument trim panel screws, noting the collars **(see illustration)**. Carefully

pull the panel away to release the pegs from the grommets **(see illustration)**.

18 Carefully pull the sidelight bulb holder out, then carefully pull the bulb out of the holder **(see illustration)**.

19 Fit the new bulb, then fit the holder into the headlight.

20 Check the operation of the sidelight.

21 Fit the trim panel.

MT-03 models

Headlight

22 Turn the handlebars to full right lock.

23 Disconnect the headlight wiring connector **(see illustration)**.

24 Pull the rubber cover off **(see illustration)**. Release the bulb holder by twisting it anti-clockwise and withdraw the bulb, bearing in mind the information in the **Note** above **(see illustrations)**.

7.24a Remove the cover . . .

7.24b . . . then release the bulb holder . . .

7.24c . . . and remove the bulb

7.29 Sidelight bulb holder (arrowed)

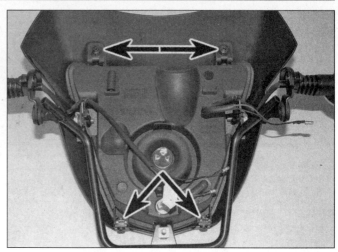

8.3 Undo the screws (arrowed) and remove the cowl

25 Fit the new bulb and secure it with the holder. Fit the rubber cover.
26 Connect the headlight wiring connector.
27 Check the operation of the headlight.

Sidelight

28 Turn the handlebars to full right lock.

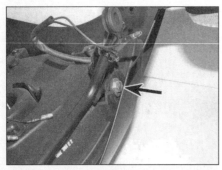

8.4a Unscrew the bolt (arrowed) on each side . . .

29 Carefully pull the sidelight bulb holder out, then carefully pull the bulb out of the holder **(see illustration)**.
30 Fit the new bulb, then fit the holder into the headlight.
31 Check the operation of the sidelight.

8 Headlight

Removal

XT-R and XT-X models

1 Remove the front cowl assembly (see Chapter 7). Remove the instrument cluster (see Section 15).
2 Disconnect the headlight and sidelight wiring connectors **(see illustration 7.2)**.
3 Undo the four screws and remove the cowl **(see illustration)**.

4 Unscrew the two bolts securing the headlight to its bracket, then release the beam adjuster nut and draw the headlight out **(see illustrations)**.
5 Remove the bulbs from the headlight if required (see Section 7).

XT-Z models

6 Remove the front cowl (see Chapter 7).
7 Disconnect the headlight wiring connectors and/or remove the bulbs as required (see Section 7).
8 Unscrew the bolts securing the headlight to its bracket and draw it out **(see illustration)**.

MT-03 models

9 Unscrew the two bolts securing the left-hand turn signal bracket and draw it off the headlight, noting how the peg locates in the hole, and either support it to one side or disconnect the wiring connector and remove

8.4b . . . then release the adjuster block (arrowed) and remove the headlight

8.8 Unscrew the bolts and remove the headlight

8.9a Unscrew the two bolts (arrowed) . . .

8.9b . . . collecting the nut with the top bolt and noting how the peg (arrowed) locates . . .

8.9c . . . and the arrangement of the grommets and collars

8.10a Draw the headlight off the peg . . .

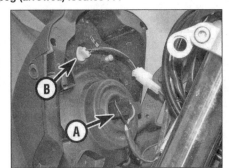

8.10b . . . then disconnect the wiring connector (A) and remove the sidelight (B)

it **(see illustrations)**. Note the arrangement of the nuts, collars and grommets with the top bolts and the washers, collars and grommets with the bottom bolts **(see illustration)**.

10 Unscrew the bottom bolt securing the right-hand turn signal bracket, then draw the headlight off the peg and disconnect the headlight wiring connector and pull the sidelight bulb holder out **(see illustrations)**.

11 Remove the bulb from the headlight if required (see Section 7).

Installation

12 Installation is the reverse of removal. Make sure all the wiring is correctly routed, connected and secured. Check the operation

of the headlight and sidelight. Check the headlight aim.

Headlight aim

Note: *An improperly adjusted headlight may cause problems for oncoming traffic or provide poor, unsafe illumination of the road ahead. Before adjusting the headlight aim, be sure to consult with local traffic laws and regulations – for UK models refer to MOT Test Checks in the Reference section.*

13 The headlight beam can adjusted vertically. Before making any adjustment, check that the tyre pressures are correct and the suspension is adjusted as required. Make any adjustments to the headlight aim with the machine on level ground, with the fuel tank half full and with

an assistant sitting on the seat. If the bike is usually ridden with a passenger on the back, have a second assistant to do this.

14 On XT-R and XT-X models adjustment is made by turning the adjuster screw under the front of the headlight **(see illustration)** – turn it clockwise to lower the beam and anti-clockwise to raise it.

15 On XT-Z models adjustment is made by turning the adjuster screw on the back of the headlight **(see illustration)** – turn it clockwise to raise the beam and anti-clockwise to lower it.

16 On MT-03 models adjustment is made by turning the adjuster screw on the back of the headlight **(see illustration)** – turn it clockwise to lower the beam and anti-clockwise to raise it.

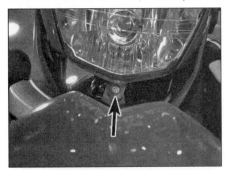

8.14 Headlight beam adjuster (arrowed) – XT-R and XT-X

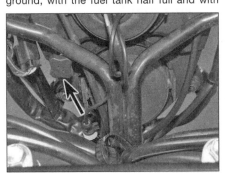

8.15 Headlight beam adjuster (arrowed) – XT-Z

8.16 Headlight beam adjuster (arrowed) – MT-03

9.1 Undo the screws (arrowed) and remove the lens

9.2 Release the bulb from the tail light

9.6a Unscrew the bolt (arrowed) on the underside . . .

9 Brake/tail light bulb and licence plate bulb

Note: *It is a good idea to use a paper towel or dry cloth when handling the new bulb to prevent injury if it breaks, and to increase bulb life.*

Brake/tail light bulb

XT-R and XT-X models

1 Undo the screws and remove the lens **(see illustration)**.
2 Carefully push the bulb in and turn it anti-clockwise to release it from the holder **(see illustration)**.
3 Line up the pins on the new bulb with the slots in the holder, then push the bulb in

and turn it clockwise, making sure it locates correctly.
4 Fit the lens – take care not to overtighten the screws as it is easy to strip the threads or crack the lens.

XT-Z models

5 The tail light contains LEDs which cannot be replaced with new ones. If the tests detailed in Section 6, Steps 8 and 10 prove that an LED is faulty replace the tail light unit with a new one (see Section 10).

MT-03 models

6 Unscrew the bolts securing the tail light assembly and displace it **(see illustrations)**.
7 Turn the bulb holder anti-clockwise to release it from the tail light **(see illustration)**.
8 Carefully push the bulb in and turn it anti-clockwise to release it from the holder **(see illustration)**.

9 Line up the pins on the new bulb with the slots in the holder, then push the bulb in and turn it clockwise, making sure it locates correctly.
10 Fit the bulb holder and turn it clockwise to secure it.
11 Fit the tail light.

Licence plate light bulb

XT-Z models

12 Carefully pull the bulb holder out **(see illustration)**. Pull the bulb out of its socket and replace it with a new one **(see illustration)**.
13 Fit the bulb holder.

MT-03 models

14 Unscrew the nuts and bolts securing the licence plate light cover on the underside of the rear mudguard and remove the cover **(see illustration)**.

9.6b . . . and the bolt (arrowed) on each side and displace the tail light assembly

9.7 Release the bulb holder . . .

9.8 . . . and remove the bulb

9.12a Pull the bulb holder out . . .

9.12b . . . and remove the bulb

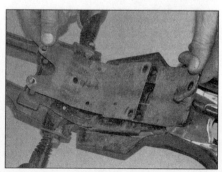

9.14 Remove the covers . . .

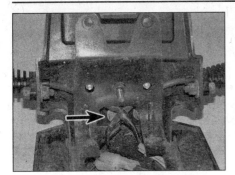

9.15 . . . to access the bulb holder (arrowed)

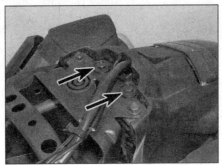

10.3a Unscrew the bolts (arrowed) . . .

10.3b . . . and pivot the assembly down

15 Carefully pull the bulb holder out (see illustration). Carefully pull the bulb out of its socket and replace it with a new one.
16 Fit the bulb holder, then fit the cover.

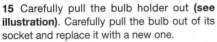

10 Tail light

Removal

XT-R and XT-X models

1 Remove the seat, grab rails and rear cowl (see Chapter 7).
2 Disconnect the wiring connectors and free the wiring from the tie and guide (see illustration 6.7a).

3 Unscrew the two bolts and pivot the licence plate assembly down (see illustrations).
4 Unscrew the nuts, remove the washers, and draw the tail light out (see illustration). Note the collars in the grommets.

XT-Z models

5 Remove the seat, grab rails, seat panels and luggage rack covers (see Chapter 7).
6 Disconnect the tail light assembly wiring connectors (see illustration 6.8).
7 Undo the screws and remove the tail light/licence plate assembly, drawing the wiring through (see illustrations). Note the collars in the underside of the luggage rack and the top of the tail light assembly and remove them for safekeeping if loose (see illustration).
8 Release the wiring ties and draw the tail light

wiring out, noting its routing. Undo the screws securing the tail light cover and remove it, then undo the tail light screws and remove the light (see illustration).

MT-03 models

9 Remove the seats (see Chapter 7).
10 Disconnect the tail light wiring connectors and free the wiring from any ties (see illustration 6.7b).
11 Unscrew the bolts securing the tail light assembly (see illustrations 9.6a and b). Remove the assembly, drawing the wiring through (see illustration).
12 Unscrew the nuts and bolts securing the tail light cover on the underside of the rear mudguard and remove the cover (see illustration 9.14).

10.4 Unscrew the nuts (arrowed) and remove the tail light

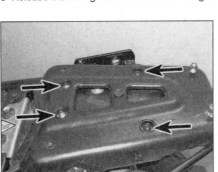

10.7a Undo the screws (arrowed) . . .

10.7b . . . and remove the tail assembly

10.7c Note the collars (arrowed), and those on the tail light holder, and remove them for safekeeping if loose

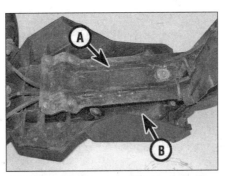

10.8 Remove the cover (A) to access the tail light (B), then undo its screws

10.11 Removing the tail light assembly

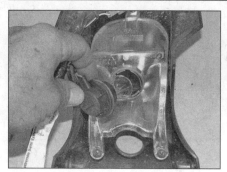

10.13 Release the bulb holder . . .

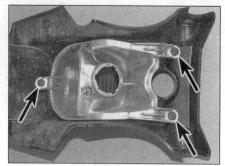

10.14 . . . then undo the screws (arrowed)

13 Turn the bulb holder anti-clockwise to release it from the tail light **(see illustration)**.
14 Undo the screws and remove the tail light **(see illustration)**.

Installation

15 Installation is the reverse of removal. Check the operation of the tail and brake lights.

11 Turn signal circuit check

1 Most turn signal problems are the result of a burned out bulb or corroded socket. This is especially true when the turn signals function on one side (although possibly too quickly), but fail to work on the other side. If this is the case, first check the bulbs, the sockets and the wiring connectors. If all the turn signals fail to work, check the sidelight fuse (see Section 5), then the relay (see below). If it is good, the problem lies in the wiring or connectors, or the switch. Refer to Section 19 for the switch testing procedures, and also to the wiring diagrams at the end of this Chapter.
2 On XT-R and XT-X models remove the right-hand side panel (see Chapter 7). On XT-Z and MT-03 models remove the seat(s) (see Chapter 7). Disconnect the relay wiring connector **(see illustrations)**.
3 Check for battery voltage at the brown wire terminal on the loom side of the connector with the ignition ON. If no voltage is present,

check the wiring from the relay to the ignition switch for continuity.
4 If voltage was present, short between the brown and brown/white wire terminals on the connector using a jumper wire. Turn the ignition ON and operate the turn signal switch, first in one direction, then the other. If the turn signal lights come on in each direction (they won't flash), the relay is confirmed faulty.
5 If none of the lights come on, check the brown/white wire for continuity to the left-hand switch housing, and repair or renew the wiring or connectors as required.
6 If all is good so far, or if some of the lights work but not all, check the wiring for the lights concerned between the left-hand switch housing and the turn signals themselves. Repair or renew the wiring or connectors as necessary.

12 Turn signal bulbs

Note: *It is a good idea to use a paper towel or dry cloth when handling the new bulb to prevent injury if the bulb should break and to increase bulb life.*
1 Undo the screw securing the lens and detach it from the housing, noting how it fits **(see illustrations)**.
2 Push the bulb into the holder and twist it

11.2a Turn signal relay (arrowed) – XT-R and XT-X models

11.2b Turn signal relay (arrowed) – XT-Z models

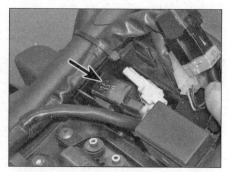

11.2c On MT-03 models displace the headlight and cooling fan relays to access the turn signal relay (arrowed)

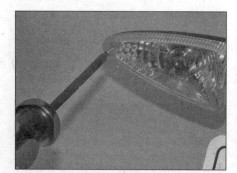

12.1a Undo the screw on the front of the lens on XT-Z models . . .

12.1b . . . and on the back on all other models . . .

12.1c . . . and detach the lens . . .

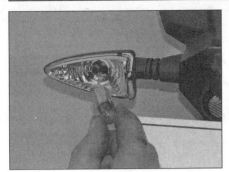

12.2 . . . then remove the bulb

12.4 Make sure the tab (arrowed) locates correctly

8 Installation is the reverse of removal. Make sure the rubber plate and mounting plate locate correctly. Check the operation of the turn signals.

XT-Z models

Front

9 Trace the wiring from the turn signal and disconnect it at the connector **(see illustration)**.
10 Unscrew the nut, withdraw the bolt and remove the turn signal, noting the collar and taking care as you draw the wiring through **(see illustrations)**.
11 Installation is the reverse of removal. Check the operation of the turn signals.

Rear

12 Remove the seat, grab rails, seat panels and luggage rack covers (see Chapter 7).
13 Disconnect the tail light assembly wiring connectors **(see illustration 6.8)**.
14 Undo the screws and remove the tail light/ licence plate assembly, drawing the wiring through **(see illustrations 10.7a and b)**. Note the collars in the underside of the luggage rack and the top of the tail light assembly and remove them for safekeeping if loose **(see illustration 10.7c)**.
15 Undo the screws securing the tail light cover and remove it **(see illustration 10.8)**. Release the wiring ties and draw the turn signal wiring out, noting its routing.
16 Unscrew the nut, withdraw the bolt and remove the turn signal, noting the collar and taking care as you draw the wiring through **(see illustration)**.

anti-clockwise to remove it **(see illustration)**. Check the socket terminals for corrosion and clean them if necessary.
3 Line up the pins of the new bulb with the slots in the socket, then push the bulb in and turn it clockwise until it locks into place.
4 Fit the lens onto the housing, making sure it locates correctly, and secure it with the screw **(see illustration)**. Do not over-tighten the screw as it is easy to strip the threads or crack the lens.

13 Turn signal assemblies

XT-R and XT-X models
Front

1 Trace the wiring from the turn signal and disconnect it at the connectors, turning the handlebars to full lock for access.

2 Undo the screw and remove the turn signal, taking care as you draw the wiring through **(see illustration)**.
3 Installation is the reverse of removal. Check the operation of the turn signals.

Rear

4 Remove the seat, grab rails and rear cowl (see Chapter 7).
5 Trace the wiring from the turn signal and disconnect it at the connectors, and free the wiring from the tie and guide **(see illustration 6.7a)**.
6 Unscrew the two bolts and pivot the licence plate assembly down **(see illustrations 10.3a and b)**.
7 Unscrew the nut and remove the washer **(see illustration)**. Withdraw the bolt and remove the turn signal and mounting plate, taking care as you draw the wiring through. Remove the rubber plug if required, noting the sleeve for the bolt fitted in it.

13.2 Front turn signal screw (arrowed)

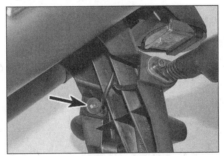

13.7 Unscrew the nut (arrowed) and remove the washer from the inside, then withdraw the bolt

13.9 Front turn signal wiring connector (arrowed)

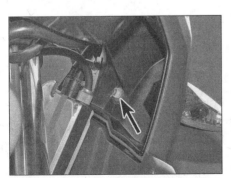

13.10a Unscrew the nut (arrowed) on the inside . . .

13.10b . . . then withdraw the bolt (arrowed) and remove the turn signal

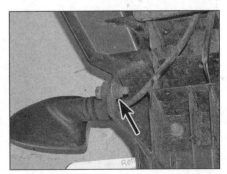

13.16 Unscrew the nut (arrowed), withdraw the bolt and remove the turn signal

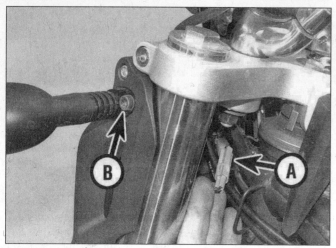

13.18 Disconnect the wiring connector (A), then unscrew the bolt (B)

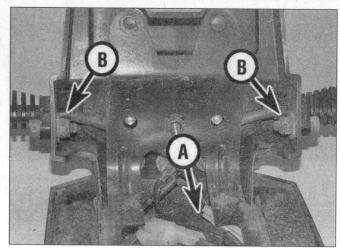

13.25 Turn signal wiring connectors (A) and mounting nuts/bolts (B)

17 Installation is the reverse of removal. Check the operation of the turn signals.

MT-03 models

Front

18 Trace the wiring from the turn signal and disconnect it at the connectors **(see illustration)**.

19 Unscrew the nut, withdraw the bolt and remove the turn signal, taking care as you draw the wiring through.

20 Installation is the reverse of removal. Check the operation of the turn signals.

Rear

21 Remove the seats (see Chapter 7).

22 Disconnect the tail light wiring connectors and free the wiring from any ties **(see illustration 6.7b)**.

23 Unscrew the bolts securing the tail light assembly **(see illustrations 9.6a and b)**. Remove the assembly, drawing the wiring through **(see illustration 10.11)**.

24 Unscrew the nuts and bolts securing the tail light cover on the underside of the

rear mudguard and remove the cover **(see illustration 9.14)**.

25 Disconnect the wiring connector **(see illustration)**.

26 Unscrew the nut, withdraw the bolt and remove the turn signal, noting the collar and taking care as you draw the wiring through.

27 Installation is the reverse of removal. Check the operation of the turn signals.

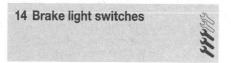

14 Brake light switches

Circuit check

1 Before checking the switches, and if not already done, check the brake light circuit (see Section 6).

Front brake lever switch

2 On XT-R and XT-X models remove the fuel tank (see Chapter 4). Trace the wiring from the

switch and disconnect it at the connector **(see illustration)**.

3 On XT-Z and MT-03 models disconnect the wiring connectors from the switch **(see illustration)**.

4 Using a continuity tester, connect the probes to the terminals on the switch side of the connector on XT-R and XT-X models, and to the terminals on the switch on XT-Z and MT-03 models. With the brake lever at rest, there should be no continuity. With the lever applied, there should be continuity. If the results are not as stated remove the switch (see below) and check the plunger for damage. Replace the switch with a new one if necessary (see below).

5 If the switch is good, check for voltage at the brown wire terminal on the loom side of the connector, with the ignition switch ON – there should be battery voltage. If there's no voltage present, check the wiring between the connector and the ignition switch (see the wiring diagrams at the end of this Chapter). If voltage is present, check the yellow wire on

14.2 Trace the wiring and disconnect the relevant connector

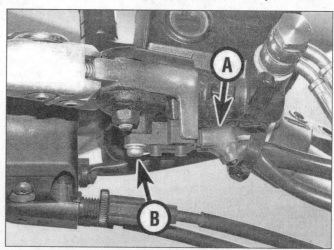

14.3 Brake light switch wiring connectors (A) and screw (B)

XT-R and XT-X models or yellow/green wire on XT-Z and MT-03 models for continuity to the brake light wiring connector, referring to the relevant wiring diagram. Repair or renew the wiring as necessary.

Rear brake pedal switch

6 On XT-R and XT-X models the rear brake light switch is on the inside of the right-hand footrest bracket **(see illustration 14.13)**. On XT-Z and MT-03 models the switch is hydraulic and is threaded into the top of the master cylinder **(see illustration 14.17a or b)**. Trace the wiring from the switch and disconnect it at the connector **(see illustrations)** – to access it, on XT models remove the seat (see Chapter 7), and on MT-03 models remove the fuel tank if required (see Chapter 4).

7 Using a continuity tester, connect the probes to the terminals on the switch side of the wiring connector. With the brake pedal at rest, there should be no continuity. With the pedal applied, there should be continuity. If the switch does not behave as described, replace it with a new one, although on XT-R and XT-X models check first that the switch is adjusted correctly (see Chapter 1, Section 10).

8 If the switch is good, check for voltage at the brown wire terminal on the loom side of the connector, with the ignition switch ON – there should be battery voltage. If there's no voltage present, check the wiring between the connector and the ignition switch (see the wiring diagrams at the end of this Chapter). If voltage is present, check the yellow wire on XT-R and XT-X models or yellow/green wire on XT-Z and MT-03 models for continuity to the brake light wiring connector, referring to the relevant wiring diagram. Repair or renew the wiring as necessary.

Switch replacement

Front brake lever switch

9 On XT-R and XT-X models remove the fuel tank (see Chapter 4). Trace the wiring from the switch and disconnect it at the connector **(see**

14.6a Rear brake light switch wiring connector (arrowed) – XT-R and XT-X

illustration 14.2). Feed the wiring back to the switch, noting its routing and releasing it from any ties. Press the switch retaining clip up from the underside using a small screwdriver and draw the switch out of its housing **(see illustration)**.

10 On XT-Z and MT-03 models disconnect the wiring connectors from the switch **(see illustration 14.3)**. Undo the screw, noting the washers, and remove the switch.

11 Installation is the reverse of removal. On XT-R and XT-X models make sure the clip on the switch is correctly located in its hole.

Rear brake pedal switch

XT-R and XT-X models

12 On XT-R and XT-X models the rear brake light switch is on the inside of the right-hand footrest bracket **(see illustration 14.13)**. Remove the seat (see Chapter 7), then trace the wiring from the switch and disconnect it at the connector **(see illustration 14.6a)**. Feed the wiring down to the switch, releasing it from any ties and noting its routing.

13 Unhook the switch spring from the pedal **(see illustration)**.

14 Thread the switch out of its adjustment nut, then remove the nut form the mounting.

15 Installation is the reverse of removal. Connect the wiring connector – make sure the wiring is correctly routed and secured by

14.6b On XT-Z displace the starter relay to access the wiring connector (arrowed)

14.6c Rear brake light switch wiring connector (arrowed) – MT-03

any ties. Make sure the brake light is activated just before the rear brake pedal takes effect. If adjustment is necessary, hold the switch body and turn the adjustment nut as required until the brake light is activated correctly – if the brake light comes on too late or not at all, turn the ring clockwise (when looked at from the top) so the switch threads up the nut. If the brake light comes on too soon or is permanently on, turn the ring anti-clockwise so the switch threads down the nut.

XT-Z and MT-03 models

16 The switch is hydraulic and is threaded into the top of the master cylinder **(see**

14.9 Press up on the clip (arrowed) and withdraw the switch

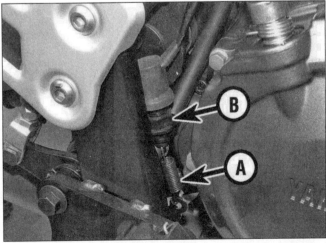

14.13 Unhook the spring (A), then hold the nut (B) and unscrew the switch

14.17a Rear brake light switch (arrowed) – XT-Z

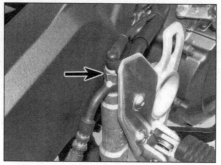

14.17b Rear brake light switch (arrowed) – MT-03

illustration 14.17). Trace the wiring from the switch and disconnect it at the connector (see illustration 14.6b or c) – to access it, on XT-Z models remove the seat (see Chapter 7), and on MT-03 models remove the fuel tank if required (see Chapter 4). Feed the wiring down to the switch, releasing it from any ties and noting its routing.

17 Unscrew the switch and detach the banjo union, noting its alignment with the master cylinder (see illustrations). Once disconnected, seal the banjo union – a good way of doing this is to place a piece of rubber over each side of the union (we used some rubber blanking caps), and clamp them in place using a spring clamp. Alternatively wrap plastic foodwrap around the banjo union and secure the hose in an upright position to minimise fluid loss. Discard the sealing washers, as new ones must be fitted on reassembly.

18 Connect the brake hose to the master cylinder, using new sealing washers on each side of the banjo fitting, and aligning it as noted on removal (see illustration 14.17a or b). Fit the brake light switch and tighten it to the torque setting specified at the beginning of the Chapter. Connect the wiring connector – make sure the wiring is correctly routed and secured by any ties.

19 Refer to Chapter 6 and bleed the rear brake.

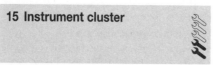

15 Instrument cluster

Check

1 There are no test details for the individual instruments.

2 If there is a problem with the instrument cluster, first check the fuses (see Section 5), then check the wiring connector(s) is/are secure and that all wires and terminals are securely connected – refer below for access. Make sure the power supply to the cluster is good by checking for battery voltage at the red/white and red/green wire terminals with the ignition ON. Also check for continuity to earth in the black/white wire.

3 Next refer to Section 2 and to the Wiring Diagrams at the end of the Chapter and check the wiring and connectors in the relevant circuit. Also check the other components relevant to the circuit, e.g. neutral switch, dimmer switch, turn signals, fuel level sensor.

4 If there is a problem with the speedometer check the sensor (see Chapter 4).

Removal

XT-R and XT-X models

5 Undo the bolt on each side and lift the instrument assembly, then free the wiring clip from the bracket and disconnect the wiring connector (see illustrations).

6 If required undo the screws and detach the bracket (see illustration). Check the condition of the rubber grommets and replace them with new ones if necessary.

XT-Z models

7 Remove the headlight (see Section 8).

8 Undo the screws and lift the instrument cluster off the bracket, then disconnect the wiring connector (see illustrations). Check the condition of the rubber grommets and replace them with new ones if necessary.

15.5a Unscrew the bolt (arrowed) on each side . . .

15.5b . . . then lift the instrument cluster, release the wiring clip (arrowed) . . .

15.5c . . . and disconnect the wiring connector

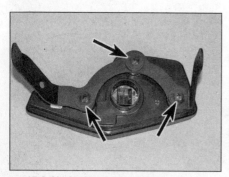

15.6 Undo the screws (arrowed) and detach the bracket

15.8a Undo the screws (arrowed) . . .

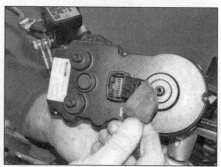

15.8b . . . lift the cluster off the bracket and disconnect the wiring

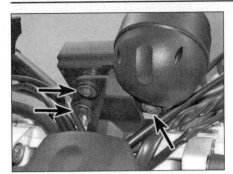

15.9 Undo the screws (arrowed), lift the cluster off the bracket and disconnect the wiring

MT-03 models

9 Undo the screws and lift the instrument cluster off the bracket, then disconnect the wiring connector **(see illustration)**. If access to the screws is impossible with the tools available displace the headlight (see Section 8). Check the condition of the rubber grommets and replace them with new ones if necessary.

Installation

10 Installation is the reverse of removal. On XT-R and XT-X models make sure the pins on the bracket seat in the cut-outs **(see illustration 15.5b)**.

16 Instrument and warning light LEDs

1 All instrument and warning lights are LEDs. Remove the instrument cluster (see Section 15). Check the relevant LED by connecting a 12 volt battery to the relevant wire terminals in the instrument cluster socket as given in the table – the LED should come on. If it doesn't, replace the instrument cluster with a new one.

	Battery positive (+) lead	Battery negative (–) lead
Instrument lights	Red/white or red/green	Black/white
Turn signal (left)	Dark brown	Black/white
Turn signal (right)	Green	Black/white
High beam	Yellow	Black/white
Neutral	Red/white	Light green
Coolant temperature	Red/white	Black/white
Fuel level (XT-R, XT-X and MT-03)	Red/white	Black/white
Engine trouble	Red/white	Black/white

2 To test the immobilser LED connect the positive (+) probe of a continuity tester to the black/white wire terminal and the negative (–) to the green/blue wire terminal – there should be continuity. Reverse the probes – there should be no continuity. Do not connect a battery to these terminals..

3 If the LED is good check the component and the circuit relevant to that LED, referring to the relevant Section.

17 Fuel gauge or warning light and level sensor

 Warning: Refer to the precautions given in Section 1 before starting work.

1 The circuit consists of the sensor mounted on the fuel pump inside the tank and the warning light on XT-R, XT-X and MT-03 models or gauge on XT-Z models in the instrument cluster. The warning light or gauge segments should come on for a seconds when the ignition is switched ON, then go out – this serves as a check that the circuit is working correctly. If not, on XT-R, XT-X and MT-03 check the LED (see Section 16). The warning light comes on and stays on when the level of fuel in the tank drops to the reserve level (see Chapter 4 specifications).

2 If a fault occurs, the warning light will be seen to flash four times (short circuit) or eight times (open circuit) depending on the problem and then go out for 3 seconds on XT-R and XT-X and MT-03 models, and the gauge segments will flash on XT-Z models, and this will repeat until the ignition is switched OFF. If the system malfunctions, refer to Chapter 4 to access the fuel pump wiring connectors and check the connector with the green/white and black wires – make sure the wiring terminals and connectors are all secure.

3 Using an ohmmeter or continuity tester, on XT-R, XT-X and MT-03 models check there is either continuity (or a small resistance) or no continuity (or a high resistance) between the green/white and black wire terminals in the sensor wiring connector socket on the underside of the pump according to the quantity of fuel in the tank, and on XT-Z models check the resistance between the terminals is between 20 ohms (full tank) and 140 ohms (empty tank) – if required remove the pump (see Chapter 4) and check the pump float manually **(see illustrations)**. If not, the sensor is faulty and a new pump will have to be fitted – individual components are not available.

4 If the sensor is good, disconnect the instrument cluster wiring connector (see Section 15), and check for continuity in the green/white wire between the level sensor and instrument cluster. Also check for continuity to earth in the black wire. If there is no continuity check the circuit and the connectors for faults.

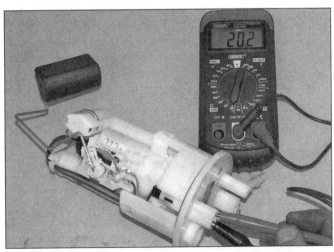

17.3a Check the resistance with the float in the full position . . .

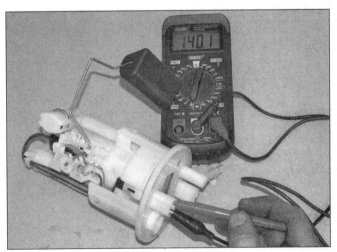

17.3b . . . and the empty position

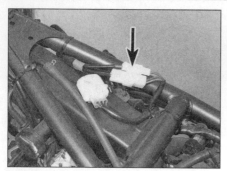

18.2a Ignition switch wiring connectors (arrowed) – XT-R and XT-X

18.2b Ignition switch wiring connectors – XT-Z

18.2c Ignition switch wiring connectors – MT-03

5 Connect the instrument cluster wiring connector, then turn the ignition ON. Check for voltage at the level sensor connector green/white wire. If no voltage is present, and all other instrument functions are good, have the instrument cluster checked by a Yamaha dealer.

18 Ignition switch

Warning: To prevent the risk of short circuits, disconnect the battery negative (–) lead before making any ignition switch checks.

Check

1 Remove the fuel tank (see Chapter 4).
2 Trace the wiring from the ignition switch and disconnect it at the connectors **(see illustrations)**.
3 Using an ohmmeter or a continuity tester, check the continuity of the connector terminal pairs (see the wiring diagrams at the end of this Chapter). Continuity should exist between the terminals connected by a solid line on the

diagram when the switch is in the indicated position.
4 If the switch fails the test, check for continuity in the wiring between the connector and the switch, and check the terminals on the switch. If necessary replace the switch with a new one.
5 If the switch is good, check for battery voltage at the red wire terminal on the loom side of the connector. If there is none, check for continuity in the wire to the starter relay (Section 25), and check the main fuse (Section 5).

Removal

6 Remove the fuel tank (see Chapter 4).
7 Trace the wiring from the ignition switch and disconnect it at the connectors **(see illustration 18.2a, b or c)**. Feed the wiring back to the switch, freeing it from any clips and ties and noting its routing.
8 On XT-R and XT-X models remove the headlight (see Section 8). The switch is secured by shear-head bolts, which have to be drifted round until loose using a punch **(see illustration)**. If better access if required remove the top yoke (see Chapter 1, Section 13, and follow the relevant steps).

18.8 Ignition switch bolts (arrowed) – XT-R and XT-X

9 On XT-Z and MT-03 models remove the shroud from the switch **(see illustration)**. The switch is secured by shear-head bolts, which have to be drifted round until loose using a punch **(see illustration)**.

Installation

10 Installation is the reverse of removal. Fit new bolts and tighten them until the heads shear off. Make sure the wiring connectors are correctly routed and securely connected.

18.9a Undo the screw on each side and remove the shroud . . .

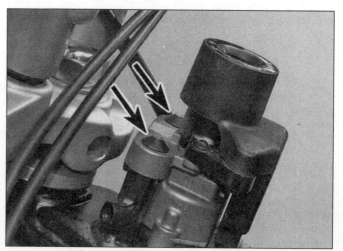

18.9b . . . to access the switch bolts (arrowed)

19 Handlebar switches

Check

1 Generally speaking, the switches are reliable and trouble-free. Most troubles, when they do occur, are caused by dirty or corroded contacts, but wear and breakage of internal parts is a possibility that should not be overlooked. If breakage does occur, the entire switch and related wiring harness will have to be replaced with a new one, as individual parts are not available.

2 The switches can be checked for continuity using an ohmmeter or a continuity test light. Disconnect the battery negative (–) lead, which will prevent the possibility of a short circuit, before making the checks.

3 Remove the fuel tank (see Chapter 4).

4 Trace the wiring from the relevant switch and disconnect it at the connector (see illustrations).

5 Check for continuity between the terminals of the switch connector with the switch in the various positions (i.e. switch off – no continuity, switch on – continuity) – see the wiring diagrams at the end of this Chapter. Continuity should exist between the terminals connected by a solid line on the diagram when the switch is in the indicated position.

6 If the continuity check indicates a problem exists, displace the switch housing and spray the switch contacts with electrical contact cleaner (there is no need to remove the switch completely). If they are accessible, the contacts can be scraped clean with a knife or polished with crocus cloth. If switch components are damaged or broken, it will be obvious when the switch is disassembled.

19.4a Wiring connectors – XT-R and XT-X models, trace the wiring to the relevant connector

Removal

7 Remove the fuel tank (see Chapter 4).

8 Trace the wiring from the relevant switch and disconnect it at the connector. Feed the wiring back to the switch, freeing it from any clips and ties and noting its routing. On XT-Z and MT-03 models when removing the right-hand switch disconnect the wiring connectors from the brake light switch (see illustration 14.3) and when removing the left-hand switch disconnect the wiring connectors from the clutch switch (see illustration 22.3).

9 To remove the right-hand switch, refer to Chapter 4 for removal of the throttle cables from the switch (there is no need to detach them from the throttle body, which involves detaching the switch housing from the handlebars).

10 To remove the left-hand switch undo the switch housing screws and free it from the handlebar by separating the halves (see illustration).

Installation

11 Installation is the reverse of removal.

19.4b Switch wiring connectors – XT-Z models

Make sure the locating pin in the switch housing locates in the hole in the handlebar. Refer to Chapter 4 for installation of the throttle cables and right-hand switch housing.

20 Neutral switch

1 The neutral switch is part of the starter safety circuit (see Chapter 1).

Check

2 Before checking the electrical circuit, check whether the neutral LED in the instrument cluster comes on momentarily when the ignition is switched on – if it does the LED is proved good; if it doesn't check it (Section 16).

3 The switch is located in the left-hand side of the transmission casing below the front sprocket cover – for best access remove the gearchange lever (see Chapter 5) and the front sprocket cover (see Chapter 6). Slacken the

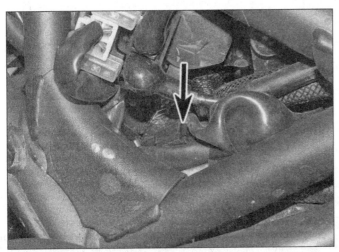

19.4c Switch wiring connectors – MT-03 models, displace the starter relay for best access

19.10 Left-hand switch housing screws (arrowed)

20.3 Slacken the screw (arrowed) and detach the wire

20.10 Unscrew the bolts and remove the switch

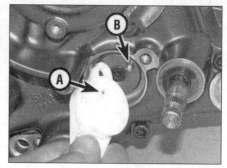

20.11a Check the contact (A) and the plunger (B) . . .

20.11b . . . and make sure the plunger moves in and springs back out

20.13 Fit a new O-ring smeared with grease

wire terminal screw and detach the wire **(see illustration)**.

4 Make sure the transmission is in neutral. With the connector disconnected and the ignition switch ON, the neutral light should be out. If not, the wire between the connector and instrument cluster must be earthed (grounded) at some point.

5 Check for continuity between the switch terminal and the crankcase. With the transmission in neutral, there should be continuity. With the transmission in gear, there should be no continuity. If the tests prove otherwise, then remove the switch (see below) and check whether the plunger or contact plate in the selector drum is bent or damaged, or whether there is damage or excessive wear to the contacts on the switch face.

6 If the continuity tests prove the switch is good, check for voltage at the wire terminal with the ignition on. If there's no voltage

present, check the wire between the switch and the relay unit (see the wiring diagrams at the end of this Chapter).

7 If the switch is good, check the other components (sidestand switch, clutch switch and diodes) and their wiring and connectors in the starter circuit as described in the relevant sections of this Chapter. If all components are good, check the wiring between the various components. Repair or renew the wiring as required.

Removal and installation

8 The switch is located in the left-hand side of the transmission casing below the front sprocket cover – for best access remove the gearchange lever (see Chapter 5) and the front sprocket cover (see Chapter 6). Stand the bike upright – if it is on the sidestand you will have to drain some oil before removing the switch (see Chapter 1).

9 Undo the wire terminal screw and detach the wire **(see illustration 20.3)**.

10 Clean the area around the switch. Undo the bolts and remove the switch **(see illustration)**. Discard the O-ring – a new one must be used.

11 Check the contact on the inner face of the switch and the plunger in the end of the selector drum **(see illustrations)**. Make sure the plunger moves in and out smoothly.

12 Clean the threads of the switch bolts.

13 Fit the switch using a new O-ring smeared with grease **(see illustration)**. Apply a suitable non-permanent thread locking compound to the screws and tighten them **(see illustration 20.10)**.

14 Fit the connector under the screw then tighten the screw **(see illustration 20.3)**. Check the operation of the switch.

15 Install the front sprocket cover (see Chapter 6) and the gearchange lever (see Chapter 5) if removed.

21 Sidestand switch

1 The sidestand switch is mounted on the stand bracket **(see illustrations)**. The switch is part of the starter safety circuit (see Chapter 1).

Check

2 To access the wiring connector on XT-R and XT-X models remove the left-hand side panel (see Chapter 7), on XT-Z models draw the rubber boot housing the connectors out

21.1a Sidestand switch (arrowed) – XT-R and XT-X models

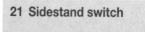

21.1b Sidestand switch (arrowed) – XT-Z models

21.1c Sidestand switch (arrowed) – MT-03 models

21.3a Alternator, CKP sensor, neutral switch and sidestand switch wiring connectors (arrowed) – XT-R and XT-X models

21.3b Alternator, CKP sensor, neutral switch and sidestand switch wiring connectors (arrowed) – XT-Z models

21.3c Alternator, CKP sensor, neutral switch and sidestand switch wiring connectors (arrowed) – MT-03 models

from behind the rear brake master cylinder reservoir, and on MT-03 models displace the regulator/rectifier (see Section 30).

3 Trace the wiring from the switch and disconnect it at the connector **(see illustrations)**.

4 Check the operation of the switch using an ohmmeter or continuity tester. Connect the meter between the terminals on the switch side of the connector. With the sidestand up there should be continuity, and with it down there should be no continuity. Make sure the switch plunger is clean and not stuck, and that it moves freely and smoothly in and out of the switch under spring pressure **(see illustration)**.

5 If the switch does not perform as expected, it is faulty and must be replaced with a new one. If the switch is good, check the other components (clutch switch, neutral switch and diodes) and their wiring and connectors in the starter circuit as described in the relevant sections of this Chapter. If all components are good, check the wiring between the various components (see the wiring diagrams at the end of this Chapter). Repair or renew the wiring as required.

Replacement

6 To access the wiring connector on XT-R and XT-X models remove the left-hand side panel (see Chapter 7), on XT-Z models draw the rubber boot out from behind the rear brake master cylinder reservoir, and on MT-03 models displace the regulator/rectifier (see Section 30).

7 Trace the wiring from the switch and disconnect it at the connector **(see illustration 21.3a, b or c)**. Feed the wiring back

to the switch, freeing it from any clips and ties and noting its routing.

8 Undo the nuts on the inner side, then withdraw the bolts and remove the switch **(see illustration 21.1a, b or c)**.

9 Fit the new switch and tighten the nuts.

10 Feed the wiring up to its connector, making sure it is correctly routed and secured by any clips and ties.

11 Reconnect the wiring connector and check the operation of the switch.

12 On XT-R and XT-X models install the left-hand side panel (see Chapter 7), on XT-Z models position the rubber boot behind the rear brake master cylinder reservoir, and on MT-03 models refit the regulator/rectifier (see Section 30).

22 Clutch switch

1 The clutch switch is mounted in or under the clutch lever bracket, depending on model. The switch is part of the starter safety circuit (see Chapter 1).

Check

2 On XT-R and XT-X models trace the wiring from the switch and disconnect it at the connector **(see illustration 14.2)**.

3 On XT-Z and MT-03 models disconnect the wiring connector from the switch **(see illustration)**.

4 Using a continuity tester, connect the probes

to the terminals on the switch side of the connector on XT-R and XT-X models, and to the terminals on the switch on XT-Z and MT-03 models. With the lever at rest, there should be no continuity. With the lever applied, there should be continuity. If the switch does not behave as described, replace it with a new one (see below). If the results are not as stated remove the switch (see below) and check the plunger for damage. Replace the switch with a new one if necessary.

5 If the switch is good, check the other components (sidestand switch, neutral switch and diodes) and their wiring and connectors in the starter circuit as described in the relevant sections of this Chapter. If all components are good, check the wiring between the various components (see the wiring diagrams at the end of this Chapter).

Replacement

6 On XT-R and XT-X models trace the wiring from the switch and disconnect it at the connector **(see illustration 14.2)**. Feed the wiring back to the switch, noting its routing and releasing it from any ties. Press the switch retaining clip up from the underside using a small screwdriver and draw the switch out of its housing **(see illustration)**.

7 On XT-Z and MT-03 models and disconnect the wiring connector from the switch **(see illustration 22.3)**. Undo the screw and remove the switch.

8 Installation is the reverse of removal. On XT-R and XT-X models make sure the clip on the switch is correctly located in its hole.

21.4 Make sure the plunger works properly

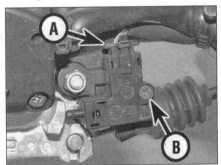

22.3 Clutch switch wiring connector (A) and screw (B)

22.6 Press up on the clip (arrowed) and withdraw the switch

23.3a Relay unit (arrowed) – XT-R and XT-X models

23.3b Relay unit (arrowed) – XT-Z models

23.3c On MT-03 models unscrew the bolts (arrowed) and remove the box . . .

23 Relay unit and diodes

1 The relay unit contains the fuel pump relay and the starter circuit cut-off relay and its associated diodes.

Starter circuit cut-off relay and diodes

2 The starter circuit cut-off relay and its associated diodes are part of the safety circuit which prevents or stops the engine running if the transmission is in gear whilst the sidestand is down, and prevents the engine from starting if the transmission is in gear unless the sidestand is up and the clutch lever is pulled in.

3 Make sure the ignition is OFF. To access the relay unit on XT-R and XT-X models remove the right-hand side panel (see Chapter 7), on XT-Z models remove the seat (see Chapter 7), and on MT-03 models remove the battery (see Section 3), then remove the battery box (see illustrations).

4 Disconnect the battery negative (–) lead (see Section 3), then displace the relay and disconnect the wiring connector (see

23.3d . . . to access the relay unit (arrowed)

illustration). Move the relay assembly to the bench for testing.

5 To check the operation of the relay, using an ohmmeter or continuity tester, connect the positive (+) probe to the blue/white wire terminal on the relay unit and the negative (–) probe to the blue/black wire terminal (see illustration). There should be no continuity. Using a fully-charged 12V battery and some jumper leads, connect the positive (+) terminal of the battery to the red/black wire terminal on the relay unit, and the negative (–) terminal to the black/yellow wire terminal. There should

23.4 Displace the relay and disconnect the wiring

now be continuity between the blue/white and blue/black wire terminals. If the relay does not test as described, replace the relay unit with a new one.

6 The diodes contained within the relay assembly can be checked by performing a continuity test – diodes should show continuity in one direction and no continuity when the meter or tester probes are reversed. Connect the multimeter (set to ohms) or continuity tester across the wire terminals for the diode being tested, and perform the tests in the table (see illustration). If any diode shows the

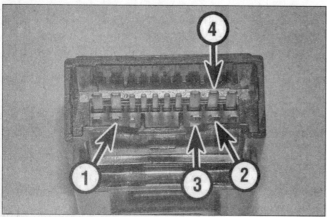

23.5 Starter circuit relay test connections

1 Blue/white wire terminal – meter positive
2 Blue/black wire terminal – meter negative
3 Red/black wire terminal – battery positive
4 Black/yellow wire terminal – battery negative

23.6 Diode test connections

1 Light blue wire terminal
2 Black/yellow wire terminal
3 Blue/yellow wire terminal
4 Blue/green wire terminal
5 Light green wire terminal

same condition in both directions it is faulty, and the relay unit must be replaced with a new one.

Positive probe (+)	Negative probe (–)	Result
1 (Light blue)	2 (Black/yellow)	No continuity
2 (Black/yellow)	1 (Light blue)	Continuity
1 (Light blue)	3 (Blue/yellow)	No continuity
3 (Blue/yellow)	1 (Light blue)	Continuity
4 (Blue/green)	3 (Blue/yellow)	No continuity
3 (Blue/yellow)	4 (Blue/green)	Continuity
1 (Light blue)	5 (Light green)	No continuity
5 (Light green)	1 (Light blue)	Continuity

7 If the cut-off relay and diodes are good, but the starting system fault still exists, check all other components in the starting circuit (i.e. the neutral switch, side stand switch, clutch switch, starter switch and starter relay) as described in the relevant Sections of this Chapter. If all components are good, check the wiring between the various components (see *Wiring Diagrams* at the end of this Chapter).
8 Installation is the reverse of removal.

Fuel pump relay

9 Refer to Chapter 4, Section 4.

24 Horn

Check

1 On XT-R and XT-X models the horn is above the radiator on the right-hand side **(see illustration)** – remove the right-hand fuel tank cover (see Chapter 7). On XT-Z models the horn is below the radiator on the right-hand side **(see illustration)** – remove the right-hand radiator cover (see Chapter 7). On MT-03 models the horn is on the left-hand end of the radiator **(see illustration)**.
2 Disconnect the wiring connectors from the horn. Check them for loose wires. Using two jumper wires, apply voltage from a fully-charged 12V battery directly to the terminals on the horn, positive (+) to the pink

24.1a Horn wiring connectors (A) and mounting bolt (B) – XT-R and XT-X models

wire terminal, negative (–) to black. If the horn doesn't sound, replace it with a new one.
3 If the horn works check for voltage at the pink wire connector with the ignition ON, and with the horn button pressed. If voltage is present, check the black wire for continuity to earth.
4 If no voltage was present, check the pink wire for continuity between the horn and the horn button.
5 If all the wiring and connectors are good, check the horn button contacts in the switch housing (see Section 19).

Replacement

6 Refer to Step 1 for location.
7 Disconnect the wiring connectors from the horn. Unscrew the bolt and remove the horn.
8 Install the horn, connect the wiring, and check that it works.

25 Starter relay

Check

1 If the starter circuit is faulty, first check the ignition fuse (see Section 5).
2 On XT-R and XT-X models the starter relay is located behind the left-hand side panel **(see illustration)** – remove the panel for access (see Chapter 7). On XT-Z models the

24.1b Horn wiring connectors (A) and mounting bolt (B) – XT-Z models

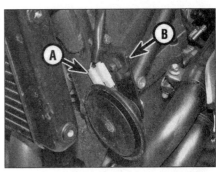
24.1c Horn wiring connectors (A) and mounting bolt (B) – MT-03 models

starter relay is located under the seat **(see illustration)** – remove the seat for access (see Chapter 7). On MT-03 models the starter relay is located under the fuel tank on the left-hand side **(see illustration)** – remove the tank for access (see Chapter 4).
3 Lift the rubber terminal cover and unscrew the bolt securing the black starter motor lead; position the lead away from the relay terminal. With the ignition switch ON, the engine kill switch in the RUN position, and the transmission in neutral, press the starter switch. The relay should be heard to click.
4 If the relay doesn't click, switch off the ignition and remove the relay as described below; test it as follows. First check the resistance of the coil by connecting an ohmmeter across the red/white and blue/white

25.2a Starter relay (arrowed) – XT-R and XT-X models

25.2b Starter relay (arrowed) – XT-Z models

25.2c Starter relay (arrowed) – MT-03 models

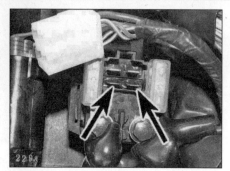

25.4 Measure the resistance between the terminals (arrowed)

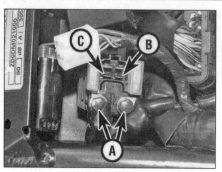

25.5 Connect the continuity tester to terminals A, connect the battery+ to B and the battery– to C

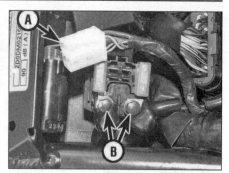

25.11 Disconnect the wiring connector (A) then unscrew the bolts (B) and detach the leads

wire terminals **(see illustration)** – it should be as specified at the beginning of the chapter.
5 Now connect a continuity tester across the relay's starter motor and battery lead terminals **(see illustration)**. There should be no continuity. Using a fully-charged 12 volt battery and two insulated jumper wires, connect the positive (+) terminal of the battery to the red/white wire terminal on the relay, and the negative (–) terminal to the blue/white wire terminal. At this point the relay should be heard to click and the multimeter read 0 ohms (continuity). If this is the case the relay is proved good. If the relay does not click when battery voltage is applied and indicates no continuity (infinite resistance) across its terminals, it is faulty and must be replaced with a new one.
6 If the relay is good, check the main lead from the battery to the relay, and the lead from the relay to the starter motor – check that the

terminals and connectors at each end are tight and corrosion-free.
7 Next check the wiring from the switch housing to the relay wiring connector, referring to Section 2 and to the wiring Diagrams at the end of the chapter, and then check the switches (see Section 19).
8 If all appears good check the neutral switch, clutch switch, sidestand switch and diodes as described in the relevant sections of this Chapter. If all components are good, check the wiring between the various components (see the wiring diagrams at the end of this Chapter).

Replacement

9 On XT-R and XT-X models the starter relay is located behind the left-hand side panel **(see illustration 25.2a)** – remove the panel for access (see Chapter 7). On XT-Z models the starter relay is located under the seat

(see illustration 25.2b) – remove the seat for access (see Chapter 7). On MT-03 models the starter relay is located under the fuel tank on the left-hand side **(see illustration 25.2c)** – remove the tank for access (see Chapter 4).
10 Disconnect the battery terminals, remembering to disconnect the negative (–) terminal first (see Section 3).
11 Disconnect the relay wiring connector **(see illustration)**. Lift the insulating cover and unscrew the bolts securing the starter motor and battery leads to the relay and detach the leads. Remove the relay from its rubber sleeve. If the relay is being replaced with a new one, remove the main fuse and its spare.
12 Installation is the reverse of removal. Make sure the terminal bolts are securely tightened. Do not forget to fit the main fuse and its spare into the relay, if removed. Connect the negative (–) lead last when reconnecting the battery.

26 Starter motor removal and installation

Removal

1 Disconnect the battery negative (–) lead (see Section 3). The starter motor is mounted on the top of the crankcase.
2 Displace the crankcase breather chamber from its bracket – if required detach one of the hoses to give more freedom of movement and access, or detach both the hoses and remove the chamber **(see illustration)**.
3 Peel back the rubber terminal cover on the starter motor. Undo the nut securing the starter lead to the motor and detach the lead – if the terminal is corroded spray it with some penetrating fluid and leave it for a while before attempting to undo it **(see illustration)**.
4 Unscrew the two bolts securing the starter motor to the crankcase, noting the earth lead secured by the rear bolt, and remove the breather chamber bracket **(see illustration)**. Slide the starter motor out and remove it **(see illustration)**.
5 Remove the O-ring on the end of the starter motor and discard it as a new one must be used **(see illustration 26.6)**.

26.2 Displace or remove the breather chamber as required

26.3 Pull back the terminal cover then undo the nut and detach the lead

26.4a Unscrew the two bolts . . .

26.4b . . . and remove the starter motor

26.6 Fit a new O-ring and lubricate it

27.4 Note the alignment marks or make your own between the housing and the covers

27.5 Release the circlip and remove the gear

Installation

6 Fit a new O-ring onto the end of the starter motor, making sure it is seated in its groove **(see illustration)**. Apply a smear of engine oil to the O-ring.

7 Manoeuvre the motor into position and slide it into the crankcase **(see illustration 26.4b)**. Ensure that the starter motor gear teeth mesh correctly. Fit the breather chamber bracket and the earth lead and tighten the mounting bolts to the torque setting specified at the beginning of the chapter **(see illustration 26.4a)**.

8 Connect the starter lead to the motor and secure it with the nut **(see illustration 26.3)**. Fit the rubber cover over the terminal.

8 Fit the crankcase breather chamber onto its bracket and connect the hoses if detached **(see illustration 26.2)**.

10 Connect the battery negative (–) lead.

27 Starter motor overhaul

Check

1 Remove the starter motor (see Section 26). Cover the body in some rag and clamp the motor in a soft-jawed vice – do not over-tighten it.

2 Using a fully-charged 12 volt battery and two insulated jumper wires, connect the positive (+) terminal of the battery to the protruding terminal on the starter motor, and the negative (–) terminal to one of the motor's mounting lugs. At this point the starter motor should spin. If this is the case the motor is proved good, though it is worth overhauling it if you suspect it of not working properly under load. If the motor does not spin, disassemble it for inspection.

Disassembly

3 Remove the starter motor (see Section 26).

4 Note any alignment marks between the main housing and the front and rear covers, or make your own if they aren't clear **(see illustration)**.

5 Release the circlip securing the drive gear on the shaft **(see illustration)**. Mark the outer face of the gear then slide it off. Note that a new circlip should be used when fitting the gear.

6 Unscrew the two long bolts and remove the front cover **(see illustrations)**. Note the sealing ring. Remove the tabbed washer from the cover and slide the insulating washer and shim(s) from the front end of the armature, noting the number of shims and their correct fitted order **(see illustrations 27.24 and 25b)**.

7 Remove the rear cover **(see illustration)**. Note the sealing ring. Remove the shim(s) from the rear end of the armature noting how many are fitted **(see illustration 27.23a)**.

8 Withdraw the armature from the main housing noting that there will be some resistance from the pull of the magnets set in the housing **(see illustration)**.

27.6a Unscrew and remove the two bolts (arrowed) . . .

27.6b . . . then remove the front cover

27.7 Remove the rear cover

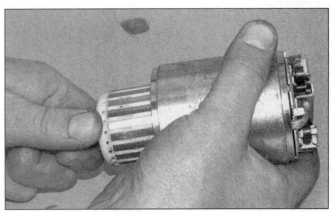

27.8 Draw the armature out of the housing

27.10a Unscrew the nut and remove the washers . . .

27.10b . . . then remove the brushplate assembly and terminal bolt . . .

27.11 . . . and the brushplate seat

9 At this stage check for continuity between the terminal bolt and each insulated brush – there should be continuity (zero resistance). Check for continuity between the terminal bolt and the housing – there should be no continuity (infinite resistance).

10 Noting the correct fitted location of each component, unscrew the nut from the terminal bolt and remove the plain washer, the one large and two small insulating washers **(see illustration)**. Remove the brushplate assembly **(see illustration)**.

11 Remove the brushplate seat, noting how it locates **(see illustration)**.

Inspection

12 The parts of the starter motor that are most likely to require attention are the brushes. Measure the length of each brush and compare the results to the length listed in this Chapter's Specifications **(see illustration)**. If any of the

brushes are worn beyond the service limit, fit a new brush set and brushplate. If the brushes are not worn excessively, nor cracked, chipped, or otherwise damaged, they may be reused.

13 Inspect the commutator bars on the armature for scoring, scratches and discoloration **(see illustration)**. The commutator can be cleaned and polished with crocus cloth, but do not use sandpaper or emery paper **(see illustration)**. After cleaning, wipe away any residue with a cloth soaked in electrical system cleaner or denatured alcohol.

14 Using an ohmmeter or a continuity test light, check for continuity between the commutator bars **(see illustration)**. Continuity should exist between each bar and all of the others. Also, check for continuity between the commutator bars and the armature shaft **(see illustration)**. There should be no continuity

(infinite resistance) between the commutator and the shaft. If the checks indicate otherwise, the armature is defective and a new starter motor must be obtained – the armature is not available separately.

15 Check the gear for worn, cracked, chipped and broken teeth. If any are found check the teeth of the damper gear and if necessary the idle/reduction gear via the starter orifice in the back of the engine. If any gear is damaged or worn replace it with a new one.

16 Inspect the front and rear covers for signs of cracks or wear. Check the oil seal and the needle bearing in the front cover and the bush in the rear cover for wear and damage – the seal, bearing, bush and covers are not listed as being available separately so if necessary a new starter motor must be fitted **(see illustration)**.

17 Inspect the magnets in the main housing and the housing itself for cracks.

18 Check the housing sealing rings for signs

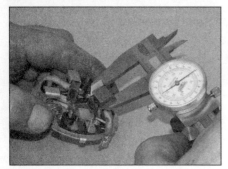

27.12 Measure the length of each brush

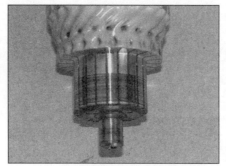

27.13a Check the bars for wear and damage . . .

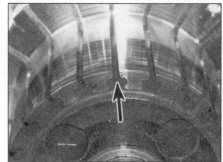

27.13b . . . and make sure the mica (arrowed) is below the surface of the bars

27.14a There should be continuity between the bars . . .

27.14b . . . and no continuity between the bars and the shaft

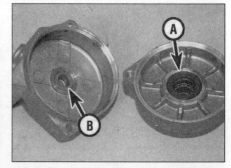

27.16 Check the bearing and seal (A) in the front cover and the bush (B) in the rear cover

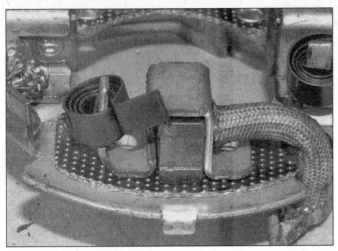

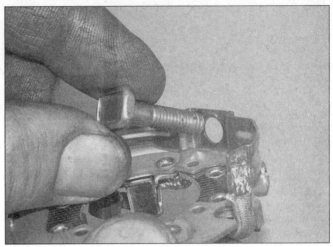

27.19 Push each brush into its housing and place the spring end as shown to keep them retracted

27.20a Fit the terminal bolt . . .

of deformation and deterioration and replace them with new ones if necessary.

Reassembly

19 Slide the brushes all the way back into their housings and locate the brush spring ends onto the tops of the brushes so they are held retracted **(see illustration)**. Fit the brushplate seat into the housing **(see illustration 27.11)**.

20 Fit the terminal bolt through the insulated brush holder then fit the, insulator piece **(see illustrations)**. Fit the brushplate assembly into the housing, locating the tab in the cut-out and making sure the insulated wires are in their guides.

21 Fit the O-ring down over the bolt and press it into place between the bolt and the cover **(see illustration)**. Slide the small insulating washers onto the terminal bolt, followed by the large insulating washer and the plain washer **(see illustration)**. Fit the nut onto the terminal bolt and tighten it securely.

22 Carefully insert the armature into the housing, keeping a strong hold on both against the draw of the magnets, and keeping the brushplate in position as the commutator fits through it **(see illustration)**. Lift the brush springs of the brushes, push the brushes against the commutator, and set the spring ends against the brushes **(see illustration)**. Check the armature turns.

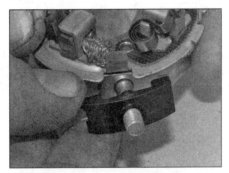

27.20b . . . and the insulator piece . . .

27.20c . . . then fit the brushplate assembly onto the housing . . .

27.20d . . . making sure it locates correctly

27.21a Fit the O-ring over the bolt and against the housing . . .

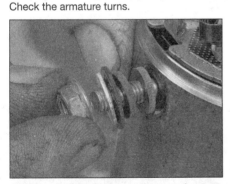

27.21b . . . then fit the washers and nut as shown

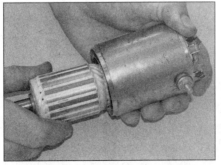

27.22a Guide the armature into the housing . . .

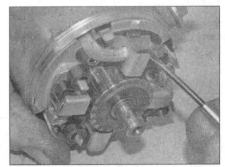

27.22b . . . then relocate the spring ends onto the brushes

27.23a Fit the shims . . .

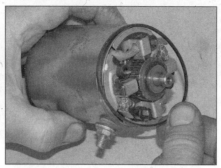

27.23b . . . and the sealing ring . . .

27.23c . . . then fit the rear cover

27.24 Fit the tabbed washer into the cover

27.25a Fit the sealing ring . . .

27.25b . . . and the shims and insulating washer . . .

27.25c . . . then fit the front cover

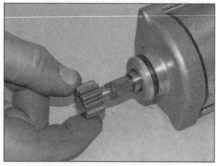

27.27a Slide the gear on . . .

27.27b . . . and secure it with a new circlip

23 Fit the shim(s) onto the rear of the armature shaft **(see illustration)**. Apply a smear of grease to the end of the shaft. Fit the sealing ring onto the rear of the housing **(see illustration)**. Fit the rear cover, aligning the marks between the cover and housing **(see illustration)**.
24 Apply a smear of grease to the front cover oil seal lip. Fit the tabbed washer into the cover so that its teeth are correctly located between the cover ribs **(see illustration)**.
25 Fit the sealing ring onto the front of the housing **(see illustration)**. Slide the shim(s) onto the front end of the armature shaft then fit the insulating washer **(see illustration)**. Slide the front cover into position, aligning the marks made on removal **(see illustration)**.
26 Check the marks made on removal are correctly aligned then fit the long bolts and tighten them **(see illustration 27.4)**.

27 Slide the gear onto the shaft with the mark made on removal facing out and secure it with a new circlip, making sure it seats correctly in the groove **(see illustrations)**.
28 Install the starter motor (see Section 26).

28 Charging system testing

1 If the performance of the charging system is suspect, the system as a whole should be checked first, followed by testing of the individual components. **Note:** *Before beginning the checks, make sure the battery is fully charged and that all system connections are clean and tight.*
2 Checking the output of the charging system and the performance of the various

components within the charging system requires the use of a multimeter (with voltage, current, and resistance functions). If a multimeter is not available, the job of checking the charging system should be left to a Yamaha dealer.
3 When making the checks, follow the procedures carefully to prevent incorrect connections or short circuits resulting in irreparable damage to electrical system components.

Regulated output test

4 On XT models remove the seat (see Chapter 7). On MT-03 models remove the fuel tank (see Chapter 4). Start the engine and warm it up.
5 To check the regulated (DC) voltage output, allow the engine to idle. Connect a multimeter set to the 0-20 volts DC scale across the terminals of the battery with the positive (+)

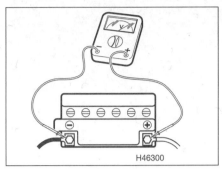

28.5 Checking regulated voltage output – connect the meter as shown

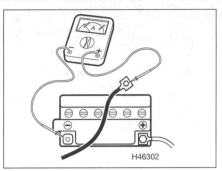

28.8 Checking the charging system leakage rate – connect the meter as shown

meter probe to battery positive (+) terminal and the negative (–) meter probe to battery negative (–) terminal **(see illustration)**.

6 Slowly increase the engine speed to 5000 rpm and note the reading obtained. Compare the result with the Specification at the beginning of this Chapter. If the regulated voltage output is outside the specification, check the alternator and the regulator (see Sections 29 and 30).

HAYNES HINT	*Clues to a faulty regulator are constantly blowing bulbs, with brightness varying considerably with engine speed, and battery overheating.*

Leakage test

Caution: Always connect an ammeter in series, never in parallel with the battery, otherwise it will be damaged. Do not turn the ignition ON or operate the starter motor when the ammeter is connected – a sudden surge in current will blow the meter's fuse.

7 Ensure the ignition is OFF, then disconnect the battery negative (–) lead (see Section 3).

8 Set the multimeter to the Amps function and connect its negative (–) probe to the battery negative (–) terminal, and positive (+) probe to the disconnected negative (–) lead **(see illustration)**. Always set the meter to a high amps range initially and then bring it down to the mA (milli Amps) range; if there is a

high current flow in the circuit it may blow the meter's fuse.

9 Battery current leakage should not exceed the maximum limit (see Specifications). If a higher leakage rate is shown there is a short circuit in the wiring, although if an after-market immobiliser or alarm is fitted, its current draw should be taken into account. Disconnect the meter and reconnect the battery negative (–) lead.

10 If leakage is indicated, refer to *Wiring Diagrams* at the end of this Chapter to systematically disconnect individual electrical components and repeat the test until the source is identified.

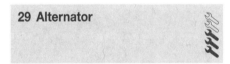

29 Alternator

Check

1 To access the wiring connector on XT-R and XT-X models remove the left-hand side panel (see Chapter 7), on XT-Z models draw the rubber boot housing the connectors out from behind the rear brake master cylinder reservoir, and on MT-03 models displace the regulator/rectifier (see Section 30).

2 Trace the wiring from the alternator cover on the left-hand side of the engine and disconnect it at the 3-pin connector with the white wires **(see illustration 21.3a, b or c)**. Check the connector terminals for corrosion and security.

3 Using a multimeter set to the ohms x 1 (ohmmeter) scale measure the resistance of the stator coils between each pair of white wire terminals on the alternator side of the connector, taking a total of three readings, then check for continuity between each terminal and ground (earth).

4 If the coil windings are in good condition the reading(s) should be within the range shown in the Specifications at the start of this Chapter, and there should be no continuity (infinite resistance) between the terminals and ground (earth). If not, the alternator stator coil assembly is at fault and should be replaced with a new one. **Note:** *Before condemning the stator coils, check the fault is not due to damaged wiring between the connector and the coils.*

Removal

5 Drain the engine oil (see Chapter 1).

6 To access the wiring connector on XT-R and XT-X models remove the left-hand side panel (see Chapter 7), on XT-Z models draw the rubber boot housing the connectors out from behind the rear brake master cylinder reservoir, and on MT-03 models displace the regulator rectifier (see Section 30). On XT-Z models remove the left-hand radiator cover (see Chapter 7).

7 Remove the starter motor (see Section 26).

8 Remove the front sprocket cover (see Chapter 6).

9 Remove the gearchange lever (see Chapter 5).

10 Trace the wiring from the alternator cover on the left-hand side of the engine and disconnect it at the connectors **(see illustration 21.3a, b or c)**. Also slacken the neutral switch wire terminal screw and detach the wire **(see illustration 20.3)**. Slacken the wiring guide bolts and draw the wire out **(see illustration)**.

11 Unscrew the starter damper gear cover bolts and remove the cover, on XT-Z models along with the exhaust shield **(see illustration)**. Remove and discard the gasket. Remove the dowel from either the cover or the crankcase if loose. Remove the outer washer, the damper gear and the inner washer **(see illustration)**.

12 Working in a criss-cross pattern, evenly

29.10 Unscrew the bolts (arrowed) to release the guide and free the wire

29.11a Unscrew the bolts (arrowed) and remove the cover, and on XT-Z models (shown) the shield

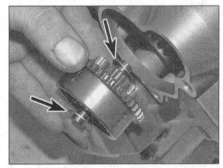

29.11b Remove the damper gear with its washers (arrowed)

29.13 Withdraw the shaft and remove the gear

29.14 Using a rotor strap to hold the rotor while unscrewing the nut

slacken the alternator cover bolts. Draw the cover off the engine, noting that it will be restrained by the force of the rotor magnets, and be prepared to catch any residual oil. Remove and discard the gasket **(see illustration 29.24)**. Remove the four dowels from either the cover or the crankcase if loose, noting the O-rings with two of them where fitted.

29.15a Keep the rotor nut on the shaft to protect it and prevent the rotor flying off

29.15b If using a legged puller locate the legs as shown

13 Withdraw the idle/reduction gear shaft and remove the gear **(see illustration)**.
14 To slacken the rotor nut it is necessary to stop the rotor from turning. The best way is to use a commercially available rotor strap, taking care to avoid the raised triggers for the crankshaft position sensor on the outside of the rotor **(see illustration)**. If one is not available, try placing the transmission in gear

and having an assistant apply the rear brake hard. Slacken the nut, then thread it up to the end of the crankshaft so it is flush – leaving it in place will help protect the end against the puller and also stop the rotor dropping off the end when it releases.

15 To remove the rotor from the shaft it is necessary to use a rotor puller (Yamaha part No.90890-01362), or its commercially available equivalent, or a suitable three-legged puller – on the engine photographed the rotor was exceptionally tight, and it was necessary to use an hydraulic puller as well as applying heat to the rotor hub. A few taps on the end of the tensioned puller bolt with a hammer can also help jolt the rotor off, but avoid hitting it hard. If the Yamaha tool or its equivalent is being used, thread the puller bolts into the threaded holes in the rotor, then hold the rotor and tighten the puller bolt until the rotor is displaced from the shaft. If a legged puller is used locate the legs behind the flat flange in the inner face of the rotor, then hold the rotor and tighten the puller bolt until the rotor is displaced from the shaft **(see illustrations)**.

29.15c Tighten the puller bolt until the rotor is displaced . . .

29.15d . . . and use localised heat if necessary

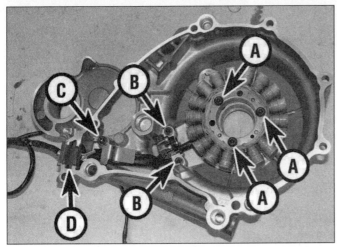

29.16 Unscrew the stator bolts (A), the CKP sensor bolts (B), wiring clamp bolt (C) and free the grommet (D)

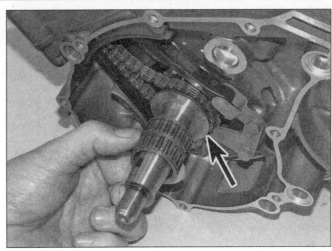

29.18a Slide the thrust washer (arrowed) and bearing onto the shaft . . .

Remove the puller. Thread the rotor nut off the crankshaft and remove the washer. Remove the rotor. Remove the Woodruff key from its slot in the crankshaft (see illustration 29.20b). If the starter driven gear did not come away with the rotor, slide it off the end of the crankshaft along with the needle bearing, and the thrust washer (see illustrations 29.18b and a). If required detach the starter clutch from the rotor (see Chapter 2).

16 To remove the stator from the cover, unscrew its bolts and the bolts securing the crankshaft position sensor and the screw securing the wiring clamp, then remove the assembly, noting how the clamp and the rubber wiring grommet fit (see illustrations).

Installation

17 Clean the threads of the stator, wiring clamp and CKP sensor bolts. Fit the stator, wiring clamp and CKP sensor into the cover,

aligning the rubber wiring grommet with the groove (see illustration 29.16). Apply a suitable non-permanent thread locking compound to the stator, clamp and sensor bolts, and tighten them to the torque setting specified at the beginning of the Chapter. Apply a suitable sealant to the wiring grommet, then press it into the cut-out in the cover.

18 Smear some clean oil onto the inner un-tapered section of the crankshaft that the starter driven gear runs on. Slide the thrust washer and the needle bearing onto the crankshaft (see illustration). Fit the driven gear over the needle bearing (see illustration).

19 If removed fit the starter clutch onto the rotor (see Chapter 2).

20 Clean the tapered end of the crankshaft and the corresponding mating surface on the inside of the rotor with a suitable solvent (see illustration). Fit the Woodruff key into its slot in the crankshaft if removed (see illustration).

29.18b . . . then fit the gear onto the bearing

21 Make sure that no metal objects have attached themselves to the magnet on the inside of the rotor. Slide the rotor onto the shaft, making sure the groove on the inside is aligned with and fits over the Woodruff key, and turn the driven gear clockwise as you do so to spread the starter clutch sprags and

29.20a Clean the tapered section . . .

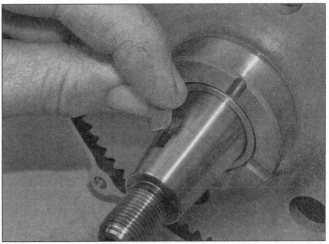

29.20b . . . then fit the Woodruff key

29.21a Slide the rotor onto the shaft, aligning the cut-out with the Woodruff key . . .

29.21b . . . and turning the gear to ease entry

29.22a Fit the nut and washer . . .

allow the hub to enter **(see illustrations)**. Make sure the Woodruff key does not become dislodged when installing the rotor.

22 Fit the nut with its washer and tighten it to the specified torque setting, using the method employed on removal to prevent the rotor from turning **(see illustrations)**.

23 Lubricate the idle/reduction gear shaft,

then position the gear and insert the shaft **(see illustration 29.13)**.

24 Fit the four dowels into the crankcase if removed, along with the two O-rings where fitted, then locate a new gasket onto them **(see illustration)**. Smear a suitable sealant onto the wiring grommet. Fit the alternator cover, noting that the rotor magnets will forcibly draw the cover/stator on, making sure

it locates onto the dowels. Tighten the cover bolts evenly in a criss-cross sequence to the specified torque.

25 Check the bearing and bush in the damper gear cover **(see illustration)**. Fit the starter damper gear inner washer, the damper gear and the outer washer **(see illustration 29.11b)**. Fit the dowel into the crankcase if removed, then locate a new gasket onto it **(see illustration)**.

29.22b . . . and tighten the nut to the specified torque

29.24 Make sure the dowels (arrowed) are in place, then fit the new gasket

29.25a Check the bearing and bush (arrowed) and fit a new cover if necessary

29.25b Fit a new gasket onto the dowel

Fit the cover, along with the exhaust shield on XT-Z models, and tighten the bolts to the specified torque (see illustration 29.11a).

26 Reconnect the wiring at the connectors, not forgetting the neutral switch wire (see illustration 21.3a, b or c). Tighten the neutral switch wire guide bolts (see illustration 29.10).

27 Install the remaining components (Steps 9 to 6).

28 Replenish the engine oil (see Chapter 1).

30 Regulator/rectifier

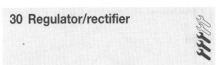

Check

1 No test details are given for the regulator/rectifier. If having checked the charging system as in Section 28 there is obviously a problem, and the alternator stator and the wiring is all good, the regulator/rectifier unit is probably faulty. Take it to a Yamaha dealer for confirmation of its condition before replacing it with a new one.

Removal and installation

2 On XT-R and XT-X models the regulator/rectifier is behind the left-hand side panel (see illustration) – remove the panel (see Chapter 7).

30.2a Regulator/rectifier (arrowed) – XT-R and XT-X models

On XT-Z models the regulator/rectifier is on the left-hand end of the radiator (see illustration) – remove the left-hand radiator panel (see Chapter 7). On MT-03 models the regulator/rectifier is below the swingarm (see illustration).

3 Disconnect the wiring connector.

4 Unscrew the two bolts securing the regulator/rectifier, noting the arrangement of the bracket, washers, collars and grommets on XT-Z models, and noting the washers on MT-03 models, and remove it.

5 Fit the new unit and tighten its bolts. Connect the wiring connector, making sure it is pushed fully into place.

6 Install the remaining components as required according to model.

30.2b Regulator/rectifier (arrowed) – XT-Z models

30.2c Regulator/rectifier (arrowed) – MT-03 models

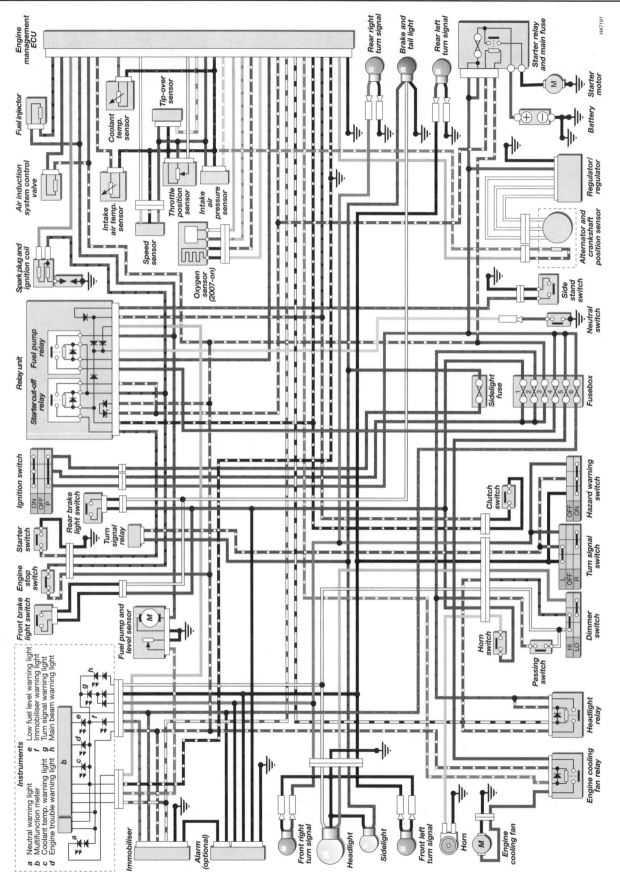

H47191

XT-R and XT-X models
(for fuse details see Chapter 8 specifications)

Engine management ECU

Fuel injector

Coolant temp. sensor

Tip-over sensor

Air induction system control valve

Intake air temp. sensor

Throttle position sensor

Intake air pressure sensor

Speed sensor

Spark plug and ignition coil

Oxygen sensor (2007-on)

Relay unit
Fuel pump relay
Start cut-off relay

Ignition switch
ON
OFF
P

Rear brake light switch

Starter switch

Turn signal relay

Engine stop switch

Front brake light switch

Fuel pump and level sensor

Instruments
a Neutral warning light
b Multifunction meter
c Coolant temp. warning light
d Engine trouble warning light
e Low fuel level warning light
f Immobiliser warning light
g Turn signal warning light
h Main beam warning light

Immobiliser

Alarm (optional)

Front right turn signal

Headlight

Sidelight

Front left turn signal

Horn

Engine cooling fan

Rear right turn signal

Brake and tail light

Rear left turn signal

Starter relay and main fuse

Starter motor

Battery

Regulator/regulator

Alternator and crankshaft position sensor

Side stand switch

Neutral switch

Sidelight fuse

Fusebox
1 2 3 4 5 6

Hazard warning switch
OFF
ON

Clutch switch

Turn signal switch
L
OFF
R

Dimmer switch
HI
LO

Horn switch

Passing switch

Headlight relay

Engine cooling fan relay

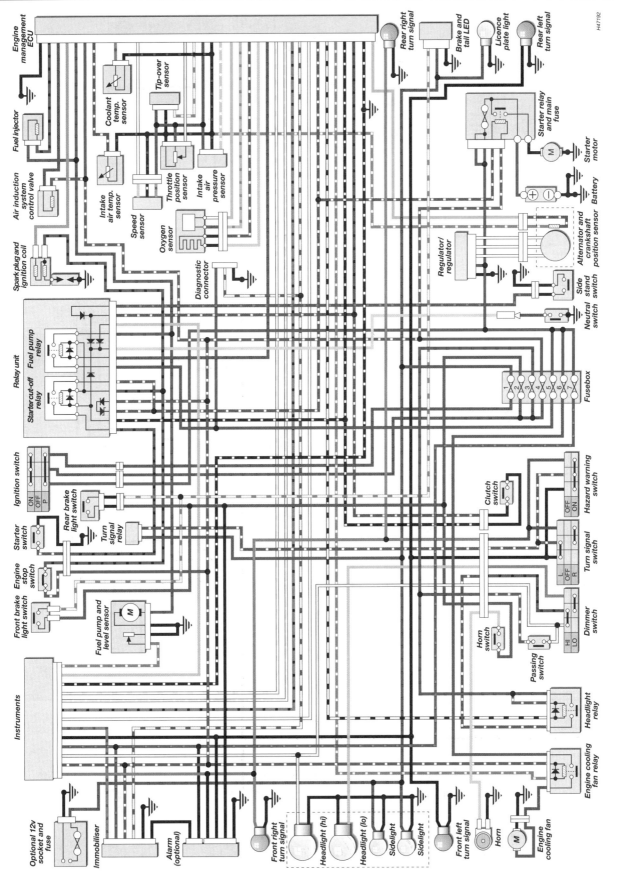

H47192

XT-Z models
(for fuse details see Chapter 8 specifications)

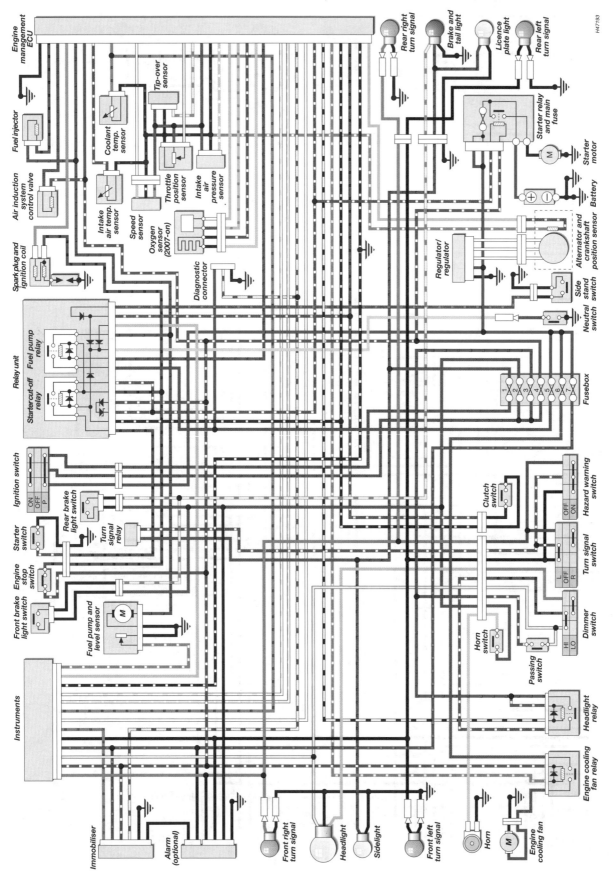

H47193

MT-03 models
(for fuse details see Chapter 8 specifications)

Reference

Tools and Workshop Tips | REF•2

● Building up a tool kit and equipping your workshop ● Using tools ● Understanding bearing, seal, fastener and chain sizes and markings ● Repair techniques

Security | REF•20

● Locks and chains ● U-locks ● Disc locks ● Alarms and immobilisers ● Security marking systems ● Tips on how to prevent bike theft

Lubricants and fluids | REF•23

● Engine oils ● Transmission (gear) oils ● Coolant/anti-freeze ● Fork oils and suspension fluids ● Brake/clutch fluids ● Spray lubes, degreasers and solvents

Conversion Factors | REF•26

34 Nm x 0.738
= 25 lbf ft

● Formulae for conversion of the metric (SI) units used throughout the manual into Imperial measures

MOT Test Checks | REF•27

● A guide to the UK MOT test ● Which items are tested ● How to prepare your motorcycle for the test and perform a pre-test check

Storage | REF•32

● How to prepare your motorcycle for going into storage and protect essential systems ● How to get the motorcycle back on the road

Fault Finding | REF•35

● Common faults and their likely causes ● Links to main chapters for testing and repair procedures

Technical Terms Explained | REF•44

● Component names, technical terms and common abbreviations explained

Index | REF•48

Buying tools

A toolkit is a fundamental requirement for servicing and repairing a motorcycle. Although there will be an initial expense in building up enough tools for servicing, this will soon be offset by the savings made by doing the job yourself. As experience and confidence grow, additional tools can be added to enable the repair and overhaul of the motorcycle. Many of the specialist tools are expensive and not often used so it may be preferable to hire them, or for a group of friends or motorcycle club to join in the purchase.

As a rule, it is better to buy more expensive, good quality tools. Cheaper tools are likely to wear out faster and need to be renewed more often, nullifying the original saving.

> **Warning: To avoid the risk of a poor quality tool breaking in use, causing injury or damage to the component being worked on, always aim to purchase tools which meet the relevant national safety standards.**

The following lists of tools do not represent the manufacturer's service tools, but serve as a guide to help the owner decide which tools are needed for this level of work. In addition, items such as an electric drill, hacksaw, files, soldering iron and a workbench equipped with a vice, may be needed. Although not classed as tools, a selection of bolts, screws, nuts, washers and pieces of tubing always come in useful.

For more information about tools, refer to the Haynes *Motorcycle Workshop Practice Techbook* (Bk. No. 3470).

Manufacturer's service tools

Inevitably certain tasks require the use of a service tool. Where possible an alternative tool or method of approach is recommended, but sometimes there is no option if personal injury or damage to the component is to be avoided. Where required, service tools are referred to in the relevant procedure.

Service tools can usually only be purchased from a motorcycle dealer and are identified by a part number. Some of the commonly-used tools, such as rotor pullers, are available in aftermarket form from mail-order motorcycle tool and accessory suppliers.

Maintenance and minor repair tools

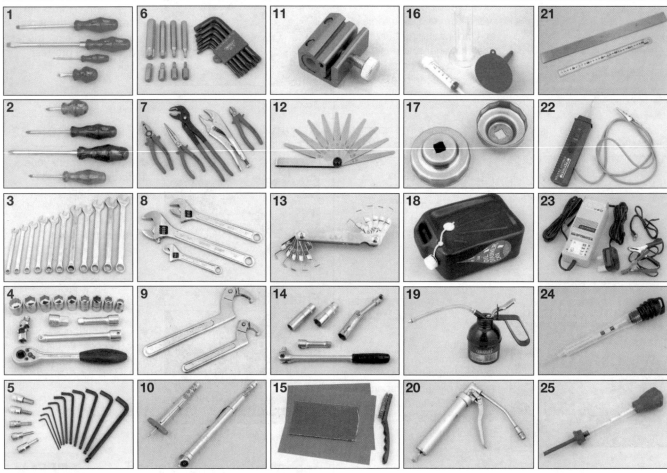

1 Set of flat-bladed screwdrivers
2 Set of Phillips head screwdrivers
3 Combination open-end and ring spanners
4 Socket set (3/8 inch or 1/2 inch drive)
5 Set of Allen keys or bits

6 Set of Torx keys or bits
7 Pliers, cutters and self-locking grips (Mole grips)
8 Adjustable spanners
9 C-spanners
10 Tread depth gauge and tyre pressure gauge

11 Cable oiler clamp
12 Feeler gauges
13 Spark plug gap measuring tool
14 Spark plug spanner or deep plug sockets
15 Wire brush and emery paper

16 Calibrated syringe, measuring vessel and funnel
17 Oil filter adapters
18 Oil drainer can or tray
19 Pump type oil can
20 Grease gun

21 Straight-edge and steel rule
22 Continuity tester
23 Battery charger
24 Hydrometer (for battery specific gravity check)
25 Anti-freeze tester (for liquid-cooled engines)

Repair and overhaul tools

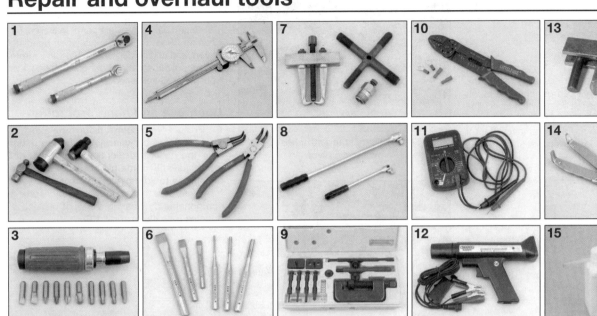

1 Torque wrench
  (small and mid-ranges)
2 Conventional, plastic or
  soft-faced hammers
3 Impact driver set

4 Vernier gauge
5 Circlip pliers (internal and
  external, or combination)
6 Set of cold chisels
  and punches

7 Selection of pullers
8 Breaker bars
9 Chain breaking/
  riveting tool set

10 Wire stripper and
   crimper tool
11 Multimeter (measures
   amps, volts and ohms)
12 Stroboscope (for
   dynamic timing checks)

13 Hose clamp
   (wingnut type shown)
14 Clutch holding tool
15 One-man brake/clutch
   bleeder kit

Specialist tools

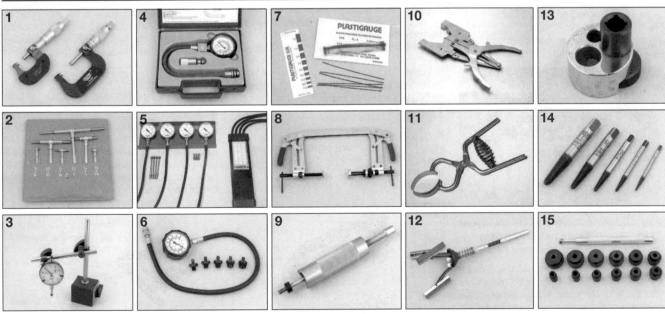

1 Micrometers
  (external type)
2 Telescoping gauges
3 Dial gauge

4 Cylinder
  compression gauge
5 Vacuum gauges (left) or
  manometer (right)
6 Oil pressure gauge

7 Plastigauge kit
8 Valve spring compressor
  (4-stroke engines)
9 Piston pin drawbolt tool

10 Piston ring removal and
   installation tool
11 Piston ring clamp
12 Cylinder bore hone
   (stone type shown)

13 Stud extractor
14 Screw extractor set
15 Bearing driver set

1 Workshop equipment and facilities

The workbench

● Work is made much easier by raising the bike up on a ramp - components are much more accessible if raised to waist level. The hydraulic or pneumatic types seen in the dealer's workshop are a sound investment if you undertake a lot of repairs or overhauls **(see illustration 1.1)**.

1.1 Hydraulic motorcycle ramp

● If raised off ground level, the bike must be supported on the ramp to avoid it falling. Most ramps incorporate a front wheel locating clamp which can be adjusted to suit different diameter wheels. When tightening the clamp, take care not to mark the wheel rim or damage the tyre - use wood blocks on each side to prevent this.
● Secure the bike to the ramp using tie-downs **(see illustration 1.2)**. If the bike has only a sidestand, and hence leans at a dangerous angle when raised, support the bike on an auxiliary stand.

1.2 Tie-downs are used around the passenger footrests to secure the bike

● Auxiliary (paddock) stands are widely available from mail order companies or motorcycle dealers and attach either to the wheel axle or swingarm pivot **(see illustration 1.3)**. If the motorcycle has a centrestand, you can support it under the crankcase to prevent it toppling whilst either wheel is removed **(see illustration 1.4)**.

1.3 This auxiliary stand attaches to the swingarm pivot

1.4 Always use a block of wood between the engine and jack head when supporting the engine in this way

Fumes and fire

● Refer to the Safety first! page at the beginning of the manual for full details. Make sure your workshop is equipped with a fire extinguisher suitable for fuel-related fires (Class B fire - flammable liquids) - it is not sufficient to have a water-filled extinguisher.
● Always ensure adequate ventilation is available. Unless an exhaust gas extraction system is available for use, ensure that the engine is run outside of the workshop.
● If working on the fuel system, make sure the workshop is ventilated to avoid a build-up of fumes. This applies equally to fume build-up when charging a battery. Do not smoke or allow anyone else to smoke in the workshop.

Fluids

● If you need to drain fuel from the tank, store it in an approved container marked as suitable for the storage of petrol (gasoline) **(see illustration 1.5)**. Do not store fuel in glass jars or bottles.

1.5 Use an approved can only for storing petrol (gasoline)

● Use proprietary engine degreasers or solvents which have a high flash-point, such as paraffin (kerosene), for cleaning off oil, grease and dirt - never use petrol (gasoline) for cleaning. Wear rubber gloves when handling solvent and engine degreaser. The fumes from certain solvents can be dangerous - always work in a well-ventilated area.

Dust, eye and hand protection

● Protect your lungs from inhalation of dust particles by wearing a filtering mask over the nose and mouth. Many frictional materials still contain asbestos which is dangerous to your health. Protect your eyes from spouts of liquid and sprung components by wearing a pair of protective goggles **(see illustration 1.6)**.

1.6 A fire extinguisher, goggles, mask and protective gloves should be at hand in the workshop

● Protect your hands from contact with solvents, fuel and oils by wearing rubber gloves. Alternatively apply a barrier cream to your hands before starting work. If handling hot components or fluids, wear suitable gloves to protect your hands from scalding and burns.

What to do with old fluids

● Old cleaning solvent, fuel, coolant and oils should not be poured down domestic drains or onto the ground. Package the fluid up in old oil containers, label it accordingly, and take it to a garage or disposal facility. Contact your local authority for location of such sites or ring the oil care hotline.

OIL CARE FOLLOW THE CODE

Note: It is illegal and anti-social to dump oil down the drain. To find the location of your local oil recycling bank in the UK, call 08708 506 506 or visit www.oilbankline. org.uk

In the USA, note that any oil supplier must accept used oil for recycling.

2 Fasteners -
screws, bolts and nuts

Fastener types and applications

Bolts and screws

● Fastener head types are either of hexagonal, Torx or splined design, with internal and external versions of each type **(see illustrations 2.1 and 2.2)**; splined head fasteners are not in common use on motorcycles. The conventional slotted or Phillips head design is used for certain screws. Bolt or screw length is always measured from the underside of the head to the end of the item **(see illustration 2.11)**.

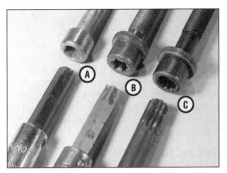

2.1 Internal hexagon/Allen (A), Torx (B) and splined (C) fasteners, with corresponding bits

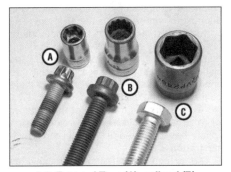

2.2 External Torx (A), splined (B) and hexagon (C) fasteners, with corresponding sockets

● Certain fasteners on the motorcycle have a tensile marking on their heads, the higher the marking the stronger the fastener. High tensile fasteners generally carry a 10 or higher marking. Never replace a high tensile fastener with one of a lower tensile strength.

Washers (see illustration 2.3)

● Plain washers are used between a fastener head and a component to prevent damage to the component or to spread the load when torque is applied. Plain washers can also be used as spacers or shims in certain assemblies. Copper or aluminium plain washers are often used as sealing washers on drain plugs.

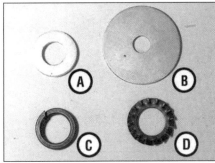

2.3 Plain washer (A), penny washer (B), spring washer (C) and serrated washer (D)

● The split-ring spring washer works by applying axial tension between the fastener head and component. If flattened, it is fatigued and must be renewed. If a plain (flat) washer is used on the fastener, position the spring washer between the fastener and the plain washer.

● Serrated star type washers dig into the fastener and component faces, preventing loosening. They are often used on electrical earth (ground) connections to the frame.

● Cone type washers (sometimes called Belleville) are conical and when tightened apply axial tension between the fastener head and component. They must be installed with the dished side against the component and often carry an OUTSIDE marking on their outer face. If flattened, they are fatigued and must be renewed.

● Tab washers are used to lock plain nuts or bolts on a shaft. A portion of the tab washer is bent up hard against one flat of the nut or bolt to prevent it loosening. Due to the tab washer being deformed in use, a new tab washer should be used every time it is disturbed.

● Wave washers are used to take up endfloat on a shaft. They provide light springing and prevent excessive side-to-side play of a component. Can be found on rocker arm shafts.

Nuts and split pins

● Conventional plain nuts are usually six-sided **(see illustration 2.4)**. They are sized by thread diameter and pitch. High tensile nuts carry a number on one end to denote their tensile strength.

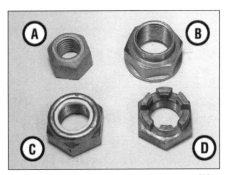

2.4 Plain nut (A), shouldered locknut (B), nylon insert nut (C) and castellated nut (D)

● Self-locking nuts either have a nylon insert, or two spring metal tabs, or a shoulder which is staked into a groove in the shaft - their advantage over conventional plain nuts is a resistance to loosening due to vibration. The nylon insert type can be used a number of times, but must be renewed when the friction of the nylon insert is reduced, ie when the nut spins freely on the shaft. The spring tab type can be reused unless the tabs are damaged. The shouldered type must be renewed every time it is disturbed.

● Split pins (cotter pins) are used to lock a castellated nut to a shaft or to prevent slackening of a plain nut. Common applications are wheel axles and brake torque arms. Because the split pin arms are deformed to lock around the nut a new split pin must always be used on installation - always fit the correct size split pin which will fit snugly in the shaft hole. Make sure the split pin arms are correctly located around the nut **(see illustrations 2.5 and 2.6)**.

2.5 Bend split pin (cotter pin) arms as shown (arrows) to secure a castellated nut

2.6 Bend split pin (cotter pin) arms as shown to secure a plain nut

Caution: If the castellated nut slots do not align with the shaft hole after tightening to the torque setting, tighten the nut until the next slot aligns with the hole - never slacken the nut to align its slot.

● R-pins (shaped like the letter R), or slip pins as they are sometimes called, are sprung and can be reused if they are otherwise in good condition. Always install R-pins with their closed end facing forwards **(see illustration 2.7)**.

2.7 Correct fitting of R-pin. Arrow indicates forward direction

Circlips (see illustration 2.8)

● Circlips (sometimes called snap-rings) are used to retain components on a shaft or in a housing and have corresponding external or internal ears to permit removal. Parallel-sided (machined) circlips can be installed either way round in their groove, whereas stamped circlips (which have a chamfered edge on one face) must be installed with the chamfer facing away from the direction of thrust load **(see illustration 2.9)**.

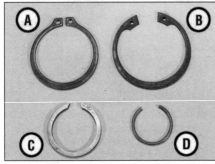

2.8 External stamped circlip (A), internal stamped circlip (B), machined circlip (C) and wire circlip (D)

● Always use circlip pliers to remove and install circlips; expand or compress them just enough to remove them. After installation, rotate the circlip in its groove to ensure it is securely seated. If installing a circlip on a splined shaft, always align its opening with a shaft channel to ensure the circlip ends are well supported and unlikely to catch **(see illustration 2.10)**.

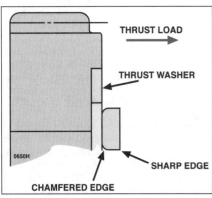

2.9 Correct fitting of a stamped circlip

THRUST LOAD

THRUST WASHER

SHARP EDGE

CHAMFERED EDGE

0650H

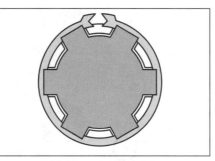

2.10 Align circlip opening with shaft channel

● Circlips can wear due to the thrust of components and become loose in their grooves, with the subsequent danger of becoming dislodged in operation. For this reason, renewal is advised every time a circlip is disturbed.

● Wire circlips are commonly used as piston pin retaining clips. If a removal tang is provided, long-nosed pliers can be used to dislodge them, otherwise careful use of a small flat-bladed screwdriver is necessary. Wire circlips should be renewed every time they are disturbed.

Thread diameter and pitch

● Diameter of a male thread (screw, bolt or stud) is the outside diameter of the threaded portion **(see illustration 2.11)**. Most motorcycle manufacturers use the ISO (International Standards Organisation) metric system expressed in millimetres, eg M6 refers to a 6 mm diameter thread. Sizing is the same for nuts, except that the thread diameter is measured across the valleys of the nut.

● Pitch is the distance between the peaks of the thread **(see illustration 2.11)**. It is expressed in millimetres, thus a common bolt size may be expressed as 6.0 x 1.0 mm (6 mm thread diameter and 1 mm pitch). Generally pitch increases in proportion to thread diameter, although there are always exceptions.

● Thread diameter and pitch are related for conventional fastener applications and the accompanying table can be used as a guide. Additionally, the AF (Across Flats), spanner or socket size dimension of the bolt or nut **(see illustration 2.11)** is linked to thread and pitch specification. Thread pitch can be measured with a thread gauge **(see illustration 2.12)**.

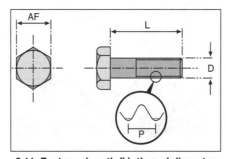

2.11 Fastener length (L), thread diameter (D), thread pitch (P) and head size (AF)

AF

L

D

P

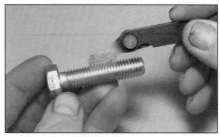

2.12 Using a thread gauge to measure pitch

AF size	Thread diameter x pitch (mm)
8 mm	M5 x 0.8
8 mm	M6 x 1.0
10 mm	M6 x 1.0
12 mm	M8 x 1.25
14 mm	M10 x 1.25
17 mm	M12 x 1.25

● The threads of most fasteners are of the right-hand type, ie they are turned clockwise to tighten and anti-clockwise to loosen. The reverse situation applies to left-hand thread fasteners, which are turned anti-clockwise to tighten and clockwise to loosen. Left-hand threads are used where rotation of a component might loosen a conventional right-hand thread fastener.

Seized fasteners

● Corrosion of external fasteners due to water or reaction between two dissimilar metals can occur over a period of time. It will build up sooner in wet conditions or in countries where salt is used on the roads during the winter. If a fastener is severely corroded it is likely that normal methods of removal will fail and result in its head being ruined. When you attempt removal, the fastener thread should be heard to crack free and unscrew easily - if it doesn't, stop there before damaging something.

● A smart tap on the head of the fastener will often succeed in breaking free corrosion which has occurred in the threads **(see illustration 2.13)**.

● An aerosol penetrating fluid (such as WD-40) applied the night beforehand may work its way down into the thread and ease removal. Depending on the location, you may be able to make up a Plasticine well around the fastener head and fill it with penetrating fluid.

2.13 A sharp tap on the head of a fastener will often break free a corroded thread

● If you are working on an engine internal component, corrosion will most likely not be a problem due to the well lubricated environment. However, components can be very tight and an impact driver is a useful tool in freeing them (see illustration 2.14).

2.14 Using an impact driver to free a fastener

● Where corrosion has occurred between dissimilar metals (eg steel and aluminium alloy), the application of heat to the fastener head will create a disproportionate expansion rate between the two metals and break the seizure caused by the corrosion. Whether heat can be applied depends on the location of the fastener - any surrounding components likely to be damaged must first be removed (see illustration 2.15). Heat can be applied using a paint stripper heat gun or clothes iron, or by immersing the component in boiling water - wear protective gloves to prevent scalding or burns to the hands.

2.15 Using heat to free a seized fastener

● As a last resort, it is possible to use a hammer and cold chisel to work the fastener head unscrewed (see illustration 2.16). This will damage the fastener, but more importantly extreme care must be taken not to damage the surrounding component.

Caution: Remember that the component being secured is generally of more value than the bolt, nut or screw - when the fastener is freed, do not unscrew it with force, instead work the fastener back and forth when resistance is felt to prevent thread damage.

2.16 Using a hammer and chisel to free a seized fastener

Broken fasteners and damaged heads

● If the shank of a broken bolt or screw is accessible you can grip it with self-locking grips. The knurled wheel type stud extractor tool or self-gripping stud puller tool is particularly useful for removing the long studs which screw into the cylinder mouth surface of the crankcase or bolts and screws from which the head has broken off (see illustration 2.17). Studs can also be removed by locking two nuts together on the threaded end of the stud and using a spanner on the lower nut (see illustration 2.18).

2.17 Using a stud extractor tool to remove a broken crankcase stud

2.18 Two nuts can be locked together to unscrew a stud from a component

● A bolt or screw which has broken off below or level with the casing must be extracted using a screw extractor set. Centre punch the fastener to centralise the drill bit, then drill a hole in the fastener (see illustration 2.19). Select a drill bit which is approximately half to three-quarters the

2.19 When using a screw extractor, first drill a hole in the fastener . . .

diameter of the fastener and drill to a depth which will accommodate the extractor. Use the largest size extractor possible, but avoid leaving too small a wall thickness otherwise the extractor will merely force the fastener walls outwards wedging it in the casing thread.

● If a spiral type extractor is used, thread it anti-clockwise into the fastener. As it is screwed in, it will grip the fastener and unscrew it from the casing (see illustration 2.20).

2.20 . . . then thread the extractor anti-clockwise into the fastener

● If a taper type extractor is used, tap it into the fastener so that it is firmly wedged in place. Unscrew the extractor (anti-clockwise) to draw the fastener out.

 Warning: Stud extractors are very hard and may break off in the fastener if care is not taken - ask an engineer about spark erosion if this happens.

● Alternatively, the broken bolt/screw can be drilled out and the hole retapped for an oversize bolt/screw or a diamond-section thread insert. It is essential that the drilling is carried out squarely and to the correct depth, otherwise the casing may be ruined - if in doubt, entrust the work to an engineer.

● Bolts and nuts with rounded corners cause the correct size spanner or socket to slip when force is applied. Of the types of spanner/socket available always use a six-point type rather than an eight or twelve-point type - better grip

2.21 Comparison of surface drive ring spanner (left) with 12-point type (right)

is obtained. Surface drive spanners grip the middle of the hex flats, rather than the corners, and are thus good in cases of damaged heads **(see illustration 2.21)**.

● Slotted-head or Phillips-head screws are often damaged by the use of the wrong size screwdriver. Allen-head and Torx-head screws are much less likely to sustain damage. If enough of the screw head is exposed you can use a hacksaw to cut a slot in its head and then use a conventional flat-bladed screwdriver to remove it. Alternatively use a hammer and cold chisel to tap the head of the fastener around to slacken it. Always replace damaged fasteners with new ones, preferably Torx or Allen-head type.

HAYNES HiNT

A dab of valve grinding compound between the screw head and screw-driver tip will often give a good grip.

Thread repair

● Threads (particularly those in aluminium alloy components) can be damaged by overtightening, being assembled with dirt in the threads, or from a component working loose and vibrating. Eventually the thread will fail completely, and it will be impossible to tighten the fastener.

● If a thread is damaged or clogged with old locking compound it can be renovated with a thread repair tool (thread chaser) **(see illustrations 2.22 and 2.23)**; special thread

2.22 A thread repair tool being used to correct an internal thread

2.23 A thread repair tool being used to correct an external thread

chasers are available for spark plug hole threads. The tool will not cut a new thread, but clean and true the original thread. Make sure that you use the correct diameter and pitch tool. Similarly, external threads can be cleaned up with a die or a thread restorer file **(see illustration 2.24)**.

2.24 Using a thread restorer file

● It is possible to drill out the old thread and retap the component to the next thread size. This will work where there is enough surrounding material and a new bolt or screw can be obtained. Sometimes, however, this is not possible - such as where the bolt/screw passes through another component which must also be suitably modified, also in cases where a spark plug or oil drain plug cannot be obtained in a larger diameter thread size.

● The diamond-section thread insert (often known by its popular trade name of Heli-Coil) is a simple and effective method of renewing the thread and retaining the original size. A kit can be purchased which contains the tap, insert and installing tool **(see illustration 2.25)**. Drill out the damaged thread with the size drill specified **(see illustration 2.26)**. Carefully retap the thread **(see illustration 2.27)**. Install the

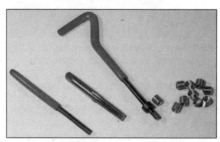

2.25 Obtain a thread insert kit to suit the thread diameter and pitch required

2.26 To install a thread insert, first drill out the original thread . . .

2.27 . . . tap a new thread . . .

2.28 . . . fit insert on the installing tool . . .

2.29 . . . and thread into the component . . .

2.30 . . . break off the tang when complete

insert on the installing tool and thread it slowly into place using a light downward pressure **(see illustrations 2.28 and 2.29)**. When positioned between a 1/4 and 1/2 turn below the surface withdraw the installing tool and use the break-off tool to press down on the tang, breaking it off **(see illustration 2.30)**.

● There are epoxy thread repair kits on the market which can rebuild stripped internal threads, although this repair should not be used on high load-bearing components.

Thread locking and sealing compounds

● Locking compounds are used in locations where the fastener is prone to loosening due to vibration or on important safety-related items which might cause loss of control of the motorcycle if they fail. It is also used where important fasteners cannot be secured by other means such as lockwashers or split pins.

● Before applying locking compound, make sure that the threads (internal and external) are clean and dry with all old compound removed. Select a compound to suit the component being secured - a non-permanent general locking and sealing type is suitable for most applications, but a high strength type is needed for permanent fixing of studs in castings. Apply a drop or two of the compound to the first few threads of the fastener, then thread it into place and tighten to the specified torque. Do not apply excessive thread locking compound otherwise the thread may be damaged on subsequent removal.

● Certain fasteners are impregnated with a dry film type coating of locking compound on their threads. Always renew this type of fastener if disturbed.

● Anti-seize compounds, such as copper-based greases, can be applied to protect threads from seizure due to extreme heat and corrosion. A common instance is spark plug threads and exhaust system fasteners.

3 Measuring tools and gauges

Feeler gauges

● Feeler gauges (or blades) are used for measuring small gaps and clearances **(see illustration 3.1)**. They can also be used to measure endfloat (sideplay) of a component on a shaft where access is not possible with a dial gauge.

● Feeler gauge sets should be treated with care and not bent or damaged. They are etched with their size on one face. Keep them clean and very lightly oiled to prevent corrosion build-up.

3.1 Feeler gauges are used for measuring small gaps and clearances - thickness is marked on one face of gauge

● When measuring a clearance, select a gauge which is a light sliding fit between the two components. You may need to use two gauges together to measure the clearance accurately.

Micrometers

● A micrometer is a precision tool capable of measuring to 0.01 or 0.001 of a millimetre. It should always be stored in its case and not in the general toolbox. It must be kept clean and never dropped, otherwise its frame or measuring anvils could be distorted resulting in inaccurate readings.

● External micrometers are used for measuring outside diameters of components and have many more applications than internal micrometers. Micrometers are available in different size ranges, eg 0 to 25 mm, 25 to 50 mm, and upwards in 25 mm steps; some large micrometers have interchangeable anvils to allow a range of measurements to be taken. Generally the largest precision measurement you are likely to take on a motorcycle is the piston diameter.

● Internal micrometers (or bore micrometers) are used for measuring inside diameters, such as valve guides and cylinder bores. Telescoping gauges and small hole gauges are used in conjunction with an external micrometer, whereas the more expensive internal micrometers have their own measuring device.

External micrometer

Note: *The conventional analogue type instrument is described. Although much easier to read, digital micrometers are considerably more expensive.*

● Always check the calibration of the micrometer before use. With the anvils closed (0 to 25 mm type) or set over a test gauge (for

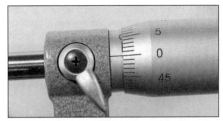

3.2 Check micrometer calibration before use

the larger types) the scale should read zero **(see illustration 3.2)**; make sure that the anvils (and test piece) are clean first. Any discrepancy can be adjusted by referring to the instructions supplied with the tool. Remember that the micrometer is a precision measuring tool - don't force the anvils closed, use the ratchet (4) on the end of the micrometer to close it. In this way, a measured force is always applied.

● To use, first make sure that the item being measured is clean. Place the anvil (1) of the micrometer against the item and use the thimble (2) to bring the spindle (3) lightly into contact with the other side of the item **(see illustration 3.3)**. Don't tighten the thimble down because this will damage the micrometer - instead use the ratchet (4) on the end of the micrometer. The ratchet mechanism applies a measured force preventing damage to the instrument.

● The micrometer is read by referring to the linear scale on the sleeve and the annular scale on the thimble. Read off the sleeve first to obtain the base measurement, then add the fine measurement from the thimble to obtain the overall reading. The linear scale on the sleeve represents the measuring range of the micrometer (eg 0 to 25 mm). The annular scale

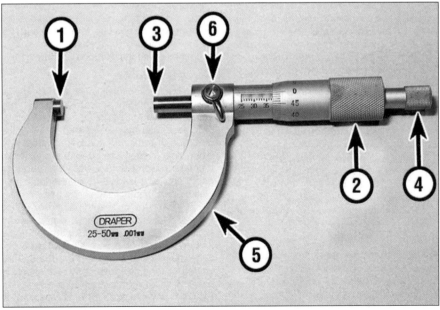

3.3 Micrometer component parts

1 Anvil	3 Spindle	5 Frame
2 Thimble	4 Ratchet	6 Locking lever

on the thimble will be in graduations of 0.01 mm (or as marked on the frame) - one full revolution of the thimble will move 0.5 mm on the linear scale. Take the reading where the datum line on the sleeve intersects the thimble's scale. Always position the eye directly above the scale otherwise an inaccurate reading will result.

In the example shown the item measures 2.95 mm **(see illustration 3.4)**:

Linear scale	2.00 mm
Linear scale	0.50 mm
Annular scale	0.45 mm
Total figure	**2.95 mm**

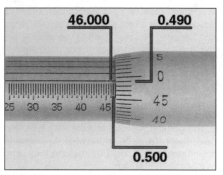

3.5 Micrometer reading of 46.99 mm on linear and annular scales . . .

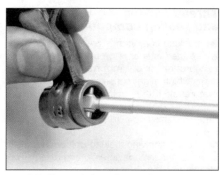

3.7 Expand the telescoping gauge in the bore, lock its position . . .

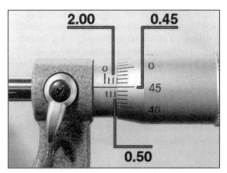

3.4 Micrometer reading of 2.95 mm

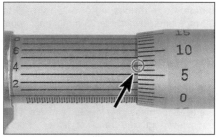

3.6 . . . and 0.004 mm on vernier scale

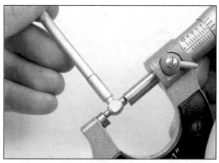

3.8 . . . then measure the gauge with a micrometer

Most micrometers have a locking lever (6) on the frame to hold the setting in place, allowing the item to be removed from the micrometer.

● Some micrometers have a vernier scale on their sleeve, providing an even finer measurement to be taken, in 0.001 increments of a millimetre. Take the sleeve and thimble measurement as described above, then check which graduation on the vernier scale aligns with that of the annular scale on the thimble **Note:** *The eye must be perpendicular to the scale when taking the vernier reading - if necessary rotate the body of the micrometer to ensure this.* Multiply the vernier scale figure by 0.001 and add it to the base and fine measurement figures.

In the example shown the item measures 46.994 mm **(see illustrations 3.5 and 3.6)**:

Linear scale (base)	46.000 mm
Linear scale (base)	00.500 mm
Annular scale (fine)	00.490 mm
Vernier scale	00.004 mm
Total figure	**46.994 mm**

Internal micrometer

● Internal micrometers are available for measuring bore diameters, but are expensive and unlikely to be available for home use. It is suggested that a set of telescoping gauges and small hole gauges, both of which must be used with an external micrometer, will suffice for taking internal measurements on a motorcycle.

● Telescoping gauges can be used to

measure internal diameters of components. Select a gauge with the correct size range, make sure its ends are clean and insert it into the bore. Expand the gauge, then lock its position and withdraw it from the bore **(see illustration 3.7)**. Measure across the gauge ends with a micrometer **(see illustration 3.8)**.

● Very small diameter bores (such as valve guides) are measured with a small hole gauge. Once adjusted to a slip-fit inside the component, its position is locked and the gauge withdrawn for measurement with a micrometer **(see illustrations 3.9 and 3.10)**.

Vernier caliper

Note: *The conventional linear and dial gauge type instruments are described. Digital types are easier to read, but are far more expensive.*

● The vernier caliper does not provide the precision of a micrometer, but is versatile in being able to measure internal and external diameters. Some types also incorporate a depth gauge. It is ideal for measuring clutch plate friction material and spring free lengths.

● To use the conventional linear scale vernier, slacken off the vernier clamp screws (1) and set its jaws over (2), or inside (3), the item to be measured **(see illustration 3.11)**. Slide the jaw into contact, using the thumbwheel (4) for fine movement of the sliding scale (5) then tighten the clamp screws (1). Read off the main scale (6) where the zero on the sliding scale (5) intersects it, taking the whole number to the left of the zero; this provides the base measurement. View along the sliding scale and select the division which

3.9 Expand the small hole gauge in the bore, lock its position . . .

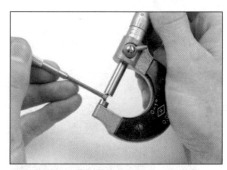

3.10 . . . then measure the gauge with a micrometer

lines up exactly with any of the divisions on the main scale, noting that the divisions usually represents 0.02 of a millimetre. Add this fine measurement to the base measurement to obtain the total reading.

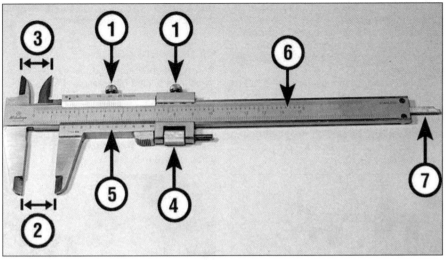

3.11 Vernier component parts (linear gauge)

1 Clamp screws	3 Internal jaws	5 Sliding scale	7 Depth gauge
2 External jaws	4 Thumbwheel	6 Main scale	

In the example shown the item measures 55.92 mm **(see illustration 3.12)**:

Base measurement	55.00 mm
Fine measurement	00.92 mm
Total figure	**55.92 mm**

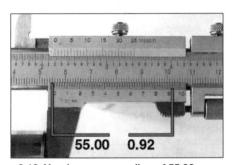

3.12 Vernier gauge reading of 55.92 mm

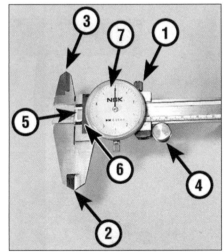

3.13 Vernier component parts (dial gauge)

1 Clamp screw	5 Main scale
2 External jaws	6 Sliding scale
3 Internal jaws	7 Dial gauge
4 Thumbwheel	

● Some vernier calipers are equipped with a dial gauge for fine measurement. Before use, check that the jaws are clean, then close them fully and check that the dial gauge reads zero. If necessary adjust the gauge ring accordingly. Slacken the vernier clamp screw (1) and set its jaws over (2), or inside (3), the item to be measured **(see illustration 3.13)**. Slide the jaws into contact, using the thumbwheel (4) for fine movement. Read off the main scale (5) where the edge of the sliding scale (6) intersects it, taking the whole number to the left of the zero; this provides the base measurement. Read off the needle position on the dial gauge (7) scale to provide the fine measurement; each division represents 0.05 of a millimetre. Add this fine measurement to the base measurement to obtain the total reading.

In the example shown the item measures 55.95 mm **(see illustration 3.14)**:

Base measurement	55.00 mm
Fine measurement	00.95 mm
Total figure	**55.95 mm**

3.14 Vernier gauge reading of 55.95 mm

Plastigauge

● Plastigauge is a plastic material which can be compressed between two surfaces to measure the oil clearance between them. The width of the compressed Plastigauge is measured against a calibrated scale to determine the clearance.

● Common uses of Plastigauge are for measuring the clearance between crankshaft journal and main bearing inserts, between crankshaft journal and big-end bearing inserts, and between camshaft and bearing surfaces. The following example describes big-end oil clearance measurement.

● Handle the Plastigauge material carefully to prevent distortion. Using a sharp knife, cut a length which corresponds with the width of the bearing being measured and place it carefully across the journal so that it is parallel with the shaft **(see illustration 3.15)**. Carefully install both bearing shells and the connecting rod. Without rotating the rod on the journal tighten its bolts or nuts (as applicable) to the specified torque. The connecting rod and bearings are then disassembled and the crushed Plastigauge examined.

3.15 Plastigauge placed across shaft journal

● Using the scale provided in the Plastigauge kit, measure the width of the material to determine the oil clearance **(see illustration 3.16)**. Always remove all traces of Plastigauge after use using your fingernails.

> *Caution: Arriving at the correct clearance demands that the assembly is torqued correctly, according to the settings and sequence (where applicable) provided by the motorcycle manufacturer.*

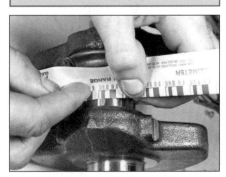

3.16 Measuring the width of the crushed Plastigauge

Dial gauge or DTI (Dial Test Indicator)

● A dial gauge can be used to accurately measure small amounts of movement. Typical uses are measuring shaft runout or shaft endfloat (sideplay) and setting piston position for ignition timing on two-strokes. A dial gauge set usually comes with a range of different probes and adapters and mounting equipment.
● The gauge needle must point to zero when at rest. Rotate the ring around its periphery to zero the gauge.
● Check that the gauge is capable of reading the extent of movement in the work. Most gauges have a small dial set in the face which records whole millimetres of movement as well as the fine scale around the face periphery which is calibrated in 0.01 mm divisions. Read off the small dial first to obtain the base measurement, then add the measurement from the fine scale to obtain the total reading.

In the example shown the gauge reads 1.48 mm (see illustration 3.17):

Base measurement	1.00 mm
Fine measurement	0.48 mm
Total figure	**1.48 mm**

3.17 Dial gauge reading of 1.48 mm

● If measuring shaft runout, the shaft must be supported in vee-blocks and the gauge mounted on a stand perpendicular to the shaft. Rest the tip of the gauge against the centre of the shaft and rotate the shaft slowly whilst watching the gauge reading (see illustration 3.18). Take several measurements along the length of the shaft and record the

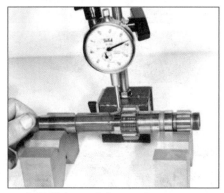

3.18 Using a dial gauge to measure shaft runout

maximum gauge reading as the amount of runout in the shaft. **Note:** *The reading obtained will be total runout at that point - some manufacturers specify that the runout figure is halved to compare with their specified runout limit.*
● Endfloat (sideplay) measurement requires that the gauge is mounted securely to the surrounding component with its probe touching the end of the shaft. Using hand pressure, push and pull on the shaft noting the maximum endfloat recorded on the gauge (see illustration 3.19).

3.19 Using a dial gauge to measure shaft endfloat

● A dial gauge with suitable adapters can be used to determine piston position BTDC on two-stroke engines for the purposes of ignition timing. The gauge, adapter and suitable length probe are installed in the place of the spark plug and the gauge zeroed at TDC. If the piston position is specified as 1.14 mm BTDC, rotate the engine back to 2.00 mm BTDC, then slowly forwards to 1.14 mm BTDC.

Cylinder compression gauges

● A compression gauge is used for measuring cylinder compression. Either the rubber-cone type or the threaded adapter type can be used. The latter is preferred to ensure a perfect seal against the cylinder head. A 0 to 300 psi (0 to 20 Bar) type gauge (for petrol/gasoline engines) will be suitable for motorcycles.
● The spark plug is removed and the gauge either held hard against the cylinder head (cone type) or the gauge adapter screwed into the cylinder head (threaded type) (see illustration 3.20). Cylinder compression is measured with the engine turning over, but not running - carry out the compression test as described in

3.20 Using a rubber-cone type cylinder compression gauge

Fault Finding Equipment. The gauge will hold the reading until manually released.

Oil pressure gauge

● An oil pressure gauge is used for measuring engine oil pressure. Most gauges come with a set of adapters to fit the thread of the take-off point (see illustration 3.21). If the take-off point specified by the motorcycle manufacturer is an external oil pipe union, make sure that the specified replacement union is used to prevent oil starvation.

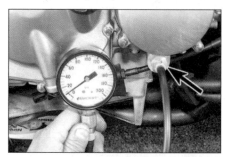

3.21 Oil pressure gauge and take-off point adapter (arrow)

● Oil pressure is measured with the engine running (at a specific rpm) and often the manufacturer will specify pressure limits for a cold and hot engine.

Straight-edge and surface plate

● If checking the gasket face of a component for warpage, place a steel rule or precision straight-edge across the gasket face and measure any gap between the straight-edge and component with feeler gauges (see illustration 3.22). Check diagonally across the component and between mounting holes (see illustration 3.23).

3.22 Use a straight-edge and feeler gauges to check for warpage

3.23 Check for warpage in these directions

● Checking individual components for warpage, such as clutch plain (metal) plates, requires a perfectly flat plate or piece or plate glass and feeler gauges.

4 Torque and leverage

What is torque?

● Torque describes the twisting force about a shaft. The amount of torque applied is determined by the distance from the centre of the shaft to the end of the lever and the amount of force being applied to the end of the lever; distance multiplied by force equals torque.

● The manufacturer applies a measured torque to a bolt or nut to ensure that it will not slacken in use and to hold two components securely together without movement in the joint. The actual torque setting depends on the thread size, bolt or nut material and the composition of the components being held.

● Too little torque may cause the fastener to loosen due to vibration, whereas too much torque will distort the joint faces of the component or cause the fastener to shear off. Always stick to the specified torque setting.

Using a torque wrench

● Check the calibration of the torque wrench and make sure it has a suitable range for the job. Torque wrenches are available in Nm (Newton-metres), kgf m (kilograms-force metre), lbf ft (pounds-feet), lbf in (inch-pounds). Do not confuse lbf ft with lbf in.

● Adjust the tool to the desired torque on the scale **(see illustration 4.1)**. If your torque wrench is not calibrated in the units specified, carefully convert the figure (see *Conversion Factors*). A manufacturer sometimes gives a torque setting as a range (8 to 10 Nm) rather than a single figure - in this case set the tool midway between the two settings. The same torque may be expressed as 9 Nm ± 1 Nm. Some torque wrenches have a method of locking the setting so that it isn't inadvertently altered during use.

4.1 Set the torque wrench index mark to the setting required, in this case 12 Nm

● Install the bolts/nuts in their correct location and secure them lightly. Their threads must be clean and free of any old locking compound. Unless specified the threads and flange should be dry - oiled threads are necessary in certain circumstances and the manufacturer will take this into account in the specified torque figure. Similarly, the manufacturer may also specify the application of thread-locking compound.

● Tighten the fasteners in the specified sequence until the torque wrench clicks, indicating that the torque setting has been reached. Apply the torque again to double-check the setting. Where different thread diameter fasteners secure the component, as a rule tighten the larger diameter ones first.

● When the torque wrench has been finished with, release the lock (where applicable) and fully back off its setting to zero - do not leave the torque wrench tensioned. Also, do not use a torque wrench for slackening a fastener.

Angle-tightening

● Manufacturers often specify a figure in degrees for final tightening of a fastener. This usually follows tightening to a specific torque setting.

● A degree disc can be set and attached to the socket **(see illustration 4.2)** or a protractor can be used to mark the angle of movement on the bolt/nut head and the surrounding casting **(see illustration 4.3)**.

4.2 Angle tightening can be accomplished with a torque-angle gauge . . .

4.3 . . . or by marking the angle on the surrounding component

Loosening sequences

● Where more than one bolt/nut secures a component, loosen each fastener evenly a little at a time. In this way, not all the stress of the joint is held by one fastener and the components are not likely to distort.

● If a tightening sequence is provided, work in the REVERSE of this, but if not, work from the outside in, in a criss-cross sequence **(see illustration 4.4)**.

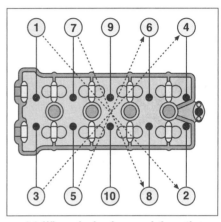

4.4 When slackening, work from the outside inwards

Tightening sequences

● If a component is held by more than one fastener it is important that the retaining bolts/nuts are tightened evenly to prevent uneven stress build-up and distortion of sealing faces. This is especially important on high-compression joints such as the cylinder head.

● A sequence is usually provided by the manufacturer, either in a diagram or actually marked in the casting. If not, always start in the centre and work outwards in a criss-cross pattern **(see illustration 4.5)**. Start off by securing all bolts/nuts finger-tight, then set the torque wrench and tighten each fastener by a small amount in sequence until the final torque is reached. By following this practice,

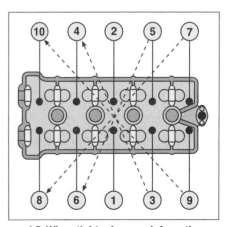

4.5 When tightening, work from the inside outwards

the joint will be held evenly and will not be distorted. Important joints, such as the cylinder head and big-end fasteners often have two- or three-stage torque settings.

Applying leverage

● Use tools at the correct angle. Position a socket wrench or spanner on the bolt/nut so that you pull it towards you when loosening. If this can't be done, push the spanner without curling your fingers around it **(see illustration 4.6)** - the spanner may slip or the fastener loosen suddenly, resulting in your fingers being crushed against a component.

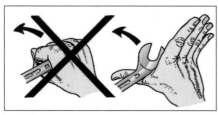

4.6 If you can't pull on the spanner to loosen a fastener, push with your hand open

● Additional leverage is gained by extending the length of the lever. The best way to do this is to use a breaker bar instead of the regular length tool, or to slip a length of tubing over the end of the spanner or socket wrench.
● If additional leverage will not work, the fastener head is either damaged or firmly corroded in place (see *Fasteners*).

5 Bearings

Bearing removal and installation

Drivers and sockets

● Before removing a bearing, always inspect the casing to see which way it must be driven out - some casings will have retaining plates or a cast step. Also check for any identifying markings on the bearing and if installed to a certain depth, measure this at this stage. Some roller bearings are sealed on one side - take note of the original fitted position.
● Bearings can be driven out of a casing using a bearing driver tool (with the correct size head) or a socket of the correct diameter. Select the driver head or socket so that it contacts the outer race of the bearing, not the balls/rollers or inner race. Always support the casing around the bearing housing with wood blocks, otherwise there is a risk of fracture. The bearing is driven out with a few blows on the driver or socket from a heavy mallet. Unless access is severely restricted (as with wheel bearings), a pin-punch is not recommended unless it is moved around the bearing to keep it square in its housing.

● The same equipment can be used to install bearings. Make sure the bearing housing is supported on wood blocks and line up the bearing in its housing. Fit the bearing as noted on removal - generally they are installed with their marked side facing outwards. Tap the bearing squarely into its housing using a driver or socket which bears only on the bearing's outer race - contact with the bearing balls/rollers or inner race will destroy it **(see illustrations 5.1 and 5.2)**.
● Check that the bearing inner race and balls/rollers rotate freely.

5.1 Using a bearing driver against the bearing's outer race

5.2 Using a large socket against the bearing's outer race

Pullers and slide-hammers

● Where a bearing is pressed on a shaft a puller will be required to extract it **(see illustration 5.3)**. Make sure that the puller clamp or legs fit securely behind the bearing and are unlikely to slip out. If pulling a bearing

5.3 This bearing puller clamps behind the bearing and pressure is applied to the shaft end to draw the bearing off

off a gear shaft for example, you may have to locate the puller behind a gear pinion if there is no access to the race and draw the gear pinion off the shaft as well **(see illustration 5.4)**.

> *Caution: Ensure that the puller's centre bolt locates securely against the end of the shaft and will not slip when pressure is applied. Also ensure that puller does not damage the shaft end.*

5.4 Where no access is available to the rear of the bearing, it is sometimes possible to draw off the adjacent component

● Operate the puller so that its centre bolt exerts pressure on the shaft end and draws the bearing off the shaft.
● When installing the bearing on the shaft, tap only on the bearing's inner race - contact with the balls/rollers or outer race with destroy the bearing. Use a socket or length of tubing as a drift which fits over the shaft end **(see illustration 5.5)**.

5.5 When installing a bearing on a shaft use a piece of tubing which bears only on the bearing's inner race

● Where a bearing locates in a blind hole in a casing, it cannot be driven or pulled out as described above. A slide-hammer with knife-edged bearing puller attachment will be required. The puller attachment passes through the bearing and when tightened expands to fit firmly behind the bearing **(see illustration 5.6)**. By operating the slide-hammer part of the tool the bearing is jarred out of its housing **(see illustration 5.7)**.
● It is possible, if the bearing is of reasonable weight, for it to drop out of its housing if the casing is heated as described opposite. If this

5.6 Expand the bearing puller so that it locks behind the bearing . . .

5.7 . . . attach the slide hammer to the bearing puller

method is attempted, first prepare a work surface which will enable the casing to be tapped face down to help dislodge the bearing - a wood surface is ideal since it will not damage the casing's gasket surface. Wearing protective gloves, tap the heated casing several times against the work surface to dislodge the bearing under its own weight **(see illustration 5.8)**.

5.8 Tapping a casing face down on wood blocks can often dislodge a bearing

● Bearings can be installed in blind holes using the driver or socket method described above.

Drawbolts

● Where a bearing or bush is set in the eye of a component, such as a suspension linkage arm or connecting rod small-end, removal by drift may damage the component. Furthermore, a rubber bushing in a shock absorber eye cannot successfully be driven out of position. If access is available to a engineering press, the task is straightforward. If not, a drawbolt can be fabricated to extract the bearing or bush.

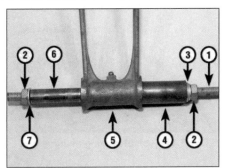

5.9 Drawbolt component parts assembled on a suspension arm

1 Bolt or length of threaded bar
2 Nuts
3 Washer (external diameter greater than tubing internal diameter)
4 Tubing (internal diameter sufficient to accommodate bearing)
5 Suspension arm with bearing
6 Tubing (external diameter slightly smaller than bearing)
7 Washer (external diameter slightly smaller than bearing)

5.10 Drawing the bearing out of the suspension arm

● To extract the bearing/bush you will need a long bolt with nut (or piece of threaded bar with two nuts), a piece of tubing which has an internal diameter larger than the bearing/bush, another piece of tubing which has an external diameter slightly smaller than the bearing/bush, and a selection of washers **(see illustrations 5.9 and 5.10)**. Note that the pieces of tubing must be of the same length, or longer, than the bearing/bush.
● The same kit (without the pieces of tubing) can be used to draw the new bearing/bush back into place **(see illustration 5.11)**.

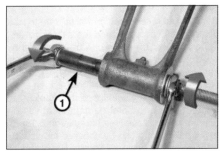

5.11 Installing a new bearing (1) in the suspension arm

Temperature change

● If the bearing's outer race is a tight fit in the casing, the aluminium casing can be heated to release its grip on the bearing. Aluminium will expand at a greater rate than the steel bearing outer race. There are several ways to do this, but avoid any localised extreme heat (such as a blow torch) - aluminium alloy has a low melting point.
● Approved methods of heating a casing are using a domestic oven (heated to 100°C) or immersing the casing in boiling water **(see illustration 5.12)**. Low temperature range localised heat sources such as a paint stripper heat gun or clothes iron can also be used **(see illustration 5.13)**. Alternatively, soak a rag in boiling water, wring it out and wrap it around the bearing housing.

> ⚠ **Warning: All of these methods require care in use to prevent scalding and burns to the hands. Wear protective gloves when handling hot components.**

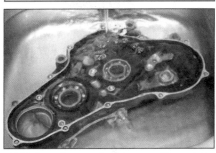

5.12 A casing can be immersed in a sink of boiling water to aid bearing removal

5.13 Using a localised heat source to aid bearing removal

● If heating the whole casing note that plastic components, such as the neutral switch, may suffer - remove them beforehand.
● After heating, remove the bearing as described above. You may find that the expansion is sufficient for the bearing to fall out of the casing under its own weight or with a light tap on the driver or socket.
● If necessary, the casing can be heated to aid bearing installation, and this is sometimes the recommended procedure if the motorcycle manufacturer has designed the housing and bearing fit with this intention.

● Installation of bearings can be eased by placing them in a freezer the night before installation. The steel bearing will contract slightly, allowing easy insertion in its housing. This is often useful when installing steering head outer races in the frame.

Bearing types and markings

● Plain shell bearings, ball bearings, needle roller bearings and tapered roller bearings will all be found on motorcycles (see illustrations 5.14 and 5.15). The ball and roller types are usually caged between an inner and outer race, but uncaged variations may be found.

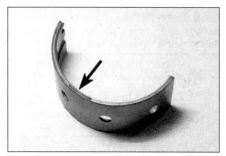

5.14 Shell bearings are either plain or grooved. They are usually identified by colour code (arrow)

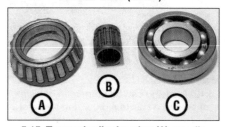

5.15 Tapered roller bearing (A), needle roller bearing (B) and ball journal bearing (C)

● Shell bearings (often called inserts) are usually found at the crankshaft main and connecting rod big-end where they are good at coping with high loads. They are made of a phosphor-bronze material and are impregnated with self-lubricating properties.
● Ball bearings and needle roller bearings consist of a steel inner and outer race with the balls or rollers between the races. They require constant lubrication by oil or grease and are good at coping with axial loads. Taper roller bearings consist of rollers set in a tapered cage set on the inner race; the outer race is separate. They are good at coping with axial loads and prevent movement along the shaft - a typical application is in the steering head.
● Bearing manufacturers produce bearings to ISO size standards and stamp one face of the bearing to indicate its internal and external diameter, load capacity and type (see illustration 5.16).
● Metal bushes are usually of phosphor-bronze material. Rubber bushes are used in suspension mounting eyes. Fibre bushes have also been used in suspension pivots.

5.16 Typical bearing marking

Bearing fault finding

● If a bearing outer race has spun in its housing, the housing material will be damaged. You can use a bearing locking compound to bond the outer race in place if damage is not too severe.
● Shell bearings will fail due to damage of their working surface, as a result of lack of lubrication, corrosion or abrasive particles in the oil (see illustration 5.17). Small particles of dirt in the oil may embed in the bearing material whereas larger particles will score the bearing and shaft journal. If a number of short journeys are made, insufficient heat will be generated to drive off condensation which has built up on the bearings.

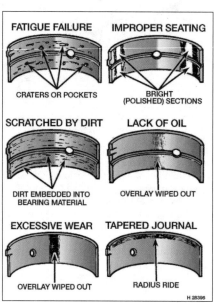

5.17 Typical bearing failures

● Ball and roller bearings will fail due to lack of lubrication or damage to the balls or rollers. Tapered-roller bearings can be damaged by overloading them. Unless the bearing is sealed on both sides, wash it in paraffin (kerosene) to remove all old grease then allow it to dry. Make a visual inspection looking to dented balls or rollers, damaged cages and worn or pitted races (see illustration 5.18).
● A ball bearing can be checked for wear by listening to it when spun. Apply a film of light oil to the bearing and hold it close to the ear - hold the outer race with one hand and spin the inner

5.18 Example of ball journal bearing with damaged balls and cages

5.19 Hold outer race and listen to inner race when spun

race with the other hand (see illustration 5.19). The bearing should be almost silent when spun; if it grates or rattles it is worn.

6 Oil seals

Oil seal removal and installation

● Oil seals should be renewed every time a component is dismantled. This is because the seal lips will become set to the sealing surface and will not necessarily reseal.
● Oil seals can be prised out of position using a large flat-bladed screwdriver (see illustration 6.1). In the case of crankcase seals, check first that the seal is not lipped on the inside, preventing its removal with the crankcases joined.

6.1 Prise out oil seals with a large flat-bladed screwdriver

● New seals are usually installed with their marked face (containing the seal reference code) outwards and the spring side towards the fluid being retained. In certain cases, such as a two-stroke engine crankshaft seal, a double lipped seal may be used due to there being fluid or gas on each side of the joint.

● Use a bearing driver or socket which bears only on the outer hard edge of the seal to install it in the casing - tapping on the inner edge will damage the sealing lip.

Oil seal types and markings

● Oil seals are usually of the single-lipped type. Double-lipped seals are found where a liquid or gas is on both sides of the joint.
● Oil seals can harden and lose their sealing ability if the motorcycle has been in storage for a long period - renewal is the only solution.
● Oil seal manufacturers also conform to the ISO markings for seal size - these are moulded into the outer face of the seal (see illustration 6.2).

6.2 These oil seal markings indicate inside diameter, outside diameter and seal thickness

7 Gaskets and sealants

Types of gasket and sealant

● Gaskets are used to seal the mating surfaces between components and keep lubricants, fluids, vacuum or pressure contained within the assembly. Aluminium gaskets are sometimes found at the cylinder joints, but most gaskets are paper-based. If the mating surfaces of the components being joined are undamaged the gasket can be installed dry, although a dab of sealant or grease will be useful to hold it in place during assembly.
● RTV (Room Temperature Vulcanising) silicone rubber sealants cure when exposed to moisture in the atmosphere. These sealants are good at filling pits or irregular gasket faces, but will tend to be forced out of the joint under very high torque. They can be used to replace a paper gasket, but first make sure that the width of the paper gasket is not essential to the shimming of internal components. RTV sealants should not be used on components containing petrol (gasoline).
● Non-hardening, semi-hardening and hard setting liquid gasket compounds can be used with a gasket or between a metal-to-metal joint. Select the sealant to suit the application: universal non-hardening sealant can be used on virtually all joints; semi-hardening on joint faces which are rough or damaged; hard setting sealant on joints which require a permanent bond and are subjected to high temperature and pressure. **Note:** *Check first if the paper gasket has a bead of sealant*

impregnated in its surface before applying additional sealant.
● When choosing a sealant, make sure it is suitable for the application, particularly if being applied in a high-temperature area or in the vicinity of fuel. Certain manufacturers produce sealants in either clear, silver or black colours to match the finish of the engine. This has a particular application on motorcycles where much of the engine is exposed.
● Do not over-apply sealant. That which is squeezed out on the outside of the joint can be wiped off, whereas an excess of sealant on the inside can break off and clog oilways.

Breaking a sealed joint

● Age, heat, pressure and the use of hard setting sealant can cause two components to stick together so tightly that they are difficult to separate using finger pressure alone. Do not resort to using levers unless there is a pry point provided for this purpose (see illustration 7.1) or else the gasket surfaces will be damaged.
● Use a soft-faced hammer (see illustration 7.2) or a wood block and conventional hammer to strike the component near the mating surface. Avoid hammering against cast extremities since they may break off. If this method fails, try using a wood wedge between the two components.

Caution: If the joint will not separate, double-check that you have removed all the fasteners.

7.1 If a pry point is provided, apply gently pressure with a flat-bladed screwdriver

7.2 Tap around the joint with a soft-faced mallet if necessary - don't strike cooling fins

Removal of old gasket and sealant

● Paper gaskets will most likely come away complete, leaving only a few traces stuck on

Most components have one or two hollow locating dowels between the two gasket faces. If a dowel cannot be removed, do not resort to gripping it with pliers - it will almost certainly be distorted. Install a close-fitting socket or Phillips screwdriver into the dowel and then grip the outer edge of the dowel to free it.

the sealing faces of the components. It is imperative that all traces are removed to ensure correct sealing of the new gasket.
● Very carefully scrape all traces of gasket away making sure that the sealing surfaces are not gouged or scored by the scraper (see illustrations 7.3, 7.4 and 7.5). Stubborn deposits can be removed by spraying with an aerosol gasket remover. Final preparation of

7.3 Paper gaskets can be scraped off with a gasket scraper tool . . .

7.4 . . . a knife blade . . .

7.5 . . . or a household scraper

7.6 Fine abrasive paper is wrapped around a flat file to clean up the gasket face

7.7 A kitchen scourer can be used on stubborn deposits

the gasket surface can be made with very fine abrasive paper or a plastic kitchen scourer **(see illustrations 7.6 and 7.7)**.

● Old sealant can be scraped or peeled off components, depending on the type originally used. Note that gasket removal compounds are available to avoid scraping the components clean; make sure the gasket remover suits the type of sealant used.

8 Chains

Breaking and joining final drive chains

● Drive chains for all but small bikes are continuous and do not have a clip-type connecting link. The chain must be broken using a chain breaker tool and the new chain securely riveted together using a new soft rivet-type link. Never use a clip-type connecting link instead of a rivet-type link, except in an emergency. Various chain breaking and riveting tools are available, either as separate tools or combined as illustrated in the accompanying photographs - read the instructions supplied with the tool carefully.

> ⚠ **Warning: The need to rivet the new link pins correctly cannot be overstressed - loss of control of the motorcycle is very likely to result if the chain breaks in use.**

● Rotate the chain and look for the soft link. The soft link pins look like they have been

8.1 Tighten the chain breaker to push the pin out of the link . . .

8.2 . . . withdraw the pin, remove the tool . . .

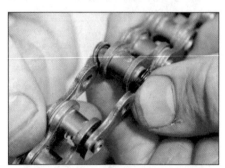

8.3 . . . and separate the chain link

deeply centre-punched instead of peened over like all the other pins **(see illustration 8.9)** and its sideplate may be a different colour. Position the soft link midway between the sprockets and assemble the chain breaker tool over one of the soft link pins **(see illustration 8.1)**. Operate the tool to push the pin out through the chain **(see illustration 8.2)**. On an O-ring chain, remove the O-rings **(see illustration 8.3)**. Carry out the same procedure on the other soft link pin.

> *Caution: Certain soft link pins (particularly on the larger chains) may require their ends to be filed or ground off before they can be pressed out using the tool.*

● Check that you have the correct size and strength (standard or heavy duty) new soft link - do not reuse the old link. Look for the size marking on the chain sideplates **(see illustration 8.10)**.

● Position the chain ends so that they are engaged over the rear sprocket. On an O-ring

8.4 Insert the new soft link, with O-rings, through the chain ends . . .

8.5 . . . install the O-rings over the pin ends . . .

8.6 . . . followed by the sideplate

chain, install a new O-ring over each pin of the link and insert the link through the two chain ends **(see illustration 8.4)**. Install a new O-ring over the end of each pin, followed by the sideplate (with the chain manufacturer's marking facing outwards) **(see illustrations 8.5 and 8.6)**. On an unsealed chain, insert the link through the two chain ends, then install the sideplate with the chain manufacturer's marking facing outwards.

● Note that it may not be possible to install the sideplate using finger pressure alone. If using a joining tool, assemble it so that the plates of the tool clamp the link and press the sideplate over the pins **(see illustration 8.7)**. Otherwise, use two small sockets placed over

8.7 Push the sideplate into position using a clamp

8.8 Assemble the chain riveting tool over one pin at a time and tighten it fully

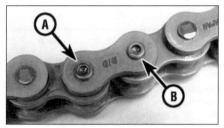

8.9 Pin end correctly riveted (A), pin end unriveted (B)

the rivet ends and two pieces of the wood between a G-clamp. Operate the clamp to press the sideplate over the pins.

● Assemble the joining tool over one pin (following the maker's instructions) and tighten the tool down to spread the pin end securely **(see illustrations 8.8 and 8.9)**. Do the same on the other pin.

 Warning: Check that the pin ends are secure and that there is no danger of the sideplate coming loose. If the pin ends are cracked the soft link must be renewed.

Final drive chain sizing

● Chains are sized using a three digit number, followed by a suffix to denote the chain type **(see illustration 8.10)**. Chain type is either standard or heavy duty (thicker sideplates), and also unsealed or O-ring/X-ring type.

● The first digit of the number relates to the pitch of the chain, ie the distance from the centre of one pin to the centre of the next pin **(see illustration 8.11)**. Pitch is expressed in eighths of an inch, as follows:

8.10 Typical chain size and type marking

8.11 Chain dimensions

| Sizes commencing with a 4 (eg 428) have a pitch of 1/2 inch (12.7 mm) |
| Sizes commencing with a 5 (eg 520) have a pitch of 5/8 inch (15.9 mm) |
| Sizes commencing with a 6 (eg 630) have a pitch of 3/4 inch (19.1 mm) |

● The second and third digits of the chain size relate to the width of the rollers, again in imperial units, eg the 525 shown has 5/16 inch (7.94 mm) rollers **(see illustration 8.11)**.

9 Hoses

Clamping to prevent flow

● Small-bore flexible hoses can be clamped to prevent fluid flow whilst a component is worked on. Whichever method is used, ensure that the hose material is not permanently distorted or damaged by the clamp.

a) A brake hose clamp available from auto accessory shops **(see illustration 9.1)**.
b) A wingnut type hose clamp **(see illustration 9.2)**.

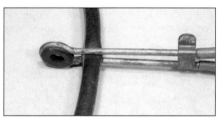

9.1 Hoses can be clamped with an automotive brake hose clamp . . .

9.2 . . . a wingnut type hose clamp . . .

c) Two sockets placed each side of the hose and held with straight-jawed self-locking grips **(see illustration 9.3)**.
d) Thick card each side of the hose held between straight-jawed self-locking grips **(see illustration 9.4)**.

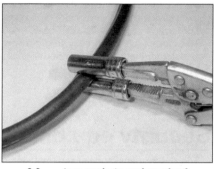

9.3 . . . two sockets and a pair of self-locking grips . . .

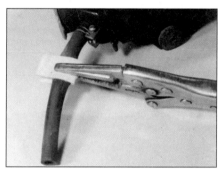

9.4 . . . or thick card and self-locking grips

Freeing and fitting hoses

● Always make sure the hose clamp is moved well clear of the hose end. Grip the hose with your hand and rotate it whilst pulling it off the union. If the hose has hardened due to age and will not move, slit it with a sharp knife and peel its ends off the union **(see illustration 9.5)**.

● Resist the temptation to use grease or soap on the unions to aid installation; although it helps the hose slip over the union it will equally aid the escape of fluid from the joint. It is preferable to soften the hose ends in hot water and wet the inside surface of the hose with water or a fluid which will evaporate.

9.5 Cutting a coolant hose free with a sharp knife

Introduction

In less time than it takes to read this introduction, a thief could steal your motorcycle. Returning only to find your bike has gone is one of the worst feelings in the world. Even if the motorcycle is insured against theft, once you've got over the initial shock, you will have the inconvenience of dealing with the police and your insurance company.

The motorcycle is an easy target for the professional thief and the joyrider alike and the official figures on motorcycle theft make for depressing reading; on average a motorcycle is stolen every 16 minutes in the UK!

Motorcycle thefts fall into two categories, those stolen 'to order' and those taken by opportunists. The thief stealing to order will be on the look out for a specific make and model and will go to extraordinary lengths to obtain that motorcycle. The opportunist thief on the other hand will look for easy targets which can be stolen with the minimum of effort and risk.

Whilst it is never going to be possible to make your machine 100% secure, it is estimated that around half of all stolen motorcycles are taken by opportunist thieves. Remember that the opportunist thief is always on the look out for the easy option: if there are two similar motorcycles parked side-by-side, they will target the one with the lowest level of security. By taking a few precautions, you can reduce the chances of your motorcycle being stolen.

Security equipment

There are many specialised motorcycle security devices available and the following text summarises their applications and their good and bad points.

Once you have decided on the type of security equipment which best suits your needs, we recommended that you read one of the many equipment tests regularly carried out by the motorcycle press. These tests compare the products from all the major manufacturers and give impartial ratings on their effectiveness, value-for-money and ease of use.

No one item of security equipment can provide complete protection. It is highly recommended that two or more of the items described below are combined to increase the security of your motorcycle (a lock and chain plus an alarm system is just about ideal). The more security measures fitted to the bike, the less likely it is to be stolen.

will be supplied with a carry bag which can be strapped to the pillion seat.

● Heavy-duty chains and locks are an excellent security measure (see illustration 1). Whenever the motorcycle is parked, use the lock and chain to secure the machine to a solid, immovable object such as a post or railings. This will prevent the machine from being ridden away or being lifted into the back of a van.

● When fitting the chain, always ensure the chain is routed around the motorcycle frame or swingarm (see illustrations 2 and 3). Never merely pass the chain around one of the wheel rims; a thief may unbolt the wheel and lift the rest of the machine into a van, leaving you with just the wheel! Try to avoid having excess chain free, thus making it difficult to use cutting tools, and keep the chain and lock off the ground to prevent thieves attacking it with a cold chisel. Position the lock so that its lock barrel is facing downwards; this will make it harder for the thief to attack the lock mechanism.

Ensure the lock and chain you buy is of good quality and long enough to shackle your bike to a solid object

Lock and chain

Pros: *Very flexible to use; can be used to secure the motorcycle to almost any immovable object. On some locks and chains, the lock can be used on its own as a disc lock (see below).*

Cons: *Can be very heavy and awkward to carry on the motorcycle, although some types*

Pass the chain through the bike's frame, rather than just through a wheel . . .

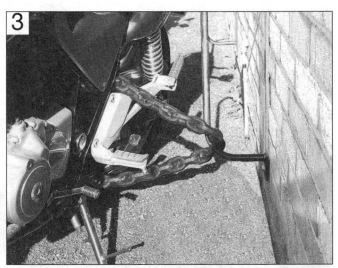

. . . and loop it around a solid object

U-locks

Pros: *Highly effective deterrent which can be used to secure the bike to a post or railings. Most U-locks come with a carrier which allows the lock to be easily carried on the bike.*

Cons: *Not as flexible to use as a lock and chain.*

● These are solid locks which are similar in use to a lock and chain. U-locks are lighter than a lock and chain but not so flexible to use. The length and shape of the lock shackle limit the objects to which the bike can be secured **(see illustration 4)**.

Disc locks

Pros: *Small, light and very easy to carry; most can be stored underneath the seat.*

Cons: *Does not prevent the motorcycle being lifted into a van. Can be very embarrassing if you*

U-locks can be used to secure the bike to a solid object – ensure you purchase one which is long enough

forget to remove the lock before attempting to ride off!

● Disc locks are designed to be attached to the front brake disc. The lock passes through one of the holes in the disc and prevents the wheel rotating by jamming against the fork/brake caliper **(see illustration 5)**. Some are equipped with an alarm siren which sounds if the disc lock is moved; this not only acts as a theft deterrent but also as a handy reminder if you try to move the bike with the lock still fitted.

● Combining the disc lock with a length of cable which can be looped around a post or railings provides an additional measure of security **(see illustration 6)**.

Alarms and immobilisers

Pros: *Once installed it is completely hassle-free to use. If the system is 'Thatcham' or 'Sold Secure-approved', insurance companies may give you a discount.*

Cons: *Can be expensive to buy and complex to install. No system will prevent the motorcycle from being lifted into a van and taken away.*

● Electronic alarms and immobilisers are available to suit a variety of budgets. There are three different types of system available: pure alarms, pure immobilisers, and the more expensive systems which are combined alarm/immobilisers **(see illustration 7)**.
● An alarm system is designed to emit an audible warning if the motorcycle is being tampered with.
● An immobiliser prevents the motorcycle being started and ridden away by disabling its electrical systems.
● When purchasing an alarm/immobiliser system, check the cost of installing the system unless you are able to do it yourself. If the motorcycle is not used regularly, another consideration is the current drain of the system. All alarm/immobiliser systems are powered by the motorcycle's battery; purchasing a system with a very low current drain could prevent the battery losing its charge whilst the motorcycle is not being used.

A typical disc lock attached through one of the holes in the disc

A disc lock combined with a security cable provides additional protection

A typical alarm/immobiliser system

Indelible markings can be applied to most areas of the bike – always apply the manufacturer's sticker to warn off thieves

Chemically-etched code numbers can be applied to main body panels . . .

. . . again, always ensure that the kit manufacturer's sticker is applied in a prominent position

Security marking kits

Pros: *Very cheap and effective deterrent. Many insurance companies will give you a discount on your insurance premium if a recognised security marking kit is used on your motorcycle.*

Cons: *Does not prevent the motorcycle being stolen by joyriders.*

● There are many different types of security marking kits available. The idea is to mark as many parts of the motorcycle as possible with a unique security number **(see illustrations 8, 9 and 10)**. A form will be included with the kit to register your personal details and those of the motorcycle with the kit manufacturer. This register is made available to the police to help them trace the rightful owner of any motorcycle or components which they recover should all other forms of identification have been removed. Always apply the warning stickers provided with the kit to deter thieves.

Ground anchors, wheel clamps and security posts

Pros: *An excellent form of security which will deter all but the most determined of thieves.*

Cons: *Awkward to install and can be expensive.*

● Whilst the motorcycle is at home, it is a good idea to attach it securely to the floor or a solid wall, even if it is kept in a securely locked garage. Various types of ground anchors, security posts and wheel clamps are available for this purpose **(see illustration 11)**. These security devices are either bolted to a solid concrete or brick structure or can be cemented into the ground.

Permanent ground anchors provide an excellent level of security when the bike is at home

Security at home

A high percentage of motorcycle thefts are from the owner's home. Here are some things to consider whenever your motorcycle is at home:

✔ Where possible, always keep the motorcycle in a securely locked garage. Never rely solely on the standard lock on the garage door, these are usual hopelessly inadequate. Fit an additional locking mechanism to the door and consider having the garage alarmed. A security light, activated by a movement sensor, is also a good investment.

✔ Always secure the motorcycle to the ground or a wall, even if it is inside a securely locked garage.

✔ Do not regularly leave the motorcycle outside your home, try to keep it out of sight wherever possible. If a garage is not available, fit a motorcycle cover over the bike to disguise its true identity.

✔ It is not uncommon for thieves to follow a motorcyclist home to find out where the bike is kept. They will then return at a later date. Be aware of this whenever you are returning

home on your motorcycle. If you suspect you are being followed, do not return home, instead ride to a garage or shop and stop as a precaution.

✔ When selling a motorcycle, do not provide your home address or the location where the bike is normally kept. Arrange to meet the buyer at a location away from your home. Thieves have been known to pose as potential buyers to find out where motorcycles are kept and then return later to steal them.

Security away from the home

As well as fitting security equipment to your motorcycle here are a few general rules to follow whenever you park your motorcycle.

✔ Park in a busy, public place.

✔ Use car parks which incorporate security features, such as CCTV.

✔ At night, park in a well-lit area, preferably directly underneath a street light.

✔ Engage the steering lock.

✔ Secure the motorcycle to a solid, immovable object such as a post or railings with an additional lock. If this is not possible,

secure the bike to a friend's motorcycle. Some public parking places provide security loops for motorcycles.

✔ Never leave your helmet or luggage attached to the motorcycle. Take them with you at all times.

Lubricants and fluids

A wide range of lubricants, fluids and cleaning agents is available for motor-cycles. This is a guide as to what is available, its applications and properties.

Four-stroke engine oil

● Engine oil is without doubt the most important component of any four-stroke engine. Modern motorcycle engines place a lot of demands on their oil and choosing the right type is essential. Using an unsuitable oil will lead to an increased rate of engine wear and could result in serious engine damage. Before purchasing oil, always check the recommended oil specification given by the manufacturer. The manufacturer will state a recommended 'type or classification' and also a specific 'viscosity' range for engine oil.

● The oil 'type or classification' is identified by its API (American Petroleum Institute) rating. The API rating will be in the form of two letters, e.g. SG. The S identifies the oil as being suitable for use in a petrol (gasoline) engine (S stands for spark ignition) and the second letter, ranging from A to J, identifies the oil's performance rating. The later this letter, the higher the specification of the oil; for example API SG oil exceeds the requirements of API SF oil. **Note:** *On some oils there may also be a second rating consisting of another two letters, the first letter being C, e.g. API SF/CD. This rating indicates the oil is also suitable for use in a diesel engines (the C stands for compression ignition) and is thus of no relevance for motorcycle use.*

● The 'viscosity' of the oil is identified by its SAE (Society of Automotive Engineers) rating. All modern engines require multigrade oils and the SAE rating will consist of two numbers, the first followed by a W, e.g. 10W/40. The first number indicates the viscosity rating of the oil at low temperatures (W stands for winter – tested at –20°C) and the second number represents the viscosity of the oil at high temperatures (tested at 100°C). The lower the number, the thinner the oil. For example an oil with an SAE 10W/40 rating will give better cold starting and running than an SAE 15W/40 oil.

● As well as ensuring the 'type' and 'viscosity' of the oil match the recommendations, another consideration to make when buying engine oil is whether to purchase a standard mineral-based oil, a semi-synthetic oil (also known as a synthetic blend or synthetic-based oil) or a fully-synthetic oil. Although all oils will have a similar rating and viscosity, their cost will vary considerably; mineral-based oils are the cheapest, the fully-synthetic oils the most expensive with the semi-synthetic oils falling somewhere in-between. This decision is very much up to the owner, but it should be noted that modern synthetic oils have far better lubricating and cleaning qualities than traditional mineral-based oils and tend to retain these properties for far longer. Bearing in mind the operating conditions inside a modern, high-revving motorcycle engine it is highly recommended that a fully synthetic oil is used. The extra expense at each service could save you money in the long term by preventing premature engine wear.

● As a final note always ensure that the oil is specifically designed for use in motorcycle engines. Engine oils designed primarily for use in car engines sometimes contain additives or friction modifiers which could cause clutch slip on a motorcycle fitted with a wet-clutch.

Two-stroke engine oil

● Modern two-stroke engines, with their high power outputs, place high demands on their oil. If engine seizure is to be avoided it is essential that a high-quality oil is used. Two-stroke oils differ hugely from four-stroke oils. The oil lubricates only the crankshaft and piston(s) (the transmission has its own lubricating oil) and is used on a total-loss basis where it is burnt completely during the combustion process.

● The Japanese have recently introduced a classification system for two-stroke oils, the JASO rating. This rating is in the form of two letters, either FA, FB or FC – FA is the lowest classification and FC the highest. Ensure the oil being used meets or exceeds the recommended rating specified by the manufacturer.

● As well as ensuring the oil rating matches the recommendation, another consideration to make when buying engine oil is whether to purchase a standard mineral-based oil, a semi-synthetic oil (also known as a synthetic blend or synthetic-based oil) or a fully-synthetic oil. The cost of each type of oil varies considerably; mineral-based oils are the cheapest, the fully-synthetic oils the most expensive with the semi-synthetic oils falling somewhere in-between. This decision is very much up to the owner, but it should be noted that modern synthetic oils have far better lubricating properties and burn cleaner than traditional mineral-based oils. It is therefore recommended that a fully synthetic oil is used. The extra expense could save you money in the long term by preventing premature engine wear, engine performance will be improved, carbon deposits and exhaust smoke will be reduced.

● Always ensure that the oil is specifically designed for use in an injector system. Many high quality two-stroke oils are designed for competition use and need to be pre-mixed with fuel. These oils are of a much higher viscosity and are not designed to flow through the injector pumps used on road-going two-stroke motorcycles.

Transmission (gear) oil

● On a two-stroke engine, the transmission and clutch are lubricated by their own separate oil bath which must be changed in accordance with the Maintenance Schedule.
● Although the engine and transmission units of most four-strokes use a common lubrication supply, there are some exceptions where the engine and gearbox have separate oil reservoirs and a dry clutch is used.
● Motorcycle manufacturers will either recommend a monograde transmission oil or a four-stroke multigrade engine oil to lubricate the transmission.
● Transmission oils, or gear oils as they are often called, are designed specifically for use in transmission systems. The viscosity of these oils is represented by an SAE number, but the scale of measurement applied is different to that used to grade engine oils. As a rough guide a SAE90 gear oil will be of the same viscosity as an SAE50 engine oil.

Shaft drive oil

● On models equipped with shaft final drive, the shaft drive gears are will have their own oil supply. The manufacturer will state a recommended 'type or classification' and also a specific 'viscosity' range in the same manner as for four-stroke engine oil.
● Gear oil classification is given by the number which follows the API GL (GL standing for gear lubricant) rating, the higher the number, the higher the specification of the oil, e.g. API GL5 oil is a higher specification than API GL4 oil. Ensure the oil meets or

exceeds the classification specified and is of the correct viscosity. The viscosity of gear oils is also represented by an SAE number but the scale of measurement used is different to that used to grade engine oils. As a rough guide an SAE90 gear oil will be of the same viscosity as an SAE50 engine oil.
● If the use of an EP (Extreme Pressure) gear oil is specified, ensure the oil purchased is suitable.

Fork oil and suspension fluid

● Conventional telescopic front forks are hydraulic and require fork oil to work. To ensure the forks function correctly, the fork oil must be changed in accordance with the Maintenance Schedule.
● Fork oil is available in a variety of viscosities, identified by their SAE rating; fork oil ratings vary from light (SAE 5) to heavy (SAE 30). When purchasing fork oil, ensure the viscosity rating matches that specified by the manufacturer.
● Some lubricant manufacturers also produce a range of high-quality suspension fluids which are very similar to fork oil but are designed mainly for competition use. These fluids may have a different viscosity rating system which is not to be confused with the SAE rating of normal fork oil. Refer to the manufacturer's instructions if in any doubt.

Brake and clutch fluid

● All disc brake systems and some clutch systems are hydraulically operated. To ensure correct operation, the hydraulic fluid must be changed in accordance with the Maintenance Schedule.
● Brake and clutch fluid is classified by its DOT rating with most motorcycle manufacturers specifying DOT 3 or 4 fluid. Both fluid types are glycol-based and can be mixed together without adverse effect; DOT 4 fluid exceeds the requirements of DOT 3

fluid. Although it is safe to use DOT 4 fluid in a system designed for use with DOT 3 fluid, never use DOT 3 fluid in a system which specifies the use of DOT 4 as this will adversely affect the system's performance. The type required for the system will be marked on the fluid reservoir cap.
● Some manufacturers also produce a DOT 5 hydraulic fluid. DOT 5 hydraulic fluid is silicone-based and is not compatible with the glycol-based DOT 3 and 4 fluids. Never mix DOT 5 fluid with DOT 3 or 4 fluid as this will seriously affect the performance of the hydraulic system.

Coolant/antifreeze

● When purchasing coolant/antifreeze, always ensure it is suitable for use in an aluminium engine and contains corrosion inhibitors to prevent possible blockages of the internal coolant passages of the system. As a general rule, most coolants are designed to be used neat and should not be diluted whereas antifreeze can be mixed with distilled water to provide a coolant solution of the required strength. Refer to the manufacturer's instructions on the bottle.
● Ensure the coolant is changed in accordance with the Maintenance Schedule.

Chain lube

● Chain lube is an aerosol-type spray lubricant specifically designed for use on motorcycle final drive chains. Chain lube has two functions, to minimise friction between the final drive chain and sprockets and to prevent corrosion of the chain. Regular use of a good-quality chain lube will extend the life of the drive chain and sprockets and thus maximise the power being transmitted from the transmission to the rear wheel.
● When using chain lube, always allow some time for the solvents in the lube to evaporate before riding the motorcycle. This will minimise the amount of lube which will

'fling' off from the chain when the motorcycle is used. If the motorcycle is equipped with an 'O-ring' chain, ensure the chain lube is labelled as being suitable for use on 'O-ring' chains.

Degreasers and solvents

● There are many different types of solvents and degreasers available to remove the grime and grease which accumulate around the motorcycle during normal use. Degreasers and solvents are usually available as an aerosol-type spray or as a liquid which you apply with a brush. Always closely follow the manufacturer's instructions and wear eye protection during use. Be aware that many solvents are flammable and may give off noxious fumes; take adequate precautions when using them (see Safety First!).

● For general cleaning, use one of the many solvents or degreasers available from most motorcycle accessory shops. These solvents are usually applied then left for a certain time before being washed off with water.

Brake cleaner is a solvent specifically designed to remove all traces of oil, grease and dust from braking system components. Brake cleaner is designed to evaporate quickly and leaves behind no residue.

Carburettor cleaner is an aerosol-type solvent specifically designed to clear carburettor blockages and break down the hard deposits and gum often found inside carburettors during overhaul.

Contact cleaner is an aerosol-type solvent designed for cleaning electrical components. The cleaner will remove all traces of oil and dirt from components such as switch contacts or fouled spark plugs and then dry, leaving behind no residue.

Gasket remover is an aerosol-type solvent designed for removing stubborn gaskets from engine components during overhaul. Gasket remover will minimise the amount of scraping required to remove the gasket and therefore reduce the risk of damage to the mating surface.

Spray lubricants

● Aerosol-based spray lubricants are widely available and are excellent for lubricating lever pivots and exposed cables and switches. Try to use a lubricant which is of the dry-film type as the fluid evaporates, leaving behind a dry-film of lubricant. Lubricants which leave behind an oily residue will attract dust and dirt which will increase the rate of wear of the cable/lever.

● Most lubricants also act as a moisture dispersant and a penetrating fluid. This means they can also be used to 'dry out' electrical components such as wiring connectors or switches as well as helping to free seized fasteners.

Greases

● Grease is used to lubricate many of the pivot-points. A good-quality multi-purpose grease is suitable for most applications but some manufacturers will specify the use of specialist greases for use on components such as swingarm and suspension linkage bushes. These specialist greases can be purchased from most motorcycle (or car) accessory shops; commonly specified types include molybdenum disulphide grease, lithium-based grease, graphite-based grease, silicone-based grease and high-temperature copper-based grease.

Gasket sealing compounds

● Gasket sealing compounds can be used in conjunction with gaskets, to improve their sealing capabilities, or on their own to seal metal-to-metal joints. Depending on their type, sealing compounds either set hard or stay relatively soft and pliable.

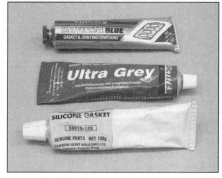

● When purchasing a gasket sealing compound, ensure that it is designed specifically for use on an internal combustion engine. General multi-purpose sealants available from DIY stores may appear visibly similar but they are not designed to withstand the extreme heat or contact with fuel and oil encountered when used on an engine (see 'Tools and Workshop Tips' for further information).

Thread locking compound

● Thread locking compounds are used to secure certain threaded fasteners in position to prevent them from loosening due to vibration. Thread locking compounds can be purchased from most motorcycle (and car) accessory shops. Ensure the threads of the both components are completely clean and dry before sparingly applying the locking compound (see 'Tools and Workshop Tips' for further information).

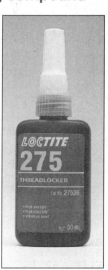

Fuel additives

● Fuel additives which protect and clean the fuel system components are widely available. These additives are designed to remove all traces of deposits that build up on the carburettors/injectors and prevent wear, helping the fuel system to operate more efficiently. If a fuel additive is being used, check that it is suitable for use with your motorcycle, especially if your motorcycle is equipped with a catalytic converter.

● Octane boosters are also available. These additives are designed to improve the performance of highly-tuned engines being run on normal pump-fuel and are of no real use on standard motorcycles.

Length (distance)

Inches (in)	x 25.4	= Millimetres (mm)	x 0.0394	= Inches (in)
Feet (ft)	x 0.305	= Metres (m)	x 3.281	= Feet (ft)
Miles	x 1.609	= Kilometres (km)	x 0.621	= Miles

Volume (capacity)

Cubic inches (cu in; in³)	x 16.387	= Cubic centimetres (cc; cm³)	x 0.061	= Cubic inches (cu in; in³)
Imperial pints (Imp pt)	x 0.568	= Litres (l)	x 1.76	= Imperial pints (Imp pt)
Imperial quarts (Imp qt)	x 1.137	= Litres (l)	x 0.88	= Imperial quarts (Imp qt)
Imperial quarts (Imp qt)	x 1.201	= US quarts (US qt)	x 0.833	= Imperial quarts (Imp qt)
US quarts (US qt)	x 0.946	= Litres (l)	x 1.057	= US quarts (US qt)
Imperial gallons (Imp gal)	x 4.546	= Litres (l)	x 0.22	= Imperial gallons (Imp gal)
Imperial gallons (Imp gal)	x 1.201	= US gallons (US gal)	x 0.833	= Imperial gallons (Imp gal)
US gallons (US gal)	x 3.785	= Litres (l)	x 0.264	= US gallons (US gal)

Mass (weight)

Ounces (oz)	x 28.35	= Grams (g)	x 0.035	= Ounces (oz)
Pounds (lb)	x 0.454	= Kilograms (kg)	x 2.205	= Pounds (lb)

Force

Ounces-force (ozf; oz)	x 0.278	= Newtons (N)	x 3.6	= Ounces-force (ozf; oz)
Pounds-force (lbf; lb)	x 4.448	= Newtons (N)	x 0.225	= Pounds-force (lbf; lb)
Newtons (N)	x 0.1	= Kilograms-force (kgf; kg)	x 9.81	= Newtons (N)

Pressure

Pounds-force per square inch (psi; lbf/in²; lb/in²)	x 0.070	= Kilograms-force per square centimetre (kgf/cm²; kg/cm²)	x 14.223	= Pounds-force per square inch (psi; lbf/in²; lb/in²)
Pounds-force per square inch (psi; lbf/in²; lb/in²)	x 0.068	= Atmospheres (atm)	x 14.696	= Pounds-force per square inch (psi; lbf/in²; lb/in²)
Pounds-force per square inch (psi; lbf/in²; lb/in²)	x 0.069	= Bars	x 14.5	= Pounds-force per square inch (psi; lbf/in²; lb/in²)
Pounds-force per square inch (psi; lbf/in²; lb/in²)	x 6.895	= Kilopascals (kPa)	x 0.145	= Pounds-force per square inch (psi; lbf/in²; lb/in²)
Kilopascals (kPa)	x 0.01	= Kilograms-force per square centimetre (kgf/cm²; kg/cm²)	x 98.1	= Kilopascals (kPa)
Millibar (mbar)	x 100	= Pascals (Pa)	x 0.01	= Millibar (mbar)
Millibar (mbar)	x 0.0145	= Pounds-force per square inch (psi; lbf/in²; lb/in²)	x 68.947	= Millibar (mbar)
Millibar (mbar)	x 0.75	= Millimetres of mercury (mmHg)	x 1.333	= Millibar (mbar)
Millibar (mbar)	x 0.401	= Inches of water (inH₂O)	x 2.491	= Millibar (mbar)
Millimetres of mercury (mmHg)	x 0.535	= Inches of water (inH₂O)	x 1.868	= Millimetres of mercury (mmHg)
Inches of water (inH₂O)	x 0.036	= Pounds-force per square inch (psi; lbf/in²; lb/in²)	x 27.68	= Inches of water (inH₂O)

Torque (moment of force)

Pounds-force inches (lbf in; lb in)	x 1.152	= Kilograms-force centimetre (kgf cm; kg cm)	x 0.868	= Pounds-force inches (lbf in; lb in)
Pounds-force inches (lbf in; lb in)	x 0.113	= Newton metres (Nm)	x 8.85	= Pounds-force inches (lbf in; lb in)
Pounds-force inches (lbf in; lb in)	x 0.083	= Pounds-force feet (lbf ft; lb ft)	x 12	= Pounds-force inches (lbf in; lb in)
Pounds-force feet (lbf ft; lb ft)	x 0.138	= Kilograms-force metres (kgf m; kg m)	x 7.233	= Pounds-force feet (lbf ft; lb ft)
Pounds-force feet (lbf ft; lb ft)	x 1.356	= Newton metres (Nm)	x 0.738	= Pounds-force feet (lbf ft; lb ft)
Newton metres (Nm)	x 0.102	= Kilograms-force metres (kgf m; kg m)	x 9.804	= Newton metres (Nm)

Power

Horsepower (hp)	x 745.7	= Watts (W)	x 0.0013	= Horsepower (hp)

Velocity (speed)

Miles per hour (miles/hr; mph)	x 1.609	= Kilometres per hour (km/hr; kph)	x 0.621	= Miles per hour (miles/hr; mph)

Fuel consumption*

Miles per gallon (mpg)	x 0.354	= Kilometres per litre (km/l)	x 2.825	= Miles per gallon (mpg)

Temperature

Degrees Fahrenheit = (°C x 1.8) + 32   Degrees Celsius (Degrees Centigrade; °C) = (°F - 32) x 0.56

* It is common practice to convert from miles per gallon (mpg) to litres/100 kilometres (l/100km), where mpg x l/100 km = 282

About the MOT Test

In the UK, all vehicles more than three years old are subject to an annual test to ensure that they meet minimum safety requirements. A current test certificate must be issued before a machine can be used on public roads, and is required before a road fund licence can be issued. Riding without a current test certificate will also invalidate your insurance.

For most owners, the MOT test is an annual cause for anxiety, and this is largely due to owners not being sure what needs to be checked prior to submitting the motorcycle for testing. The simple answer is that a fully roadworthy motorcycle will have no difficulty in passing the test.

This is a guide to getting your motorcycle through the MOT test. Obviously it will not be possible to examine the motorcycle to the same standard as the professional MOT tester, particularly in view of the equipment required for some of the checks. However, working through the following procedures will enable you to identify any problem areas before submitting the motorcycle for the test.

It has only been possible to summarise the test requirements here, based on the regulations in force at the time of printing. Test standards are becoming increasingly stringent, although there are some exemptions for older vehicles. More information about the MOT test can be obtained from the TSO publications, *How Safe is your Motorcycle* and *The MOT Inspection Manual for Motorcycle Testing*.

Many of the checks require that one of the wheels is raised off the ground. If the motorcycle doesn't have a centre stand, note that an auxiliary stand will be required. Additionally, the help of an assistant may prove useful.

Certain exceptions apply to machines under 50 cc, machines without a lighting system, and Classic bikes - if in doubt about any of the requirements listed below seek confirmation from an MOT tester prior to submitting the motorcycle for the test.

Check that the frame number is clearly visible.

Electrical System

Lights, turn signals, horn and reflector

✔ With the ignition on, check the operation of the following electrical components. **Note:** *The electrical components on certain small-capacity machines are powered by the generator, requiring that the engine is run for this check.*

a) *Headlight and tail light. Check that both illuminate in the low and high beam switch positions.*

b) *Position lights. Check that the front position (or sidelight) and tail light illuminate in this switch position.*

c) *Turn signals. Check that all flash at the correct rate, and that the warning light(s) function correctly. Check that the turn signal switch works correctly.*

d) *Hazard warning system (where fitted). Check that all four turn signals flash in this switch position.*

e) *Brake stop light. Check that the light comes on when the front and rear brakes are independently applied. Models first used on or after 1st April 1986 must have a brake light switch on each brake.*

f) *Horn. Check that the sound is continuous and of reasonable volume.*

✔ Check that there is a red reflector on the rear of the machine, either mounted separately or as part of the tail light lens.

✔ Check the condition of the headlight, tail light and turn signal lenses.

Headlight beam height

✔ The MOT tester will perform a headlight beam height check using specialised beam setting equipment **(see illustration 1)**. This equipment will not be available to the home mechanic, but if you suspect that the headlight is incorrectly set or may have been maladjusted in the past, you can perform a rough test as follows.

✔ Position the bike in a straight line facing a brick wall. The bike must be off its stand, upright and with a rider seated. Measure the height from the ground to the centre of the headlight and mark a horizontal line on the wall at this height. Position the motorcycle 3.8 metres from the wall and draw a vertical

Headlight beam height checking equipment

line up the wall central to the centreline of the motorcycle. Switch to dipped beam and check that the beam pattern falls slightly lower than the horizontal line and to the left of the vertical line **(see illustration 2)**.

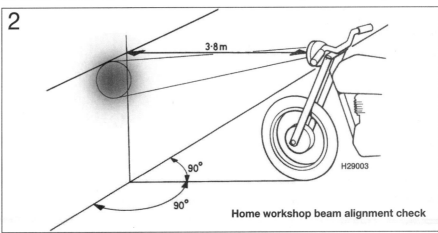

Home workshop beam alignment check

Exhaust System and Final Drive

Exhaust

✔ Check that the exhaust mountings are secure and that the system does not foul any of the rear suspension components.
✔ Start the motorcycle. When the revs are increased, check that the exhaust is neither holed nor leaking from any of its joints. On a linked system, check that the collector box is not leaking due to corrosion.

✔ Note that the exhaust decibel level ("loudness" of the exhaust) is assessed at the discretion of the tester. If the motorcycle was first used on or after 1st January 1985 the silencer must carry the BSAU 193 stamp, or a marking relating to its make and model, or be of OE (original equipment) manufacture. If the silencer is marked NOT FOR ROAD USE, RACING USE ONLY or similar, it will fail the MOT.

Final drive

✔ On chain or belt drive machines, check that the chain/belt is in good condition and does not have excessive slack. Also check that the sprocket is securely mounted on the rear wheel hub. Check that the chain/belt guard is in place.
✔ On shaft drive bikes, check for oil leaking from the drive unit and fouling the rear tyre.

Steering and Suspension

Steering

✔ With the front wheel raised off the ground, rotate the steering from lock to lock. The handlebar or switches must not contact the fuel tank or be close enough to trap the rider's hand. Problems can be caused by damaged lock stops on the lower yoke and frame, or by the fitting of non-standard handlebars.
✔ When performing the lock to lock check, also ensure that the steering moves freely without drag or notchiness. Steering movement can be impaired by poorly routed cables, or by overtight head bearings or worn bearings. The tester will perform a check of the steering head bearing lower race by mounting the front wheel on a surface plate, then performing a lock to lock check with the weight of the machine on the lower bearing **(see illustration 3)**.
✔ Grasp the fork sliders (lower legs) and attempt to push and pull on the forks **(see**

Front wheel mounted on a surface plate for steering head bearing lower race check

illustration 4). Any play in the steering head bearings will be felt. Note that in extreme cases, wear of the front fork bushes can be misinterpreted for head bearing play.
✔ Check that the handlebars are securely mounted.
✔ Check that the handlebar grip rubbers are secure. They should by bonded to the bar left end and to the throttle cable pulley on the right end.

Front suspension

✔ With the motorcycle off the stand, hold the front brake on and pump the front forks up and down **(see illustration 5)**. Check that they are adequately damped.

Checking the steering head bearings for freeplay

Hold the front brake on and pump the front forks up and down to check operation

Inspect the area around the fork dust seal for oil leakage (arrow)

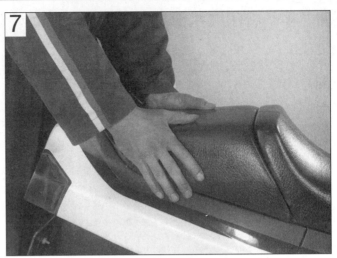

Bounce the rear of the motorcycle to check rear suspension operation

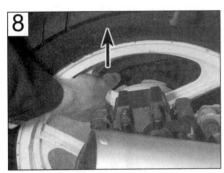

Checking for rear suspension linkage play

✔ Inspect the area above and around the front fork oil seals **(see illustration 6)**. There should be no sign of oil on the fork tube (stanchion) nor leaking down the slider (lower leg). On models so equipped, check that there is no oil leaking from the anti-dive units.

✔ On models with swingarm front suspension, check that there is no freeplay in the linkage when moved from side to side.

Rear suspension

✔ With the motorcycle off the stand and an assistant supporting the motorcycle by its handlebars, bounce the rear suspension **(see illustration 7)**. Check that the suspension components do not foul on any of the cycle parts and check that the shock absorber(s) provide adequate damping.

✔ Visually inspect the shock absorber(s) and check that there is no sign of oil leakage from its damper. This is somewhat restricted on certain single shock models due to the location of the shock absorber.

✔ With the rear wheel raised off the ground, grasp the wheel at the highest point and attempt to pull it up **(see illustration 8)**. Any play in the swingarm pivot or suspension linkage bearings will be felt as movement. **Note:** *Do not confuse play with actual suspension movement.* Failure to lubricate suspension linkage bearings can lead to bearing failure **(see illustration 9)**.

✔ With the rear wheel raised off the ground, grasp the swingarm ends and attempt to move the swingarm from side to side and forwards and backwards - any play indicates wear of the swingarm pivot bearings **(see illustration 10)**.

Worn suspension linkage pivots (arrows) are usually the cause of play in the rear suspension

Grasp the swingarm at the ends to check for play in its pivot bearings

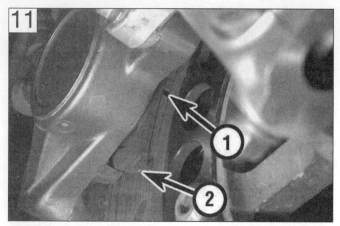

Brake pad wear can usually be viewed without removing the caliper. Most pads have wear indicator grooves (1) and some also have indicator tangs (2)

On drum brakes, check the angle of the operating lever with the brake fully applied. Most drum brakes have a wear indicator pointer and scale.

Brakes, Wheels and Tyres

Brakes

✔ With the wheel raised off the ground, apply the brake then free it off, and check that the wheel is about to revolve freely without brake drag.

✔ On disc brakes, examine the disc itself. Check that it is securely mounted and not cracked.

✔ On disc brakes, view the pad material through the caliper mouth and check that the pads are not worn down beyond the limit **(see illustration 11)**.

✔ On drum brakes, check that when the brake is applied the angle between the operating lever and cable or rod is not too great **(see illustration 12)**. Check also that the operating lever doesn't foul any other components.

✔ On disc brakes, examine the flexible hoses from top to bottom. Have an assistant hold the brake on so that the fluid in the hose is under pressure, and check that there is no sign of fluid leakage, bulges or cracking. If there are any metal brake pipes or unions, check that these are free from corrosion and damage. Where a brake-linked anti-dive system is fitted, check the hoses to the anti-dive in a similar manner.

✔ Check that the rear brake torque arm is secure and that its fasteners are secured by self-locking nuts or castellated nuts with split-pins or R-pins **(see illustration 13)**.

✔ On models with ABS, check that the self-check warning light in the instrument panel works.

✔ The MOT tester will perform a test of the motorcycle's braking efficiency based on a calculation of rider and motorcycle weight. Although this cannot be carried out at home, you can at least ensure that the braking systems are properly maintained. For hydraulic disc brakes, check the fluid level, lever/pedal feel (bleed of air if its spongy) and pad material. For drum brakes, check adjustment, cable or rod operation and shoe lining thickness.

Wheels and tyres

✔ Check the wheel condition. Cast wheels should be free from cracks and if of the built-up design, all fasteners should be secure. Spoked wheels should be checked for broken, corroded, loose or bent spokes.

✔ With the wheel raised off the ground, spin the wheel and visually check that the tyre and wheel run true. Check that the tyre does not foul the suspension or mudguards.

✔ With the wheel raised off the ground, grasp the wheel and attempt to move it about the axle (spindle) **(see illustration 14)**. Any play felt here indicates wheel bearing failure.

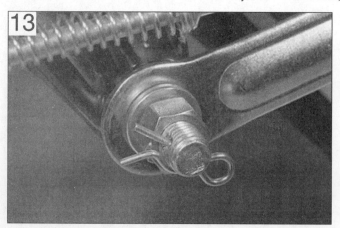

Brake torque arm must be properly secured at both ends

Check for wheel bearing play by trying to move the wheel about the axle (spindle)

Checking the tyre tread depth

Tyre direction of rotation arrow can be found on tyre sidewall

Castellated type wheel axle (spindle) nut must be secured by a split pin or R-pin

Two straightedges are used to check wheel alignment

✔ Check the tyre tread depth, tread condition and sidewall condition **(see illustration 15)**.

✔ Check the tyre type. Front and rear tyre types must be compatible and be suitable for road use. Tyres marked NOT FOR ROAD USE, COMPETITION USE ONLY or similar, will fail the MOT.

✔ If the tyre sidewall carries a direction of rotation arrow, this must be pointing in the direction of normal wheel rotation **(see illustration 16)**.

✔ Check that the wheel axle (spindle) nuts (where applicable) are properly secured. A self-locking nut or castellated nut with a split-pin or R-pin can be used **(see illustration 17)**.

✔ Wheel alignment is checked with the motorcycle off the stand and a rider seated. With the front wheel pointing straight ahead, two perfectly straight lengths of metal or wood and placed against the sidewalls of both tyres **(see illustration 18)**. The gap each side of the front tyre must be equidistant on both sides. Incorrect wheel alignment may be due to a cocked rear wheel (often as the result of poor chain adjustment) or in extreme cases, a bent frame.

General checks and condition

✔ Check the security of all major fasteners, bodypanels, seat, fairings (where fitted) and mudguards.

✔ Check that the rider and pillion footrests, handlebar levers and brake pedal are securely mounted.

✔ Check for corrosion on the frame or any load-bearing components. If severe, this may affect the structure, particularly under stress.

Sidecars

A motorcycle fitted with a sidecar requires additional checks relating to the stability of the machine and security of attachment and swivel joints, plus specific wheel alignment (toe-in) requirements. Additionally, tyre and lighting requirements differ from conventional motorcycle use. Owners are advised to check MOT test requirements with an official test centre.

Preparing for storage

Before you start

If repairs or an overhaul is needed, see that this is carried out now rather than left until you want to ride the bike again.

Give the bike a good wash and scrub all dirt from its underside. Make sure the bike dries completely before preparing for storage.

Engine

● Remove the spark plug(s) and lubricate the cylinder bores with approximately a teaspoon of motor oil using a spout-type oil can **(see illustration 1)**. Reinstall the spark plug(s). Crank the engine over a couple of times to coat the piston rings and bores with oil. If the bike has a kickstart, use this to turn the engine over. If not, flick the kill switch to the OFF position and crank the engine over on the starter **(see illustration 2)**. If the nature on the ignition system prevents the starter operating with the kill switch in the OFF position,

remove the spark plugs and fit them back in their caps; ensure that the plugs are earthed (grounded) against the cylinder head when the starter is operated **(see illustration 3)**.

⚠ **Warning: It is important that the plugs are earthed (grounded) away from the spark plug holes otherwise there is a risk of atomised fuel from the cylinders igniting.**

HAYNES HiNT *On a single cylinder four-stroke engine, you can seal the combustion chamber completely by positioning the piston at TDC on the compression stroke.*

● Drain the carburettor(s) otherwise there is a risk of jets becoming blocked by gum deposits from the fuel **(see illustration 4)**.

● If the bike is going into long-term storage, consider adding a fuel stabiliser to the fuel in the tank. If the tank is drained completely, corrosion of its internal surfaces may occur if left unprotected for a long period. The tank can be treated with a rust preventative especially for this purpose. Alternatively, remove the tank and pour half a litre of motor oil into it, install the filler cap and shake the tank to coat its internals with oil before draining off the excess. The same effect can also be achieved by spraying WD40 or a similar water-dispersant around the inside of the tank via its flexible nozzle.

● Make sure the cooling system contains the correct mix of antifreeze. Antifreeze also contains important corrosion inhibitors.

● The air intakes and exhaust can be sealed off by covering or plugging the openings. Ensure that you do not seal in any condensation; run the engine until it is hot,

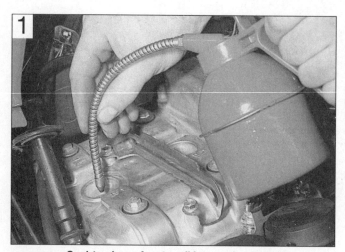

Squirt a drop of motor oil into each cylinder

Flick the kill switch to OFF . . .

. . . and ensure that the metal bodies of the plugs (arrows) are earthed against the cylinder head

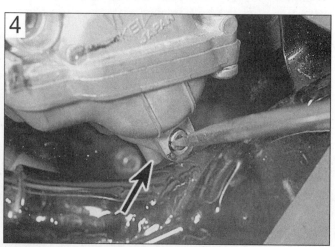

Connect a hose to the carburettor float chamber drain stub (arrow) and unscrew the drain screw

Exhausts can be sealed off with a plastic bag

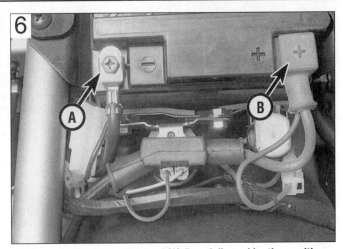

Disconnect the negative lead (A) first, followed by the positive lead (B)

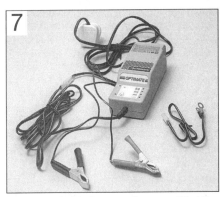

Use a suitable battery charger - this kit also assess battery condition

● Check the electrolyte level and top up if necessary (conventional refillable batteries). Clean the terminals.
● Store the battery off the motorcycle and away from any sources of fire. Position a wooden block under the battery if it is to sit on the ground.
● Give the battery a trickle charge for a few hours every month **(see illustration 7)**.

Tyres

● Place the bike on its centrestand or an auxiliary stand which will support the motorcycle in an upright position. Position wood blocks under the tyres to keep them off the ground and to provide insulation from damp. If the bike is being put into long-term storage, ideally both tyres should be off the ground; not only will this protect the tyres, but will also ensure that no load is placed on the steering head or wheel bearings.
● Deflate each tyre by 5 to 10 psi, no more or the beads may unseat from the rim, making subsequent inflation difficult on tubeless tyres.

Pivots and controls

● Lubricate all lever, pedal, stand and

footrest pivot points. If grease nipples are fitted to the rear suspension components, apply lubricant to the pivots.
● Lubricate all control cables.

Cycle components

● Apply a wax protectant to all painted and plastic components. Wipe off any excess, but don't polish to a shine. Where fitted, clean the screen with soap and water.
● Coat metal parts with Vaseline (petroleum jelly). When applying this to the fork tubes, do not compress the forks otherwise the seals will rot from contact with the Vaseline.
● Apply a vinyl cleaner to the seat.

Storage conditions

● Aim to store the bike in a shed or garage which does not leak and is free from damp.
● Drape an old blanket or bedspread over the bike to protect it from dust and direct contact with sunlight (which will fade paint). This also hides the bike from prying eyes. Beware of tight-fitting plastic covers which may allow condensation to form and settle on the bike.

then switch off and allow to cool. Tape a piece of thick plastic over the silencer end(s) **(see illustration 5)**. Note that some advocate pouring a tablespoon of motor oil into the silencer(s) before sealing them off.

Battery

● Remove it from the bike - in extreme cases of cold the battery may freeze and crack its case **(see illustration 6)**.

Getting back on the road

Engine and transmission

● Change the oil and replace the oil filter. If this was done prior to storage, check that the oil hasn't emulsified - a thick whitish substance which occurs through condensation.
● Remove the spark plugs. Using a spout-type oil can, squirt a few drops of oil into the cylinder(s). This will provide initial lubrication as the piston rings and bores comes back into contact. Service the spark plugs, or fit new ones, and install them in the engine.

● Check that the clutch isn't stuck on. The plates can stick together if left standing for some time, preventing clutch operation. Engage a gear and try rocking the bike back and forth with the clutch lever held against the handlebar. If this doesn't work on cable-operated clutches, hold the clutch lever back against the handlebar with a strong elastic band or cable tie for a couple of hours **(see illustration 8)**.
● If the air intakes or silencer end(s) were blocked off, remove the bung or cover used.
● If the fuel tank was coated with a rust

Hold clutch lever back against the handlebar with elastic bands or a cable tie

preventative, oil or a stabiliser added to the fuel, drain and flush the tank and dispose of the fuel sensibly. If no action was taken with the fuel tank prior to storage, it is advised that the old fuel is disposed of since it will go off over a period of time. Refill the fuel tank with fresh fuel.

Frame and running gear

● Oil all pivot points and cables.
● Check the tyre pressures. They will definitely need inflating if pressures were reduced for storage.
● Lubricate the final drive chain (where applicable).
● Remove any protective coating applied to the fork tubes (stanchions) since this may well destroy the fork seals. If the fork tubes weren't protected and have picked up rust spots, remove them with very fine abrasive paper and refinish with metal polish.
● Check that both brakes operate correctly. Apply each brake hard and check that it's not possible to move the motorcycle forwards, then check that the brake frees off again once released. Brake caliper pistons can stick due to corrosion around the piston head, or on the sliding caliper types, due to corrosion of the slider pins. If the brake doesn't free after repeated operation, take the caliper off for examination. Similarly drum brakes can stick due to a seized operating cam, cable or rod linkage.
● If the motorcycle has been in long-term storage, renew the brake fluid and clutch fluid (where applicable).
● Depending on where the bike has been stored, the wiring, cables and hoses may have been nibbled by rodents. Make a visual check and investigate disturbed wiring loom tape.

Battery

● If the battery has been previously removal and given top up charges it can simply be reconnected. Remember to connect the positive cable first and the negative cable last.
● On conventional refillable batteries, if the battery has not received any attention, remove it from the motorcycle and check its electrolyte level. Top up if necessary then charge the battery. If the battery fails to hold a charge and a visual checks show heavy white sulphation of the plates, the battery is probably defective and must be renewed. This is particularly likely if the battery is old. Confirm battery condition with a specific gravity check.
● On sealed (MF) batteries, if the battery has not received any attention, remove it from the motorcycle and charge it according to the information on the battery case - if the battery fails to hold a charge it must be renewed.

Starting procedure

● If a kickstart is fitted, turn the engine over a couple of times with the ignition OFF to distribute oil around the engine. If no kickstart is fitted, flick the engine kill switch OFF and the ignition ON and crank the engine over a couple of times to work oil around the upper cylinder components. If the nature of the ignition system is such that the starter won't work with the kill switch OFF, remove the spark plugs, fit them back into their caps and earth (ground) their bodies on the cylinder head. Reinstall the spark plugs afterwards.
● Switch the kill switch to RUN, operate the choke and start the engine. If the engine won't start don't continue cranking the engine - not only will this flatten the battery, but the starter motor will overheat. Switch the ignition off and try again later. If the engine refuses to start, go through the fault finding procedures in this manual. **Note:** *If the bike has been in storage for a long time, old fuel or a carburettor blockage may be the problem. Gum deposits in carburettors can block jets - if a carburettor cleaner doesn't prove successful the carburettors must be dismantled for cleaning.*

● Once the engine has started, check that the lights, turn signals and horn work properly.

● Treat the bike gently for the first ride and check all fluid levels on completion. Settle the bike back into the maintenance schedule.

This Section provides an easy reference-guide to the more common faults that are likely to afflict your machine. Obviously, the opportunities are almost limitless for faults to occur as a result of obscure failures, and to try and cover all eventualities would require a book. Indeed, a number have been written on the subject.

Successful troubleshooting is not a mysterious 'black art' but the application of a bit of knowledge combined with a systematic and logical approach to the problem. Approach any troubleshooting by first accurately identifying the symptom and then checking through the list of possible causes, starting with the simplest or most obvious and progressing in stages to the most complex.

Take nothing for granted, but above all apply liberal quantities of common sense.

The main symptom of a fault is given in the text as a major heading below which are listed the various systems or areas which may contain the fault. Details of each possible cause for a fault and the remedial action to be taken are given, in brief, in the paragraphs below each heading. Further information should be sought in the relevant Chapter.

1 Engine doesn't start or is difficult to start
- [ ] Starter motor doesn't rotate
- [ ] Starter motor rotates but engine does not turn over
- [ ] Starter works but engine won't turn over (seized)
- [ ] No fuel flow
- [ ] Engine flooded
- [ ] No spark or weak spark
- [ ] Compression low
- [ ] Stalls after starting
- [ ] Rough idle

2 Poor running at low speed
- [ ] Spark weak
- [ ] Fuel/air mixture incorrect
- [ ] Compression low
- [ ] Poor acceleration

3 Poor running or no power at high speed
- [ ] Firing incorrect
- [ ] Fuel/air mixture incorrect
- [ ] Compression low
- [ ] Knocking or pinking
- [ ] Miscellaneous causes

4 Overheating
- [ ] Engine overheats
- [ ] Firing incorrect
- [ ] Fuel/air mixture incorrect
- [ ] Compression too high
- [ ] Engine load excessive
- [ ] Lubrication inadequate
- [ ] Miscellaneous causes

5 Clutch problems
- [ ] Clutch slipping
- [ ] Clutch not disengaging completely

6 Gearchanging problems
- [ ] Doesn't go into gear, or lever doesn't return
- [ ] Jumps out of gear
- [ ] Overselects

7 Abnormal engine noise
- [ ] Knocking or pinking
- [ ] Piston slap or rattling
- [ ] Valve noise
- [ ] Other noise

8 Abnormal driveline noise
- [ ] Clutch noise
- [ ] Transmission noise
- [ ] Final drive noise

9 Abnormal frame and suspension noise
- [ ] Front end noise
- [ ] Shock absorber noise
- [ ] Brake noise

10 Excessive exhaust smoke
- [ ] White smoke
- [ ] Black smoke
- [ ] Brown smoke

11 Poor handling or stability
- [ ] Handlebar hard to turn
- [ ] Handlebar shakes or vibrates excessively
- [ ] Handlebar pulls to one side
- [ ] Poor shock absorbing qualities

12 Braking problems
- [ ] Brakes are spongy, don't hold
- [ ] Brake lever or pedal pulsates
- [ ] Brakes drag

13 Electrical problems
- [ ] Battery dead or weak
- [ ] Battery overcharged

1 Engine doesn't start or is difficult to start

Starter motor doesn't rotate

- ☐ Engine kill switch OFF.
- ☐ Main fuse blown (Chapter 8).
- ☐ Battery voltage low. Check and recharge battery (Chapter 8).
- ☐ Starter motor defective. Make sure the wiring to the starter is secure. Make sure the starter relay clicks when the start button is pushed. If the relay clicks, then the fault is in the wiring or motor (see Chapter 8).
- ☐ Starter switch not contacting. The contacts could be wet, corroded or dirty. Disassemble and clean the switch (Chapter 8).
- ☐ Wiring open or shorted. Check all wiring connections and harnesses to make sure that they are dry, tight and not corroded. Also check for broken or frayed wires that can cause a short to ground (earth) (see Wiring diagrams, Chapter 8).
- ☐ Ignition switch defective. Check the switch and replace with a new one if it is defective (see Chapter 8).
- ☐ Engine kill switch defective. Check for wet, dirty or corroded contacts. Clean or replace the switch with a new one as necessary (see Chapter 8).
- ☐ Faulty neutral switch, sidestand switch or clutch switch. Check the wiring to each switch and the switch itself (see Chapter 8).
- ☐ Faulty starter circuit cut-off relay or diodes (Chapter 8).
- ☐ Fuel injection system shutdown due to system fault (Chapter 4).

Starter motor rotates but engine does not turn over

- ☐ Starter clutch defective. Inspect and repair or replace with a new one (see Chapter 2).
- ☐ Damaged idler or starter gears. Inspect and replace the damaged parts (see Chapter 2).

Starter works but engine won't turn over (seized)

- ☐ Seized engine caused by one or more internally damaged components. Failure due to wear, abuse or lack of lubrication. Damage can include seized valves, rockers, camshaft, piston, crankshaft, connecting rod bearings, or transmission gears or bearings. Refer to Chapter 2 for engine disassembly.

No fuel flow

- ☐ No fuel in tank.
- ☐ Fuel tank breather hose obstructed.
- ☐ Faulty fuel pump relay. Check the relay (see Chapter 4).
- ☐ Fuel pump faulty, or the fuel filter is blocked (see Chapter 4).
- ☐ Fuel hose clogged. Remove the fuel hose and carefully blow through it. Check the fuel filter for damage.
- ☐ Fuel rail or injector clogged. For all of the injectors to be clogged, either a very bad batch of fuel with an unusual additive has been used, or some other foreign material has entered the tank. In some cases, if a machine has been unused for several months, the fuel turns to a varnish-like liquid which can cause an injector needle to stick to its seat. Drain the tank and clean the fuel system (Chapter 4).

Engine flooded

- ☐ Injector needle valve worn or stuck open. A piece of dirt, rust or other debris can cause the needle to seat improperly, causing excess fuel to be admitted to the throttle body. In this case, the injector should be cleaned and the needle and seat inspected (see Chapter 4). If the needle and seat are worn, then the leaking will persist and the parts should be replaced with new ones.
- ☐ Starting technique incorrect. Under normal circumstances (i.e. if all the components of the fuel injection system are good) the machine should start with the throttle closed.

No spark or weak spark

- ☐ Ignition switch OFF.
- ☐ Engine kill switch turned to the OFF position.
- ☐ Ignition or kill switch shorted. This is usually caused by water, corrosion, damage or excessive wear. The switches can be disassembled and cleaned with electrical contact cleaner. If cleaning does not help, replace the switches (see Chapter 8).
- ☐ Battery voltage low. Check and recharge the battery as necessary (Chapter 8).
- ☐ Spark plug cap not making good contact. Make sure that the cap fits snugly over the plug.
- ☐ Spark plug dirty, defective or worn out. Identify reason for fouled plug using spark plug condition chart on the inside back cover and follow the plug maintenance procedures (see Chapter 1).
- ☐ Incorrect spark plug. Wrong type or heat range. Check and install correct plug (see Chapter 1).
- ☐ Ignition coil defective. Test and replace with new one if necessary (Chapter 4).
- ☐ Fuel injection system shutdown due to system fault (Chapter 4).
- ☐ Crankshaft position (CKP) sensor defective (see Chapter 4).
- ☐ Engine control unit (ECU) defective (see Chapter 4).
- ☐ Wiring shorted or broken between:
    - a) Ignition switch and engine kill switch (or blown fuse)
    - b) ECU and engine kill switch
    - c) ECU and ignition coil
    - d) ECU and CKP sensor
- ☐ Make sure that all wiring connections are clean, dry and tight. Look for chafed and broken wires (see Chapters 4 and 8).

Compression low

- ☐ Spark plug loose. Remove the plug and inspect the threads. Reinstall and tighten securely (see Chapter 1).
- ☐ Cylinder head not sufficiently tightened down. If the cylinder head is suspected of being loose, then there's a chance that the gasket or head is damaged if the problem has persisted for any length of time. The head bolts should be tightened to the proper torque and in the correct sequence (Chapter 2).
- ☐ Improper valve clearance. This means that the valve is not closing completely and compression pressure is leaking past the valve. Check and adjust the valve clearances (Chapter 1).
- ☐ Cylinder and/or piston worn. Excessive wear will cause compression pressure to leak past the rings. This is usually accompanied by worn rings as well. A top-end overhaul is necessary (Chapter 2).
- ☐ Piston rings worn, weak, broken, or sticking. Broken or sticking piston rings usually indicate a lubrication or fuelling problem that causes excess carbon deposits to form on the pistons and rings. Top-end overhaul is necessary (Chapter 2).
- ☐ Piston ring-to-groove clearance excessive. This is caused by excessive wear of the piston ring lands. Piston renewal is necessary (Chapter 2).
- ☐ Cylinder head gasket damaged. If the head is allowed to become loose, or if excessive carbon build-up on the piston crown and combustion chamber causes extremely high compression, the head gasket may leak. Retorquing the head is not always sufficient to restore the seal, so a new gasket is necessary (Chapter 2).
- ☐ Cylinder head warped. This is caused by overheating or improperly tightened head bolts. Machine shop resurfacing or head renewal is necessary (Chapter 2).
- ☐ Valve spring broken or weak. Caused by component failure or wear; the springs must be renewed (Chapter 2).
- ☐ Valve not seating properly. This is caused by a bent valve (from over-revving or improper valve adjustment), burned valve or seat (incorrect air/fuel mixture) or an accumulation of carbon deposits on the seat. The valves must be cleaned and/or renewed and the seats serviced (Chapter 2).

1 Engine doesn't start or is difficult to start (continued)

Stalls after starting

- [ ] Faulty fast idle system. Check the operation of the fast idle unit (see Chapter 4).
- [ ] Engine idle speed incorrect. Turn idle adjusting screw until the engine idles at the specified rpm (Chapter 1).
- [ ] Ignition malfunction (see Chapter 4).
- [ ] Fuel injection system malfunction (see Chapter 4).
- [ ] Fuel contaminated. The fuel can be contaminated with either dirt or water, or can change chemically if the machine has been unused for several months. Drain the tank and fuel system (Chapter 4).
- [ ] Intake air leak. Check for loose throttle body-to-intake manifold connections, loose or damaged AIS vacuum hose or throttle body vacuum hoses (Chapter 4).

Rough idle

- [ ] Idle speed incorrect (see Chapter 1).
- [ ] Ignition fault (see Chapter 4).
- [ ] Fuel injection system malfunction (see Chapter 4).
- [ ] Fuel contaminated. The fuel can be contaminated with either dirt or water, or can change chemically if the machine has been unused for several months. Drain the tank and the fuel system (Chapter 4).
- [ ] Intake air leak. Check for loose throttle body-to-intake manifold connections, loose or damaged AIS vacuum hose or throttle body vacuum hoses (Chapter 4).
- [ ] Air filter clogged. Clean the air filter element or replace it with a new one (Chapter 1).

2 Poor running at low speeds

Spark weak

- [ ] Battery voltage low. Check and recharge battery (see Chapter 8).
- [ ] Spark plug cap not making good contact. Make sure that the cap fits snugly over the plug.
- [ ] Spark plug dirty, defective or worn out. Locate reason for fouled plug using spark plug condition chart on the inside back cover and follow the plug maintenance procedures (see Chapter 1).
- [ ] Incorrect spark plug. Wrong type or heat range. Check and install correct plug (see Chapter 1).
- [ ] Ignition coil defective. Test and replace with new one if necessary (see Chapter 4).

Fuel/air mixture incorrect

- [ ] Fuel tank breather hose obstructed.
- [ ] Fuel pump faulty, or the fuel filter is blocked (see Chapter 4).
- [ ] Fuel hose clogged. Remove the fuel hose and carefully blow through it. Check the fuel filter for damage.
- [ ] Fuel rail or injector clogged. Check the fuel filter. In some cases, if a machine has been unused for several months, the fuel turns to a varnish-like liquid which can cause an injector needle to stick to its seat. Drain the tank and fuel system (Chapter 4).
- [ ] Intake air leak. Check for loose throttle body-to-intake duct joint, loose or damaged IAP sensor vacuum hose (Chapter 4).
- [ ] Air filter clogged. Clean the air filter element or replace it with a new one (Chapter 1).

Compression low

Check by performing a compression test (see Chapter 2).

- [ ] Spark plug loose. Remove the plug and inspect the threads. Reinstall and tighten securely (see Chapter 1).
- [ ] Cylinder head not sufficiently tightened down. If the cylinder head is suspected of being loose, then there's a chance that the gasket or head is damaged if the problem has persisted for any length of time. The head bolts should be tightened to the proper torque and in the correct sequence (Chapter 2).
- [ ] Improper valve clearance. This means that the valve is not closing completely and compression pressure is leaking past the valve. Check and adjust the valve clearances (Chapter 1).

- [ ] Cylinder and/or piston worn. Excessive wear will cause compression pressure to leak past the rings. This is usually accompanied by worn rings as well. A top-end overhaul is necessary (Chapter 2).
- [ ] Piston rings worn, weak, broken, or sticking. Broken or sticking piston rings usually indicate a lubrication or fuelling problem that causes excess carbon deposits to form on the pistons and rings. Top-end overhaul is necessary (Chapter 2).
- [ ] Piston ring-to-groove clearance excessive. This is caused by excessive wear of the piston ring lands. Piston renewal is necessary (Chapter 2).
- [ ] Cylinder head gasket damaged. If the head is allowed to become loose, or if excessive carbon build-up on the piston crown and combustion chamber causes extremely high compression, the head gasket may leak. Retorquing the head is not always sufficient to restore the seal, so a new gasket is necessary (Chapter 2).
- [ ] Cylinder head warped. This is caused by overheating or improperly tightened head bolts. Machine shop resurfacing or head renewal is necessary (Chapter 2).
- [ ] Valve spring broken or weak. Caused by component failure or wear; the springs must be renewed (Chapter 2).
- [ ] Valve not seating properly. This is caused by a bent valve (from over-revving or improper valve adjustment), burned valve or seat (improper fuelling) or an accumulation of carbon deposits on the seat (from fuelling or lubrication problems). The valves must be cleaned and/or renewed and the seats serviced (Chapter 2).

Poor acceleration

- [ ] Timing not advancing. The crankshaft position sensor (CKP) or the engine control unit (ECU) may be defective (see Chapter 4). If so, they must be renewed.
- [ ] Engine oil viscosity too high. Using a heavier oil than that recommended in Chapter 1 can damage the oil pump or lubrication system and cause drag on the engine.
- [ ] Brakes dragging. Usually caused by debris which has entered the brake caliper piston seals, or from a warped disc or bent axle (see Chapter 6).

3 Poor running or no power at high speed

Firing incorrect

- ☐ Spark plug cap not making good contact. Make sure that the cap fits snugly over the plug and that the wiring is secure.
- ☐ Spark plug dirty, defective or worn out. Identify reason for fouled plug using spark plug condition chart on the inside back cover and follow the plug maintenance procedures (see Chapter 1).
- ☐ Incorrect spark plug. Wrong type or heat range. Check and install correct plug (see Chapter 1).
- ☐ Ignition coil defective. Test and replace with new one if necessary (see Chapter 4).
- ☐ Faulty ECU (engine control unit) (see Chapter 4).

Fuel/air mixture incorrect

- ☐ Fuel tank breather hose obstructed.
- ☐ Fuel pump faulty, or the fuel filter is blocked (see Chapter 4).
- ☐ Fuel hose clogged. Remove the fuel hose and carefully blow through it. Check the fuel filter for damage.
- ☐ Fuel rail or injector clogged. Check the fuel filter. In some cases, if a machine has been unused for several months, the fuel turns to a varnish-like liquid which can cause an injector needle to stick to its seat. Drain the tank and fuel system (Chapter 4).
- ☐ Intake air leak. Check for loose throttle body-to-intake duct joint, loose or damaged IAP sensor vacuum hose (Chapter 4).
- ☐ Air filter clogged. Clean the air filter element or replace it with a new one (Chapter 1).

Compression low

Check by performing a compression test (see Chapter 2).
- ☐ Spark plug loose. Remove the plug and inspect the threads. Reinstall and tighten securely (see Chapter 1).
- ☐ Cylinder head not sufficiently tightened down. If the cylinder head is suspected of being loose, then there's a chance that the gasket or head is damaged if the problem has persisted for any length of time. The head bolts should be tightened to the proper torque and in the correct sequence (Chapter 2).
- ☐ Improper valve clearance. This means that the valve is not closing completely and compression pressure is leaking past the valve. Check and adjust the valve clearances (Chapter 1).
- ☐ Cylinder and/or piston worn. Excessive wear will cause compression pressure to leak past the rings. This is usually accompanied by worn rings as well. A top-end overhaul is necessary (Chapter 2).
- ☐ Piston rings worn, weak, broken, or sticking. Broken or sticking piston rings usually indicate a lubrication or fuelling problem that causes excess carbon deposits to form on the pistons and rings. Top-end overhaul is necessary (Chapter 2).
- ☐ Piston ring-to-groove clearance excessive. This is caused by excessive wear of the piston ring lands. Piston renewal is necessary (Chapter 2).

- ☐ Cylinder head gasket damaged. If a head is allowed to become loose, or if excessive carbon build-up on the piston crown and combustion chamber causes extremely high compression, the head gasket may leak. Retorquing the head is not always sufficient to restore the seal, so a new gasket is necessary (Chapter 2).
- ☐ Cylinder head warped. This is caused by overheating or improperly tightened head bolts. Machine shop resurfacing or head renewal is necessary (Chapter 2).
- ☐ Valve spring broken or weak. Caused by component failure or wear; the springs must be replaced with new ones (Chapter 2).
- ☐ Valve not seating properly. This is caused by a bent valve (from over-revving or improper valve adjustment), burned valve or seat (improper fuelling) or an accumulation of carbon deposits on the seat (from fuelling or lubrication problems). The valves must be cleaned and/or renewed and the seats serviced (Chapter 2).

Knocking or pinking

- ☐ Carbon build-up in combustion chamber. Use of a fuel additive that will dissolve the adhesive bonding the carbon particles to the piston crown and chamber is the easiest way to remove the build-up. Otherwise, the cylinder head will have to be removed and decarbonised (Chapter 2).
- ☐ Incorrect or poor quality fuel. Old or improper grades of fuel can cause detonation. This causes the piston to rattle, thus the knocking or pinking sound. Drain old fuel and always use the recommended fuel grade.
- ☐ Spark plug heat range incorrect. Uncontrolled detonation indicates the plug heat range is too hot. The plug in effect becomes a glow plug, raising cylinder temperatures. Install the proper heat range plug (Chapter 1).
- ☐ Improper air/fuel mixture. This will cause the engine to run hot, which leads to detonation. A blockage in the fuel system or an air leak can cause this imbalance (see Chapter 4).

Miscellaneous causes

- ☐ Throttle valve doesn't open fully. Adjust the throttle twistgrip freeplay (see Chapter 1).
- ☐ Clutch slipping due loose or worn clutch components (see Chapter 2).
- ☐ Timing not advancing. The crankshaft position sensor (CKP) or the engine control unit (ECU) may be defective (see Chapter 4). If so, they must be replaced with new ones.
- ☐ Engine oil viscosity too high. Using a heavier oil than the one recommended in Chapter 1 can damage the oil pump or lubrication system and cause drag on the engine.
- ☐ Brakes dragging. Usually caused by debris which has entered the brake caliper piston seals, or from a warped disc or bent axle (see Chapter 6).

4 Overheating

Engine overheats

- [ ] Coolant level low. Check and add coolant (see *Pre-ride checks*).
- [ ] Leak in cooling system. Check cooling system hoses and radiator for leaks and other damage. Repair or renew parts as necessary (see Chapter 3).
- [ ] Faulty thermostat. Check and renew as described in Chapter 3.
- [ ] Faulty radiator cap. Remove the cap and have it pressure tested.
- [ ] Coolant passages clogged. Drain, flush and refill with fresh coolant (Chapter 1).
- [ ] Water pump defective. Remove the pump and check the components (see Chapter 3).
- [ ] Clogged or damaged radiator fins (see Chapter 3).
- [ ] Faulty cooling fan, fan relay or ECT sensor (see Chapter 3).

Firing incorrect

- [ ] Spark plug dirty, defective or worn out. Identify reason for fouled plug using spark plug condition chart on the inside back cover and follow the plug maintenance procedures (see Chapter 1).
- [ ] Incorrect spark plug. Wrong type or heat range. Check and install correct plug (see Chapter 1).
- [ ] Ignition coil defective. Test and replace with a new one if necessary (see Chapter 4).
- [ ] Faulty ECU (engine control unit) (see Chapter 4).

Fuel/air mixture incorrect

- [ ] Fuel tank breather hose obstructed.
- [ ] Fuel pump faulty, or the fuel filter is blocked (see Chapter 4).
- [ ] Fuel hose clogged. Remove the fuel hose and carefully blow through it. Check the fuel filter for damage.
- [ ] Fuel rail or injector clogged. Check the fuel filter. In some cases, if a machine has been unused for several months, the fuel turns to a varnish-like liquid which can cause an injector needle to stick to its seat. Drain the tank and fuel system (Chapter 4).
- [ ] Intake air leak. Check for loose throttle body-to-intake manifold connections, loose or damaged IAP sensor vacuum hose (Chapter 4).
- [ ] Air filter clogged. Clean the air filter element or replace it with a new one (Chapter 1).

Compression too high

Check by performing a compression test (see Chapter 2).

- [ ] Carbon build-up in combustion chamber. Use of a fuel additive that will dissolve the adhesive bonding the carbon particles to the piston crown and chamber is the easiest way to remove the build-up. Otherwise, the cylinder head will have to be removed and decarbonised (Chapter 2).
- [ ] Improperly machined head surface or installation of incorrect gasket during engine assembly.

Engine load excessive

- [ ] Clutch slipping due to loose or worn clutch components (see Chapter 2).
- [ ] Engine oil level too high. Too much oil will cause pressurisation of the crankcase and inefficient engine operation. Check Specifications and drain to proper level (Chapter 1 and *Pre-ride checks*).
- [ ] Engine oil viscosity too high. Using a heavier oil than the one recommended in Chapter 1 can damage the oil pump or lubrication system as well as cause drag on the engine.
- [ ] Brakes dragging. Usually caused by debris which has entered the brake caliper piston seals, or from a warped disc or bent axle (see Chapter 6).

Lubrication inadequate

- [ ] Engine oil level too low. Friction caused by intermittent lack of lubrication or from oil that is overworked can cause overheating. The oil provides a definite cooling function in the engine. Check the oil level (see *Pre-ride checks*).
- [ ] Low engine oil pressure. Check the pressure (see Chapter 2).
- [ ] Blocked oil filter (see Chapter 2).

Miscellaneous causes

- [ ] Modification to exhaust system. Most aftermarket exhaust systems cause the engine to run leaner, which make them run hotter. When installing an accessory exhaust system, always check with the manufacturer/supplier as to whether the fuel system requires adjustment.

5 Clutch problems

Clutch slipping

- [ ] Insufficient clutch cable freeplay. Check and adjust (see Chapter 1).
- [ ] Clutch plates worn or warped. Overhaul the clutch assembly (see Chapter 2).
- [ ] Clutch springs broken or weak. Old or heat-damaged (from slipping clutch) springs should be renewed (Chapter 2).
- [ ] Faulty clutch release mechanism. Replace any defective parts with new ones (see Chapter 2).
- [ ] Clutch centre or housing unevenly worn. This causes improper engagement of the plates. Replace the damaged or worn parts (see Chapter 2).
- [ ] Incorrect oil used in engine. Oils designed for car engines often contain friction modifiers which if used in an engine with a wet clutch can promote clutch slip. Always use an oil designed for motorcycle engines (see *Pre-ride checks*).

Clutch not disengaging completely

- [ ] Excessive clutch cable freeplay. Check and adjust (see Chapter 1).
- [ ] Clutch plates warped or damaged. This will cause clutch drag, which in turn will cause the machine to creep. Overhaul the clutch assembly (see Chapter 2).
- [ ] Clutch springs fatigued or broken. Check and renew the springs (see Chapter 2).
- [ ] Engine oil deteriorated. Old, thin oil will not provide proper lubrication for the plates, causing the clutch to drag. Renew the oil and filter (see Chapter 1).
- [ ] Engine oil viscosity too high. Using a heavier oil than recommended in Chapter 1 can cause the plates to stick together. Change to the correct weight oil.
- [ ] Clutch housing bearing seized on the transmission input shaft. Lack of lubrication, severe wear or damage can cause the bearing to seize. Overhaul of the clutch, and perhaps transmission, may be necessary to repair the damage (see Chapter 2).
- [ ] Faulty clutch release mechanism. Renew any defective parts (see Chapter 2).
- [ ] Loose clutch centre nut. Causes housing and centre misalignment putting a drag on the engine. Engagement adjustment continually varies. Overhaul the clutch assembly (see Chapter 2).

6 Gearchanging problems

Doesn't go into gear or lever doesn't return

☐ Clutch not disengaging (see above).

☐ Gearchange mechanism stopper arm spring weak or broken, or arm roller broken or worn. Replace the spring or arm with a new one (see Chapter 2).

☐ Selector fork(s) bent, worn or seized. Overhaul the transmission (see Chapter 2).

☐ Gear(s) stuck on shaft. Most often caused by a lack of lubrication or excessive wear in transmission bearings and bushes. Overhaul the transmission (see Chapter 2).

☐ Selector drum binding. Caused by lubrication failure or excessive wear. Replace the drum and/or its bearing with a new one (see Chapter 2).

☐ Gearchange mechanism return spring weak or broken (see Chapter 2).

☐ Gearchange linkage arm broken. Splines stripped out of arm or shaft, caused by a loose linkage arm pinch bolt or from dropping the machine (see Chapter 2).

Jumps out of gear

☐ Selector fork(s) worn (see Chapter 2).

☐ Selector fork groove(s) in selector drum worn (see Chapter 2).

☐ Gear pinion dogs or dog slots worn or damaged. The gear pinions should be inspected and renewed. No attempt should be made to repair the worn parts.

Overselects

☐ Gearchange mechanism stopper arm spring weak or broken, or arm roller broken or worn. Renew the spring or arm (see Chapter 2).

☐ Gearchange mechanism return spring weak or broken (see Chapter 2).

7 Abnormal engine noise

Knocking or pinking

☐ Carbon build-up in combustion chamber. Use of a fuel additive that will dissolve the adhesive bonding the carbon particles to the piston crown and chamber is the easiest way to remove the build-up. Otherwise, the cylinder head will have to be removed and decarbonised (Chapter 2).

☐ Incorrect or poor quality fuel. Old or improper grades of fuel can cause detonation. This causes the piston to rattle, thus the knocking or pinking sound. Drain old fuel and always use the recommended fuel grade.

☐ Spark plug heat range incorrect. Uncontrolled detonation indicates the plug heat range is too hot. The plug in effect becomes a glow plug, raising cylinder temperatures. Install the proper heat range plug (Chapter 1).

☐ Improper air/fuel mixture. This will cause the engine to run hot, which leads to detonation. A blockage in the fuel system or an air leak can cause this imbalance (see Chapter 4).

Piston slap or rattling

☐ Cylinder-to-piston clearance excessive. Cylinder and/or piston worn, usually accompanied by worn rings as well. A top-end overhaul is necessary (see Chapter 2).

☐ Piston ring(s) worn, broken or sticking. Overhaul the top-end (see Chapter 2).

☐ Piston pin, piston pin bore or connecting rod small-end worn from high mileage or seized due to lack of lubrication (see Chapter 2).

☐ Piston seizure damage. Usually from lack of lubrication or overheating. Replace the piston and cylinder block (see Chapter 2).

☐ Connecting rod big-end clearance excessive. Caused by excessive wear or lack of lubrication. Replace worn parts.

☐ Connecting rod bent. Caused by over-revving, trying to start a badly flooded engine or from ingesting a foreign object into the combustion chamber. Replace the damaged parts (Chapter 2).

Valve noise

☐ Incorrect valve clearances – check and adjust (see Chapter 1).

☐ Valve spring broken or weak. Check and replace weak valve springs with new ones (see Chapter 2).

☐ Camshaft or camshaft bearings worn or damaged. Lubrication failure at high rpm is usually the cause of damage due to insufficient oil or failure to change the oil at the recommended intervals. Since there are no replaceable bearings in the head, the head itself will have to be replaced with a new one (see Chapter 2).

Other noise

☐ Cylinder head gasket leaking. Check around the joint for blowing with the engine running.

☐ Exhaust pipe leaking at cylinder head connection. Caused by incorrect fit of pipe, loose exhaust flange or damaged gasket. All exhaust system fasteners should be tightened evenly and carefully to avoid leaks (see Chapter 4).

☐ Crankshaft runout excessive. Caused by a bent crankshaft (from over-revving) or damage from an upper cylinder component failure. Can also be attributed to dropping the machine on either of the crankshaft ends.

☐ Engine mounting bolts loose – ensure all the bolts are tightened to the specified torque settings (see Chapter 2).

☐ Crankshaft bearings worn (see Chapter 2).

☐ Cam chain rattle, due to worn chain or defective tensioner. Also worn chain tensioner/guide blades (see Chapter 2).

8 Abnormal driveline noise

Clutch noise

- ☐ Clutch housing/friction plate clearance excessive (Chapter 2).
- ☐ Wear between the clutch housing splines and input shaft splines (Chapter 2).
- ☐ Worn release bearing (Chapter 2).

Transmission noise

- ☐ Bearings worn. Also includes the possibility that the shafts are worn. Overhaul the transmission (Chapter 2).
- ☐ Gears worn or chipped (Chapter 2).
- ☐ Metal chips jammed in gear teeth. Probably pieces from a broken clutch, gear or selector mechanism that were picked up by the gears. This will cause early bearing failure (Chapter 2).
- ☐ Engine oil level too low. Causes a howl from transmission. Also affects engine power and clutch operation (*Pre-ride checks*).

Final drive noise

- ☐ Chain not adjusted properly (Chapter 1).
- ☐ Front or rear sprocket loose. Tighten fasteners (Chapter 6).
- ☐ Sprockets and/or chain worn. Fit new sprockets and chain (Chapter 6).
- ☐ Rear sprocket warped. Fit a new sprocket (Chapter 6).
- ☐ Rubber dampers in rear sprocket coupling worn (Chapter 6).

9 Abnormal frame and suspension noise

Front end noise

- ☐ Low fluid level or improper viscosity oil in forks. This can sound like spurting and is usually accompanied by irregular fork action (Chapter 5).
- ☐ Spring weak or broken. Makes a clicking or scraping sound. Fork oil, when drained, will have a lot of metal particles in it (Chapter 5).
- ☐ Steering head bearings loose or damaged. Clicks when braking. Check and adjust or replace with new ones as necessary (Chapters 1 and 5).
- ☐ Fork yoke clamp bolts loose – ensure all the bolts are tightened to the specified torque (Chapter 5).
- ☐ Forks bent. Good possibility if machine has been dropped. Replace the fork tubes (Chapter 5).
- ☐ Front axle or axle pinch bolts loose. Tighten them to the specified torque (Chapter 6).
- ☐ Loose or worn wheel bearings. Check and replace with new ones as needed (Chapters 1 and 6).

Shock absorber noise

- ☐ Fluid level incorrect. Indicates a leak caused by defective seal. Shock will be covered with oil. Replace shock with a new one or seek advice on repair from a suspension specialist (Chapter 5).
- ☐ Defective shock absorber with internal damage. This is in the body of the shock and can't be remedied. The shock must be replaced with a new one or rebuilt (Chapter 5).
- ☐ Bent or damaged shock body or mounts. Check the mounts. If the shock absorber itself is damaged replace it with a new one (Chapter 5).
- ☐ Loose or worn suspension linkage components (XT models only). Check and replace with new ones as necessary (Chapter 5).

Brake noise

- ☐ Squeal caused by pad shim not installed or positioned correctly (where fitted) (Chapter 6).
- ☐ Squeal caused by dust on brake pads. Usually found in combination with glazed pads. Clean using brake cleaning solvent (Chapter 6).
- ☐ Pads glazed. Caused by excessive heat from prolonged hard use or from contamination. DO NOT use sandpaper, emery cloth, carborundum cloth or any other abrasive to roughen the pad surfaces as abrasives will stay in the pad material and damage the disc. A very fine flat file can be used, but new pads is the best remedy (Chapter 6).
- ☐ Contamination of brake pads. Oil or brake fluid can cause the brake pads to chatter or squeal. Fit new pads. Identify the cause of the contamination, especially check the caliper piston seals for leaking fluid. Clean disc thoroughly with brake system cleaner (Chapter 6).
- ☐ Disc warped. Can cause a chattering, clicking or intermittent squeal. Usually accompanied by a pulsating lever and uneven braking. Replace the disc with new one (Chapter 6).
- ☐ Loose or worn wheel bearings. Check and replace with new ones as needed (Chapters 1 and 6).

10 Excessive exhaust smoke

White smoke

- ☐ Piston rings worn or broken, causing oil from the crankcase to be pulled past the piston into the combustion chamber. Replace the rings with new ones (Chapter 2).
- ☐ Cylinder worn or scored. Caused by overheating or oil starvation. Install a new cylinder block and piston and rings (Chapter 2).
- ☐ Valve stem oil seal damaged or worn. Replace the oil seals with new ones (Chapter 2).
- ☐ Valve guide worn. Perform a complete valve job (Chapter 2).
- ☐ Engine oil level too high, which causes the oil to be forced past the rings. Drain oil to the proper level (see Chapter 1 and *Pre-ride checks*).
- ☐ Head gasket broken between oil return and cylinder. Causes oil to be pulled into the combustion chamber. Replace the head gasket with a new one and check the head for warpage (Chapter 2).
- ☐ Abnormal crankcase pressurisation which forces oil past the rings, usually caused by a clogged breather.

Black smoke

- ☐ Air filter clogged. Clean the air filter element or replace it with a new one (Chapter 1).
- ☐ Fuel injection system malfunction (Chapter 4).

Brown smoke

- ☐ Air filter poorly sealed or not installed (Chapter 1).
- ☐ Fuel injection system malfunction (Chapter 4).

11 Poor handling or stability

Handlebars hard to turn

☐ Steering head bearing adjuster nut too tight. Check adjustment as described in Chapter 1.

☐ Bearings damaged. Roughness can be felt as the bars are turned from side-to-side. Replace the bearings with new ones (Chapter 5).

☐ Races dented or worn. Denting results from wear in only one position (e.g., straight ahead), from a collision or hitting a pothole or from dropping the machine. Replace the bearings with new ones (Chapter 5).

☐ Steering stem lubrication inadequate. Causes are grease getting hard from age or being washed out by high pressure car washes. Disassemble steering head and repack bearings (Chapter 5).

☐ Steering stem bent. Caused by a collision, hitting a pothole or by dropping the machine. Replace damaged part. Don't try to straighten the steering stem (Chapter 5).

☐ Front tyre air pressure too low (*Pre-ride checks*).

Handlebar shakes or vibrates excessively

☐ Tyres worn or out of balance (Chapter 6).

☐ Swingarm bearings worn. Replace the bearings with new ones (Chapter 5).

☐ Wheel rim(s) warped or damaged. Inspect wheels for runout (Chapter 6).

☐ Wheel bearings worn. Worn front or rear wheel bearings can cause poor tracking. Worn front bearings will cause wobble (Chapters 1 and 6).

☐ Fork yoke clamp bolts or handlebar clamp bolts loose. Tighten them to the specified torque (Chapter 5).

☐ Engine mounting bolts loose. Will cause excessive vibration with increased engine rpm – ensure all the bolts are tightened to the specified torque settings (see Chapter 2).

Machine pulls to one side

☐ Frame bent. Definitely suspect this if the machine has been dropped. May or may not be accompanied by cracking near the steering head, swingarm mountings or engine mountings. Replace the frame with a new one (Chapter 5).

☐ Wheels out of alignment. Caused by improper location of axle spacers or from bent steering stem or frame (Chapter 5).

☐ Forks bent. Disassemble the forks and replace the damaged parts (Chapter 5).

☐ Swingarm bent or twisted. Replace the arm with a new one (Chapter 5).

☐ Fork oil level uneven. Check and add or drain as necessary (Chapter 5).

Poor shock absorbing qualities

☐ Too hard:
   a) Suspension settings incorrect.
   b) Fork oil level excessive (Chapter 5).
   c) Fork oil viscosity too high. Use a lighter oil (see the Specifications in Chapter 5).
   d) Fork tube bent. Causes a harsh, sticking feeling (Chapter 5).
   e) Fork internal damage (Chapter 5).
   f) Shock shaft or body bent or damaged (Chapter 5).
   g) Shock internal damage.
   h) Tyre pressure too high (Pre-ride checks).

☐ Too soft:
   a) Suspension settings incorrect.
   b) Fork oil level too low (Chapter 5).
   c) Fork oil viscosity too light (Chapter 5).
   d) Fork springs weak or broken (Chapter 5).
   e) Fork or shock oil leaking (Chapter 5).
   f) Shock internal damage (Chapter 5).

12 Braking problems

Brakes
are spongy, don't hold

☐ Low brake fluid level (see *Pre-ride checks*).
☐ Air in hydraulic system. Caused by inattention to master cylinder fluid level or by leakage. Locate problem and bleed brakes (Chapter 6).
☐ Pad or disc worn (Chapters 1 and 6).
☐ Contaminated pads. Caused by contamination with oil, grease, brake fluid, etc. Fit new pads. Identify the cause of the contamination, especially check the caliper piston seals for leaking fluid. Clean disc thoroughly with brake system cleaner (Chapter 6).
☐ Brake fluid deteriorated. Fluid is old or contaminated. Drain system, replenish with new fluid and bleed the system (Chapter 6).
☐ Master cylinder internal seals worn or damaged causing fluid to bypass (Chapter 6).
☐ Master cylinder bore scratched by foreign material or broken spring. Fit a new master cylinder (Chapter 6).
☐ Disc warped. Replace disc with new one (Chapter 6).

Brake lever or pedal pulsates

☐ Disc warped. Replace disc with new one (Chapter 6).
☐ Axle bent. Replace axle with new one (Chapter 6).
☐ Brake caliper bolts loose – tighten the bolts to the specified torque (Chapter 6).
☐ Wheel warped or otherwise damaged (Chapter 6).
☐ Wheel bearings damaged or worn (Chapters 1 and 6).

Brakes drag

☐ Master cylinder piston seized. Caused by wear or damage to piston or cylinder bore (Chapter 6).
☐ Lever balky or stuck. Check pivot and lubricate (Chapter 6).
☐ Brake caliper piston seized in bore. Caused by corrosion or ingestion of dirt past deteriorated seal (Chapter 6).
☐ Caliper sticking on slider pins due to corrosion (sliding type caliper only). Clean and lubricate pins and check dust boots (Chapter 6).
☐ Brake pad damaged. Pad material separated from backing plate. Usually caused by faulty manufacturing process or from contact with chemicals. Fit new pads (Chapter 6).
☐ Pads improperly installed (Chapter 6).
☐ Brake caliper incorrectly installed (Chapter 6).

13 Electrical problems

Battery dead or weak

☐ Battery faulty. Caused by sulphated plates which are shorted through sedimentation. Confirm by terminal voltage check (Chapter 8).
☐ Broken battery terminal making only occasional contact.
☐ Battery leads making poor contact (Chapter 8).
☐ Load excessive. Caused by addition of high wattage lights or other electrical accessories.
☐ Ignition switch defective. Switch either grounds (earths) internally or fails to shut off system. Renew the switch (Chapter 8).
☐ Regulator/rectifier defective (Chapter 8).
☐ Alternator stator coil open or shorted (Chapter 8).

☐ Charging system fault. Check for excessive current leakage (Chapter 8).
☐ Wiring faulty. Wiring grounded (earthed) or connections loose in ignition, charging or lighting circuits (Chapter 8).

Battery overcharged

☐ Regulator/rectifier defective. Overcharging is noticed when battery gets excessively warm (Chapter 8).
☐ Battery faulty. Confirm with battery terminal voltage check (Chapter 8).
☐ Battery amperage too low, wrong type or size of battery. Install manufacturer's specified amp-hour battery to handle charging load (Chapter 8).

A

ABS (Anti-lock braking system) A system, usually electronically controlled, that senses incipient wheel lockup during braking and relieves hydraulic pressure at wheel which is about to skid.

Aftermarket Components suitable for the motorcycle, but not produced by the motorcycle manufacturer.

Allen key A hexagonal wrench which fits into a recessed hexagonal hole.

Alternating current (ac) Current produced by an alternator. Requires converting to direct current by a rectifier for charging purposes.

Alternator Converts mechanical energy from the engine into electrical energy to charge the battery and power the electrical system.

Ampere (amp) A unit of measurement for the flow of electrical current. Current = Volts ÷ Ohms.

Ampere-hour (Ah) Measure of battery capacity.

Angle-tightening A torque expressed in degrees. Often follows a conventional tightening torque for cylinder head or main bearing fasteners **(see illustration)**.

Angle-tightening cylinder head bolts

Antifreeze A substance (usually ethylene glycol) mixed with water, and added to the cooling system, to prevent freezing of the coolant in winter. Antifreeze also contains chemicals to inhibit corrosion and the formation of rust and other deposits that would tend to clog the radiator and coolant passages and reduce cooling efficiency.

Anti-dive System attached to the fork lower leg (slider) to prevent fork dive when braking hard.

Anti-seize compound A coating that reduces the risk of seizing on fasteners that are subjected to high temperatures, such as exhaust clamp bolts and nuts.

API American Petroleum Institute. A quality standard for 4-stroke motor oils.

Asbestos A natural fibrous mineral with great heat resistance, commonly used in the composition of brake friction materials. Asbestos is a health hazard and the dust created by brake systems should never be inhaled or ingested.

ATF Automatic Transmission Fluid. Often used in front forks.

ATU Automatic Timing Unit. Mechanical device for advancing the ignition timing on early engines.

ATV All Terrain Vehicle. Often called a Quad.

Axial play Side-to-side movement.

Axle A shaft on which a wheel revolves. Also known as a spindle.

B

Backlash The amount of movement between meshed components when one component is held still. Usually applies to gear teeth.

Ball bearing A bearing consisting of a hardened inner and outer race with hardened steel balls between the two races.

Bearings Used between two working surfaces to prevent wear of the components and a build-up of heat. Four types of bearing are commonly used on motorcycles: plain shell bearings, ball bearings, tapered roller bearings and needle roller bearings.

Bevel gears Used to turn the drive through 90º. Typical applications are shaft final drive and camshaft drive **(see illustration)**.

Bevel gears are used to turn the drive through 90°

BHP Brake Horsepower. The British measurement for engine power output. Power output is now usually expressed in kilowatts (kW).

Bias-belted tyre Similar construction to radial tyre, but with outer belt running at an angle to the wheel rim.

Big-end bearing The bearing in the end of the connecting rod that's attached to the crankshaft.

Bleeding The process of removing air from an hydraulic system via a bleed nipple or bleed screw.

Bottom-end A description of an engine's crankcase components and all components contained there-in.

BTDC Before Top Dead Centre in terms of piston position. Ignition timing is often expressed in terms of degrees or millimetres BTDC.

Bush A cylindrical metal or rubber component used between two moving parts.

Burr Rough edge left on a component after machining or as a result of excessive wear.

C

Cam chain The chain which takes drive from the crankshaft to the camshaft(s).

Canister The main component in an evaporative emission control system (California market only); contains activated charcoal granules to trap vapours from the fuel system rather than allowing them to vent to the atmosphere.

Castellated Resembling the parapets along the top of a castle wall. For example, a castellated wheel axle or spindle nut.

Catalytic converter A device in the exhaust system of some machines which converts certain pollutants in the exhaust gases into less harmful substances.

Charging system Description of the components which charge the battery, ie the alternator, rectifier and regulator.

Circlip A ring-shaped clip used to prevent endwise movement of cylindrical parts and shafts. An internal circlip is installed in a groove in a housing; an external circlip fits into a groove on the outside of a cylindrical piece such as a shaft. Also known as a snap-ring.

Clearance The amount of space between two parts. For example, between a piston and a cylinder, between a bearing and a journal, etc.

Coil spring A spiral of elastic steel found in various sizes throughout a vehicle, for example as a springing medium in the suspension and in the valve train.

Compression Reduction in volume, and increase in pressure and temperature, of a gas, caused by squeezing it into a smaller space.

Compression damping Controls the speed the suspension compresses when hitting a bump.

Compression ratio The relationship between cylinder volume when the piston is at top dead centre and cylinder volume when the piston is at bottom dead centre.

Continuity The uninterrupted path in the flow of electricity. Little or no measurable resistance.

Continuity tester Self-powered bleeper or test light which indicates continuity.

Cp Candlepower. Bulb rating commonly found on US motorcycles.

Crossply tyre Tyre plies arranged in a criss-cross pattern. Usually four or six plies used, hence 4PR or 6PR in tyre size codes.

Cush drive Rubber damper segments fitted between the rear wheel and final drive sprocket to absorb transmission shocks **(see illustration)**.

Cush drive rubbers dampen out transmission shocks

D

Degree disc Calibrated disc for measuring piston position. Expressed in degrees.

Dial gauge Clock-type gauge with adapters for measuring runout and piston position. Expressed in mm or inches.

Diaphragm The rubber membrane in a master cylinder or carburettor which seals the upper chamber.

Diaphragm spring A single sprung plate often used in clutches.

Direct current (dc) Current produced by a dc generator.

Decarbonisation The process of removing carbon deposits - typically from the combustion chamber, valves and exhaust port/system.

Detonation Destructive and damaging explosion of fuel/air mixture in combustion chamber instead of controlled burning.

Diode An electrical valve which only allows current to flow in one direction. Commonly used in rectifiers and starter interlock systems.

Disc valve (or rotary valve) A induction system used on some two-stroke engines.

Double-overhead camshaft (DOHC) An engine that uses two overhead camshafts, one for the intake valves and one for the exhaust valves.

Drivebelt A toothed belt used to transmit drive to the rear wheel on some motorcycles. A drivebelt has also been used to drive the camshafts. Drivebelts are usually made of Kevlar.

Driveshaft Any shaft used to transmit motion. Commonly used when referring to the final driveshaft on shaft drive motorcycles.

E

Earth return The return path of an electrical circuit, utilising the motorcycle's frame.

ECU (Electronic Control Unit) A computer which controls (for instance) an ignition system, or an anti-lock braking system.

EGO Exhaust Gas Oxygen sensor. Sometimes called a Lambda sensor.

Electrolyte The fluid in a lead-acid battery.

EMS (Engine Management System) A computer controlled system which manages the fuel injection and the ignition systems in an integrated fashion.

Endfloat The amount of lengthways movement between two parts. As applied to a crankshaft, the distance that the crankshaft can move side-to-side in the crankcase.

Endless chain A chain having no joining link. Common use for cam chains and final drive chains.

EP (Extreme Pressure) Oil type used in locations where high loads are applied, such as between gear teeth.

Evaporative emission control system Describes a charcoal filled canister which stores fuel vapours from the tank rather than allowing them to vent to the atmosphere. Usually only fitted to California models and referred to as an EVAP system.

Expansion chamber Section of two-stroke engine exhaust system so designed to improve engine efficiency and boost power.

F

Feeler blade or gauge A thin strip or blade of hardened steel, ground to an exact thickness, used to check or measure clearances between parts.

Final drive Description of the drive from the transmission to the rear wheel. Usually by chain or shaft, but sometimes by belt.

Firing order The order in which the engine cylinders fire, or deliver their power strokes, beginning with the number one cylinder.

Flooding Term used to describe a high fuel level in the carburettor float chambers, leading to fuel overflow. Also refers to excess fuel in the combustion chamber due to incorrect starting technique.

Free length The no-load state of a component when measured. Clutch, valve and fork spring lengths are measured at rest, without any preload.

Freeplay The amount of travel before any action takes place. The looseness in a linkage, or an assembly of parts, between the initial application of force and actual movement. For example, the distance the rear brake pedal moves before the rear brake is actuated.

Fuel injection The fuel/air mixture is metered electronically and directed into the engine intake ports (indirect injection) or into the cylinders (direct injection). Sensors supply information on engine speed and conditions.

Fuel/air mixture The charge of fuel and air going into the engine. See **Stoichiometric ratio**.

Fuse An electrical device which protects a circuit against accidental overload. The typical fuse contains a soft piece of metal which is calibrated to melt at a predetermined current flow (expressed as amps) and break the circuit.

G

Gap The distance the spark must travel in jumping from the centre electrode to the side electrode in a spark plug. Also refers to the distance between the ignition rotor and the pickup coil in an electronic ignition system.

Gasket Any thin, soft material - usually cork, cardboard, asbestos or soft metal - installed between two metal surfaces to ensure a good seal. For instance, the cylinder head gasket seals the joint between the block and the cylinder head.

Gauge An instrument panel display used to monitor engine conditions. A gauge with a movable pointer on a dial or a fixed scale is an analogue gauge. A gauge with a numerical readout is called a digital gauge.

Gear ratios The drive ratio of a pair of gears in a gearbox, calculated on their number of teeth.

Glaze-busting see **Honing**

Grinding Process for renovating the valve face and valve seat contact area in the cylinder head.

Gudgeon pin The shaft which connects the connecting rod small-end with the piston. Often called a piston pin or wrist pin.

H

Helical gears Gear teeth are slightly curved and produce less gear noise that straight-cut gears. Often used for primary drives.

Installing a Helicoil thread insert in a cylinder head

Helicoil A thread insert repair system. Commonly used as a repair for stripped spark plug threads **(see illustration)**.

Honing A process used to break down the glaze on a cylinder bore (also called glaze-busting). Can also be carried out to roughen a rebored cylinder to aid ring bedding-in.

HT (High Tension) Description of the electrical circuit from the secondary winding of the ignition coil to the spark plug.

Hydraulic A liquid filled system used to transmit pressure from one component to another. Common uses on motorcycles are brakes and clutches.

Hydrometer An instrument for measuring the specific gravity of a lead-acid battery.

Hygroscopic Water absorbing. In motorcycle applications, braking efficiency will be reduced if DOT 3 or 4 hydraulic fluid absorbs water from the air - care must be taken to keep new brake fluid in tightly sealed containers.

I

lbf ft Pounds-force feet. An imperial unit of torque. Sometimes written as ft-lbs.

lbf in Pound-force inch. An imperial unit of torque, applied to components where a very low torque is required. Sometimes written as in-lbs.

IC Abbreviation for Integrated Circuit.

Ignition advance Means of increasing the timing of the spark at higher engine speeds. Done by mechanical means (ATU) on early engines or electronically by the ignition control unit on later engines.

Ignition timing The moment at which the spark plug fires, expressed in the number of crankshaft degrees before the piston reaches the top of its stroke, or in the number of millimetres before the piston reaches the top of its stroke.

Infinity (∞) Description of an open-circuit electrical state, where no continuity exists.

Inverted forks (upside down forks) The sliders or lower legs are held in the yokes and the fork tubes or stanchions are connected to the wheel axle (spindle). Less unsprung weight and stiffer construction than conventional forks.

J

JASO Quality standard for 2-stroke oils.

Joule The unit of electrical energy.

Journal The bearing surface of a shaft.

K

Kickstart Mechanical means of turning the engine over for starting purposes. Only usually fitted to mopeds, small capacity motorcycles and off-road motorcycles.

Kill switch Handebar-mounted switch for emergency ignition cut-out. Cuts the ignition circuit on all models, and additionally prevent starter motor operation on others.

km Symbol for kilometre.

kmh Abbreviation for kilometres per hour.

L

Lambda (λ) sensor A sensor fitted in the exhaust system to measure the exhaust gas oxygen content (excess air factor).

Lapping see **Grinding**.
LCD Abbreviation for Liquid Crystal Display.
LED Abbreviation for Light Emitting Diode.
Liner A steel cylinder liner inserted in a aluminium alloy cylinder block.
Locknut A nut used to lock an adjustment nut, or other threaded component, in place.
Lockstops The lugs on the lower triple clamp (yoke) which abut those on the frame, preventing handlebar-to-fuel tank contact.
Lockwasher A form of washer designed to prevent an attaching nut from working loose.
LT Low Tension Description of the electrical circuit from the power supply to the primary winding of the ignition coil.

M

Main bearings The bearings between the crankshaft and crankcase.
Maintenance-free (MF) battery A sealed battery which cannot be topped up.
Manometer Mercury-filled calibrated tubes used to measure intake tract vacuum. Used to synchronise carburettors on multi-cylinder engines.
Micrometer A precision measuring instrument that measures component outside diameters **(see illustration)**.

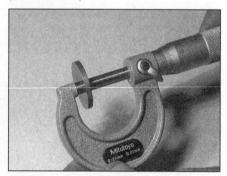

Tappet shims are measured with a micrometer

MON (Motor Octane Number) A measure of a fuel's resistance to knock.
Monograde oil An oil with a single viscosity, eg SAE80W.
Monoshock A single suspension unit linking the swingarm or suspension linkage to the frame.
mph Abbreviation for miles per hour.
Multigrade oil Having a wide viscosity range (eg 10W40). The W stands for Winter, thus the viscosity ranges from SAE10 when cold to SAE40 when hot.
Multimeter An electrical test instrument with the capability to measure voltage, current and resistance. Some meters also incorporate a continuity tester and buzzer.

N

Needle roller bearing Inner race of caged needle rollers and hardened outer race. Examples of uncaged needle rollers can be found on some engines. Commonly used in rear suspension applications and in two-stroke engines.
Nm Newton metres.
NOx Oxides of Nitrogen. A common toxic pollutant emitted by petrol engines at higher temperatures.

O

Octane The measure of a fuel's resistance to knock.
OE (Original Equipment) Relates to components fitted to a motorcycle as standard or replacement parts supplied by the motorcycle manufacturer.
Ohm The unit of electrical resistance. Ohms = Volts ÷ Current.
Ohmmeter An instrument for measuring electrical resistance.
Oil cooler System for diverting engine oil outside of the engine to a radiator for cooling purposes.
Oil injection A system of two-stroke engine lubrication where oil is pump-fed to the engine in accordance with throttle position.
Open-circuit An electrical condition where there is a break in the flow of electricity - no continuity (high resistance).
O-ring A type of sealing ring made of a special rubber-like material; in use, the O-ring is compressed into a groove to provide the sealing action.
Oversize (OS) Term used for piston and ring size options fitted to a rebored cylinder.
Overhead cam (sohc) engine An engine with single camshaft located on top of the cylinder head.
Overhead valve (ohv) engine An engine with the valves located in the cylinder head, but with the camshaft located in the engine block or crankcase.
Oxygen sensor A device installed in the exhaust system which senses the oxygen content in the exhaust and converts this information into an electric current. Also called a Lambda sensor.

P

Plastigauge A thin strip of plastic thread, available in different sizes, used for measuring clearances. For example, a strip of Plastigauge is laid across a bearing journal. The parts are assembled and dismantled; the width of the crushed strip indicates the clearance between journal and bearing.
Polarity Either negative or positive earth (ground), determined by which battery lead is connected to the frame (earth return). Modern motorcycles are usually negative earth.
Pre-ignition A situation where the fuel/air mixture ignites before the spark plug fires. Often due to a hot spot in the combustion chamber caused by carbon build-up. Engine has a tendency to 'run-on'.
Pre-load (suspension) The amount a spring is compressed when in the unloaded state. Preload can be applied by gas, spacer or mechanical adjuster.
Premix The method of engine lubrication on older two-stroke engines. Engine oil is mixed with the petrol in the fuel tank in a specific ratio. The fuel/oil mix is sometimes referred to as "petroil".
Primary drive Description of the drive from the crankshaft to the clutch. Usually by gear or chain.
PS Pfedestärke - a German interpretation of BHP.
PSI Pounds-force per square inch. Imperial measurement of tyre pressure and cylinder pressure measurement.
PTFE Polytetrafluroethylene. A low friction substance.

Pulse secondary air injection system A process of promoting the burning of excess fuel present in the exhaust gases by routing fresh air into the exhaust ports.

Q

Quartz halogen bulb Tungsten filament surrounded by a halogen gas. Typically used for the headlight **(see illustration)**.

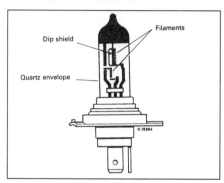

Quartz halogen headlight bulb construction

R

Rack-and-pinion A pinion gear on the end of a shaft that mates with a rack (think of a geared wheel opened up and laid flat). Sometimes used in clutch operating systems.
Radial play Up and down movement about a shaft.
Radial ply tyres Tyre plies run across the tyre (from bead to bead) and around the circumference of the tyre. Less resistant to tread distortion than other tyre types.
Radiator A liquid-to-air heat transfer device designed to reduce the temperature of the coolant in a liquid cooled engine.
Rake A feature of steering geometry - the angle of the steering head in relation to the vertical **(see illustration)**.

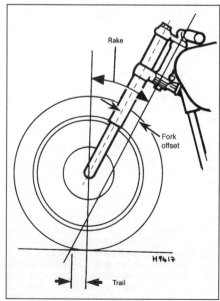

Steering geometry

Rebore Providing a new working surface to the cylinder bore by boring out the old surface. Necessitates the use of oversize piston and rings.

Rebound damping A means of controlling the oscillation of a suspension unit spring after it has been compressed. Resists the spring's natural tendency to bounce back after being compressed.

Rectifier Device for converting the ac output of an alternator into dc for battery charging.

Reed valve An induction system commonly used on two-stroke engines.

Regulator Device for maintaining the charging voltage from the generator or alternator within a specified range.

Relay A electrical device used to switch heavy current on and off by using a low current auxiliary circuit.

Resistance Measured in ohms. An electrical component's ability to pass electrical current.

RON (Research Octane Number) A measure of a fuel's resistance to knock.

rpm revolutions per minute.

Runout The amount of wobble (in-and-out movement) of a wheel or shaft as it's rotated. The amount a shaft rotates 'out-of-true'. The out-of-round condition of a rotating part.

S

SAE (Society of Automotive Engineers) A standard for the viscosity of a fluid.

Sealant A liquid or paste used to prevent leakage at a joint. Sometimes used in conjunction with a gasket.

Service limit Term for the point where a component is no longer useable and must be renewed.

Shaft drive A method of transmitting drive from the transmission to the rear wheel.

Shell bearings Plain bearings consisting of two shell halves. Most often used as big-end and main bearings in a four-stroke engine. Often called bearing inserts.

Shim Thin spacer, commonly used to adjust the clearance or relative positions between two parts. For example, shims inserted into or under tappets or followers to control valve clearances. Clearance is adjusted by changing the thickness of the shim.

Short-circuit An electrical condition where current shorts to earth (ground) bypassing the circuit components.

Skimming Process to correct warpage or repair a damaged surface, eg on brake discs or drums.

Slide-hammer A special puller that screws into or hooks onto a component such as a shaft or bearing; a heavy sliding handle on the shaft bottoms against the end of the shaft to knock the component free.

Small-end bearing The bearing in the upper end of the connecting rod at its joint with the gudgeon pin.

Spalling Damage to camshaft lobes or bearing journals shown as pitting of the working surface.

Specific gravity (SG) The state of charge of the electrolyte in a lead-acid battery. A measure of the electrolyte's density compared with water.

Straight-cut gears Common type gear used on gearbox shafts and for oil pump and water pump drives.

Stanchion The inner sliding part of the front forks, held by the yokes. Often called a fork tube.

Stoichiometric ratio The optimum chemical air/fuel ratio for a petrol engine, said to be 14.7 parts of air to 1 part of fuel.

Sulphuric acid The liquid (electrolyte) used in a lead-acid battery. Poisonous and extremely corrosive.

Surface grinding (lapping) Process to correct a warped gasket face, commonly used on cylinder heads.

T

Tapered-roller bearing Tapered inner race of caged needle rollers and separate tapered outer race. Examples of taper roller bearings can be found on steering heads.

Tappet A cylindrical component which transmits motion from the cam to the valve stem, either directly or via a pushrod and rocker arm. Also called a cam follower.

TCS Traction Control System. An electronically-controlled system which senses wheel spin and reduces engine speed accordingly.

TDC Top Dead Centre denotes that the piston is at its highest point in the cylinder.

Thread-locking compound Solution applied to fastener threads to prevent slackening. Select type to suit application.

Thrust washer A washer positioned between two moving components on a shaft. For example, between gear pinions on gearshaft.

Timing chain See **Cam Chain.**

Timing light Stroboscopic lamp for carrying out ignition timing checks with the engine running.

Top-end A description of an engine's cylinder block, head and valve gear components.

Torque Turning or twisting force about a shaft.

Torque setting A prescribed tightness specified by the motorcycle manufacturer to ensure that the bolt or nut is secured correctly. Undertightening can result in the bolt or nut coming loose or a surface not being sealed. Overtightening can result in stripped threads, distortion or damage to the component being retained.

Torx key A six-point wrench.

Tracer A stripe of a second colour applied to a wire insulator to distinguish that wire from another one with the same colour insulator. For example, Br/W is often used to denote a brown insulator with a white tracer.

Trail A feature of steering geometry. Distance from the steering head axis to the tyre's central contact point.

Triple clamps The cast components which extend from the steering head and support the fork stanchions or tubes. Often called fork yokes.

Turbocharger A centrifugal device, driven by exhaust gases, that pressurises the intake air. Normally used to increase the power output from a given engine displacement.

TWI Abbreviation for Tyre Wear Indicator. Indicates the location of the tread depth indicator bars on tyres.

U

Universal joint or U-joint (UJ) A double-pivoted connection for transmitting power from a driving to a driven shaft through an angle. Typically found in shaft drive assemblies.

Unsprung weight Anything not supported by the bike's suspension (ie the wheel, tyres, brakes, final drive and bottom (moving) part of the suspension).

V

Vacuum gauges Clock-type gauges for measuring intake tract vacuum. Used for carburettor synchronisation on multi-cylinder engines.

Valve A device through which the flow of liquid, gas or vacuum may be stopped, started or regulated by a moveable part that opens, shuts or partially obstructs one or more ports or passageways. The intake and exhaust valves in the cylinder head are of the poppet type.

Valve clearance The clearance between the valve tip (the end of the valve stem) and the rocker arm or tappet/follower. The valve clearance is measured when the valve is closed. The correct clearance is important - if too small the valve won't close fully and will burn out, whereas if too large noisy operation will result.

Valve lift The amount a valve is lifted off its seat by the camshaft lobe.

Valve timing The exact setting for the opening and closing of the valves in relation to piston position.

Vernier caliper A precision measuring instrument that measures inside and outside dimensions. Not quite as accurate as a micrometer, but more convenient.

VIN Vehicle Identification Number. Term for the bike's engine and frame numbers.

Viscosity The thickness of a liquid or its resistance to flow.

Volt A unit for expressing electrical "pressure" in a circuit. Volts = current x ohms.

W

Water pump A mechanically-driven device for moving coolant around the engine.

Watt A unit for expressing electrical power. Watts = volts x current.

Wear limit see **Service limit**

Wet liner A liquid-cooled engine design where the pistons run in liners which are directly surrounded by coolant **(see illustration)**.

Wet liner arrangement

Wheelbase Distance from the centre of the front wheel to the centre of the rear wheel.

Wiring harness or loom Describes the electrical wires running the length of the motorcycle and enclosed in tape or plastic sheathing. Wiring coming off the main harness is usually referred to as a sub harness.

Woodruff key A key of semi-circular or square section used to locate a gear to a shaft. Often used to locate the alternator rotor on the crankshaft.

Wrist pin Another name for gudgeon or piston pin.

Note: *References throughout this index are in the form - "Chapter number" • "Page number"*

A

Acknowledgements – 0•8
Air filter – 1•27
  housing – 4•15
Air induction system (AIS) – 1•12, 4•25
Air pressure sensor – 4•12
Air temperature sensor – 4•12
Alternator – 8•31
Asbestos – 0•10

B

Balancer shaft – 2•48
  bearings – 2•45
  gears – 2•36
Battery – 0•10, 1•27
  charging – 8•5
  removal, installation and inspection – 8•4
Bearing seal lips lubricant – 1•2
Big-end bearing – 2•45
Bike spec – 0•17 *et seq*
Bleeding brake system and fluid
  change – 6•16
Block – 2•23
Bodywork – 7•1 *et seq*
  cockpit covers – 7•6
  cowl – 7•2, 7•4, 7•7
  fork protector – 7•3
  fuel tank covers – 7•2, 7•5, 7•8
  general information – 7•1
  grab-rails – 7•2, 7•5, 7•7
  luggage rack covers – 7•5
  mirrors – 7•5, 7•7, 7•8
  mudguards – 7•3, 7•6, 7•8
  rack covers – 7•5
  radiator covers – 7•6, 7•8
  seats – 7•2, 7•5, 7•7
  seat panels – 7•5
  side panels – 7•2
  sump guard – 7•7
Bolts – 1•27
Brake caliper(s) – 6•6, 6•12
Brake disc(s) – 6•9, 6•13
Brake fluid – 1•2, 6•1
  bleeding – 6•16
  change – 1•22, 6•16
  levels – 0•14
Brake hoses and fitings – 1•22, 6•15
Brake lever
  pivot and piston tip lubricant – 1•2
  switch – 8•16, 8•17
Brake light – 8•8
  circuit check – 8•16
  switches – 8•16
Brake master cylinder – 6•9, 6•14
Brake pads – 6•3, 6•11
  wear check – 1•22
Brake pedal – 5•3
  lubricant – 1•2
  switch – 8•17
Brake system – 1•20
  bleeding and fluid change – 6•16
  check – 1•20
Brake/tail light bulb – 8•12
Brakes, wheels and final drive – 6•1 *et seq*
  brake fluid – 1•2, 6•1
  brake fluid change – 6•16
  caliper(s) – 6•6, 6•12
  chain – 6•23
  chain lubricant – 1•2
  disc(s) – 6•9, 6•13

drive chain – 6•23, REF.18
drive chain lubricant – 1•2
general information – 6•3
hoses and fittings – 1•22, 6•15
master cylinder – 6•9, 6•14
pads – 6•3, 6•11
sprocket coupling bearing – 6•22
sprocket coupling/rubber dampers – 6•25
sprockets – 6•24
tyre pressures – 0•16
tyres – 6•22
wheel alignment check – 6•17
wheel bearings – 6•20, 6•21
wheel inspection and repair – 6•17
wheels – 6•18, 6•19
Bulbs – 8•1
Buying spare parts – 0•9

C

Cables
  clutch – 2•33
  lubrication – 1•2, 1•26
  throttle – 1•12, 4•20
Caliper(s) – 6•6, 6•12
Cam chain – 2•17
  tensioner – 2•11
Camshaft – 2•12
Catalytic converter – 4•26
Chain – 0•13, 1•8, 6•23, REF•18
  lubricant – 1•2
Charging system testing – 8•30
Clutch – 1•13, 2•28
  cable – 2•33
  lever pivot lubricant – 1•2
  switch – 8•23
Cockpit covers – 7•6
Coil – 4•27
Connecting rod – 2•46
  big-end bearing – 2•45
Continuity checks – 8•3
Conversion factors – REF•26
Cooling system – 1•17, 3•1 *et seq*
  coolant type – 1•2
  draining – 1•19
  ECT sensor – 3•3
  fan and relay – 3•2
  flushing – 1•20
  general information – 3•2
  hoses and unions – 3•10
  level – 0•11
  pressure cap check – 3•6
  radiator – 3•4
  refilling – 1•20
  reservoir – 3•9
  temperature sensor – 3•3, 4•13
  temperature warning light – 3•3
  thermostat – 3•4
  type – 1•2
  water pump – 3•6
Cowl – 7•2, 7•4, 7•7
Crankcases – 2•44
  cover – 2•33
  separation and reassembly – 2•42
Crankshaft – 2•46
  crankshaft position (CKP) sensor – 4•12
  main bearings – 2•45
Cut-off relay and diodes – 8•24
Cylinder block – 2•23
Cylinder compression check – 2•6
Cylinder head – 2•18, 2•19

D

Daily (pre-ride checks) – 0•11 *et seq*
  brake fluid levels – 0•14
  chain – 0•13
  coolant level – 0•11
  drive chain – 0•13
  engine oil level – 0•12
  fuel – 0•15
  legal – 0•15
  lighting – 0•15
  oil level – 0•12
  safety – 0•15
  signalling – 0•15
  steering – 0•13
  suspension – 0•13
  tyres – 0•16
Dimensions – 0•17
Diodes – 8•24
Disc(s) – 6•9, 6•13
Downpipe – 4•22, 4•23, 4•24
Drive chain – 0•13, 1•8, 6•23
  lubricant – 1•2
  staking methods – REF•18

E

Earth (ground) checks – 8•4
Electrical system – 8•1 *et seq*
  alternator – 8•31
  battery charging – 8•5
  battery removal, installation and
    inspection – 8•4
  brake lever switch – 8•16, 8•17
  brake light – 8•8
  brake light circuit check – 8•16
  brake light switches – 8•16
  brake pedal switch – 8•17
  brake/tail light bulb – 8•12
  bulbs – 8•1
  charging system testing – 8•30
  clutch switch – 8•23
  continuity checks – 8•3
  earth (ground) checks – 8•4
  fault finding – 8•2
  fuel gauge or warning light and level
    sensor – 8•19
  fuses – 8•6
  general information – 8•2
  handlebar switches – 8•21
  headlight – 8•7, 8•8, 8•9, 8•10
  headlight aim – 8•11
  horn – 8•25
  ignition switch – 8•20
  instrument cluster – 8•18
  instrument LEDs – 8•19
  leakage test – 8•30
  licence plate light – 8•8
  licence plate light bulb – 8•12
  lighting system check – 8•7
  neutral switch – 8•21
  regulated output test – 8•30
  regulator/rectifier – 8•35
  relay unit and diodes – 8•24
  sidelight(s) – 8•7, 8•9, 8•10
  sidestand switch – 8•22
  starter circuit cut-off relay and diodes – 8•24
  starter motor overhaul – 8•27
  starter motor removal and installation – 8•26
  starter relay – 8•25
  switch continuity checks – 8•3
  switches – 8•16, 8•17, 8•20, 8•21, 8•22, 8•23

tail light – 8•8, 8•13
tail light bulb – 8•12
turn signal assemblies – 8•15
turn signal bulbs – 8•14
turn signal circuit check – 8•14
voltage checks – 8•3
warning light LEDs – 8•19
wiring continuity checks – 8•3
wiring diagrams – 8•36 et seq
Electricity – 0•10
Electronic control unit (ECU) – 4•28
Engine coolant temperature (ECT) sensor – 3•3, 4•13
Engine management system – 4•1 et seq
air filter housing – 4•15
air induction system (AIS) – 4•25
catalytic converter – 4•26
code re-registering key registration procedure – 4•29
components – 4•11
coolant temperature sensor – 4•13
crankshaft position (CKP) sensor – 4•12
description – 4•8
downpipe – 4•22, 4•23, 4•24
electronic control unit (ECU) – 4•28, 4•29
exhaust system – 4•21
fast idle unit – 4•20
fault codes – 4•9
fault diagnosis – 4•8
fault diagnosis (immobiliser) – 4•30
fuel pressure check – 4•6
fuel pump and relay – 4•6
fuel rail and injector – 4•19
fuel system – 4•3
fuel system diagnostic codes and data – 4•10
fuel tank – 4•3
fuel tank storage, cleaning and repair – 4•6
general information and precautions – 4•3
ignition coil – 4•27
ignition system – 4•3
ignition system check – 4•27
ignition timing – 4•28
immobiliser system – 4•29
injector – 4•19
intake air pressure (IAP) sensor – 4•12
intake air temperature (IAT) sensor – 4•12
intermediate pipe – 4•23, 4•25
key registration – 4•29
oxygen (O2) sensor – 4•15
silencer – 4•21, 4•22, 4•24
spark plug cap – 4•27
spark plugs – 1•1
speed sensor – 4•14
throttle body – 4•18
throttle cables – 4•20
throttle position (TP) sensor – 4•13
timing – 4•28
tip-over sensor – 4•13
troubleshooting procedure immobiliser – 4•30
Engine numbers – 0•9
Engine oil – 1•2, 1•14
level – 0•12
Engine, clutch and transmission – 2•1 et seq
balancer shaft – 2•48
balancer shaft bearings – 2•45
balancer shaft gears – 2•36
bearings – 2•44
big-end bearing – 2•45
block – 2•23
cam chain – 2•17
cam chain tensioner – 2•11
camshaft – 2•12
clutch – 2•28
clutch cable – 2•33
component access – 2•6
connecting rod – 2•46

connecting rod (big-end) bearing – 2•45
crankcase cover – 2•33
crankcase separation and reassembly – 2•42
crankcases – 2•44
crankshaft – 2•46
crankshaft (main) bearings – 2•45
cylinder block – 2•23
cylinder compression check – 2•6
cylinder head – 2•18, 2•19
engine disassembly and reassembly – 2•11
engine oil pressure check – 2•6
engine removal and installation – 2•7
engine wear assessment – 2•6
gearchange mechanism – 2•41
general information – 2•5
input shaft – 2•50
main bearings – 2•45
oil pump and strainer – 2•38
operations possible with the engine in the frame – 2•6
operations requiring engine removal – 2•6
output shaft – 2•52
output shaft oil seal – 2•48
piston – 2•24
piston rings – 2•26
primary drive gears – 2•36
rocker arms – 2•12
running-in procedure – 2•55
selector drum and forks – 2•54
starter clutch and gears – 2•27
tensioner blade and guide blade – 2•17
transmission assembly – 2•48
transmission shaft bearings – 2•45
transmission shaft overhaul – 2•50
valve clearances – 1•1
valves overhaul – 2•19
water pump gears – 2•36
Exhaust system – 4•21

F

Fast idle unit – 4•20
Fault Finding – REF• 35 et seq
electrical system – 8•2
immobiliser – 4•30
Filter
air – 1•27, 4•15
oil – 1•14
Fire – 0•10
Fluids – 1•2
Footrests – 5•3
pivots lubricant – 1•2
Forks
adjustment – 5•24
oil – 5•1
oil change – 1•24, 5•9
overhaul – 5•10
protector – 7•3
removal and installation – 5•8
Frame and suspension – 5•1 et seq
brake pedal – 5•3
footrests – 5•3
fork oil – 5•1
fork oil change – 5•9
fork overhaul – 5•10
fork removal and installation – 5•8
forks adjustment – 5•24
frame numbers – 0•9
frame inspection and repair – 5•3
gearchange lever – 5•5
general information – 5•3
handlebars – 5•5
levers – 5•7
shock absorber – 5•16
shock absorber adjustment – 5•14
shock absorber disposal – 5•18

sidestand – 5•5
steering head bearings – 5•15
steering stem – 5•13
suspension adjustment – 5•23
suspension linkage – 5•18
swingarm – 5•19
Fuel gauge or warning light and level sensor – 8•19
Fuel pressure check – 4•6
Fuel pump and relay – 4•6
Fuel rail and injector – 4•19
Fuel system – 1•12, 4•3
diagnostic codes and data – 4•10
Fuel tank – 4•3
covers – 7•2, 7•5, 7•8
storage, cleaning and repair – 4•6
Fumes – 0•10
Fuses – 8•6

G

Gearbox see Transmission
Gearchange
lever – 5•5
lever lubricant – 1•2
mechanism – 2•41
selector drum and forks – 2•54
Grab-rails – 7•2, 7•5, 7•7

H

Handlebars – 5•5
switches – 8•21
Headlight – 8•7, 8•8, 8•9, 8•10
aim – 8•11
Horn – 8•25
Hoses and fittings
brake system – 1•22, 6•15
cooling system – 3•10

I

Identification numbers – 0•9
Idle speed – 1•11
Ignition system – 4•3
check – 4•27
coil – 4•27
key registration (immobiliser) – 4•29
switch – 8•20
Ignition timing – 4•28
Immobiliser system – 4•29
fault diagnosis – 4•30
troubleshooting procedure – 4•30
Injector – 4•19
Input shaft – 2•50
Instrument cluster – 8•18
LEDs – 8•19
Intake air pressure (IAP) sensor – 4•12
Intake air temperature (IAT) sensor – 4•12
Intermediate pipe removal – 4•23, 4•25

K

Key registration (immobiliser) – 4•29

L

Leakage test – 8•30
Legal and safety – 0•15
Levers – 5•7
brake – 8•16, 8•17
gearchange – 5•5
pivot lubricant – 1•2
Licence plate light – 8•8
bulb – 8•12
Lighting and signalling – 0•15
check – 8•7
Lubricants and fluids – 1•2, REF• 23 et seq
Lubrication – 1•26
Luggage rack covers – 7•5

M

Main bearings – 2•45
Maintenance schedule – 1•3
Master cylinder
  brake – 6•9, 6•14
Mirrors – 7•5, 7•7, 7•8
MOT Test Checks – REF• 27 *et seq*
Mudguards – 7•3, 7•6, 7•8

N

Neutral switch – 8•21
Nuts and bolts – 1•27

O

Oil
  engine – 0•12, 1•2, 1•14
  fork – 5•1
Oil filter – 1•14
Oil pressure check – 2•6
Oil pump and strainer – 2•38
Output shaft – 2•52
  oil seal – 2•48
Oxygen (O2) sensor – 4•15

P

Pads – 6•3, 6•11
  wear check – 1•22
Parts – 0•9
Pedal
  brake – 5•3, 8•17
Piston – 2•24
Piston rings – 2•26
Pivot points lubrication – 1•26
Pre-ride checks – 0•11 *et seq*
Pressure cap check – 3•6
Primary drive gears – 2•36

R

Rack covers – 7•5
Radiator – 3•4
  covers – 7•6, 7•8
Regulator/rectifier – 8•35
  output test – 8•30
Relay unit and diodes – 8•24
  fan – 3•2
  fuel pump – 4•6
Rocker arms – 2•12
Routine maintenance and
  servicing – 1•1 *et seq*
  air filter – 1•27
  air induction system – 1•12
  battery – 1•27
  bearing seal lips lubricant – 1•2
  bolts – 1•27
  brake fluid – 1•2
  brake fluid change – 1•22
  brake hoses – 1•22
  brake lever pivot and piston tip lubricant – 1•2
  brake pedal lubricant – 1•2
  brake system – 1•20
  cables lubrication – 1•2, 1•26
  chain and sprockets – 1•8
  chain lubricant – 1•2
  clutch – 1•13
  clutch lever pivot lubricant – 1•2
  coolant – 1•2
  cooling system – 1•17
  drive chain and sprockets – 1•8

drive chain lubricant – 1•2
engine oil – 1•2, 1•14
filter – 1•14
fluids – 1•2
footrest pivots lubricant – 1•2
fork oil change – 1•24
fuel system – 1•12
gearchange lever lubricant – 1•2
idle speed – 1•11
lever pivot lubricant – 1•2
lubricants and fluids – 1•2
lubrication – 1•26
maintenance schedule – 1•3
nuts and bolts – 1•27
oil – 1•2, 1•14
oil filter – 1•14
pad wear check – 1•22
pivot points lubrication – 1•26
sidestand and starter safety circuit – 1•27
sidestand pivot lubricant – 1•2
spark plug check and adjustment – 1•10
spark plug type – 1•1
starter safety circuit – 1•27
steering head bearings – 1•24
steering head bearings lubricant – 1•2
steering head freeplay check and
  adjustment – 1•24
steering head lubrication – 1•26
suspension – 1•23
suspension lubrication – 1•24
throttle cables – 1•12
throttle twistgrip lubricant – 1•2
tyre pressures – 0•16
tyres – 1•23
valve clearances – 1•1, 1•30
wheel bearings – 1•23
wheels – 1•22
Running-in procedure – 2•55

S

Safety first! – 0•10, 0•15
Seats – 7•2, 7•5, 7•7
  panels – 7•5
Security – REF• 20 *et seq*
Selector drum and forks – 2•54
Shock absorber – 5•16
  adjustment – 5•14
  disposal – 5•18
Side panels – 7•2
Sidelight(s) – 8•7, 8•9, 8•10
Sidestand – 5•5
  pivot lubricant – 1•2
  starter safety circuit – 1•27
  switch – 8•22
Signalling – 0•15
Silencer removal – 4•21, 4•22, 4•24
Spare parts – 0•9
Spark plug
  cap – 4•27
  check and adjustment – 1•10
  type – 1•1
Speed sensor – 4•14
Sprockets – 6•24
  coupling bearing – 6•22
  coupling/rubber dampers – 6•25
Starter circuit cut-off relay and diodes – 8•24
Starter clutch and gears – 2•27
Starter motor
  overhaul – 8•27
  removal and installation – 8•26

Starter relay – 8•25
Starter safety circuit – 1•27
Steering – 0•13
Steering head
  bearings – 1•24, 5•15
  bearings lubrication – 1•2, 1•26
  freeplay check and adjustment – 1•24
Steering stem – 5•13
Storage – REF• 32 *et seq*
Sump guard – 7•7
Suspension – 0•13, 1•23
  adjustment – 5•23
  linkage – 5•18
  lubrication – 1•24
Swingarm – 5•19
Switches
  brake lever – 8•16, 8•17
  brake pedal – 8•17
  clutch – 8•23
  continuity checks – 8•3
  handlebar – 8•21
  ignition – 8•20
  neutral – 8•21
  sidestand – 8•22

T

Tail light – 8•8, 8•13
  bulb – 8•12
Temperature sensor – 3•3, 4•12, 4•13
Temperature warning light – 3•3
Tensioner blade and guide blade – 2•17
Thermostat – 3•4
Throttle body – 4•18
Throttle cables – 1•12, 4•20
Throttle position (TP) sensor – 4•13
Throttle twistgrip lubricant – 1•2
Timing – 4•28
Tip-over sensor – 4•13
Tools and Workshop Tips – REF• 2 *et seq*
Transmission assembly – 2•48
  bearings – 2•45
  overhaul – 2•50
Turn signal assemblies – 8•15
  bulbs – 8•14
  circuit check – 8•14
Tyres – 0•16, 1•23, 6•22
  care – 0•16
  pressures – 0•16
  tread depth – 0•16

V

Valve
  clearances – 1•1, 1•30
  overhaul – 2•19
Voltage checks – 8•3

W

Warning light – 3•3
  LEDs – 8•19
Water pump – 3•6
  gears – 2•36
  seal and bearing replacement – 3•7
Weights – 0•17
Wheels – 1•22, 6•18, 6•19
  alignment check – 6•17
  bearings – 1•23, •20, 6•21
  inspection and repair – 6•17
Wiring continuity checks – 8•3
Wiring diagrams – 8•36 *et seq*

Haynes Motorcycle Manuals – The Complete List

Title	Book No
APRILIA RS50 (99 - 06) & RS125 (93 - 06)	4298
Aprilia RSV1000 Mille (98 - 03)	♦ 4255
Aprilia SR50	4755
BMW 2-valve Twins (70 - 96)	♦ 0249
BMW F650	♦ 4761
BMW K100 & 75 2-valve Models (83 - 96)	♦ 1373
BMW R850, 1100 & 1150 4-valve Twins (93 - 04)	♦ 3466
BMW R1200 (04 - 06)	♦ 4598
BSA Bantam (48 - 71)	0117
BSA Unit Singles (58 - 72)	0127
BSA Pre-unit Singles (54 - 61)	0326
BSA A7 & A10 Twins (47 - 62)	0121
BSA A50 & A65 Twins (62 - 73)	0155
Chinese Scooters	4768
DUCATI 600, 620, 750 and 900 2-valve V-Twins (91 - 05)	♦ 3290
Ducati MK III & Desmo Singles (69 - 76)	◊ 0445
Ducati 748, 916 & 996 4-valve V-Twins (94 - 01)	♦ 3756
GILERA Runner, DNA, Ice & SKP/Stalker (97 - 07)	4163
HARLEY-DAVIDSON Sportsters (70 - 08)	♦ 2534
Harley-Davidson Shovelhead and Evolution Big Twins (70 - 99)	♦ 2536
Harley-Davidson Twin Cam 88 (99 - 03)	♦ 2478
HONDA NB, ND, NP & NS50 Melody (81 - 85)	♦ 0622
Honda NE/NB50 Vision & SA50 Vision Met-in (85 - 95)	◊ 1278
Honda MB, MBX, MT & MTX50 (80 - 93)	0731
Honda C50, C70 & C90 (67 - 03)	0324
Honda XR80/100R & CRF80/100F (85 - 04)	2218
Honda XL/XR 80, 100, 125, 185 & 200 2-valve Models (78 - 87)	0566
Honda H100 & H100S Singles (80 - 92)	◊ 0734
Honda CB/CD125T & CM125C Twins (77 - 88)	0571
Honda CG125 (76 - 07)	◊ 0433
Honda NS125 (86 - 93)	3056
Honda CBR125R (04 - 07)	4620
Honda MBX/MTX125 & MTX200 (83 - 93)	◊ 1132
Honda CD/CM185 200T & CM250C 2-valve Twins (77 - 85)	0572
Honda XL/XR 250 & 500 (78 - 84)	0567
Honda XR250L, XR250R & XR400R (86 - 03)	2219
Honda CB250 & CB400N Super Dreams (78 - 84)	◊ 0540
Honda CR Motocross Bikes (86 - 01)	2222
Honda CRF250 & CRF450 (02 - 06)	2630
Honda CBR400RR Fours (88 - 99)	◊ ♦ 3552
Honda VFR400 (NC30) & RVF400 (NC35) V-Fours (89 - 98)	◊ ♦ 3496
Honda CB500 (93 - 02) & CBF500 03 - 08	◊ 3753
Honda CB400 & CB550 Fours (73 - 77)	0262
Honda CX/GL500 & 650 V-Twins (78 - 86)	0442
Honda CBX550 Four (82 - 86)	◊ 0940
Honda XL600R & XR600R (83 - 08)	♦ 2183
Honda XL600/650V Transalp & XRV750 Africa Twin (87 to 07)	♦ 3919
Honda CBR600F1 & 1000F Fours (87 - 96)	♦ 1730
Honda CBR600F2 & F3 Fours (91 - 98)	♦ 2070
Honda CBR600F4 (99 - 06)	♦ 3911
Honda CB600F Hornet & CBF600 (98 - 06)	◊ ♦ 3915
Honda CBR600RR (03 - 06)	♦ 4590
Honda CB650 sohc Fours (78 - 84)	0665
Honda NTV600 Revere, NTV650 and NT650V Deauville (88 - 05)	◊ ♦ 3243
Honda Shadow VT600 & 750 (USA) (88 - 03)	2312
Honda CB750 sohc Four (69 - 79)	0131
Honda V45/65 Sabre & Magna (82 - 88)	0820
Honda VFR750 & 700 V-Fours (86 - 97)	♦ 2101
Honda VFR800 V-Fours (97 - 01)	♦ 3703
Honda VFR800 V-Tec V-Fours (02 - 05)	♦ 4196
Honda CB750 & CB900 dohc Fours (78 - 84)	0535
Honda VTR1000 (FireStorm, Super Hawk) & XL1000V (Varadero) (97 - 08)	♦ 3744
Honda CBR900RR FireBlade (92 - 99)	♦ 2161
Honda CBR900RR FireBlade (00 - 03)	♦ 4060
Honda CBR1000RR Fireblade (04 - 07)	♦ 4604
Honda CBR1100XX Super Blackbird (97 - 07)	♦ 3901
Honda ST1100 Pan European V-Fours (90 - 02)	♦ 3384
Honda Shadow VT1100 (USA) (85 - 98)	2313
Honda GL1000 Gold Wing (75 - 79)	0309

Title	Book No
Honda GL1100 Gold Wing (79 - 81)	0669
Honda Gold Wing 1200 (USA) (84 - 87)	2199
Honda Gold Wing 1500 (USA) (88 - 00)	2225
KAWASAKI AE/AR 50 & 80 (81 - 95)	1007
Kawasaki KC, KE & KH100 (75 - 99)	1371
Kawasaki KMX125 & 200 (86 - 02)	◊ 3046
Kawasaki 250, 350 & 400 Triples (72 - 79)	0134
Kawasaki 400 & 440 Twins (74 - 81)	0281
Kawasaki 400, 500 & 550 Fours (79 - 91)	0910
Kawasaki EN450 & 500 Twins (Ltd/Vulcan) (85 - 07)	2053
Kawasaki EX500 (GPZ500S) & ER500 (ER-5) (87 - 08)	♦ 2052
Kawasaki ZX600 (ZZ-R600 & Ninja ZX-6) (90 - 06)	♦ 2146
Kawasaki ZX-6R Ninja Fours (95 - 02)	♦ 3541
Kawasaki ZX-6R (03 - 06)	♦ 4742
Kawasaki ZX600 (GPZ600R, GPX600R, Ninja 600R & RX) & ZX750 (GPX750R, Ninja 750R)	♦ 1780
Kawasaki 650 Four (76 - 78)	0373
Kawasaki Vulcan 700/750 & 800 (85 - 04)	♦ 2457
Kawasaki 750 Air-cooled Fours (80 - 91)	0574
Kawasaki ZR550 & 750 Zephyr Fours (90 - 97)	♦ 3382
Kawasaki Z750 & Z1000 (03 - 08)	♦ 4762
Kawasaki ZX750 (Ninja ZX-7 & ZXR750) Fours (89 - 96)	♦ 2054
Kawasaki Ninja ZX-7R & ZX-9R (94 - 04)	♦ 3721
Kawasaki 900 & 1000 Fours (73 - 77)	0222
Kawasaki ZX900, 1000 & 1100 Liquid-cooled Fours (83 - 97)	♦ 1681
KTM EXC Enduro & SX Motocross (00 - 07)	♦ 4629
MOTO GUZZI 750, 850 & 1000 V-Twins (74 - 78)	0339
MZ ETZ Models (81 - 95)	◊ 1680
NORTON 500, 600, 650 & 750 Twins (57 - 70)	0187
Norton Commando (68 - 77)	0125
PEUGEOT Speedfight, Trekker & Vivacity Scooters (96 - 08)	◊ 3920
PIAGGIO (Vespa) Scooters (91 - 06)	◊ 3492
SUZUKI GT, ZR & TS50 (77 - 90)	◊ 0799
Suzuki TS50X (84 - 00)	◊ 1599
Suzuki 100, 125, 185 & 250 Air-cooled Trail bikes (79 - 89)	0797
Suzuki GP100 & 125 Singles (78 - 93)	◊ 0576
Suzuki GS, GN, GZ & DR125 Singles (82 - 05)	0888
Suzuki GSX-R600/750 (06 - 09)	♦ 4790
Suzuki 250 & 350 Twins (68 - 78)	0120
Suzuki GT250X7, GT200X5 & SB200 Twins (78 - 83)	◊ 0469
Suzuki GS/GSX250, 400 & 450 Twins (79 - 85)	0736
Suzuki GS500 Twin (89 - 06)	♦ 3238
Suzuki GS550 (77 - 82) & GS750 Fours (76 - 79)	0363
Suzuki GS/GSX550 4-valve Fours (83 - 88)	1133
Suzuki SV650 & SV650S (99 - 08)	♦ 3912
Suzuki GSX-R600 & 750 (96 - 00)	♦ 3553
Suzuki GSX-R600 (01 - 03), GSX-R750 (00 - 03) & GSX-R1000 (01 - 02)	♦ 3986
Suzuki GSX-R600/750 (04 - 05) & GSX-R1000 (03 - 06)	♦ 4382
Suzuki GSF600, 650 & 1200 Bandit Fours (95 - 06)	♦ 3367
Suzuki Intruder, Marauder, Volusia & Boulevard (85 - 06)	♦ 2618
Suzuki GS850 Fours (78 - 88)	0536
Suzuki GS1000 Four (77 - 79)	0484
Suzuki GSX-R750, GSX-R1100 (85 - 92), GSX600F, GSX750F, GSX1100F (Katana) Fours	♦ 2055
Suzuki GSX600/750F & GSX750 (98 - 02)	♦ 3987
Suzuki GS/GSX1000, 1100 & 1150 4-valve Fours (79 - 88)	0737
Suzuki TL1000S/R & DL1000 V-Strom (97 - 04)	♦ 4083
Suzuki GSF650/1250 (05 - 09)	♦ 4798
Suzuki GSX1300R Hayabusa (99 - 04)	♦ 4184
Suzuki GSX1400 (02 - 07)	♦ 4758
TRIUMPH Tiger Cub & Terrier (52 - 68)	0414
Triumph 350 & 500 Unit Twins (58 - 73)	0137
Triumph Pre-Unit Twins (47 - 62)	0251
Triumph 650 & 750 2-valve Unit Twins (63 - 83)	0122
Triumph Trident & BSA Rocket 3 (69 - 75)	0136
Triumph Bonneville (01 - 07)	♦ 4364
Triumph Daytona, Speed Triple, Sprint & Tiger (97 - 05)	♦ 3755
Triumph Triples and Fours (carburettor engines) (91 - 04)	♦ 2162
VESPA P/PX125, 150 & 200 Scooters (78 - 06)	0707
Vespa Scooters (59 - 78)	0126
YAMAHA DT50 & 80 Trail Bikes (78 - 95)	◊ 0800
Yamaha T50 & 80 Townmate (83 - 95)	◊ 1247

Title	Book No
Yamaha YB100 Singles (73 - 91)	◊ 0474
Yamaha RS/RXS100 & 125 Singles (74 - 95)	0331
Yamaha RD & DT125LC (82 - 95)	◊ 0887
Yamaha TZR125 (87 - 93) & DT125R (88 - 07)	◊ 1655
Yamaha TY50, 80, 125 & 175 (74 - 84)	◊ 0464
Yamaha XT & SR125 (82 - 03)	◊ 1021
Yamaha YBR125	4797
Yamaha Trail Bikes (81 - 00)	2350
Yamaha 2-stroke Motocross Bikes 1986 - 2006	2662
Yamaha YZ & WR 4-stroke Motocross Bikes (98 - 08)	2689
Yamaha 250 & 350 Twins (70 - 79)	0040
Yamaha XS250, 360 & 400 sohc Twins (75 - 84)	0378
Yamaha RD250 & 350LC Twins (80 - 82)	0803
Yamaha RD350 YPVS Twins (83 - 95)	1158
Yamaha RD400 Twin (75 - 79)	0333
Yamaha XT, TT & SR500 Singles (75 - 83)	0342
Yamaha XZ550 Vision V-Twins (82 - 85)	0821
Yamaha FJ, FZ, XJ & YX600 Radian (84 - 92)	2100
Yamaha XJ600S (Diversion, Seca II) & XJ600N Fours (92 - 03)	♦ 2145
Yamaha YZF600R Thundercat & FZS600 Fazer (96 - 03)	♦ 3702
Yamaha FZ-6 Fazer (04 - 07)	♦ 4751
Yamaha YZF-R6 (99 - 02)	♦ 3900
Yamaha YZF-R6 (03 - 05)	♦ 4601
Yamaha 650 Twins (70 - 83)	0341
Yamaha XJ650 & 750 Fours (80 - 84)	0738
Yamaha XS750 & 850 Triples (76 - 85)	0340
Yamaha TDM850, TRX850 & XTZ750 (89 - 99)	◊ ♦ 3540
Yamaha YZF750R & YZF1000R Thunderace (93 - 00)	♦ 3720
Yamaha FZR600, 750 & 1000 Fours (87 - 96)	♦ 2056
Yamaha XV (Virago) V-Twins (81 - 03)	♦ 0802
Yamaha XVS650 & 1100 Drag Star/V-Star (97 - 05)	♦ 4195
Yamaha XJ900F Fours (83 - 94)	♦ 3239
Yamaha XJ900S Diversion (94 - 01)	♦ 3739
Yamaha YZF-R1 (98 - 03)	♦ 3754
Yamaha YZF-R1 (04 - 06)	♦ 4605
Yamaha FZS1000 Fazer (01 - 05)	♦ 4287
Yamaha FJ1100 & 1200 Fours (84 - 96)	♦ 2057
Yamaha XJR1200 & 1300 (95 - 06)	♦ 3981
Yamaha V-Max (85 - 03)	♦ 4072

ATVs

Title	Book No
Honda ATC70, 90, 110, 185 & 200 (71 - 85)	0565
Honda Rancher, Recon & TRX250EX ATVs	2553
Honda TRX300 Shaft Drive ATVs (88 - 00)	2125
Honda Foreman (95 - 07)	2465
Honda TRX300EX, TRX400EX & TRX450R/ER ATVs (93 - 06)	2318
Kawasaki Bayou 220/250/300 & Prairie 300 ATVs (86 - 03)	2351
Polaris ATVs (85 - 97)	2302
Polaris ATVs (98 - 06)	2508
Yamaha YFS200 Blaster ATV (88 - 06)	2317
Yamaha YFB250 Timberwolf ATVs (92 - 00)	2217
Yamaha YFM350 & YFM400 (ER and Big Bear) ATVs (87 - 03)	2126
Yamaha Banshee and Warrior ATVs (87 - 03)	2314
Yamaha Kodiak and Grizzly ATVs (93 - 05)	2567
ATV Basics	10450

TECHBOOK SERIES

Title	Book No
Twist and Go (automatic transmission) Scooters Service and Repair Manual	4082
Motorcycle Basics TechBook (2nd Edition)	3515
Motorcycle Electrical TechBook (3rd Edition)	3471
Motorcycle Fuel Systems TechBook	3514
Motorcycle Maintenance TechBook	4071
Motorcycle Modifying	4272
Motorcycle Workshop Practice TechBook (2nd Edition)	3470

◊ = not available in the USA   ♦ = Superbike

The manuals on this page are available through good motorcycle dealers and accessory shops.
In case of difficulty, contact: **Haynes Publishing**
(UK) **+44 1963 442030**   (USA) **+1 805 498 6703**
(SV) **+46 18 124016**
(Australia/New Zealand) **+61 3 9763 8100**

Preserving Our Motoring Heritage

< *The Model J Duesenberg Derham Tourster. Only eight of these magnificent cars were ever built – this is the only example to be found outside the United States of America*

Almost every car you've ever loved, loathed or desired is gathered under one roof at the Haynes Motor Museum. Over 300 immaculately presented cars and motorbikes represent every aspect of our motoring heritage, from elegant reminders of bygone days, such as the superb Model J Duesenberg to curiosities like the bug-eyed BMW Isetta. There are also many old friends and flames. Perhaps you remember the 1959 Ford Popular that you did your courting in? The magnificent 'Red Collection' is a spectacle of classic sports cars including AC, Alfa Romeo, Austin Healey, Ferrari, Lamborghini, Maserati, MG, Riley, Porsche and Triumph.

A Perfect Day Out

Each and every vehicle at the Haynes Motor Museum has played its part in the history and culture of Motoring. Today, they make a wonderful spectacle and a great day out for all the family. Bring the kids, bring Mum and Dad, but above all bring your camera to capture those golden memories for ever. You will also find an impressive array of motoring memorabilia, a comfortable 70 seat video cinema and one of the most extensive transport book shops in Britain. The Pit Stop Cafe serves everything from a cup of tea to wholesome, home-made meals or, if you prefer, you can enjoy the large picnic area nestled in the beautiful rural surroundings of Somerset.

> *John Haynes O.B.E., Founder and Chairman of the museum at the wheel of a Haynes Light 12.*

< *The 1936 490cc sohc-engined International Norton – well known for its racing success*

The Museum is situated on the A359 Yeovil to Frome road at Sparkford, just off the A303 in Somerset. It is about 40 miles south of Bristol, and 25 minutes drive from the M5 intersection at Taunton.

Open 9.30am - 5.30pm (10.00am - 4.00pm Winter) 7 days a week, *except Christmas Day, Boxing Day and New Years Day*

Special rates available for schools, coach parties and outings Charitable Trust No. 292048